W9-AJU-925

MOON HANDBOOKS®

MEXICO CITY

THIRD EDITION

CHRIS HUMPHREY

AVALON TRAVEL

To Toluca

Parque Nacional
Cerro de la
Estrella

CERRO DE LA
ESTRELLA

Tlahuac

AV TLAHUAC

AV TLAHUAC

ARNESES

CIRCUITO INTERIOR

PURISIMA

PLAYA PIE DE LA CUESTA

Iztapalapa

CALZ DE LA VIGA

AV TASQUEÑA

PLUTARCO ELIAS CALLES

AV POPOCATEPETL

TERMINAL CENTRAL
DEL SUR (TASQUEÑA)

CANAL DE MIRAMONTES

CALZ DE TLALPAN

CALZ DE TALPAN

CUMBRES DE MALTRATA

EJE CENTRAL

ANGEL URRAZA

AV DIVISION DEL NORTE

AV MIGUEL ANGEL DE QUEVEDO

COYOACÁN

Coyoacán

MUSEO
ANAHUACALLI

To Cuernavaca
and Taxco

AV UNIVERSIDAD

Del Valle

DIAG SAN ANTONIO

WORLD TRADE CENTER

Nápoles

JOSÉ MARIA RICO

FÉLIX CUEVAS

Mixcoac

INSURGENTES SUR

AV UNIVERSIDAD

REVOLUCIÓN

CIRCUITO INTERIOR

San Ángel
SAN ÁNGEL

PEDRO HENRIQUEZ UREÑA

COPILCO

CIUDAD
UNIVERSITARIA

INSURGENTES SUR

AV AZTECAS

ESTADIO
AZTECA

ANILLO PERIFÉRICO

0   0.5 mi

0   0.5 km

To Cuernavaca
and Taxco

ALTA TENSIÓN

CENTENARIO

CALZ DE LAS AGUILAS

DE LOS LEONES

To Desierto de
los Leones

CALZ AL DESIERTO

AV TOLUCA

To Los
Dinamos

To San Nicolás
Totolapan and
El Ajusco

CENTRO HISTÓRICO

REPÚBLICA DE CHILE

REPÚBLICA DE HONDURAS

APARTADO

REPÚBLICA DE PERU

L VALLE

REPÚBLICA DE BRASIL

REPÚBLICA DE ARGENTINA

REPÚBLICA DE BOLIVIA

RODRIGUEZ PUEBLA

LEONA VICARIO

MARGIL

REPÚBLICA DE COLOMBIA

HOSTERÍA SANTO DOMINGO ▼

TEMPLO DE SANTO DOMINGO ♦

GENERAL M ALEMÁN

Plaza de Santo Domingo

SECRETARÍA DE EDUCACIÓN PÚBLICA

REPÚBLICA DE VENEZUELA

CICERO CENTENARIO ★

PALMA

INTERNET LAFOEL ★

IGLESIA DE LA ENSEÑANZA

SN ILDEFONSO

CASA DE LOS CONDES HERAS Y SOTO ★

SUPER SOYA ▼

HOTEL CATEDRAL

ANTIGUO COLEGIO DE SAN ILDEFONSO

SAN ANTONIO

HOSTEL CATEDRAL

GALERÍA SHCP ★

CENTRO CULTURAL DE ESPAÑA

CASA DE LAS SIRENAS ▼

TEMPLO MAYOR ★

MUSEO DEL TEMPLO MAYOR ★

JUSTO SIERRA

É LA ... NCA

PANADERÍA Y CAFETERÍA VASCONIA ▼

LOS BISQUETS OBREGÓN ▼

REPÚBLICA DE GUATEMALA

MIXCALCO

POLLOS GILI ★

NACIONAL MONTE DE PIEDAD

CATHEDRAL

LIC VERDAD

EX-SANTA TERESA ★

HOTEL GILLOW ●

SAGRARIO

PALACIO DEL ARZOBISPADO ★

CASA DE LA IMPRENTA

MUSEO JOSÉ LUIS CUEVAS ★

HOTEL ZAMORA/ CAFÉ POPULAR ●

HOLIDAY INN SELECT ▼

MONEDA

IGLESIA LA PROFESA ★

EL CARDENAL ▼

● HOSTAL MONEDA

ACADEMIA DE SAN CARLOS ★

IGLESIA DE LA SANTÍSIMA TRINIDAD ♦

EDIFICIO LONGORIO ★

FCO I MADERO

BEST WESTERN HOTEL MAJESTIC ▼

LA CASA DE LA MONEDA ★

E ZAPATA

SINO ÑOL

PALMA

RL REY DEL PAVO ▼

Plaza de la Constitución

SOLEDAD

LORETO

SANTÍSIMA

16 DE SEPTIEMBRE

PALACIO NACIONAL

SUPER SOYA ▼

★ ZÓCALO

Ⓜ Zócalo

ASA DEL CONDE MATEO DE VALPARAÍSO ★

PERVERT LOUNGE

RESTAURANT EL EHDEN ★

ALHÓNDIGA

MooN

HOTEL MONTE CARLO ●

EX-CONVENTO DE LA MERCED ★

MUSEO DE LA CIUDAD ★

MANZANARES

CORREO MAYOR

LAS CRUCES

JESÚS MARÍA

TALAVERA

ROLDAN

SANTO TOMÁS

ANILLO DE CIRCUVALACIÓN

IGLESIA JESÚS NAZARENO ♦

HOSPITAL DE JESÚS NAZARENO ★

5 DE FEBRERO

20 DE NOVIEMBRE

JOSÉ MARÍA PINO SUÁREZ

REGINA

MISIONEROS

RESTAURANT AL ANDALÚZ ▼

RESTAURANT ▼ DON CHON

To Mercado de Sonora and Mercado de la Merced

X-CLAUSTRO E SOR JUANA

SAN JERONIMO

Pino Suárez Ⓜ Ⓜ

SAN PABLO

© AVALON TRAVEL PUBLISHING, INC

SISTEMA
DE TRANSPORTE
® COLECTIVO

RED DEL METRO

CONTENTS

Discover Mexico City

Explore Mexico City

Know Mexico City

Maps

MAP SYMBOLS

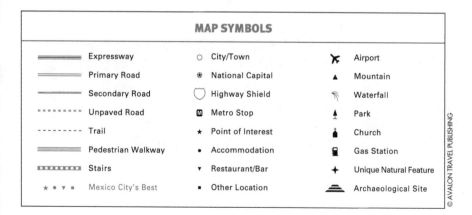

Expressway	○ City/Town	✈	Airport
Primary Road	⊛ National Capital	▲	Mountain
Secondary Road	◯ Highway Shield	⇗	Waterfall
Unpaved Road	Ⓜ Metro Stop	⚲	Park
Trail	★ Point of Interest	⚱	Church
Pedestrian Walkway	• Accommodation	⛽	Gas Station
Stairs	▼ Restaurant/Bar	✦	Unique Natural Feature
★ • ▼ ■ Mexico City's Best	■ Other Location	⛰	Archaeological Site

© AVALON TRAVEL PUBLISHING

Discover
Mexico City

Mexico City—also known as La Ciudad, La Capital, México, el Distrito Federal, or simply "De Efe" (D.F.) for short—often astounds first-time visitors with its disarming combination of Old World charm and New World sophistication. The city lures visitors with a long list of superlatives—it's the oldest and highest city in North America, one of the largest in the world, and the only metropolis with three UNESCO World Heritage Sites within its city limits.

Despite its epic sprawl, it can be a remarkably attractive city, at least in certain areas—the downtown Centro Histórico, lined with colonial mansions and churches; broad, elegant Paseo de la Reforma, lined with office buildings and first-class hotels; the art deco architecture, galleries, and cafés of the Roma and Condesa neighborhoods; and the quiet cobblestone streets of Coyoacán and San Ángel in the south.

Museum-lovers could spend days, even weeks, touring all the different exhibits of art, history, archaeology, and popular culture. Architect enthusiasts can see every kind of building from 2000-year-old pyramids to Latin America's highest skyscraper. And lovers of the good life won't want to miss the fantastic food and the epic, dawn-chasing nightlife for which the city is famous.

But it's the little discoveries that are addictive. A cantina in continuous operation for seven decades, a used bookshop specializing in 19th-century engravings, street-corner vendors selling blue-corn *quesadillas,* a colonial-era *plazuela* (little plaza) seemingly lost to all but local inhabitants—all conspire to pull you under the city's spell.

At the same time, Mexico City sometimes seems as if it's hurtling from one disaster to the next. The city is reportedly sinking at a rate of several inches per year as wells suck the water table dry beneath the spongy lake bed upon which the city was laid out in the 16th century. The legendary air pollution has improved noticeably in the last few years, but it's still pretty bad. Nearly one-fifth of Mexico's population lives in the capital's metro area, and every bus from the provinces brings in yet more fortune-seekers, unfazed by the occasional 7.0 temblor.

Crazed? Definitely. But the amazing thing is how well the city works, how it reaches well beyond mere survival. You can zip across town by underground Metro or glide slowly around the Centro Histórico in a *bicitaxi* (pedicab). Dig into a steaming chile-and-cheese tamale served by a sidewalk vendor for $.35 while standing outside a $200-a-night hotel. Catch a classic Mexican film at a local *cineclub,* then stroll through one of Latin America's most beautiful urban parks. Climb aboard a brightly painted *trajinera* (Mexican-style gondola) and disappear down the shaded waterways of Xochimilco. Aztec temples and Catholic cathedrals, punk rockers and mariachi serenaders, poverty-stricken slums and walled villas; they're all part of the phantasmagoric heart of *mexicanidad* (Mexicanness) that is Mexico City. The longer you stay, the more intriguing it all seems to become.

Mexico City has always been huge and vibrant, but in the decades that the country lived under a one-party political system and a closed economy, it also had a provincial feel, closed off from the rest of the world. No longer. Visitors these days will find dozens of upscale restaurants serving world-class Mexican and international food, as well as unexpected fusions of the two. Galleries are showing the latest experimental art, Mexican cinema is on the rise, and young writers are producing all sorts of new fiction—much of it inspired by the streets of the city itself. The city has reinvented itself a thousand times since it was founded by the Aztecs in 1325, and it's at it again.

Many casual visitors to Mexico arrive in the capital by plane, take one look at the traffic and air pollution, and make an immediate beeline for the nearest exit, heading to the coastal resorts, colonial cities, or, basically, anywhere else. It's their loss. As huge and environmentally challenged as it is, Mexico City is one of the most fascinating and vibrant cauldrons of humanity in the world, and anyone with a taste for cities can't afford to miss it.

Traveling to Mexico City is extremely easy. Visas are not required for tourists from the U.S., Canada, and nearly 40 countries in Europe and Latin America, meaning you can easily arrange a last-minute trip to D.F. should the mood strike your fancy.

WHAT TO TAKE

Everyone has their own taste for what sort of clothing and accoutrements they like to bring traveling with them, but a few points bear keeping in mind when packing your bag. Mexico City might be technically located in the tropics, but it's not very tropical. At 2,100 meters above sea level, the climate is much, much cooler than Cancún. So make sure you bring a light jacket, even in summer, for the evenings, and in winter be prepared for it to be positively chilly at night. The rainy season in Mexico City is usually between April and October, but rains can hit all year, so a pocket umbrella isn't a bad idea (although you can buy them there very cheaply). Warmer clothes are needed for visiting the mountain countryside around the city, near Valle de Bravo for example. Bring sunscreen and a hat when the weather is sunny (most of the time), especially if you plan a day trip to somewhere like Teotihuacán.

Not only is the climate very different in Mexico City than in the beach towns, but so is the style of dress. This is a huge, busy, working city—you're not going to see a lot of people walking around in shorts and sandals. You will definitely draw attention to yourself if that's what you wear. Think of yourself visiting a big city anywhere in Europe or North America, and pack accordingly. Women will want to dress relatively conservatively for touring the city, if only to keep the occasional catcalls to a minimum.

A photocopy of your passport and of your visa paper (given to you when you arrive at the airport) are always good to have, but leave the originals in your hotel. The easiest way to get cash is with an ATM card. All the major Mexican banks are owned by foreign companies, and their ATM machines are hooked up to most international networks and offer up-to-the-minute exchange rates. Don't travel with too much cash (or valuables in general), but having, say, a 500-peso note tucked away is not a bad idea in case of emergencies. Beware of toting around expensive-looking cameras as they are a temptation to would-be thieves. It's best to keep it in a bag when you aren't using it. Also sometimes useful are 20- or 50-peso Ladatel telephone cards, which work at the ubiquitous pay phone. Ladatel cards are sold at magazine stands and convenience stores, such as Oxxo and Sanborns.

WHEN TO GO

Pretty much any time of year is a good time to go to Mexico City. Because this is a mainly urban environment, most sights are not particularly weather-dependent. Sometimes visiting Mexico City during the April–October rainy season can be wet, but it's not difficult to come prepared with an umbrella or rain jacket. Temperatures are cooler in the winter but fairly moderate all year round. In terms of air pollution, it tends to get a bit worse during the colder, drier winter months (thermal inversions are not uncommon), but good and bad days are possible throughout the year. In general, pollution is lighter (logically enough) when it's windy.

There's no tourist season per se in Mexico City, but it's often nice to go during Mexican holidays, when many residents are away on vacation and the city is less congested. The Christmas holidays and Semana Santa (Easter Week) are great times to visit.

SAFETY

Mexico City has a well-deserved reputation as a city with a lot of crime. While some people will be put off by this, the truth is that it's no more dangerous than any city in Latin America, or indeed, most of the world. And like any big city, knowing where you can and can't go and what you can and can't do will make you a whole lot safer. Tourists can very easily stay out of harm's way by simply sticking to the neighborhoods described in this book. Most crime takes place well away from tourist destinations, where foreign visitors are un-likely to venture. A large number of tourist robberies happen when foreigners flag a taxi off the street; always get a safe *sitio* (radio) taxi instead. The other common place to get robbed is on a crowded Metro car, so don't bring valu-ables with you, and watch out for pickpockets. Be wary of strangers who approach you, as tourist scams, though not common, are not unheard of. But try not to be so suspicious that you cut yourself off from meeting Mexicans, who tend to be more open and friendly than many foreigners are used to. In general, pay attention to your surroundings and use your judgment to stay out of trouble's way.

Flying into Mexico City for the first time, across what seems to be an endless sea of urbanity, is a daunting experience. But even a first-time visitor shouldn't have too hard a time getting oriented. A large part of the buildings you see from above are actually not even in the D.F. but in the sprawling *área conurbada* outside the city limits. Within Mexico City proper, almost all the attractions, hotels, restaurants, and other services of interest to visitors are located within an area in the southwest part of the city roughly defined on the east by the Calzada de Tlalpan avenue, on the north by Paseo de la Reforma, and the west and south by the Periférico ring highway.

CENTRO HISTÓRICO

If you go to only one place in Mexico City, it should unquestionably be the Zócalo, Mexico City's downtown square, which has been the city's—and indeed the entire country's—epicenter since the time of the Aztec empire. Surrounding the huge, unadorned square is evidence of the country's past: the ruins of the Aztec Templo Mayor (Great Temple); the massive, sumptuous Catedral; the red, volcanic-brick Palacio Nacional; and ornate colonial palaces and churches packed into the surrounding blocks. Inside the Palacio is the famed mural by Diego Rivera where a visitor can take in the sweep of Mexico's history in one dazzling display of artistry. But make sure you take the time to see more than just the tourist sites of the Centro. Part of its charm is that it's still a living, thriving neighborhood, full of ordinary city people going about their daily business—a hustling, bustling crowd of noisy street vendors hawking all variety of wares, bicycle taxis, traffic policemen, political protestors, Aztec dancers, and tourists from across the globe.

PASEO DE LA REFORMA

As the population of Mexico City grew and began to expand beyond the limits of the Centro, the city designed and built its first suburbs along the broad European-style Paseo de la Reforma avenue. The original 19th-century mansions now house embassies and swank restaurants, and are surrounded by high-rise bank offices and luxury hotels. The western end of the avenue is punctuated by the Torre Mayor, Latin America's tallest building, at 225 meters. While tourist destinations in this neighborhood are limited to the imposing Monumento de la Revolución and two art museums, visitors will often find themselves here to visit one of the embassies, banks, or airline offices—or to shop in the many stores of the Zona Rosa district, just south of Reforma.

IN AND AROUND CHAPULTEPEC

Just past the Torre Mayor on Paseo de la Reforma begins Chapultepec, formerly the private preserve of Aztec rulers and, later, of the Spanish colonial elite. Now it's a leafy park centered on a small hill topped by a castle. The park is great place for a peaceful stroll in the trees or an afternoon picnic. Right across from the park is the world-famous Museo Nacional de Antropología e Historia, a treasure trove of exhibits on Mexico's rich legacy of indigenous cultures. Nearby are two of the country's best art museums, the Museo de Arte Moderno and the Museo Rufino Tamayo. North of Chapultepec is the wealthy neighborhood of Polanco, a sort of Rodeo Drive for Mexico City, replete with chic fashion shops, pricey (but very good) restaurants, and upscale night spots.

INSURGENTES SUR

Two of the city's most happening *colonias,* not well known by many tourists but immensely popular with the local and expatriate younger crowds, are the Condesa and Roma, both not far south of Paseo de la Reforma, on the west and east side, respectively, of Avenida Insurgentes. The 1920s-era Condesa, centered on the lush Parque México, is home to a couple of dozen upscale cafés, restaurants, and bars in converted art deco–style houses. The Roma is similar but a bit more bohemian in flavor, with lots of art galleries, coffeehouses, and alternative night spots. The Casa Lamm cultural center, housed in an elegant Porfiriato-era mansion, is a popular destination in the Roma. Both neighborhoods are great places to walk around safely, with fine architecture and many tree-filled parks.

SOUTHERN MEXICO CITY

Formerly rural villages that were long ago surrounded by the ever-growing city, Coyoacán and San Ángel still retain the flavor of past years, with cobblestone streets, quiet plazas, and colonial-era mansions and churches. Both are popular weekend destinations for foreigners and Mexicans alike for their bustling art and handicrafts markets and festive ambiance. Tourists will find much to busy themselves with, including several museums dedicated to renowned artist couple Diego Rivera and Frida Kahlo. Make sure you take at least a half day to fully enjoy strolling around these tranquil neighborhoods and sampling some of the good food offered in their numerous restaurants. Further to the south, past the sprawling campus of the national university, are the famed *chinampas,* the floating gardens of Xochimilco, the breadbasket of the Aztec empire and now a popular destination for revelers hosting parties on boats that cruise the ancient canals.

NORTHERN MEXICO CITY

Situated on a hill known as Cerro Tepayac in the north part of the city is the Basílica de Nuestra Señora de Guadalupe, the most sacred shrine in the country. Some 15 million pilgrims come here each year to pray beneath the cloak of Juan Diego, an indigenous man who saw an apparition of the Virgin on the hilltop in 1531 and miraculously ended up with an image of her in his cloak to prove the truth of his story to church authorities. On December 12, the day of the miracle, the shrine is packed with worshipers from across Mexico who come to see *la virgen morenita* (the little dark-skinned virgin). Not far from the Basílica are the little-visited Aztec ruins of Santa Cecilia Acatitlán, as well as the smaller pre-Aztec pyramid of Tenayuca.

PARKS NEAR MEXICO CITY

For a dose of fresh air and pine trees, head up to the mountains ringing the southern and western parts of the city. On the flanks of El Ajusco (3,930 meters), mountain bikers and hikers will find the community-managed forest reserve San Nicolás Totolopan, with over 150 kilometers of well-maintained trails to roam. Desierto de los Leones is another forested park great for hiking and biking, with a beautiful 18th-century monastery secluded in a grove of pine trees. On the highway to Toluca is a third park, La Marquesa. One great excuse to visit La Marquesa is to sample the delicious and inexpensive *antojitos,* like mushroom soup and *quesadillas* sold in the many roadside restaurants in the park.

EXCURSIONS FROM MEXICO CITY

Mexico City is a fascinating place to visit in and of itself, but it has the added bonus of being located in the heartland of Mexico, with all manner of destinations within an easy day or overnight trip. Colonial Mexico buffs will find plenty to keep them busy in the cities of Puebla, Cuernavaca, and Taxco. There you'll encounter ornate churches and 17th-century mansions, museums of colonial and prehispanic culture and art, handicraft and jewelry markets, and superlative cuisine. For a more relaxed, small-town feel, check out Tepoztlán, Malinalco, or Valle de Bravo—all set amidst beautiful mountain country and with a stronger indigenous influence than the bigger cities. Outdoor aficionados can choose between climbing glacier-covered volcanoes, world-class hiking and mountain biking amid high pine forest, hundreds of rock climbing routes, and horseback trips to the monarch butterfly sanctuaries.

Two days isn't a whole lot of time for one of the biggest cities in the world, but the amount of fun you can have in Mexico City in just a weekend is impressive. A weekend is certainly long enough to get you hooked and to get you to start planning your next trip. These days you can purchase last-minute airline tickets from the U.S. sometimes for as low as $250, making D.F. a reasonable alternative to going to New York City, Miami, or San Francisco for the weekend—especially when you factor in lower hotel and restaurant costs.

DAY 1, MORNING

Start in the heart of the city, at the Zócalo, surrounded on all sides by some of the most important monuments in Mexico. Dominating the view is the Catedral Metropolitana. It is well worth your while to take an hour or so to admire both its architectural grandeur and the collection of religious art tucked into the seemingly endless alcoves and side altars. Right next door are the ruins of the Aztec Templo Mayor, along with the Museo del Templo Mayor, which has exhibits on art and artifacts found during its excavation. If you like the

look of the red-brick Palacio Nacional, also on the Zócalo, step inside to see Diego Rivera's famous murals. After seeing these three sights at a leisurely pace, you'll be starting to work up an appetite, so walk a couple of blocks west of the Zócalo and stop for lunch at either El Cardenal or Hostería Santo Domingo.

DAY 1, AFTERNOON

After the *comida,* walk west on Calle Tacuba, which dates from Aztec times and is lined with ornate colonial mansions. Across the busy Eje Central av-

Volcán Ajusco looming above the Periférico

enue, just past the Venetian-style Palacio Postal, is the imposing Palacio de Bellas Artes. Stop in to admire the art nouveau/art deco architecture, the impressive Tiffany glass curtain, and the political murals. Just beyond is the Alameda, Mexico City's first public park, a fine place to take a rest on a bench and watch the world go by. If you've got more energy to spare, finish up the day with a visit to the eclectic applied-arts collection at the Museo de Franz Mayer or switch to shopping mode and visit the FONART store, just off the Alameda, or the handicrafts market at La Ciudadela, just south of the Alameda on Calle Balderas.

DAY 1, EVENING

With only one weekend night out in Mexico City to live it up, you might as well do it in style. So put on some respectable duds and head over to Hacienda de los Morales in Polanco, where you can savor sublime Mexican cooking in the refined atmosphere of a 16th-century hacienda. For late-night entertainment, the options are many: salsa dancing, old-school cantinas, hipster lounges, queer clubs, political cabaret shows, you name it. But if you have to pick one place to get a taste of the soul of Mexico City's nightlife, it's got to be Plaza Garibaldi. Make your way through the crowd of revelers mingling with mariachi musicians crowding this little square in the Centro, and grab a table in the venerable Salón Tenampa. Buy a bottle of your favorite drink, pay one of the roving bands to strike up a classic old *bolero* tune, and join the fun.

DAY 2, MORNING

You'll be feeling a little groggy, so start off with a solid breakfast. One good option is Café Los Asombros at the El Péndulo bookstores in the Condesa or the Zona Rosa, where you can ease into the day with a big omelet filled with spinach, mushrooms, and goat cheese; a tall glass of juice; and an *espresso cortado*. Suitably fortified, head to the world-famous Museo Nacional de Antropología e Historia along Paseo de la Reforma for an hour or

two. Don't even think of trying to see all the exhibit halls or you'll be spent for the day. Afterward, de-program with a walk across the street through the leafy Parque Chapultepec, with a short detour up to the hilltop castle/museum to check out the views over the city.

DAY 2, AFTERNOON/EVENING

Sunday afternoon is a great time to head down to the former colonial-era village of Coyoacán, in the south part of the city. Amble around the twin plazas, thronged with handicraft vendors and locals out enjoying the weekend. A few blocks away along quiet cobblestone streets are the houses of the conquistador Cortés and his much-maligned lover and interpreter, La Malinche, as well as the Museo Frida Kahlo, dedicated to Mexico's best-known woman artist. After you're done touring, top off your weekend with another good meal—this time at one of the many great restaurants in the hip Condesa district. A good choice is El Zorzal, where you can dig into a juicy Argentine steak with red wine, empanadas, and a big bowl of salad.

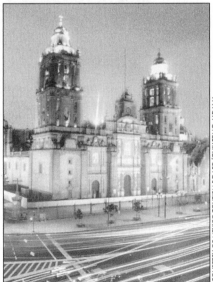

night view of Catedral Metropolitana

COURTESY OF MEXICO TOURISM BOARD/GUILLERMO ALDANA

A week is really the perfect amount of time for a trip to Mexico City. You'll have plenty of time to tour the major sights and even a few less-frequented destinations without running yourself ragged, leaving yourself enough energy to spend a couple of evenings enjoying the city's great nightlife. You'll also be able to take a couple of days to visit one of the many towns set amidst the lovely countryside surrounding the capital.

Day 1

Dedicate an entire day to taking in the Centro Histórico, taking the time to explore some of the lesser-known sites. Just north of the Templo Mayor is the Antiguo Colegio de San Ildefonso, a gracefully built religious school from the 16th century that now shows a variety of cultural exhibits; it also has some of first murals by Rivera, Orozco, and the other great painters of the early 20th century decorating the walls. Take a stroll through the Plaza Santo Domingo to watch the low-budget scribes writing missives for hire on their venerable old printing presses. For an aerial view of the Centro and the rest of the city, pay a nominal fee to ride up to the 38th floor of the Torre Latinoamericano office building, where there is an observation platform.

Day 2

In Chapultepec Park, take in the Museo Nacional de Antropología e Historia, and two top-quality modern art museums—the Museo Nacional de Arte Moderno and the Museo Rufino Tamayo. If the park greenery appeals, take the time for a leisurely stroll, perhaps stopping into the zoo or just grabbing a bench by the lake and watching the day go by. After you've had your fill of Chapultepec, spend a couple of hours to tour either the chichi shopping and restaurant district of Polanco, or the more bohemian, relaxed Roma neighborhood, filled with old Porfiriato-era mansions, coffeehouses, and bookstores.

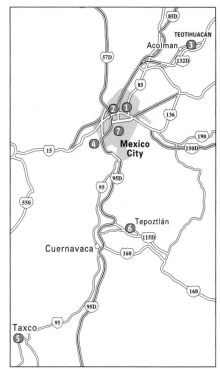

Day 3

The ancient ruins of Teotihuacán, located just northeast of Mexico City, are without doubt the most popular day-trip destination for tourists, and with good reason. This huge city, built by an unknown civilization over 2000 years ago, leaves

lucha libre

Cruz Azul, or Pumas club teams—or, if you're lucky, there might be a national team match. If you'd prefer a slightly more unusual sport, check out *lucha libre,* Mexico's colorful and melodramatic version of professional wrestling. To get yourself some exercise, take a jaunt up to the parks at Ajusco or La Marquesa, where you can breathe crisp mountain air and hike around trails through the pine forest.

DAYS 5–6

Set aside two days to take an overnight trip to one of myriad destinations in Central Mexico. Everyone will have their own destinations of choice, but one great place to go for first-time visitors is the famed silver city of Taxco, perched precariously on a steep, lush mountainside in the state of Guerrero, south of Mexico City. Apart from shopping for the trademark silver jewelry and other handicrafts, the picturesque town has several museums worth visiting and plenty of good restaurants. On your way back to Mexico City the next day, take a short detour to Tepoztlán near Cuernavaca to visit the beautiful convent and hike up to a prehispanic hilltop temple just outside of town.

visitors in awe of the towering pyramids, grand avenues, and stone carvings. The blazing sun and arid landscape can be exhausting, so come prepared with water and a hat. If you've got some energy left on the way back into town, stop off at Acolman, a magnificent early colonial monastery with indigenous motifs carved into the church facade.

DAY 4

After being such a dedicated sightseer, a day without any touristy destinations might be in order. One option might be to catch an event of some variety. For example, you could catch a soccer match at one of Mexico City's three stadiums, where you can join in the cheering for the America,

DAY 7

Spend your last day in Mexico City in the south of town, touring the colonial-era neighborhoods of Coyoacán and San Ángel, visiting different art and history museums, or just walking around the narrow, mansion-lined streets and enjoying the ambiance. Any day is a good day to go, but it's worth going on a Saturday for the Bazar Sábado, one of the finest arts-and-crafts markets in the city, held on the plaza in San Ángel. Further south is Xochimilco, where you can rent a *trajinera* to paddle you around the ancient Aztec canals.

© KEITH DANNEMILLER

Mexico's indigenous roots and culture are present in every part of D.F.—from the remnants of ancient Aztec capital in the Centro Histórico to the archaeological and anthropological treasures in the world-renowned Museo Nacional de Antropología e Historia. A visitor could easily spend a week on a tour of just cultural and archaeological sites.

CENTRO HISTÓRICO

The crown of the Centro's Aztec past is of course the Templo Mayor, just off the northeast side of the Zócalo. Walking around the pathways through the ruins feels like—is, really—tapping into Mexico City's very foundation. Inside the adjacent museum are some 7,000 artifacts from the site, including the famous eight-ton circular stone adorned with carvings of the moon goddess Coyolxuahqui. Remnants of the ancient Aztec capital are found in the unlikeliest spots around the Centro, like the serpent's head cornerstone of the colonial palace that houses the Museo de la Ciudad. For a taste of indigenous culture, literally, head over to the Fonda Don Chon, a humble little eatery on a backstreet that specializes in all sorts of well-prepared Aztec delicacies, like *gusanos de maguey* (cactus worms) or *venado con huitlacoche* (deer meat with corn fungus)—definitely for the brave, but good.

© ELENA PAPPAS

statue in front of the Museo Nacional de Antropología e Historia

CHAPULTEPEC

A lengthy stop at the Museo Nacional de Antropología e Historia in Chapultepec is obligatory for those with a strong interest in Mexico's indigenous cultures. If you could actually take the time to read and digest all the information in the 23 halls of the vast museum (impossible!), you'd be a world-class expert. Outside the museum you can see some of that culture in action, watching the trapezelike spectacle of the *voladores de Papantla*, costumed indigenous men from Veracruz who swing around a tall pole with ropes around their feet. Just across the street, the hill underneath the Castillo de Chapultepec was a sacred shrine of the Aztecs for the water that sprung from its base, and although you can't see them now, the portraits of Aztec emperors were carved in the hillside, à la Mt. Rushmore.

SOUTHERN MEXICO CITY

A couple of millennia ago, the area just south of the national university was the site of the first urban settlement in the Valle de México, Cuicuilco. Although it was destroyed by a volcanic eruption, the ruins of Cuicuilco are still there, poking up out of a hardened lava field right at the intersection of Avenida Insurgentes and the Periférico Sur, easily accessible for a short visit. Further east is Cerro de la Estrella, a small volcanic cone where the Aztecs used to light their 52-year fire, which they believed renewed the world. Nowadays the hill is the site of the city's biggest annual Passion Play reenactment during Semana Santa (Holy Week). Also worth seeing in the south is the Museo Anahuacalli, built by Mexican painter Diego Rivera to resemble a Mesoamerican pyramid and filled with his collection of prehispanic artifacts.

NORTHERN MEXICO CITY

Not exactly indigenous, properly speaking, the Basílica de Guadalupe, Mexico's most popular religious shrine, nonetheless has a deep connection to Mexico's prehispanic past. It's hard to believe it was a coincidence that *la virgen morena* (the dark-skinned virgin) appeared on the hill of Tepayac, site of the Aztec shrine to the goddess Tonantzin, almost five centuries ago. It's an amazing sight to witness the humble people from across

Mexico, many of them indigenous, thronging the Basílica, waiting their turn to pray in front of the Virgin. Also in northern Mexico City are two archeological sites, the pre-Aztec pyramid of Tenayuca, dating to at least the 11th century, and the larger Aztec pyramid, Santa Cecilia Acatitlán.

AROUND MEXICO CITY

Most people will make a beeline to Teotihuacán as their first destination outside the city, as well they should. But the adventurous might want to stop at a much less frequented but surprisingly extensive ruin not far away: the Baños de Nezahualcóyotl, on a mountainside near Texcoco. Other ruins not far from Mexico City include the hilltop city of Xochicalco, near Cuernavaca, and the warrior shrine carved into solid rock outside Malinalco. Those interested in Cuauhtémoc, the last Aztec ruler, might want to make a pilgrimage to Ixcateopan, a remote village in the Guerrero mountains, a two-hour drive from Taxco. This was Cuauhtémoc's birthplace, and if you believe local legend, it is also the place where his body was buried after he was killed by the Spanish.

carved serpent head, Templo Mayor

As the crown jewel of the Spanish empire in the New World, Mexico City is filled with monuments to its colonial years. A traveler would be hard pressed to find anywhere in the Americas with more colonial monuments per square meter than the Centro Histórico. Whether you are interested in the architecture or the history, Mexico City has a wealth of interesting colonial sights to explore.

CENTRO HISTÓRICO

Both the Catedral and the Palacio Nacional are classics of religious and civic architecture, but that's just the tip of the iceberg. For a well-hidden display of the flights that religious art took in the baroque era, take a peek into the 18th-century Iglesia de la Enseñanza, with nine dazzling gold-leafed *retablos* (altar pieces) crammed inside the small church. Keep your eyes peeled for the lovely architecture of the old mansions that earned Mexico City its colonial-era sobriquet of *la ciudad de los palacios* (the city of palaces)—like the Palacio de Iturbide, on Moneda, or Casa de los Condes Heras y Soto, at the corner of Chile and Donceles. Three blocks south of the Zócalo you can see the final resting place of

© ELENA PAPPAS

The Catedral can be seen in the background of the Templo Mayor.

the man who started it all, Hernán Cortés—the enigmatic and much-maligned Spaniard who conquered Mexico—marked by a simple plaque near the altar of the Iglesia de Jesús Nazareno, reputedly the spot where he first met Aztec Emperor Moctezuma on that fateful day in 1519.

REFORMA/CHAPULTEPEC

For those interested in the history of the Spanish conquest, it's possible to trace the route of the Spanish soldiers as they fled the city in panic during the *noche triste* (sad night) in 1520 after an attack by the Aztecs. Follow Calle Tacuba west from the Zócalo, and once past the Alameda you'll be atop what was once the Aztec causeway across the lake, over which the Spaniards ran for their lives. A few kilometers west still stands (if you can believe it) the burned-out trunk of the Árbol de la Noche Triste, the very same tree that Cortés leaned against and wept when the remaining soldiers reached the mainland to regroup and relaunch their conquest. For a taste of what wealthy Spaniards must have lived like at the height of their empire, take a tour (Sundays only) of the Casa de la Bola, an opulent mansion just south of Chapultepec and restored with period furniture and decorations.

SOUTHERN MEXICO CITY

A trip to the neighborhood of Coyoacán offers a taste of what a colonial suburb might have felt like, with narrow cobblestone streets winding around twin plazas, and with centuries-old churches and houses on all sides. This is where

Cortés had his palace and where he installed La Malinche, the woman who served as his interpreter and lover, and who is an emblematic and enigmatic figure in Mexican history. Similar to Coyoacán, but considerably smaller and less visited, is Tlalpan, situated around a very fine little plaza hidden off backstreets near the highway exit to Cuernavaca. Up in the mountains south of the city, in the park of Desierto de los Leones, is a lovely colonial monastery built as a retreat in the forests by Carmelite monks in the late 18th century.

AROUND MEXICO CITY

Puebla, just over the mountains to the east of Mexico City, was a key Spanish city during the colonial era and is filled with myriad monuments from that time. The Catedral is one of the finest in Mexico, and there's plenty of churches and museums to see, as well as more unusual sites like the Harry Potter–style Biblioteca Palafoxiana (a library). Nearby is Cholula, with even more colonial churches, and Huejotzingo, an early 16th-century monastery with fantastical stone carvings. If you've got a car and feel like an adventure, follow the dirt road beyond Cholula through the village of San Nicolás de los Ranchos up to the Paso de Cortés, the high pass between the great volcanoes of Popocatépetl and Ixtaccíhuatl, the vantage point from where Cortés first saw the Aztec capital of Tenochtitlán below.

a fountain in Coyoacán

COURTESY OF MEXICO TOURISM BOARD/CARLOS SANCHEZ

Any visitor to Mexico will immediately notice the explosions of color everywhere, from the wild decals on a minibus to the elaborate and macabre candy decorations for Día de los Muertos (Day of the Dead). So it's no surprise to find that Mexico City is filled with a variety of art, from postmodern performance art to indigenous-influenced paintings and sculpture. Apart from the museums, art galleries, and sights listed in this book, Metro riders should be sure to keep their eye out for an eclectic selection of painting and photography exhibits in different stations. They change all the time; to find out what's up currently, see www.metro.df.gob.mx/cultura/index.html.

CENTRO HISTÓRICO

Most art lovers will already know all about the famed Diego Rivera mural in the Palacio Nacional, but not as frequently seen are the more than 100 murals by Rivera covering three stories of the Secretaría de Educación Pública building, plenty to sate even the most die-hard fan of the master. For an odd but often very good selection of modern Mexican art, stop into the Galería SCHP, right behind the Catedral; it's a gallery run by the Mexican tax authorities that shows works by artists in lieu of their tax debt—a creative solution indeed.

A good selection of modern art can be found at the Museo José Luis Cuevas, just off the Zócalo, while younger, more alternative artists are frequently on display at the nearby Centro de Arte Alternativo Ex-Santa Teresa and the Laboratorio de Arte Alameda, near the Alameda park.

CHAPULTEPEC

Right on Paseo de la Reforma are two of the premier modern art museums in Mexico City, the Museo Rufino Tamayo and the Museo de Arte Moderno. The Tamayo, founded by the Oaxacan artist famed for his intense use of color, contains his own work, as well as work from his private collection, including paintings by Salvador Dalí, Max Ernst, Willem de Kooning, Joan Miró, and Andy Warhol. The Arte Moderno is one of the best places to see the Mexican greats from the 20th century, in-

cluding Tamayo, Rivera, Siquieros, Dr. Atl, Frida Kahlo, photographer Manuel Álvarez Bravo, and more. A number of high-end galleries are found in Polanco, right north of Chapultepec, where you can see works by more recent artists, like Vicente Rojo and Francisco Toledo.

INSURGENTES SUR

The Roma and Condesa neighborhoods were wealthy enclaves a hundred years ago. They have since declined and are now on their way up again, fast-becoming the epicenter of Mexico City's current art scene. It's here where you'll find galleries like Nina Menocal, Galería OMR, and Art & Idea, showing new artists from Mexico, Latin America, and across the globe. Attending openings at these galleries is a great way to meet people in the local art world. The Casa Lamm, in the Roma, is a cultural institute of sorts. It has exhibits, offers a number of art courses, and features a top-notch library. Architecture fans can't miss the Casa Barragán, the house designed by Luis Barragán; it was recently designated a UNESCO World Heritage Site.

SOUTHERN MEXICO CITY

Coyoacán is home to the Museo Frida Kahlo, a must-see for aficionados of the great artist and wife of Diego Rivera. This unusual blue house contains the kitchen, study, and living rooms as the

La Giganta at the Museo José Luis Cuevas

artist kept them, and on the walls hang a number of paintings by herself, her husband, and other modern artists, as well as many indigenous handicrafts and artworks. Her husband's counterpart is the Museo Estudio Diego Rivera, in San Ángel. For an even larger collection of works by Kahlo and Rivera, head to the Museo Dolores Olmedo, in a beautiful colonial building in Xochimilco. Another top-notch art museum is the Museo de Arte Carrillo Gil, in San Ángel, with a collection of Mexico's modernists to rival the Arte Moderno in Chapultepec.

Explore Mexico City

Sights

Considering its rich culture and eventful history, it's no surprise that Mexico City has an almost overwhelming number of destinations to interest visitors. Start off down in the Centro, the ancient island capital of the Aztecs, where you can walk to the spot where Cortés and Moctezuma met that fateful day in 1519, and then see the result of that meeting a couple of blocks away in the ruins of the Templo Mayor, right next to the Catedral.

There's hundreds of ornate buildings from the colonial era in the Centro and throughout the city, from old monasteries to baroque churches and sumptuous palaces built by silver barons—even haciendas that used to be on farmland but now sit stranded within the city, islands of the past. And there's plenty of ingenious modern architecture to see too, like the modernist buildings at the national university, covered in three-dimensional murals, or a little gem of a house built by architect Luis Barragán, declared a UNESCO World Heritage Site in 2004.

But Mexico City isn't just about seeing monuments and buildings. This is one of the most vibrant cities in the world, with one of the most colorful arrays of cultures and subcultures you're ever likely to run across. Check out the ancient printing presses, where low-budget scribes still write love letters for hire on the Plaza Santo Domingo; go listen to sequined mariachis at Garibaldi; or go watch the faithful pray at the feet of Mexico's most sacred national symbol, La Virgen de Guadalupe.

Mexico City's Best

Look for **N** to find the sights you can't miss.

N **Must-see Square:** Since it was founded as the ancient Aztec island capital Tenochtitlán in 1325, the **Zócalo,** a broad, empty square, has been the center of the city. The square is surrounded by some of the most important monuments in the city: the ruins of the Aztec Templo Mayor, the Catedral, and the Palacio Nacional (page 27).

N **Best View:** Take an elevator ride up to the top of the 142-meter **Torre Latinoamericana,** located right next to Bellas Artes in the Centro. From the 38th floor observation deck, with coin-operated telescopes, catch a bird's-eye view of the rooftops of central Mexico City, and if air quality permits, the surrounding mountains (page 35).

N **Best Murals:** A block north of the Zócalo is the **Antiguo Colegio de San Ildefonso,** where the mural movement began in 1922. Here a group of talented young painters, including Diego Rivera, José Clemente Orozco, and David Alfaro Siqueiros, decorated the walls of this exceptionally beautiful colonial-era building with their murals (page 37).

N **Most Ornate Colonial Art:** A small church just off the Zócalo, **Iglesia de la Enseñanza,** has a fine carved facade. But the real reason for a visit here is for the nine baroque *retablos* (altarpieces) lining the walls inside the church (page 39).

N **Best Museum:** One of the finest museums of its kind in the world, the **Museo Nacional de Antropología e Historia** is a seemingly endless collection of archaeological artifacts, from the huge and austere carved stone Olmec heads to the dazzlingly artwork of the Zapotecs (page 58).

N **Best Neighborhood Park:** In the hip Colonia Condesa, **Parque México** is an oval-shaped little eden, just a couple of blocks from the bustling Avenida Insurgentes. Bring a newspaper or book, grab a coffee at one of the corner cafés, and take a bench on one of the quiet walkways (page 67).

A *trajinera* glides down a canal at Xochimilco.

N **Best Hidden Gem:** Just west of the Condesa, the **Casa de la Bola** still stands in the Tacubaya neighborhood, which used to be a wealthy suburb hundreds of years ago. Step off the busy avenues through the almost hidden front door of this 17th-century home and you'll be transported back to those years in an instant (page 68).

N **Best Walking Route:** In the center of Coyoacán you'll find lovely cobblestone streets lined with colonial mansions in all directions. One of the best routes is the stroll between two beautiful and quiet little squares, **Plaza y Capilla de la Conchita** (page 73) and **Parque Santa Catarina** (page 74).

N **Best Place for a Boat Ride:** For a true Mexican-style party, take an afternoon trip down to **Xochimilco** in the south of the city. Here you can rent a *trajinera* (small boat) that will take you and your friends for a relaxed ride along tree-lined canals. Mariachis will float by on their own boats, happy to strike up a cheery tune for a small fee (page 77).

N **Best Place to Get Some Fresh Air:** The pine-forested mountains of **Desierto de los Leones** is a great place to take a long walk through the woods or go horseback riding. Set in a forest grove in the park is a lovely old monastery, now open for tourists to visit (page 84).

Mexico City is a fantastic city to walk in. Basically all the neighborhoods covered in this book are excellent for wandering on foot, although moving between them sometimes requires a taxi, bus, or Metro ride. In particular, places like the Centro, Roma, Condesa, and Coyoacán are perfect for strolling through at a relaxed pace, with narrow streets, parks, and plenty of fine historic architecture. And the weather is almost always amenable, with daytime temperatures usually in the comfortable 65–75° F (although you might want an umbrella in case of an afternoon shower in the spring–summer rainy season).

TIPS FOR TOURING

Mexico City's 2,240-meter elevation makes it one of the highest capitals in the world. If you're bothered by the altitude, go easy on strenuous activity for the first couple of days. Headaches, mild fatigue, and mild stomach upset may be symptoms of altitude sickness; doctors suggest staying away from alcoholic drinks and eating lightly for those first days.

Two different types of government-sponsored tours provide very good and reasonably priced ways to see the city and learn more about it.

Turibus (www.turibus.com.mx) is a new bus service that makes circuits frequently throughout the day among the main tourist neighborhoods in the city on bright red double-decker buses. A one-day pass costs $10, and you can get on and off as many times as you like. Three-day passes are $18. The buses, which start their circuit right in front of the Auditorio Nacional, run 9 A.M.–9 P.M. daily.

Paseos Culturales offers very informative tours in Mexico City and other parts of the country. The tours are guided by experts in archeology and history and are run by the Instituto Nacional de Antropología e Historia (INAH, tel. 5553-2365 or 5553-3822, www.inah.gob.mx). Mexico City trips typically cost $22 per day (8 A.M.–2 P.M.), with transportation, guide, and entrance fee to sites included. Examples of frequent tours include the streets of the Centro Histórico, colonial-era convents in the city, and the Templo Mayor and Palacio Nacional. All the prescheduled trips are in Spanish, but special trips can be arranged with English-speaking guides for groups (minimum 10 people). At last check, information on the tours was only on the Spanish version of the website, not on the English version.

Centro Histórico

When the Aztecs first arrived in the Valle de México, they were forced to settle on a small island in the center of the great lake, as most of the more desirable land on the lake's shores was already populated by other tribes. This small island, known as Tenochtitlán, became the Aztec capital, and later the center of Spanish Mexico. As the centuries passed and the lakes and canals were gradually filled in and covered over, the Centro was physically joined to the rest of the city, but the rough outlines of the old island are still apparent, bordered on the west by Eje Central Lázaro Cárdenas, the north by Eje 1 Norte, the south by Avenida Izazaga or San Pablo, and the east by Avenida Circunvalación.

The downtown area, centered on the broad, wide-open Zócalo, is jam-packed with centuries-old palaces and churches—some crumbling to bits, others recently renovated—as well as museums, banks, and one of the city's main shopping districts. In any European city, an ancient central area would have long since been renovated, cleaned up, and gentrified, but despite the oft-stated plans of successive city governments, the Centro remains a chaotic place of crowded sidewalks, street vendors, political rallies, tourists both Mexican and foreign, peasants from the countryside, bustling office workers, and who knows who else. Not for nothing do locals jokingly call it the "Centro Histérico" (Hysterical Center).

In the summer of 2001, President Vicente Fox and Mexico City Mayor Andrés Manuel López Obrador jointly announced a plan to "rescue" the Centro. While the Centro is still fairly rough around the edges, especially once you get out of the main touristed areas, improvements are noticeable in the few years since the plan was announced. Particularly impressive is the transformation of Avenida Juárez on the south side of the Alameda, where a new Sheraton hotel (the only real luxury hotel in the downtown area) and a widened pedestrian walkway has anchored the redevelopment of the area. A number of colonial-era Centro buildings are also being renovated; for an example of one, take a look at the Centro Cultural de España at Guatemala 18, behind the Catedral.

But rest assured that the Centro will not soon lose its disheveled charm. This is still a living neighborhood, with busy commercial and residential districts, especially east and north of the Zócalo, populated by a thriving lower-middle class community renowned throughout Mexico for their street smarts and cynical good humor, and the reputed origin of many classic Mexican slang words. Taxis throng, buses honk, vendors hawk their wares at the top of their lungs, and pedestrians scurry in all directions. And just when you're being overwhelmed with the relentless urbanity of it all, you'll step off the street into the cool, blissfully calm courtyard of some colonial palace covered with marvelous stone carvings and wonder how this spot could be in the middle of such a city.

No matter how short your stay, at least a brief visit to the Centro is obligatory to taste the ambience of Mexico's ancient capital.

ORIENTATION

The Centro is a compact area, and its narrow streets and traffic make driving a major headache, so walking is unquestionably the best way to go. Should all the pavement-pounding wear you out, consider hopping onto one of the many bicycle taxis cruising round the Centro; they will charge $2–3 to peddle you from one destination to the next.

The sites in this section are divided into five walking tours, the first around the Zócalo and the other four through the neighborhoods in

each direction from the Zócalo. Needless to say, readers will have their own ideas of what they would like to visit and should arrange their walks accordingly.

Watching Your Step

Most tourists will likely limit their explorations to the few blocks surrounding the Zócalo and the streets running west toward the Alameda park. Many historic buildings are in this district, and the streets are cleaner and less crowded than in other parts of the Centro. The area southwest of the Zócalo, between Avenidas Madero and Izazaga, is a bit run-down and bustling with small businesses, but it hides a few minor treasures of colonial and 19th-century architecture, and it is generally safe for walking around.

But not too far beyond these areas, the neighborhoods generally take a turn for the dirtier and more crowded. Not all foreign (or even Mexican) visitors will feel comfortable on some blocks to the north of the Zócalo past República de Venezuela, northwest between the Plaza Santo Domingo and Plaza Garibaldi, and east past Loreto and Jesús María. It's not necessarily dangerous to venture out in these directions, in the day at least, but go with your wits (and not your camera) about you. It's not a great idea to walk past the north side of Eje 1 Norte (into the Tepito neighborhood, famed as the haunt of smugglers and thieves), east of Eje 1 Oriente Circunvalación, and south of Fray Servando Teresa de Mier. The only reason to venture out this way would be to get a taste of the seamier side of street life in the Centro, as almost all of the main historical sites are close to the Zócalo.

Getting There and Getting Away

If you're not staying in a downtown hotel already, chances are you'll be somewhere near Paseo de la Reforma, Polanco, or another neighborhood to the west and south. The easiest and quickest way to get to the Centro is via Metro to one of the downtown stations: Zócalo (obviously the most central), Allende, Bellas Artes, San Juan de Letrán, Salto de Agua, Isabel la Católica, Pino Suárez, or Garibaldi.

By car, you can reach the Centro Histórico either (from the west) along Paseo de la Reforma, then turning onto Avenida Juárez past the Alameda, and crossing into the Centro on Avenida Madero; or (from the south) by coming up Eje Central Lázaro Cárdenas and taking a right turn (east) on Avenida Madero. It's a bit less expensive to park the car in one of the lots on the south side of the Alameda (for example, on Revillagigedo, Luis Moya, or Dolores Streets) than in lots closer to the Zócalo. Two decent parking lots in the Centro which can be entered and left easily, even in traffic, can be found on Avenida Cinco de Mayo between Isabel la Católica and Bolívar just west of Café La Blanca, and on República del Salvador just east of Bolívar.

If you come downtown in a taxi, probably the easiest place to get off is at the corner of Juárez and the Eje Central, right in front of the Palacio de Bellas Artes. During the day, traffic can be heavy closer in toward the Zócalo, making it easier to get out and walk.

HISTORY

Until the mid-19th century, Mexico City essentially *was* the Centro Histórico. It was in this roughly 10-kilometer square area, surrounded by the shallow waters of Lago Texcoco, that the Aztecs first founded Tenochtitlán in the early 14th century, and in turn it was where the Spaniards erected their colonial capital after the conquest in 1521.

The Aztec city was divided into four *calpulli,* self-governing districts grouping several different clans, located in each quadrant of the city. At the intersection of the four districts was the broad central square, flanked by the Templo Mayor complex and the palaces of the Aztec nobility. Four causeways connected the island city to the mainland: Tacuba, to the west; Tenayuca, northwest; Tepeyac, to the north; and Ixtapalapa, to the south.

Although its buildings were utterly destroyed during the Spanish siege, the basic street plan of the old city was nonetheless mostly preserved by Alonso García Bravo, who supervised the construction of the new colonial capital in 1521–1522. The Aztec central square became the new Plaza Mayor, with the government palaces and the Catedral alongside. Many of the wealthier conquistadors built their mansions along Calle Tacuba, to the west of the plaza, while the powerful missionary orders erected huge complexes all over the city. The poor, both mestizo and Amerindian, were left to their own devices to raise ramshackle warrens of shacks to the east and south of downtown (areas more prone to flooding during the annual rainy season).

By the time of independence from Spain, city authorities had relocated the markets from the Plaza Mayor to La Merced, a neighborhood surrounding the convent of the same name a few blocks southeast of the plaza. La Merced was Mexico's largest marketplace until the Central de Abastos opened in 1992. Commerce also began invading the streets around Plaza Santo Domingo and near Tacuba, northwest of the Zócalo, driving the wealthiest residents to the new "in" street farther south, Plateros, now named Francisco I. Madero.

Armed by the Reform Laws of 1857, which dispossessed the once-mighty religious orders of their properties, city planners ordered the destruction of large chunks of the Centro's many convents and monasteries to lay down new streets such as Cinco de Mayo, Gante, Belisario Domínguez, and others, giving the Centro the street plan it has today.

When Mexico City finally started expanding beyond the boundaries of the original island, and as Lago Texcoco began seriously shrinking in the mid-19th century, the city's elite were not slow to flee the increasingly crowded Centro to the new suburbs. By the end of the Mexican Revolution, in 1920, most of the wealthiest families had long since relocated to the mansions along Paseo de la Reforma or the Roma. The largest merchants and textile producers in La Merced—many of whom were Syrians, Lebanese, and Jews—had by the 1940s moved out to Roma, Condesa, and later Polanco.

The colonial mansions in the Centro were quickly taken over by the flood of new immigrants coming in from the countryside in the boom years after World War II. But rather than housing one family, as before, the erstwhile palaces now sheltered whole communities. The rent freeze in the 1940s sealed the fate of the Centro, as all the landlords got out as soon as possible and left their buildings to decay.

Successive city governments have promised great things with regard to renovating and rejuvenating the Centro, particularly after it was declared a World Heritage Site by UNESCO in 1987. Progress, however, has been very limited, and city officials are forthright in saying they simply have no money for major work. Much of the downtown area is still inhabited by low-income families and small-scale retail businesses, although the recent spate of colonial building renovations and an upswing in property values in the Centro may point to the beginnings of a regentrification. But if that does happen—and it's a big "if"—you can be sure the Centro will never lose its manic, magic urban energy.

IN AND AROUND THE ZÓCALO

The Zócalo

Also called the Plaza de la Constitución, the Zócalo is the second-largest public plaza in the world after Red Square in Moscow. For most of the past two centuries it was lined with trees and grass (as are most plazas in Mexico). Now it's completely empty, save for the flagpole in the center. Although certainly a bit spartan, this massive open square in the very center of one of the most crowded environments on the globe makes a powerful spatial statement. Mexicans regularly fill the plaza for political rallies and protest demonstrations, or just to enjoy a sunny afternoon.

The Zócalo has formed the heart of Mexico City since the founding of the original Tenochtitlán in 1325. During the height of the Aztec empire, the space frequently served as a site for dances and celebrations, in addition to being the second most important market in the city. On the northeast corner towered the Templo Mayor, while the palaces of Aztec rulers lined the sides of the plaza. The causeways leading off the island of

THE EMPTY PEDESTAL

Shortly after independence from Spain in 1821, Mexico City's central square acquired its popular name, Zócalo, which is also often used for the main plazas in many other Mexican towns. Historians agree the name derives from a pedestal (*zócalo* is an Arabic-derived Spanish word) that stood empty on the plaza for many years in the 19th century, but they disagree on what did or did not stand on the pedestal.

One camp maintains that the mercurial dictator Santa Anna ordered a monument to independence from Spain built in the 1830s, but that in the chaos of his erratic administration, only the pedestal was built.

Others say the pedestal was originally occupied by *El Caballito,* that peripatetic equestrian statue of Spanish King Carlos IV now standing in front of the Museo Nacional de Arte. The statue was originally erected in the plaza in 1803, but it was hastily removed shortly after the independence movement triumphed, leaving the pedestal behind. Perhaps Santa Anna didn't even get the pedestal built but merely wanted to use the one left behind from *El Caballito.*

Either way, the pedestal is long gone, but the name remains.

Tenochtitlán to the north, west, and south began at the plaza and are now paved over by the avenues of República de Brasil, Tacuba, and 20 de Noviembre, respectively.

After the Spanish took over the Zócalo during the colonial years, the import merchants of El Parian market and secondhand traders of El Baratillo flea market filled the space. As in Aztec times, the square remained the city's main meeting place and was a center of constant activity. By the end of the 18th century, the Zócalo was surrounded by the same buildings that flank it today: the Catedral Metropolitana on the north side, the Palacio Virreinal (now Palacio Nacional) on the east, the Palacio del Ayuntamiento (City Hall) on the south, and the merchants' arcades on the west. The only new building raised since that time is a second city hall building, the easterly of the two, built between 1941 and 1948. Just off the southeast corner of the Zócalo stood the smaller Plaza Volador, which housed a market of its own and also served as the city's bullfighting ring. The Suprema Corte de Justicia (Supreme Court) building now occupies this spot.

The liberal-minded Emperor Maximilian banished the markets and tried to create his vision of a Parisian park in Mexico, replete with tree-lined walks, benches, and a wrought-iron kiosk in the center. With many modifications, the trees remained through the years of Porfirio Díaz, who

EL GRITO

To see the Zócalo at its most vibrant (or most chaotic, depending on your point of view), join the thousands of Mexicans who gather each year to watch the president stand on the balcony of the Palacio Nacional and shout *¡Viva México!* just before midnight each September 15, commemorating Padre Hidalgo's famous launch of the struggle for independence from Spain in 1810.

For the first decades after independence in 1821, Hidalgo was reviled by many (particularly Mexico's elite) as a rabble rouser, and his ill-fated rebellion was hardly the stuff of official myth. But in 1896 the legendary dictator Porfirio Díaz saw fit to rehabilitate Hidalgo by shouting the first official *Grito* in Mexican history. According to historians, Hidalgo's original shout was *"Vive la Virgen de Guadalupe y mueran los gachupines!"* (Long live the Virgin of Guadalupe and death to the Spaniards!), but Díaz thought it more diplomatic to shout, *"¡Viva México! ¡Vivan los héroes de la Patria! ¡Viva la República!"*

It may seem odd that the *Grito* happens on September 15 at midnight, when Independence Day is September 16. As it turns out, Don Porfirio took a slight liberty with the dates, since his birthday was September 15.

The *Grito* has since become one of the main political ceremonies of the year. The scene in the square during and after the *Grito* is reminiscent of New Year's Eve in Times Square, *a la mexicana*. If you go, be fully prepared to be plastered by the harmless shaving cream everyone is throwing around in jest.

took pains to cultivate European styles. To achieve its current vaguely social-realist monumental style, the Zócalo was cleared shortly after the 1910–1920 revolution, perhaps in homage to the Soviet Red Square.

Now a towering flagpole in the center is the square's only ornamentation. In strict military drill, a contingent of goose-stepping guards, in full battle gear, issue from the Palacio Nacional and then raise (in the morning) or lower (at sunset) a huge Mexican flag daily. The folding of the gigantic tricolor takes a half-dozen soldiers a full 15 minutes to accomplish and is accompanied by a fanfare of drums, bugles, and flugelhorns.

The city government has considered adding a row of trees along one side of the plaza, but that's yet to transpire. Even if it does, the Zócalo is unlikely ever to become just another one of the innumerable tree-lined plazas in Mexican cities, if only because Mexicans love taking advantage of this irresistible void in the center of one of the most populated cities on earth. Every day the plaza gathers a crowd of locals, tourists, street vendors, political activists, beggars, people looking for work, Aztec dancers, clowns, and much else besides.

The **Aztec dancers** perform most days, but always on weekends and also on certain celebration dates: August 13, the day Tenochtitlán fell to the Spaniards; September 21, the fall equinox; November 1 and 2, Días de los Muertos; December 21, the winter solstice; March 21, the spring equinox; and June 21, the summer solstice.

For good, wide-angle views of the square, have a meal at the balcony restaurant of the Hotel Majestic or Holiday Inn on the west side. The Hotel Majestic won't let you stay just for drinks, unless you're very persuasive and it's not crowded, but the Holiday Inn is more relaxed.

The *portales* (archways) on the southwest side of the plaza often shelter temporary displays of paintings or photography.

The government has installed a tourist information booth on the Zócalo, on the west side of the Catedral (left side as you face it); there, you can find maps and other information.

Catedral Metropolitana

In some ways the Zócalo, impressive though it may be, is but a stage for the magnificent Catedral. The government and private palaces pressed up against one another on the other three sides of the plaza seem merely the audience, as it were, to the Catedral's immense architectural performance.

The largest colonial cathedral in the Americas, the current Catedral stands on the site of a more humble chapel built by the Spanish conquistadors in 1524, immediately following the conquest of Tenochtitlán. Intended to symbolically replace the Aztec Templo Mayor, the first church was erected with the rubble of the temple and other buildings destroyed during the Spanish assault.

The rather modest size of Mexico's first cathedral prompted the colonists to develop plans for a structure more suitable to their idea of the city's greatness. Work on the foundations alone

took 42 years, and the church would end up taking fully two and a half centuries to complete, from 1573 to 1813.

Because the Catedral took so long to build, different architects and changing architectural fashions left their mark in the building's interior and exterior ornamentation, which include elements of gothic, baroque, churrigueresque, and neoclassical styles. Despite the apparently eclectic mix, the church's styles come together with remarkable harmony. The north side of the Catedral, facing the plaza, is a perfect example: The exuberant baroque facades of the main church and the adjacent Sagrario chapel seem tempered and balanced by the more austere neoclassical flanking towers and central clock tower, built in the late 18th and early 19th centuries.

Exterior: Built in the shape of a Latin cross, the cathedral's floor plan measures 109 meters

BENEATH THE CATEDRAL

Recent archaeological and geological studies indicate that the Catedral is built over the site of a small spring, which may be why Aztecs chose the location as the center of their city when they first moved to the small island of Tenochtitlán. Thus, in what could be construed as unintended Aztec revenge on the Spanish for building the cathedral with stones from their destroyed temple, the Catedral stands on particularly weak, fissured ground.

Over the centuries the massive weight of the cathedral has forced the ground beneath to compress. The Catedral's slight tilt, easily visible if you look at the monument from the opposite side of the Zócalo, indicates how this geologic handicap has placed stress on its structure. Because of the irregularity of the soil, the compression has occurred unevenly, causing some parts of the building to sink more than others.

In a vain effort to halt the subsidence, a steel grid was placed underneath the cathedral's floor in 1940, and when that didn't help, new pilings were sunk to supposedly firmer subsoil 40 meters below the church. That didn't stop the sinking either, and by 1988 government authorities had wrapped the cathedral's columns in metal bands

and erected braces and scaffolding to ensure the building didn't collapse outright.

At the same time, architectural engineers began an excavation project beneath the foundation, drilling 32 holes 25 meters deep and carefully digging to the side in selected spots. The theory was to cause "high points" in the subsoil to collapse, and thus allow the cathedral to settle evenly. This was the same technique used at the famously leaning tower at Pisa, in Italy.

By late 1999, engineers estimated that different points of the cathedral floor were sinking at a maximum differential of 4–6 millimeters per year, rather than a previously measured 1.8 centimeters. The floor of the building is now about as close to "true" as it was in the 1930s. And as the fissures in the subsoil close, the sinking rate will continue to slow, meaning the cathedral's structure is likely to undergo less stress than in previous years.

As a result of the project, much of the scaffolding that has for years impeded the full admiration of one of the greatest example of Catholic architecture in the world has been removed, although metal supporting bands remain around the columns.

long and 54 meters wide. The rear-facing northern facade was the first to be completed, followed by the eastern and western side facades, all done in Renaissance style, with just a few suggestions of baroque flair. The baroque front facade, finished in 1689, has one principal entrance and two side entrances, each flanked with columns and topped with a sculpted marble relief on the second level. In niches between the columns adjacent to the central portal are statues of St. Pedro and St. Pablo, while St. Andrés and St. Jaime above frame a relief depicting the Asunción de la Virgen (Assumption of the Virgin).

The side towers, measuring 67 meters, were designed by Mexican architect José Damián Ortiz de Castro and completed in 1790, while the central clock tower and dome were finished by Valenciana architect Manuel Tolsá in 1813.

Interior: The cathedral's cavernous interior contains a total of five naves, 14 side chapels, a central choir, and a sacristy, as well as a quantity of artistic detail that is almost impossible to fully absorb.

Upon entering the cathedral, visitors first come upon the golden Altar de Perdón (the Altar of Forgiveness) in the central nave, carved by Andalusian Jerónimo de Balbás. The altar, along with the choir behind it, was damaged in a 1967 fire but has since been restored. The sculpted black Christ at the center of the altar has taken the place of a painting of the Virgen María, destroyed in the fire. The baroque choir, designed by Juan de Rojas, is made of cedar, while the metal latticework is a mix of gold, silver, and copper; it was cast in China.

The central altar at the front of the Catedral, the Altar de los Reyes (Altar of the Kings) houses a 25-meter-high golden *retablo* (altarpiece) decorated in such ornate baroque complexity that it's difficult for the eye even to begin to notice individual sculptures. The carvings, showing a veritable army of saints, cherubim, and other religious figures, were executed by Jerónimo de Balbás, while Francisco Martínez was responsible for covering the work in gold leaf. Note the odd, squared-off *estípite* columns, one of the first uses of churrigueresque elements in Mexico. The two paintings, both by Mexican

painter Juan Rodríguez Juárez (1675–1728), depict the Three Wise Men paying homage to the baby Jesús (below) and the Asunción de la Virgen (above).

The 14 side chapels all date from the 17th century. The Capilla de los Ángeles is particularly impressive artistically, with its high baroque altarpiece and painting of San Miguel. The Capilla de San Felipe de Jesús is dedicated to Mexico's first saint, a missionary martyred in Japan, and contains a vase with the remains of Mexican Emperor Agustín de Iturbide (1783–1824), the country's often denigrated leader in defeating the Spaniards in the war of independence.

Sagrario

Adjacent to the main church is the Sagrario, built between 1749 and 1768 by Spaniard Lorenzo Rodríguez. The white sculpted front of the Sagrario, considered by many to be the definitive churrigueresque facade in Mexico (though other art historians place the churrigueresque facade of the cathedral in Zacatecas at the top), is offset

© ELENA PAPPAS

The Catedral (background) was built in part with stones taken from the Aztec Templo Mayor (foreground).

by flanking walls made with blocks of deep red *tezontle,* a volcanic stone. Closed for 10 years for repairs, the Sagrario reopened its doors in 2001 and now holds regular Masses. The bare, rather unimaginative altars (the originals were destroyed long ago by fire) don't compare to the magnificent exterior. A replica of the Virgen de Guadalupe painting is worth taking a look at, especially if you don't have the time or inclination to make the trip up to see the original at the Basílica de Guadalupe in the north of the city.

Templo Mayor de Tenochtitlán

At the time Cortés first laid eyes on the Templo Mayor (Teocalli to the Aztecs) in 1519, the holiest shrine in Tenochtitlán had been rebuilt at least six times and consisted of a walled complex of 78 buildings built on different levels, crowned with two tall pyramids. One was intended to symbolize the sacred hill of Coatepec, birthplace of the capricious and violent god Huitzilopochtli, while the other represented the hill of Tonacatepetl and was dedicated to the rain god Tlaloc. Each pyramid, in turn, was crowned with a small temple containing statues of the two gods. The Spanish conquistadors, on first entering the temples, were overwhelmed with righteous disgust at the gloomy atmosphere and insisted to the captive Emperor Moctezuma II that the temples be destroyed.

To the Aztecs, the ritual sacrifices in the temple complex represented a key event in their mythology—namely, when the new god Huitzilopochtli slew his sister Coyolxuahqui, the moon goddess, on Coatepec, and cast her body down to the foot of the hill. Some anthropologists have suggested this myth represented a changeover in Aztec politics from a society dominated by women to one ruled by men.

The rubble of the temple, which was razed during the battle for Tenochtitlán, served as building material for the cathedral and other buildings when the Spaniards rebuilt the city, and the remains of the temple were buried over and mostly forgotten. In 1911, 1933, and 1948, minor archaeological work uncovered remnants of the temple and some sculptures. Then in 1978 workers excavating for the Metro uncovered by chance an eight-ton round rock slab covered with carvings of the moon goddess Coyolxuahqui. The carving is now on display in the temple museum.

This magnificent work of art, found behind the Catedral near the corner of the streets República de Argentina and República de Guatemala, prompted authorities to begin a major archaeological project. After demolishing four city blocks over several years of excavations, archaeologists had uncovered a wealth of artifacts from the Aztec era.

A path leads visitors around the reconstructed foundations of the temple to view sculptures and faded murals. The **Museo de Templo Mayor** (entrance on Seminario 8, on the east side of the Catedral, tel. 5542-4943 or 5542-4784, www.conaculta.gob.mx/templomayor, 9 A.M.–5 P.M. Tues.–Sun., $4 admission to ruins and museum, $3.50 extra for a video camera), alongside the temple, displays a model of the Aztec city and some 7,000 artifacts found at the site, including life-sized statues of eagle warriors standing menacingly over the skulls of their victims. The museum is an oddly spartan building designed by Pedro Ramírez Vázquez of Museo de Antropología fame.

Palacio Nacional

Originally one of Hernán Cortés's many residences, this palace of red *tezontle* blocks stands on the site of Aztec Emperor Moctezuma II's castle, on the east side of the Zócalo. Martín Cortés, son of the conquistador, sold the palace to the crown in 1562, after which it became the Palacio Virreinal (Viceregal Palace), the main seat of colonial authority in Nueva España. Prochurch, antiviceroy rioters destroyed the first building in 1624, and the current palace was built in 1628. Emperor Maximilian modified it significantly during his brief reign (1864–1867), giving it much of its current European flavor. President Plutarco Elias Calles ordered the addition of a third floor and further modifications to the facade in 1926.

In 1810 Padre Miguel Hidalgo rang the bell now hanging above the main entrance as he uttered his *grito* (shout) for Mexican independence

© ELENA PAPPAS

fountain inside the Palacio Nacional

Though the Palacio (9 A.M.–5 P.M. daily, free admission) is the official residence of the Mexican president, recent presidents have opted to spend most of their time in a second residence, known as Los Pinos, in the Bosque de Chapultepec.

Visitors are required to show a photo identification on entering the building. A driver's license will do if you don't want to bring your passport. No flash photography is allowed. The restrooms on the ground floor make a convenient, clean pit stop in your downtown tour.

Nacional Monte de Piedad

On the west side of the Zócalo, this government-run pawnshop (whose name means Mountain of Mercy) has for more than two centuries offered low-interest loans to the needy. In times of economic crisis—not an uncommon situation during the last 30 years in Mexico—people line the surrounding blocks waiting to put their jewelry, musical instruments, and other personal possessions in hock for a loan.

Monte de Piedad (7 Calle Monte de Piedad, tel. 5518-2206, 8:30 A.M.–6 P.M. Mon.–Fri., 8:30 A.M.–1 P.M. Sat.) sits over the site of another of Cortés's palaces, which in turn was built on the remains of Moctezuma I's residence. Cortés's huge original palace, which covered several city blocks, was divided up and sold in 1615, and the current structure was built in 1775 by Pedro Romero de Terreros, owner of the fabulously wealthy Regla silver mines near Pachuca. After independence from Spain, the government took over the building.

Lining the sidewalk along the same block as Monte de Piedad are dozens of men and women standing in front of private pawn shops, their windows filled with jewelry and trinkets, calling out to the passing crowd *"¿Algo le vende?"* (Something to sell?).

from Spain in the Guanajuato town of Dolores. President Porfirio Díaz moved the bell to the palace in 1896 and started the tradition of ringing the bell every year on September 15, just before midnight.

Between 1929 and 1935, Diego Rivera painted one of his best-known murals on the walls above the palace's central staircase. Divided into three parts, the mural is Rivera's vision of Mexican history, arranged chronologically right to left. The right-hand panel shows Aztec life before the conquest, while the central wall traces Mexico's history from the brutal conquest and colonial era, through independence from Spain, to the bloody revolution in 1910–1920. The left-hand mural depicts Rivera's socialist view of Mexico's capitalist milieu and the inevitable workers' revolution yet to come.

On the walls of the 2nd-floor corridor, Rivera painted a further eight mural panels between 1941 and 1952 to illustrate idealized aspects of Mexico's prehispanic life, and a ninth depicts the arrival of Cortés.

WEST OF THE ZÓCALO

The corridor of streets between the Zócalo and the Alameda was, during most of the city's post-Aztec history, the Centro Histórico's most posh district. Although the city's wealthy have long since departed this neighborhood, it remains a more upscale area than other parts of the city center, and it is a favorite place for visitors to tour on foot.

While some older buildings have deteriorated or been replaced by poorly made modern structures or parking lots, much of the architecture remains remarkably intact. Because of its storied history and constant development, the buildings in this neighborhood—the colonial churches of La Profesa and San Francisco, the baroque Palacio de Iturbide and Casa de los Azulejos, the neoclassical Palacio de Minería, and the all-over-the-board Palacio Postal—represent a cross-section of the city's architectural styles. The Museo Nacional de Arte is worth a visit, both to admire the fine building and to tour the museum's collection of Mexican art, and several cafés and bars offer places to rest after tromping around. Unlike many other parts of the Centro, these streets are generally safe after dark and are no problem at all during the day.

West on Tacuba from the Zócalo

Walk from the Zócalo on Calle Tacuba, the route of one of the ancient Aztec causeways that used to leave the island city. One block west, take a one-block detour north on República de Chile to the corner of Donceles to admire one of the finest colonial palaces in the city, the **Casa de los Condes de Heras y Soto.** With exceptionally well-carved reliefs decorating the exterior, the building houses the offices of the Fideicomiso del Centro Histórico, an organization dedicated to restoring the downtown area. Visitors may enter and admire the courtyard 9 A.M.–6 P.M. Mon.–Fri. Around the corner, the block of Donceles between República de Chile and Palma is a secondhand book emporium of sorts, with around 10 shops on both sides of the street.

Further along Tacuba, you'll pass the pedestrian street Calle Motolinía. Depending on how much the city government has been cracking down on *ambulantes,* or street vendors, a lively market sometimes fills the block of Motolinía between Tacuba and Cinco de Mayo. Just before Avenida Bolívar, you'll pass the **Ex-Convento y Iglesia de Santa Clara,** which now houses the Biblioteca del Congreso (Library of Congress) and is open to the public.

Plaza Manuel Tolsá

Just before Tacuba reaches the Eje Central, there is a small square flanked by two imposing neoclassical buildings and crowned with a bronze equestrian statue of Spanish King Carlos IV. The statue and one of the buildings are the works of Manuel Tolsá, an architect and artist from Valencia, Spain, who came to Mexico City in 1791 to direct the Academia de San Carlos. On the plaza is the Museo Nacional de Arte, one of the premier colonial art museums in Mexico (See the *Arts and Entertainment* chapter for details).

El Caballito (The Little Horse), as the equestrian statue of Spanish King Carlos IV in Roman garb is popularly known, is probably Tolsá's best-known work. The peripatetic *El Caballito* has traveled around the city with some frequency since it was cast in 1803. Originally it stood in the center of the Zócalo, but after independence from Spain it was then moved to the courtyard of the national university. Then it was moved again to the mouth of Paseo de Bucareli, west of the Alameda. As the city grew and the statue began to look a bit lost amidst all the traffic, the city moved it to its current location in 1979. The huge, bright yellow sculpture now at the beginning of Bucareli is meant to be an abstract vision of the original, although it's not easy to see the resemblance.

Tolsá was a disciple of a severe though elegant neoclassicism, and he strongly rejected the more ornate baroque styles favored in Mexico City up to that time. Dozens of his works, including buildings, paintings, and his oddly cold neoclassical altarpieces (such as those in the La Profesa and Santo Domingo churches), can be seen throughout the city. The frenetically productive Tolsá also found time to finish the Mexico City and Aguascalientes Cathedrals, supervise drainage and running water projects, and lay out Mexico City's first civil cemetery.

Across the street from *El Caballito* is Tolsá's three-story **Palacio de Minería,** built between 1797 and 1813 to house offices governing the colony's most important industry. The building now serves as the engineering school of UNAM, the national university. On one side is a small museum (10 A.M.–7 P.M. Tues.–Sun., admission $1.50) dedicated to Tolsá's life and work. In the main entrance to the building is a collection of meteorites from around Mexico. Guided tours of the entire building in English or Spanish, for a minimum of 10 people, can be arranged by calling tel. 5623-2962.

In a small garden across Palacio and in front of the Museo del Ejército, you'll see three large bronze sculptures of Nezahualcóyotl, Iztcoatl, and Totoquihuatzin—the creators of the Mesoamerican Triple Alliance, which ruled the Valle de México before the arrival of the Spaniards. In the entryway of the museum stands a fourth bronze of the heroic warrior and last Aztec Emperor Cuauhtémoc. The sculptures were fashioned by Mexican artist José Faustino Contreras for Mexico's pavilion at the Paris Universal Exposition in 1898. Contreras badly burned his feet with molten bronze as he cast the Cuauhtémoc piece—a gruesome coincidence, considering that the Spanish had burned the feet of Cuauhtémoc in an effort to force him to reveal the whereabouts of hidden gold.

Palacio Postal

Normally a post office wouldn't make it as a tourist destination, but the old Mexico City "postal palace" is an unusual case. At the corner of Eje Central and Tacuba, the building is a gothic/arabesque palace, with neoclassical, baroque, and art deco elements thrown in for good measure. In a word, eclectic. Designed in 1908 by Italian architect Adamo Boari, who also designed the Palacio de Bellas Artes across the street, the post office (8 A.M.–9 P.M. Mon.–Fri., 8 A.M.–6 P.M. Sat.) is made of a very light, almost translucent stone called *chiluca*. The exterior is covered with all sorts of fine detail, such as the wicked little iron dragon light fixtures and a wealth of stone carving around the windows and at the edge of the roof. The spacious interior is laden with different kinds of marble and much fine metalwork.

Casa de los Azulejos

Two blocks south of the Palacio Postal on Madero is an exceptionally lovely tile-covered colonial mansion known as Casa de los Azulejos (House of Tiles). Originally built in the 16th century, it wasn't until the mid-18th century that the owners covered the exterior with blue Talavera tile

© CHRIS HUMPHREY

ornate central staircase of the Palacio Postal

Sights

from the State of Puebla. As legend has it, the son of one of the owners added the tiles to live down an insult from his father, who told him he would "never build a house of tiles," meaning that he would never amount to anything. Between 1891 and 1914 the house was home to the Jockey Club, the city's most exclusive social club at the time. During the Revolution, the Zapatista army occupied the building, and in 1919 Walter and Frank Sanborn opened a soda fountain, the first of what is now a national chain known simply as Sanborns. The atmospheric patio cafeteria inside is a popular place for Mexicans and foreigners alike to have a meal in luxurious surroundings. Take a walk upstairs to view José Clemente Orozco's 1925 staircase mural *Omniciencia* and to see the porcelain art on the upper floor surrounding the patio.

Ⓜ Torre Latinoamericana

To really get a feel for the immensity of Mexico City, air quality permitting, take an elevator ride to the top of the tallest building in the downtown area (9:30 A.M.–10:30 P.M. daily, admission $3.50 adults, $2.50 kids 11 and under). Although not particularly attractive architecturally, the 182-meter-tall blue and gray tower, built between 1948 and 1956 at the corner of Eje Central and Avenida Madero, is specially designed to handle the earthquake-prone and flexible subsoil. Avoid weekends, when the small area at the top is packed and you'd be lucky to get an open spot to peer through the fence at the city below. Apart from the views across the valley, the tower affords a unique bird's-eye view of the layout of the downtown area. Should you have a particular inclination for seeing fish at high altitude, check out the aquarium on the 38th floor; it costs $2.50 adults, $2 kids 11 and under.

Iglesia y Ex-Convento de San Francisco

Near the western end of Madero, butting up against the back of the Torre Latinoamericana, are the sad, boxed-in remains of what was one of the greatest convents in Mexico City, San Francisco. Built on the site of Moctezuma II's famed

© ELENA PAPPAS

On Avenida Madero is the old Ex-Convento de San Francisco, one of the Centro's many colonial monasteries.

zoo, the Convento de San Francisco and its associated chapels once covered the entire area now enclosed by Bolívar, Madero, Eje Central, and Venustiano Carranza.

After the passing of reform legislation against the Catholic Church in 1857, the Convento de San Francisco, along with other convents in Mexico City, saw their property seized and much of it destroyed to make way for the construction of new roads.

The main Iglesia de San Francisco is actually the third church built on this location, as earlier ones sank in the soft subsoil and had to be torn down. As visitors will notice from the steps leading *down* to the church, the third doesn't appear to be faring much better than the first two.

The church's main facade, dating from 1710, is walled in and thus cannot be seen. Visitors enter by walking through the smaller Capilla de Balvanera, which offers an impressive late baroque facade and a gilded altarpiece dedicated

Sights

to the Virgin. The main church, with a neoclassical, gilded altarpiece and several religious paintings, may be reached through a side door in the Capilla de Balvanera.

Though you wouldn't guess from its uninteresting exterior, the Methodist church at Calle Gante 5 is actually the remains of the San Francisco cloister. The church officials are usually quite friendly and allow visitors to take a look at the old cloister. And on Venustiano Carranza, the Panadería Ideal bakery was built using some of the old walls of the convent. City restoration officials have plans to reconnect some parts of the convent that are now sealed off and open them to the public. Although little progress has been made, a small square has been cleared between the Capilla de Balvanera and the back of the Torre Latinoamerica.

Palacio de Iturbide

Continuing down Madero toward the Zócalo stands a former colonial palace, built in 1780 by a Mexico City *alcalde* (mayor), Conde de San Mateo Valparaíso. Fine stone carvings cover the outside of the *tezontle*-block building. Short-lived Mexican Emperor Iturbide occupied the palace in 1822; hence its current name. After serving as a hotel for many years, the mansion (10 A.M.–7 P.M. Wed.–Mon.) was purchased by Banamex and was restored in 1965. It now houses bank offices as well as a free art museum. The revolving exhibits consist mainly of Mexican paintings, sometimes quite interesting, but it's worth looking in regardless to admire the four-story interior courtyard.

Casa Borda

A block further east on Madero is the Casa Borda, another 18th-century palace, this one built by Taxco silver magnate José de Borda. In postindependence Mexico it served variously as public baths and one of Mexico City's first movie theaters before being bought by Banca Serfín in 1988. A free museum (10 A.M.–6 P.M. Tues.–Sun.) set in a small room just inside the building has displays of Amerindian clothing. Visitors cannot see the interior of the building, but the carved exterior is impressive enough.

Iglesia de la Profesa (San Felipe Neri)

Two blocks west of the Zócalo, on Madero at the corner of Isabel la Católica, stands a hulking 18th-century church popularly known as La Profesa. It doesn't compare to some of the more ornate churches in the Centro, but church buffs might want to stop in. Built in 1720 by the Jesuits, the church was turned over to the order of San Felipe in 1767 when the Jesuits were expelled from New Spain. It has since been officially named San Felipe Neri, but everyone still refers to it as La Profesa (The Professed, a euphemism for a nun).

The early baroque facade is somewhat subdued compared to the flights of fancy decorating later churches. The interior is unusually compact, almost square in layout, with a neoclassical altarpiece by Manuel Tolsá. Several of the colonial religious paintings on the walls and in the adjacent art gallery, particularly those by famed painter Cristóbal de Villalpando, are worth a look.

NORTH OF THE ZÓCALO

The blocks directly behind the Catedral contain several colonial buildings of note, including the churches of Santo Domingo and the ultrabaroque masterpiece La Enseñanza. The Antiguo Colegio de San Ildefonso, now a museum and cultural center, is worth visiting both to admire what is considered a classic example of colonial architecture and to see the first place where Mexico's renowned muralists began their art revolution in 1922. And the walls of the Secretaría de Educación Pública, housed in a former convent, are covered with more than 100 mural panels by Diego Rivera, making it a must-see for Rivera aficionados.

Those with an interest in the market life in Mexico City might walk farther north to check out Mercado Lagunilla and environs. The name derives from a small lake formerly at this location that divided the Aztec capital city from the neighboring market center of Tlatelolco. If you're feeling particularly brave, head across Eje 1 Norte into the Tepito "thieves' market" (see sidebar, *El*

Barrio Bravo de Tepito, in the *Shopping* chapter). On Sundays there's a well-known street market of furniture and old collectibles (not stolen goods!), some of it fascinating slices of old Mexico City life, along the eastern *lateral* (side lane) of Paseo de la Reforma just north of the Eje 1 Norte, and on a few side streets heading off Reforma east into Tepito. If you've got a hankering for mariachi, Mexico's national music form, take a walk northwest from the Zócalo to Plaza Garibaldi on the Eje Central to see the many bands hanging out on the square.

While it's no problem walking this area during the day, it's best not to head over this way after dark. You might get away with it around Plaza Santo Domingo, but if you wandered into the streets around Garibaldi or Lagunilla at night you might as well hold out your wallet and save the omnipresent *rateros* ("ratters," or thieves, in Mexican slang) the trouble of asking.

Antiguo Colegio de San Ildefonso

Running along the north side of the Templo Mayor is the imposing red-brick facade, divided by three baroque portals, of the Antiguo Colegio de San Ildefonso, first begun by Jesuit friars in 1588. Originally it was only a small school, but the Jesuits steadily expanded the building and the number of students until 1767, when the Spanish crown expelled the Jesuit order from New Spain and seized their properties. Shortly thereafter it served as a law school and medical school before undergoing a mid-19th-century conversion into the Preparatoria Nacional, an institute that groomed students for the Universidad Nacional.

In 1922, shortly after the end of the Mexican revolution, idealistic Education Minister José Vasconcelos hired a number of young, then-unknown Mexican artists to paint the walls of the Antiguo Colegio with murals depicting their vision of the revolutionary nation, thus beginning the mural movement that would become so important to 20th-century Mexican art. Diego Rivera, José Clemente Orozco, David Alfaro Siqueiros, Fermín Revueltas, Ramón Alva de la Canal, Fernando Leal, and Jean Charlot all painted different sections of the old school. On

dancers from the Yucatán at the Antiguo Colegio de San Ildefonso

several occasions while the painters worked, the school had to be barred and guarded by the police to protect the artists and murals from citizens who disagreed with the artists' sensibilities and leftist ideals.

At the entrance to the Patio Principal (Main Patio), you'll see the first mural painted, Alva de la Canal's *El desembarque de los españoles y la cruz plantada en tierras nuevas,* depicting the beginning of *mestizaje* (the cultural and genetic mixing of the Spanish and Indian peoples) and the birth of modern Mexico. Directly in front is *Alegoría de la Virgen de Guadalupe,* by Revueltas. The Orozco murals on the walls of the main patio are famed for their intensity, particularly *Cortés y la Malinche,* showing the conquistador and his lover/interpreter naked and holding hands.

In the Anfiteatro Bolívar, an addition built in 1911 at the front of the school and intended to copy the rest of the building's baroque style,

Sights

Diego Rivera painted his first mural, *La creación*. He had just returned from living in Europe, and the artistic influence of the Old Continent can easily be spotted in the cubist elements and hints of Italian fresco style seen in the mural. Rivera's early interest in Asian symbolism is also apparent in the way an angel in the mural holds his hands in a classic Zen meditation pose. (A preliminary sketch for this detail in the private Gelman Collection is labeled *Wisdom,* indicating that the hand gesture was no coincidence.)

In 1992 the Antiguo Colegio was converted into a museum and cultural center (Justo Sierra 16, tel. 5792-5223 or 5702-6378, 10 A.M.–6 P.M. Sun.–Fri., 10 A.M.–9 P.M. Sat., admission $4), and it often hosts exhibits and events of cultural interest. On weekends, music and dance groups from around Mexico frequently hold concerts in one of the two large courtyards. A small café on the 2nd floor of the main patio is a fine spot to take a rest and drink in the atmosphere along with refreshments.

Centro Cultural de España

Until a couple of years ago, this beautiful little gem of an early colonial palace right behind the Catedral was a crumbing ruin. But the Mexico City government ceded it to the Spanish government, who in turn undertook a careful and loving restoration of the old *casona* (old mansion). The two-story, narrow house belonged to one of the original conquistadors and had been gradually modified and rebuilt over the centuries, housing lawyers, workshops, and stores of various types. Inaugurated in 2002 by the king of Spain himself, the building now serves as a Spanish-run cultural center (Guatemala 18, tel. 5521-1920, www.centro-culturalesp.org.mx, hours vary but usually 10 A.M.–8 P.M. Tues.–Wed., 10 A.M.–11 P.M. Thurs.–Sat.). Shows are of both Mexican and Spanish artists and include younger, more experimental artists, as well as more established artists. It's definitely worth a look, both to admire the building and to see what show is currently up. They have a small café upstairs and a gift shop downstairs.

Templo y Plaza de Santo Domingo

This ancient plaza, three blocks north of the Zócalo, is the site of the first monastery in Mexico and was the second-most important square in the city during the colonial period. Today, the Portales de los Evangelistas archways on the south side of the square are lined with low-budget scribes with mechanical printing presses who have been ghost-writing love letters and legal documents since the late 19th century. A crowd of street sellers usually surrounds the statue, their wares displayed on blankets. It's a lively scene in all, well worth taking a seat and watching the world of Mexico City flow by. The center of the plaza contains a statue of independence heroine La Corregidora Josefa Ortiz de Domínguez.

The first church was erected on the square in 1530, then a second in 1556. The existing Templo de Santo Domingo, on the plaza's north side, was built between 1717 and 1736. The baroque

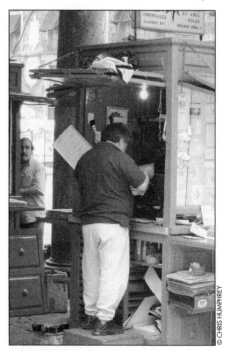

printing the old-school way in Plaza de Santo Domingo

© CHRIS HUMPHREY

facade has statues of San Francisco and San Agustín on either side of the main door, a marble relief of Santo Domingo de Guzmán above, and another relief of the Virgin Mary on the top. Inside is a neoclassical altarpiece sculpted by Manuel Tolsá early in the 19th century to take the place of an earlier baroque piece. The two side *retablos* are done in the ultrabaroque churrigueresque style and date from the early 18th century.

Directly opposite the square is the **Palacio de la Escuela de Medicina** (9 A.M.–5 P.M. daily, admission $2). Built between 1732 and 1736 by Pedro de Arrieta, the same architect who designed Iglesia La Profesa and worked on the Catedral, this palace first housed the dreaded Inquisition Tribunal before becoming a medical school in 1854. Although not dramatic on first glance, Arrieta's corner entrance was considered highly unusual in its time, as were the odd "hanging" arches in the interior courtyard. Visitors can pay $2 to see the medicine museum or just take a quick free look inside to admire the courtyard.

Secretaría de Educación Pública

The Education Secretariat, not to be missed by Diego Rivera fans for its multitude of murals by the master, is housed in two separate but attached buildings: a former customs house at Brasil 31, facing the Plaza Santo Domingo, and the **Ex-Convento de la Encarnación,** with its entrance at Argentina 28. Built in 1729 (against the wishes of the nuns next door, who thought it would block their light), the customs house contains a Davíd Alfaro Siqueiros mural titled *Patricios and Patricidas* (Patricians and Patricide) in its main stairwell. The mural, begun in 1945 and completed in 1971, was continually interrupted by the artist's political work and temporary imprisonment.

While the Siqueiros mural is impressive, it's hard to compete with the ex-convent next door, where 124 Diego Rivera mural panels cover wall space that extends three stories high and two city blocks long. Rivera's work was commissioned by Education Secretary José Vasconcelos, who had been given the convent to serve as the secretariat's offices.

Rivera gave the nicknames Patio de Trabajo (Work Patio) and Patio de Fiesta (Party Patio) for the two courtyards, and filled each with images related to the two themes between 1923 and 1928. The 1st floor of the Patio de Trabajo depicts various industries, as well as religious themes, while the 2nd floor is dedicated to science and intellectual pursuits. Whether because of the topics or some other consideration, the 2nd-floor murals consist of *grisallas,* or gray tones. On the stairwell to the 3rd level is a self-portrait of Rivera.

The bottom level of the second courtyard, true to its nickname, depicts popular festival activities in Mexico, including scenes from Day of the Dead, the Danza del Venado (Deer Dance), and (demonstrating Rivera's socialist beliefs) Labor Day. The murals on the north side of the courtyard were painted by Rivera students Jean Charlot and Amado de la Cueva. Walls on the 2nd floor carry the coats of arms of different Mexican states, painted by Charlot and de la Cueva, while the 3rd floor features some superb Rivera murals dedicated to *corridos,* or traditional storytelling ballads. Particularly noteworthy are *En el arsenal* (In the Arsenal), which shows Frida Kahlo handing out weapons, and *La Balada de Emiliano Zapata* (The Ballad of Emiliano Zapata).

The ex-convent (9 A.M.–5 P.M. Mon.–Fri., free admission) is a quiet, restful place to enjoy the murals, or to take a seat and rest from sightseeing. The chapel of the convent, though reputedly lovely, is closed to visitors.

Iglesia de la Enseñanza

On your way back to the Zócalo from Plaza Santo Domingo, take a detour left on Donceles to a church with an unusually narrow facade that now exhibits a severe backward tilt because of ground subsidence. Built in the 1770s as the Templo de Nuestra Señora del Pilar—but referred to as La Enseñanza (The Teaching) because it was founded by the Marianists, a teaching order—the former church has an impressive late baroque facade. But the real reason to visit the church is for the nine ultrabaroque, gilt *retablos* crammed into the small interior space.

M Sights

Infrequently visited, La Enseñanza (Donceles 104) is one of the Centro's hidden treasures and merits a few minutes' visit to marvel at the dazzling display inside. The church is packed on the feast day of its patron saint, Pilar, on October 12.

Plaza Garibaldi

Once a neighborhood square, this little plaza on Eje Central became a nightlife hotspot in the 1920s with the establishment of the Salón Tenampa and its mariachi band led by Cirilo Marmolejo. Because of the success of the bar and the group, the plaza became a magnet for mariachi musicians. Now you can see mariachi bands strolling around Garibaldi looking for clients at all hours of the afternoon or night. On weekend nights, competing groups line Eje Central between the Alameda and Garibaldi, relentlessly chasing down cars that slow down, trying to pick up gigs for private parties (roughly $200 per hour but very negotiable—the groups will arrange their own transport to and from the gig).

Groups will be glad to strike up a tune for you right there on the square for a rather steep $10 per song, perhaps less if you bargain well. Or you can venture into one of the many nearby bars and put back a couple of tequilas to get properly into the spirit of things.

With its recent facelift (to install a parking lot and subway station underneath the square), Garibaldi is not too daunting during the afternoon for the average tourist. It's not uncommon to see a group of foreigners having a couple of beers in one of the taco restaurants and enjoying the activity around them on the northeast corner of the plaza. But if you really want to see Garibaldi in full swing, and you are in the mood for a night of partying *a la mexicana,* show up sometime after 10 P.M. (preferably later) on a weekend night with a group of friends and make your rounds of the bars. Although most bars at Garibaldi see their share of tourists and are generally okay, a couple of dives are to be avoided, so look before you leap. Under no circumstances should you walk on the backstreets around Garibaldi after dark, as you will promptly get robbed. Ask the bar to call you a *sitio* (taxi). If you need to walk back to

downtown after dark, walk down Eje Central to Tacuba before turning east toward the Zócalo. (For more information on Garibaldi nightlife, see the *Arts and Entertainment* chapter.)

SOUTH OF THE ZÓCALO

Although not as frequented as other parts of the Centro, the blocks between the Zócalo and Avenida Izazaga hide several unique colonial buildings well worth taking a couple of hours to tour. Along Avenida Pino Suárez, which once was the old Aztec causeway leading south off the island capital, you'll find the Iglesia de Jesús Nazareno. The church is on the spot where Cortés and Moctezuma first met when the conquistadors arrived in Mexico City, and it is also the site of Cortés's tomb. Across the street stands the Museo de la Ciudad, housed in an imposing colonial mansion. Farther south is the Ex-Convento de San Jerónimo, the colonial convent where Mexican poet Sor Juana wrote much of her famed verse, and nearby is the Templo de Regina Coeli, rivaled only by La Enseñanza for the quality of its interior baroque artwork.

Walking south from Avenida Madero, you'll notice the streets start to get a bit shabbier and commercial after Calle Mesones. While walking south of here during the day is no problem, it's best not to venture south of Mesones after dark.

Museo de la Ciudad de México

Three blocks south of the Zócalo on Avenida Pino Suárez, at the corner of Avenida República del Salvador, sits a colonial-era mansion that now serves as a small city museum (Av. Pino Suárez 30, tel. 5542-0487, 10 A.M.–6 P.M. daily, free admission). Historians surmise that one of the conquistadors built a house on the site shortly after the conquest, as the building's cornerstone is an impressive serpent head probably taken from the Templo Mayor after its destruction by the Spanish.

The Conde de Calimaya ordered the construction of the current high baroque mansion in 1781. The richly carved main portal leads to a quiet patio with a fountain on one side, overseen by a stone sculpture of a mermaid strumming a guitar. On the 2nd floor you can see the restored office of one of the 19th-century occupants, as well as a small chapel to the Virgen de Guadalupe with three colonial-era religious paintings.

The museum's permanent exhibit displays some paintings and sketches of the city, but of more interest are the building itself, the rooms upstairs, and the frequently revolving displays of artwork (sometimes surprisingly alternative). Musical and cultural events are often hosted on weekends.

Iglesia y Hospital de Jesús Nazareno

The unadorned red brick Iglesia de Jesús Nazareno, diagonally across Avenida Pino Suárez from the Museo de la Ciudad, is the final resting place of that much-maligned conquistador Hernán Cortés. Perhaps reflecting the less-than-glorious image modern Mexicans have of Cortés, his tomb is marked only by a small plaque at the front of the bare church (7 A.M.–8 P.M. Mon.–Sat., 7 A.M.–1 P.M. and 5–8 P.M. Sun.), to the left of the altar. Legend has it that at the same corner where the church now stands, Aztec Emperor Moctezuma II first met Cortés as the conquistadors rode into Tenochtitlán for the first time. A plaque on the rear of the church, facing Avenida Pino Suárez, commemorates the event. The ceiling of the *coro* (choir seating area) bears a José Clemente Orozco mural, *El apocalipsis.*

Half a block south on Avenida Pino Suárez from the church is the Hospital de Jesús, one of the oldest buildings still standing in Mexico City, now hidden by a modern facade. Take a walk through the unremarkable entrance into a tranquil two-story colonial courtyard, filled with plants and a fountain in the center. Past the central staircase, where there is a bust of Cortés, you'll come to a second courtyard. Cortés ordered its construction in 1524 to tend to soldiers who were wounded fighting the Aztecs. Amazingly, the building (much modified since Cortés's time) still functions as a hospital, but tourists are free to walk in and around the courtyards—there's very little activity in the hallways. Judging from the lack of patients, you're probably better off going to one of the better hospitals in Polanco or elsewhere if you had a medical problem, but in an emergency, the *urgencias* at the Hospital de Jesús (Av. Pino Suárez 35, tel. 5542-6501 or 5542-6507) is open all night and is convenient to Centro stays.

Ex-Convento de San Jerónimo

It was in this convent, during the late 17th century, where Mexican nun and poet Sor Juana Inés de la Cruz wrote much of her remarkable, passionate verse, and it is under the chapel inside the old convent where she is buried. The remains of the convent have now been converted into a small, private university with a humanist focus called the Universidad del Claustro de Sor Juana (Izazaga 92, tel. 5709-4066 or 5709-4126, www.ucsj.edu.mx). Although it's a bit off the usual tourist path, visitors are free to tour the school grounds (particularly the beautiful two-story cloister) and see the old chapel, where Sor Juana and the other nuns of the convent are buried. The chapel is now used for school theater productions and has been mostly stripped of its ornamentation, leaving it eerily bare.

The convent was originally founded in 1585 through the efforts of Isabel de Barrios (daughter of conquistador Andrés de Barrios) and her second husband, Diego de Guzmán. The couple's four daughters and one cousin eventually became nuns in the convent. The chapel, dedicated in 1626, has a somewhat severe renaissance facade on the north side.

By the middle of the 19th century, when it was closed by the Reform Laws, the convent had at least 200 permanent residents. After the nuns' expulsion, different parts of the convent were used variously as army barracks, a hospital, a stable, a hotel, dozens of private homes, and even a legendary 1940s night spot called La Smyrna. Prompted by the complaints of people appalled that the burial site of a woman who is practically Mexico's national poet was being thus abused, government authorities intervened and expropriated the property in 1975, and shortly thereafter the university opened.

Visitors should bring some sort of photo identification to leave at the front gate entrance at Avenida Izazaga 92.

Near the chapel inside the university compound is the **Museo de la Indumentaria Mexicana** (10 A.M.–6 P.M. Mon.–Fri., free admission), which has rotating displays on traditional Amerindian and mestizo clothing from a large private collection belonging to photographer/folklorist Luis Marquéz Ramay.

Templo de Regina Coeli

A hidden treasure of religious art in the Centro Histórico, this 17th-century church (corner of Bolívar and Regina) doesn't look overly spectacular on the outside, although the sculptures and reliefs are attractive enough. But inside, the church houses five separate carved, gilded *retablos,* masterpieces of late baroque colonial art. The principal altar, dedicated to the Regina Coeli and dating to 1671, has an oil painting of the Virgin in the center and a statue of San José with the baby Jesus above. The *estípite* columns, characteristic of the churrigueresque style of the church, are dazzlingly complex and fluid. The four side altars are dedicated to the Virgen de la Fuente, Virgen de Guadalupe, Virgen de la Soledad, and San Francisco de Asís.

The Convento de Regina Coeli began construction in 1573, and the church was completed in 1636. As with so many convents, the Regina Coeli was partitioned after the 19th-century Reform Laws, and the eastern part became the Hospital Concepción Beistegui, which is now a rundown senior citizens' home.

Templo de San Agustín

Two blocks north of the Regina Coeli church and one block east, look for the massive Templo de San Agustín (corner of Isabel la Católica and República de Uruguay), along with what remains of the Augustinian convent. The church, built in 1692 on the site of an earlier, destroyed chapel, has an imposing front entrance topped with a sculpted relief of San Agustín sheltering several monks, flanked by double rows of Solomonic-style twisted columns. After the Reform, Mexico's government converted the church into the Biblioteca Nacional (National Library). The library has

long since moved on, and the church itself is in a woeful state, evidenced by its dramatic east-to-west tilt. Only a small chapel (República de El Salvador 76) on the south side is open to the public.

Casa del Conde Mateo del Valparaíso

A block north of the Templo de San Agustín (Isabel la Católica at Venustiano Carranza) stands a two-story private palace with a 3rd-story corner tower, built between 1769 and 1772 under the direction of architect Francisco Guerrero Torres. Sculpted reliefs decorate the tower and the area above the main entrance. Originally owned by the same count who built the Palacio de Iturbide on Avenida Madero, this palace is now owned by Banamex and forms part of the bank's central offices.

Visitors can go into part of the old building through a Banamex branch in the adjacent building (itself an amusing modernist retake on the colonial palace, done in *tezontle*-flecked concrete).

EAST OF THE ZÓCALO

In the few blocks behind the Palacio Nacional and Templo Mayor are several important and not frequently visited museums housed in buildings dating from the colonial area. Most of the sites are inexpensive or free and can easily be visited in an hour or two. A very good modern art museum on Academia, three blocks from the Zócalo, is **Museo José Luis Cuevas** (see the *Arts and Entertainment* chapter).

It's not recommended that tourists wander too far off—more than about four blocks from the Zócalo—in an easterly direction, toward Avenida Circunvalación or Avenida San Pablo. Although much honest business goes on in these neighborhoods, which form part of La Merced market district, prostitutes patrol the main avenues while more suspicious-looking types walk the backstreets. This is not a place to go around toting a camera and looking lost. But all the sites listed below, with the exception of the Ex-Convento de la Merced and the Merced and Sonora markets, are close to the Zócalo and quite safe to walk to.

Palacio del Arzobispado

Facing the Palacio Nacional from the Zócalo, take the street heading east from the left (north) side of the Palace, known as Calle Moneda because the mint was for years located there. On the left side of the street, you'll find the former Palacio del Arzobispado (Archbishop's Palace), now a museum run by the Finance Secretariat (Moneda 4, tel. 5228-1241, www.shcp.gob.mx/dgpcap/apa_index.html, 10 A.M.–5 P.M. Tues.–Sun., admission $1). Built in the 1530s, it remained the seat of ecclesiastical authority in Mexico until 1867, when it was seized by the Juárez government along with most other church property.

With the remains of an Aztec palace in the basement, the building is one of the most historic in the city and is worth a visit in its own right, but it also houses a sizeable collection of Mexican art given by artists or collectors to the government in lieu of tax payments. These include works by such greats as Diego Rivera and Rufino Tamayo, as well as contemporary artists such as Benjamín Domínguez and Vicente Rojo. Some rooms also contain modest displays of colonial art and artifacts. Free concerts and theater productions are held every Sunday between noon and 2 P.M.—get there before noon, as it often fills up, and the doors are closed until the show finishes.

Casa de la Imprenta

In this modest house at the corner of Calle Moneda and Calle Licenciado Primo de Verdad, early colonists cranked up the first printing machine in the Americas in 1536. Apart from a model of the press, the house (tel. 5522-1535, 10 A.M.–5 P.M. Mon.–Sat., free admission) contains a small exhibit of Aztec artifacts and occasional temporary exhibits.

La Casa de la Moneda

At Moneda 13, just past the north wall of the Palacio Nacional, stands a colonial-era building where the silver riches of Mexico's mines were once counted before being sent on to the Spanish crown's treasury each year by ship. The building, modified repeatedly over the centuries, served as Mexico's mint from the late 16th century until 1865, when Emperor Maximilian I converted it into a natural history museum. Since 1966 it has served as the **Museo Nacional de las Culturas** (tel. 5542-0187, 9:30 A.M.–5:45 P.M. daily, free admission), a museum for the cultures of the world. Mexican artist Rufino Tamayo painted the mural in the entranceway. While the permanent exhibit is nothing to write home about, occasional temporary shows can be worth a look. As admission to the museum is free, you could spend just a few minutes walking around the rambling old building, even if the exhibits aren't of interest. The museum has a good, government-run bookstore with plenty of historical and cultural books, postcards, posters, and other assorted trinkets.

Academia San Carlos

Once the principal art school in Spanish America, the Academia de San Carlos began life early in the colonial era as a hospital, but it was occupied by the academy in 1790. To help train sculpture students, master artists made plaster copies of some of the great works of European art, such as *Venus de Milo* and *David,* and these casts line the school's two-story courtyard today. Visitors are free to look inside the school (Academia at Moneda, tel. 5522-3102, 9 A.M.–2 P.M. and 5–8 P.M. Mon.–Fri.), which is now run by UNAM, the national university. A fee is charged to take pictures. The school frequently mounts art exhibits by young Mexican artists.

Iglesia de la Santísima Trinidad

Popularly known simply as La Santísima, this is another little baroque masterpiece tucked away in the backstreets of the Centro, at the corner of the scruffy pedestrian streets Emiliano Zapata and La Santísima. Built between 1755 and 1783, La Santísima is one of the most important churrigueresque churches in the city, along with the Sagrario. The main facade, decorated with busts of the 12 apostles and a symbol of La Santísima Trinidad (the Holy Trinity), is stunning, and the deep relief carvings on the side entrance are also exceptional. The original altarpiece is long gone, so don't worry too much if the church happens to be closed up when you go by.

© CHRIS HUMPHREY

A hidden colonial gem, Iglesia de la Santísima Trinidad is located on a side street east of the Zócalo.

Ex-Convento de la Merced

Lost amid rundown streets a 15-minute walk southeast of the Zócalo is this convent, a gem of colonial architecture—although one in a sorry state of disrepair and at last report closed to the public. One hopes that this changes soon, and that resources are found to rehabilitate the convent so that it can be reopened to the public.

The convent is considered by some to have the most beautifully sculpted cloister in all of the Americas. The two stories of sculpted columns and arches around the patio of the cloister will cause rapture in those with an affinity for the best of Latin colonial religious architecture. The lower level was finished in 1656 in a somewhat reserved baroque that includes sculptures of various saints and biblical allusions decorating the stonework above the arches. Thirteen striking *portales,* with scalloped arches in the Arab-influenced Mudejar style, line each side of the top floor and represent Jesus and the 12 Apostles.

Unfortunately, much of the convent aside from the cloister was destroyed after the Reform Laws of 1857 allowed the government to expropriate church property, and the remains have further decayed. Probably because it is in a rough neighborhood that is unlikely to draw many tourists, the cloister is closed to the public and appears to be slowly decaying. The walls and sculptures all show signs of water and earthquake damage in urgent need of repair.

I once managed to chat with the guard at the site, and he kindly let me in to look around for a few minutes as he lamented the decay of the cloister. I tried again later with no luck, so feel free to go by and check, but don't expect to get in anytime soon.

Mercado de la Merced and Mercado de Sonora

One of the largest retail and wholesale markets in Mexico, La Merced (6 A.M.–6 P.M. daily) covers an entire block between the streets of Santa Escuela, General Anaya, Rosario, and Cerrada del Rosario in Colonia Merced Balbuena, near the Ex-Convento de la Merced and just outside of Metro Merced. For most of the nearly two centuries since independence from Spain, La Merced was the city's principal marketplace and was the centerpiece of a bustling commercial neighborhood. In 1983 the city inaugurated the Central de Abastos farther south, and it soon superceded La Merced in the wholesale business. But La Merced is still going strong, and many *capitalinos* (citizens of the capital) still consider it the quintessential Mexico City market.

Across Avenida Fray Servando Teresa de Mier from La Merced is Mercado Sonora (6 A.M.–6 P.M. daily), the so-called "witches' market." Mexicans flock here to buy herbal remedies, love potions, talismans, and other assorted psychospiritual balms. The market also does a booming trade in endangered plants and animals, for which it is routinely raided by the police.

Beware of walking the backstreets around the two markets, as the neighborhood is rough and dirty.

AROUND THE ALAMEDA CENTRAL

West of Eje Central Lázaro Cárdenas, the older colonial architecture of the Centro Histórico is interspersed with many modern structures, and the city blocks begin to lengthen. Attractions in this area include one of the city's oldest and largest parks, the architectural gem Palacio de Bellas Artes, a small museum housing Diego Rivera's famed mural set in the Alameda, La Ciudadela handicraft market, and assorted smaller plazas and historic churches.

Palacio de Bellas Artes

Looming over the eastern end of the Alameda Central is the huge, domed Palace of Fine Arts (corner of Av. Juárez and Eje Central, tel. 5512-2593, ext. 193). The white palace, fronted on the south side by a park with marble benches and on the other three by broad avenues, is all the more impressive because of the empty space all around it. Construction began in 1904, during the presidency of Porfirio Díaz, under the supervision of Italian architect Adamo Boari. Boari planned for the building to be a masterpiece of art nouveau architecture, but, frustrated by inter-ruptions wrought by the decade-long Mexican Revolution, he left Mexico in 1916, having completed only the grand facades.

One of Boari's Mexican apprentices, Federico Mariscal, took over the design in 1932 and finished off the interior of the building as well as the impressive cupolas in art deco. The exterior decoration mixes classical Greco-Roman statuary with Aztec motifs such as serpent heads and representations of Aztec warriors, most of it sculpted by Italian artists. For the main auditorium inside, Mexican painter Gerardo Murillo, also known as Dr. Atl, designed a huge stained-glass stage curtain (cortina de cristal) depicting the Ixtaccíhuatl and Popocatépetl volcanoes. Tiffany Studios of New York assembled more than a million pieces of glass to realize the design. The building was completed in 1934.

From west to east, the building consists of the entrance vestibule and reception rooms; the large mezzanine and stairwells, beneath the Palacio's three cupolas, plus art galleries; the theater and associated service rooms; and backstage areas and scenery workshops. Only the first two sections are open to the public on a daily basis (except Monday, when Bellas Artes is closed). The theater is reserved for performances—except on Sunday

---

RIVERA AND ROCKEFELLER

When in 1933 Nelson Rockefeller decided he wanted a mural for the new RCA Building at Rockefeller Center, New York, he commissioned Diego Rivera (after receiving refusals from Picasso and Matisse) to carry out the work. Thumbing his nose at the Western world's primary proponent of free enterprise, Rivera chose to depict the modern worker at a symbolic junction of science, industry, capitalism, and socialism in a work provisionally titled *Man at the Crossroads Looking with Hope and High Vision to the Choosing of a New and Better Future.*

Among several influential world personalities portrayed in the fresco—including Edsel Ford, Jean Harlow, and Charlie Chaplin—Rivera included a figure of Russian Communist leader Vladimir Lenin. When Rivera steadfastly refused Rockefeller's request to remove Lenin's portrait, Rockefeller had the entire fresco chiseled off the wall.

In 1934, Rivera reproduced the mural on an interior wall of the third level of the Palacio de Bellas Artes, where it can be seen today under the title *Man, Controller of the Universe.* In the second version he included not only Lenin, but Marx, Engels, and Trotsky. Taking revenge one step further, Rivera added a portrait of John D. Rockefeller Jr. standing in a nightclub and surrounded by sleek women. Just above Rockefeller's head stretches a microscopic view of a swirl of bacteria, said to represent venereal diseases.

morning, when the public may visit—and the backstage areas and workshops are usually off limits to all but performers and staff.

The massive marble building is so heavy that it has already settled more than four and a half meters into the old lakebed. The exterior ornamentation of the Palacio has suffered from air pollution and neglect, particularly the copper-laminated cupolas, which are considered the best examples of art deco in Mexico.

Aside from admiring the interior architecture, you can visit the 2nd and 3rd floors of the mezzanine to view massive social-political works by Mexico's most famous muralists. Davíd Alfaro Siqueiros's 1944–1945 *Nueva democracia* (New Democracy), on the north wall of the 3rd level, is probably the most striking and clearly designed. Siqueiros's wife served as the model for the bare-breasted, helmeted woman breaking out of chains in the mural. For this painting, which is the central panel of a larger triptych, Siqueiros used pyroxilin, a commercial enamel used for airplanes and automobiles. Four other Siqueiros panels can also be seen on this floor. Diego Rivera's 1934 *El hombre contralor del Universo* (Man, Controller of the Universe) occupies another wall. On the south wall, José Clemente Orozco's 1934–1935 *La katharsis* depicts a confrontation of the mechanistic world with humanity in a swirl of guns, machines, and tortured human faces. Less interesting murals by Rufino Tamayo and Juan O'Gorman cover the remaining walls.

On the 2nd floor of the mezzanine you'll see more murals by less-famous Mexican artists Roberto Montenegro, Jorge González Camarena, and Manuel Rodríguez Lozano. Camarena's 1963 *Humanidad librándose* (Humanity Liberating Itself) is especially worth noting. Like Siqueiros, Camarena's approach to color and line was bold and bright, almost psychedelic, but he had a much greater range of technique, which he could turn from abstraction to realism or superrealism. Also on this floor are a couple of galleries used for well-curated temporary exhibits.

The 4th floor of Bellas Artes, the **Museo de Arquitectura** (www.museobellasartes.artte.com) exhibits building floor plans, photos, and other archived memorabilia related to Mexico City's historic buildings, including many older structures that have disappeared from Roma, Juárez, San Rafael, Tacubaya, and other *barrios* (neighborhoods).

The massive lobby, mezzanine, and galleries are open to the public 10 A.M.–6 P.M. Tue.–Sun.; admission to the mezzanine and galleries is $2.75, free on Sunday. On Sunday mornings visitors are also permitted to enter the theater to see the lighted Tiffany glass curtain. Off the north side of the lobby is a very pleasant and slightly upscale café. Ticket windows downstairs offer advance sales for the Orquestra Sinfónica Nacional (National Symphonic Orchestra) and for the famous Ballet Folklórico (see the *Arts and Entertainment* chapter for details). Other concerts and events are scheduled regularly.

Right next to the northwest corner of the Palacio is the Metro Bellas Artes subway station. The French government recently paid for a renovation of the Metro entrance, giving it the full art nouveau treatment like the famed Metro station entrances of Paris.

Alameda Central

When the Spanish conquered Tenochtitlán, the area now occupied by the Alameda Central was an Aztec *tianguis* (open-air market). Spanish Viceroy Don Luis de Velasco, as part of a plan to develop what was then the western edge of the city, ordered the construction of the first Alameda—named for the *álamos* (poplar trees) originally planted throughout—between 1592 and 1595. More than 400 years later it is one of the most traditional and well-proportioned city parks in all of Mexico, and it so beloved by Mexicans that parks of all sizes throughout the country take the name "Alameda" in homage.

The original park covered only about half the current area, from the Palacio de Bellas Artes to the park's Hemiciclo de Juárez. The newer western half took the place of an unadorned public square built during the Spanish Inquisition and known as El Quemadero (The Burning Place), as this was where "infidels" were tortured and burned at the stake with much public ceremony.

The inquisitors wore special conical hats and yellow shirts emblazoned with devils, flames, alligators, and snakes painted by the top religious artists of the era. By the 1760s, the Inquisition was all but over in Mexico, and in 1770 Viceroy Marqués de Croix ordered the expansion of the park over El Quemadero.

The de Croix expansion was further amplified in 1791 by the Conde de Revillagigedo, who erected a wood fence around the perimeter in an attempt to reserve the park for the exclusive use of the aristocracy. But that didn't last long: the Alameda hosted the main popular celebration of Mexican independence in 1821, and when megalomaniac President Santa Anna rode triumphantly into Mexico City in 1846, he ordered the fountains of the Alameda filled with booze.

A French designer installed five classical fountains inspired by Greco-Roman mythology, and more statuary, both classical and modern, was added in the 19th century. Gas lamps were erected in 1868, to be replaced by electric lighting in 1892, by which time the park had become a popular spot for all classes of Mexicans. Most of what you can see in the park today, from the starburst pathways set around fountains to the band kiosk, dates to the 19th and early 20th centuries.

The Alameda remains a favorite place for local romantics during the week and for a Sunday afternoon stroll with the family. Aside from being a pleasant place to walk and observe Mexican park life at its finest, the park features a couple of monuments worth visiting in and of themselves. Standing at the south side of the park, facing Avenida Juárez, is the **Hemiciclo de Benito Juárez,** a semicircle of eight marble Doric columns joined at the top. Inaugurated by dictator Porfirio Díaz in September 1910, the monument was intended to commemorate 100 years of independence from Spain but wasn't completed till 1919. Four columns stand on each side of a central obelisk topped with a statue of Juárez holding a copy of the Mexican constitution. The mythical Greek goddess Glory places a laurel crown on his head as Victory stands by with brandished sword.

Although any day of the week is a good time for a stroll through the leafy Alameda, the park is at its most festive on Sunday, when many food and trinket vendors set up along the pathways. An excellent children's puppet theater sometimes performs along the north side of the park, toward the Hotel de Cortés, around the middle of the day on Sunday, and occasionally a live symphonic ensemble mounts the kiosk to perform. Check out the new *policías charros,* horseback policemen in full black cowboy regalia, complete with a broad sombrero.

During the Christmas season the park is dotted with Santa Claus displays and other Christmas scenery, most of it oriented toward children; between Christmas and January 6, Día de los Reyes, the themes switch to the Three Kings.

Avenida Juárez opposite the south side of the Alameda has undergone major improvements in recent years, with the sidewalks widened for pedestrians and formerly vacant lots filled in with luxury hotels. Take a quick glance in the **Museo Corpus Cristi** (Juárez 44, 9:30 A.M.–6 P.M. daily, free admission). This former Templo de Corpus Cristi was recently renovated and now hosts rotating art exhibits.

Churches of the Plaza de la Santa Veracruz

This small plaza on the north side of Avenida Hidalgo, opposite the Alameda Central, is surrounded by four small architectural and artistic gems. At the south end of the plaza, which lies a couple of meters below the level of Avenida Hidalgo because of soil subsidence, stands dark **Iglesia de la Santa Veracruz** (10:30 A.M.–1:30 P.M. and 4:30–6:30 P.M. daily). Reportedly, the original church that once stood here was built by order of chief conquistador Hernán Cortés in 1521 to celebrate the arrival of his ships at Veracruz in 1519, making it the oldest church in Mexico City. The oldest sections of the present structure date to 1730, while the southern facade was redone in 1759 and 1764 in the baroque style. Neoclassical architect Manuel Tolsá—who, ironically enough, abhorred baroque architecture—is entombed inside.

© CHRIS HUMPHREY

Iglesia de la Santa Veracruz on the Alameda

At the opposite end of the plaza, **Iglesia de San Juan de Dios** (10:30 A.M.–1:30 P.M. and 4:30–6:30 P.M. daily) was completed in 1729 and features a unique concave facade. Inside is a figure of one of the most sought-after saints in the city, San Antonio de Padua. Local myth says San Antonio will help supplicants obtain a fiancée; to win the saint's favor, you must offer only coins obtained from strangers.

The other two colonial buildings, a hospital and a two-story mansion, now house the Museo Franz Mayer and the Museo Nacional de la Estampa (see the *Arts and Entertainment* chapter for more information).

Hotel Cortés (Ex-Hospicio de San Nicolás Tolentino de los Ermitaños de San Agustín)

Built in 1730 as an Augustinian hospice dedicated to providing shelter and food for the poor, this dark building with a baroque facade of *tezontle* block became a hostel for traveling trades-

men in 1860 and was completely refurbished and reopened as a hotel in 1943. Mexican and foreign visitors alike stop off for late breakfast or lunch in the cool stone courtyard of the hotel, which stands at the west end of Avenida Hidalgo near Paseo de la Reforma (see the *Accommodations* chapter for more information).

Museo Mural Diego Rivera

Opposite the southwest corner of Alameda Central, facing a smaller garden plaza, a small, modern museum (10 A.M.–6 P.M. Tues.–Sun., admission $1.50) houses the famous Diego Rivera mural called *Sueño de una tarde dominical en la Alameda Central* (Dream of a Sunday Afternoon in the Alameda Central). Rivera created this huge work for the lobby of the Hotel Del Prado in 1947–1948. Mexico City's 1985 earthquake damaged the hotel beyond repair, but the mural survived and was moved to this museum built especially to exhibit the work in 1986. Also on display are various photos showing the work in progress, as well as the effects of the quake on the Hotel Del Prado.

Dominating the museum's back wall, the 15-by 4-meter mural's park scene portrays many famous Mexican personalities—including Hernán Cortés; Porfirio Díaz; Francisco I. Madero; General Antonio López de Santa Anna (handing the "keys" to Mexico to American General Winfield Scott); and Emperor Maximilian and his wife, Carlota. In the center of the cartoonlike mural, José Guadalupe Posadas, Mexico's most well-known engraver, walks arm in arm with La Calavera Catrina (see Museo Nacional de la Estampa in the *Arts and Entertainment* chapter), who is decked out in a feathered hat and serpent-headed boa. To the right of the *calavera* (skeleton) stands Frida Kahlo, holding in her left hand the Taoist yin-yang symbol. A self-portrait of Diego Rivera as a young boy stands in front of Kahlo.

To commemorate the many people who died during the 1985 quake, the Mexico City government established the rectangular **Jardín de la Solidaridad** (Solidarity Garden) in front of the museum. The plaza lies on the former site of the Hotel Regis, which was destroyed during the cataclysm.

Templo de San Hipólito

At the corner of Calle de Zarco and Avenida Hidalgo, slightly west of Paseo de la Reforma, this church was founded a year after the so-called *noche triste* (sad night) of June 30, 1520, when Cortés's Spanish troops came under heavy Aztec attack and were forced to flee the city. Reputedly Cortés vowed to build a church at this spot, the beginning of the Aztec causeway leaving the island, when he returned. A small plaque in a corner of the church courtyard commemorates the infamous event. Cortés returned in 1521, took the city after a three-month siege, razed it, and captured the Aztec Emperor Cuauhtémoc. The church was completely redone in 1577, when America's first mental hospital—Hospital de San Hipólito—was attached.

Worth a brief look is the church's dark *tezontle* and stone three-stage early baroque facade, topped by slender bell towers uniquely twisted so that their corners face toward the front.

Plaza de San Fernando

Two and a half blocks west of the Templo de San Hipólito, on the north side of Puente de Alvarado, sits the small, narrow landscaped Plaza de San Fernando, with a statue of Mexican independence hero Vicente Guerrero (1782–1831). On the east side is the **Panteón Histórico de San Fernando,** an old cemetery (8 A.M.–3 P.M. daily) extending from San Fernando's east side. Most of the grave markers—some grand tombs, others mere headstones—date to the 19th century. Revered Mexican President Benito Juárez is interred in a marble tomb surrounded with Greek columns. Atop the tomb is a marble sculpture of Juárez himself, dressed in Greco-Roman robes and dying in his mother's arms. Buried alongside the great hero are his wife and children. Many of the other gravesites and tombs contain military heroes from the 19th and early 20th centuries, including Vicente Guerrero, Ignacio Comonfort, Melchor Ocampo, Tomás Mejía, and Miguel Miramón.

The **Iglesia de San Fernando** can be seen just beyond the north end of the plaza. Franciscans from Querétaro established the San Fernando

Casa de Cultura of Tamaulipas, located near La Ciudadela, is one of the many restored colonial mansions in the Centro.

© CHRIS HUMPHREY

church and convent in 1734 to serve as a headquarters for the missionary effort. A century later the convent was badly damaged by an earthquake, and the city razed the ruin in 1862. Around that same time, the convent's surrounding orchards and pasturelands were divided and sold off to create Colonia Guerrero, named, of course, for Vicente. Once an elegant neighborhood, Guerrero is nowadays a bit run down.

La Ciudadela

Built as a tobacco factory in the 18th century, this thick-walled quadrangle served as a military barracks during the Mexican Revolution and is today home to the **Biblioteca de México** (Library of Mexico).

In the same building, the **Centro de la Imagen** (tel. 9172-4724, www.conaculta.gob.mx/cimagen, 11 A.M.–6 P.M. Mon.–Fri.) contains studios, classrooms, a library, and a bookshop—all specializing in photography. The center issues a quarterly journal, *Luna Córnea,* which may be purchased in Imagen's bookshop. They also manage an exhibition space dedicated to Mexican photography.

The complex is located six blocks south of the Alameda Central, on the west side of Avenida Balderas opposite Metro Balderas. The area surrounding La Ciudadela is sometimes referred to as "Plaza de la Ciudadela," although the plaza just north of the complex is also called "Plaza José María Morelos." Chess aficionados will find dozens of intent-looking men playing the game of kings under a tent in the park. You can rent a chess set for $.20 an hour, but if you like to play timed games, bring your own clock because they don't rent them.

On the same side of Balderas, two blocks north at Calle Ayuntamiento, the **Centro Artesenal La Ciudadela,** also called Mercado de Artesanías de la Ciudadela, is one of the better places to buy Mexican handicrafts in the center of the city. (See the *Shopping* chapter for further information.)

Just across Avenida Balderas from the Ciudadela market is **Parque Carlos Pacheco,** a small quiet square surrounded by a number of colonial buildings, including the restored **Casa de Cultura of Tamaulipas,** on Calle Pugibet.

Plaza de San Juan

This recently renovated small plaza, north of the TelMex tower and west of the Eje Central, was the center of a relatively major market area during the late colonial and early postcolonial eras. In an effort to revitalize the rather run-down neighborhood surrounding Plaza de San Juan, the city government lent money for the restoration of not only the plaza, but adjacent historic buildings and a handicrafts market, **Mercado de Artesanías San Juan,** which sits on the east side of the plaza. The district around the plaza consists mostly of shops selling housing accessories. (See the *Shopping* chapter for more information.)

Facing the north end of the plaza is the **Basílica de San José de Nuestra Señora del Sagrado,** a small twin-towered church originally built in 1772 and rebuilt after earthquakes in 1857 and 1985.

Opposite the northwest corner of the plaza stands an imposing Republican-era building erected by the **Compañía Cigarrera Mexicana** back when Mexico City was a major tobacco entrepôt. Nowadays the building is subdivided into office space.

The San Juan de Letrán Metro station is only two blocks northeast of the Plaza de San Juan, on the corner of República de Uruguay and Eje Central Lázaro Cárdenas.

TLATELOLCO/PLAZA DE LAS TRES CULTURAS

Just northwest of the Centro Histórico, this plaza is so named (Plaza of the Three Cultures) because around it are the ruins of an ancient Aztec temple, the renovated 16th-century Iglesia de Santiago Tlatelolco, and a huge 1960s-era apartment complex—thus presenting three cultures in one wide-angle view. Walkways wind through the temple ruins, which contain the walls of 18 structures.

On the southeast side of the ruins stand the colonial church and adjacent Ex-Convento de San Buenaventura. The old monastery was founded in 1535 as one of the principal schools where children of Aztec nobility were educated in the ways of Catholicism and the Western world. The existing structure, now part of the Foreign Relations Secretariat, was built in the 1660s, while the unadorned church was built shortly thereafter.

The plaza can be reached by walking about a kilometer or so either from the Garibaldi or Tlatelolco Metro stations (the latter is a bit closer), or by driving or taking a taxi north on the Eje Central and getting off at the corner of Ricardo Flores Magón. From here the plaza is a short walk through the building complex to the northeast.

History

The plaza sits over the site of Tlatelolco, once a small island appended to Tenochtitlán and the market center of the Aztec empire. A group of Aztec dissidents, unhappy with the growing empire's power structure, established themselves here in the late 14th century. The island was allowed a degree of autonomy until 1473, when its leaders were executed and the island was annexed by Tenochtitlán.

When Cortés first arrived, Tlatelolco was a massive market complex trading in goods from as far away as Guatemala. Hundreds of products were bought, sold, or bartered (usually the latter) by thousands of people each day. Merchandise was grouped by category in specific areas, and government appointees oversaw the transactions. According to the memoirs of Cortés himself, the market traded more fabrics each day than did the great markets of Granada at that time. At the center of the market stood the main temple, with twin pyramids dedicated to Tlaloc and Huitzilopochtli as in Tenochtitlán. The ruins seen today are the remains of this temple.

Over the centuries, Tlatelolco has been the location of an unusual number of bloody tragedies. It was here that the fanatical defense of the Aztecs under Cuauhtémoc came to its gory finale, with thousands of Aztecs run through with Spanish steel. Again in the colonial period, during grain riots in 1692, an unknown number of poor protesters were killed on the square.

But when Mexicans hear the word Tlatelolco today, the first thing they think of was the massacre that took place on the plaza the night of October 2, 1968. In the preceding weeks, a series of student protests had swept Mexico City. While the protests posed no immediate threat to the government, they took place shortly before the 1968 Olympics, and President Gustavo Díaz Ordaz did not want students causing any embarrassing problems. As the protests continued, the police responded with increasing violence.

Because of the perceived overreaction, the protests grew stronger, and on September 18 the Army occupied UNAM, the national university. Students continued to hold smaller demonstrations in different parts of the city and ended up at Tlatelolco the night of October 2. Exactly how the violence started remains a matter of great dispute. The government insists that protesters had guns and started the shootout, while many others hold that gun-toting government agents planted among the protesters provoked the army into opening fire.

However it started, it ended with several hundred protesters dead, and hundreds more wounded and under arrest. The student protests were indeed halted, and the Olympics took place without a hitch, but in the end it was a Pyrrhic victory, for the Tlatelolco massacre was in many ways the birth of the opposition to the long-ruling Institutional Revolutionary Party (PRI). By all accounts it was this brutal overreaction on the part of the government that, for many Mexicans, unmasked the dictatorship. The full truth about what happened that night will likely never be known, but it remains a touchstone event for modern Mexico.

As if the massacre weren't enough, the government-built Tlatelolco housing complex around the plaza was severely damaged during the 1985 earthquake. The Nuevo León building, in which residents had been complaining for months about evidence of shoddy construction, collapsed in a heap, killing an estimated thousand people who lived in it. Other buildings suffered heavy damage, and to this day the residents are engaged in a long-standing legal battle with the government over the state of the complex. Considering the Nuevo León collapse, and looking at the dramatic tilt and large cracks visible in many of the buildings, it's no surprise they want the government to pay for repairs.

Sights

Paseo de la Reforma and Zona Rosa

Designed by Emperor Maximilian to resemble Paris's famous Champs Elysées, the Paseo de la Reforma (often shortened to "Reforma") is Mexico City's grandest avenue, a broad boulevard that's home to the Bolsa Mexicana de Valores (Mexican Stock Exchange) as well as numerous banks, stock brokerage firms, and office buildings. Foreign visitors will likely find themselves on Paseo de la Reforma at some point during their visit, either on their way to Chapultepec or the Zona Rosa, or to avail themselves of the avenue's many banks, exchange houses, airline offices, hotels, and nearby embassies. South of Reforma lies the Zona Rosa shopping and restaurant district, much frequented by tourists, and on the avenue's north side is the imposing Monumento a la Revolución and two interesting and not oft-visited museums, El Chopo and San Carlos. A bit farther north are San Rafael and Santa María de la Ribera, two formerly wealthy neighborhoods now on the downside but still replete with historical buildings.

HISTORY

For the 20-odd years after Maximilian first laid it out, Reforma remained a narrow street running through open fields, while Avenida Bucareli was the principal avenue outside the downtown area and the address of choice for the city's upper crust.

But under the francophile dictator Porfirio Díaz, Reforma assumed the Parisian grandeur Maximilian had intended. Díaz ordered the laying out of a broad central avenue flanked by side lanes *(laterales),* and the city's elite flocked to build their new palaces (only a few of which remain standing) along what was to quickly become the most fashionable district in town.

Díaz decorated three of the avenue's five *glorietas* (traffic circles) with sculptures of (from east to west) Spanish King Carlos IV, explorer Cristóbal Colón (known to Anglos as Christopher Columbus), and Aztec Emperor Cuauhtémoc. A fourth *glorieta* was crowned with the Monumento de la Independencia. Díaz also

lined the boulevard with 70-odd busts of lesser figures of the late-19th-century elite, most of which are still standing.

Historian Michael Johns, author of the well-written and engrossing *The City of Mexico in the Age of Díaz,* commented on the Porfiriato development of Reforma:

> *[The monuments] narrated a history of Mexico that aimed to reconcile the ideas and events of a real past with the ideals and needs of an inexperienced ruling class that was trying to guide a new nation. That story all but ignored Mexico's past as a colony while praising the European world that Spain had introduced it to.*

The *colonias,* or neighborhoods, that grew up along either side of Reforma, first Colonia Juárez to the south and then Colonia Cuauhtémoc to the north, were filled with mansions owned by Mexico's richest citizens, often built in bizarre, eclectic combinations of different European styles.

© CHRIS HUMPHREY

North of the Cuauhtémoc statue is the Monumento a la Madre, a social-realist sculpture dedicated to the mothers of Mexico.

In the 1950s the cafés and bars in a triangular section of Colonia Juárez bordered by the avenues Insurgentes, Reforma, and Florencia became the gathering spot of choice for the city's cultural elite—including famed writers Carlos Fuentes and Carlos Monsiváis and composer Agustín Lara, to name only three of the most prominent. The district was soon the hip spot to be seen at night, and Mexican newspaper columnists soon christened it "la Zona Rosa" (the Pink Zone, perhaps in reference to the pinkish glow given off by the red neon lights).

PASEO DE LA REFORMA

The central section of Reforma, between the Alameda and Chapultepec, features an eight-lane middle avenue and two-lane parallel side streets, punctuated with five *glorietas,* each with a monument in the center.

Although Reforma has expanded over the years to the northeast as far as La Villa de Guadalupe, and westward to the Toluca highway exit, the sights described in this section are along the original, century-old boulevard. Distances along the spacious walkways on Reforma are farther than they might appear, so it's best to try to arrive fairly close to your destination before walking.

Several Metro stations can be found near Reforma: Metro Hidalgo is close to the eastern end and the Monumento de Colón; Metro Insurgentes is next to the Zona Rosa; and Metro Chapultepec is at the avenue's western end, near Chapultepec Park. For destinations close to the Monumento a la Revolución, get off at Metro Revolución, which is on Avenida Puente de Alvarado, a few blocks north of the monument.

Pesero buses run the entire central stretch of Paseo de la Reforma, beginning at the Hidalgo Metro station and going west past the Chapultepec museums to the Auditorio Nacional. These are perhaps the most convenient way of moving up and down Reforma.

Should you have a car, plenty of metered parking places can be found both in the Zona Rosa and on side streets off the north side of Reforma. The *transitos* (traffic police, dressed in brown)

take great pleasure in slapping metal boots on the wheels of cars who haven't fed the parking meters, so beware. Traffic tends to flow pretty well along Reforma day and night (unless you hit a protest march), but it can get tied up in the middle of the Zona Rosa, especially on Friday and Saturday nights.

Paseo de la Reforma Monuments

The **King Carlos IV statue** that originally marked the start of Reforma has since moved downtown, and in its place stands a bright yellow, modernist interpretation of the horse-riding king—so highly stylized as to be unrecognizable. The lettering on the sculpture, "Torre El Caballito," refers to the adjacent office building, suggesting the piece can't stand on its own merits.

Cast in 1877 by French sculptor Charles Cordier, the **Monumento de Colón** still stands, despite the best efforts of political protesters who in an annual ritual sling ropes around the statue and try to pull it down. Once the protesters managed to snap off one of the Great Mariner's thumbs, but the city promptly reattached it.

At the intersection of the city's two most important avenues, Insurgentes and Reforma, stands a statue of the Aztec Emperor **Cuauhtémoc** (Attacking Eagle), who fought in a desperate last stand against the Spaniards before the fall of Tenochtitlán. It is the work of Mexican sculptors Francisco Jiménez and Ramón Agea.

The *glorieta* beyond Cuauhtémoc has a single, tall palm tree in the center, while the next one southwest contains Mexico's **Monumento de la Independencia.** This 32-meter-high column, topped with the winged *Ángel de la Independencia,* was formally inaugurated by Porfirio Díaz on September 16, 1910, shortly before his overthrow and the start of the Revolution. The gold-sheathed angel, one of the city's landmark symbols, is the site of frequent political rallies and spontaneous street celebrations whenever the beloved *tricolor* (as Mexico's national soccer team is known) pulls off a victory. It's best to avoid such victory parties—the crowd is normally nonaggressive, if boisterous, but occasionally people have been beaten up or robbed amidst the celebration.

After dodging the traffic to cross Reforma, you can walk up the steps of the monument's base, pass through a door into the foot of the column, and walk around a small passageway wherein the remains of 12 heroes from the independence struggle are stored in three niches: Miguel Hidalgo, José María Morelos, Ignacio Allende, Nicolás Bravo, Mariano Matamoros, Juan Aldama, Mariano Jiménez, Leona Vicario, Vicente Guerrero (whose remains are also supposed to be interred in a tomb at the Panteón Histórico de San Fernando), Francisco Javier Mina, Guadalupe Victoria, and Andrés Quintana Roo. All in all it's a bit spooky, particularly the faceless skull of Hidalgo in the second niche. It's open 9 A.M.–6 P.M. daily; admission is free.

At the westernmost *glorieta* stands a circular fountain and a statue of the Greek goddess **Diana Cazadora** (Diana the Huntress), aiming a bow. Raised in 1942, the naked and voluptuous Diana stirred such a scandal that the sculptor, Juan Francisco Olabuíbel, was forced to add bronze undergarments to her loins. Olabuíbel later confessed he had attached the covering using only three weak solders, and the underwear was removed in 1967. Reputedly at the behest of the prudish wife of one of Mexico's presidents, Diana was again deemed too provocative for such a prominent monument, and the statue was temporarily relocated to a small park off Insurgentes. It was returned to the *glorieta* in 1992.

Punctuating the end of the Reforma business strip is the tallest building in Mexico, and indeed all of Latin America: the 55-story office building **Torre Mayor Chapultepec.** The tower, fronted with a curved wall of grey-green glass and soaring 225 meters high, has a slanted roof that looks for the world like the tip of a flat-head screwdriver. At last report, visitors were allowed to take elevators up to an observation post for $7, but this is reputedly not going to continue. If you are nearby, it might be worth stopping in the building to ask, as the views are stupendous (on a semiclear day, at least).

ZONA ROSA

A trendy area of bohemian bars and cafés in the '50s, the Zona Rosa is still one of the city's principal shopping and entertainment districts, though it's not as chic as it was in its earlier heydays. Many tourists will look around at the chain stores, fast-food restaurants, beggars, and young men offering to take them to "nightclubs with pretty ladies" and wonder why they came in the first place.

That said, the Zona Rosa is still a pleasant place to grab a cup of java in a European-style café or visit the one of the smart boutiques in the neighborhood. The Zona Rosa hotels are of good quality and are conveniently located for touring the city. You'll find music stores and bookshops, gift shops, restaurants, nightclubs, major hotels, airlines, and banks in the area. There's an antiques market on Londrés and a good selection of Mexican handicrafts for sale

the statue Diana Cazadora (Diana the Huntress) on Paseo de la Reforma

COURTESY OF MEXICO TOURISM BOARD/CARLOS SANCHEZ

at **Mercado Insurgentes** (in the first block east of Florencia between Liverpool and Londrés). Many of the shopkeepers in the area speak English; some accept U.S. dollars. Calles Copenhagen and Génova are pedestrian-only streets full of shops and sidewalk cafés. (For more information, see the *Shopping* chapter.)

The Zona Rosa isn't all shopping and restaurants, however, and in fact today the area holds more than its share of "men's clubs," a euphemism for clubs that feature erotic dancing. Increasingly it's also becoming a center for gay nightlife in Mexico City, as evidenced by the numerous clubs and bars with the rainbow flag hanging out front.

AROUND THE MONUMENTO A LA REVOLUCIÓN

The lower-middle class neighborhood around the Monumento a la Revolución, between Avenida Puente de Alvarado and Paseo de la Reforma, is slightly run down but contains several budget hotels and two points of tourist interest: the Monumento a la Revolución and Museo San Carlos.

Monumento a la Revolución

This massive marble and basalt monument to Mexico's bloody 1910–1920 revolution was begun by Porfirio Díaz to house his puppet Congress. Designed by an (inevitable) European architect who clearly aimed for an art deco structure, the building ran into massive cost overruns, and once the revolution began, it was left as an empty hulk and stayed that way for more than 20 years. When the government was on the verge of destroying the unfinished structure, Mexican architect Carlos Obregón Santacilia proposed to convert the shell into a monument to the revolution.

With the additions of several unsmiling, heroic proletariat statues on the corners, evidently influenced by the socialist realism of Russia and the Eastern Bloc, work was completed in 1938. Crypts within the "feet" of the monument hold the remains of revolutionary heroes Venustiano Carranza, Francisco I. Madero, Francisco "Pan-

cho" Villa, Plutarco Elias Calles, and Lázaro Cárdenas. It's a little ironic that the five men should end up buried in the same place, as they all despised and plotted against one another.

On weekends 10 A.M.–5:30 P.M., visitors may pass through the crypt of Plutarco Elias Calles and ride an elevator to the *mirador*, or viewpoint, in the monument's dome. And below the grand ramp running up to the eastern side of the monument lies the **Museo de la Revolución** (9 A.M.– 5 P.M. Tue.–Sat., 9 A.M.–3 P.M. Sun., admission $1), where there is a small collection of photos and memorabilia related to the revolution.

On the northeast side of the plaza, the art deco **Frontón Nacional** contains a wooden court where jai alai—the world's fastest ball game—was played until a 1995 workers' strike closed it down.

SANTA MARÍA DE LA RIBERA AND SAN RAFAEL

West of Avenida Insurgentes and on either side of Avenida San Cosme (the extension of Avenida Tacuba) are these two *colonias* dating from the mid-19th century. Built for the wealthy residents of Mexico City eager to flee the growing squalidness of the downtown area, the streets of Santa María and San Rafael (both named for the ranches on which they were built) are lined with dozens of old mansions, some in sorry states of disrepair, others beautifully restored. Both neighborhoods are resolutely lower-middle class these days, although some predict they will soon be on the upswing again, particularly San Rafael. If you've got an extra afternoon for wandering, it's worth taking a stroll through this area to enjoy a corner of Mexico City that isn't visited much by foreigners. The Alameda of Santa María is a particularly fine spot, evocative of life in the city from years past. The unusually designed art museum **Museo El Chopo** is also in Santa Maria (see the *Arts and Entertainment* chapter for details).

La Alameda de Santa María

The center of Santa María is the lovely Alameda, a leafy, tranquil park with an unusual brightly colored arabesque-style kiosk in the middle, built

© CHRIS HUMPHREY

the Eiffelesque Museo El Chopo

in 1904. On weekends the park is replete with local families out for an afternoon stroll, boys playing soccer, or young couples seeking out a quiet nook. On the west side of the Alameda is UNAM's **Museo de Geología** (tel. 5547-3900, 10 A.M.–5 P.M. Tues.–Sun.) housed in a beautiful old mansion. The displays of meteorites, fossils, and some impressive mammoth skeletons, as well as the opportunity to wander around the old building, are well worth the $1 admission charge. Check out the imposing art nouveau wrought-iron staircase in the entryway. Guided tours of the museum can be arranged by calling ahead and are even available in English if the museum director (who speaks English) is around.

Árbol de la Noche Triste

On the night of the *noche triste,* June 30, 1520, the Aztecs revolted and expelled the Spanish conquistadors from Tenochtitlán, driving them out of the city in the middle of the night along the Tacuba causeway, killing many and sending the rest fleeing for their lives. The story goes that when the remaining band of conquistadors finally managed to get to the far end of the causeway, on dry land again, Cortés leaned up against a tree and cried. And then—a testament to the will of this ferociously determined soldier—he pulled himself together and asked his company only one thing: Did the carpenter survive? It turns out he had. And so Cortés immediately began his next move, the building of a fleet of brigantines that the Spaniards used to launch an amphibious assault on the city, eventually taking it.

If you can believe it, the tree that Cortés cried against still exists. It's along Avenida Mexico-Tacuba (which is the extension of Avenida Puente de Alvarado/San Cosme), between Metro stations Cuitlahuac and Popotla. The burnt-out, destroyed tree trunk, with a small bust of Cortés nestled inside and surrounded by a metal fence, is not much of a sight to see itself. But anyone with a fascination with Mexican history will feel a shiver at the legendary spot. If you go by Metro, get off at the Popotla station, but better yet, hop a *microbus* (minibus) or take a taxi along Avenida Mexico-Tacuba and imagine yourself on the ancient Aztec causeway. Along the route you'll see a few old churches, the imposing Colegio Militar, and several old mansions from the years when this was the spot for wealthy residents to have their country homes.

San Rafael

South of Avenida Mexico-Tacuba is Colonia San Rafael, another once-upscale neighborhood that has slid into decline. In recent years younger, bohemian Mexicans, along with a smattering of expatriates, have begun moving into San Rafael, which could signal a regentrification of the neighborhood. To get a taste for the old *casonas* for which San Rafael was famous, take a walk down Calle Sadi Carnot, Avenida Mexico-Tacuba, and Monumento a la Madre, near the intersection of Insurgentes and Paseo de la Reforma. Numbers 33 and 35 are fine old mansions, and at 57 is the Universidad del Valle (tel. 5628-6375), partly housed in a restored palace.

In and Around Chapultepec

Five kilometers west of the Zócalo along Paseo de la Reforma, Bosque de Chapultepec is filled with some of the city's finest museums, green grass and trees, small lakes, and plenty of families out for a stroll, especially on Sunday. At the eastern edge of the park, crowning a 60-meter bluff, is the 18th-century Castillo de Chapultepec, a city landmark.

Generations of *capitalinos* have used Bosque de Chapultepec's six square kilometers of trees and meadows to escape the travails of the city. On weekends the grass is covered with families out for a picnic, lovers seeking secluded spots, and all manner of random folks out for a breath of fresh air. During the week the park is usually much more *tranquilo*. The main section of the park is closed on Monday.

Just north of Chapultepec is the wealthy neighborhood of Polanco, filled with upscale hotels, restaurants, and boutiques. To the south is Tacubaya, a rundown neighborhood with a couple of interesting museums housed in mansions from the area's more genteel past.

Chapultepec is home to one of the finest anthropology museums in the world, the Museo Nacional de Antropología e Historia. Two of Mexico's premier modern art museums, Museo de Arte Moderno and Museo de Arte Contemporáneo Internacional Rufino Tamayo, are both located in the Chapultepec along Paseo de la Reforma (see the *Arts and Entertainment* chapter for details).

HISTORY

The hill and forests of Chapultepec ("Grasshopper Hill" in Náhuatl, the language of the Aztecs) have occupied a special place in Mexican history since the beginning of the Aztec era. On arriving in the Valle de México in the early 13th century from their original homeland in northern Mexico, the small band of Aztecs, unwelcomed by the valley's other inhabitants, found a temporary home on Chapultepec, and it was there that they held their first "New Fire" ceremony in the valley. Shortly thereafter, the Aztecs suffered their first great defeat on Chapultepec at the hands of the neighboring Tepanecs, who forced the tribe to serve as slave-mercenaries.

Once the Aztecs had emerged from servitude to dominate the valley, Chapultepec became the hunting grounds and summer retreat of successive Aztec rulers. Aztec ally Nezahualcóyotl, the famed poet-king of Texcoco, had his own palace on the hill. In 1465, with the inauguration of the first aqueduct, it also became the principal water supply for the island city of Tenochtitlán. Aztec leaders ordered their likenesses carved into the side of the hill; the fragments of these carvings still exist today, although they are not visible to the public. The caves on the side of the rocky bluff were thought to be the sacred resting place of the last ruler of the Toltecs, whom the Aztecs believed to be their predecessors.

During the Spanish invasion of Mexico, a group of Spanish soldiers attacked an Aztec garrison at Chapultepec in 1521; they then destroyed the aqueduct and cut Tenochtitlán's water supply in preparation for the subsequent siege of the city. The aqueduct was quickly repaired after the conquest, and in 1537 King Carlos V of Spain declared the forests around Chapultepec a protected area for "the good of the population," making it Mexico's first designated nature preserve.

Not that the colonial public was allowed to frolic in the woods, of course: it remained the favored retreat for the Spanish viceroys and governing elite. It was finally turned into a public park by President Lázaro Cárdenas in the 1930s.

Toward the end of the 19th century, the Chapultepec springs that supplied the city with *agua gorda* (literally "fat water," meaning rich in minerals) for more than 400 years finally dried up because of the drainage of the valley's lakes and the sinking level of groundwater. The only remaining traces of Chapultepec's once-great water system are the Baños de Moctezuma, now a concrete pool surrounded by a fence, and the grievously mistreated colonial fountain outside the Chapultepec Metro station, where the aqueduct began. Most of the aqueduct itself was destroyed around the beginning of the 20th century, but 22 of its original 904 arches still stand, looking a bit forlorn, along Avenida Chapultepec, near the Sevilla Metro station.

ORIENTATION

Chapultepec Park extends from the eastern entrance on Paseo de la Reforma several kilometers to the west and is bordered on the south by Avenida Constituyentes and on the north (for much of the way at least) by Paseo de la Reforma. The park is divided into three sections: the first closest to downtown and containing most of the museums and sites of interest for tourists, and the second and third west of the Periférico, with an amusement park, children's museum, two restaurants, and plenty of spots for picnics or a jog.

There's a tourist information booth (9 A.M.–6 P.M. Tues.–Sun.) right in front of the Museo Nacional de Antropología that can help visitors with basic questions in English and Spanish.

Getting There and Away

The first section of Chapultepec is accessible easily enough from the Chapultepec or Auditorio Metro stations. The Chapultepec station works better for El Castillo and the two art museums, while Auditorio is closer to the zoo. The Museo Nacional de Antropología lies more or less midway between the two stations. If you prefer to take a bus, hop one of the *peseros* marked Auditorio near the Hidalgo Metro station, at the western end of the Alameda. These run as far as the Auditorio Nacional. The public is not allowed to drive in the first section, though you may see the occasional park vehicle.

To get to the second section, catch a *pesero* marked La Feria, Papalote from the Chapultepec Metro station. *Peseros* to the third section also leave from Chapultepec Metro and are marked Panteón Dolores. Several roads cut through the second and third sections, making all the sites there accessible by car.

PRIMERA SECCIÓN (FIRST SECTION)

Closest to downtown and with most of Chapultepec's favorite sights, the Primera Sección (5 A.M.–4:30 P.M. Tue.–Sun.) is where most tourists are likely to end up. Here you'll find Cerro Chapultepec itself, crowned by the castle, as well as the zoo and three museums: Museo Nacional de Antropología, Museo de Arte Moderno, and Museo Rufino Tamayo. The grounds around Cerro Chapultepec, particularly to the south toward Avenida Constituyentes, have long shady paths perfect for strolling, cycling, or in-line skating. A small train leaves from near the castle for regular 20-minute narrated (in Spanish) tours around the park for $1. Rent a bicycle to cruise the park near the Paseo de la Reforma entrance for $3.50 per hour.

On the **Lago Mayor** (Bigger Lake) and **Lago Menor** (Smaller Lake), swans and ducks mingle with canoes and rowboats. Rent a rowboat for a paddle around the lake for $1 per hour. The ballet *Swan Lake,* complete with live swans, is presented on an small island in Lago Mayor on weekends in February and March. In the verdant **Jardín de la Tercera Edad** (literally, Garden of the Third Age), the city's senior citizens practice aerobics, yoga, tai chi, and other fitness activities.

On the southwestern edge of the first section, surrounded by extensive grounds, stands the presidential mansion **Los Pinos.** Don't try hopping fences over that way unless you want to cause an international incident.

Bicycles and in-line skates are allowed in the first section of the park, but pets and alcoholic drinks are not.

M Museo Nacional de Antropología e Historia

The largest museum in Latin America, and one of the great anthropological museums of the world, the Museo de Antropología is a must-see for most foreign visitors to Mexico City. The museum recounts the crossing of the first hunter-gatherers from Asia onto the North American continent and has magnificent archaeological

The Tlaloc rain god statue in front of the Museo Nacional de Antropología e Historia was originally on a hillside east of Mexico City near Texacoco.

exhibits from early Mesoamerican societies as well as ethnological displays on Mexico's current Amerindian groups.

Apart from its archaeological and anthropological treasures, Pedro Ramírez Vásquez's building itself is an impressive work of art, with its understated exterior and dramatic central patio. In the middle of the patio, a sheer curtain of water flows from a huge overhang supported by a single concrete column. The column is covered with sculpted reliefs depicting events in Mexican history. Out front is a massive sculpture of Tlaloc, the Aztec god of rain; the sculpture came from a mountainside east of Mexico City.

The museum is laid out in two floors, with 23 exhibition rooms. Each room on the 1st floor is dedicated to the archaeology of particular geographic areas or cultures throughout Mexican history. Casual visitors may want to skip the first two rooms, which are dedicated to the profession of anthropology and Mesoamerica in general, and move directly to the "Origins" room. Here begins the chronological tracing of different civ-

ilizations that grew up in Mexico over the centuries, including Teotihuacanos, Toltecs, Olmecs, Zapotecs, and others, right up to the Aztecs. Many of the finest pieces of prehispanic art anywhere in the world are found in the rooms on this floor. Upstairs, rooms focus on the anthropology and ethnography of different indigenous groups in Mexico today, including the Huichol, Cora, Purépecha, Otomí, Nahua, and different groups from the Sierra de Puebla, Oaxaca, and Gulf of Mexico regions. The exhibits are exhaustively labeled in both Spanish and English, providing a veritable university course of anthropology for those who take the time to read them all.

A full day is required to get an adequate tour of the museum, and many people with a serious interest in Mexican history spend two. But don't be daunted: if you have just a casual interest in the subject, two or three hours of popping in and out of different halls will give you an excellent taste. Take in the museum's 20-minute orientation film before setting out to tour the five kilometers of walkways, patios, and exhibit halls. If you need to catch your breath, have a snack at the lower-level café or check out the well-stocked bookstore (both English and Spanish titles are available). Rent headsets with taped information (in English or Spanish) for $6—a good value to save your eyes from getting tired due to reading labels all day.

The museum (Paseo de la Reforma, just west of the Museo Rufino Tamayo, tel. 5553-6285 or 5553-6554, www.mna.inah.gob.mx, 9 A.M.– 7 P.M. Tues.–Sat., 10 A.M.–6 P.M. Sun., admission $4, or $10 with a camera) is best avoided on weekends, especially Sundays, when it is usually mobbed. **Note:** No flash photography is allowed. If you don't want to pay the fee, you can check your cameras and anything else not needed at the entrance.

Outside the museum, the vertiginous *voladores* perform daily. These men, who hail from the eastern state of Veracruz, perform their traditional indigenous ceremony, which entails climbing up a tall pole, hanging upside down with their feet attached to a rope, and gradually descending to the ground as the rope unwinds. Those who watch the show should contribute a small amount to the performers.

The *voladores* perform throughout the afternoon Tuesday–Sunday.

El Castillo de Chapultepec

Standing at attention atop Cerro Chapultepec, the original Castillo was built by Viceroy Bernardo de Gálvez in 1785. While Chapultepec was historically the "weekend" home of Aztecs and viceroys, the previous villas had been on the southern side of the hill, near Chapultepec's spring, while a temple (first Aztec, then Catholic) crowned the hilltop. Evidently Viceroy de Gálvez had defensive considerations in mind when he decided to build atop the hill. As it would happen, El Castillo—at that time housing the nation's military college—would be the last, and ultimately unsuccessful, bastion of defense against the U.S. Army during its 1847 invasion of Mexico City.

The castle took its current shape during the brief rule of Emperor Maximilian (1863–1867). Feeling uncomfortable in the tradition-laden Palacio Nacional downtown, Maximilian declared El Castillo to be his official residence, and he and his wife, Carlota, set about remodeling it to their liking during 1865 and 1866 in a vain effort to re-create a little corner of Europe that

El Castillo de Chapultepec

might shut out the problems of Maximilian's disastrous government. Mexicans heaped criticism on their short-lived emperor for spending so much money on the grand salons, flowered terraces, and rooftop garden.

After Maximilian and Carlota were overthrown by Benito Juárez, the castle was converted to the Mexican presidential residence. In 1876 Porfirio Díaz moved in, and under the dictator the castle's interior reached new heights of sumptuousness. President Lázaro Cárdenas, disliking the elaborate palace, moved to the more modest residence of Los Pinos in 1939, and the castle became a national history museum.

Perhaps because of its multiple historical roles, El Castillo looks as though it can't decide whether it's a Gothic fortress or a Mediterranean palace. The two-story gray stone building is divided into two distinct sections. The Alcázar, formerly the living quarters of Maximilian and Díaz, is a series of rooms and terraces laid out around a central courtyard. The different rooms are filled with 19th-century furniture, artwork, and musical instruments. The patios, once open to the air, have been covered with glass to protect the antiques and art inside. The Alcázar was closed for a year in 1999–2000 for restoration and to allow archaeologists access to the grounds below the building to learn more about the past of this key location in Mexican history.

The more stolid, heavy-looking main wing of the castle houses the **Museo Nacional de Historia** (tel. 5241-3100, www.mnh.inah.gob.mx), chronicling the nation's turbulent history between conquest and the Revolution. An extensive collection of artifacts, documents, and paintings of modern Mexican history is displayed in 20 rooms on both floors. Among the noteworthy art objects are murals by Juan O'Gorman (of Mexican history), Davíd Alfaro Siqueiros (of Revolutionary leaders), and José Clemente Orozco (of Benito Juárez).

Outside the castle (10 A.M.–5 P.M. Tue.–Sun., admission $4), a side terrace garden makes a quiet place to sit, rest, and admire the views (air quality permitting). Just down the stairs from the terrace is a small, dingy snack shop (good for soft drinks at least).

Monumento de los Niños Héroes

Right below the castle at the foot of Cerro Chapultepec, this six-towered monument commemorates a heroic though ultimately doomed defense of the castle against invading U.S. troops during the Mexican-American War. On September 13, 1847, when it was clear the Americans would take the castle, six military cadets—Juan de la Barrera, Juan Escutia, Fernando Montes de Oca, Vicente Suárez, Francisco Marquéz, and Agustín Melgar—reputedly wrapped themselves in Mexican flags and jumped to their deaths from the castle ramparts rather than surrender. Their deaths are honored by six tall columns, each topped with a black eagle. On September 13, the Mexican president holds a solemn national ceremony honoring the cadets.

Behind the main monument, right up against the edge of the hill, is a smaller monument, a semicircle with paintings of each of the six cadets. Right behind the fence here, archaeologists have made some fascinating discoveries in recent years, including Aztec carvings in the rock and burials dating from the era of Teotihuacán, around the time of Christ. At the moment the area is closed to the public, but it may be opened in the future.

Zoológico de Chapultepec

The Chapultepec Zoo (9 A.M.–4:15 P.M. Tues.–Sun., admission free) houses about 1,600 animals of 270 species, the most famous of which are a family of pandas. As zoos go it's relatively humane, giving most animals plenty of room to roam. If you're tired of walking take the minitrain from the station in the center of the zoo. Admission to the zoo is free, but there is a small charge for the train ride. Next to the zoo is the park's botanical gardens.

Also next door is the **Casa del Lago** (tel. 5211-6093, www.casadellago.unam.mx), a cultural center run by UNAM that often shows art exhibits and holds cultural events.

Baños de Moctezuma

Around on the south side of Cerro Chapultepec, following the paved road from behind the Niños Héroes monument, lie the dilapidated remains of the Baños de Moctezuma. Legend has it

Moctezuma once threw treasure into the well on the south side of hill to placate Tlaloc, the Aztec rain god, when the city was flooded. As a result, treasure hunters from across the centuries have dug all around the area—so far, in vain. Even though the baths aren't much to see nowadays, it's worth wandering over that way to enjoy walking in a quieter part of the park.

Just above the *baños* one can see channels cut into the rock where the old springs welled up, supplying Mexico City with much of its drinking water for centuries. Up until the mid-20th century, water still rose here, but it's now long gone.

SEGUNDA SECCIÓN (SECOND SECTION)

On the west side of the Periférico highway lies Chapultepec's second section. The main attractions here include a children's museum, an amusement park, and two upscale restaurants: Café del Lago and Café del Bosque. Mexico City residents seeking a place to exercise near the city frequent the meadows and stands of trees to jog and kick a soccer ball on weekends. Just up an old flight of steps in front of the roller coaster are several large, circular old water storage tanks that have been filled in with dirt and now serve as impromptu soccer fields.

La Feria de Chapultepec

This amusement park (10 A.M.–9 P.M. daily, admission $7) is in the western section of the park, on the far side of the Periférico from El Castillo. It's easy to spot—just look for the towering *montaña rusa,* (Russian mountain, as roller coasters are known here).

TERCERA SECCIÓN (THIRD SECTION)

Past the Panteón Dolores is the newest section of Chapultepec, added only in the 1970s as the city expanded to the west. The third section is a jum-ble of ravines, meadows, patches of forest, and a few caves, not really developed for visitors beyond a few picnic tables set up by the roadside. Aside from the grounds of the horse club, it's unfortunately not the safest place to go walking or jogging—better to stick to the first and second sections.

Lienzo Charro

Charreadas—the Mexican equivalent of the rodeo, but with considerably more finesse and pageantry—are held in the *charro* ring from time to time throughout the year. For current scheduling, contact the Asociación Nacional de la Charrería (Av. Constituyentes 500, tel. 5277-8706, www.nacionaldecharros.com).

POLANCO

Opposite the Paseo de la Reforma from the first section of Chapultepec is Polanco, a Rodeo Drive–style area replete with modern high-rises, hotels, elegant shops, art galleries, embassies, and fine restaurants. Originally land belonging to a colonial silkworm farm known as Hacienda de los Morales, Polanco was subdivided and developed in the late 1930s and early 1940s and was for years the most exclusive neighborhood in Mexico City. While it is still the highest-end shopping district, many of the superrich have moved farther west to Tecamachalco or Lomas.

Polanco may not have many tourist sites as such, but if you're after upscale lodgings, top-quality dining, and all the shopping you can handle, this is the place. Just be sure not to forget your wallet. Polanco is also home to many foreign embassies, so you may find yourself coming this way if you plan to travel elsewhere in Latin America from Mexico City. A perennial favorite among foreign visitors to Mexico City is **Hacienda de los Morales,** a superb restaurant specializing in traditional Mexican cuisine housed in the original 16th-century hacienda in the area (see the *Restaurants* chapter for more details).

Insurgentes Sur

Along both sides of Avenida Insurgentes Sur, between the Zona Rosa and San Ángel, lies a series of residential neighborhoods, including Roma, Condesa, Del Valle, Nápoles, and Mixcoac. While only the Roma merits a visit in its own right, due to its Porfiriato-era mansions and tranquil parks, both Roma and Condesa are two of the most happening neighborhoods in the city, filled with young people of all sorts attracted to restaurants, cafés, art galleries, and cosmopolitan nightlife. The Condesa boasts the trendiest restaurant district in the city.

ROMA

A tree-lined residential neighborhood between Avenida Cuauhtémoc and Insurgentes, south of Avenida Chapultepec, the Roma was the most upscale area of the city when it was built in the early 20th century, and in recent years it has once again become fashionable. Many of the old mansions, left to decay over the decades, have been renovated by wealthy residents with a taste for the neighborhood's genteel ambience, while others now house cafés and art galleries.

While the Roma does not have many tourist sights apart from the Casa Lamm cultural center, visitors may enjoy a couple of hours strolling the quiet, leafy streets lined with Porfiriato-era mansions. Most casual tourists will want to walk around the Roma for an hour or two, visit the Casa Lamm, and have a cup of coffee or a meal in one of a number of good restaurants before returning to their home or hotel. But those who like bohemian-style neighborhoods may like to dally among the bookshops, cafés, and quiet streets. There's a street market with all sorts of art and collectibles on the walkway in the middle of the main street in the Roma, Álvaro Obregón, between Frontera and Orizaba on weekends until 5 P.M.

Since the Roma began its resurgence during the late 1980s and 1990s, it has become Mexico City's premier location for contemporary art galleries. (See the *Arts and Entertainment* chapter for gallery listings.)

THE LONG AND NOT SO WINDING ROAD

An appropriately hyperbolic avenue for this city of excess, Insurgentes stretches a full 45 kilometers in length, from just short of Ecatepec in the northeast, at the exit to Pachuca, across the entire valley to Tlalpan and the highway to Cuernavaca in the south. By one counting (a local one, admittedly), it's the longest avenue in the world.

Lengthy Insurgentes came into being in the 1950s, shortly after the construction of the new university complex south of San Ángel, as the city government linked up dozens of smaller, unconnected roads to form the avenue.

Traffic on Insurgentes is proverbial. One of the jokes going around says the city government should hang strings of garlic on lampposts up and down Insurgentes to improve circulation. At the intersection with Avenida Mixcoac, one of the dozens of tangled traffic interchanges that turn into battle zones along Insurgentes during the afternoon, 15,000 cars pass per minute during peak hours.

While in the U.S. or Europe such a traffic artery would be given over exclusively to vehicles, millions of pedestrians swarm on and around Insurgentes day and night. It's practically an elongated city in its own right, a sort of urban epiphany, a literal cross-section of Mexico City life. The avenue passes through 60 of the city's 300-odd *colonias* and five of its 16 *delegaciones*. At last count, Insurgentes claimed 217 restaurants, 172 bars, 97 banks, 30 department stores, 12 gas stations, 8 Metro stations, 4 federal secretariat offices, the headquarters of the Institutional Revolutionary Party (PRI), and UNAM (the national university), to name only a few of the most prominent *avenida*-dwellers.

LA ROMITA

The "shameful daughter of the Colonia Roma," as one early chronicler labeled it, La Romita is a tiny corner of the Roma Norte, near the Metro Chapultepec station, with a singularly bad reputation. La Romita was actually the original native village in the area, long predating the building of the Roma (in the early 20th century). In fact, the original Roma developers fought a lengthy battle to try to incorporate what is now La Romita into their neighborhood plans, while the locals resisted tooth and nail.

From this inauspicious beginning, the plaza and little chapel of La Romita were off limits for the wealthy families of the Roma, who feared getting robbed by La Romita's many *rateros* (literally, "ratters," i.e., thieves). La Romita even boasted two legendary female thieves during the 1930s and 1940s, Plácida Hernández and the ominously named "La Loba" (The She-Wolf).

But the most famed crooks to come out of La Romita managed to take their dirty deeds to another level altogether. During the 1940s a gang known as Los Halcones, led by a thug named Arturo "El Negro" Durazo, controlled part of La Romita's turf. Durazo befriended a more bookish type by the name of José "Pepito" López Portillo and made sure no harm came to the young man.

López Portillo went on to a career in politics and arrived at the presidency (1976–1982). In Mexico one does not forget past favors lightly, so López Portillo made his old protector Durazo the police chief of Mexico City. Thus began a reign of official terror, bringing the routine corruption of the city police to new lows of venality, until El Negro was ousted and imprisoned by the administration of President Miguel de la Madrid.

Los Halcones and their ilk are long gone, but in La Romita their aura somehow lingers. Trying to find the little square and church, just a few meters from Avenida Cuauhtémoc but only reached by a couple of narrow side streets, is no easy task. When you ask a local where the plaza is, the first reply is invariably to warn you about getting robbed. But on one recent afternoon, the only people in the shady little plaza were a young mother and her baby, and an old man eager to tell a foreign visitor stories of La Romita's legendary past. Of course, there were also three suspicious-looking young men huddled together in the alley next to the church, looking at the visitor with interest. . . .

Orientation

The Roma has Metro stations at each of its four corners, clockwise from the northwest: Metro Insurgentes, Metro Cuauhtémoc, Metro Centro Médico, and Metro Chilpancingo. For the Roma Norte, where most visitors will likely be going, Metro Insurgentes is the closest.

By bus from the Centro, take a *pesero* to Insurgentes, and change on another bus going south on Insurgentes. Get off just past the large traffic circle, about one kilometer south of Reforma. The Roma is on the left (east) side of Insurgentes.

If you're in the Zona Rosa, it's just a 10-minute walk over to the Roma. Follow the pedestrian street Génova to the Insurgentes Metro roundabout, go straight underneath, and come out the other side, and you'll be on Calle Jalapa in the Roma Norte (North Roma).

History

The land on which the Roma now stands is thought to have originally been "grown" from *chinampas,* the floating islands made of twigs, earth, and compost that were built on the lake for agricultural purposes, and which eventually became solid chunks of land. After the conquest, it became part of the estate granted by the Spanish crown to Hernán Cortés in 1529, and by the early 20th century, it was owned by descendents of the Conde de Miravalle.

The Roma was planned and developed by a group of foreigners operating together as the Compañía de Terrenos de la Calzada de Chapultepec. The principal partners were Edward Walter Orrin (British owner of a Mexican traveling circus) and U.S. engineer Casius Clay Lamm and his sons. Porfirio Díaz Jr. also participated, which no doubt eased government approval. With the city growing rapidly westward, especially around the newly chic Paseo de la Reforma, the wealthy were clamoring to move out of the crumbling downtown and into better neighborhoods.

In 1903 the Díaz administration gave permission to Orrin, Lamm, and crew to divide up the land into lots and committed itself to provide public services to the new development. Construction began immediately, and the Roma quickly became the chosen place to live for the second-level elite, as it were: wealthy families eager to move out of the decaying Centro but unable to afford building on Paseo de la Reforma.

In the 1930s, the neighboring Condesa district became fashionable, and by the 1940s and 1950s, the Roma was slipping into decay. Many of the "better" families moved on to newer developments farther west in Polanco or Lomas, while poorer families migrating to Mexico City began to take over the old mansions and turn them into apartment buildings.

Nonetheless Roma remained trendy, but for the genteel poverty favored by many Mexican artists and intelligentsia. Because so many writers have lived in the Roma, several important Mexican novels take place in the neighborhood, including *Batallas en el desierto,* by José Emilio Pacheco; *Agua quemada,* by Carlos Fuentes; *Manifestación de silencios,* by Arturo Azuela; and more recently *El vampiro de la colonia Roma,* by Luis Zapata.

The few remaining wealthy residents of the Roma fled after the devastating 1985 earthquake. Because it was built on soft, unstable subsoil, the quake rocked the Roma, toppling hundreds of new, shoddily built apartments and houses, killing hundreds of neighborhood residents and leaving 15,000 homeless.

In part because the rents fell sharply in the Roma after the earthquake, a resurgence of sorts has been under way since the early 1990s. A younger crowd of artists and other urban hipsters, as well as the wealthy who want to be associated with them, have been moving back in and renovating many of the crumbling old mansions, particularly in the Roma Norte between Álvaro Obregón and Avenida Chapultepec.

Around Plaza Río de Janeiro

For a stroll around the Roma, the best place to start is the old heart of the neighborhood, Plaza Río de Janeiro (originally called Plaza Roma), just a few blocks southeast of the Insurgentes Metro station.

Although a couple of remarkably ugly towers now scar the park's skyline, one can still enjoy the graceful mansions around the stately park, with its fountain and a replica of Michelangelo's *David* statue in the center. One building worth a look is **La Casa de las Brujas** (Witches' House), as the Edificio Río de Janeiro is popularly known. It's not hard to spot the striking red-brick castle, built in 1908, on the east side of the park. Note the "face" formed by the windows right on the top floor of the corner tower, and the art deco entranceway, which was added in the 1930s.

A block north of the park, at Orizaba 24 at the corner of Puebla, is the **Casa Universitária del Libro** (10 A.M.–3 P.M. and 5–8 P.M. Mon.–Fri.), the offices of a small publishing house run by UNAM. During working hours, visitors may sign in and tour a small museum in the renovated mansion, which affords an opportunity to view the lovely wood interior and exceptional stained-glass windows of the central atrium.

The blocks between Plaza Río de Janeiro and Álvaro Obregón are dotted with mansions built in the early 20th century, decorated in a variety of eclectic styles. A few noteworthy examples:

Tabasco 133, at the corner of Córdoba: a 1917 mansion with fine iron grillwork and stone carvings over the windows.

Colima 145 at Córdoba: a squat facade with subtle art nouveau stone details.

Colima 168: a Venetian-style palace with pink trim.

Álvaro Obregón and Orizaba: the reserved, elegant Edificio Balmori, overshadowed by a monstrous concrete tower right next door.

Three blocks south of Álvaro Obregón on Orizaba is another tranquil small park called Plaza Luis Cabrera, the setting for part of José Emilio Pacheco's classic short story, *La batallas en el desierto.*

Casa Lamm

If you have time only for a brief visit to the Roma, at least make sure to take a look around Casa Lamm, a cultural center with an art gallery, a wonderful bookstore, and restaurant all situated in a beautifully restored 1911 mansion at Álvaro Obregón 99, at the corner of Orizaba. Whether you're interested in seeing the art exhibits or not, the mansion is worth visiting to get an idea of how people lived in the heyday of the Roma.

It was built by Lewis Lamm, son of one of Roma's founders, but the architect never got around to living there and instead rented it for years to a religious orphanage. In 1939 the house was sold to a private family who lived in it until 1990, saving the building from the depredations faced by other Roma mansions.

In 1993 Casa Lamm was renovated and opened as a private cultural institute (tel. 5514-4899, www.lamm.com.mx) that holds frequent exhibits and events and teaches a couple of dozen university-level courses each year on art, literature, music, politics, and society. Courses cost $200–800 per four-month semester. A program of guided visits to 10 different art galleries in the city over the course of a semester costs $250. Look on their website or call for more information.

Since it was opened, the Casa Lamm has mounted regular exhibits of all variety of art, but in 1999 the institute received stewardship of a large collection of art amassed by Mexican media giant Televisa. This collection had formerly been housed in the now-closed Centro de Arte Contemporáneo in Polanco. The collection contains hundreds of works by many famed Mexican and international artists, including Sergio Hernández, María Izquierdo, Francisco Toledo, Jasper Johns, Gerhard Richter, Manuel Álvarez Bravo, Tina Modotti, and Guillermo Kahlo (photographer and father of Frida).

Casa Lamm built a new wing in the courtyard to house a small exhibit space (tel. 5511-0899, www.galeriacasalamm.com.mx, 10 A.M.–6 P.M. Tues.–Sun.) with rotating art displays. The visiting exhibits will continue as well, both in the atrium upstairs in the main house and in the annex. There is no charge to visit the exhibits. Downstairs is the **Biblioteca de Arte** (10 A.M.–7 P.M.), an art library.

On the ground floor of the main house is **Librería Pegaso** (tel. 5208-0171 or 5208-0174, 10 A.M.–8 P.M. daily), one of the most user-friendly bookstores in Mexico City, with free coffee and comfy couches in the middle of the store to relax on. The store has an extensive selection of titles, many in English, and the art book collection is particularly good. All-day browsing is tolerated.

An odd-looking, glassed-in porch structure built into the corner of the old *casona* houses the **Restaurante Lamm,** which has very good international cuisine (see the *Restaurants* chapter for more details).

CONDESA

Until the mid-1980s, this leafy, quiet *colonia* of attractive art deco–era buildings was an upper-middle class preserve populated predominantly by Jewish families who moved there from the Centro decades past. The Condesa was not badly damaged in the 1985 earthquake, but many of the older Condesa families joined the exodus to newer suburbs farther west outside of the downtown area. And as with the Roma, the sudden drop in rents and increase in apartment openings led to a recolonization of sorts, this time with actors, gays, artists, journalists, and other bohemian types, who appreciate the local parks, attractive apartment buildings, and many restaurants and bars. In recent years the number of restaurants has exploded, and rents have swung up dramatically (my old three-bedroom apartment on Parque México, which I first rented for $300 a month in 1996, now goes for $1100); consequently, the neighborhood is once again becoming more upscale.

One website with lots of information on the Condesa is www.coloniacondesa.com.mx.

History

After the Roma began filling up with mansions in the 1920s, the next neighborhood to develop was the Condesa, to the south and west of the Roma. Originally part of a hacienda owned by an old *casona* with a funny new hat at the end of Avenida Veracruz in the Condesa

© CHRIS HUMPHREY

Parque México called Hipódromo Condesa (because of the former horsetrack), and the section west of Nuevo León known as the Condesa, which is where most of the restaurants are located. Many people now think of both parts simply as the Condesa.

The closest Metro station for the Hipódromo Condesa is Metro Chilpancingo, while the nearest to the restaurant district in the Condesa is Metro Patriotismo. If you drive to the Condesa, Parque México is a good place to park your car, as spots are usually available. The streets around the restaurant zone are more congested.

Sights

Despite the growing popularity of the Condesa among young Mexicans and foreigners as a place to live and hang out, there's not a whole lot for most visitors to do apart from eating out at one of the (generally pricey) restaurants. But if you feel like seeing something besides colonial churches and museums, you might consider walking around **M Parque México** and surrounding streets for a couple of hours, or relaxing on a bench with a book or your journal in the park.

The large, oval-shaped park, built on the site of a horsetrack, is filled with remarkably lush, almost tropical vegetation, and it is a wonderful oasis of clean air in the midst of the city. If you're a runner, you might consider joining the many locals who get their daily exercise jogging, in-line skating, or just walking their dogs around the park. The *camellón*-filled central pedestrian walkway along Avenida Amsterdam, which forms a larger oval around the park one block away, is also a good place to run.

While the hype of the Condesa as the most pristine art deco neighborhood outside of Miami's South Beach is overblown, there are several elegant deco/functionalist apartment houses facing Parque México. Near the north end of the park, right next to the Suburbia department store at the corner of Sonora, is **Edificio Basurto,** named in honor of its architect (José Basurto), who was also one of the developers of the Condesa. For a brief time after its construction in the 1920s, this was the tallest building in Mexico City. It's hard to appreciate the architecture from the

the Condesa de Miravalle (hence the name), the land had nothing on it but open pastures and a defunct horseracing track when a street plan was drawn up in 1924.

Rather than destroy the old racetrack, Mexican developers José Basurto and José de la Lama incorporated the shape into their street plan, giving us the oval Avenida Amsterdam, with Parque México in the middle. Many of the wealthier Catholic and Jewish families still living in the Centro began moving into Condesa in the 1930s and 1940s. The time period is reflected in the architecture, with art deco stylings on some of the older buildings.

Orientation

The Condesa is bordered on the east by Insurgentes Sur, on the south by Eje 3 Sur Baja California, on the west by Avenida Patriotismo (a section of the Circuito Interior), and on the north by the Roma Norte. The neighborhood itself is divided in two, the eastern half around outside, but the circular atrium and apartments have clean, crisp lines.

Parque México is divided by two streets, Michoacán (in the middle) and Sonora (at the north end). Follow Michoacán four blocks to the west, across Nuevo León and Tamaulipas, and you'll find yourself in the middle of the Condesa restaurant and café zone. Following Sonora west from Parque México will take you across Nuevo León to **Parque España,** a second, smaller park; it's not as nice as Parque México, because it's stranded next to a major avenue. Beyond Parque España is the stately Avenida Veracruz, which is still a bit run down in places but is quickly being gentrified.

TACUBAYA

Now an unlovely neighborhood of elevated highways and rather dirty backstreets west of Condesa, the sorely mistreated Colonia Tacubaya is one of the oldest settlement areas in the Valle de México. Although it's certainly not atop the list for tourists with a limited time in the city, those who have a more leisurely schedule or who live in Mexico City might enjoy a day walking around the Tacubaya for a taste of an unusual corner of the city.

Tacubaya is situated at the edge of the long-gone lake, right where several small rivers come out of the hills; its name derives from an Aztec word meaning "where one drinks water." The area was controlled by the Tepanecas when the Aztecs arrived in the valley, but the intruders soon saw fit to conquer this strategic location. After the arrival of the Spanish, Tacubaya became one of the favored places for the colonial elite to live because of its fresh air, clean water, and myriad orchards. For a brief time in the 17th century, when the downtown area was flooded for a period of five years, it was the colony's capital. Tacubaya was also the birthplace of Mexican industry, with the construction of mills along the Becerra, Tacubaya, and de la Piedad Rivers. Only one mill, the Santo Domingo, still exists today, but it contains private homes and is not open for visitors.

Apart from the Casa de la Bola and the Museo Casa Barragán, the Museo Nacional de la Car-

tografía—an obscure army-run museum housed in a former 16th-century Franciscan convent—is also in the Tacubaya (see the *Arts and Entertainment* chapter for details).

Casa de la Bola and Parque Lira

This medium-sized park is a little corner of leafy tranquility amid the avenues of Tacubaya. It is easily reached from Metro Tacubaya or via taxi along Avenida Parque Lira or Avenida Observatorio. Giving a magnificent taste of what life was like in Tacubaya during its era of colonial glory is the Casa de la Bola, an unusual and little-known museum in an old mansion in a corner of the park. Step off the noisy avenues through the doors of the Casa de la Bola, and the blissfully calm courtyard and garden will make the city seem a distant dream.

Built in the early 17th century, this lovely mansion (Av. Parque Lira 136, tel. 5515-8825, 11 A.M.–5 P.M. Sun. or by appointment, admission $2.50) was first the home of Mexico's grand inquisitor, after which it changed hands frequently over the years before its last owner, Antonio Haghenbeck y de la Lama, donated it to the government in the 1940s. Haghenbeck maintained the two-story house much as it had looked during the colonial era, supplementing the decor with his own unusually rich tastes, judging from all the fine furniture, tapestries, and artwork inside. Visitors see the house through a guided tour.

At the northern end of Parque Lira is the **Delegación Miguel Hidalgo building,** the administrative offices for this part of the city. Evidently a former colonial hacienda, the sprawling red-brick complex has the **Capilla de Nuestra Señora de Guadalupe** on site.

Across Avenida Parque Lira, a several-block walk through the San Miguel Chapultepec neighborhood, is the first still-operating art gallery in Mexico City, **Galería de Arte Mexicano** (Gobernador Rafael Rebollar 43, tel. 5273-1261, artgam@prodigy.net.mx).

Museo Casa Barragán

A museum dedicated to Luis Barragán, one of Mexico's greatest architects, is in a house that Barragán built near Metro Constituyentes—it's well worth a visit for architecture fans. At **Museo Casa Barragán** (Av. General Francisco Ramírez 14, tel. 5272-4945, tours by prior appointment only 10 A.M.–2 P.M. and 4–6 P.M. Mon.–Fri., 10 A.M.–1 P.M. Sat., admission $7) visitors are taken on guided tours that are available in Spanish, English, and French. The museum, declared a UNESCO World Heritage Site in 2004, is a house built in 1947 by Barragán for himself. Located near the Constituyentes Metro station, the museum was left exactly how Barragán left it when he died in 1988. The house's interior is a fascinating display of Barragán's powerful use of simple, unadorned lines and powerful, bright primary colors. The rear of the extra-tall main room is covered with a large window facing a small interior garden.

Born in 1902, Barragán was seduced early in his career by the more international styles prominent in Europe, as he lived there between the wars. However, he was increasingly influenced by the stylistic traditions of his own country, as well as of the Mediterranean, and by the late 1940s he had developed his own unique vision. In particular his technique relied on imposing walls conceived as pure planes but enlivened with bright colors; he also used natural materials, such as adobe, timber, or even water. He emphasized the importance of gardens as a crucial space and liked to describe himself as primarily a landscape architect.

NÁPOLES, DEL VALLE, AND MIXCOAC

Until the 1940s, south of what was then the Río de la Piedad (and is now the Viaducto highway, covering the now-entubed river), there was nothing but open fields with a few scattered country houses until you reached San Ángel. But with the construction of Avenida Insurgentes, the Nápoles and Del Valle middle class neighborhoods were developed. Farther south is Mixcoac, a former village which has long since been overtaken by the city, though it still has a couple of quiet squares and colonial buildings. Apart from visiting the Polyforum Siqueiros or passing along Insurgentes to get to San Ángel, casual tourists won't find much reason to come down this way.

Metro Chilpancingo is the southernmost Metro station along Insurgentes, so to get anywhere between the Condesa and San Ángel along Insurgentes, hop any one of the constantly passing *peseros* marked "San Ángel" (going south) or "Reforma/La Raza" (going north). Metro Mixcoac, on Avenida Revolución, is a short walk from the Mixcoac neighborhood.

Políforo Cultural Siqueiros

On Insurgentes Sur south of the Viaducto, in the shadow of the monstrous 50-story World Trade Center de México, is this eye-catching, geometric building covered with huge mural paintings inside and outside by Mexican artist Davíd Alfaro Siqueiros.

The Polyforum was the brainchild of ex-revolutionary and later businessman Manuel Suárez y Suárez, who originally conceived of the building for a location in Cuernavaca. But seeing the unique structure and the murals begun by Siqueiros, President Gustavo Díaz Ordaz convinced Suárez to relocate it to its present site.

The 12-sided building was designed to resemble a diamond sitting on four pillars. Inside are eight facets, and three horizontal levels. The first is the entrance, with a small, free museum about the Polyforum, while in the center, but set down a level, is a 500-seat circular theater often used for drama productions. For upcoming show information, call the Polyforum (Insurgentes Sur 701, tel. 5536-4520, 9 A.M.–7 P.M. daily, mural viewing $1.25, museum free).

Upstairs is the main forum hall, frequently used for major events, particularly by the leftist Democratic Revolution Party (PRD), which perhaps feels an affinity for the socialist beliefs expressed in the monumental, three-dimensional mural created by Siqueiros inside the hall, titled *La marcha de la Humanidad* (The March of Humanity). At 11:30 A.M., 12:45 P.M., and 5 P.M. on weekends only, visitors can attend a sound-and-light show ($3.50) narrated by a recording of Siqueiros, describing his vision in the mural.

Nápoles and Del Valle

South of the World Trade Center along Insurgentes are the Nápoles (west of Insurgentes) and

Mexico City is full of hidden parks and colonial churches, such as Capilla San Lorenzo Martír in Colonia Del Valle.

© CHRIS HUMPHREY

Del Valle (east of Insurgentes) neighborhoods, residential areas developed in the 1950s. At the north end are two major stadiums, the **Estadio Azul** soccer stadium, and right next door the **Plaza de Toros México,** the largest bullfighting ring in the Americas. Farther south, between Eje 6 Sur and Eje 7 Sur, is **Parque Hundido** (Sunken Park), a large leafy park along Insurgentes, set below street level. The gravel and dirt paths of the park, lined with about 50 reproductions of prehispanic sculptures, are a good place for a jog—as with Parque México in the Condesa, the trees seem to help keep out the fumes from traffic on nearby Insurgentes.

Across Insurgentes from Parque Hundido is the smaller **Parque San Lorenzo,** another tree-filled park. This one boasts a couple of basketball courts and the 16th-century chapel **Capilla San Lorenzo Martír** dedicated to San Lorenzo Martír, with a bare facade and a worn brick bell tower.

Mixcoac

Another one of the many "lost" neighborhoods populating unlikely corners of Mexico City, Mixcoac is a small oasis of cobblestone streets and colonial buildings hidden between the noisy avenues of Insurgentes and Patriotismo. The only sight, per se, in the neighborhood is the **Instituto de Mora** (Plaza Valentín Gómez Farías 12, tel. 5598-3777, www.institutomora.edu.mx, 8 A.M.–7 P.M. Mon.–Fri., 8 A.M.–3:30 P.M. Sat.), a library specializing in the history of Mexico, Latin America, and the United States. Housed in what was briefly the home of ex-president Valentín Gómez Farías, the library is a wonderful place for anyone interested in history (and who can read Spanish). There's a peaceful garden to sit and read in and a small cafeteria to buy coffee or snacks. In front of the building is a quiet, tree-filled square, and across the street is the colonial-era **Iglesia de San Juan.**

Several blocks south from the Instituto Mora, across Avenida Felix Cuevas, is what was the old center of Mixcoac, a remarkably quiet pedestrian area with three interconnecting plazas. Three buildings of note here are the **Casa de Cultura Juan Rulfo,** housed in what was the old Palacio Municipal; the 17th-century **Parroquia de Santo Domingo de Guzmán** church and adjacent convent complex; and the **Universidad Panamericana,** housed in what was an 18th-century textile factory and hacienda. In the archways of a building right opposite the university is **Café Los Arcos,** a sidewalk coffee shop invariably filled with students; it makes a great spot for a soft drink or coffee.

By public transportation, the easiest way to get to Mixcoac is to go by Metro to the Mixcoac station and walk from there.

Southern Mexico City

COYOACÁN

Eight kilometers south of the Centro, Coyoacán was once a walled colonial village separated from Mexico City proper by farmland and lakes, and it remains one of the most traditional neighborhoods in the Distrito Federal. The plazas and narrow cobbled streets of Coyoacán, once part of huge haciendas and convents, are marvelous places for visitors to stroll and appreciate the neighborhood's relaxed ambience. Not for nothing was Coyoacán voted the fifth most liveable neighborhood in North America (ahead of Rittenhouse, Philadelphia, and behind Camden, Maine—go figure) according to a 2004 survey held by the Project on Public Spaces.

After the Centro Histórico, Coyoacán might be the most tour-worthy part of in the city—even if it didn't contain the highly popular Museo Frida Kahlo (which it does). Visitors who think that nearby San Ángel is too pricey or "precious" often find Coyoacán more to their taste.

Coyoacán life is centered on its twin main plazas, Jardín del Centenario and Jardín Hidalgo. On weekends the plazas fill with all manner of street vendors, musicians, and passersby—so many that it can be difficult to find room to walk. Casual tourists may wish to avoid the mad throng on weekends, but it's also when all the handicraft vendors come out and free concerts on the bandstand take place. Take a break from walking at one of the plaza cafés under brightly colored awnings, while organ grinders play beneath towering Indian laurel trees.

Most attractions lie within easy walking distance of the two plazas. For tourist information, go through the main doorway of the Casa Municipal, on the north side of Jardín del Centenario, and immediately on your right you'll find the Centro de Información y Servicios Turísticos de Coyoacán (tel. 5658-0221, 8 A.M.–8 P.M. daily). At the northwest corner of the plaza is a Banamex, where you can change money or use the ATM if needed.

History

When the conquistadors arrived in Coyoacán in the early 16th century, it was populated by Aztecs, who called the area Coyohuacan, a Náhuatl name meaning "place of coyotes." Hernán Cortés and his troops were very well received in Coyoacán by the area's earlier inhabitants, the Tepanecas, who resented the oppressive Aztec domination of their homelands. At that time Lago de Texcoco extended all the way south to Coyoacán, and Cortés chose the lakeside port as the spot for his headquarters during the conquest of Tenochtitlán, the Aztec capital. As the reconstruction of the conquered capital was under way, Cortés installed himself in Coyoacán and made it the first capital of Nueva España between 1521 and 1523. Coyoacán's current Casa Municipal sits at the north end of Jardín del Centenario on the site of one of Cortés's many former residences.

After Mexican independence from Spain, one of the most notable local historic events occurred on August 20, 1847, when the Convento de Churubusco became the scene of a fierce battle between Mexican troops and invading U.S. forces during the Mexican-American War.

In 1923, the famous Escuela de Pintura al Aire Libre (Open Air School of Painting) was founded in the former Hacienda de San Pedro Mártir, thus establishing Coyoacán as an artists' colony. Later in the 20th century, Coyoacán offered refuge to two world-renowned exiles, Romania's King Carol and Russia's Leon Trotsky.

Coyoacán became part of the Distrito Federal upon the ratification of Mexico's 1857 constitution. Today, the Delegación Coyoacán (much bigger than the colonial neighborhood that tourists visit) extends over 60 square kilometers and is bisected by three waterways, including the channeled Río Churubusco, the partially channeled Río Chiquito, and the Canal Nacional. Around 640,000 residents live in Coyoacán, making it the fourth most populous of the D.F.'s 16 *delegaciónes*.

Getting There

To get to Coyoacán from the city center, take the Línea 3 Metro to the Miguel Ángel de Quevedo station and hop a *pesero* heading east on Avenida M. A. de Quevedo, telling the driver that you want to get off at Calle Tres Cruces. Walk north along Tres Cruces, which becomes Calle Centenario and reaches the west side of Jardín Centenario after five blocks. Two other Línea 3 Metro possibilities are the Coyoacán and Viveros stations, each about a 20-minute walk from the plazas. Another way to combine bus and Metro would be to catch a Línea 2 Metro to the Tasqueña station, southeast of Coyoacán, and from there hop a *pesero* directly to Plaza Centenario, Coyoacán. This takes a little longer but allows you to avoid having to walk into Coyoacán.

Jardín Hidalgo and Casa Municipal

Bordered east, west, and north by Calles Carillo Puerto, Caballocalco, and B. Domínguez, Coyoacán's lovely *zócalo* (square) is a traditional

Parroquia de San Juan Batista in Jardín Hidalgo, Coyoacán

COURTESY OF MEXICO TOURISM BOARD/CARLOS SANCHEZ

rectangle centered around a 19th-century kiosk. The kiosk features a stained-glass cupola topped by a bronze republican eagle. Along the north side of the plaza lies the Casa Municipal, which houses local and federal government offices on the site of a former Cortés residence. An attached chapel contains Diego Rosales frescoes narrating local history, while the Sala de Cabildos (Council Hall) features an elaborate mural by the painter Aurora Reyes.

Parroquia y Ex-Convento de San Juan Bautista

Built in 1589 by Dominican friars (and later transferred to the Franciscans), this parish church and former convent looms over the southeast corner of Jardín Hidalgo. The plastered early baroque facade is original, while the interior has been beautifully reconstructed. In one of the church's three naves, the Capilla de Rosario contains an ornate baroque *retablo* from the end of the 17th century.

Jardín del Centenario

This smaller plaza to the west of Jardín Hidalgo is centered around a fountain and bronze sculptures of two coyotes, a reference to the literal meaning of the name Coyoacán. The south side of the verdant plaza is lined with cafés and restaurants, including the very well-known Café El Parnaso, considered the perfect place for a philosophical chat over a cup of coffee. Just off the square is the Museo Nacional de Culturas Populares, a cultural museum on Avenida Hidalgo, worth a look to see what the current exhibit is (see the *Arts and Entertainment* chapter for details).

Acuario Acuavida Coyoacán

Facing the north side of the Plaza del Centenario, this public aquarium (tel. 5659-2060, 10 A.M.–8 P.M. Tues.–Fri., 10 A.M.–10 P.M. Sat. and Sun., admission $2 for adults, $1 for children 3–11) offers exhibits of fishes, reptiles, live corals, aquatic plants, and other waterbound life, including the only freshwater manta ray in captivity in the Americas. The jungle courtyard is popular with kids, and refreshments are available.

Calle de la Higuera

Behind the Parroquia San Juan Bautista, this street heading southeast away from the plaza is lined with beautifully renovated colonial homes, including **Casa Colorada,** site of the first Spanish military encampment in the Valle de México.

A little farther southeast, Calle de la Higuera passes the **Ⓜ Plaza y Capilla de la Conchita.** A chapel constructed here in 1521 by order of Cortés was thought to have been the first Christian building in the city. Although officially known as Capilla de la Purísima Concepción, the chapel and surrounding garden are more commonly known by the affectionate nickname La Conchita (The Little Shell). The chapel is thought to be next to a spot where springs once provided water for Tenochititlán, now Mexico City proper.

A controversial piece of Hernán Cortés's past can be found just off Plaza de la Conchita at the **Casa de la Malinche,** the former house of the conqueror's Indian lover/interpreter. A complex woman, originally enslaved by rival tribes before being taken by Cortés, Malintzin (her Indian name) played a crucial role in the conquest of the Aztec empire, offering Cortés subtle advice along with her interpretations. She is reviled by many modern Mexicans for helping Cortés, to the point that the term *malinchista* refers to any Mexican (but particularly women) who idealizes foreigners and puts down Mexico.

Casa de los Camilos, on the right at the corner of the next block, was built in the 17th century as the residence and hospice of the Camillians, a religious order founded by San Camilo de Lelis (1550–1614), patron saint of hospitals and the sick. The stone-block structure's small, but the unique door, made of black stone, is worth a look.

On the opposite side of the street, the **Jardín Frida Kahlo** is dedicated to the famous Coyoacán painter. A statue of Kahlo contemplates the garden that carries her name. A fountain completes the picture.

Running north along the west side of Jardín Frida Kahlo, tree-shaded **Calle de Fernández Leal** boasts a string of attractive country mansions and houses built around the beginning of the 20th century and typical of residential Coyoacán.

Museo Frida Kahlo

One of the most popular sights in Coyoacán, the Museo Frida Kahlo is a startlingly blue early-20th-century house in which the world-famous artist was born to a German father and Mexican mother in 1907. In recent years acclaimed by critics and collectors worldwide, Kahlo painted for years in the shadow of her famed muralist husband, Diego Rivera. She suffered a crippling injury in her early years, and her art suggests a stoic life full of pain and self-absorption. She lived with Rivera off and on for 25 years until her death in 1954. Perhaps because the work she created seems to have transcended her difficult circumstances, Kahlo has become an emblem for contemporary female artists.

A selection of Kahlo's personal art collection is on display—including excellent prehispanic artifacts and Mexican folk art (including jewelry and clothes, most of it inspired by Amerindian designs, which Kahlo herself wore) as well as works by well-known artists José María Velasco, Paul Klee, and, of course, her husband, Rivera. Particularly interesting are Kahlo's self-portraits, which combine her own self-examination along with a fascination with communist ideology and Amerindian folkways. For a larger exhibit of Kahlo's own paintings, head to the Museo Dolores Olmedo in Xochimilco. Kahlo was said to have had a love affair with Leon Trotsky, whose own museum is nearby. The garden at this museum (Londrés 247, tel. 5554-5999, 10 A.M.–6 P.M. Tues.–Sun., admission $3) is a quiet spot to sit and write a letter or drink in the atmosphere. A small gift shop and café are on the premises. Cameras aren't allowed inside the museum.

Museo León Trotsky

Leon Trotsky's house looks like a fortress—which is the function it served (albeit unsuccessfully) for this exiled Russian bolshevik. Having lost to Josef Stalin in a struggle for rulership over the Soviet Union, Trotsky left the USSR in 1929 under the threat of execution. At the invitation of Diego Rivera and Frida Kahlo, he came to Mexico in 1937 to seek asylum and, after having an affair with Kahlo, he moved to this building, just around the corner from Kahlo's home.

Trotsky, living in justifiable paranoia of Stalin, seldom left his house, in an effort to protect himself from assassination attempts. But to no avail—in 1940, a Spanish Stalinist named Ramón Mercader convinced Trotsky to allow him in the house and promptly stabbed him with an ice pick as Trotsky looked the other way. The room in which he was killed has been left untouched; every paper and book remains in the same position. Among other artifacts on display are photographs of Trotsky; his wife, Natalia; and Rivera and Kahlo. Some visitors find the veneration expressed by the museum tour guides toward some of Trotsky's daily objects ("This was the spoon he stirred his coffee with!") a bit over the top.

The museum (Río Churubusco 410, tel. 5658-8732, 10 A.M.–5 P.M. Tues.–Sun., admission $2.50) is also headquarters for the **Instituto del Derecho de Asilo y las Libertades Públicas** (IDALP, Institute for the Right of Asylum and Public Liberties), founded in 1990, and for the **Biblioteca Rafael Galván,** housing a collection of books focused on social themes. The IDALP (Viena 45, around the corner from the main museum entrance) organizes occasional expositions, conferences, and art activities.

M Parque Santa Catarina

A few blocks west of Parque Centenario along Calle Francisco Sosa is a beautiful small square, fronted by the brightly painted **Capilla de Santa Catarina** as well as several restored colonial-era houses. On one side is the **Casa de Cultura de Coyoacán** (Francisco Sosa 202, tel. 5658-7826), which often holds cultural events and art exhibits. It's worth taking a peek in to admire the rambling old hacienda or take a rest in the lush gardens in back. Heading back toward the center of Coyoacán you'll find the **Instituto Italiano di Cultura** (Francisco Sosa 77, tel. 5554-0044), also with art exhibits and other events.

Viveros de Coyoacán

Although once they were the private nurseries (*viveros*) and orchards of Miguel Ángel de Quevedo, since nationalization under President Venustiano Carranza, this wide expanse of green has become a cool park (6 A.M.–7 P.M. daily) where you might want to go for a walk or a jog.

SAN ÁNGEL

During the colonial era, the village of San Ángel attracted wealthy Spaniards who found the pleasant climate and rural ambience perfect for their estates and summer homes. Nine kilometers from the Centro, today it's a posh and attractive suburb that the spreading city has grown to meet. You'll still find cobblestone streets with marvelous old colonial-era homes and haciendas now inhabited by the wealthy. The Saturday art market is a favorite spot for tourists and Mexicans alike to go gift shopping.

A small tourist office in the **Centro Cultural de San Ángel** (Av. Revolución and Madero, tel. 5277-6955) can answer questions about touring the *colonia*. You can also join a free **walking tour** around San Ángel here each Saturday at noon, 2 P.M., and 4 P.M. One of Mexico's best modern Mexican art museums, Museo de Art Carrillo Gil, as well as the more general Museo Soumaya and the Museo Estudio Diego Rivera (details in the *Arts and Entertainment* chapter), are all a short walk from the center of San Ángel.

Getting There

San Ángel is easily accessible from downtown via Metro or bus. The closest Metro station to San Ángel is M. A. Quevedo. From this station, take a *pesero* marked "San Ángel." Tell the driver you want to go to Plaza San Jacinto. Just about any of the many buses heading down Insurgentes from Reforma will drop you off a short walk from San Ángel. Get off at Avenida La Paz—ask the driver to let you know when to get off if you're not sure. Some of these buses continue south along Insurgentes to UNAM, Pedregal, and Cuicuilco.

Driving from central Mexico City, the quickest way to reach San Ángel is either via the Periférico ring highway from Paseo de la Reforma or via Avenida Revolución. Although it has stoplights, Revolución is often faster than the Periférico, especially if traffic is heavy.

Plaza San Jacinto

A short walk up the hill from Avenida Revolución along Calle Madero is this fine colonial plaza surrounded by period architecture. Although just a couple of blocks from a sea of traffic and asphalt, by sitting in one of the relaxed plaza cafés, one can still imagine San Ángel as a village isolated from Mexico City. On Saturday, 9 A.M.–6 P.M., local artists offer their works for sale, turning the plaza into a *jardín del arte* (art garden).

The **Iglesia de San Jacinto** on the west side of the plaza was at one time part of a Dominican monastery built between 1564 and 1614. Notable are the principal *retablo* inside and the carved stone *cruz atrial* (atrium cross) standing in front of the church. The beautiful walled gardens in front of the church are a favorite venue for weekend wedding parties.

Opposite the southeast side of the plaza, amid a row of shops and cafés, **Baños Colonial** (6 A.M.–8 P.M. Mon.–Fri., 6 A.M.–8:30 P.M. Sat., 6 A.M.–5:30 P.M. Sun.) is an old bath/steam establishment where you can shower for $.75, take a public Turkish bath for $3.50, or pay $5 for a private steam. An attached soda fountain sells soft drinks and fresh juices.

A plaque on the square commemorates the execution of Irish American U.S. soldiers (by order of General Zachary Taylor) who switched sides during the 1847 U.S. invasion to fight for Mexico.

Casa del Risco

Also known as the Casa del Mirador, this late-17th-century house on the north side of Plaza San Jacinto encloses a museum, a library, and two courtyards (10 A.M.–5 P.M. Tues.–Sun, free admission). The displays at the Museo Colonial Casa del Risco illustrate the fascination with European lifestyles felt by wealthy Mexicans in the colonial era. Upstairs in the Salón Barroco is a display of Mexican baroque art from the 17th century, mostly religious art and furniture. Two rooms feature portraits of European kings and nobility, and another room displays some collected art from the 19th and early 20th centuries. There's one large room downstairs where temporary exhibits of contemporary

Mexican artists are mounted. Also in the building is the colonial library **Centro Cultural y Biblioteca Isidro Fabela.**

A large wall fountain in the eastern courtyard is decorated with whole Talavera plates (along with a few Spanish, English, and Japanese ones), interspersed with hand-painted tiles and seashells.

Bazar Sábado

On Saturday one of the finest craft and art markets in Mexico sets up in a 17th-century stone edifice along the northwest side of the Plaza San Jacinto. Talented artisans sell handcrafted items such as jewelry, pottery, leather, and clothing in the two-story plaza. Some of the more successful artists selling the highest quality crafts maintain regular shops here. Spurred by the success of the market, artists without a stall inside have taken to spreading out their wares across the plaza, making the entire area one big art market. Bargaining is not well received inside the main market, but haggle all you wish outside. Snacks are available at the patio. It's open Saturday only, 10 A.M.–7 P.M.

Walk west and north of the Bazar Sábado along the cobblestone streets to view some of the neighborhood's most sumptuous ex-colonial mansions.

Ex-Convento e Iglesia del Carmen

At this Carmelite ex-monastery (Av. Revolución right near the intersection of Av. La Paz, 10 A.M.–4:45 P.M. Tues.–Sun., admission $2), built between 1615 and 1626, you'll find a diverse collection of colonial art by such maestros as Cristóbal de Villalpando, Juan Correa, and Juan Becerra, along with colonial furniture displays. Even more amazing is the basement crypt containing mummified remains of priests, nuns, and nobility, discovered during a building project.

The adjacent church, built in the usual Latin cross floor plan, contains colonial-era *retablos* of some interest.

Plaza Loreto

A bit further south of the center of San Ángel is Plaza Loreto, a shopping mall built in an unusual and interesting fashion around what was formerly a colonial-era mill once owned by

Hernán Cortés himself. Later, it was the biggest paper factory in Latin America. Apart from the many high-end shops (mainly for clothing, but also music, books, and much else), you'll now find several restaurants and snack shops, as well as a movie theater. Live concerts or performances are often held in the plaza on weekends. Plaza Loreto is also home to a small but interesting art museum, Museo Soumaya, with works by Degas, Renoir, Camine Claudel, and Miró, as well as colonial-era Latin American art.

UNIVERSIDAD NACIONAL AUTÓNOMA DE MÉXICO (UNAM)

Founded in 1551 by special charter from the king of Spain, this is the oldest university in the Western Hemisphere. The original campus was in Mexico City's Centro, but in the early 1950s it was moved to its present site southwest of the city center. So vast is the present campus of the **Universidad Nacional Autónoma de México** (UNAM)—covering 7.3 million square meters, much of it green areas—that it is referred to as the Ciudad Universitaria (University City).

With an enrollment of nearly half a million students and a teaching staff of 25,000, this is the largest campus in the Americas. UNAM has a reputation for teaching left-leaning theories and as a center for political activism. The famed 1968 student riots, which ended in the bloodbath at Tlaltelolco, began among students from UNAM. In 1999, a group of students went on strike and closed the university for nine months. The strike was initially triggered by a government plan to raise the miniscule tuition, but it quickly broadened to a more general antigovernment and antiglobalization protest. The strike was eventually broken up when the government sent in the police (a major taboo at the fiercely independent UNAM) in the wee hours of the morning, catching groups of strikers who were still asleep.

The modern buildings—many covered with elaborate murals—were built between 1950 and 1955 by Carlos Lazo. The campus is divided into two sections, with the northern part con-

taining most of the faculty buildings. Sprawling over a huge area of lava fields, the university is laid out in groups of faculties *(facultades)* centered on the **Rectoría** administration building, whose south wall is covered with a three-dimensional Davíd Alfaro Siqueiros mural. Next to the Rectoría is the library, with an impressive Juan O'Gorman mosaic on Mexico's past and future. Just south of the Rectoría is the **Museo Universitario de Ciencias y Artes CU** (tel. 5622-0206, www.muca.unam.mx, 10 A.M.–7 P.M. Mon.–Fri., 10 A.M.–6 P.M. weekends), with free revolving exhibits. Right next to the museum are two bookstores, **El Sótano** and **Librería UNAM.**

Across Insurgentes from the Rectoría complex, the **Estadio Olímpico**—a broad, open stadium designed to mimic one of the many volcanic cones in the area—has a Rivera mosaic over the main entrance. Home to the UNAM Pumas soccer club, the stadium has a reputation for the rowdiest fans in the city. If you go to a game and can understand a bit of Spanish, you'll enjoy hearing the crowd chanting creative (and often profane) songs and mercilessly razzing the opposing team and fans.

For information about the university, stop in to the **Dirección General de Orientación** (9 A.M.–5 P.M. Mon.–Fri., www.unam.edu.mx), an office on the south side of the large lawn just below the library.

The southern part of the campus is centered on the **Centro Cultural Universitario,** a collection of arts buildings and theaters. Here is the **Sala Nezahualcóyotl,** considered to have the finest acoustics in the country. In the middle of the complex is a café where you can grab some refreshments and the **Librería Julio Torri** bookstore. Just south of the Centro Cultural is the **Unidad Bibliográfica** (tel. 5622-6814, 9 A.M.–8 P.M. Mon.–Fri.), which houses part of the national library and the **Hemeroteca Nacional,** which is far and away the most comprehensive collection of newspapers and magazines in the country. Next to the library is the **Espacio Escultórico,** a collection of huge, colorful, and bizarre metal sculptures rising out of a field of lava. The maze of trails through the shrubs around the sculptures is a favorite spot for students to go find a quiet nook to read, play music, or even do a bit of rock climbing.

Getting to Ciudad Universitaria

The most direct way to reach University City is by bus traveling on Insurgentes Sur (Insurgentes passes the campus, on the east side of the road, and the stadium, on the west). The bus stops close to both sides, so it's an easy walk to the central part of the campus. Because of the amount of space the university takes up, walking around is feasible only in the north, main section. The closest Metro stop to the central area of campus is Copilco, but it's still a couple of kilometers' walk from there.

Cuicuilco

Although only a few round ruins remain to be seen, the structures at Cuicuilco once housed a settlement of 20,000. The city was built in approximately 600 B.C. and the ceremonial center was active 600–200 B.C. The main "pyramid" (actually a rare round circular platform) measures 118 meters in diameter and 18 meters tall and was topped with a ceremonial altar. Volcán Xitle, which looms to the south, buried the base

of the pyramid, along with the rest of the ceremonial center, with lava. Much of the lava has been removed, making it possible to see the construction of the pyramid. Excavations continue around the base of the pyramid.

Take a look at the small museum nearby for information about the people and a few artifacts found at the site (tel. 5606-9758, 9 A.M.–5 P.M. Mon.–Sat., admission $2.50), along with descriptive paintings. Note the image of the fierce fire and volcano god. Guided visits (in Spanish) are available 9 A.M.–1 P.M. Mon.–Fri. It's easy to get here from the Ciudad Universitaria—take a bus marked "Cuicuilco" traveling south on Insurgentes. The site is south of the intersection of Insurgentes and Periférico Sur.

XOCHIMILCO

According to the Códice Ramírez, Xochimilco ("place where flowers grow") was originally founded on an island in Lago de Xochimilco in 919 B.C. by a Náhuatl-speaking tribe that called themselves Xochimilcas. Semi-independent of the Aztecs, they fought many wars with neighboring tribes before the Spanish conquest. Today,

A *trajinera* glides down a canal at Xochimilco.

the central *colonia* of Xochimilco serves as a living museum for prehispanic Mexico City, conserving the ancient canals and *chinampas* (floating gardens) of a long-lost lifestyle. Hiring a boat to cruise the canals and have a floating party is a favorite weekend pastime for Mexico City residents.

Most visitors see only a small portion of the 189 kilometers of canals comprising Xochimilco, usually amidst a number of other party boats full of revelers. But in the farther reaches of the canals reside at least 150 species of endemic birds and another 70-odd migratory species that dally here in the winter months. The birds can be best seen on some of the quieter canals, where mariachi and radio music is prohibited to leave the birds (and a few humans!) in peace to enjoy the pastoral surroundings.

Although the *chinampas* and canals of Xochimilco are protected by UNESCO for their unique character, the international organization has recently threatened to rescind their designation because of constant urban encroachment. In part because of UNESCO's prodding, the city government announced plans to invest $17 million in restoring natural areas in 2005, but time will tell how effective the resources are.

Canals and Chinampas

Long before the Spanish arrived, the Xochimilcas had developed an imaginative solution to the difficulties of farming in the Valle de México. As the lowlying lake water could not easily be directed to the higher land on the islands and shoreline of Lago de Xochimilco, the Aztecs brought the soil to the lake and—assembling reeds, tree limbs, and soil—built the floating islands (the word *chinampa* means "terrain fenced by interwoven sticks"), on which they planted their crops. The bottom soil proved to be extremely fertile, yielding two or three harvests a year, and as more *chinampas* were created, the lake was broken into a series of canals. Early European visitors often referred to Xochimilco as "the Venice of Mexico," although the setting is far more rural and agricultural than Venice.

The Spaniards spared Xochimilco after the conquest because the area produced much of the city's food. Vegetables and flowers continue to

grow on the *chinampas* today, and floriculture is the region's principle source of income. **Mercado Xóchitl** in the center of town, **Mercado de Plantas Madreselva** in the south of town, and **Mercado de Flores, Plantas y Hortilizas** next to the Parque Ecológico are the main plant markets. Native flora can be seen along the banks of the canals, including bulrushes, pepper trees, camphor, *jarilla, toloache,* and Mexican poppy.

Of the estimated 40,000 *chinampas* found in Xochimilco at the beginning of the 18th century, only 15,000 were left when the 20th century began. Canoe vendors began serving snacks to weekend visitors around 1920, followed quickly by the first restaurants on the embarcaderos. Around this same time, traditional *trajineras,* poled barges used for transporting local cargo along the canals, were transformed into tour boats by the addition of seats, tables, tarp roofs, and flower-festooned facades (nowadays heavily painted, wired-together bunches of bulrushes). In 1987 UNESCO named Xochimilco a World Heritage Site to publicize its cultural importance.

Canal Touring

The Xochimilco canals are a popular spot for locals and visitors alike to rent colorful *trajineras turísticas,* drinking and picnicking onboard for an afternoon while the boatmen propel the craft down the canals with a long pole. Four sizes of *trajineras* are available, from the *toldo amarillo* (yellow tarp), with a capacity of four people for $6 per hour, up to the *toldo verde* (green tarp), holding up to 18 people for $17 per hour. Although prices are posted and are the same for each boat, it is sometimes possible to negotiate cheaper rates, especially during the week. Each of these boats has a name—usually a woman's name, such as Lupita or Julieta—so if you have a favorite it's easy to find the same boat and boatman on subsequent visits.

The main landings for *trajineras,* Embarcadero Caltonga and Embarcadero Nativitas, can be found near the center of town and the Parroquia de San Bernardino. An hour's rental is the minimum, but it's better to spend two or three hours to get farther out into the canals, see more, and have a more relaxing time. Be sure to confirm the price *before* you board. Also, give the boat a look; some are nicer than others.

A cheaper alternative would be to share a *lancha colectiva* (collective boat), which holds up to 60 people for $1 per person. These much larger boats run only on Sunday and holidays and leave only from Embarcadero Salitre and Embarcadero Caltongo. Food service is available on all the boats for around $2–3 per dish. Of course it wouldn't be Mexican without the availability of live music, and, like the price of boat hire, the rates are regulated and publicly posted: a mariachi number costs $4 (a bargain compared to Plaza Garibaldi), a *norteña* song is $3, marimba $2, and *salterio* (Mexican zither) or *acordeón* $2.

Lots of souvenir stalls, as well as vendors on foot, sell blankets and trinkets at each of the piers. During the week, it's almost empty, so visit then if you want a peaceful ride. On the other hand, if you want to see how the Mexicans most enjoy Xochimilco, the weekend would be the time to go.

Xochimilco is 24 kilometers southeast of the Zócalo. Take Metro Línea 2 as far as Tasqueña, then board the Tren Ligero (light train, or streetcar) to the Embarcadero station. From there follow the signs to the piers, which are about six short blocks to the northeast. Or take a "Xochimilco" bus or *pesero* from the Metro Tasqueña station all the way to the end of the line, which will put you in almost the same spot as the Tren Ligero. If you're driving, avoid Sunday, when traffic in Xochimilco can be very heavy.

Parroquia de San Bernardino de Siena

In the center of town, not far from the main embarcaderos, rises this enormous parish church (at Violeta and Pino, about 100 meters northeast of the Mercado Xóchitl), which was founded by Franciscans in 1535 but only inaugurated in 1590. The strong, stable architectural style has been described as "military monastic," with plain buttressed walls and ornate *portadas* (doorways). Exterior decoration mixes Greco-Roman, gothic, and native motifs, while the interior of the attached convent shows Moorish influences. Inside, the principal *retablo* and 12 side *retablos* are authentic, late 16th-century jewels of art.

Mercado Xóchitl

This traditional municipal market (5:30 A.M.– 6 P.M. daily), founded in 1957, stocks everything from fresh produce to clay, leather, and cane *artesanías*. It's southwest of the Parroquia, in a block bounded by Calles Madero, 16 de Septiembre, Guerrero, and Morelos.

Parque Ecológico de Xochimilco (PEX)

This educational/recreational park got its start in 1989 as part of the Ecological Rescue Plan for Xochimilco, an ambitious strategy to include water reclamation, agricultural reactivation, and historical and archaeological studies—all based on the traditional *chinampero* systems.

PEX covers about 300 hectares distributed into three areas, including the 13-hectare Mercado de Flores, Plantas y Hortilizas—reportedly the largest horticultural market in Latin America and the third largest in the world. A second part, the 67-hectare Deportivo Ecológico Cuemanco, is dedicated to water sports, leaving the 189-hectare Parque Ecológico de Xochimilco, or PEX.

About a quarter of the PEX (9 A.M.–6 P.M. Tues.–Sun. in summer, 10 A.M.–7 P.M. in winter, admission $1.70 adults, $0.70 over age 60, $0.30 under age 12) consists of lakes, *ciénegas* (underground springs), and canals. Wide gravel and asphalt walking paths wind through the park, making this a great place to get some exercise and relatively fresh air. One path leads through the flower-lined Paseo de las Flores. A *chinampería* demonstrates how *chinampa* cultivation works. In addition to viewing natural and cultivated flora, visitors have a good chance of spotting herons, cormorants, egrets, ducks, and other waterfowl.

If you don't want to walk, a truck-pulled "train" takes visitors around the park frequently throughout the day. *Trajineras* are available on weekends. You can also rent mountain bikes and paddleboats any day of the week. Guards patrol the park, and it seems to be a very safe place to get out for some exercise.

A museum near the front of the park offers historical, cultural, and natural history exhibits. There are also several children's playgrounds on the premises.

TLALPAN AND CERRO DE LA ESTRELLA

Most casual tourists will content themselves with taking a day trip to Coyoacán or San Ángel, or perhaps picnicking on the canals at Xochimilco. Two other sights in the southern part of the city, the quaint colonial neighborhood of Tlalpan and the Aztec ceremonial site at Cerro de la Estrella, may be of interest for those with more time on their hands.

Tlalpan

For a taste of what Coyoacán and San Ángel might have looked like in decades past, consider taking a trip down to the old center of Tlalpan. It's a bit off the beaten path—hard to find amidst a maze of streets located just south of the Periférico highway, not far from where the Cuernavaca highway comes into the city—and there's not much in the way of sights per se. But those who make the trip will enjoy the odd feeling of being in a small colonial town (which is of course what Tlalpan was until not too long ago) hidden away in the middle of Mexico City. There are a couple of restaurants right around the plaza with well-prepared meals, offering a convenient excuse to make the trip. Tlalpan is also a particularly relaxed place to come during the September 15 Independence Day celebration, which is a mob scene in the Centro.

The epicenter of Tlalpan is the **Plaza de la Constitución,** an especially lovely square; it's not very big but is filled with tall trees, creating a verdant canopy over the top. A kiosk punctuates the middle, with benches on all sides invariably filled with locals passing the time in this time-honored Mexican fashion. On the east side of the plaza is the **Iglesia de San Agustín de las Cuevas,** surrounded by well-kept gardens and lawn. On the south side of the square is the grey stone neoclassical municipal building, with the front wall under the archways covered by historical murals. Behind the municipal building, in the same block, is the **Mercado de la Paz,** a large, airy market built in the old style: fun to wander around and also good for low-priced food if you're on a budget. Far better though, if you can afford it, to sit down and eat in style at either the Ar-gentine steak house **1900** on the north side of the plaza, or the **La Jaliscience,** a traditional cantina with very well-cooked Mexican classics (see the *Restaurants* chapter for more details).

Without your own car, the easiest way to get to Tlalpan is by taxi, which can take anywhere from 30 minutes to two hours (but usually a bit under an hour) from the central part of the city, depending on traffic. By public transport, catch a *pesero* from either Izazaga or Tasqueña metro stops. Look for buses with signs in the front window that say "Centro de Tlalpan."

Cerro de la Estrella

In the midst of Ixtapalapa, a sprawling, dirty, and rough region in the southeastern part of the capital, a conical volcano rises up from the valley floor. This was the ancient sacred site where the Aztecs performed the New Flame ceremony that marked the beginning of each 52-year cycle in their calendar. Nowadays the mountain, which is technically protected as a national park, is the location of Mexico's biggest annual Passion Play, an elaborate reenactment of Jesus' crucifixion every Easter. The event attracts literally hundreds of thousands of people from across Mexico and the globe—quite a chaotic scene. If you go see it, take good care to watch out for pickpockets, as they are rife in the crowds.

The rest of the year, however, Cerro de la Estrella is a quiet, somewhat unkempt park with lots of graffiti but with superlative views out across the eastern and southern parts of the valley and of the surrounding volcanos. The entrance road goes part of the way up the hill to a parking lot and small, not very interesting museum, and from there, it's another 30 minutes' walk up to the top. The path passes through groves of eucalyptus trees, along with a whole lot of exercise equipment improvised out of tree trunks and the like used by local health enthusiasts. On top are the remains of a reconstructed Aztec pyramid and a white cross. It's best to go on weekends, when there are lots of people around. The nearest Metro stop is Cerro de la Estrella, and from there it takes about 20 minutes to walk to the museum and parking lot. If you're driving, look for the entrance off of Eje 8 Sur Calzada Ixtapalapa.

Northern Mexico City

BASÍLICA DE NUESTRA SEÑORA DE GUADALUPE

The church of Mexico's patron saint sees about 15 million visitors a year, and it's by far the most popular religious shrine in the country. It was here that Juan Diego (an Aztec nobleman named Cuauhtaoctzin before converting to Christianity) reported seeing his vision of the Virgen María on December 9, 1531, on the top of Cerro Tepeyac, a hill not far north of downtown Mexico City.

There has been a succession of chapels and *basílicas* on the hill, the most recent a very modern one. Whatever your religious proclivities, there's no denying that the latest *basílica* has all the mystical aura of an airport terminal. For a slightly surreal religious experience, take a conveyor-belt ride behind the altar to see the image of the Virgen. The conveyor belt was put there so there wouldn't be a traffic jam of the reverent below the image. The succession of faithful are an amazing cross-section of Mexican life, from the most humble countryside indigenous campesino to upper-class Mexico City residents. A religious art museum at the rear of the older 18th-century *basílica* contains oil paintings and sculptures of the colonial period, including works by such famed masters as Cabrera, Villalpando, Correa, and Echave.

The original chapel at Tepeyac, built on the hilltop in the late 17th century over the site of the old temple to the Aztec mother goddess Tonanztin, is reached by a walking path that winds up through the hillside gardens.

In the days running up to December 12, the highways around Mexico City are filled with a steady stream of pilgrims trudging or bicycling along the side of the road on their way to the *basílica*. The night of the 12th is a crowded spectacle almost beyond imagining, a unique focus of Mexico's spiritual and national character. Unless you wish to pay your respects to the Virgin, or unless you have a particular fascination with checking out a huge crowd *a la mexicana*, it's best to avoid the *basílica* during most of the month of December.

the roof of the new Basílica, with the older church in the foreground

Technically, the range of hills north of Tepeyac, known as the Sierra de Guadalupe, are protected as a national park. Unfortunately the hills are almost totally denuded of trees and would make for fairly desolate hiking. Because some of the neighborhoods surrounding and creeping up the sides of the hills are poor and rough, it's not recommended to venture into the range.

The easiest way to reach the *basílica* is to take the Metro to the Basílica station and walk the short distance to the church. The gardens and pathways leading up to the hilltop chapel are a relaxing place for a stroll.

History

As the legend has it, Mexico City Bishop Juan de Zumárraga refused to believe Juan Diego's story that he had seen the Virgen on December

MORE MYSTERIES OF THE VIRGEN DE GUADALUPE

While modern historians might be quick to point to the historical situation at the time of the Guadalupe apparition to explain the "miracle," certain aspects of the original supposed spontaneous printing of the Virgen are less easy to explain away.

The color image appears to be painted onto a 2.2- by 1-meter piece of *ayate*—a paperlike cloth made from leaves of the agave using prehispanic technology. While *ayate* was used by the Aztecs for their codices, it is a very difficult material on which to paint a detailed image such as this one. This anomaly alone is in fact one of the elements that convinced many of the validity of the miracle. Furthermore, after 116 years of leaving the cloth in the open, exposed to the elements and the hands of thousands of pilgrims, followed by another 352 years in a glass case, the image has retained most of its unusually brilliant colors. A reproduction done on *ayate* in the 17th century lasted only 30 years. And despite years of scientific investigation, the origin of the blue and skin-colored pigments remains a mystery.

Computer studies of the Virgen's eyes in the painting have suggested that several minute figures lie hidden within, figures who some have interpreted as Juan Diego, Bishop Zumárraga, and others.

9 and demanded further evidence of his vision. On December 12 Juan had a second vision of the Virgen; this time, she was surrounded by roses. This image was miraculously imprinted upon Juan Diego's cloak, and when he brought this to Zumárraga, the bishop was convinced of the miracle. After years of controversy, including a bizarre allegation by former Abbot Guillermo Shulenburg (of all people) that Juan Diego never existed, Pope John Paul II declared Juan Diego a Catholic saint in 2002.

Historians like to point out that Cerro Tepeyac was coincidentally, or perhaps not, the site of a temple dedicated to a major Aztec female deity, Tonantzin. Unsurprisingly, most Amerindian inhabitants of Mexico referred to the Virgen as Tonantzin well into the 17th century. It's also curious to note that the first Virgen de Guadalupe shrine was founded in a remote corner of the Spanish province of Extremadura, the home of many *conquistadores,* including Hernán Cortés. The Extremadura Virgen is also dark and appeared in the 14th century, during the height of the conflict when the Spaniards were reconquering southern Spain from the darker-skinned Moors.

Whatever you make of the unusual coincidences surrounding the apparition, the New World Virgen de Guadalupe was an immediate success with Mexico's Amerindians and dramatically helped the Spanish missionaries with their work of conversion. Over the years *la virgen morena* (the dark-skinned virgin, one of Guadalupe's epithets) has grown into the most revered religious figure in Mexico and is considered the protector of all Mexicans—the one who provides hope when all hope is lost. The number of miracles attributed to the icon of the Virgen runs into the many thousands, and her festival day of December 12 is the country's most important religious holiday.

The first church was a simple chapel built on the hilltop, where Juan Diego lived the rest of his days. The current hilltop chapel was built at the end of the 17th century, which is also when construction began on the first *basílica* at the foot of the hill. Completed in 1709, by the 1970s the basílica was sinking into the soft subsoil and could no longer accommodate the steady stream of pilgrims. So the modern *basílica,* designed by Pedro Ramírez Vásquez (of Museo Nacional de Antropología fame), was constructed in 1976 and is now the main place of worship at the site.

TENAYUCA AND SANTA CECILIA ACATITLÁN

Pirámide de Tenayuca

On the northern edge of Mexico City, technically in the State of Mexico suburb, Tlalnepantla, stands a pre-Aztec pyramid known as Tenayuca. Two parallel stairways climb the large, wide base and lead to temples on top. Occupied since at least the 11th century, six structures were raised here, each built over the other at 52-year intervals. Studies of the ruins indicate that the site was once occupied by Teotihuacáns at one point in time. The nicely landscaped grounds have an attached small museum (10 A.M.–4:45 P.M. Tues.–Sun., admission $2).

To get to Tenayuca, go to the Metro La Raza station, then switch to a *pesero* marked "Pirámide."

Pirámide Santa Cecilia Acatitlán

A little farther north of Tenayuca in a *colonia* known as Santa Cecilia is the more interesting, but less visited, pyramid of Acatitlán. In the Náhuatl language, Acatitlán means "place between the reeds," no doubt in reference to a time when the environs of Mexico City were much wetter. This archaeological site dates to the late postclassic period (A.D. 1300–1521) and is thought to have been a ceremonial center where Tláloc and Huitzilopochtli, the Mesoamerican gods of rain and war/sun, respectively, were worshiped. The adjacent Parroquia de Santa Cecilia bears a large number of stones taken from the pyramid's base; with the arrival of the Spanish, Amerindian temples were usually ransacked, and the materials were used for building Spanish churches and colonial houses.

The temple that tops the small, steeply sloped pyramid is one of the only intact pyramid temples in Mexico and is considered the most authentically restored. The first archaeological exploration of this site was carried out in 1923, and in 1961, archaeologist Eduardo Pareyón restored the pyramid's foundation. The work of this Mexican researcher has special merit, because he reconstructed the upper temple that crowns the foundation after carrying out extensive research on the codices and archaeological materials (such as clay scale models) available. You can climb the steep steps to the top and walk inside the temple to see how these rooms were constructed, with wooden roofs, panels with embedded nails, an entrance with a wooden lintel, a bench, and a mezzanine or loft inside. On the outside, the temple is flanked by ceremonial arms. The entrance displays a carved sacrificial stone.

INAH-sponsored plaques on the grounds chronicle the history and architecture of Acatitlán in Spanish, English, and Náhuatl. Near the entrance to the grounds, the **Museo de la Escultura** (10 A.M.–4:45 P.M. Tues.–Sun., admission $2) contains sculpture from the late postclassic period (A.D. 1300–1521). Many of the carved stone figures on display represent flora and fauna, which no doubt had a direct relation to the Mesoamericans' daily lives. Anthropomorphic art in the museum tends toward the gruesome; a large stone receptacle, for example, is decorated in relief with various elements and symbols of human sacrifice—hearts and severed arms, hands, and ears, which no doubt went into the stone bowl as offerings to Aztec gods. The museum building itself is a former Porfiriato home made of simple stone block and brick. A few rooms have been set aside to exhibit rustic antique furniture of the era, representing how the more common people of the era lived.

To get there from Tenayuca, either hop a taxi or get on a bus heading north along the Tenayuca-Santa Cecilia road, and ask the driver where to get off.

Parks Near Mexico City

After a lengthy dose of Mexico City, visitors and expatriates will likely feel the need for a counterbalancing dose of fresh air and nature. The mountains ringing the southwest corner of the valley are home to four adjacent parks perfect for picnicking, hiking, and mountain biking. The parks enclose pine and oak forests from about 2,500 meters to the top of the hills marking the edge of the Valle de México.

⋈ DESIERTO DE LOS LEONES

Decreed Mexico's first national park in 1917, Desierto de los Leones is neither a desert nor populated with lions, but is a pine and oak forest covering almost 1,529 hectares of mountainside and centered on the remains of an early-18th-century monastery. Picnickers frequent the groves and gardens around the semiruined Carmelite monastery, while hikers and mountain bikers roam the dirt roads and trails in the hills above. The woods around Desierto de los Leones are well patrolled, particularly on weekends, making it the safest and most recommendable park near Mexico City for hiking and biking. Regardless, ask one of the *vigilantes* (guards) at the monastery what the current situation is in the surrounding woods. Severe forest fires in 1998 ripped through parts of the Desierto, and burnt-out patches can still be seen in the upper reaches of the forest. The woods around the convent, however, were not touched by the fires.

The road into the park, **Camino al Desierto,** runs from the Toluca highway near the neighborhood of Cuajimalpa to San Ángel. Unless you're in the south of the city, the best way in for those driving motor vehicles is via the Toluca highway. A bus runs from the Metro Barranca del Muerto station up to the monastery, on Saturday and Sunday only, 6 A.M.–5 P.M. Bikers without a car would have to hire a taxi from the city, which would cost $10–15 at least. Two gates at either end of the park collect a $1 entrance fee from drivers 7 A.M.–6 P.M.

The Monastery

Desiertos were Carmelite monasteries first built in Spain in forests, meant to isolate the monks from the travails of urban life. The name is thought to be an allusion to Christ's 40 days in the desert. Started in 1606, Desierto de los Leones was the first such monastery built in the Americas. An earthquake destroyed the original building in 1711, and the current monastery was erected in 1722. The Carmelites moved away in 1801 to their present location in Mt. Niscongo above Tenancingo, in the State of México.

Although there were likely some mountain lions in the area when the monastery was in operation, the second half of the monastery's name is thought to derive from the León family, who acted as the order's representative in affairs with the Spanish crown for many years.

Today the old monastery is a museum (10 A.M.–7 P.M. Tues.–Sun., admission $0.50). Parts are a bit decrepit, but the main building is in good condition and features a lovely chapel. One large room has been converted into a restaurant, open for breakfast and lunch. On Sundays a crowd is usually milling around the hallways, but the gardens behind are quiet, restful corners. Dotting the woods around the monastery are 8 of the original 10 hermitages.

For suggestions on where to take more lengthy hikes and mountain bike rides, see the *Recreation* chapter.

LA MARQUESA AND VICINITY

Just as the Mexico City-Toluca highway crosses the pass leaving the valley and starts its descent into the State of México, the road passes through Parque Nacional La Marquesa, in a high valley surrounded by pine forest. Here visitors can find plenty of space to stretch out a blanket, kick around a soccer ball, bike offroad, buy fresh trout, and generally laze around and enjoy the clean, fresh air and greenery.

The forests above La Marquesa, particularly the trails around Valle de los Conejos, are filled with great single-track mountain bike trails, but unfortunately a few robberies have been reported here in recent years. Rock climbers, however, will be glad to hear of a rock pitch called Peñasco de los Perros, in the northwest part of La Marquesa, which is quite safe all week long (see the *Recreation* chapter for details).

If you feel the stomach rumbling when at La Marquesa, be sure to enjoy local specialties such as *barbacoa* (pit-baked sheep meat), *sopa de hongo* (mushroom soup), and *quesadillas de flor de calabaza,* (squash flower and cheese in a corn tortilla), as well as fresh rabbit and trout, served at the innumerable roadside restaurants.

To get to La Marquesa without a car, visitors can catch a *pesero* bus at either Tacubaya or Juanacatlán Metro stations up to the park for $2, taking 45–75 minutes, depending on traffic. The last bus returns to Mexico City at around 8 P.M.

As well, you can go to the Observatorio bus station and catch an intercity bus to Tenancingo or Chalma, and get off at La Marquesa.

Valle de los Conejos

A grassy area behind a small group of roadside restaurants about three kilometers south of La Marquesa, on the two-lane highway leading to Malinalco, Valle de los Conejos is a good spot to picnic on a sunny afternoon in the broad meadows or to bring a mountain bike and explore the forests above. If you don't have wheels, the easiest way out is to take a *pesero* from Metro Juanacatlán, or go to Observatorio bus station and take a bus marked "Chalma" or "Tenancingo," telling the driver you'd like to get off at Valle de los Conejos. About five kilometers southwest of Valle de los Conejos is Valle del Potrero, another grassy meadow in

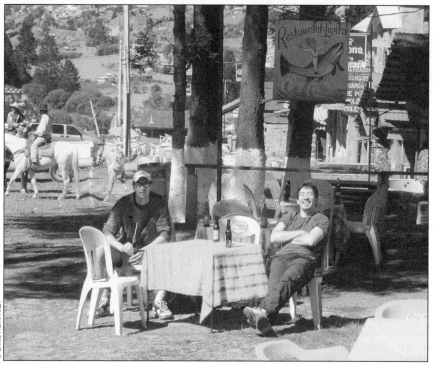

© CHRIS HUMPHREY

enjoying a cold *viki* (Victoria beer) on a hot day, Valle de los Conejos the forest. Both places have horses to rent (usually around $10 an hour) and plenty of restaurants with tasty local food.

AJUSCO

The volcanic peak of El Ajusco (3,930 meters) looms large over the southern end of the valley of Mexico, visible to anyone looking down Insurgentes to the south on a semiclear day. Easily reached from downtown, the fields around the base of Ajusco are popular for weekend picknickers, who make good use of the soccer fields, horseback riding, dirt-bike tracks, and many small rustic restaurants.

To get to Ajusco by car, get on Periférico Sur and look for the turnoff to Reino Aventura amusement park (there are lots of signs). The road, also called Camino al Ajusco, winds steadily uphill, past the amusement park on the left, through several kilometers of gradually less urban neighborhoods into fields and forest at the base of Volcán Ajusco. Here you'll find dozens of small stands selling tacos, quesadillas, *barbacoa,* and other munchies in the grassy meadows along the roadside. As the road approaches Ajusco, it forks and ends up making a complete circle around the mountain in about 20 kilometers, a popular route for road cyclists on weekends. To get to Ajusco by bus, the easiest way is to go to Metro Tasqueña; from there, take the light rail *(tren ligero)* to the Estadio Azteca stop. Here look for a *pesero* marked "Ruta 39," which goes up to Ajusco for $.50. The last one back down to the city leaves Ajusco around 9 P.M. Alternatively, you can catch a *pesero* at Metro CU and transfer to the Route 39 bus.

While the forested hills around Ajusco are great for hiking and mountain biking, it's generally not safe to go wandering too far from frequently visited areas, as robberies are reported with regularity. However, a local *ejido* (communal farm), **San Nicolás Totolapan,** has cordoned off about 2,300 hectares of hillside crossed with dozens of kilometers of dirt roads and trails. It ranges in altitude from 2,700 meters at the entrance (Km 11.5 on the Ajusco highway) up to 3,740 meters at its highest point, Montaña Neze-

huiloya. The *ejido* patrols the forest, making it quite safe for hiking and biking. (See the *Recreation* chapter for details on hiking and biking at San Nicolás.)

LOS DINAMOS

A deep gorge in the southwest corner of the Valle de México, Los Dinamos comprises 2,293 hectares of communally protected forest and offers some of the best rock climbing in the Mexico City region. The name refers to four generators *(dinamos),* only two of which are in operation, along the narrow Río Magdalena valley.

While the meadows and forest along the valley make a fine spot to pass a sunny afternoon biking on the single-track trails, the forest is best enjoyed on weekends, when mounted police from the Magdalena Contreras *delegación* patrol the area. The area around the Segundo (Second) Dinamo, in particular, has been cleaned up and turned into an ecological park that's quite safe on weekends. But it's best not to wander too far from the beaten path, particularly in the forest above the Cuarto (Fourth) Dinamo. Nearby is some very good rock climbing (see the *Recreation* chapter for details).

To reach Los Dinamos by car, take the Periférico Sur to the Magdalena Contreras exit, just west of the Ajusco exit. Follow the signs to "Contreras" and "Los Dinamos" through Santa Teresa and Magdalena Contreras to the edge of the forest, three kilometers from the Periférico. A paved road continues up the left side of the valley, reaching the Segundo Dinamo in three kilometers and the Cuarto Dinamo, four kilometers farther.

Those without a private vehicle can hop on the Metro to the Miguel Ángel de Quevedo or the Copilco stations, and from there look for the microbuses to Contreras. Get off at the end of the line, a small square faced on one side by food and handicraft shops and on the other by the 18th-century Santa María Magdalena Contreras chapel, with a fine guilded *retablo.* From this square, special buses continue farther up the road, on weekends only, stopping just short of the Cuarto Dinamo. During the week, visitors have to walk or hire a taxi from the Contreras bus stop.

Restaurants

Coming to Mexico City for the sole purpose of dining your time away here, with maybe a little sightseeing in between meals, is a perfectly legitimate excuse for a trip. The variety of different cuisines available in D.F. is astounding, from the perfect hole-in-the-wall taco joint with the flaming habanero sauce where you can stuff yourself and wash it all down with an ice-cold Victoria beer for $2, to Asian-Mexican fusion dishes like shrimp with wasabi and tequila sauce served in a sleek glassed-in dining room surrounded by Mexico City power brokers. Traditional cuisine from every region in Mexico abounds in D.F., such as *cochinita pibil* (tender pork dish) from the Yucatán, moles from Oaxaca and Puebla, and seafood Veracruz or Mazatlán style, flown in fresh daily from the coast. There are Spanish tapas bars, world-class French cuisine, sushi everywhere (from fast food to $20 a roll), and Argentine steakhouses that seem to open every week.

The quality and number of higher-end Mexican and international restaurants in Mexico City has been increasing dramatically in recent years. These sorts of places were so rare until 20 years ago that they could survive with mediocre, expensive food and snooty waiters. No longer. The growing number of Mexicans with enough disposable income to dine out regularly has led to a proliferation of restaurants catering to their clients' more international tastes and openness to seeing traditional Mexican food reinvented in unexpected ways.

The Condesa district, not far south of Paseo de la Reforma along Avenida Insurgentes, was

Mexico City's Best

☒ **Best Traditional Mexican:** An impossible choice, but **Hostería Santo Domingo** in the Centro is a great place to start. Try their famed *chiles en nogada,* chiles stuffed with a mix of shredded beef, raisins, olives and almonds, bathed in a cream and nut sauce, or the *mole poblano* (page 97).

☒ **Best Coffee:** For a bit of tradition with your java, head to **La Habana.** The simple tables are always filled with journalists and literary types poring over newspapers with cigarettes and coffee underneath huge 1950s-era photos of Havana, Cuba. If you really want a jolt, try the wickedly strong *café campechano* (page 103).

☒ **Best Hangover Helper:** A little too much tequila last night? Proceed directly to **La Polar,** a cantina where you can wolf down a steaming bowl of *birria* (a hearty meat soup), along with a bunch of other bleary-eyed folks on weekends (page 103).

☒ **Classiest Atmosphere:** A perennial favorite for tourists and Mexicans alike, **Hacienda de los Morales** is a mansion built in the 16th century on farmland now in the middle of the Polanco district. The dining rooms are set around lovely patios and gardens, and the Mexican cuisine is excellent (try the succulent *cabrito,* kid goat) (page 106).

☒ **Best Steak:** Argentinian restaurant **El Zorzal** cooks up a flavorful and tender *arrachera* steak and fantastic spinach-and-cheese *empanada* to go along with it (page 107).

☒ **Best Taco Joint:** Choosing one taco joint out of the thousands in Mexico City is a cruel task, but you could definitely do worse than

panadería

El Tizoncito. Grab a stool and order a few *tacos al pastor* (page 109).

☒ **Best Seafood:** Some of the finest seafood in the city is served at **Contramar,** a high-end restaurant in the Roma open for lunch only. The deep-fried shrimp tacos make a great starter, and for a main course try the juicy *filete contramar,* a fish fillet served on a wooden platter with four different sauces (page 110).

☒ **Best Place to Eat-and-Be-Seen:** Really anywhere in the center of the uber-hip Condesa restaurant district will do, but **Garufa** was one of the first and is still one of the best. Grab a sidewalk table to watch the crowds of beautiful people while you savor a creative pasta dish (page 111).

☒ **Best Tapas and Wine:** Mediterranean-style **Tierra de Vinos** is a preserve of fine dining tucked into a nondescript storefront in the Roma. The wine selection is perhaps the best in the city, and the *tapas* and main dishes whipped up by the Catalán chef are superb (page 113).

the epicenter of this culinary renaissance starting in the early 1990s, when cafés and restaurants gradually took over part of what had been a quiet residential neighborhood. But the Condesa is just the most concentrated; you'll find creative new restaurants in Polanco, Roma, the Centro, Coyoacán, San Ángel, and elsewhere.

The turnover is high in restaurants of all types and all price ranges, but that's because the demands of the clients are high too, as in New York or any other great dining city. If a restaurant—whether they serve humble *comida corridas* (set meals) or inch-thick cuts of Argentine beef—has been around more than three years and it's still got a crowd during meal hours, it's bound to be good. It's an eater's market.

WHEN TO EAT

Capitalinos (citizens of the capital) used to have two kinds of breakfasts, an early one, called *desayuno*, eaten shortly after rising, and a second, called *almuerzo* that was usually taken about 11 A.M. Nowadays most people just have one breakfast, whenever they get up and go. The multicourse main meal of the day, *la comida*, is usually somewhere between 2 and 5 P.M. The *comida* is where Mexicans pack on most of the day's calories. The large afternoon *comida* will sustain most Mexicans till at least 8 P.M. or so, when it's time for *cena*, traditionally a light evening meal usually consisting of *pan dulce* (Mexican pastries) with tea or coffee. While the light evening meal is still eaten by many Mexicans, an increasing number have a heartier dinners in the American style, especially in Mexico City.

WHERE TO EAT

At the more humble end of the dining scale comes the venerable *puesto,* or street stand, most often located in areas where there's lots of foot traffic, like outside a Metro station. The most common *puesto* is of course the omnipresent taco stand, but those selling *tortas,* an inexpensive Mexican-style sandwich, are a close second.

Another economical choice is any *lonchería* or *comedor,* which are small, café-style places that usually serve *almuerzo* (late breakfast or early lunch) and *comida* (midday meal). Hours are typically 11 A.M.–5 P.M., and the staple is invariably an inexpensive *comida corrida* with some variety: a beverage, an entrée or two, side dishes, and possibly dessert. Travelers who discover them often become completely hooked and find themselves becoming connoisseurs of the best *corrida* eateries in their vicinity.

Taquerías, logically enough, are simple sitdown eateries (sometimes with stools only) specializing in tacos. In Mexico City you can often spot a *taquería* by a spit of meat at the entrance for making *tacos al pastor* (marinated pork), a local favorite.

More formal meals are available at *restaurantes,* which tend to serve *plato fuertes* (main dishes) rather than *antojitos* (snacks). Male, uniformed waiter service and the use of tablecloths often distinguish *restaurantes* from simpler venues.

One of the most convivial places for an evening meal in Mexico City is the cantina. Unlike in many other towns in Mexico, the cantinas of Mexico City often welcome both women and men. Food at cantinas can be very good and relatively inexpensive, and service is often exemplary. Some cantinas offer free *botanas* (snacks) when you order drinks for a couple of hours in the afternoon and (sometimes) early evening.

ORDERING AND PAYING

You really don't need that much Spanish to get by in a Mexican restaurant. Stating what you want, and adding *"por favor"* (please), will usually do the trick (e.g., *"dos cervezas, por favor,"* (two beers, please). The menu is called *el menú* or *la carta*. As a last resort, you can always point to what you want on the menu.

La cuenta is the bill. A tip *(propina)* of 10–15 percent is expected at any restaurant with table service; look to see if it's already been added to the bill before placing it on the table. In small *comedores, fondas,* or *taquerías,* tips are not expected.

MEXICAN COOKING

What follows is merely intended to give a taste, as it were, of the myriad pleasures of Mexican food, with more suggestions for further culinary explorations. A comprehensive review would require years of (admittedly very pleasurable) research and an entire book, or series of books, to expound upon. You'll find a dozen such books at any decent library or bookstore, and even more cookbooks. Or you can check out websites like www.comida.com.mx (a description and history of Mexican food, Spanish only) or http://cocinamexicana.com.mx (Mexican cooking recipes, in English and Spanish).

For those Americans who have never been to Mexico, or only to tourist areas, don't expect to find any burritos around here, or fajitas, or tacos stuffed with everything but the kitchen sink—those are Northern Mexican specialties that have been adopted with gusto by Tex-Mex restaurants in the States. Mexico City cuisine is far-ranging and constantly changing, but one thing it definitely is not is Tex-Mex.

Tomatoes and chili peppers are staples of Mexican cuisine.

COURTESY OF MEXICO TOURISM BOARD/CARLOS SANCHEZ

Tortillas

A Mexican meal is not a meal without tortillas, the round, flat, pancakelike disks that are eaten with nearly any nondessert dish, including salads, meats, seafood, beans, and vegetables. Many foreigners may have an automatic desire to fill a tortilla full of their main meal and eat it like a burrito. Think again. The idea is to grasp a utensil in one hand and the tortilla with the other, and after having a bite of the main meal, have a bite off the end of the rolled-up tortilla.

Both corn and wheat tortillas are consumed in great quantity, although *capitalinos* clearly have an overall preference for corn tortillas. Some Mexicans claim meat and poultry dishes taste best with flour tortillas while vegetable dishes go best with corn. Restaurants sometimes offer a choice of the two; if you order tortillas without specifying, you may get *"¿De harina o de maíz?"* (Flour or corn?) as a response.

Incidentally, a tortilla has two sides—an inside and an outside—that dictate which direction the tortilla is best folded when wrapping it

around food. The side with the thinner layer—sometimes called the *pancita,* or belly—should face the inside when folding the tortilla. If you notice the outside of your tortilla cracking, with pieces peeling off onto the table, you've probably folded it with the *pancita* outside instead of inside.

Breakfasts

The most common *desayuno* for the majority of Mexicans is simply *pan dulce* and/or *bolillos* (torpedo-shaped, European-style rolls) with coffee and/or milk. Cereal is also sometimes eaten for *desayuno,* e.g., *avena* (oatmeal), *crema de trigo* (cream of wheat), or *hojuelas de maíz* (corn flakes). Another favorite *desayuno* on the run is a *tamal* (steamed corn meal stuffed with a bit of meat or cheese) and a cup of *atole,* a hot, corn-based drink, sold in the morning throughout the city by street vendors out of big steel containers. Another economic choice is *molletes,* a split *bolillo* spread with mashed beans and melted cheese, served with salsa on the side.

The heavier eggs-and-frijoles dishes known

widely as "Mexican breakfasts" in the U.S. and Canada come in a variety of ways, including *huevos revueltos* (scrambled eggs), *huevos duros* (hard-boiled eggs), *huevos tibios* (coddled eggs, not soft-boiled, as sometimes translated), *huevos escafaldos* (soft-boiled eggs), *huevos estrellados* or *huevos fritos* (eggs fried sunny side up), *huevos a la mexicana* (eggs scrambled with chopped tomato, onion, and chile), *huevos rancheros* (fried eggs served on a tortilla), and *huevos divorciados* (two *huevos estrellados* separated by beans, each egg usually topped with a different salsa). One of the cheapest and most filling *almuerzos* is *chilaquiles,* tortilla chips in a chile gravy with crumbled cheese on top, a favorite hangover remedy. Eggs and/or chicken can be added to *chilaquiles* as options.

Main Meals

The main dish, or *el plato fuerte,* of any meal can be a grander version of an *antojito,* a regional specialty (*mole poblano,* for example), or something the *cocineros* (cooks) dream up themselves. Typical entrées are centered on meats, seafood, or poultry. Common meats include *carne de res* (beef), *puerco* (pork), and *cabrito* (kid goat). *Venado* (deer) and *conejo* (rabbit) are often found in rural areas in Central Mexico but less so in the city itself. Poultry dishes include *pollo* (chicken), *pavo* or *guajolote* (turkey), and, less frequently, *pato* (duck) and *codorniz* (quail).

All of these can all be cooked in an astonishing variety of ways in Mexico City, with literally hundreds of different kind of salsas and preparation techniques. Both chicken and beef are often prepared *a la mexicana,* with chopped tomatoes, onions, and serrano chile peppers. The name is because the colors of the three vegetables match those of the national flag. Another popular meat dish is a *tampiqueña,* a cut of beef surrounded by a full plate guacamole, frijoles, fried cheese, and an *enchilada. Puntas de res* are beef tips, frequently served in a smokey *chipotle* sauce. *Arrachera* denotes a flank steak, more tender and of better quality (and hence a bit more expensive) than regular beef. *Milanesa* is any kind of breaded meal, frequently pork or beef but sometimes veal as well; it's usually served in better restaurants.

One of the best-known Mexican specialties are the many varieties of *mole* (MO-lay), thick brown sauces from the states of Puebla and Oaxaca usually served over chicken or turkey. The sauce is typically made from a lengthy list of ingredients that may include unsweetened chocolate, sesame seeds, and chiles. A similar but green-hued sauce made with pumpkin seeds is called *pipián.* Both are ancient dishes dating to Mexico's prehispanic cultures.

Another Puebla specialty is *chiles en nogada,* big *poblano* chiles stuffed with a mix of shredded beef, raisins, olives, and almonds and bathed in a cream and nut sauce. *Chiles rellenos* are similar but stuffed with rice and/or cheese and fried in a bean sauce. From the southern Yucatán state comes dishes like *cochinita pibil,* a way of cooking tender pork with oranges, garlic and cumin. A favorite in the Central Mexican highlands is *barbacoa* (barbequed lamb).

Seafood runs the gamut, from succulent *huachinango* (red snapper) from the coast to *trucha* (trout) from mountain streams near the

fruit sellers in front of the **Sagrario**

city. Fish can be cooked myriad ways, including *al mojo de ajo* (with garlic), *empanizado* (breaded), *empapelado* (in foil), *a la veracruzana* (with a tomato and olive sauce), or just plain old *frito* (fried). *Camarón* (shrimp) and other shellfish are often served as *cocteles* (cocktails, steamed or boiled and served with lime and salsa), *en sus conchas* (in the shell), as ceviche (raw fish or shellfish marinated in lime juice, onions, and chiles until "cooked" by the acidic juices), or many other ways. Upscale restaurants sometimes cook shrimp in a tequila sauce.

Vegetables and salads are very common in Mexico, and much of what you'll see is exactly what you'd find at home, only usually a whole lot more flavorful, since most Mexican produce isn't industrially farmed (not yet at least). A few vegetables you might not have seen before include the light and delicate *flor de calabaza* (squash flower), dark green and chewy *nopal* (cactus petals), and trufflelike delicate *huitlacoche* (sometimes spelled *cuitlacoche,* a blue-black fungus that grows on fresh corn). *Maíz* (corn) is the grain of choice in Mexico (not wheat), and apart from serving as the basis for many foods, *elotes* (ears of corn) are often sold hot and fresh by street vendors, topped with mayonnaise and chile pepper if you don't ask otherwise. *Chayote* is a native vegetable that looks sort of like a pear and is frequently used as the base for a cream soup.

Salsas and Condiments

Any restaurant, café, *cafetería, lonchería, taquería,* or *comedor* will offer a variety of salsas. Sometimes only certain salsas are served with certain dishes, while at other times one, two, or even three salsas are stationed on every table. Often each place has its own unique salsa recipes—canned or bottled salsas are rarely used. The one ingredient common to all salsas is chile peppers, varying in heat from mild to incendiary.

There are as many types of salsas as there are Mexican dishes—red, green, yellow, brown, hot, mild, salty, sweet, thick, thin, blended, and chunky. It would take a separate book to describe them all. The most typical is the *salsa casera* (house salsa), a simple, fresh concoction of chopped chiles, onions, and tomatoes mixed with salt, lime juice, and cilantro. This is what you usually get with the free basket of *totopos* (tortilla chips), which are served at the beginning of many Mexican restaurant meals. Another common offering

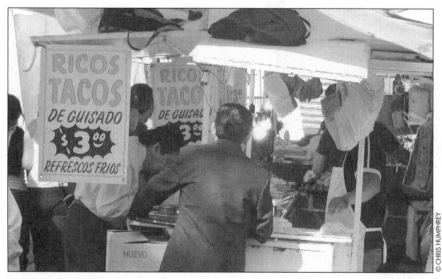

bueno, bonito, y barrato—tacos for a quarter each

ANTOJITOS

This word literally means "little whims," thus implying snacks to many people. However, the word also refers to any food that can be ordered, served, and eaten quickly—in other words, Mexican fast food. Visitors who identify these terms with dishes at Mexican restaurants in their home countries are sometimes confused by the different shapes and forms they may take in Mexico. Tacos can be rolled as well as folded, and enchiladas can be folded or stacked as well as rolled; shape is irrelevant. An enchilada (literally, "chilied") is any *antojito* made with a tortilla dipped or cooked in a chile sauce; an *entomada* (or *entomatada*) is the equivalent made with tomatoes, while the *enfrijolada* is the same made with a thin bean sauce.

Common Antojitos

alambre—a stir fry of sorts, with chopped beef, onions, peppers, and bacon and served with tortillas

birria—lamb or goat stew in a sauce spiced with chiles, cinnamon, cloves, cumin, and oregano

burrito—a flour tortilla rolled around meat, beans, or seafood fillings; rather rare in Mexico City

carnitas—braised pork, chopped into thin slices and eaten with tortillas, guacamole, and various salsas

cecina—a type of cured beef pounded flat and served with beans, fresh cheese, avocado, *nopal* cactus, and corn tortillas

chalupa—a crisp, whole tortilla topped with beans, meat, etc. (also known as a tostada); or a thicker, canoe-shaped cornmeal tortilla filled with the same

chile relleno—a mild poblano chile stuffed with cheese, deep-fried in egg batter, and covered with a sauce of tomatoes, onions, and chiles

chimichanga—tortilla (usually flour) with beans, ham, and cheese

enchilada—a corn tortilla dipped in chile sauce, then folded or rolled around a filling of meat, chicken, seafood, or cheese and baked in an oven

enfrijolada—same as enchilada except dipped in a sauce of thinned refried beans instead of chile sauce

entomatada—same as enchilada except dipped in a tomato sauce instead of chile sauce

flauta—a small corn tortilla roll, usually stuffed with beef or chicken and fried

gordita—a small, thick, corn tortilla stuffed with a spicy meat mixture; a common street-vendor offering

huarache—literally, "sandal;" a large, flat, thick, oval-shaped tortilla topped with fried meat and chiles; a common street-vendor offering

machaca—a northern dish of dried, shredded beef served with flour tortillas and guacamole, or also sometimes mixed in with scrambled eggs as a hearty breakfast

menudo—a thick soup made with cows' feet and stomachs (and less commonly, intestines) and garnished with *chiles de árbol*, oregano, and fresh chopped onion; reputedly a sure hangover cure

pancita—the Mexico City equivalent of *menudo*

picadillo—a spicy salad of chopped or ground meat with chiles and onions (also known as *salpicón*)

pozole—hominy stew made with pork or chicken and garnished with radishes, oregano, onions, chile powder, salt, and lime

quesadilla—a flour tortilla folded over sliced cheese and grilled; some cooks can add *chiles rajas* (pepper strips), *flor de calabaza* (squash flower), *champiñones* (mushrooms), or *huitlacoche* (a trufflelike fungus that grows on fresh corn) on request

sincronizada—deep-fried corn tortilla with beans, ham, and cheese, topped with guacamole

sope—a small, thick, round corn cake with dimpled edges, topped with a spicy meat mixture and crumbled cheese

taco—a corn tortilla folded or rolled around anything and eaten with the hands; *tacos al pastor,* made with thin slivers of spit-cooked pork marinated in reddish *adobo* sauce, are the most popular Mexico City variation

tamal—cornmeal *(masa)* dough wrapped in a corn husk and steamed; sometimes stuffed with cheese, chile strips, corn, olives, pork, or turkey; popularly seen on street corners (plural: tamales)

torta—a Mexican-style sandwich made with *pan telera,* a large, flat roll; *jamón* (ham) and *pollo* (chicken) are common is *salsa verde* (green salsa), made with a base of tomatillos, a small, tart, green tomatolike vegetable. Some salsas are quite *picante* (spicy hot), so it's always a good idea to test a bit before pouring the stuff over everything on your plate. Smokey chipotle salsas are often an interesting change from the hotter stuff.

Sliced, pickled chiles and carrots are sometimes served on the side as a condiment, especially with tacos and *tortas,* and are called *rajas.* In Mexico City's few Sonoran restaurants you may see a bowl of *chiltepines* (sometimes spelled *chilpetines* or *chiles pequines*), small, round, fiery red peppers. The kick of the *chiltepín* is exceeded only by that of the habañero, the world's hottest pepper and a regular table condiment at restaurants featuring dishes from the State of Yucatán.

Salt *(sal)* is usually on the table, although it's rarely needed, since Mexican dishes tend to be prepared with plenty of salt. Black pepper is *pimiento negro,* and if it's not on the table it's normally available for the asking. *Limones* are not lemons but limes (and counterintuitively enough for English-speakers, lemon is *lima!*), and they are served in almost all but the most upscale restaurants.

In *taquerías,* guacamole (mashed avocado blended with onions, chiles, salt, and other optional ingredients) is frequently served as a condiment. In restaurants it may be served as a salad or with tortilla chips. "Guacamole" sometimes refers to a very spicy paste of tomatillos and green habañero chiles that may resemble avocado guacamole—always taste before heaping it on your plate.

Vegetarians

It's difficult but not impossible to practice a vegetarian regime in Mexico City. Lacto-vegetarians can eat quesadillas, but ask for corn tortillas, which do not contain lard (most flour tortillas do) or *enchiladas de queso* (cheese enchiladas). With some luck, you'll stumble across restaurants that can prepare a variety of interesting cheese dishes, including *queso fundido con champiñones* (melted cheese with mushrooms, eaten with tortillas) and quesadillas made with *flor de calabaza.* Some places make beans without lard *(sin manteca),*

but you'll have to ask to find out. Many Mexico City restaurants offer pizza, usually offered in vegetarian versions (often called *pizza margherita*). You'll also find vegetarian/health food stores (usually called *tiendas naturistas*) with small dining sections as well as bulk foods.

Ovo-lacto-vegetarians can add egg dishes and flan to their menus. Vegans for the most part will do best to prepare their own food. Look for shops with signs reading *semillas* (seeds) to pin down a good selection of nuts and dried beans. Of course you'll find plenty of fresh fruits and vegetables in markets and grocery stores. The ever-present fruit juice stands are a great place to get all sorts of fruit combinations, along with carrots, beets, granola, and whatever else you feel like throwing in.

Soup

The general menu term for soup is *sopa* (no, that's not the word for soap), although a thick soup with lots of ingredients is usually a *caldo.* Frequently a *crema,* or cream of vegetable soup, is one of the soup options with a *comida corrida.* *Menudo*—a soup made with hominy *(nixtamal),* cow's feet, and stomach (or, less commonly, intestine) in a savory, reddish-brown broth served with chopped onions, chiles, and crumbled oregano—is seen throughout Mexico and is highly prized as a hangover remedy. Mexico City has its own version of *menudo,* and it's called *pancita* (little stomach). *Pozole*—eaten since Aztec times, when it was known as *pozolli*—is a thick stew made with a much lighter-colored broth and filled with corn and some kind of meat.

Other tasty soups include *sopa de tortillas, sopa azteca,* and *sopa tlapeña,* all featuring varying combinations of artfully seasoned chicken broth garnished with *totopos* (tortilla wedges) and sliced avocado. *Sopa de hongo* (mushroom soup) is a favorite at the many village restaurants in the mountains around Mexico City.

Cheese

Mexicans produce a great variety of cheeses. Among the most commonly used are *queso cotijo* (also called *queso añejo*), *queso chihuahua* (called *queso menonita* in the State of Chihuahua), *queso manchego, queso oaxaqueño,* and *queso asadero.*

Queso menonita or *queso chihuahua* (Mennonite, or Chihuahuan, cheese) is a mild, white cheddar produced in wheels by Mennonite colonists in Chihuahua and Durango. Spanish import (though also made in Mexico) *queso manchego* is similar but usually softer. *Queso asadero* (griller cheese) is a braided cheese somewhat similar to Armenian string cheese, made by combining sour milk with fresh milk. *Chihuahua* is a common ingredient in dishes stuffed with cheese, such as enchiladas or *chiles rellenos,* that won't receive high, direct heat. *Asadero* melts well at high temperatures without burning or separating, and as such is well suited to *chile con queso* (hot, blended chile-cheese dip), *queso fundido* (hot melted cheese topped with chorizo or mushrooms), and other dishes in which the cheese is directly exposed to high heat. *Queso oaxaqueño,* also called *quesillo,* is a lump-style cheese similar to *asadero* but a little softer—close to mozzarella. It's popular in *tortas.*

Cotija or *añejo* is a crumbly aged cheese that resists melting and is commonly used as a topping for enchiladas and beans; the flavor and texture is somewhat like a cross between feta and parmesan.

Occasionally you'll also come across *panela,* an extra-rich cheese made from heavy cream, usually sliced and served as a side dish all its own.

Bread and Pan Dulce

The most common bread *(pan)* you'll encounter is the *bolillo* (little ball), a small torpedo-shaped roll, usually rather hard on the outside. *Pan telera* ("scissor bread," so named for the two clefts on top) resemble *bolillos* but are larger and flatter; they're mainly used for making *tortas,* the ubiquitous Mexican sandwich.

Sweetened breads or pastries are known as *pan dulce* (sweet bread). Common types of *pan dulce* include *buñuelos* (crisp, round, flat pastries fried and coated with cinnamon sugar), *campechanas* (flaky, sugar-glazed puff pastries), *canastas* (thick, round, fruit-filled cookies), *capirotada* (bread pudding), *cortadillos* (cake squares topped with jelly and finely shredded coconut), *cuernitos* (small crescent rolls rolled in cinnamon sugar), or just straight-ahead *galletas* (cookies), to name a few.

Mexican Drinks

Apart from the usual array of soft drinks and alcohols, Mexico has a number of unique beverages well worth sampling during your stay. *Licuados* are similar to American smoothies—fruit blended with water, ice, honey or sugar, and sometimes milk or raw eggs to produce something like a fruit shake. One of the great joys of traveling or living in Mexico is to wander to a nearby street-corner *licuado* stand and order a mix with whatever fruits strike your fancy for under $1. In Mexico, *tuna* (not the fish, but the prickly-pear cactus fruit) *licuados* are particularly delicious. Other tasty and nutritious additives include oats *(avena)* and wheat germ *(germen de trigo).* Most places that make *licuados* also offer fruit juices such as orange juice *(jugo de naranja)* or carrot juice *(jugo de zanahoria).*

Aguas frescas are the colorful beverages sold from huge glass jars in markets and occasionally on the streets. They're made by boiling the pulp of

COOKING METHODS

Entrées, whether meat, poultry, or seafood, are most commonly prepared in one of the following styles:

adobo, adobada—marinated or stewed in a sauce of vinegar, chiles, and spices; often reddened by the addition of annatto seed extract
a la parrilla—broiled or grilled
a la veracruzana—seafood, often *huachinango* (red snapper), cooked with tomatoes, onions, chiles, and olives
albóndigas—meatballs
al carbón—charcoal-grilled
al mojo de ajo—in a garlic sauce
al pastor—slowly roasted on a vertical spit
al vapor—steamed
asado/asada—grilled
barbacoa—pit-roasted
con arroz—with rice
empanizada—breaded
encebollado—cooked with onions
enpapelada—baked in parchment
frito—fried
guisado—in a spicy stew

various fruits, grains, or seeds with water, then straining it and adding large chunks of ice. *Arroz* (rice), *horchata* (melon-seed), and *jamaica* (hibiscus flower) are three of the tastiest *aguas. Licuados* and *aguas frescas* are often sold from colorful storefronts invariably named La Flor de Michoacán or La Michoacana.

Local soft drinks include Boing and Jarritos, as well as an apple-flavored soft drink called Manzanita. Less common, but very good, is Peñafiel, a flavored mineral water drink.

Coffee is everywhere in Mexico (they grow lots of it in Veracruz and Chiapas), but a particularly Mexican version of the brew is *café de olla* flavored with cinnamon, clove, or other spices. *Café con leche* is the Mexican version of café au lait (coffee and hot milk mixed in near-equal proportions). *Café con crema* (coffee with cream) is not as available; when it is, it usually means nondairy powdered creamer.

Centuries ago, Mesoamericans mixed honey and spices with a bitter extract of the cacao bean to produce *atolli,* a warm chocolate drink popular among the upper classes. Today hot chocolate is still commonly found on Mexican menus. It's usually served very sweet and may contain cinnamon, ground almonds, and other flavorings.

Desserts and Sweets

The most popular of Mexican desserts, or *postres,* is a delicious egg custard called *flan.* It's listed on virtually every tourist restaurant menu, along with *helado* (ice cream). Other sweet alternatives include pastries found in *panaderías* (bakeries) and the frosty offerings at *paleterías.* Strictly speaking, a *paletería* serves only *paletas,* fruit-flavored ice on sticks (like American popsicles but with a much wider range of flavors), but many also serve *nieve* (literally, "snow"), flavored grated ice served in bowls or cones like ice cream.

Another street-vendor sweet is *churros,* a sweet fried pastry that's something like a doughnut stick sprinkled with sugar and cinnamon. To complete the full sugar dose, dunk it in a glass of hot chocolate. If this sounds even slightly appealing, you must visit the Churrería El Moro, on Eje Central between Uruguay and V. Carranza, where you'll find the city's best *churros* 24 hours a day.

CHILANGO COOKING

Although most Mexican dishes commonly served in Mexico City had their culinary origins outside the capital, a few have been claimed as the city's own. One common dish in this category includes *barbacoa,* lamb that has been wrapped in *maguey* leaves and slowly pit-barbecued. Some restaurants serve *barbacoa* with a *salsa borracha,* a sauce made with chiles and *pulque.*

Another *capitalino* dish is *budín azteca,* in which tortillas, chicken, puréed tomatillos, roasted chiles, cheese, and various seasonings are baked in a *cazuela,* or earthenware bowl—basically a casserole version of *chilaquiles.* Economic necessity in the infamous market ghetto of Tepito gave birth to *migas,* literally "crumbs," made by frying broken pieces of dried tortilla with eggs, onions, chiles, and whatever else is available.

Caldo tlalpeño, originally from the village of Tlalpan, now a suburb of southern Mexico City, is a very popular soup made by stewing chicken in a broth flavored with *chipotles* (smoked jalapeños) and served with garnishes of cilantro and avocado. This smoky-flavored *caldo* has become a menu standard throughout Mexico.

Street vendors sell a wide variety of foods that originated in the Mexican countryside but which have taken on their own Mexico City style. *Tacos al pastor,* made with layers of meat marinated in orange-red *adobo* sauce and cooked on a vertical spit, have become so ubiquitous in the capital that *al pastor* is now considered a D.F. specialty. On many street corners in the Centro, you'll also see steel washtubs filled with steaming *tamales* that tend to be larger than those you might encounter in Mexican villages. Served with a hot cup of *atole*—a drink made with cornmeal and chocolate—a Mexico City tamal makes a filling breakfast for only around $0.70. Other common street foods, especially in the Centro, include *huaraches* and *sopes.*

Centro Histórico

Downtown Mexico City is crammed with restaurants of all types, with plenty of choices for travelers in all price ranges. The emphasis among almost all of the Centro eateries is Mexican cuisine in all its myriad variations, varying from some great hole-in-the-wall taco joints to veritable pageants of traditional Mexican dishes served in renovated colonial mansions.

TACOS, TORTAS, AND SNACKS

On the east end of Plaza Manuel Tolsá, near the Museo Nacional de Arte, **Taco Inn** (Tacuba 10, 8 A.M.–11 P.M. daily, $4–6 for a big plate of tacos) is an upscale taco restaurant with hygienically prepared tacos and other *antojitos* at slightly higher-than-normal prices (for tacos). The steaming *café de olla,* served in ceramic mugs, is excellent.

A more traditional taco spot, infrequently visited by tourists but mobbed by locals, is **Tacos Beatriz** (Uruguay 30, 10 A.M.–4:45 P.M. daily). This little hole-in-the-wall might seem less than appealing at first, but step inside and you'll see that the cheerful ladies running it keep everything clean, and the tacos are delicious and cheap. *Tacos de carnitas* (braised pork) are a specialty, as are *tacos de chichacharrón con aguacate* (pork rinds with avocado).

Lonchería Vasconia (corner of Tacuba and Palma, 7:30 A.M.–9 P.M. Mon.–Sat., 7:30 A.M.–8 P.M. Sun.), attached to the bakery of the same name, serves *tacos al pastor* and roast chicken; a good place for a quick, inexpensive bite to eat.

Turkey-lovers should stop by **El Rey del Pavo** (Palma 32, 11 A.M.–6:30 P.M. Mon.–Sat.), where you can get a full meal for $3–4, or tasty turkey *tortas* topped with guacamole for $1.40 each in a funky but clean cafeteria-style restaurant.

Gili Pollos (corner of Cinco de Mayo and Isabel la Católica, noon–8 P.M. daily) offers delicious and inexpensive roast chickens and chicken tacos in a modest corner storefront, with stools for the clients. Those familiar with Iberian Spanish slang will catch the off-color pun in the name.

Café El Alcatraz (Av. Madero right behind Iglesia La Profesa, 1–6 P.M. Mon.–Sat.) offers a few tables set on a terrace below street level where you can rest from your tour with a snack or soda.

MEXICAN

At the 1930-vintage **Café La Blanca** (Cinco de Mayo 40, 7 A.M.–11 P.M. daily, entrées $2–5) the simple tables and Formica counter, topped with plastic placemats, are always filled with men poring over newspapers while sipping strong coffee. The reliable though unexceptional menu focuses on Mexican specialties at very reasonable prices (one of the main attractions). Breakfasts are a good deal here. Lithographs on the walls depict Mexico City of yesteryear.

If you'd like to try *comida yucateca* (food from the Yucatán region), head over to **Coox Hanal** (Isabel la Católica 83, tel. 5709-3613, 9 A.M.–5 P.M. daily, entrées $3–5) a breakfast and lunch joint always swarming with locals gobbling down the restaurant's inexpensive specialties such as *sopa de lima* (lemon soup), *panuchos* (fried tortilla filled with beans and topped with chicken and onions), or *papadzules* (tortilla with eggs and tomato sauce). It's invariably packed around 3 P.M.

While most **Sanborns** (Av. Madero 4, tel. 5512-9820, 7 A.M.–11 P.M. daily, entrées $3–6) feel somewhat like a Mexican-style Denny's, the historic original restaurant on Madero is an exception. Set in the two-story courtyard of the Casa de los Azulejos, a 16th-century palace covered in blue tiles, the spacious restaurant is always packed with businessmen, politicians, tourists, and others. The Mexican menu is unexceptional but hygienic and reasonably priced.

M Hostería Santo Domingo (Belisario Dominguez 72, tel. 5510-1434, 9 A.M.–9 P.M. daily, entrées $3–7) has been serving classic Mexican dishes since 1860. The *chiles en nogada* are superb, considered by some to be the best in the city, and the *mole poblano* is also legendary. Musicians frequently serenade diners.

On weekends expect a long wait for a table, particularly during the middle of the afternoon.

Set in a converted 17th-century colonial mansion, **Café Tacuba** (Tacuba 28, tel. 5521-2048, 8 A.M.–11 P.M. daily, entrées $3–8) serves well-prepared, traditional Mexican meal amid historic ambience. The restaurant is very popular with both Mexicans and visitors and has been in operation since 1912, although lately they seem to be resting on their laurels a bit. It's so well-known there's even a famous Mexican rock band named in its honor. One good choice, *cuatro cositas* (four little things), comes with a large, moist, and tasty tamal filled with cheese and fresh *epazote,* an *enchilada Tacuba* (chicken rolled up in a corn tortilla bathed in a house sauce), rice, beans, and guacamole. Be prepared to wait for your meal as the service can be terrible.

Another top-notch Mexican restaurant, with very reasonable prices, is **El Cardenal** (Palma 23, tel. 5521-8815, www.elcardenal.com.mx, 9 A.M.–7 P.M. daily, entrées $5–11), serving traditionally prepared Mexican dishes such as sea bass in barbecue sauce or beef tips in *chipotle,* as well as a number of seasonal specialties like *chiles en nogada* (August–September) and *bacaloa* (November–December) in a quietly elegant dining room.

La Casa de las Sirenas (behind the Catedral at Av. República de Guatemala 32, tel. 5704-3345 or 5704-3225, 8 A.M.–11 P.M. Mon.–Sat., 9 A.M.–6 P.M. Sun., entrées $8–15) makes an excellent choice for a relaxing (though not cheap) midday meal while sightseeing. The restaurant serves well-prepared Mexican classics such as *mole poblano, chiles en nogada,* and *pozole,* all pricey but good. It's on the second and third floors of a colonial-era mansion; the second floor patio is favored by Mexico City politicians who work in the Centro and are fond of taking their power lunches here.

Another "power lunch" favorite is **Los Girasoles** (on the pedestrian-only Calle Xicotencatl, east end of Plaza Manuel Tolsá off Tacuba, tel. 5510-0630, 1:30 P.M.–midnight Mon.–Sat., 1:30 P.M.–8 P.M. Sun., entrées $8–15), a formal restaurant frequented by senators and their staff

from the federal Senate next door. The menu offers some interesting *nueva cocina* specialties, such as *tacos de pato* (duck tacos) and trout cooked in mezcal sauce.

In a spacious, peaceful dining room in an old building on the northwest corner of the Zócalo, **Mexico Viejo** (Tacuba 87, tel. 5510-3748, 8 A.M.–9 P.M. Mon.–Sat., 9 A.M.–6 P.M. Sun., entrées $4–10) is a popular spot with foreign and Mexican tourists visiting the downtown area. The extensive menu (available in English) offers specialties such as *crepas huitlacoche* and *chilaquiles con pollo.* It also has a reasonably priced *comida del día* (meal of the day). Breakfasts are good and not expensive.

For culinary adventure-seekers after a taste of exotic pre-Hispanic cuisine, including *gusanos de maguey* (cactus worms), *venado con huitlacoche* (deer meat with corn fungus), or other Aztec delicacies, try the famed **Fonda de Don Chon** (Regina 160, tel. 5542 0873, noon–6 P.M. Mon.–Sat., entrées $3–8) southeast of the Zócalo. The surrounding neighborhood is rather run-down, so watch your step heading over this way.

CANTINAS

If you'd like to take in a little history with a meal or cold *cerveza,* stop in at **Bar La Ópera** (Av. 5 de Mayo 10, tel. 5512-8959, 1– 11:30 P.M. Mon.– Sat., 1–5:30 P.M. Sun., entrées $6–12), where Pancho Villa left bullet holes in the ceiling while riding around inside on his horse during the Revolution. This dark, baroque cavern of a place was built with plenty of wood and huge, mirrored booths big enough to hold large parties of revelers (or conceal couples deep in the recesses). The menu is large and the food is good. Try the seafood *paella,* or the *favada asturiana,* a hearty Spanish meat and bean dish. They also have a set menu of the day during the afternoon meal.

For a *torta* or shrimp cocktail, and a mug of cold beer to wash it down, drop into **Salón Corona** (Bolívar 24, tel. 5512-9007, 8 A.M.– 11:30 P.M. daily) a family restaurant/cantina in business since 1928. Large *tarros* (mugs) of draft Corona—light, dark, or mixed together (*campechana*)—cost $1.50. The *caldo de camarón* (shrimp stew) comes in a glass and is excellent. This a very popular spot on Sunday afternoons, when many other downtown spots are closed, and anytime there's a soccer game on TV.

If you'd like to eat in an old-style cantina, check out **El Gallo de Oro** (Carranza 35 at the corner of Bolivar, noon–10 P.M. Mon.–Fri., noon–7 P.M. Sat.). Another very good cantina is the well-lit, friendly **La Mascota** (Mesones 20, noon–11 P.M. daily). Both places offer *botanas,* snacks offered free with drinks during the late afternoon, or multicourse fixed meals. Most people come for the free *botanas,* usually a choice of seven different plates like meatballs in *chipotle* sauce or *carnitas.*

SEAFOOD

Refined, quiet **El Danubio** (Uruguay 3, just off Eje Central, tel. 5512-0912, 1–10 P.M. daily, entrées $6–12) is the place to go for top-quality seafood downtown at midrange prices. Some say it has the best seafood in the city. The weekday *comida corrida* (served 2–5 P.M. only) is a bargain at $8.

BISQUETS

Café El Popular (with two branches downtown, both on Cinco de Mayo, one at Cinco de Mayo 50 near the Zócalo, 24 hours daily, and the other at Cinco de Mayo 10, next to Bar La Ópera, 8 A.M.–1 A.M. daily, entrées $2–6). El Popular is an example of the gradually disappearing *bisquet* café or *café chino*—operated by Chinese families and once popular in the 1940s and 1950s in Mexico City. The menu is unspectacular but reliable. The branch of El Popular nearer the Zócalo is smaller and has more character, though you may have to wait briefly by the cash register for an open table.

Another popular *bisquet* restaurant is **Los Bisquets Obregón** (Tacuba 85 near Palma, 7:30 A.M.–10 P.M. daily, entrées $2–6), a branch of the famous diner in the Roma neighborhood. On weekends there's often a line for

tables, a testament to the reliable, reasonably priced meals.

FOOD WITH A VIEW

Umbrella-shaded tables on the restaurant veranda on the top floor of the historic **Best Western Hotel Majestic** (Madero 73 at Monte de Piedad, tel. 5521-8600, 8 A.M.–11 P.M. daily, entrées $7–15) look east out over the Zócalo, affording good views of the Catedral, Sagrario, Palacio Nacional, and the twice-daily flag ceremonies in the center of the plaza. Prices are moderate, considering the view, and the food is quite respectable if not the most exciting in the capital. The *pollo almendrado* (chicken baked in a tasty almond sauce) and *crema de queso Sonora* (a rich Sonoran cheese soup) are both hearty and good. If you're just dropping by for dessert, try the *crepas de cajeta al tequila* (crepes in a goat-milk caramel and tequila sauce). The **Holiday Inn** also has a rooftop restaurant overlooking the Zócalo.

VEGETARIAN

Decent vegetarian meals can be found at the dinerlike **Vegetarianos del Centro** (Filomeno Mata 13 near Cinco de Mayo, tel. 5510-0113, 8 A.M.–8 P.M. Mon.–Sat., 9 A.M.–8 P.M. Sun., $5 for set meal). A fixed vegetarian menu is served every day, or you can order dishes à la carte, including stuffed avocados, baked potatoes, and lots of egg dishes, all at low prices.

Another veggie place worth trying is **Comedor Vegetariano** (Motolinía 31, 2nd floor, 1–6 P.M. daily, $4 for set meal). Don't be deterred by the somewhat dingy entranceway—the restaurant itself is clean, and the food good and inexpensive.

The chain of health food store/lunch counters serves For vegetarian *tortas, comida corridas,* and juices, head to the lunch counters at one of the three downtown branches of the chain health food store **Super Soya** (16 de Septiembre 79, 11 A.M.–8 P.M. daily, Brasil 11, 9 A.M.– 8:30 P.M. Mon.–Fri., 10 A.M.–7 P.M. weekends, and Bolívar 31-A, 9 A.M.–9 P.M. Mon.–Sat., 9 A.M.–7 P.M. Sun.).

MIDDLE EASTERN

Three blocks southeast of the Zócalo is **El Ehden** (Venustiano Carranza 148, 2nd floor, tel. 5542-2320, noon–6 P.M. daily, entrées $3–5) a cafeteria-style restaurant run by a Lebanese woman and her Mexican husband. They serve a wide selection of Middle Eastern dishes, including stuffed grape leaves, hummus, falafel, *baba ganoush,* tabouli, and more.

Considered to have some of the best Middle Eastern food in the city, but tucked into a not altogether pleasant neighborhood about seven blocks southeast of the Zócalo, is **Al Andaluz** (Mesones 171, between Las Cruces and Jesús María, tel. 5522-2528, 9 A.M.–6 P.M. daily, entrées $4–8). The restaurant, which caters principally to the Arab community who work in the neighborhood textile trade, is hidden in a cozy, renovated, two-story colonial house, an oasis from the surrounding streets. Specialties include *baba ganoush, shwarma,* hummus, and *kepa bola* (this last a mix of wheat, ground beef, and onion). Top off your meal with a cup of strong Arab coffee. Prices are very reasonable and the quality is excellent. Because of the location, Al Andaluz is not frequented by tourists.

SPANISH

A gathering place for Spaniards living in Mexico, the **Casino Español** (Isabel la Católica 31, tel. 5521-8894, 1–6 P.M. daily, *comida del día* $11) is housed in a sumptuous early 20th-century building. Open only for lunch, the Casino's restaurant serves an excellent Spanish-style *comida del día* with five dishes, as well as a selection of specialties from the menu. The Casino is particularly popular on weekends.

COFFEE, SWEETS, AND BREAD

For a late-night treat, head for the 1935-vintage **Churrería El Moro** (Eje Central 42 between Uruguay and V. Carranza, tel. 5512-0896, 24 hours daily). Warning: *Churros,* deep-fried, sugary pastries meant to be dipped in hot chocolate before eating, can be very addictive.

Mexico City's *panaderías* offer dozens of sweet treats to please the palate.

Two bakeries next to one another on Av. 16 de Septiembre near Eje Central, **Pastelería La Ideal** and **El Globo** (both 7 P.M.–8 P.M. daily) offer huge selections of pastries, both European and Mexican style.

Founded in 1927, the original **Panadería Ideal,** west of Eje Central on the north side of República de Uruguay, may be the ultimate Mexican bakery. It's worth a visit just to see the marvelous cakes on display and the seemingly endless variety of *pan dulce.*

At the corner of Tacuba and Palma it's hard to miss **Panadería y Pastelería Vasconia** (7 P.M.–8 P.M. daily), a good bakery with a huge selection. Pick up a tray and tongs and serve yourself, then sit down and have some coffee at one of the tables inside.

Just off Madero, the upscale **Café El Passaje** (Gante 6, 9 A.M.–9 P.M. Mon.–Sat.) serves espresso drinks and sweet treats The tables, some set up on the pedestrian-only street and some inside, are a fine place to sip a cup and read one of the international or Mexican papers sold at the café.

Café Emir (Uruguay 45, 9 A.M.–6 P.M. Mon.–Sat.) serves a good strong cup of java to drink at its collection of small tables.

Alameda Central

The area around the Alameda can't claim a great profusion of restaurants, although there are several worth seeking out if you're in the area.

TACOS, TORTAS, AND SNACKS

Those who appreciate good street vendor *tacos de guisado* should go the two stands on Av. Balderas just south of the corner of Juárez, where you can feast for a dollar or two.

MEXICAN

Fonda Santa Anita (southwest of the Alameda at Humboldt 48, tel. 5518-4609, 1:30–6 P.M. daily, entrées $3–6) is a traditional Mexican restaurant offering tasty home-cooked stan-

At Sanborns Café, you can count on the same menu items and prices as at the main cafeteria at Casa de Los Azulejos in Centro Histórico, shown above.

dards at inexpensive to moderate prices. The multicourse *comida corridas* are an excellent value at $6 with a choice of entrée, served in a cheerfully decorated dining room.

Right next to the FONART handicraft shop, near the Metro Hidalgo station, is a 24-hour **Sanborns Café.** At the southeast corner of López and Juárez streets, you'll find yet another branch of **Sanborns,** open daily for breakfast, lunch, and dinner.

For a more upscale meal, try the **Café del Palacio** (corner of Av. Juárez and the Eje Central, 11 A.M.–7 P.M. daily, or until later during evening shows, entrées $8–12) inside the Palacio de Bellas Artes. Despite the good quality and elegant ambience, prices are quite reasonable. A *menú* including an appetizer, main course (such as grilled red snapper or steak), salad, and drinks costs $16. If you just want a snack, try a pâté, quiche, or *cazuelitas de salpicón,* a dish of beans, shredded beef, onion, potato, lettuce, olive oil, and vinegar. This is also a fine spot to enjoy a strong espresso and dessert.

CANTINAS

Since 1933, **Cantina La Única de Guerrero** (Guerrero 258 at Marte, tel. 5526-6854, 10 A.M.–10 P.M. Mon.–Sat., noon–8 P.M. Sunday, entrées $3–8) has preserved a legacy of culinary tradition that many other city cantinas aspire to. Popular with writers and intellectuals, "La Única" (also commonly known as "La U de G") dispenses good *caldo de camarón* (shrimp stew), as well as its trademark *cabrito al horno* (kid goat) and plenty of other cantina favorites besides, but no free *botanas.* Live *salterio* (Mexican zither) music is played from 3 P.M. onward, with an emphasis on sad *valses* (waltzes). To find it, go a block south of Avenida Ricardo Flores Magón on Guerrero, turn right (west) at Martes, and look for the cantina at the southwest corner of the intersection.

Salón Cantina La Victoria (Magnolia 3 at Eje Central Lázaro Cárdenas, tel. 5526-3667, noon–11 P.M. Mon.–Sat., noon–8 P.M. Sun., $3–8) specializes in regional dishes from many parts of Mexico. It offers a choice of seven daily platters. Two blocks south of the Metro Plaza Garibaldi on the west side of Eje Central.

Although La Única and La Victoria are anything but rough themselves, this isn't a great neighborhood for an after-dark stroll, so consider using taxi service at night when going to or from these cantinas.

MARKETS

Inexpensive *comida corridas* can be found at a number of simple lunch restaurants in the **Mercado San Juan,** (off Calle Pugibet, 7 A.M.–5 P.M. daily).

VEGETARIAN

On the east side of Dolores—one-half block south of the Alameda between Avenida Juárez and Calle Independencia—basic, inexpensive **Centro Naturista de México** is a vegetarian restaurant and health-food store featuring a daily buffet.

CHINESE

South of the Alameda, a small Chinatown runs along Calle Dolores north of Calle Artículo 123. An attempt is under way to create a pedestrian walkway here with decorations and street lamps, but so far this hasn't kept cars off the street. In this area you'll find **Restaurant Bar Nuevo Cantón, Restaurant Bar Chung King, Restaurant Bar Oriental, Restaurant Tong Fong, Restaurant Bar Shang Hai, Cuatro Mares,** and **Restaurant Hong King,** all serving reasonable Cantonese food. Shanghai and Tong Fong are two of the better ones. **Dinastia Lee,** on Calle Dolores, is more of a *café chino,* serving *bisquets,* chop suey, and Mexican breakfasts.

ITALIAN

Friendly and with inexpensive but mediocre food, **Cafe Trevi** (Colón 1 at the western end of the Alameda, tel. 5512-3020, 8 A.M.–11:30 P.M. daily, entrées $2.50–5) has been in operation since 1955, serving pizza, pasta, breakfasts, and snacks. There's also a full bar.

Paseo de la Reforma and Zona Rosa

Restaurants in the Zona Rosa and around Reforma are generally more upscale than in the Centro Histórico or Alameda Central, and prices are accordingly higher. Visitors can choose from several international cuisine styles as well as upscale Mexican fare. But those on a budget need not fear: Lower-priced meals can be found in the surrounding neighborhoods, particularly at the markets and in little *comida corrida* eateries. McDonald's, KFC, and other fast-food chains have outlets in the Zona Rosa for those desperate for a taste of Americana.

TACOS, TORTAS, AND SNACKS

Just off the pedestrian-only Calle Génova in the Zona Rosa, **Taco Inn** (Hamburgo 96, 7 A.M.–4 A.M. daily, $4–6 for a big plate of tacos) has rather pricey but very good tacos.

Its long hours make it convenient for breakfast as well as a late-night snack.

MEXICAN

El Mixteco (on the west side of the Lotería Nacional building at the corner of Thomas A. Edison, lunches until 4 P.M. Mon.–Fri., entrées $2–5) is a classic little hole-in-the-wall spot specializing in cuisine from the Mixtec region of Oaxaca, including *tlayuda,* (a tortilla with salsa, onions, shredded beef, and special sauce), *tazajo* (a beef or shrimp dish), and exotica such as *chapulines* (grasshoppers). It offers a *comida corrida* with a fresh-squeezed fruit drink for $4.50.

A more upscale option is the all-time Zona Rosa favorite, **Fonda del Refugio** (Liverpool 166, tel. 5525-8128, 1 P.M.–midnight Mon.–Sat.,

1–10 P.M. Sun., entrées $6–12) serving traditional Mexican dishes such as *chiles en nogada* and *tacos de huitlacoche,* along with imaginative daily specials such as *albóndigas chipotle* (meatballs with chipotle chile sauce) in the quiet, relaxed ambience of an old two-story colonial house. The restaurant displays the folk art collection of the late Judit van Beuren, a writer who founded the restaurant in the 1950s. If you have a hard time with the Spanish menu, ask for the English version.

At the corner of Avenida Cuauhtémoc and Morelos, at the eastern edge of the Reforma area, is the legendary coffeehouse and restaurant **M La Habana** (Morelos 62, tel. 5535-2620, 8 A.M.–midnight Mon.–Sat., entrées $3–7), frequented by generations of journalists who work in the surrounding blocks. This is a wonderful spot to enjoy a strong cup of coffee and a good breakfast or lunch at leisure. They offer good set menus for both meals. I'm a huge fan of the *huevos con machaca* (eggs with dried, shredded beef in a spicy sauce), but there are plenty of other options. The Formica and plastic decor comes straight from the 1950s, along with the old photos of Cuba on the walls. When government bribery of journalists was more common than it is nowadays, the men's room of La Habana was reputedly where most of the *chayotes* (a slang word for payoffs made for flattering stories) were passed along. Yet another historical legend has it that a young Fidel Castro planned his return to Cuba on the legendary ship *Granma* sitting at the tables here. Ground or whole-bean Veracruz coffee can be purchased to go.

guacamole, a couple of enchiladas, and other fixings, for $10.

For very possibly the best *birria* (lamb stew) in Mexico City, stop off at **M La Polar** (Guillermo Prieto 129, at the corner of the Circuito Interior, tel. 5546-5066, 9 A.M.–midnight daily and until 2 A.M. Fri., entrées $3–7) in the San Rafael neighborhood. This classic, old-style cantina has several rooms, usually filled with crowds of Mexicans enjoying their legendary bowls of *birria,* a stew of shredded lamb in a spicy broth, served with tortillas, onion, salsa, and avocado. *Birria* is famed as a great hangover cure, to which the bleary-eyed crowds on Saturday and Sunday around noon can attest. La Polar also has beer on tap, and entertainment is provided by roving *norteña* and mariachi bands. It also serves *birria* to go from a take-out window.

Behind the Hotel Melía Reforma, **Cantina Latino** (Antonio Caso 17, tel. 5564-0800, 11 A.M.–midnight Mon.–Fri., 11 A.M.–6 P.M. Sat., entrées $4–7) is a large bar/restaurant with high-backed wooden booths popular for business lunches. The menu has a heavy emphasis on meats, including *arrachera* steaks, *cabrito, chistorra,* and a selection of Spanish hams and sausages (no free *botanas* here). It also has a full bar.

El Picadero (Morelos 65, between Bucareli and Abraham González, tel. 5535-2620, 1–10:30 P.M. Mon.–Sat.) is a small, lively cantina that serves a selection of more than 40 *botanas,* from *nopal* stuffed with cheese, Veracruz-style fish fillet, or *panuchos.* Keep ordering drinks ($3 beer, $4 most mixed drinks) and the *botanas* keep coming.

CANTINAS

In the center of the Zona Rosa is **Bohemio's** (Londrés 142, tel. 5514-0790, 1 P.M.–1 A.M. Mon.–Sat., entrées $6–12), a somewhat upscale cantina that stays entertaining and rowdy nonetheless, with live Mexican music and many pitchers of light and dark Kloster beer swinging among the crowded tables. The food is traditional Mexican and of good quality. Try the *tampiqueña,* a piece of tender beef served with

SEAFOOD

Clean and inexpensive **Mariscos del Camaronero** (Ignacio Ramírez 21B, north of Paseo de la Reforma, 10 A.M.–10 P.M. Mon.–Sat., entrées $2–5) serves tasty shrimp and fish tacos, ceviche, and seafood cocktails.

A few blocks farther north, past the Monumento a la Revolución, is **Restaurante El Delfín** (Arriaga 7, 10 A.M.–7 P.M. daily, entrées $2–5), with similar, inexpensive fare.

MARKETS

The lowest-priced meals around Reforma are, predictably, to be found in the markets. While the Zona Rosa's **Mercado Insurgentes** (9 A.M.–7 P.M. Mon.–Sat., 10 A.M.–3 P.M. Sun.), in the first block east of Florencia between Liverpool and Londrés, is mainly dedicated to handicrafts, one corner of the market has a number of hygienic *comida corrida* stands where a meal will set you back around $3.

Directly behind the U.S. embassy on Río Lerma, **Mercado Cuauhtémoc** is a regular neighborhood market, though it is a touch pricier than most because of the relatively upscale clientele. The food stands inside serve tasty *comidas corridas* for $2–4 and *antojitos* for $1–3; they are open during the week until 6 P.M. and on weekends until 4 P.M.

VEGETARIAN

Yug (Varsovia 3 at Paseo de la Reforma, tel. 5533-3296, 7 A.M.–10 P.M. Mon.–Fri., 8 A.M.–8 P.M. Sat., 1–8 P.M. Sun., entrées $3–6) goes beyond the standard health-store ambience of most D.F. veggie restaurants to serve vegetarian crepes, potato latkes, and a variety of fruit and vegetable juices.

North of Reforma, **Restaurante Vegetariano Las Fuentes** (Río Pánuco 127, at Río Tiber, tel. 5525-7095, 8 A.M.–6 P.M. daily, entrées $3–6) offers good breakfasts and *comidas corridas.*

ARGENTINE

A very good and reasonably priced Argentine restaurant popular with the middle-class crowd who work and live in the Cuauhtémoc neighborhood north of Reforma is **Quebracho** (Río Lerma 175, tel. 5208-3999, 1–11 P.M. daily, entrées $7–13). It's located on a pleasant block where several sidewalk cafés have opened in the past couple of years. The tender *arrachera* steak for $11 is a reliable choice, and try the cream-of-spinach side dish.

The chain restaurant **La Mansión** (Hamburgo 77, tel. 5514-3425, 1–11 P.M. Tues.–Sat., 1–9 P.M.

Sun., entrées $9–16) serves hearty Argentine-style steaks, empanadas, and wine.

ASIAN

If you're looking for Japanese cuisine, try **Daikoku** (Río Pánuco 170, at Río Nilo, tel. 5525-6520, 1–11 P.M. daily, entrées $7–12), a couple of blocks north of Reforma. Japanese people living in Mexico City say they favor the sushi and sashimi in this restaurant over any other in the capital.

Sushi Itto (Hamburgo 141, tel. 5525-2635, 1–10:30 P.M. daily, entrées $4–6) whips up (very quickly) sushi of the mass-produced variety, but it's reliable and hygienic, and the miso soup is tasty.

In the middle of the Zona Rosa, **Luau's** (Niza 38, tel. 5525-7474, noon–11 P.M. Mon.–Sat., noon–6 P.M. Sun., entrées $7–9) serves decent Cantonese food amid an amusingly kitsch decor. House specialties include *cha siu* (barbecued pork) and the ever-popular *chow mein cantonés.* The hearty multicourse set meals are a good value.

FRENCH

A block and a half north of Reforma, near the British embassy, **Les Moustaches** (Río Sena 88, tel. 5533-3390, 1–11:30 P.M. Mon.–Sat., entrées $20–30) is a very posh restaurant in a converted old *casona* (old mansion). The service and authentic French food are top-notch, although you certainly pay for the quality. Specialties include duck in a green-olive sauce and chicory-leaf salad with goat cheese. Soft piano music adds to the ambience.

Champs Elysees (Paseo de la Reforma 316, between Estocolmo and Amberes, tel. 5533-3698, 1–11 P.M. Mon.–Sat., $17–28) is frequently recommended for its exemplary foie gras and *confit de pato* (duck confit). Attached to the restaurant is a deli with fresh baguettes and a selection of French wines and other specialties.

At the Casa de Francia, a cultural organization run by the French Embassy, is **Cordon Bleu** (Havre 15, tel. 5208-0660, 9 A.M.–6 P.M. Mon.–Sat., $30 for a set meal with wine). The quality of the food is very good, and the setting—with an outdoor patio—is more relaxed and informal than the above restaurants. The set meal with wine during the day is not cheap, but it is good and filling.

INTERNATIONAL

Difficult to classify, but well worth visiting if you're tired of *tortas* and *comida corridas* for lunch, is **Café Mangia** (Río Sena 85, 8 A.M.–6 P.M. Mon.–Fri., set meals $6–8), a deli-style restaurant catering to the local office-and-embassy crowd with breakfasts such as croissants stuffed with egg, cheddar cheese, avocado, and bacon, or eggs scrambled with gruyère cheese for $2–5. Italian sandwiches are $4–8. They also have good daily set meals, often with some type of pasta.

ITALIAN

La Gondola Restaurante (Génova 21, tel. 5514-0743, 1–11 P.M. daily, entrées $10–20) has been serving Italian food for many years. If you'd like to dine alfresco, arrive before 8 P.M., or you probably won't get a table. The veal scallopini with lemon is tangy and tender, and the fettuccine alfredo is creamy and sweet. The restaurant offers a decent wine selection.

BASQUE

Tezka (Hotel Royal Zona, Amberes 78, tel. 5228-9918, ext. 5067, 1:30–11 P.M. Mon.–Fri., 1:30–6 P.M. Sat., entrées $20–30) is an upscale new hotel restaurant specializing in Basque cuisine. For those who don't know, the Basque region is a part of northwest Spain and southwest France and is known for its fierce independent streak, unusual language, and top-notch food. Be prepared to drop a pretty penny here, but the quality is superb, with specialties such as venison ($25), lamb in coffee ($25), or a tasting menu for $40. The chef learned his trade in the legendary Basque food mecca, San Sebastián.

STEAKS

Angus (Copenhague 31, between Hamburgo and Reforma, tel. 5208-2828, 1 P.M.–midnight daily, entrées $15–30) is a perennial favorite with the upper-class business crowd. Here you will certainly sate your craving for meat in short order—even the potatoes come with ham in them. The waitresses, dressed in skimpy Santa Fe–style cowgirl outfits, seem puzzled that one could want a plain potato.

COFFEE, SWEETS, AND BREAD

Near the corner of Florencia in the Zona Rosa is **Salón de Té Auseba** (Hamburgo 179, 8 A.M.–10:30 P.M. Mon.–Sat., 11 A.M.–10:30 P.M. Sun.), a great, old-school, quiet spot to sit and relax in the comfortable 1950s-style vinyl chairs and recharge with small sandwiches, pastries, and strong coffee.

Starbucks, inevitably, has arrived to Mexico City, and if you just can't do without your double tall skinny latte, proceed directly to the branches at Hamburgo 126 in the Zona Rosa or next to the U.S. Embassy on Paseo de la Reforma.

Restaurants

Chapultepec and Polanco

As with hotels in this zone, Chapultepec and Polanco restaurants tend to be upscale and pricey, but they offer excellent quality. Polanco in particular features some of the best "ethnic" restaurants in the city. Reservations are recommended for many of these spots, particularly during the afternoon meal hours, and most credit cards are accepted.

TACOS, TORTAS, AND SNACKS

Those after a quick *torta* or *comida corrida* in Polanco can head over to **Las Tortugas** (Presidente Mazaryk 249, at Arquimedes, tel. 5280-1290, 9 A.M.–11 P.M. daily, $3–6 per *torta*). They're not the cheapest *tortas,* but they are hearty and good. They deliver within Polanco. Another decent spot is **Doña Torta** (in the center of the Polanco shopping district, at Virgilio 4, tel. 5281-6521).

Grab an inexpensive Lebanese-style snack of stuffed grape leaves, falafel, or *tacos arabes* (tacos with meat cut from a rotating spit) at **Yamil** (Virgilio 9, tel. 8589-8142, 1–6 P.M. daily).

MEXICAN

Next to the Periférico, the superlative restaurant **M Hacienda de los Morales** (Vázquez de Mella 525, tel. 5281-4703 or 5281-4554, 1 P.M.–midnight daily, entrées $15–30) dates from the 16th century and was originally a silk-producing hacienda (hence the name—from *moral,* the mulberry tree groves in which the worms lived) in what was then a rural area west of Mexico City. The city has long since surrounded the hacienda, but this oasis of colonial calm is renowned for its Mexican cuisine, good service, and beautiful gardens. Well-prepared Mexican specialties include *chiles en nogada* (meat-stuffed chiles *poblanos* in a cream and nut sauce), shrimp in tequila sauce, and *cabrito norteño* (Northern Mexican–style barbecued goat). The clientele tends to dress up to dine here, so don't come in shorts and a T-shirt.

Another very good traditional Mexican restaurant in Polanco is **Villa María** (Homero 704, tel. 5203-0306, 1:30 P.M.–midnight Mon.–Sat., 1:30 P.M.–midnight Sun., entrées $7–13). Start off with the delectable *infladitas,* a sort of miniquesadilla, or the *sopa capilla* with *queso panela,* corn, and squash flowers. The *arrachera* steak is a good main course. Live mariachi musicians stroll among the tables during dinner.

A converted mansion near the Paseo de la Reforma houses **Estoril** (Alejandro Dumas 24, tel. 5280-3414, 1–11 P.M. Mon.–Sat., entrées $10–17), favored by wealthy Mexicans who enjoy the restaurant's cool ambience, attentive service, and top-quality Mexican specialties such as *nopales rellenos de huitlacoche* (cactus pads stuffed with corn fungus—a lot better than it sounds).

DINERS

Klein's Restaurant (in the strip of eateries along Presidente Mazaryk between Alejandro Dumas and Anatole France, tel. 5281-0862, 8 A.M.–midnight Mon.–Sat., 9 A.M.–midnight Sun., entrées $4–8) is about the closest you'll come to a New York diner in Mexico (and it isn't all that close, either). Klein's serves moderately priced sandwiches and meals. The *enchiladas verdes,* with either chicken or cheese, are a filling treat for $6, and the burgers aren't bad either. It's usually packed for the 2–4 P.M. midday meal.

SEAFOOD

Los Arcos (Torcuato Tasso 330, just off Mazaryk, tel. 5254-5624, noon–10 P.M. Mon.–Sat., noon–8 P.M. Sun., entrées $10–20) is the Mexico City branch of the famed Sinaloa seafood restaurant. Fresh fish is flown in daily. Be ready to drop an easy $20–30 per person with drinks, but rest assured your stomach will thank you profusely. Be sure to try the house specialty appetizer, *callo de hacha,* a scallop dish. In Bosque de Chapultepec

Café del Lago (tel. 5515-9586, open 7:30A.M.–11 P.M. Mon.–Sat., Domingo 1030-439, 7:30 A.M.–11 P.M. Mon.–Sat., 10:30 A.M.–4 P.M. Sun., entrées $17–30) features one glass wall facing the lake. After walking through an entranceway that seems part of an elegant spaceship, you'll be seated in the spacious dining room. The restaurant is a favored haunt of Mexican politicians and others from the elite set seeking a quiet place to hold their negotiations. The contemporary Mexican food emphasizes seafood. Reservations are required.

WEEKEND BRUNCH

Even if you're not staying in Polanco but feel like a splurge, especially after an intensive Saturday night of partying, the Sunday morning buffet at the JW Grill (JW Marriott Hotel, Andrés Bello 29, tel. 5999-0000, 9:30 A.M.–3 P.M., $25) is a great way to greet the day. A mimosa is included in the price to subdue that hangover if it starts getting any ideas.

Another good brunch option is La Huerta (in the Camino Real, Av. Mariano Escobedo 700, tel. 5263-8888, 11:30 A.M.–5 P.M. Sun., $23), serving an brunch buffet with a huge array of cheeses, smoked fish, cold cuts, and half a dozen main dishes to choose from.

In Chapultepec Park, Café del Bosque (tel. 5516-4214, 8 A.M.– 6 P.M. daily, entrées $15–25) attracts a wealthy crowd, particularly for its weekend brunches (morning breakfast buffet $15, afternoon lunch buffet $21). One tasty breakfast option is the *omelette azteca* stuffed with jam, *nopal* cactus (spikes removed, rest assured!), and *tostadas*. The prime rib is a popular choice for lunch.

ARGENTINE

Rincón Argentino (Presidente Mazaryk 177, tel. 5254-8744, 1–11 P.M. daily, entrées $10–25) has some of the best Argentine food in the city, with succulent steaks, sausages, pastas, and wines. Started by an Argentine soccer star who played in Mexico for years, the cavernous, log cabin–style restaurant is always packed.

At the other end of Mazaryk, at the corner of Anatole France, is ⋈ El Zorzal, (on the triangular corner set back from the intersection of Presidente Mazaryk and Anatole France, tel. 5280-0111, 1–11 P.M. Mon.–Thurs., until midnight Fri–Sat., until 7 P.M. Sun., entrées $7–15), a branch of the original restaurant in the Condesa. The *corte criollo,* ($12) a thick, juicy steak, is delicious, as are the spinach and cheese empanadas ($4).

ASIAN

For those after authentic Chinese cuisine, never mind the bill, Chez Wok (Tennyson 117, tel. 5281-2921, 1:30–4:45 P.M. and 7:30–11 P.M. Mon.–Sat., first shift only on Sun., entrées $15–30) is the place. On the 2nd floor of a converted house at the corner of Presidente Mazaryk; you can savor a superb Peking duck, steak in orange sauce, and many other specialties from the extensive menu. Most meals are meant to be shared among two to six people. Dim sum is served on weekends only.

Sushi Grove (Av. Presidente Mazaryk 410, tel. 5281-1631, 2 P.M.–1 A.M. Tues.–Sat., 2–8 P.M. Sun., $9–12 per serving) serves sublime sushi in a stylish modern restaurant. The warm shrimp salad in Spanish-style alioli sauce ($8) is a popular choice, as are the salmon crunch sushi rolls ($10).

Restaurant Tandoor (Copernico 156, at Leibniz, tel. 5203-0045, 1–11 P.M. Mon.–Sat., 1–7 P.M. Sun., entrées $4–9) serves very good Pakistani and Indian dishes at reasonable prices in a quiet house near the Hotel Camino Real. Mexicans apparently find the taste of Indian food rather odd, as the place usually contains only foreign customers, and not very many, either. But quality, thankfully, remains high. The chicken *tandoor* is the house specialty, and vegetarians will love the *palak paneer,* a tasty spinach and cheese dish. Service is excellent.

FRENCH

Late-night cravers of wonderfully rich French cuisine will be pleased to discover Au Pied de Cochon (Presidente Inter-Continental Hotel in

Polanco, Campos Eliseos 218, tel. 5327-7756, entrées $12–30). They're open 24 hours a day, so you can enjoy the sublime French onion soup ($6) or the pig's feet in béarnaise sauce ($13) at ungodly hours of the morning.

Another top-notch French restaurant in a hotel is **Le Cirque** (Camino Real Hotel, Av. Mariano Escobedo 700, tel. 5263-8881, 1 P.M.–midnight Mon.–Sat., 2–5 P.M. Sun., entrées $20–40), serving a tasty three-course meal for $37. Or you can order from the menu: Try the rack of lamb for $38, and top it off with **fantasia del abuelo** (grandpa's fantasy), a crème brûlée topped with nuts, coffee ice cream, and hot chocolate.

INTERNATIONAL

An unusual mix of Asian and Latin cuisine is the specialty at the chic, upscale **Café Bistro MP** (A. Bello 10, tel. 5280-2506 or 5281-0592, 1:30 P.M.–midnight Mon.–Sat., 1:30–6 P.M. Sun., entrées $13–20). Enjoy dim sum, pizza, entrecôte with wasabi, or Thai sirloin with tamarind and mangos in a sleek, modern dining room decorated with Asian art.

ITALIAN

Il Punto (Emilio Castelar 213B, tel. 5280-3623, 1 P.M.–midnight Mon.–Sat., 1–6 P.M. Sun., entrées $10–25) is one of the best Italian restaurants in town. Specialties include pizzas baked in a wood oven ($17–20), *farfalle tequila* (pasta and shrimp with a tequila cream sauce, $10),

and *canelones Il Punto* (round pasta stuffed with tuna and a tomato cream sauce, $10).

Another good option is **Prego** (A. Dumas 10, tel. 5281-0203, 1 P.M.–midnight Mon.–Sat., 1–6 P.M. Sun., $10–25), in a converted mansion just off Campos Eliseos. Prego offers an extensive menu of pastas, salads, cuts of beef, and wines.

A bit less stuffy, with more of a corner trattoria feel, is **Non Solo Pasta** (Julio Verne 89, tel. 5280-9706, 1 P.M.–1 A.M. Mon.–Sat., entrées $7–10), in the center of the Polanco commercial district. Run by a friendly French expat, this is a fine, reasonably priced spot to enjoy a relaxing glass of wine with pasta.

COFFEE, SWEETS, AND BREAD

If you need a caffeine injection to revive you after touring the museums, stop in at **The Coffee Bar** (Temistocles at Presidente Mazaryk, 8:30 A.M.–10 P.M. Mon.–Sat., noon–10 P.M. Sun.). The Coffee Bar has a large selection of international magazines and newspapers. Another branch is at Presidente Mazaryk and Moliere.

The **Balmoral Tea Room,** at the Inter-Continental Presidente, is also a pleasant, though more expensive, place to relax and recharge the batteries in the finest English style.

A good place to grab a quick, tasty breakfast is **Paris Croissant** (J. Verne 89, tel. 5281-0980, 8 A.M.–7 P.M. Mon.–Fri., 9 A.M.–7 P.M. Sat.), serving stuffed croissants, crepes, omelettes, and of course good coffee.

Insurgentes Sur

Starting in the early 1990s, an increasing number of high-end restaurants have proliferated in the Condesa neighborhood. The epicenter is near the intersection of Vicente Suárez and Michoacán, where you'll find a dozen places to choose from, but eateries have also opened on nearby streets such as Tamaulipas, Montes de Oca, and Nuevo León, and a handful of others near Parque México. Emphasis is definitely international—several taco joints and the like still occupy the neighborhood, but the real attraction is the more upscale places. It's gotten to the point where local residents are getting annoyed by all the traffic on weekends, with people coming from across the city to dine in what is now one of the hippest parts of town. Many restaurants have sidewalk dining, which makes a lovely way to spend a couple of hours tucking in a fine meal and a bottle or two of wine with some friends. The nearby Roma neighborhood also has some very good restaurants, although not as many and not as concentrated as the Condesa.

TACOS, TORTAS, AND SNACKS

M **El Tizoncito** (noon–3 A.M. Sun.–Thurs., noon–4:30 A.M. Fri.–Sat.) offers two Condesa locations: a stool-and-bar, eat-and-run affair at the corner of Campeche and Tamaulipas, and a more formal sit-down restaurant two blocks east at Campeche and Cholula. Both serve delicious *tacos al pastor* ($.70 each) and a variety of other *antojitos,* along with beer and soft drinks. Prices are a bit higher than most *taquerías,* but the food is reliably hygienic.

Another excellent Condesa taco restaurant is **Taquería El Greco** (Michoacán 54, near the corner of Nuevo León, 2–10 P.M.–Sat.). The *tacos arabe* with pita bread ($2.50–5) are a popular Mexican culinary fusion of Middle Eastern and Mexican, as the regular crowds in the little restaurant will attest. The *tortas* with cheese ($2) are a good, filling value—ask them to put the guacamole sauce on it for extra fire. If there's no

room at the half-dozen small tables, you can order from the man in charge of the cutting the meat and eat them right there on the sidewalk.

A block away is **Hola's** (Amsterdam 135, at the corner of Michoacán, from early morning until 4 P.M. Mon.–Sat.), with delicious and inexpensive ($.75 each) tacos of all varieties. It even serves a couple of vegetarian tacos, believe it or not—one with spinach, and the other with squash and corn. There's a constant line of clients standing around the "taco bar" in the afternoon, calling out orders to the cheerful servers, who scoop out the fixings into fresh tortillas and add grated cheese and beans if you like.

Toma 5 (Sonora 201, one block from Insurgentes, 8 A.M.–4 A.M. daily, entrées $3–7) has decent, filling meals and *antojitos* served amid photos of old Mexican and U.S. movies. The *zorba griego* salad ($4), complete with goat cheese, spinach, lettuce, olives, walnuts, and even some pita bread on the side, is remarkably good for a place that serves mostly tacos.

One inexpensive and decent *taquería* in the Roma is **Tacos Álvaro O.** (Av. Álvaro Obregón, near the corner of Jalapa, from early afternoon until 3 A.M. daily). Try the tasty and filling *alambre,* a mix of grilled beef with green peppers, onions, and bacon served with a pile of tortillas ($3.50).

A clean, well-run fruit and *torta* stand at the corner of Avenida Álvaro Obregón and Córdoba is a great place to get an inexpensive *milanesa* (breaded pork) or chicken sandwich ($1.20) and a fresh-squeezed juice to wash it down.

MEXICAN

Restaurante-Bar La Tecla (Durango 186A, tel. 5525-4920, 1 P.M.–midnight Mon.–Sat., 1–6 P.M. Sun., $3–8) is one of the best all-Mexican restaurants in Roma. Prices are reasonable, too; a *menú de degustación* (tasting menu) is available Monday to Thursday nights for just $7. The daily set menu for both lunch and dinner is an excellent value. Main dishes include trout, steak with roquefort cheese and *huitlacoche,* or squash flower stuffed with goat cheese in a chipotle sauce.

If you're in the mood for a hearty meal but don't want to spend a whole lot of money, stop in at **Las Arracheras** (Vicente Suarez 110, at the corner of Mazatlán, 1:30–8 P.M. daily), an unpretentious eatery in the Condesa. It serves reasonably priced, good-quality *arrachera* steaks, as well as very tasty *alambres,* a stir-fry of sorts with chopped steak, green peppers, onions, and a bit of bacon for flavor, eaten with tortillas. The green salsa here, made with green tomatoes, avocado, and habañero, is hot and tasty.

Los Tamales Emporio (Álvaro Obregón 154, tel. 5574-2078, 8 A.M.–9 P.M. Mon.–Sat., 9 A.M.–5 P.M. Sun.) is an inexpensive and good-quality Mexican restaurant in the heart of Roma serving breakfast, lunch, and dinner, as well as its namesake tamales (only $1 each). Try the *oaxaqueño,* with mole and chicken; the *chiapaneco,* with mole, chicken, olives, almonds, plums, egg, and pepper; or the *yucatecos,* with gouda cheese, strips of green *poblano* peppers, and *guajillo* chile sauce.

Another restaurant specializing in *tamales* is **Flor de Lis** (Huichapán 17, tel. 5286-2229, 8:30 A.M.–9 P.M. daily). In operation in Condesa since 1918, the simple cafeteria is a great place to enjoy a top-quality tamale stuffed with mushrooms or chicken and green chiles ($2 each), or an assortment of other Mexican dishes at midrange prices.

CANTINAS

La Auténtica (corner of Álvaro Obregón and Av. Cuauhtémoc, 10 A.M.–11 P.M. daily, entrées $3–8) is exactly what its name suggests: a classic cantina of the old school, with uniformed waiters bustling around to keep the many clients well supplied with hearty traditional Mexican food and bountiful drinks to wash it down. If you're really hungry, try the monster *molcajete,* a huge bowl brimming with chorizo, beef, beans, and cheese, or the thick pork tenderloin. Service is great, the ambience is convivial, and wandering guitarists play tunes for a nominal fee.

The cantina **Bar Montejo** (Benjamín Franklin 261, on the corner of Nuevo León, 10 A.M.–midnight Mon.–Sat., entrées $3–7) offers a full bar, inexpensive and good-quality *comida yucateca* (Yucatán cuisine), and even a couple of tasty, full-bodied *yucateca* beers—Montejo and León. The service is exemplary.

Restaurant Covadonga, (in Roma Norte, at Puebla 121, tel. 5533-2701, 1 P.M.–2 A.M. Mon.–Fri., entrées $4–10) is a well-kept cantina/restaurant in a cavernous room with a bar at one end and a couple dozen tables populated mostly by men playing dominoes, but there is also an assortment of artists and random other people from the Roma. Women will feel quite comfortable here, unlike at some cantinas. Covadonga has an extensive menu filled with reasonably priced Spanish-style fish and meat dishes, appetizers such as *tortilla española,* soups, salads, and a midday set meal ($7). The paella is excellent, and so is the service by the uniformed waiters. The liquor selection is large.

An interesting updated version of a traditional Mexican restaurant/cantina, set amidst vaguely gothic decor, is **El Candelero** (Insurgentes Sur 1333, in Colonia Mixcoac, tel. 5598-9008, 1:30 P.M.–2 A.M. Thurs.–Sat., 1:30–6 P.M. Sun., entrées $5–12). Grab a table in the cozy bar or in the high-ceilinged, spacious central area and order from the menu of excellent quality Mexican specialties while enjoying the strains of the roaming mariachi or *trío* bands. A great spot for late night drinks *a la mexicana.*

SEAFOOD

M Contramar (Durango 200, in Roma, tel. 5514-9217 or 5514-3169, lunch only, 1–6 P.M. daily, entrées $10–25) serves outstanding seafood in a bright, airy dining room bustling with waiters attending the 20-odd tables. Start off with the delicious *tacos de camarón* ($7), stuffed with minced shrimp and more reminiscent of an Asian-style spring roll than a taco, then move on to the succulent *filete Contramar* ($20), served on a wooden platter and lightly coated with sauce.

Another good seafood restaurant is **La Morena** (in the center of the Condesa restaurant district, Atlixco 94, tel. 5211-0250, 1–11 P.M. Mon.–Wed., 1 P.M.–midnight or later Thurs.–Sun., entrées $10–25). The *tostada ceviche a la peruana* is a great appetizer, as are the shrimp quesadillas. For a main course try the excellent, meaty *huachinango* (red snapper).

Less chic but also very good is the long-running popular Roma restaurant, **La Embajada Jarocha** (Jalapa at Zacatecas, tel. 5584-2570, opens at 3 P.M. daily, closes at 2 A.M. Thurs.–Sat., earlier but variable on other nights, entrées $8–15). The name translates as "The Veracruz Embassy," and they specialize in seafood cooked in the styles of this eastern coastal state. *Huachinango* cooked in a variety of ways runs $15, as does a large order of lobster tacos. Live tropical music serenades diners Thurs.–Sat.

MARKETS

While Condesa has a market on the corner of Calles Tamaulipas and Michoacán, it's small and fairly pricey, which is no surprise considering the neighborhood. Far better is the **Mercado Medellín** (in Roma, bounded by Calles Medellín, Campeche, Monterrey, and Coahuila, 8 A.M.–5 P.M. daily). A spacious, well-lit market with mountains of fresh produce, Medellín is known for its excellent seafood, sold in bulk and cooked in the many market restaurants. Shrimp cocktails are a tasty treat for a mere $2.50.

BISQUETS

Roma remains a holdout for the classic Mexico City *café chino,* and the most famous of them all (and now a citywide chain), is **Bisquets Obregón** (Álvaro Obregón and Mérida, 7 A.M.–midnight daily, entrées $2–5). Because of the popularity of the original 1950s-style restaurant, a new, McDonald's-style, multistory Bisquets is now open across the street. Both serve a large menu of inexpensive Mexican meals (breakfasts are a good deal), as well as the mandatory *bisquets* and chop suey.

A block west on Álvaro Obregón, at Córdoba, are the two branches of **Café Paris** (7:30 A.M.–midnight daily, entrées $2–5), another longtime Roma favorite with bright purple booths and a similar menu to Bisquets Obregón.

INTERNATIONAL

One of the first of the trendy restaurants in Condesa, and still considered one of the best, is **M Garufa** (Michoacán 93, tel. 5286-8293, 1–11 P.M. Sun.–Thurs., 1 P.M.–1 A.M. Fri.–Sat., entrées $7–16), with tables inside and on the sidewalk. Among the excellent pastas are cannelloni with spinach or corn and *fettucini hindú,* chicken breast in a tangy yogurt-and-ginger sauce over a bed of pasta. It has great steaks too.

Similar in quality and style to Garufa, but a bit more comfortable for sitting, is **El Principio** (Tamaulipas 61, at the corner of Montes de Oca, tel. 5286-0657, 1:30 P.M.–midnight daily, entrées $7–16). The *risotto con pato,* a rice and cheese dish with shredded duck ($7), is sinfully rich.

Café Los Asombros (in the bookstore El Péndulo, at Av. Nuevo León 115, in Condesa, tel. 5286-9493, 8 A.M.–11 P.M. Mon.–Fri., 10 A.M.–11 P.M. Sat.–Sun., entrées $5–12) offers meals with a literary theme—such as beef *el pre-socrático* or *ensalada de pollo Neruda*—in a fittingly refined atmosphere. Breakfasts here are particularly good, and on weekend mornings it often has live classical music to aid your digestion. While the food is very good, service is often slow, so don't come in a hurry.

In a converted old Roma mansion is **Ixcel** (Medellín 65, tel. 5280-4055, 1:30 P.M.–midnight Mon.–Tues., 1:30 P.M.–2 A.M. Wed.–Sun., entrées $8–20), formerly a nightclub and now a very hip, popular upscale restaurant, still with something of a club feel to it. The Blue Room upstairs is particularly loungelike, if that's what you're looking for. The food is an eclectic mix of Mexican and international, including grilled shrimp with couscous, ravioli stuffed with spinach and goat cheese, duck meat tacos with plum sauce, and Vietnamese spring rolls. It's best to call ahead for a table, particularly on weekends.

Rojo Bistrot (corner of Parras and Amsterdam, tel. 5211-3705, 2–11 P.M. Mon.–Thurs., 2 P.M.–midnight Fri.–Sat., entrées $8–15) is a very comfortable, relaxed European-style café with an airy dining room as well as sidewalk seating on a quiet street corner in a residential area of the Condesa. Subdued lighting and well-chosen music give a pleasing intimate feel, and there's a small bar also. The food can sometimes be uneven—I had bad luck with the mussels last time I was there, but everyone I was with were happy with their dishes. The *magret de pato,* duck in black cherry sauce with potatoes ($13), is a popular choice.

If you've got a craving for a retro-lounge/diner complete with burgers and milkshakes, but with a decidedly hipster, upscale vibe, head to **Barracuda Dinner** (Nuevo León 4A, tel. 5211-9480, 24 hours daily, entrées $7–15). Sit either at the long bar or one of the booths with vinyl seats and take your pick among the sandwiches, burgers, breakfasts, and other treats. One good burger is the redneck, with bacon, cheddar cheese, and barbeque sauce ($8). It's a refreshing different option for late-night eats besides the ever-popular taco feast.

Housed in the Casa Lamm Cultural Center in the Roma, **Restaurante Lamm** (Álvaro Obregón 99, at the corner of Orizaba, tel. 5514-8501, 8 A.M.–midnight Tues.–Fri., 9 A.M.–2 A.M. Sat., 9 A.M.–6 A.M. Sun., entrées $7–25) is an architectural curiosity, with a glass and wood framed patio jutting into the courtyard of a 1890s stone mansion. The high-end Mexican and international cuisine is of very good quality. Choose between several kinds of pastas ($6–8), fresh tuna in tamarind sauce ($17), or giant shrimps with coconut sauce ($25).

ARGENTINE

Specializing in hearty cuts of imported steak (the *corte criollo* and the *arrachera* are both top-notch)—as well as sublime spinach-and-cheese empanadas, large salads, pastas, and wines—is **El Zorzal** (Tamaulipas at the corner of Alfonso Reyes, tel. 5273-6023, 1:30–11 P.M. Sun.–Thurs., 1:30 P.M.–midnight Fri.–Sat., entrées $7–15). A full meal with wine runs $20–35, depending on how much you indulge—well worth it for the superb quality.

A bit less expensive but still good is the newer, Uruguayan-style **Don Asado** (Michoacan right near corner of Tamaulipas, tel. 5286-0789,

2–11 P.M. Mon.–Sat., 2–7 P.M. Sun., entrées $6–12). Seating is limited in the cozy restaurant, which has reasonably priced steaks like the *bife de chorizo* ($11) and tasty wood-oven pizza ($10).

ASIAN

Nagaoka, (Arkansas 38, tel. 5543-9530, 1–10 P.M. Tues.–Sat., 1–7 P.M. Sun., entrées $6–14), in a converted house on a quiet side street in the Nápoles neighborhood, has some of the better Japanese food in the city. After walking in past the stands of bamboo at the entrance, take a seat in the peaceful dining room and enjoy the excellent sushi, *teppanyaki* (stir-fried beef and vegetables), and other dishes.

Also very good is **Sushi Kaiten** (Plaza Villa de Madrid 22, at corner of Oaxaca, tel. 5511-8390, 1:30–11 P.M. Mon.–Sat., 1:30–6 P.M. Sun., sushi plates with four rolls $2–5), a sleek, modern place on a corner in the midst of a well-populated restaurant center in the Roma. Take a seat at one of the diner-style booths, order your sushi rolls, and watch it be delivered on the slow-moving conveyer belts right to your table. Try the "moori," with breaded shrimp and crab and mango and avocado, or the "astroboy," a spicy crab tempura with asparagus and cheese.

Blossom (in Colonia Del Valle, at San Francisco 360, corner of Luz Saviñon, tel. 5523-8516, 1–11 P.M. Mon.–Sat., 1–6:30 P.M. Sun., entrées $8–20) has some of the better Chinese food in Mexico City. The zippy *filete mongol* steak, with chile and spices, runs $10, while the sumptuous *pescado blossom* (fried red snapper with shrimp and vegetables in a sweet and sour sauce) will set you back $17. The restaurant has set lunch and dinner meals costing $17.

ITALIAN

A new popular Italian restaurant, frequented as much for its hip late-night bar scene as for its food, is **Prima** (Plaza Villa de Madrid 17, tel. 5208-2029, 2–6 P.M. and 8 P.M.–1 A.M. Mon.–Sat., entrées $7–15). Good entrée choices include the risotto with mushrooms in a nebbiolo wine sauce ($12) or pizzas ($5–10). The portions are definitely on the small side, apparently to maintain the figures of the chic clientele.

On Roma's tranquil Plaza Luis Cabrera, **La Piazza,** (corner of Guanajuato and Orizaba, tel. 5264-5556, 1:30–11 P.M. Mon.–Sat., 1:30–7 P.M. Sun., entrées $5–11) serves good, if not superlative, Italian cuisine in a pleasingly relaxed ambience. If the night is balmy, take a table out on the sidewalk.

On the ground floor of a 1930s apartment building on a shady corner of Parque México in Condesa, upscale **Vucciria** (Av. México 157, tel. 5564-7441, 2–11 P.M. Sun.–Thurs., 2 P.M.–1 A.M. Fri.–Sat., entrées $8–15) specializes in *tagliata al rosmarino,* strips of sirloin on a bed of spinach ($13). Portions are not large considering the prices, but the quality is high.

For haute cuisine in the most literal sense, try **Bellini's** (Av. Insurgentes Sur at Filedelfia, in Colonia Nápoles, tel. 5628-8304 or 5628-8305, 1 P.M.–1 A.M. Mon.–Sat., 9 A.M.–11 P.M. Sun., entrées $7–12). It perches on the 45th floor of the World Trade Center de México. Sweeping views over the city accompany respectable and surprisingly moderately priced Italian food. Apart from Italian favorites such as *fettucine tres quesos* (with provolone, manchego, and roquefort cheeses), the restaurant also features an international array of dishes such as Latin American ceviche, English-style prime rib, and French foie gras. The Sunday brunch (9 A.M.–2 P.M., $16) is bountiful. Jackets and ties are required for men.

MEDITERRANEAN

Probably the best wine selection anywhere in the city is in the new **M Tierra de Vinos** (Durango 197, tel. 5208-5133, www.tierradevinos.com .mx, 11 A.M.–6 P.M. Mon.–Tues., 11–1 A.M. Wed.–Sat., entrées $10–20), located just off the Fuente de los Cibeles traffic circle in the Roma. Hard to spot because of its nondescript facade, the restaurant offers a vast array of different wines from around the world and serves superb Mediterranean cuisine (the chef is Catalán) to accompany it. They have an extensive selection of tapas, as well as full meals, such as salmon with spinach or breast of veal, each with suggested wines. The menu changes frequently. The restaurant sometimes hosts intimate jazz concerts, with the ticket (often around $60) including a complete meal with wine.

SPANISH

A ragingly popular tapas bar in the Condesa, frequented as much for people-watching as for the food and drink, is **La Pata Negra** (in the old Condesa Cinema building at the north end of Tamaulipas, tel. 5211-5563, 1 P.M.–1 A.M. Sun.–Tues., or until 2 A.M. other nights). The food is quite good and not overly expensive, with *bocatas* (mouthfuls) at $6 and tapas like garlic mushrooms for $3.50. Expect crowds most nights.

Right across the street is **Capícua** (Nuevo León 66, tel. 5211-5280, 1 P.M.–1 A.M. Mon.–Sat.), another tapas bar with similar culinary offerings but housed in a more sleek, postmodern atmosphere, with glass walls with metal chairs. Despite the somewhat chilly feel, it's also extremely popular.

VEGETARIAN

A modest lunchtime restaurant in a converted house right on Parque Mexico, **Lettuzze** (Av. Mexico 67, 1–7 P.M.) has vegetarian *comida corridas* for $5, as well as nonvegetarian ones for a bit more, and baguette sandwiches for $4.50.

COFFEE, SWEETS, AND BREAD

Café D'Carlo (Orizaba 115, 8 A.M.–10 P.M. Mon.–Fri., 8 A.M.–9 P.M. Sat.), now two blocks south from its former location, is a great little hole-in-the-wall Roma coffee shop with a few tables on the sidewalk, often filled with an interesting assortment of artist-hipster types, longtime Roma residents, and occasional expats sipping a strong espresso.

Another Roma café, serving very tasty and inexpensive breakfasts and light meals along with the coffee, is **Café Tapanco** (Orizaba 161, tel. 5564-2274, 8 A.M.–11 P.M. Mon.–Thurs.,

9 A.M.–11 P.M. Fri.–Sat., 9 A.M.–10 P.M. Sun.). Popular with local artists, this friendly café often has art displays on the wall and live events like poetry readings or acoustic music.

In the Condesa, **Café La Selva** (Vicente Suárez 38D, tel. 5211-5170, 9 A.M.–10:30 P.M. daily) is part of a socially conscious café chain serving only organically grown coffee from Chiapas collectives. It's now even opened a branch in Atlanta, Georgia. The java is wickedly strong.

For a more comfortable place to sit down, walk around the corner to the **Village Café**

(Tamaulipas 99, tel. 5211-0346, 8:30 A.M.–11 P.M. Mon.–Sat., 11 A.M.–11 P.M. Sun.), a funky little coffee shop with Beatles memorabilia and stacks of old magazines. Seating is available in two quiet rooms or at outdoor tables.

Another popular spot to while away the hours while sipping espresso and reading a newspaper or chatting with friends is **Cafemanía** (Av. México 123, at the corner of Ixtaccíhuatl, tel. 5264-0577, 9 A.M.–10 P.M. Mon.–Fri., 10 A.M.–10 P.M. Sat.–Sun., or sometimes later). Apart from coffee drinks, it also serves light meals and pastries.

Coyoacán

These neighborhoods in southern Mexico City—a mix of bohemian, working class and upper crust—offer some of the capital's finest and most traditional dining options.

TACOS, TORTAS, AND SNACKS

A neighborhood legend, attracting visitors from across the city to munch on the tasty, inexpensive Mexican specialties in a colorful tiled dining room, is **Las Lupitas** (on Francisco Sosa at the corner of Plaza Santa Catarina, about six blocks west of Jardín Centenario, 9 A.M.–5 P.M. and 7–11 P.M. Mon.–Fri., 9 A.M.–11 P.M. Sat.–Sun.). Try the *enchiladas potosinas,* one of the specialties.

Pepe Coyotes (Av. Hidalgo, half a block off the Jardín, 8 A.M.–2 A.M. daily) is a very good value, with filling tacos at reasonable prices and savory *pozole* (corn and meat stew) also.

At Calles Aguayo and Cuauhtémoc, opposite Pasaje Coyoacán, **El Tizoncito** (noon–2 A.M. Sun.–Thurs., noon–4 A.M. Fri.– Sat.) offers a delicious variety of tacos and other *antojitos* along with beer and soft drinks. Prices are a bit higher than in most *taquerías,* but the food is very reliable. The *tacos al pastor,* marinated meat cooked on a spit, are the house specialty.

A half block east of Jardín Hidalgo, on the north side of Calle de la Higuera, a cluster of semiindoor *antojito* **stands** serve quesadillas

with your choice of cheese, cheese with pepper strips, cheese with beans, potato, *panza* (beef stomach), *seso* (beef cheeks), *huitlacoche,* mushrooms, *flor de calabaza,* and chicken or beef *tinga* (spicy stew), along with *sopes* and tostadas with choice of toppings. It's all under one roof; plain cheese quesadillas start at $.60 each. Also on hand are delicious *flautas* (rolled, deep-fried tortilla with meat filling) and *pozole.*

MEXICAN

At the south end of Jardín del Centenario, **Los Danzantes** (tel. 5658-6451, noon–11 P.M. Sun.–Thurs., noon–1 A.M. Fri.–Sat., entrées $10–20) offers plaza-side tables as well as indoor seating on the ground floor of a two-story, colonial-style mansion. The Swiss-trained chef's lyrical way with food lives up to the name, which means "the dancers." The menu emphasizes Mexican fusion cuisine, offering such house specialties as *fettucine con salsa de jitomate, ostiones ahumados, y chile pasilla* (fettucine topped with a sauce of smoked oysters, tomato, and chocolate-colored dried chiles) and *pechuga rellena de queso con salsa de cabuches* (chicken breast filled with cheese and covered with the fruit of the barrel cactus). The plush bar offers a wide selection of high-quality tequilas. Prices are high, but this is one of the more culinarily interesting restaurants in the city, so foodies should find it a worthwhile splurge.

Popular, tile-faced **Fonda El Morral** (Allende 2, a little north of Jardín Hidalgo in Coyoacán, 8 A.M.–midnight Fri.–Sat., 8 A.M.–10 P.M. Sun.) specializes in regional dishes. Have a complete breakfast ($5), *antojitos* ($3–5), or entrées of fish, fowl, and beef ($8–15), all served in a colorful and festive environment. Savor the tasty handmade tortillas.

CANTINAS

Cantina La Guadalupana (Higuera just off Jardín Hidalgo, tel. 5554-6253, 10 A.M.–9:30 P.M. Mon.–Thurs., 10 A.M.–midnight Fri.–Sat., entrées $5–12) is one of the city's most traditional and popular *cantinas familiares* (family cantinas). Foreigners both male and female will feel quite comfortable here. The full menu covers all the Mexican standards.

MARKETS

Inside the **Mercado Coyoacán** (three blocks north of Jardín Hidalgo off Calle Allende), you'll find a string of *marisquerías,* countertop purveyors of fresh seafood. Popular choices include *tostada de ceviche* (crisp corn tortillas topped with ceviche), *pulpo en su tinta* (octopus cooked in its own ink), and *sopa de mariscos* (seafood soup). One particularly good place is the **Jardín del Pulpo,** at the corner of Allende and Abasolo, with ceviche and fried fish at reasonable prices. Other *comedores* are sprinkled throughout the market, and most are very clean. Off to one side of the market there's also a *sección comidas,* where you'll find big *cazuelas* bubbling with *pancita,* Mexico City's answer to *menudo.* Most market eateries are open until 5 or 6 P.M.

INTERNATIONAL

Fabio's (in an upstairs dining room at Allende 15, tel. 5554-7961, opposite the north end of Jardín Hidalgo, 8 A.M.–10 P.M. daily, entrées $6–12) serves an economical Mediterranean and Italian menu that includes pizzas, olive and eggplant appetizers, a Lebanese platter, and pastries. The restaurant has a very nice balcony overlooking the park.

El Sheik (Madrid 129, a few blocks northwest of Jardín Hidalgo, tel. 5659-3311, 8 A.M.–7 P.M. daily) serves Arab cuisine specialties such as hummus and tabouli ($3.50) or a mixed plate of goodies for $12.

URUGUAYAN

Entre Vero (Jardín Centenario 14C, tel. 5659-0066, 1:30–11 P.M. Mon.–Fri., until midnight Sat.–Sun., entrées $8–17) is a very good South American restaurant offering such delectables as a grilled vegetable platter with radicchio, eggplant, and zucchini, first grilled and then baked ($8); great pizzas ($10–14); and the standard steaks, empanadas, and pastas.

COFFEE, SWEETS, AND BREAD

Around Coyoacán's twin plazas, both residents and visitors appear to sustain themselves on a steady diet of coffee and pastries. At the corner of Caballocalco and Avenida Hidalgo, opposite the east side of Coyoacán's Jardín Hidalgo, stands a

COURTESY OF MEXICO TOURISM BOARD/CARLOS SANCHEZ

fruit market in Coyoacán

Restaurants

branch of **Panadería El Globo** (8 A.M.–7 P.M. Mon.–Sat., 10 A.M.–5 P.M. Sun.), one of Mexico City's best bakeries. Founded in 1884, El Globo now has several branches in the capital, and this is one of the fancier ones; most of the pastries come prewrapped, and there's a section dedicated to *pan rustico europeo* (rustic European breads). On the opposite corner of Avenida Hidalgo, a bakery/deli called **América** offers more economical pastries, along with wines and various other comestibles.

If you're looking for intellectual stimulation, you might find it over a cappuccino at the **Cafe El Parnaso** (tel. 5554-2225, 9 A.M.–10 P.M. Mon.–Fri., 9 A.M.–11 P.M. Sat–Sun.), a cluster of wrought-iron tables just outside the ground floor of an old three-story colonial near the southeast corner of Jardín del Centenario. The attached bookstore offers tomes covering all subjects, mostly in Spanish, as well as music CDs. Try the empanadas, filled with your choice of tuna, spinach, ground beef, or other fillings, or share a *plato combinado* piled with empanadas, *tortilla española* (thick egg and potato omelette), cheeses, and *pan dulce*.

Facing the southwest corner of Jardín del Centenario, the casual outdoor tables at **Caffe Latte** appear to rival Café El Parnaso's in popularity. Then tucked away in a small courtyard at the southeast corner of adjacent Jardín Hidalgo, **Café La Selva** is packed with coffee drinkers savoring organic, politically correct Chiapas coffee all day long.

Politics aside, some claim that tiny **El Jarocho** (Calle Cuauhtémoc 134, at the corner of Allende north of Jardín Hidalgo), serves the best Mexican coffee in Mexico City. There is no seating inside the small shop, which has been serving fresh-roasted, fresh-brewed java since 1953, but if you're lucky you'll find space on a bench outside. You can buy whole-bean coffee by the kilo and half kilo here, and it also sells *tortas*.

To get away from the plaza scene a bit, check out **Cafetería Moheli** (on the north side of Avenida Francisco Sosa west of Jardín del Centenario). Like El Parnaso, it's a popular place for those addicted to both books and caffeine.

San Ángel

Restaurants in relatively upmarket San Ángel tend to be substantially pricier than those in Coyoacán.

MEXICAN

Built in the 17th century as an opulent Carmelite monastery, and later home to Spanish viceroys—and, briefly, Emperor Maximilian and his wife, Carlota—the **San Ángel Inn** (Diego Rivera 50, tel. 5616-0973 or 5616-1527, 1 P.M.–1 A.M. Mon.–Sat., 1–10 P.M. Sun., entrées $15–25) has seen a variety of guests over its three centuries, including Santa Anna and his troops, and, during the Revolution, Emiliano Zapata and Pancho Villa. Today, though still called San Ángel Inn, it's a restaurant only. It serves very good, traditional Mexican food, though it's pricey, and the dining room is often crowded.

La Camelia (on the plaza, tel. 5616-4668, noon–9 P.M. Mon.–Wed., 10 A.M.–11 P.M. Thurs.–Sun.) serves excellent though pricey Mexican seafood dishes. Try the red snapper with a green sauce made with *hoja santa* (special herb) and cilantro for $18, or *tostada camellia* with either shrimp, octopus, or fish ceviche for $5. The seafood buffet for $12 from 2–5 P.M. on Wednesday, Friday, Saturday, and Sunday is a very good value considering the quality.

Right on Plaza San Jacinto in a two-story colonial building is **Fonda San Ángel** (San Jacinto 3, tel. 5550-1641, 9 A.M.–midnight Mon.–Sat., 10 A.M.–9 P.M. Sun., entrées $10–15), with a lovely ambience and decent (though not spectacular) food. One culinary attraction is that instead of choosing from the menu, you can pick a meat and your own mix of 15 different sauces to go with it. It's a good place to have a drink after a hot Saturday morning of shopping.

INTERNATIONAL

For light French cuisine, try **Cluny** (Av. La Paz 57, tel. 5550-7350, 1 P.M.–midnight Mon.–Sat., 1–10 P.M. Sun., crepes $7–10), with a selection of delectable crepes. You can choose between "salty" crepes, with ingredients such as chicken, corn, cheese, *huitlacoche;* or sweet ones with strawberries and cream or caramel and nuts. It also has very good salads.

Tlalpan

This quiet, modest colonial neighborhood southeast of Coyoacán has a fine little square around which are tucked a number of sidewalk cafés and restaurants. It's a ways off the main tourist track, but if you go that way, the two restaurants below are definitely worth a look.

CANTINAS

On the southeast side of the downtown square is a traditional old cantina called **La Jaliscience** (closed Mon.). The name means "the lady from Jalisco," and the place features swinging doors, sturdy wooden tables, uniformed waiters, and roving musicians. It's great for a drink and a meal in classic Mexican style. They have a rather unusual (for a cantina) house specialty: *tortas de bacalao* (cod sandwiches).

ARGENTINE

A very popular eatery on north side of the Tlalpan plaza is **Restaurante 1900** (tel. 5573-3693, 1:30–11:30 P.M. Tues.–Sat., 1:30–7 P.M. Sun., entrées $10–20), a small, simple dining room invariably bustling with diners. The *bife de chorizo* ($27) is the star of the menu, but there are a number of other less expensive and still very hearty steaks, as well as a very good *pizza mediterranea* with shrimp and calamari ($14).

Restaurants

Arts and Entertainment

In their relentless quest for diversion, *capitalinos* (citizens of the capital) have turned their city into a world-class source of art and entertainment for virtually every taste. Whether you're into modern art museums, avant-garde theater, gallery exhibitions, cult cinema, mariachi bands, dancing to every kind of music from salsa to techno, or just a great corner cantina, you'll find some part of the city dedicated to that particular form of expression.

Maybe it's the fact that living in such a determinedly urban environment already seems unhealthy, but Mexico City residents are unquestionably prone to excess. They like to have fun often, and tend to do it for several hours, if not days, at a time. Most parties really don't get going until after midnight, and if the vibe is right, staying up until the morning light is not uncommon—and not just for 20-year-olds, either.

While the suggestions in this chapter should

© ELENA PAPPAS

Mexico City's Best

M **Best Night** *a la Mexicana:* There's really no better way to plumb the depths of a night in D.F. than to spend a few hours (preferably well past midnight) in **Plaza Garibaldi.** Make your way through the throngs of revelers and mariachis out on the square and grab a table at the convivial Salon Tenampa, where the mariachi phenomenon began in the 1920s (page 120).

M **Best Salsa Dancing:** There are two places in the Centro that take salsa very seriously: **Salón Baraimas** and **Tarara.** Here you won't see a lot of heavy drinking, but you will see some outrageous moves. Both places have classes for beginners (page 121).

M **Best Underground Rock Venue:** When the *rock en español* movement got its start in the 1980s **Rockotitlán Sur** was one of the original venues showcasing that genre, and it's still at it. Head down on a weekend night to see which band might become the next Café Tacuba or Botellita de Jeréz (page 124).

M **Best Cabaret:** Unless your Spanish is really good it's not easy to catch the word play and political references, but you'll still have a blast watching the over-the-top Astrid Hadad perform her music review at **El Bataclán,** with updated versions of classic *rancheras* and *boleros* (page 125).

M **Best Dance Performance:** With its performances taking place in the ornate Palacio de Bellas Artes, **Ballet Folklórico de Amalia Hernández** is an impressive display of choreographed traditional dances from around Mexico, with elaborate costumes and great music (page 125).

M **Best Traditional Cantina:** Of the hundreds of great cantinas in this town, **Cantina la Guadalupana** in Coyoacán is a great choice. Popular with tourists and Mexicans alike, this old-school cantina has exemplary service, good food, and wandering music bands happy to strike up a tune in front of your table (page 128).

mariachis in Plaza Garibaldi

M **Best Dance Club:** For a young crowd looking to lose themselves in the loud rhythms of house and techno music, the **Pervert Lounge** is a popular choice. It has been around forever, but oddly enough (for this trendy scene) it remains a favorite (page 128).

M **Best Diego and Frida Museum:** It's a bit out of the way, but for fans of Mexico's most famous artist couple, the trip down to Xochimilco to the **Museo Dolores Olmedo Patiño** is well worth it. Housed in a lovely 16th-century *hacienda* surrounded by lush gardens, this museum was created by Olmedo out of her personal collection of works by Rivera and Kahlo (page 134).

M **Best Modern Art Museum:** Mexico City has a number of top-notch modern art museums, but one of the best is **Museo de Arte Carrillo Gil** in San Ángel. You'll find a comprehensive collection of Mexico's greatest modern artists, including Rivera, Siqueiros, Tamayo, and Toledo, as well as newer, more experimental, artists (page 138).

M **Most Unusual Art Gallery:** Not every country has an art gallery run by the tax man, but D.F. does. Right behind the Catedral is the **Galería SCHP,** which shows an eclectic selection of works donated by Mexican artists in lieu of their tax bill (page 144).

M Arts and Entertainment

give you plenty to start with, there's a whole lot more going on just waiting to be discovered by those who choose to explore. A good place to start is the entertainment listings of many local newspapers and magazines, especially *Reforma, Tiempo Libre, D.F.,* and *Chilango.*

Nightlife

LIVE MUSIC

Mexico claims a rich musical heritage, from the traditional folk *chilenas* of the southwestern states to the Latino ska of Mexico City. Because of Mexico's position between the U.S. and the rest of Latin America, an unusually vibrant cross-fertilization results in an astonishing variety of musical styles that only an ethnomusicological survey could adequately convey.

Since 1998, when Mexico City was first governed by an opposition party, the city government has been much more amenable to holding open-air concerts in the Zócalo. Recent free concerts, with at times more than 100,000 in attendance, include Manu Chao, Café Tacuba, Los Tigres del Norte, and the Afro Cuban All Stars. Concerts are also occasionally held in Parque México, in Colonia Condesa, on weekend afternoons.

While Mexico City has a fantastically vibrant music nightlife, it also has a fairly high rate of club turnover, due both to the vagaries of changing tastes as well as an increased propensity by city authorities in recent years to shut places down for code violations. I've tried to mainly include well-established places that are almost certain to stay in business for years to come, but a few newer places are here also, and there's always a chance they won't survive. Try calling ahead to check if you're in doubt, or look at the entertainment listings of local newspapers (the *Reforma* weekend pullout section is a good place to start).

Plaza Garibaldi

This little square along the east side of Eje Central Lázaro Cárdenas, a few blocks north of Bellas Artes, has been one of the main centers of traditional Mexican nightlife in the capital since

Mariachis strike up a tune in Plaza Garibaldi.

COURTESY OF MEXICO TOURISM BOARD/CARLOS SANCHEZ

Arts and Entertainment

the 1920s, when Cirilo Marmolejo and his mariachi band first took up residence at the Salón Tenampa. Marmolejo is long gone, but legions of fellow mariachis still fill Garibaldi every day and night. A foreign visitor interested in experiencing a night of partying *a la mexicana* should go to Garibaldi forthwith, preferably on a Friday or Saturday evening from about 11 P.M. onward. Just make sure you get a *sitio* (radio) cab or other type of safe ride home afterward, as the gangs of *rateros* (thieves) lingering in the back streets a couple of blocks from Garibaldi are almost as famous as the mariachis themselves. The main square, however, is quite safe.

Salón Tenampa, on the north side of the square, is still going strong every day of the week until 3 A.M. (till 4 A.M. Friday and Saturday). Two other favorites on the east side are **Guadalajara de Noche** and **Nuevo México Típico** (both 8 P.M.–2 A.M. daily, later on weekends). On the south side adjacent to Eje Central is **Tropicana** (9 P.M.–4 A.M. daily).

The adventurous tourist may wish to try *pulque,* an unusual alcoholic drink favored by the Aztecs and made from fermented agave hearts. Although not the most traditional *pulquería* in the city, **Pulquería Hermosa Hortensia** (5 P.M.–2 A.M. Wed.–Mon.), on the north side of the square, is a relatively safe place to try the drink.

While Garibaldi is in true form mainly at night, tourists may enjoy coming by on a sunny afternoon, having a beer and a couple of tacos at one of the little restaurants on the square's north side, and watching the mariachis ply their trade. A group will gladly strike up an impassioned tune for you right then and there on the square, but it's not cheap—usually $10 for a song, although sometimes you can convince them to play two for the price of one.

Música Antillana and Salones de Baile

From the lower Gulf of Mexico coast, Afro-Caribbean styles, from rumba to reggae, have made serious inroads in the Mexico City music and dance scene. Tropical *cumbias* from Colombia and salsa from New York and Puerto Rico

have also become standards in the capital, along with the Dominican specialties merengue and bachata. All of these Afro-Caribbean forms are generally referred to as *música antillana* (music from the Antilles) or *música tropical.*

The Centro has several good places to dance to tropical music. **M** **Salón Baraimas** (Filomena Mata 7, between Tacuba and 5 de Mayo in the Centro Histórico, tel. 5510-4486 or 2508-5589, starting 9 P.M. Thurs.–Sat., cover $8 men, $4 women), whips up a good mix of salsa and merengue music fueled by plenty of *mojitos* (a Cuban drink with rum and mint) and *cuba libres* (rum and coke). You can also take good salsa classes here on Friday and Saturday, starting at 6 P.M. Another good spot downtown is **M** **Tarara** (Madero 39, right above the McDonald's, tel. 5521-0102 or 5521-0123, Friday and Saturday only, $5 cover), often with live music, in a slightly more refined environment than Baraimas.

MARIACHI TRIVIA

- The word mariachi comes from the French word *mariage* (marriage). The music first became popular at weddings during the French occupation of Mexico (1862–1867).

- Mexico's first nationally known mariachi ensemble was headed by Concho Andrade in the 1920s.

- A traditional troupe features 10 performers—four violinists, three guitarists (actually *guitarrón,* guitar, and *vihuela*), and three trumpet players.

- The male mariachi's tight-fitting, silver-studded costume is inspired by Mexican *charro* (horseman) suits.

- About 20 percent of all mariachi musicians are women, whose trademark *coronela* or *china poblana* outfits feature embroidered blouses and long, billowing, brightly colored skirts.

In the Roma, **Mama Rumba** (Querétaro 230, at the corner of Monterrey, tel. 5564-6920, Tues.–Sat. until all hours, $6 cover) is a hugely popular Cuban bar with a live *son* (sort of a Cuban proto-salsa) band nightly, a lively crowd, and plenty of *mojitos*. Although the club has expanded in the last couple of years to cope with the crowds, Mama Rumba is still packed every weekend, and it can be difficult to get a table or find space on the packed dance floor. In San Ángel is **Mama Rumba Sur** (Plaza San Jacinto 23, tel. 5550-8099, 9 P.M.–3 A.M. Wed.–Sat., $5 cover), with the same owners.

More or less across the street from Mama Rumba in the Roma, and not quite as chic, is **Gran León** (Querétaro 225, tel. 5564-7110, 9 P.M.–3:30 A.M. Tues.–Sat., $5 cover), originally established by the same people who ran the famed (and now, tragically, closed) Bar León in the city center. Pepé Arévalo y sus Mulatos keep the crowd swinging their hips until the wee hours with salsa and merengue tunes. Tuesday is *danzón* night, dedicated to a dance from Veracruz. Seating is available in the main hall downstairs by the dance floor or in the smaller balcony. Check out the egg-carton soundproofing on the walls and the fake palm trees.

A more old-fashioned version of the tropical dance club, the *salón de baile* (dance salon), which reached its peak between the 1930s and 1950s in Mexico City, has managed to hang on into the 21st century. The loyal clientele tend to be lower-middle class Mexicans, but anyone who enjoys dancing is made to feel very welcome. Made famous by the Mexican film of the same name, the legendary **Salón México** (Pensador Mexicano 11, at San Juan de Dios near the Alameda, tel. 5518-0931, 9 P.M.–3:30 A.M. Thurs.–Sat., cover $3–5) was remodeled and reopened in 1993. The spacious club hosts large bands playing salsa, merengue, and sometimes *danzón*, and attracts a wide selection of Mexicans from different social classes and age groups.

Another in this vicinity, and equally legendary, is the **Salón Los Angeles** (Lerdo 206, between Ricardo Flores Magón and Estrella, tel. 5597-5181, 8 P.M.–midnight Tues.–Sun., $4 cover). The sign over the door reads *"Quién*

no conoce Los Ángeles, no conoce México," a tribute to its long-standing place in the hearts of dancing *chilangos*.

The self-proclaimed "Palacio de Baile" (Palace of Dance) of Mexico City is **Salón California** (Calz. Tlalpan 1189, tel. 5672-3317, Fri.–Sun., cover depends on event), in the Portales neighborhood well south of the Centro. It's another old-style, traditional dance hall where the clients take their dancing seriously and don't do a lot of drinking. Saturday night is usually the best salsa, while Sunday sees a raging *grupera* party. The club is just off Line 2 (blue line) of the Metro, not far from the Portales station.

A more upscale Cuban-style club can be found in Polanco at **Barfly** (1st floor of Plaza Mazaryk, a shopping center on Presidente Mazaryk between La Fontaine and A. France, Tues.–Sat., $10 cover), with a live band playing from 10 P.M. onward.

Just north of Polanco is **Salón 21** (Lago Andómaco 17, near the corner of Moliere, tel. 5255-1496 or 5255-5322). Formerly a regular dance hall, it is now only open for special events, but it often has really excellent music and a great dance floor. It's worth calling to see what's on.

La Bodeguita en Medio (Cozumel 37, tel. 5553-0246, 1–11 P.M. Mon.–Wed., 1 P.M.– 1 A.M. Thurs.–Sat., 1–5 P.M. Sun.), in the Roma, is styled after the famed Havana bar of the same name. There's no dancing here, but order a *mojito* and enjoy the small band that wanders from table to table. Another place to enjoy a drink and listen to a small Cuban band is **La Bodega** (corner of Popocatépetl and Amsterdam in the Condesa, just off Parque México, tel. 5511-7390), a relaxed bar in a beautiful old mansion.

Rancheras, Corridos, and Boleros

The most popular song forms among the middle class and among the older generation in Mexico City are *rancheras* (similar to American country and western), *corridos* (Mexican ballads), and boleros (based on a traditional Andalusian form)—sometimes collectively known as *bohemio* (bohemian). This music become very popular in the 1940s and 1950s, with *trío* bands such as Los Panchos or Los Diamantes. At any bar, cantina, or restaurant where *trovadores* (strolling musicians) play, you'll hear plenty of music of this sort. In most bars or cantinas, you can expect to pay about $3 for a song played by a guitar *trío* at your table. If you're not sure which Mexican chestnut to name, ask for anything by Mexican composer Agustín Lara.

To see a more formal show of this sort of music (or a slightly ironic version of it, at any rate), check out the legendary Paquita la del Barrio, who has her own modest club in Colonia Guerrero, **La Casa de Paquita la del Barrio** (Zarco 202, tel. 5583-8131, Thurs.–Sat. nights, $10 cover). Paquita continues the Lola Beltrán tradition of castigating men for their abuse of love through dramatic boleros. She occasionally performs at larger venues around the city, such as the Teatro Metropolitán.

Grupera

This is the latest name for a musical genre that basically has Northern Mexican origins. The name itself refers to music performed by large ensembles blending the *ranchera*-and-polka *música norteña* of groups such Los Tigres del Norte with Sinaloan *perrada* or *tambora sinaloense*. The latter is a type of brass-and-drum band music originally brought by German immigrants but adopted and adapted in Sinaloa to become the "music of the people" when string music was still for the elite; during the 1910–20 Mexican Revolution it became a rallying soundtrack for the *constitucionalistas*.

The immense popularity can be explained not only by the cheerful horn and accordion instrumentation (brass carries the quality most cherished by the Mexican mainstream, *alegría*, or joy), but—because today's *grupera* lyrics reflect the daily lives and sentiments of Mexican peasants—sometimes with a political edge. *Norteña* lyrics often chronicle the tragedies and triumphs of *mota* (marijuana) and *coca* (cocaine) *narcotraficantes* (drug runners) and illegal immigrants to the U.S. on the run from law enforcement and the Border Patrol *(la migra)*. Some *grupera* songs have been banned by the Mexican government and can be heard only from bootleg tapes that circulate at cantinas or local fiestas.

The best place in town to see this kind of music and dancing live is **Salón Pacífico** (Bucareli at Morelos, tel. 5592-2778, 9 P.M.–3:30 A.M.Fri.–Sat. only, cover $6 men, $2 women), the modestly named the "Catedral de la Quebradita." The house band, La Perla Sinaloense (The Pearl from Sinaloa), alternates with visiting acts, including a recent visit by Espuela de Oro. Be prepared for cowboy hats and boots and some acrobatic dancing.

Salón California (Calz. Tlalpan 1189, tel. 5672-3317, Sun. only from 6 P.M., cover $8), in the Portales neighborhood well south of the Centro, is better known for its tropical-music dancing, but it has a *grupera* night every Sunday until very late (don't these people have work to do?).

Rock en Español/ La Nueva Onda/Guacarock

Although lyrically descended from Latin American *nuevo canto* folk/rock music, *rock en español* takes its major musical inspiration from Anglo-American rock and Anglo-Jamaican ska. With Mexico City the premier center for the movement, this international genre has spread all over Latin America, particularly to Argentina and Brazil. *Rock en español,* also known as La Nueva Onda (The New Wave), began reaching critical popular mass in the mid-1980s; many observers speculate that the 1985 earthquake served as a major catalyst.

In the late 1980s, Botellita de Jeréz (Little Bottle of Sherry) and Maldita Vecindad (Cursed Neighborhood) began blending ska, punk, rock, jazz, and traditional Mexican elements as part of a movement within La Onda Nueva known by the descriptive *guacarock,* a reference to the mix of influences that are blended together like the ingredients in guacamole. Maldita Vecindad's first major hit was "Mojado" (Wetback), a tribute to transborder Mexican workers. Botellita has since disbanded, but Maldita Vecindad still flourishes at the center of the *guacarock* movement.

Also popular is rock fusion/art group Café Tacuba, a band that mixes alternative rock sounds with some Amerindian instrumentation and inspired live performances very much in the *guacarock* tradition. Santa Sabina adds a hint of Latin jazz improvisations to the mix, giving the band an art rock feel. All the major groups working in this medium come from D.F. or the State of México, except for ¡Tijuana No!, possibly the most political of all the recent bands (the name signifies a plea not to flee Tijuana for the U.S.). One of its CDs, *Transgresores de la ley (Lawbreakers)*, is more or less a tribute to the EZLN (Zapatista National Liberation Army) of Chiapas. Former band singer Julieta Venegas has now branched out on her own, and, with her two albums *(Aquí* and *Bueninvento)*, is quickly establishing a name for herself as an immensely talented singer/songwriter. Two excellent Mexican rap/rock bands very popular in recent years are Control Machete and Molotov. Control Machete's "Sí Señor" is the theme song to a recent Levi's ad shown in the U.S., depicting a wobbly-legged young tough with a walkman ambling through the streets of some Mexican city. Molotov's tune "Frijolero" is hilarious with a hard edge, making fun of *"gringo puñeteros"* (gringo jerkoffs) and "fucking beaners" (illegal immigrants) equally. Well, maybe not quite equally, but they slam the Mexican political system just as hard as they dis the gringos in their earlier *Todo El Poder*. They also can put on a smoking show, if you get a chance to catch them live.

Other Mexican rock groups still playing in Mexico include the venerable El Tri (kind of a Mexican Rolling Stones), CuCa, Maná (with a lead vocalist who sounds exactly like Sting), Los Jaguares, Caifanes, Plexo Solar, La Castañeda, La Barranca, El Sr. Gonzalez, La Lupita, Amantes de Lola, and Fobia. You may also come across bands who sing in Spanish but cleave more closely to Anglo styles, such as the glam/metal/goth Víctimas del Doctor Cerebro and Plastilina Mosh, or the punk/metal/rap sounds of Mauricio Garces.

None of these bands were the first in Mexico to play rock music; Los Apson and Los Locos del Ritmo created Spanish versions of Chuck Berry and Bill Haley in the 1950s, and 1960s indie garage rock produced sufficient output to fill two current CD compilations available in the

U.S., *Mexican Rock and Roll Rumble* and *Psych-Out South of the Border*.

To get an idea of what young Mexicans are listening to, watch MTV Latino (formerly MTV Internacional), the Spanish version of America's MTV music channel, available via cable or satellite throughout Mexico and in selected markets throughout the Americas, including the United States. The selections present a balance of English-language performances by groups from the U.S. or the U.K., Mexican performances in Spanish, and a good dose of Spanish-language videos from Spain and Latin America.

A number of venues in Mexico City are dedicated to modern rock music. **Bulldog** (Rubens 6, at the corner of Av. Revolución, San Juan Mixcoac, tel. 5331-4381, cover varies but usually a lot more for men than women) has live rock Friday and Saturday in a laid-back, unpretentious atmosphere inside a converted arabesque mansion.

Another popular spot to catch live rock bands is **Ⓜ Rockotitlán Sur** (Canal de Miramontes 2640, Coyoacán, tel. 5677-2439 or 5677-7374, www.rockotitlan.com, Thur.–Sat., cover usually $5–10 for men and free for women). Formerly located on Insurgentes and now near Metro Tasqueña, this was one of the original *rock en español* venues back in the 1980s, and it's still a great place to catch newer bands from Mexico and elsewhere in Latin America.

El Péndulo (Nuevo León 115, tel. 5286-9493, www.pendulo.com), in Condesa, frequently has small concerts of major bands in a coffeehouse atmosphere. Call or check their website for upcoming shows, or just walk by and look at the big sign on their building, where upcoming acts are posted.

Mexico City's **Hard Rock Café** (Campos Eliseos 278, at Paseo de la Reforma, tel. 5327-7101, www.hardrock.com) is always reliable. The club consists of a main restaurant/bar area and a separate small auditorium for live concerts. Tickets are also available through TicketMaster (tel. 5325-9000, www.ticketmaster.com.mx).

A more underground club is **Alisa** (Cuauhté-moc 91, in the Roma, tel. 5511-2100, admission $3–5), a bare room with a small stage; it can pack in a few hundred patrons on a good night. Many of the Mexican bands, mostly but not exclusively from Mexico City, play here regularly. Usually three acts play each night, Thursday through Saturday from 9 P.M. until sometime in the morning. The telephone works only intermittently, so you're better to either come by or keep an eye out for the posters plastered all over the city advertising concerts.

Larger *rockero* shows are held in the 3,000-seat **Teatro Metropolitana** (Independencia 90, tel. 5510-3448 or 5510-1045) or the even larger **Auditorio Nacional** (Paseo de la Reforma 50, tel. 5280-9250 or 5280-9979). Larger concerts are also held out at the open-air **Palacio de los Deportes** (Av. Río Churubusco at Viaducto, tel. 5237-9999), near Ciudad Deportiva Metro station. Tickets and schedules for shows at these venues are best found through TicketMaster (tel. 5325-9000, www.ticketmaster.com.mx).

Cabaret

Astrid Hadad y los Tarzanes perform amusing, politically sharp, yet respectful takeoffs on Mexico's *rancheras* and boleros in the upstairs *teatro* (theater) at **M El Bataclán** (Popocatépetl and Amsterdam, upstairs from the bar La Bodega, tel. 5511-7390), in the Condesa, on occasional weekends. Lately Hadad has taken to including a healthy dose of rumba in her repertoire as well. Hadad is worth seeing for her stage sets and costume changes alone, and her backing band is excellent. Check the weekly *Tiempo Libre* for scheduling, or call El Bataclán.

With a stronger political edge is Jesusa Rodríguez at **El Hábito** (Madrid 13, tel. 5659-1139), in Coyoacán, who puts on satirical music shows on weekends only.

You'll need proficient Spanish and a decent awareness of Mexican politics and society to catch most of what Hadad and Rodríguez are on about, but even if your Spanish isn't so hot, you'll still enjoy the show.

Folkloric Music and Dance

Música folklórica, ethnic folk music, has its roots at the local level in Mexico's rural areas, with differing *son* or song forms and instrumentation tied to particular regions of Mexico, such as the *sandunga* in Oaxaca, *jarabe* in Jalisco, *jarana* in Yucatán, *danzón* in Veracruz, or *huapango* in Tamaulipas and San Luis Potosí. Such song forms are for the most part restricted to regional festivals or, in Mexico City, at shows staged for the benefit of tourists.

The best of the latter, the **M Ballet Folklórico de Amalia Hernández** (Palacio de Bellas Artes, tel. 5512-2593, ext. 193, www .inba.gob.mx), performs regularly at the Palacio de Bellas Artes. This troupe, founded by Hernández and now managed by her daughter Norma Martínez, has accumulated 56 folk dances from around Mexico that have been choreographed for Mexico City and foreign tastes into 30 separate "ballets." The costuming, settings, and music for these performances are superb. Some of the choreography—such as the "Aztec" dances—are by nature highly speculative but also among the most dramatic. Performances at Bellas Artes are offered only two days a week, on Wednesday at 8:30 P.M. and on Sunday at 9:30 A.M. and 8:30 P.M. Tickets run $30–50, depending on seating. They sometimes play at the Teatro Hidalgo across the street also. Although the Amalia Hernández troupe is the most well known and is the permanent Bellas Artes troupe, other folkloric dance companies, such as the Compañia Nacional de Danza Folklórica, perform at Bellas Artes and elsewhere in the city.

A Mexican record label called Discos Corasón (www.corason.com) produces an excellent series of tapes and CDs focusing on folkloric music of Mexico and the Caribbean. Corasón's three-CD set *Antología del Son de México (An Anthology of Mexican Folk Music)* is a good place to start. The company was started in an apartment in the Condesa back in the 1990s by two Mexicans who were obsessed with traveling around the country and making recordings of traditional music. Their passions soon diversified to throughout the Caribbean, and they have built a wonderful collection. Discos Corasón recorded many of the old Cuban greats, and it was through their efforts that Ry Cooder ended up hearing them and helping make the phenomenal *Buena Vista Social Club* album.

Jazz/Coffeehouse

Other than the Latin jazz of hard-swinging Cuban bands in the city, it's difficult to find straight-ahead jazz ensembles in D.F. **New Orleans** (Av. Revolución 1655, tel. 5550-1908), in San Ángel, and **Pasta Jazz** (Alfonso Reyes at Saltillo, tel. 5271-9207), in Hipódromo Condesa, take a stab at it.

Los Íntimos (Querétaro 244, tel. 5264-2390, Tues.–Sun., cover usually around $10), in the Roma, often has jazz acts, as well as Cuban music or rock bands, in a small club atmosphere.

Upstairs at La Bodega restaurant is **Bataclán** (Popocatépetl and Amsterdam in the Condesa, tel. 5511-7390), a performance space with a variety of different acts during the week, from jazz/blues to vocalists to comedians. Famed performance-artist/musician Astrid Hadad regularly appears here.

Flamenco/Tango

Flamenco music has a small but strong following in the capital. One club serving up hot flamenco in the Roma is **Gitanerias** (Oaxaca 15, tel. 5514-2027, Tues.–Sun., first show at 9 P.M., second at midnight, cover $11 men, $5.50 women).

For live tango music and some excellent dancers, check out **Bar Arrabalero** at the Hotel Viena (corner of Marsella and Dinamarca, tel. 5524-4864), in Colonia Juárez near the Zona Rosa. Shows are on Friday at 9 P.M.; classes are Monday to Tuesday and Thursday to Saturday 7–9 P.M. Friday and Saturday classes charge $12 instead of $10 because of the greater experience of the instructor.

Classical Music

The **Auditorio Nacional** (Paseo de la Reforma 50, tel. 5280-9250) is a common venue for domestic and visiting international orchestras, major concerts by Mexico's top performers, or visiting international groups. The theater at the **Palacio de Bellas Artes** (tel. 5512-2593, www.inba .gob.mx), in the Centro, also hosts symphonic music from time to time, including weekly performances by the **Orquestra Sinfónica Nacional** (National Symphony Orchestra). Tickets for most events can be purchased through TicketMaster (tel. 5325-9000, www.ticketmaster .com.mx).

The national university, UNAM, hosts classical music in several venues. The **Orquestra Filarmónica de la UNAM** plays regularly at the Sala Nezahualcóyotl (tel. 5622-7125, www.agendacultural.unam.mx) and Sala Carlos Chávez (tel. 5622-7137), on the main campus. Other concerts are often held at the **Casa del Lago in Chapultepec** (tel. 5211-6093) and at **Anfiteatro Simón Bolívar** (downtown at Justo Sierra 16, within the Antiguo Colegio de San Ildefonso, tel. 5702-4221). For more information look them up on the web at http://cartelera.musica.unam.mx.

BARS AND CLUBS

Cantinas

Mexico City's older, more traditional bars are mostly men-only hangouts, but a woman arriving in the company of males will feel comfortable in all the places listed in this section. Mexico City's many cantinas are wonderful places to toss back a few *tragitos* (swallows; i.e., drinks) with friends while listening to the music of strolling *trovadores*. Since most true cantinas serve food, you'll find several cantina listings in the *Restaurants* chapter.

Two very good cantinas downtown are **Bar La India** (Salvador 42, noon–1 A.M. Mon.–Sat) and **Cantina La Mascota** (Mesones 20, noon–11 P.M. daily). Both are clean, well-lit, and comfortable for foreigners and women.

More seedy but with lots of ambience is **El Mesón del Castellano** (Bolívar 51, at República de Uruguay). Downstairs is a regular cantina, while upstairs is a dance hall with ladies hired to dance or sit and talk with male clients. The music upstairs is loud and invariably bad, but in a back room on the 2nd floor you'll find a decent billiards room where you can shoot a few games of Mexican pool and drink inexpensive beer.

Also with lots of atmosphere, although of a different variety, is **La Faena** (V. Carranza 49, tel. 5510-4417, noon–10 P.M. Sun.–Thurs., noon–2 A.M. Fri.–Sat.). This high-ceilinged bar/restaurant pays homage to the *fiesta brava*,

BAR LINGO

botanas—snacks
cantinero/cantinera—bartender
casco—"helmet," empty bottle
cerveza—beer
chela—beer (slang)
chupar—to drink (slang)
con hielo—with ice
copa—glass (for wine)
copita—"little cup," a drink
envase, botella—bottle
hasta atrás—drunk
hasta las chanclas—drunk
la cruda—"the crude," hangover
pedo—drunk (off-color slang)
sin hielo—without ice
tarro—mug (beer)
tragito—"little swallow," a drink
una fría—"a cold one"
vaso—glass (for most drinks)

bullfighting. Stylish old bullfighting costumes fill the glass cases around the room. It often has tacky live music and, bizarrely enough, some nights it gets taken over by hipsters holding alternative music events. Either way, it's an interesting, weird place to have a couple of drinks, and it's set in a beautiful though decrepit colonial-era building.

A more traditional, upscale bar in the Centro is **La Ópera** (Av. 5 de Mayo 10, tel. 5512-8959, 1–11:30 P.M. Mon.–Sat., 1–5:30 P.M. Sun.), where Pancho Villa left bullet holes in the ceiling while riding around inside on his horse during the Revolution. This dark, baroque cavern of a place was built with plenty of wood and huge, mirrored booths big enough to hold large parties of revelers. The food is very good.

In an extraordinarily baroque-styled house between República de Chile and Palma is **Cicero Centenario** (República de Cuba 79, tel. 5533-4276, 1 P.M.–1 A.M. Mon.–Sat., 1–8 P.M. Sun.). The food is good, but the main attractions are the drinks and the bands of roaming musicians. As in La Ópera, the ambience is a bit more formal than in cantinas, so don't show up in shorts. This

is a good place to go with a group of friends for a few hours of drinking, chatting, and listening to music in a lively atmosphere.

Bohemio's (Londrés 142, tel. 5514-0790, 1 P.M.–1 A.M. Mon.–Sat.) in the middle of the Zona Rosa, is a lively, little cantina that serves pitchers of beer to wash down the tasty *comida*, with live music most nights.

Another slightly yuppyish cantina, but more spacious and laid back, is **Cantina de los Remedios** (corner of Río Tiber and Río Lerma, tel. 5208-8922, 2 P.M.–1 A.M. daily). Wash down tasty *botanas* (snacks) with reasonably priced (especially during 6–10 P.M. happy hour) drinks in a convivial atmosphere, with sports on the TVs and guitarists strumming from table to table.

La Flor Asturiana (Puente de Alvarado 80, near the Monumento a la Revolución, tel. 5535-4353, noon–11 P.M. Mon.–Sat.) is a low-key neighborhood cantina with tasty *botanas* free with the drinks in the late afternoon. There is live music Wednesday through Friday from 5 P.M. onward. It's a good quiet spot for early evening drinks and snacks, particularly if you're staying at one of the nearby hotels.

More refined, but still relaxed, is **Cantina Latino** (Antonio Caso 17, a block from Reforma, tel. 5564-0800). There are no free *botanas*, but it offers tasty meat dishes such as Spanish ham, sausage, *cabrito* (kid goat), chistorra, (a type of sausage) or *arrachera* (flank steak).

Right in the center of the Condesa restaurant district is **Cantina Centenario** (Vicente Suarez 42, noon–1 A.M. Mon.–Sat.). This cantina has been gentrified somewhat in recent years by the Condesa hipster set, but it still has its contingent of regular clients and a laid-back atmosphere.

Cantina La Auténtica (corner of Álvaro Obregón and Av. Cuauhtémoc, 10 A.M.–11 P.M. daily) is a well-run, traditional cantina in the Roma. The service is great, the ambience is friendly, and wandering guitarists play tunes for a nominal fee.

Restaurant Covadonga (Puebla 121, tel. 5533-2701, 1 P.M.–2 A.M. Mon.–Fri.) is a well-kept cantina/restaurant in the Roma Norte,

Arts and Entertainment

housed in a cavernous room with a fine old bar at one end and a couple dozen tables populated mostly by men playing dominoes. Many artists and art scene followers converge at Covadonga after an exhibit opening in the neighborhood to enjoy a few drinks and the good Spanish and Mexican food.

The same owners as Cicero Centenario in the Centro also run the similar **El Candelero** (Insurgentes Sur 1333, in Colonia Mixcoac, tel. 5598-9008, 1:30 P.M.–2 A.M. Mon.–Sat., 1:30–6 P.M. Sun.). Grab a table in the cozier bar or in the high-ceilinged, spacious central area and enjoy the strains of the roaming mariachi or *trío* bands. It's a great spot for late-night drinks as well as good, traditional Mexican food.

It's hard to go wrong with the ever-popular **El Hijo del Cuervo** (Jardín Centenario 17, tel. 5658-7824, 5–11 P.M. Mon.–Wed., 1 P.M.–1 A.M. Thurs.–Sun.), which is invariably packed with more upscale Coyoacán denizens, especially on weekends.

M Cantina la Guadalupana (just off Jardín Hidalgo on Higuera, tel. 5554-6253, 10 A.M.–midnight Mon.–Sat.) is a very popular *cantina familiar* (family cantina) in Coyoacán that first opened its doors in 1932. It manages to still be authentic (complete with boozy locals) and comfortable for most foreigners. The full menu covers all the Mexican standards. Prices are a bit higher than in most cantinas.

La Jaliscience, in the old *centro* of Tlalpan, right on the *zócalo,* is similar but a bit more old-school.

Dance Clubs

Because of both the current spate of club closures by city authorities and the generally very fast turnover of clubs among the trend-conscious crowd, listing good dance clubs is a dangerous idea. Those listed in this section seem to have withstood the test of time, and hopefully, they will be around for some time. But to be sure, it's a good idea to take a look at club listings in current magazines and newspapers to check on the latest hot spots. The weekend pullout section of the daily newspaper

Reforma has a good club list with descriptions of what to expect, as do two Mexico City magazines, *D.F.* and *Chilango*. The latter also has a section in English.

A long-running popular spot is the Centro Histórico club **M Pervert Lounge** (Uruguay 70, tel. 5510-4454, 11 P.M.–5 A.M. or so Wed.–Sat., cover $6), with deejays spinning house, techno, and other club music to a young dance-happy crowd. It's a minor miracle that this place has stayed open so long, what with the ever-changing fads and the constant hassles from authorities, so they must be doing something right.

Another stalwart of D.F. nightlife, run by a group of young Brits, **El Colmillo** (Versalles 52, tel. 5592-6164, 9 P.M.–4 A.M. Thurs.–Sun., cover $5), in Colonia Juárez near the Zona Rosa, has been going strong since its inception in 1997. The club has two rooms, a straight-ahead house-music disco and bar downstairs, and a more exclusive bar upstairs. Although not as happening as it used to be, the downstairs section can still get packed on weekends.

Not far from El Comillo, and a cross between a club and a bar, is **Bar Milan** (Milan 16, just east of Insurgentes near Reforma, tel. 5592-0031, 9 P.M.–2 A.M. daily). It is a dark little bar with strange, pizzalike sculptures on the wall and groovy music (but no dance floor). On first entering, you must buy a sort of monopoly money to pay for drinks at the bar—$2.50–5, depending on what you get.

One very popular (at last report) late-night club in the Condesa is **Rioma** (Insurgentes Sur 377, tel. 5584-0613, starting at 11:30 P.M. Wed.–Sat., cover $12). Don't be put off by the strange entrance, which looks like a parking garage. The club reputedly was owned years ago (in a very different permutation, no doubt) by famed Mexican comedian Cantinflas.

Hipster Bars and Lounges

A massively popular Spanish-style tapas bar, **La Pata Negra** (in the old Condesa Cinema building at the corner of Tamaulipas and Juan Escutia, tel. 5211-5563, 1 P.M.–1 A.M. Sun.–Tues., 1 P.M.–2 A.M. Wed.–Sat.) can get packed later in the evening with Condesa hipsters.

More chilled out is **El Mitote** (Amsterdam 33, tel. 5211-9150, www.elmitote.com, 8 P.M.–1 A.M. Tues.–Sat., 1 P.M.–2 A.M. Sun.–Mon.), a comfortable bar set around several small rooms in an old Condesa house. It's a good place for a few drinks and a conversation.

Similarly relaxed but with more of a lounge vibe (they usually have a deejay spinning house music) is **Non Solo Bar** (Álavaro Obregón 130, tel. 5574-8795, 8 P.M.–3 A.M. Mon.–Sat.), in the Roma on the 2nd floor of a modest Italian restaurant, Non Solo Pasta.

Nearby in the Roma is **Red Fly** (Orizaba 145, tel. 1054-3616, until 2 A.M. Thurs.–Sat., until midnight other nights, closed Mon.), which often has live music of different varieties (jazz, hip-hop, rock) on the weekends.

An upscale spot favored by the well-dressed set in the Condesa is **Rexo** (Saltillo 1, on the corner of Nuevo León, tel. 5553-1300, Mon.–Fri. 1 P.M.–2 A.M.), a sleek glass-and-metal restaurant/bar. The martinis are strong and tasty.

El Área (Hotel Hábita, Av. Masaryk 201, tel. 5282-3100) is a modernist bar looking like a transplant from Miami to the roof of a Polanco hotel. The jet-set clientele lounge and admire each other in relaxing sofas outside, and videos are projected on a nearby building's wall.

A much more underground scene can be found in the weird little dive bar that has been colonized by young alternative hipsters called **La Perla** (República de Cuba 44, open until 4 A.M. on Thurs., hours and days may vary). Normally it has techno/house music on Thursday and a mixed bag of random music and events on Friday and Saturday.

Tequilerías

Although tequila is served in virtually every bar or cantina in the city, a few places make a point of providing a full range of Mexico's better tequilas. Because of the emphasis on quality, these can be pricey places to drink, but if you fancy yourself a tequila aficionado—or if you mean to become one—*tequilerías* are a must. In addition to the usual Jimador, Herradura (the *reposado* is my personal favorite), and Cazadores, you'll find such illustrious brands as Garañón, Los García,

Don Jesús, El Tesoro de Don Felipe, Pura Sangre, Los Corrales, Dos Amigos, Tres Mujeres, Sombrero Negro, Don Leoncio, Cimarrón, Misión Imperial, Don Tacho, Las Iguanas, Bambarria, Los Tres Alegres Compadres, La Cava del Villano, Tenoch, Las Trancas, Reserva del Patrón, Zafarrancho, El Grito, Los Valientes, Chamuco Reposado, and many more.

Behind the Catedral Metropolitana in the Centro Histórico, **Salones Tequila de la Casa de las Sirenas** (República de Guatemala 32, tel. 5704-3273, 1–11 P.M. Mon.–Thurs., 1 P.M.–2 A.M. Fri.–Sat., 1–6 P.M. Sun.) occupies three rooms of a beautiful old mansion built of volcanic stone. At last report, the bar offered more than 120 labels of tequila. Service includes all the elements for tackling your assignment: salt, *chile piquín*, and limes.

Despite its name, **Salón España** (Luis González Obregón 25, at República de Argentina, in the Centro Histórico, tel. 5702-1719, 10 A.M.–11:30 P.M. Mon.–Sat.) is a cantina devoted to Mexico's national drink. In a section of the former *convento* of La Enseñanza (see the *Sights* chapter), you'll find more than 215 brands of tequila costing $2–18 per glass. Don't be deterred by the less-than-impressive entryway; the interior is clean and orderly. Three or four different free *botanas* are served daily, along with a menu of traditional *antojitos* (snacks) and a *comida corrida* (set meal) costing only $3.50.

In the luxurious Hotel Camino Real, **María Bonita** (Mariano Escobedo 700, tel. 5203-2121, 5 P.M.–1 A.M. Mon.–Sat.) pours more than 120 kinds of tequila. If straight tequila isn't to your liking, the bartenders will mix up tequila cocktails, including a *margarita azul,* tequila sunrise, *cucaracha, iguana, chilango, México lindo,* or a *tecama.* Bolero tríos wander the floor, and there are assorted free *botanas.*

Pulquerías

Places that specialize in brewing and serving *pulque,* the fermented juice of the agave plant, could be found on virtually every street corner in the city before World War II. Nowadays they are few in number, though a few classics hold

THE LIQUID HEART OF MEXICO

Tequila is a pallid flame that passes through walls and soars over tile roofs to allay despair.

Álvaro Mútis, Tequila: Panegyric and Emblem

Mexico's national drink has been in production, in prototypical form, since at least the time of the Aztecs. The Aztecs in fact called themselves Mexicas in direct reference to the special spiritual role mescal—tequila's forerunner—played in their culture via Mextli, the god of agave (the desert plant from which mescal and tequila are derived). These names, as interpreted by the Spanish, eventually yielded "Mexico."

The first true distillers of mescal—as opposed to prehispanic forms of fermented maguey juice such as *pulque*—are thought to have been the Filipinos who accompanied the Spanish to Mexico aboard the famous Manila galleons. Although modern historians once assumed the distilling technique for tequila came from Europe, tequila stills—now as in the past—copy Southeast Asian rather than European methods of distilling, eschewing the familiar coiled piping for a simple distillation dome over the boilers.

In 1795, King Carlos IV granted the first legal concession to produce tequila to Don José María Guadalupe Cuervo. The liquor's name was taken from the Ticuila Indians of Jalisco, who mastered the technique of baking the heart of the *Agave tequiliana weber*, or **blue agave,** and extracting its juice, a process employed by tequila distilleries today. Native to Jalisco, this succulent is the only agave that produces true tequila as certified by the Mexican government. All liquors labeled "tequila" must contain at least 51 percent blue agave distillates. Contrary to the myth that all true tequila must come from Tequila, Jalisco, Mexican law enumerates specific districts in five different Mexican states where tequila may be legally produced.

Despite the fact that tequila sales are booming today, much of the tequila-making process is still carried out *a mano* (by hand). In the traditional method, the mature heart of the tequila agave, which looks like a huge pineapple and weighs 50–150 pounds, is roasted in pits for 24 hours, then shredded and ground by mule- or horse-powered mills. After the juice is extracted from the pulp and fermented in ceramic pots, it's distilled in copper stills to produce the basic tequila, which is always clear and colorless, with an alcohol content of around 40 percent.

True "gold" tequilas are produced by aging the tequila in imported oak barrels to achieve a slightly mellowed flavor. The *reposado,* or "rested," type is oak-aged for at least two months, while *añejo,* or "aged," tequila must stay in barrels at least a year. Inferior "gold" tequilas may be nothing more than the silver stuff mixed with caramel coloring—always look for *reposado* or *añejo* on the label if you want the true gold.

Dozens of tequilas populate the shelves of liquor stores and bars in Mexico. José Cuervo and Sauza are the two brands best known to most foreigners, although they often wish they've never tried them because of their bad taste. A step up is Jimador, Cazadores, and Centenario, which are decent for mixing but not so hot straight up. Some of the better makes, worth sipping to savor their flavor rather than shooting straight, include (to name just a few) Las Trancas, Don Julio, La Perseverancia, Tesoro de Don Felipe, Patrón, and my personal favorite for flavor and price, Herradura. Like all really good tequilas, Herradura uses 100 percent agave, while the less-expensive brands are only 51 percent. If it's 100 percent, it will say so on the bottle. Cuervo produces a high-end, limited-edition tequila called Reserva de la Familia that is pricey and superb.

The usual way to drink tequila is straight up from a tall, narrow shot glass *(caballito)*. Licking a few grains of salt before taking a shot and sucking a lime wedge afterward makes it go down smoother, but when it comes to a good tequila, I'm a purist, and prefer it *solo*. One zippy chaser is *sangrita* (not to be confused with *sangría,* the wine-and-fruit punch), tomato juice mixed with lime, grenadine, red chile, and salt. An old tequila standby is the much-abused margarita, a tart Tex-Mex cocktail made with tequila, lime juice, and Cointreau (usually substitute with Controy or triple sec in Mexico) and served in a salt-rimmed glass. More popular than margaritas among Mex-

Tequila is distilled from the blue agave cactus.

ican drinkers is a sort of Mexican highball, mixing tequila with Seven-Up, Squirt, or (for a real wake-up call) Red Bull.

Mescal and the Worm

The distillate of other agave plants—also known as magueys or century plants—is called mescal (sometimes spelled "mezcal"), not to be confused with the nondistilled mescal—*pulque*—prepared in prehispanic Mexico. The same roasting and distilling process is used for today's mescal as for tequila. Actually, tequila is a mescal, but no drinker calls it that, just as no one in a U.S. bar orders "whiskey" rather than specifying scotch or bourbon. Although many states in Mexico produce mescal, the best is often said to come from the State of Oaxaca.

The caterpillar-like grub or *gusano de maguey* (maguey worm) at the bottom of a bottle of mescal lives on the maguey plant itself. They're safe to eat—just about anything pickled in mescal would be—but not particularly appetizing. By the time you hit the bottom of the bottle, who cares? Maguey worms are often fried and eaten with fresh corn tortillas and salsa—a delicious appetizer.

Pulque

Let some maguey-cactus sap ferment and you have *pulque,* an ancient Mexican drink infused with more mystique than even tequila. Usually served in rustic establishments called *pulquerías,* the nutty-fla-vored, somewhat viscous liquid has an alcohol level comparable to beer and is said to be loaded with protein, vitamins, and minerals. *Pulquerías* are men-only establishments where outsiders are sometimes viewed with mild but real suspicion; it's best to enter with a regular. In Mexico City, you can easily find *pulque* at Pulquería La Hortensia, in Plaza Garibaldi. In the nearby States of Tlaxcala, Hidalgo, and México, you will also find the occasional *ambulante* (street vendor) selling the beverage, often blended with fruit or nut extracts to produce a colorful display of bottles.

Before the arrival of the Spanish, Aztec priests drank *pulque*—Mexico's first alcoholic beverage—only during religious rituals. Spanish colonization and later Mexican independence secularized and democratized the consumption of *pulque,* and by 1883 Mexico City denizens were imbibing 100,000 tons of the inebriating liquid. Under Porfirio Díaz, consumption in the capital tripled, as huge haciendas in nearby Apam, Soltepec, Omestuco, Otumba, Apizaco, and Guadalupe dedicated themselves to cultivation of the agave plant and *pulque* production. By 1905 Mexico City boasted well over a thousand *pulquerías*—one for every 300 residents. The popularity of *pulque* waned considerably after World War II, when *capitalinos* became more accustomed to beer, brandy, and tequila.

The method for making the ancient drink has varied little over the last thousand years. When an agave or *maguey* is about to flower, a *tlachiquero* (harvester) slices the top off the plant and scoops out the middle of the plant's heart (often referred to as the *piña* for its pineapple-like shape). The sweet sap of the plant will naturally accumulate in the resulting hollow. Several times daily the *tlachiquero* collects this *aguamiel* (literally, "honey water") by inserting a long tube into the hollow and siphoning the juice into a shoulder-slung sack. One *maguey* will continue to produce *aguamiel* for two or three months before drying up. Left to stand, the sweet juice will ferment on its own into *pulque,* but the process is usually helped along by adding *madre* ("mother," previously fermented *pulque*), which will turn the entire batch into *pulque* in just one day. The results must be drunk within 24 hours, before the beverage goes bad.

on. One of these, **Pulquería Las Duelistas** (Aranda 30 between Ayuntamiento and Puente de Peredo, 9 A.M.–9 P.M. Mon.–Sat.), next to Mercado San Juan in the Centro, has been serving *pulque* for more than 50 years. Especially good are the *curados* (*pulque* mixed with fruit or nut extracts). The *rockola* (jukebox) specializes in José Alfredo Jiménez, one of the great *ranchera* singers.

Other *pulquerías* include **La Hortensia** (Amargura 4, Plaza Garibaldi); **La Antigua Roma** (Allende and República de Perú), in the Centro; **La Hija de los Apaches** (Av. Cuauhtémoc 27, just south of Av. Chapultepec) and **La Reina Xóxitl** (18 de Marzo 31, Xochimilco).

Pulquerías tend to be humble establishments, so don't come expecting the same quality as cantinas—the "bathroom" is usually an open drain against the back wall, barely partitioned off. There is a predominantly male clientele in pulquerías and the environment is not always welcoming for women. One I went to behind the Palacio Nacional (it's now closed) had a curious little booth of sorts near the entrance to the bar, which was for women who might want a drink, but didn't want to come into the main bar area.

Billiards

Roma Gym Billar (Orizaba 99, in Roma Norte, tel. 5207-8441, 11 A.M.–11 P.M. Mon.–Fri., 4–11 P.M. Sat., 4–10 P.M. Sun., $3 an hour per table) is a traditional Mexican pool hall, with local men drinking beer and shooting Mexican pool beneath fluorescent lights. The tables are in good condition, and chess and backgammon sets are available also. The game of choice here, as at most Mexican billiard parlors, is "pool," wherein balls 1–15 are lined up along the side of the table and are sunk in order. Several players, rather than just two, frequently shoot this game. Second in popularity is *ocho bola,* or eight-ball, played much like it is in the United States. Also on hand are a couple of *carambola* tables, which feature three balls and no pockets; you use one ball to strike the other two, but only after it has touched three rails of the table.

In the center of Condesa, **Billares Malafama** (Michoacán 78, tel. 5553-5138, 10 A.M.–mid-night Mon.–Wed., 11 A.M.–1 A.M. Thurs.–Sat., noon–midnight Sun., $8 an hour per table) offers 12 pool tables in a converted warehouse and is filled with young Condesa hipsters every night. Come in the afternoon or early evening to avoid a wait, or sit and watch the crowd until a table opens up, enjoying the great music. They charge two hours for the price of one between 10 A.M. and 4 P.M.

In the Zona Rosa is **Brownsville Café Billar** (upstairs at Hamburgo 158, tel. 5511-9223, noon–11 P.M. Mon.–Sat.), with a dozen tables but not a lot of atmosphere.

One place downtown to shoot some pool is **Ups & Downs** (Isabel la Catolica 83, tel. 5709-1539, 10 A.M.–10 P.M. daily).

Gay and Lesbian

Mexico City has a vibrant queer subculture. It may not be as in the open as in Europe or the United States, but it's a lot more apparent than in much of Latin America. The capital's queer scene is replete with hangouts of all different styles, from old-time gay cantinas to techno discos to drag dance revues. Pamphlets such as "La Otra Guia" or "Sergay" have listings of "in" clubs and can be picked up at several of the places written up below. Most of these clubs welcome women as well as men, although the women will be heavily outnumbered.

Unfortunately, the authorities have recently been closing down nightspots all over the city in a "clean-up drive." Hangouts geared toward the queer crowd are not the only targets, but they are easy ones. Some of the information here may soon be out of date. It's best to check the Internet: www.sergay.com.mx and www.gaymex-ico.net both have information in English.

In the Mexico City queer scene you may observe a class, race, and social divide. A lighter-skinned, upper-class clientele tend to frequent the more expensive clubs, while middle- and lower-class folks who are more likely to live with their families, perhaps in the closet, frequent the cheaper joints.

The Zona Rosa, whose streets also become a cruising zone for gay men on weekend afternoons and evenings, contains a bunch of places.

DIEGO AND FRIDA (cont'd)

and society circuit around Mexico, the United States, and Europe. Their tumultuous relationship and Rivera's notorious infidelity only seemed to propel their mythic status. "I have suffered two accidents in my life," Kahlo is quoted as saying in the Malka Drucker biography, *Frida Kahlo: Torment and Triumph in Her Life and Art*. "One in which a streetcar ran over me [at age 18]. The other is Diego."

The aftermath of the streetcar accident, which included more than 30 surgical procedures and 28 plaster corsets designed to support her damaged spine, forms a recurring theme in Kahlo's famous self portraits. But more than the sometimes tortuously clinical details in these *autoretratos*, it's her iconic facial features—the batwing eyebrows; the stern, roselike mouth; and secretive, sidelong glance fixed on the viewer—that one most remembers. A pronounced sexual ambiguity is also often present. In one portrait she suggests androgyny by merging her face with Diego's, while another portrays Kahlo sporting shorn hair and a man's suit and tie. In a now-famous family photo from 1926, her hair is pulled back tightly, and she again is dressed like a man.

In spite of her preference for personal rather than overtly political themes, Kahlo's work formed a central part of the Mexican renaissance in its employment of native Mexican elements. Many of her paintings show an influence rooted in the tradition of Mexican religious folk culture, yet in a sense her work was postmodernist, since she didn't completely turn away from traditional European presentation concepts. In *The Little Deer* (1946), Kahlo superimposed her head on the body of a stag (once again blending genders), whose body is pierced by numerous arrows. The painting recalls the martyrdom of St. Sebastian—a popular European theme in medieval religious art—while evoking the *danza del venado*, a mythic deer-hunting dance ritual common among Amerindian tribes throughout Mexico.

Although she didn't participate in public works of art like the muralists—in her physical condition she could hardly be expected to mount scaffolds—Kahlo in her own way became just as influential in her promotion of Mexican cultural nationalism. She decorated her home not with European and American art and accessories, but with Mexican handicrafts and folk art. Rivera and his colleagues typically dressed in the European fashions of the day, while Kahlo, though born of a German immigrant father, most often wore Amerindian dresses, shawls, and jewelry. Although she was born in 1907, she usually gave 1910—the year the Mexican Revolution began—as her birth date.

Kahlo died in 1954, and Rivera followed her three years later. Of all the Mexican artists who have worked in the 20th century, Diego and Frida are the most loved and remembered. In spite of the dynamic couple's original living-legend status, over the last decade, Kahlo's international reputation has grown beyond that of her contemporaries, as well as that of her husband Rivera. At a recent San Francisco Museum of Modern Art exhibition of the Gelman Collection—one of the largest private collections of paintings by the Mexican Modernists—museumgoers paid scant attention to paintings by Rivera, Siqueiros, and Orozco, but they stood four deep around the Kahlo paintings.

collection of the painter's work. Not all pieces are displayed at any given time, however.

The 6,000-square-meter Hacienda La Noria also displays colonial objects and furniture. The surrounding grounds, which together with the main building encompass 37,000 square meters, are beautifully landscaped with native trees and plants. You may also see Mexican turkeys and a few unique Xoloitzcuintle dogs, a rare prehis-panic canine species that is small, dark, and hairless—a rather spooky-looking creature.

To reach the museum by public transport, take the Metro to the Tasqueña station and then board the *tren ligero* (light rail) from the metro station to La Noria streetcar terminal. From here, walk west along Avenida Guadalupe Ramírez till you come to a large three-way intersection, a distance of around 100 meters, and then make a

One longtime favorite is **El Taller/El Almacén** (Florencia 37, tel. 5533-4984 or 5207-0727, cover $6 Thurs.–Sun., free Mon.–Wed.), which is two clubs in one: upstairs is a mixed crowd, while downstairs is only men. It has popular tunes, videos, strippers, and lots of men on the make. Tuesday and weekend nights are particularly strong. This is also a good place to find out about other "in" spots.

Also in the Zona Rosa are several places along Calle Londrés, including **El Celo,** (Londrés 104, tel. 5514-4766, Wed.–Sun., cover $6) and **El Cabaretito Teatro** (Londrés 117-Bis, tel. 5207-2554, no cover). Seedier and little more like a sex club is **La Estación** (Hamburgo 234, tel. 5514-4707); there is no cover, but you have to drink at least $3 worth.

Down in the Colonia Roma, **Anyway/The Doors** (Monterrey 47, tel. 5533-1691) is another veteran D.F. queer club, with three different levels of dance floors and drag cabarets on weekend nights. Some nights one floor is reserved for women only; this is one of the few clubs in Mexico that caters to women. Not far away is the **Living Room** (Orizaba 137, tel. 5584-7403, www.living.com.mx, Fri.–Sat. only), a more upscale place with house and techno music, as well as an agreeable chill-out area upstairs.

For the hippest clubs try **Box,** (Moliere 425, tel. 5203-3356 or 5203-3365, www.boxmexico.com.mx, cover $14), in a vast warehouse at the northwestern end of Colonia Polanco. Only open on Friday and Saturday, Box is always packed mostly with young men but some women too, and it features Mexico's finest go-go dancers and occasional celebrity acts. The clientele here is more affluent than in the places downtown.

Further downmarket, **Tom's Leather Bar** (Insurgentes Sur 357, closed Mon., cover $8), in Colonia Hipódromo Condesa, has precious little leather but does boast strippers, porn videos, a dark gothic interior, a backroom, and eclectic music—the only gay bar where you might croon along with Ella Fitzgerald singing "Summertime." Farther south in Colonia Mixcoac is another supposedly leathery joint, **La Cantina del Vaquero,** (Alcegiras 26, tel. 5598-2195).

At the same address is **El Ansia** (tel. 5611-6118), an intriguing dive where, if you so choose, you may wear a numbered badge allowing potential beaux to leave notes for you in the corresponding message box.

Among the more working-class places is the **Cantina Viena** (República de Cuba 3, no cover), a bar near the Eje Central that looks just like any other Mexican cantina you might see, even down to the fact that men are the only clients. It's open daily. There are a few other gay bars nearby, some of them extremely seedy, but be wary in the dark streets. A bit further south, also near the Eje Central, is **Butterflies** (Izazaga 9, cover $6), a big club that holds the city's best drag revue by far, and it is always packed on Friday and Saturday nights.

The notorious **14,** famed for its live straight sex shows near Garibaldi, has closed for good, and **15** (Ecuador 24, tel. 8589-9966), a pale imitation, has opened nearby; no live sex, but it attracts the same mixed straight-queer crowd.

Many gays and lesbians live in the Colonia Condesa neighborhood, and a stroll through its streets or around the ellipse of Parque México is a pleasant way to spend a couple of hours. There are several gay-owned eateries in the Condesa restaurant hub centered on the streets of Tamaulipas, Vicente Suarez, and Michoacán. Places open and close so fast here that it's not worth mentioning any, but walk around and explore the options.

Finally, if after all this hedonism you are missing something spiritual in your life, you'll be welcome at Mexico City's only gay church, the **Instituto de la Comunidad Metropolitana** (Norte 77, No. 3218, in Azcapotzalco, tel. 5556-2172 or 5396-7768). It is an ecumenical chapel in the house of Father Jorge and Father Rodolfo, two priests who have been partners for more than 20 years. Mass is on Sunday at 10 A.M., 12.30 P.M., and 7 P.M. and lasts about two hours. Take the Metro to Cuitlahuac station, and from there either take a taxi to the address, or walk 100 yards down the road to Avenida Cuitlahuac and take a *pesero* heading northeast until you reach a big roundabout—the Glorieta de los Camarones. Get off just before the roundabout, turn right, and it's the first street on your right.

Tangas

Mexico City's many topless "table dance" bars (called *tangas* in D.F.) are perhaps best left for so-inclined individuals to discover on their own, but **El Closet** (Saltillo 67, in the Condesa, tel. 5286-5041, 8 P.M.–early morning Mon.–Sat.) is so well established it's practically respectable to be seen there. You'll see lots of nicely dressed middle-aged men. The Zona Rosa has *tanga* clubs on almost every other block.

A word of advice on places like this: If you don't think to ask how much drinks cost before ordering them, the bill can become very expensive very quickly.

Arts

MUSEUMS

Diego Rivera and Frida Kahlo

Diego Rivera (1886–1958) stands out as the most famous Mexican artist of the last century. No other renowned painter of the early 20th century except Picasso was considered as technically erudite as Rivera in terms of the range of his technique. According to MacKinley Helms, author of the 1941 *Modern Mexican Painters,* "[Rivera] painted in scores of styles before he developed his unmistakably personal formulas on Mexican walls." Among his Paris society friends were the artists Picasso, Braque, Gris, Modigliani, and Derain. Three places to see the more famous of Rivera's murals are all located in the Centro: the Palacio Nacional, the Secretaría de Educación Pública building, and Museo Mural Diego Rivera, on the Alameda. (See the *Sights* chapter for more information on these museums).

The **Museo Estudio Diego Rivera** (Av. Diego Rivera, at the corner of Altavista, tel. 5550-1189, 10 A.M.–6 P.M. Tues.–Sun., $2 admission), in San Ángel, designed by architectural prodigy Juan O'Gorman in 1928, was where Rivera lived and worked for a time with his wife Frida Kahlo. Rivera's life and work (reproductions only) are depicted on the ground floor of this tightly spaced, functionalist structure, while the upper floor is arranged as it might have been when Rivera was still in residence, complete with unfinished paintings on easels. At last report the museum was closed for renovations; call first to confirm that it's reopened.

Just outside of Mexico City, Rivera decorated the chapel of the Universidad de Chapingo in Texcoco with murals; it's worth a visit for the dedicated Rivera fan. (See the *Excursions* chapter for more details.)

In the U.S., the status of Rivera's wife, German-Mexican artist Frida Kahlo (1907–1954), has eclipsed that of Diego himself over the last decade. Most of Kahlo's work is held by private collectors; her tortured self-portraits fetch record auction prices, and art connoisseurs brave long lines whenever a Kahlo exhibit visits an American museum. The Museo Frida Kahlo in Coyoacán (detailed in the *Sights* chapter) is more about the artist's life and her own art collection and the Museo de Arte Moderno holds on permanent exhibit Kahlo's most famous work in Mexico, *The Two Fridas.* The best place to view Kahlo's work is the **M Museo Dolores Olmedo Patiño** (Av. México 5843, Colonia La Noria, tel. 5555-1016, 10 A.M.–6 P.M. Tues.–Sun., admission $3), which is about two kilometers west of the main docks in Xochimilco, in the far south part of the city. A lifelong friend and supporter of Diego Rivera (not to mention an occasional model for his paintings), Dolores Olmedo has donated a large part of her own house as a museum dedicated to Rivera and Kahlo. The building itself, the lovingly restored 16th-century Hacienda La Noria, is worth a visit in and of itself, even if it weren't for the collection of more than 600 prehispanic artifacts and pieces of native art, and works by Rivera (127 pieces) as well as Frida Kahlo. Although the Kahlo collection numbers only 25 pieces, this is the largest single private

DIEGO AND FRIDA

Mexico City in the 1920s stood on the threshold of a new era. Although the country had won its independence from Spain in 1821, it became obvious by the early 20th century that the economic gap between rich and poor—and the social gap between the Spanish descendant and Amerindian descendant—had only increased after the departure of the Spanish. Sparked by the populist escapades of colorful bandit-turned-revolutionary Francisco "Pancho" Villa and peasant-hero Emiliano Zapata, Mexico endured a decade of civil war before the newly established Partido Revolucionario Nacional (PNR, which later became the PRI) began steering the nation in a new, socialist-inspired direction in 1920.

The capital swarmed with optimism as the PNR vowed to make *mestizaje*—the blending of Amerindian and European patrimonies—the national zeitgeist. For Mexico, and especially for the intellectuals, artists, and academicians of Mexico City, the armed battles had ended, but the cultural struggle was just beginning.

Under the 1920–1924 presidency of Álvaro Obregón, the government decided that public works of art could play an important role in restoring a nationhood tattered by civil war. Commissioned to create a number of murals at the National Preparatory School at the University of Mexico in 1922, painter Diego Rivera took on the task of conceiving a new art medium that avoided a Eurocentric orientation and instead celebrated Mexican heritage from early Mesoamerica through the Revolution. Rivera was joined by a number of other similarly commissioned Mexican artists, who together formed the Syndicate of Technical Workers, Painters, and Sculptors. In a public tract issued by the Syndicate in 1922, fellow muralist Davíd Alfaro Siqueiros urged Mexican artists to "repudiate so-called easel painting and every kind of art favored by the ultra intellectual circles, because it is aristocratic, and praise monumental art in all its forms, because it is public property."

While the colonial art of Mexico and Latin America had from time to time incorporated Indian decorative motifs—sculpting squash foliage or pineapple patterns in stone to fill the space between religious figures on churches and cathedrals,

for example—the overall design concepts, styles, and techniques employed were always Spanish. A painted *bodegón,* or pantry scene, might contain corn and cacao instead of oranges and grapes, yet it remained the patented European still life, muted in color and devoid of human presence.

The soon-to-be-dubbed Mexican Modernist School abandoned the solemn and detached art of Europe and instead embraced bold New World imagery full of color and human activity. Looking for a medium beyond the confines of canvas and church porticoes, they settled on the vast, undecorated walls of Mexico's governmental edifices. Like the Aztecs and Maya of earlier eras, who painted on the walls of their temples and tombs, the Mexican muralists left their public buildings awash with color. And as did their Mesoamerican predecessors, they took native subjects as their inspiration. Instead of creating portraits of Spanish aristocrats, they glorified the everyday lives of the contemporary Amerindian population; in place of Franciscan friars fingering rosaries, they painted peasants tilling the soil.

Although many Mexican artists participated in the muralist movement, three names quickly came to the fore in Mexico City: Diego Rivera, Davíd Alfaro Siqueiros, and José Clemente Orozco. One of Rivera's earliest mural efforts emblazoned the courtyard of the Secretaría de Educación Pública with a series of dancing Tehuanas (natives of Tehuantepec, in Southern Mexico). This four-year project went on to incorporate many other contemporary Amerindian themes, and it eventually encompassed 124 frescoes that extended three stories high and two city blocks long. Such prodigious output, along with the predominance of native elements, had a profound effect on the Mexican art scene.

But as famous as the Mexico City murals made Rivera and his colleagues, a star-crossed romance with a teenaged National Preparatory School student named Frida Kahlo drew Rivera into a living tableau that for much of the world has symbolized the 20th-century Mexican art milieu, seemingly for all eternity. Kahlo and Rivera married in 1929 and nearly overnight became a charismatic, celebrated couple on the art

(continued on next page)

sharp left (southeast) onto Antiguo Camino Xochimilco. After another 300 meters or so, you'll come to the museum on your left, at the intersection with Avenida México.

Modern Art Museums

Postrevolutionary nationalism in Mexico inspired grand works of art in painting and mosaics on the walls of public buildings throughout the nation. Often containing social and political criticism, Mexican murals have become one of the most imitated visual art forms in the Americas. Among the country's most famous muralists are José Clemente Orozco, Diego Rivera, Davíd Alfaro Siqueiros, Jean Charlot, Rufino Tamayo, and Juan O'Gorman. One of the best places to see murals by different artists in the same location is at the Antiguo Colegio de San Ildefonso in the Centro (see the *Sights* chapter for details).

Serving as a bridge between the highly symbolic and often political art of the early 20th century and the more representational art of younger artists are two older contemporary Mexico City painters, Gunther Gerzso and José Luis Cuevas. Gerzso abandoned symbolism for intensely abstract works that today are highly collectible. Cuevas rebelled against the idea that art had to serve a higher moral or political purpose and instead invested his talents in intensely personal explorations in concept, technique, and media, producing everything from labeled vials of his own semen to elaborate metal sculptures.

Currently extremely popular on the international art scene is the Oaxaca School of painters, a movement that was kicked off by Rufino Tamayo in the 1950s and continues to the present day with the whimsical, dreamlike works of Francisco Toledo. Others from Oaxaca include Rodolfo Morales, Jorge Barrios, and Alejandro Santiago.

Apart from the museums listed in this section, the Palacio del Arzobispado, just off the Zócalo on Calle Moneda, also has an interesting collection of different Mexican modernists (see the *Sights* chapter for details).

Museo de Arte Contemporáneo Internacional Rufino Tamayo (Paseo de la Reforma at

COURTESY OF MEXICO TOURISM BOARD/CARLOS SANCHEZ

Arts and Entertainment

Juan O'Gorman's three-dimensional mural covers the main library building at Universidad Nacional Autónoma de México (UNAM).

Gandhi, tel. 5286-5889, www.museotamayo.org, 10 A.M.–6 P.M. Tues.–Sun., admission $2) was created by one of the great Mexican painters of the 20th century, a Zapotec Indian born in Oaxaca in 1899. Heavily influenced by his indigenous roots, Tamayo gained fame in the 1950s (when he was living in New York) for his dramatic use of colors, particularly the earth tones from his native state. In 1981, he and his wife, Olga, donated this museum along with a fabulous collection of modern art, consisting of his works plus the works of Salvador Dalí, Max Ernst, Gunther Gerzso, Alberto Giacometti, Willem de Kooning, René Magritte, Joan Miró, Andy Warhol, and many others. Tamayo died in 1991 at the age of 91.

A modernistic red sculpture sits in front of the odd, bunkerlike building of concrete and white marble, hidden away amid a stand of trees. World-class traveling exhibits change frequently in the 10 halls around a central patio. The museum installed a cyberlounge in 2001, dedicated to art on the Internet. The museum is east of the Museo Nacional de Antropología, on Paseo de la Reforma.

Almost across the street from the Tamayo is the **Museo de Arte Moderno** (tel. 5553-6233, www.cnca.gob.mx, 10 A.M.–6 P.M. Tues.–Sun., admission $2). It is between Paseo de la Reforma and the Monumento de los Niños Héroes (entrance on Reforma) and has a wide ranging collection of modern Mexican art. This dark glass building, designed by Pedro Ramírez Vásquez of Museo de Antropología fame, looks a bit drab on the outside, but inside are four spacious, well-lit exhibition halls off a broad central stairway. Three rooms are dedicated to rotating exhibits of sometimes excellent quality (a fine show of Cartier-Bresson photography is one recent example), while the fourth displays selections from the museum's permanent collection, including Mexican greats Diego Rivera, José Clemente Orozco, Rufino Tamayo, Dr. Atl. One of the galleries contains Frida Kahlo's largest work, *Las Dos Fridas,* in which twin portraits of the artist are joined by arteries looping from the exposed hearts of each figure. Also notable are some 1920s paintings by Ángel Zárraga.

One of Mexico's finest modern art museums, M **Museo de Arte Carrillo Gil** (Av. Revolución 1608, tel. 5550-6260, www.macg.inba.gob.mx, 10 A.M.–6 P.M. Tues.–Sun., admission $1.50) is housed in this slick building in San Ángel. Along with an excellent collection of works by Mexican greats such as Rivera, Siqueiros, Tamayo, and Toledo, the museum also shows more experimental current Mexican and international artists. The museum is a 10-minute walk from Plaza San Jacinto.

On a side street two blocks behind the Palacio Nacional is **Museo José Luis Cuevas** (Academia 13, tel. 5522-0156 or 5542-6198, 10 A.M.–5 P.M. Tues.–Sun., $1 admission, free for students with I.D.), established by one of Mexico's preeminent modern artists, José Luis Cuevas. Housed in the remodeled 16th-century Convento de Santa Inés, the museum mounts new exhibits every month or two that are drawn from the artist's private collection, which he donated to create the museum. The collection contains works by Mexican artists Francisco Toledo, Vicente Rojo, and Arnold Belkin, among others, as well as by foreign artists such as Pablo Picasso, Leonora Carrington, and Roberto Matta.

Erotica, found in a room draped in ominous black curtains on the 1st floor, contains a small display of rather tame erotic sketches by Cuevas. Several impressive Cuevas sculptures are placed throughout the museum. Particularly striking is the eight-meter-high bronze sculpture of a female figure that Cuevas designed especially for the center patio, titled *La giganta* (The Giantess).

To find the museum, walk up Calle Moneda to the corner of Academia, turn left, and look for a bright red metal sculpture marking the entrance.

Fans of the Mexican muralist movement may want to stop in **Museo Sala de Arte Público David Alfaro Siqueiros** (Tres Picos 29, tel. 5203-5888, 10 A.M.–6 P.M. Tues.–Sun., admission $1.50). Here, in a private house donated by the artist shortly before his death in 1974, you'll find a permanent exhibit of his art, as well as temporary exhibits of other contemporary art.

Plaza Loreto in San Ángel is home to **Museo Soumaya** (Plaza Loreto, Av. Revolución and Río Magdalena, tel. 5616-3731, www.soumaya

© CHRIS HUMPHREY

La Giganta at the Museo José Luis Cuevas

.com.mx, 10:30 A.M.–6:30 P.M. Thurs.–Mon., 10:30 A.M.–8:30 P.M. Wed., $1 admission), a private museum with a varied and interesting collection, including several sculptures by Rodin and paintings by Degas, Renoir, Camine Claudel, and Miró. There's also a modest collection of colonial-era Latin American art, as well as two murals by modern Mexican painter Rufino Tamayo. The museum offers free guided tours of the museum (in Spanish) on weekends at noon.

New and Alternative Art Spaces
In the shell of an old Carmelite chapel and convent, where famed 17th-century poet Sor Juana Inés de la Cruz briefly lived, is the **Centro de Arte Alternativo Ex-Santa Teresa** (Licenciado Primo de Verdad 6, just off Moneda, 10 A.M.–6 P.M. daily, free admission). Backed by the government's Instituto Nacional de Bellas Artes (INBA), this is one of the few art spaces in Mexico City dedicated to young, alternative art. It's located right next to the Templo Mayor, just off the Zócalo.

On the Alameda, in what was formerly a museum for colonial art, is the **Laboratorio de Arte Alameda** (Dr. Mora 7, tel. 5510-2793, 9 A.M.–5 P.M. Tues.–Sun., $1 admission, free Sun.) is a new art space for young artists also run by INBA. Rotating exhibits of experimental modern art (video art is prominent) are on display.

The Eiffelesque **Museo El Chopo** (Dr. Enrique González 10, tel. 5546-5484, www.chopo .unam.mx, 10 A.M.–2 P.M. and 3–7 P.M. Tues.–Sun., admission $.70.) was originally built in Germany and was moved to Mexico in pieces. This structure of girders and glass first served as the Japanese pavilion at an industrial exposition in 1910 and then was moved to its current site to become a natural history museum. UNAM, the national university, took over the building in 1973 and uses it as a forum for revolving shows of modern art, mostly by young Mexican artists. Occasional theater shows are also staged in the cavernous interior, which has the ambience of a train station but boasts wonderful light from all the colored stained glass. A small café at the museum serves coffee and snacks. At the rear of the museum is the **Cinematógrafo del Chopo,** run by UNAM and showing art movies daily.

The museum is a block from the intersection of Insurgentes and San Cosme (look for the iron towers). San Cosme is the closest Metro stop.

Museo Universitario de Ciencias y Artes Roma (Muca Roma) (Tabasco 73, tel. 5511-0925, www.muca.unam.mx, 10 A.M.–6 P.M. Mon.–Sat., free admission), near Plaza Río de Janeiro in the Roma, is a UNAM-run art space in a early-20th-century brick house. Eight rooms exhibit works of different Mexican and international artists; they are often very good.

Mexican and European Classical Art Museums

Apart from the museums listed in this section, you'll also find many colonial paintings and sculptures in the older churches around the city.

The **Museo Nacional de Arte** (Tacuba 8, tel. 5130-3400, www.munal.com.mx, 10 A.M.–5:30 P.M. Tues.–Sun., admission $3) occupies the former Palacio de Comunicaciones building on the north side of Calle Tacuba. The reserved, gray palace was finished in 1910 under the supervision of Italian architect Silvio Contri and was converted into a museum in 1982. The building's cool, beautiful interior houses an overview of Mexican art dating from the early colonial period to the mid-20th century. Among the notable artists featured are colonial painters Miguel Cabrera, Cristóbal Villalpando, and Luis Juárez; 19th-century painters Juan Cordero, José María Velasco, and Ramón Sagredo; and the 20th century's Diego Rivera, Frida Kahlo, Rufino Tamayo, and others. Guide service is free and sometimes available in English. Major renovations were under way at last report, with only a temporary exhibit open to the public, but the permanent collection is set to reopen soon.

On the corner of Puente de Alvarado and Ramos Arizpe, amidst a row of otherwise drab buildings, stands an anomalous neoclassical palace that was once the home of the Marqués de Buenavista, which now houses the **Museo San Carlos** (Av. Puente de Alvarado 50, tel. 5566-8342, www.mnsancarlos.inba.gob.mx, 10 A.M.–6 P.M. Wed.–Mon., admission $2.30, $1 for cameras, $4 for video). Although the original building plans have been lost, it's thought to have been the work

of that omnipresent Valencian architect and artist, Manuel Tolsá. The rooms of the former mansion, around the unusual oval-shaped courtyard, now house a remarkable collection of European artworks, including paintings by Rubens and Anton van Dyck, a series of sketches by Goya known as "Los Caprichos" (The Whims), and sculptures by Rodin and Manuel Vilar. Works by foreign masters who taught at the San Carlos school, such as Eugenio Landesio and Pelegrín Clavé, are also included.

King Carlos IV donated much of the art to the Academia de San Carlos when the art school opened in the late 18th century. Originally housed in the academy building in the Centro, these sculptures and paintings served as models for students learning their chosen medium. The collection was opened to public viewing during the last years of the Spanish colony, thus establishing the first public art museum in the Americas. When the quantity of visitors began to overwhelm the art school in the Centro, many of the finest works were moved to the current museum, which doesn't see a whole lot of traffic. It's a great place to look at works by some of the European masters without the crowds.

Architecture Museums

Architectural styles in Mexico City vary from ancient Aztec pyramids to flamboyantly colored, cubistic high-rise office buildings. **Colonial architecture** in the capital extends from simple early-16th-century churches to the highly ornate late baroque or churrigueresque styles that flourished in the 18th century. The **baroque** period in Spanish church architecture was a response to the Protestant Reform and formed part of a Catholic religious movement known as the *contrareforma,* during which many Catholics felt a strong need to elaborate on the mysteries of their faith. The baroque style permitted artists to experiment more freely with ornamentation, developing the twisted Solomonic column in the 17th century and the *estípite* (sections of columns and ornamentation layered vertically) in the 18th century.

As Mexican nationalism surged toward the end of the 18th century, government buildings adopted a more restrained, French-influenced **neoclassic style**, also known as Republican style. For colonial and neoclassic architecture, the Centro Histórico is far and away the best district for touring, followed by Coyoacán and San Ángel.

For a taste of **art deco** architecture, take a couple of hours to tour around the Condesa neighborhood, particularly around Parque México, which began its boom in the 1930s. Across Avenida Insurgentes in the Roma are scores of century-old mansions built in homage to the Parisian styles to which the owners aspired. Paseo de la Reforma, Polanco, and Chapultepec showcase styles of **modern architecture** created by such renowned 20th-century architects as Ricardo Legoretta, Luis Barragán, and Pedro Ramírez Vásquez.

Barragán has a museum all his own, **Museo Casa Barragán,** in the Tacubaya neighborhood, recently named a UNESCO World Heritage Site (see the *Sights* chapter for details).

On the 4th floor of the Palacios de Bellas Artes, the **Museo de Arquitectura** (corner of Av. Juárez and the Eje Central, www.museobellasartes.artte.com) is an exhibit with the building's floor plans, photos, and archived memorabilia related to Mexico City's other historic buildings, including many older structures that have disappeared from Roma, Juárez, San Rafael, Tacubaya, and other *barrios* (neighborhoods).

Museums of Mexican Popular and Indigenous Culture

Mexico has one of the richest and deepest cultures of any country in the Americas, if not the world. The cultural gumbo resulting from the country's complex history is evidenced constantly, from the dozens of indigenous languages still spoke by 10 percent of the population to the little sugar skeleton candies you'll see everywhere for Día de los Muertos (November 1).

An obligatory stop for anyone with even a passing interest in Mexican cultures is the **Museo Nacional de Antropología e Historia,** in Chapultepec, one of the finest museums of its kind anywhere (see the *Sights* chapter for details).

Mexican muralist Diego Rivera designed and built the **Museo Anahuacalli** (Calle de Museo 150, tel. 5617-4310, 10 A.M.–2 P.M. and 3–6 P.M. Tues.–Sun., admission $3), a bizarre Mesoamerican pyramid–inspired museum of volcanic stone, to contain his prodigious collection of prehispanic treasures. The museum displays 60,000 artifacts from the Zapotec, Toltec, Teotihuacán, Veracruz, Mixtec, and Aztec cultures. Upstairs a studio holds many personal belongings and sketches of Rivera, offering a window on this legendary artist's personal life. On the top floor is a terrace offering views out over the city.

The museum is in Colonia San Pablo Tepetlapa, southeast of Coyoacán, in the direction of Xochimilco. By car or taxi, follow Avenida División del Norte south from Avenida Miguel Ángel de Quevedo until you reach Calle de Museo, about a 20-minute drive. The easiest way to get there on public transportation is to go to Tasqueña Metro station and catch the *tren ligero* south to the Xotepingo stop. From there, walk 10 minutes along Avenida División del Norte until it crosses Calle de Museo.

On the north side of the Alameda, in the Plaza de la Santa Veracruz, is the **Museo Franz Mayer** (Av. Hidalgo 45, tel. 5518-2266, www.franzmayer.org.mx, 10 A.M.–5 P.M. Tue.–Sun., until 7 P.M. Wed., admission $3). This museum, housed in a 16th-century former hospital, contains the carefully and artfully displayed applied-arts collection of German financier-philanthropist Franz Mayer. The fine selection, which extends to two floors, includes 16th- through 19th-century Mexican ceramics, antique *rebozos* (Mexican shawls), religious articles, furniture, textiles, silver and gold pieces, clocks, and even full *cocinas poblanas* (tiled Puebla-style kitchens)—a real treat for fans of Mexican culinary history. The museum contains a few canvases by European Renaissance artists as well, plus temporary exhibitions of often excellent quality. A courtyard café toward the back of the museum is a quiet spot for reflection and refreshment.

Established in 1982, the **Museo Nacional de Culturas Populares** (Av. Hidalgo, half block northeast of Plaza Hidalgo, 10 A.M.–6 P.M. Tues.–Thurs., 10 A.M.–8 P.M. Fri.–Sun., donation requested) is dedicated to Mexico's diverse artistic and cultural expressions. Sometimes the shows can be very interesting, like a recent one on Día de los Muertos art from throughout the country. Visitors will encounter displays of both traditional and modern handicrafts, along with live demonstrations. Special courses and fairs with gastronomic or handicraft themes are also frequently hosted here. A cafeteria offers refreshment, while shops purvey a variety of books, magazines, and posters. One of the posters for sale in the shop is a lovely black-and-white photo of the church and plazas of Coyoacán a century ago, surrounded by farmland and countryside.

Historical Museums

The **Museo Casa de Carranza** (Río Lerma 35, tel. 5546-6494, 9 A.M.–7 P.M. Tue.–Sat., 11 A.M.–3 P.M. Sun., admission $3), in a French-inspired mansion two blocks north of Reforma, was the last home of revolutionary leader Venustiano Carranza, who stayed here for six months before his execution in Puebla on May 7, 1920. Carranza's widow was granted the house after the Revolution, and in 1942 she in turn converted it into a museum commemorating her husband. Art, period furniture, and memorabilia from Carranza's life fill the various rooms. One particularly interesting piece is an ambiguous Carranza portrait by Mexican painter Dr. Atl (Gerardo Murillo).

For a country that has been sorely treated by invading countries (one of its great holidays, Cinco de Mayo, commemorates one winning battle in a war Mexico lost), it's only appropriate that one of the best historical museums would be the **Museo Nacional de las Intervenciones** (20 de Agosto at General Anaya, right behind Metro General Anaya, tel. 5604-0699, 9 A.M.–6 P.M. Tues.–Sun., admission $3.50). The museum, two kilometers from the center of Coyoacán, is in the 17th-century **Ex-Convento de Churubusco**, where Mexican General Pedro Anaya surrendered his sword to U.S. forces in 1847. The museum's 13 rooms chronicle invasions of Mexico on the part of Spain in 1829, France in 1838, and the U.S. in 1846–47, 1914, and 1916. Administered by INAH, the museum also hosts temporary historical exhibitions, cultural extension courses, round-table discussions, conferences, and other educational/cultural activities.

In addition to weaponry, flags, paintings, lithographs, maps, photos, and documents, the casual visitor can admire large-scale dioramas depicting various battles against French and U.S. forces. The museum is of particular interest to history buffs, and all sides are treated fairly and without animosity in the displays. A plaque commemorates a group of Irish American soldiers from Texas known as the St. Patrick's Battalion, who switched sides during the 1847 invasion, in large part because of to their religious affinity with the Mexicans. Those who survived the battle for Mexico City were executed by the Americans.

(The **Museo Leon Trotsky,** dedicated to the legendary Russian revolutionary who was executed in Mexico City by Stalinist agents, and the **Casa de la Bola,** a museum in a historic mansion, are both discussed in the *Sights* chapter.)

Children's Museums

Popularly known as El Papalote, the excellent **Museo del Niño** (9 A.M.–1 P.M. and 2–6 P.M. Mon.–Fri., 10 A.M.–2 P.M. and 3–7 P.M. Sat.–Sun., tel. 5237-1881, www.papalote.org.mx, admission $3 adults, $2.50 children, free for kids under two) is a bright blue, oddly shaped building just south of the amusement park at the edge of the Periférico. On the premises are 380 "touch, play, and learn" exhibits on science, the human body, communications, and other subjects. The museum has limited capacity, meaning you may have to wait (usually not long) before being allowed into the museum. Tickets can also be bought in advance through TicketMaster (tel. 5325-9000).

Science and Technology Museums

On the square of the the little-visited Santa María de la Ribera neighborhood is UNAM's **Museo de Geología** (tel. 5547-3900, 10 A.M.–5 P.M. Tues.–Sun.), housed in a beautiful old mansion. The displays of meteorites, fossils, and some impressive mammoth skeletons, as well as the opportunity to wander around the old building, are well worth the $1 admission charge. Check out the imposing art nouveau wrought-iron staircase in the entryway. Guided tours of the museum can be arranged by calling ahead and are even available in English if the museum director (who speaks English) is around.

Seemingly lost amid a sea of concrete and traffic, right at the intersection of the Periférico and Avenida Observatorio, is this former Franciscan convent dedicated to San Diego, built in 1590 and now housing the **Museo Nacional de la Cartografía** (10 A.M.–6 P.M. Mon.–Sat., 10 A.M.–4 P.M. Sun., free admission). The red domed building with a simple facade and a small park shaded with palm trees out front has seen a turbulent history. It was taken over by the Dominicans in the late 17th century and was then closed in 1827 by the government because the convent authorities had supported the Spaniards against the Mexican independence movement. During the U.S. invasion in 1847, the church was the site of a prisoner exchange between the Mexicans and the victorious Americans. It was briefly reopened as a church in the late 19th century but was taken over by the government in 1918.

Nowadays the building houses an fascinating museum of maps (fascinating if you like maps, that is) and is run by the Mexican military. Inside are copies of old codices and many maps of Mexico City and the country as a whole, as well as mapmaking gear, such as compasses, cameras, projectors, and GPS instruments, all housed amid the bare walls of the old church. For an idea of Mexico City's prodigious growth, check out the satellite photo showing how the city has changed over 110 years.

Unless you have a particular fascination with the Mexican government's heroic progress in generating power for the country, there's not much to see in the **Museo Tecnológico** (Segunda Sección of Chapultepec Park, tel. 5516-0965, 9 A.M.–5 P.M. daily, free admission), which is dedicated to electricity generation.

Other Museums

In a former Bethlehemite hospital and chapel in the Centro across from the Palacio de Minería is the **Museo del Ejército** (10 A.M.–6 P.M. Tues.–Sat., 10 A.M.–4 P.M. Sun., free admission), dedicated to the soldiers of Mexico. The museum contains armor worn by Spanish conquistadors and Aztec soldiers, plenty of old pistols and rifles, and other assorted military paraphernalia from across the centuries. There's no entrance fee, so it's worth taking a quick look inside if you're in the area, if only to admire the interior of the old church. The museum also boasts a café and gift shop, attended by extremely efficient young soldiers.

Formerly a 16th-century Benedictine convent, the two-story building on Avenida Izazaga at Isabel la Católica is now home to the **Museo Nacional de la Charrería** (tel. 5512-2523, 10 A.M.–7 P.M. Mon.–Fri., free admission), dedicated to Mexico's passion for the *charreada* (a show of horsemanship). The humble little museum contains a few displays of the famed outfits worn by *charros* (horsemen) from Mexico, Spain, Argentina, and Venezuela, along with a collection of swords, saddles, and guns. A .44 caliber pistol once owned by Pancho Villa is the only labeled display. Historical inscriptions, however, are written in Spanish, English, and even French.

The **Museo Nacional de la Estampa** (Hidalgo 43, tel. 5521-2244, 10 A.M.–6 P.M. Tues.–Sun., admission $2), in a reconstructed 16th-century two-story mansion just off the Alameda, is filled with a large collection of printmaking paraphernalia, from the clay seals and agave leaves of precolonial times to modern metal plates. There are also many displays of the prints themselves. Among the most interesting are those that were used to illustrate books and periodicals before the popularization of photography. The latter include works by Manuel Manilla (1830–1890) and José Guadalupe Posadas (1852–1913), both of whom were famous satirical newspaper illustrators in the late 19th century.

The etchings of Aguascalientes native Posadas often feature variations of the *calavera,* or skeleton figure associated with Mexico's Day of the Dead celebration. His most famous *calavera* engraving, *Catrina,* depicts a skeleton wearing an expensive lady's hat ("Catrina" is an old-fashioned slang word used to refer to a well-dressed aristocratic woman) and is on display here, as is his noted Don Quijote skeleton. Great muralists

Rivera and Orozco, who hung around his studio as novice artists, revered Posadas as the first truly Mexican artist in the country's history.

GALLERIES

Mexico City used to be second-best to Guadalajara when it came to art, but those days are changing fast. New galleries are opening regularly, and more and more international artists are seeing D.F. as a place to be. The **Festival del Centro Histórico,** held in three weeks in March, includes a major art show. The Roma and Polanco neighborhoods, in particular, are where most art galleries are found. Check on the Internet at www.arte-mexico.com for an excellent listing of galleries with upcoming openings. The following sections highight some of the best-known galleries in the city, carrying both Mexican and international art.

Roma

Since the Roma began its resurgence during the late 1980s and 1990s, it has become Mexico City's premier location for contemporary art galleries. Most galleries hold regular opening parties; call for information on upcoming exhibitions.

Not technically in the Roma, but right nearby, in the Condesa, **Art & Idea** (Parque España 47, tel. 5211-7192, www.art-idea.com) is a nonprofit gallery with strong links to the international art scene that often shows works by both established and up-and-coming artists from Mexico and around the world.

Espacio de Arte Yvonamor Palix (Córdoba 37–7, tel. 5514-5384, by appointment only 10 A.M.–4 P.M. Mon.–Fri.) has intermittent shows, mainly installations and photography exhibits but some painting exhibits as well.

Galeria Florencia Riestra (Colima 166, tel. 5514-2537, 10 A.M.–7 P.M. Mon.–Fri., 10 A.M.–1 P.M. Sat.) is housed in a lovely 1908 Porfiriato mansion. The main rooms downstairs focus on contemporary Mexican painting and photography. Upstairs, several rooms are crammed with an eclectic collection of colonial art and antiques.

Galería OMR (Plaza Río de Janeiro 54, tel. 5511-1179 or 5207-1080, www.galeriaomr

.com, 10 A.M.–3 P.M. and 4–7 P.M. Mon.–Fri., 10 A.M.–2 P.M. Sat.) carries both Mexican and international contemporary art (mainly paintings and sculpture) in a converted mansion, with frequent group shows and monthly or bimonthly openings.

Nina Menocal (Zacatecas 93, tel. 5564-7209 or 5564-7443, ninart@mail.internet.com.mx, 9 A.M.–7 P.M. Mon.–Fri., 10 A.M.–3 P.M. Sat.) is owned by Cuban expatriates and carries contemporary Latin American art, with an emphasis on young Cuban artists.

Polanco

Polanco is the home to some of Mexico City's finest art galleries, with both Mexican and international modern art. In general, the more established artists are found in Polanco's galleries, unlike the Roma galleries, which tend to work with newer artists. Four well-known galleries in Polanco are the following: **Galería Enrique Guerrero** (Horacio 1549A, tel. 5280-2941), focusing on more established artists; **Galería Lopez Quiroga** (Aristótles 169, tel. 5280-6218, www.arte-mexico.com/eguerrero), specializing in contemporary Latin American and Mexican artists; **Galería Praxis México** (Arquimedes 175, tel. 5254-8813, www.arte-mexico.com/praxismexico), with more experimental Mexican and international art; and **Galería Juan Martín** (Dickens 33B, tel. 5280-0277, www.arte-mexico.com/juanmartin), with more established Mexican artists, such as Francisco Toledo and Vicente Rojo.

Centro

If you're a starving artist and you owe Mexico's government some back taxes, you may have a work in **M Galería SCHP** (República de Guatemala 8, www.shcp.gob.mx/dgpcap, 10 A.M.–6 P.M. daily, free admission), run by the Finance Ministry. It's housed in a colonial building right behind the Catedral. Here artists whose tax payments are delinquent may erase their tax debt by donating works of art. Those interested in seeing an eclectic collection of Mexican modern art might want to take a glance inside to see what they've got up.

THEATER

Mexico City is very rich in live theater, and if you understand Spanish you will undoubtedly find something entertaining, not to mention educational. The weekly *Tiempo Libre* is a good source of information on theater, typically devoting a dozen pages to what's playing and where. Listings are also in the weekend sections of several newspapers (*Primera Fila*, printed on Friday, by *Reforma* is particularly good) and the magazine *D.F.* The Consejo Nacional para la Cultura y las Artes (Conaculta, the National Council for Culture and the Arts) funds many plays. You can find the latest information on Conaculta shows at www.conaculta.gob.mx.

Theaters with regular programming include: **Teatro Helénico** (Av. Revolución 1500, tel. 5662-2945 or 5662-7535); **Teatro La Capilla** (Madrid 13, in Coyoacán, tel. 5659-1139); **Teatro de los Insurgentes** (Av. Insurgentes Sur 1587, tel. 5611-5048); **Teatro Juan Ruiz Alarcón** (Insurgentes Sur 3000, at UNAM's Centro Cultural Universitario, tel. 5665-0709); **Teatro San Rafael** (Virginia Fabregas 40, Colonia San Rafael, tel. 5546-1431); and **Teatro Santa Catarina** (Plaza Santa Catarina 10, in Coyoacán, tel. 5658-0560).

CINEMA

Like other megalopolises—such as New York, London, or Tokyo—Mexico City boasts a thriving cinema scene, with many world-class cinema facilities for viewing commercially distributed films (both international and Mexican), as well as institutes and clubs where films and filmmaking are dissected, critiqued, studied, and treated as a serious art form.

Film fans will find plenty of *cines* (cinemas) and *cineclubes* (film clubs) to choose from for an evening's entertainment, any night of the week. Many cinemas screen first-run American films, typically of the blockbuster genre (but a few art films sneak in as well), along with Mexican reels of all kinds.

Foreign-language films—most of them American, with lesser numbers of French, German, and Italian films—are almost always projected in the original language, with Spanish subtitling. Ticket prices differ depending on the neighborhood and the movie house. Even branches of the same cinema chain will vary their admission prices according to the location. Movie theaters operated by Cinemex, one of the capital's better chains, can vary from $2.40 general admission at one theater (Cinemex Real, on Av. Colón near Metro Hidalgo) to $3.50 at another (Cinemex Galerias, at Ocampo and Bahía de Asención, in the Centro). Compared to cinema-going in other world capitals, viewing first-run, international films in modern Mexico City facilities at these prices is already a bargain, but you can do even better if you attend showings before 6 P.M. (when there is a slight discount most days of the week) or on specified days. In general the theaters in Polanco have the best projection and sound systems—and the highest prices. Note: Almost all Mexico City movie theaters offer half-price tickets on Wednesday.

Tiempo Libre carries extensive listings for current cinema showings in the capital, along with critical reviews in Spanish. The bigger daily newspapers also carry film listings; *Reforma* offers one of the more complete ones.

At least two local chains maintain their own websites, complete with addresses and phone numbers for all cinema outlets, ticket prices, and the titles of current film screenings: www.cinemex.com.mx and www.cinepolis.com.mx. Tickets for films showing at Cinemex theaters can be booked by phone at tel. 5257-6969.

The following cinemas tend to show a preponderance of first-run American films, both independent and major studio productions, interspersed with occasional Mexican, Italian, and French films.

Cinemark Polanco (Miguel de Cervantes Saavedra 397, Polanco, tel. 5580-0506); **Cinemex Casa de Arte** (Anatole France 120, Polanco, tel. 5280-9156); **Cinemex Loreto** (Altamirano 46, Tizapán San Ángel, tel. 5550-0914); **Cinemex Palacio Chino** (Iturbide 21, Metro Hidalgo, Juárez, tel. 5512-0348); **Cinemex Plaza Insurgentes** (San Luis Potosí 214, at Insurgentes Sur, Roma, tel. 5264-7079); **Cinemex Real**

CINE MEXICANO

Mexico's first cinema opened on Avenida Plateros (now Avenida Madero) in Mexico City on August 16, 1896, a few months after the Lumière brothers had premiered their famous cinematic projection system in Paris. *Capitalinos* took to the silver screen with great enthusiasm; statistics indicate that by 1902 Mexico City boasted more than 300 cinemas and 1,000 separate screenings per year.

Popular Mexican films run the gamut, from drama to comedy to action pictures, with a high number of what might be called "cops and cowboys" films, which focus on struggles between Mexican police agencies and *narcotraficantes* (drug traffickers). As in the *narco-corridos* that celebrate the exploits of Robin Hood–like drug smugglers in song, such movies often extol smugglers' honor over police corruption. *Lucha libre* (professional Mexican wrestling, in which the opponents wear full head masks) films make up another curious subgenre of Mexican film. The longest-lasting of these is a series of B horror/detective films featuring El Santo, Mexico's most famous *luchador*, with such titles as *Santo contra los zombies (Santo Against the Zombies), Santo contra las mujeres vampiro (Santo Against the Vampire Women)*, and *Santo: la leyenda del enmascarado de plata (Santo: The Legend of the Silver Masking)*. Other Mexican productions have inserted masked wrestlers into all sorts of movie formulae.

In the 1940s and 1950s, Mexican films went through a high point known today as *la época de oro* (the golden age) for the quality of films produced. This was the era of great singer/actors such as Pedro Infante and Jorge Negrete, the dazzling actresses Maria Felix and Dolores del Río, and legendary comedian Cantínflas. Of the many top directors of the era, two of the best-known are Emilio "El Indio" Fernández and Alejandro Galindo, and cinematographer Gabriel Figueroa is considered one of the best ever in Mexico.

Mexico's cinematic tradition slipped in the 1960s and 1970s, with only a few classics shot during these years. An exception was the work of the father of cinematic surrealism, Luis Buñuel. Born in Spain in 1900, Buñuel moved to Mexico in the 1940s and directed some of his greatest cinematic works in his adopted homeland, including *Los olvidados* (1950), *Él* (1955), and *El ángel exterminador* (1962), before dying in Mexico City in 1983.

Another watershed art film made in Mexico, *El Topo* (1971), sees a nameless gunfighter travel from one bizarre village landscape to another in what could be a surreal version of a Kurosawa or Sergio Leone/Clint Eastwood epic. Alejandro Jodorowsky (Chilean-born but a Mexican resident) directed the film, wrote the story, composed most of the music, and designed both sets and costumes. Both Buñuel and Jodorowsky were major influences on American director David Lynch.

Ariel de Oro (the Mexican equivalent of the Oscar) winner *Cronos*, directed in 1992 by Guadalajara native Guillermo del Toro, employs del Toro's trademark insect imagery and fondness for religious relics to create a story of a Mexican antique dealer who comes upon a strange scarablike mechanism that promises eternal life yet leads to the inevitable tragic end.

A more international hit was 1992's *Like Water for Chocolate (Como agua para chocolate)*. Based on Laura Esquivel's recipe-studded novel of love, lust, and gustation, and adapted for the screen by her director husband Alfonso Arau, the film is considered one of the most successful transitions of Latin American literature's magic realism to the screen. *Chocolate* was filmed in Piedras Negras, Coahuila, near the U.S.–Mexico border. Two other films shot in *la frontera* that have become cult international hits include action thrillers *El Mariachi* (1992) and *Desperado* (1995), both directed by Mexican American Richard Rodriguez on shoestring budgets.

In 1995 *El Callejón de los milagros (Alley of Miracles)* not only won Mexico's Ariel de Oro but became the most critically acclaimed film in Mexican history, earning 49 cinema awards around the globe. Loosely based on a novel by renowned Egyptian author Naguib Mahfouz and directed by Jorge Fons, the film paints a complex portrait of the interwoven lives of a cantina owner, a tarot card reader, a prostitute, and a small-time landlady in downtown Mexico City. Like several other Mexican art films, it was produced by the Universidad de Guadalajara with support from the Instituto Mexicano de Cinematografía (Mexican Institute of Cinematography, or Imcine) and Fondo de Fomento a la Calidad Cinematográfica (Fund in Support of Cinematic Quality).

In recent years Mexican cinema seems to be on the upswing again, with several excellent releases that have done well both in Mexico and abroad. The 1999 film *La ley de Herodes (Herod's Law)*, directed by Luis Estrada, is an extremely entertaining political satire which, for the first time in Mexican movies, explicitly skewered the then-ruling PRI party, as well as the now-ruling PAN, the Catholic church, and much else besides. It chronicles the travails of a PRI flunky in a small village in the 1950s who is picked to be town mayor, and who proves quite adept at extorting, lying, cheating, and murdering his way to PRI glory.

But the real international breakthrough came with the brilliant *Amores perros* (dubiously translated in the English release as *Love's a Bitch*), filmed in 2000 by Alejandro González Iñárritu. The harrowing, at times painfully realistic, movie follows the stories of three groups of Mexico City residents whose lives are brought together by a horrific car accident. By far the most moving of the stories is of a lower-class youth (played by rising film start Gael García Bernal) who falls in love with his brother's wife, and who begins to make money by bringing his pet rottweiler, Coffee, to underground dog fights. The movie won more than 30 prizes around the world and was nominated for an Oscar for best foreign film.

Filmed in 2001 and released in the U.S. in 2002, *Y tu mamá también*, directed by Alfonso Cuaron, garnered plenty of foreign attention as well. The story, starring (again) García Bernal along with Diego Luna and Maribel Verdu, is a road movie of sorts with a heavy sexual emphasis, following the trip of two young friends who take an older Spanish woman with them to the beach. The movie is entertaining and marks a significant step in the pushing back of boundaries for sexual content in mainstream Mexican film. Some more recent releases include the hugely popular crime thriller *Nicotina* (2003) starring Diego Luna and *El Misterio de Trinidad* (2003), a treasure-hunting story that won several film awards in Mexico and Spain.

Arts and Entertainment

(Colón 17, Centro, tel. 5512-7718); **Cinépolis Bucareli** (Bucareli 63, Metro Balderas, tel. 5535-9002); **Lumiere Hipódromo Condesa** (Progreso 1, between Av. Jalisco and Av. Revolución, Colonia Tacubaya, tel. 5272-2649); **Lumiere Reforma** (Río Guadalquivir 104, at Paseo de la Reforma, tel. 5514-0000); **Lumiere Telmex** (Av. Cuauhtémoc 19, Colonia Roma, tel. 5525-3598); **Multimax Continental** (Av. Coyoacán 116, at Xola, Del Valle, tel. 5687-5457.)

Cineclubes

Several nonprofit venues screen smaller independent films and art films, typically for one or two nights only. One of the premier facilities is the government-supported **Cineteca Nacional** (Av. México Coyoacán 389, tel. 1253-9300). Typical admission prices are $3 general admission, $1 for students with identification. The Cineteca building contains five projection rooms, which means five different films are screened every night of the week. Also on the premises are a library and bookstore. For the latest schedule, see *Tiempo Libre* or the Friday arts section of *Reforma*. Classes in film history, such as "La historia de México, vista a través del cine" (The History of Mexico Viewed Through Cinema) and "Cine y literatura" (Cinema and Literature) are offered on weekday nights and on Saturday.

Sala José Revueltas (Insurgentes 3000, Ciudad Universitaria, tel. 5665-0709) is in the Centro Cultural Universitario complex on the national university grounds. Another nonprofit venue showing oldies and more unusual films is the **Cinematógrafo del Chopo** (Dr. Atl 37, Santa María La Ribera, tel. 5546-1245, admission $2, students $1).

Other *cineclub* showings occur in a screening room at the **Museo de Arte Carillo Gil,** in San Ángel, and at these three Centro Histórico locations: **Biblioteca de México** (La Ciudadela 4); **Biblioteca Nacional de Educación** (Leandro Valle 20); and **Salón Cinematográfico Fósforo** (San Ildefonso 43). Check newspapers for listings of upcoming movies.

LITERATURE

Elaborate hieroglyphic books and a priest-dominated literary tradition existed in the New World before the arrival of the Spaniards. But many scholars consider the fantastic chronicles of newly arrived Spanish soldiers, explorers, and priests as the first flowering of a truly Mexican literature, early expressions of what would become enduring Mexican themes: being caught between Indian and European worlds, and the fall from (or destruction of) an Edenic paradise.

Two examples of this genre, widely available in English translation, make for compelling reading. Bernal Diaz del Castillo's *Conquest of New Spain* is the memoir of a foot soldier in Cortés's military campaign against the Aztec empire. With just 400 men, superior weaponry, horses, and the help of Indian tribes in thrall to the Aztecs, the Spaniards marched into Tenochtitlán, the heart of the empire, and triumphed against an army numbering in the tens of thousands.

A very different view can be found in Bartolomé de las Casas's *Brevísima relación de la destrucción de las Indias (Brief Account of the Devastation of the Indies),* which details the astounding brutality that the invaders visited upon the people of not just the West Indies but much of what was then called the New World. De las Casas, a priest who accompanied many expeditions, raised the first voice of protest against Spanish destruction of native peoples and cultures.

The colonial era produced many authors who tried to imitate the prevailing styles in Europe. One colonial-era writer whose work has outlived that of most of her contemporaries is Sor Juana Inés de la Cruz, a remarkable nun, poet, and playwright. Her *Repuesta (The Reply),* a reply to a bishop who censured her and wrote of how women's role in the Catholic church should be severely limited, has become a feminist classic and is available in English translation, often accompanied by her poems, the best known of which is *Primer Sueño (First Dream).*

Modern Mexican writers—including Juan Rulfo, Octavio Paz, Carlos Fuentes, Mariano Azuela, Agustín Yáñez, Elena Poniatowska, and Rosario Castellanos—enjoy success outside of Mexico as well as in their native land. Rulfo's *Pedro Páramo,* published in 1955, is a hallucinatory novel well worth deciphering. Some consider it Latin America's first magical realist novel. Paz's *Labyrinth of Solitude* comprises classic essays that address the mysteries of Mexican identity. Poniatowska's *Massacre in Mexico* is an account of the 1968 killings of protesting Mexico City students by government troops. All are available in English translation. Another excellent observer of Mexican character and society is Carlos Monsiváis, whose *Rituales del Caos* is a collection of essays on life in Mexico City; it's available in Spanish only.

Two Colombian writers long residing in Mexico City, Gabriel García Marquéz and Álvaro Mútis, have also garnered international acclaim for their fiction, which is set in Latin American locales and imbued with a distinctly Latin perspective. The fact that these two literary stars have chosen to live and write in Mexico City says much about the capital's intellectual environment. Both have several works available in English translation.

Paco Ignacio Taibo II writes detective novels set in Mexico City, often from the bicultural view of a character or characters who move back and forth between Mexico and the United States. Taibo novels that are available in English translation include *De Paso, Four Hands, Just Passing Through, Some Clouds,* and *Leonardo's Bicycle.*

Of the many current Mexican writers, Guillermo Fadanelli is definitely worth a read, if your Spanish is up to it. His gritty, realistic, and funny novels and stories are set in contemporary Mexico City. Two of his better-known works are *¿Te veré en el desayuno?* and *La otra cara de Rock Hudson.* José Emilio Pacheco's novella *Las batallas en el desierto,* set in the Roma neighborhood of Mexico City, is a great read and is easy to follow, even if your Spanish is not excellent. Other current fiction writers include Sara Shefkovich, Mario González Suárez, Mario Bellatin, Mauricio Montiel, and Ignacio Padilla. Padilla's 2000 novel, *Amphytrion* (translated in English under the title *Shadow Without a Name*), got a lot of attention but has nothing to do with Mexico: it's set in Europe during World War I,

where two strangers exchange identities as a result of a chess game on a train.

One great novel that takes place mainly in Mexico City is *Los Detectives Salvajes,* by Chilean expatriate Roberto Bolaño. It's about a group of idealistic (or just weird) young poets in D.F. who call themselves the *real viceralistas,* and it offers a great portrait of one of the many subcultures of the city.

Works by all of these authors can be found in many Mexico City bookstores. Two good ones are Librería Gandhi, on the Alameda and in Coyoacán, and El Péndulo, in Condesa and the Zona Rosa. (See the *Shopping* chapter for more details.)

Festivals and Events

Like Mexicans around the country, *capitalinos* love a fiesta. Any occasion will suffice as an excuse to hold a celebration, from a birthday or promotion to a chile harvest. Add to all the civic possibilities the vast number of Mexican Catholic religious holidays, and there's potential for some kind of public fiesta at least every week of the year, if not all 365 days. Besides the national religious holidays, there are feast days for 115 Catholic saints per year, 9 or 10 each month. Any pueblo or *colonia* (neighborhood) named for a saint will usually hold a fiesta on the feast day of its namesake. Individuals named for saints will often host parties on their *día de santo* (saint's day).

The primary requisites of a fiesta are plenty of food (especially tamales, considered a festive dish), beer and liquor, music, and dancing. More elaborate celebrations include parades, exhibitions, *charreadas,* and occasional fireworks.

Some of the more memorable yearly events and public holidays observed in Mexico City are highlighted below by month. Actual dates may vary from year to year, so be sure to check with the appropriate tourist office in advance.

Government offices and some businesses close on national holidays. You may want to call ahead to find out.

January
- **New Year's Day:** January 1 is an official holiday.
- **Día de los Santos Reyes:** January 6.

February
- **Constitution Day:** February 5 is an official holiday.
- **Flag Day:** February 24 is an official holiday.

March/April
- **Feria de la Flor Más Bella del Ejido:** Xochimilco celebrates its floriculture, its main claim to fame for at least 400 years. Among the events are a beauty contest; cooking demos; exhibitions of agriculture, cattle, and handicrafts; and a contest for the best-decorated *trajinera* (gondola). Dates vary from year to year.
- **Día de San José:** Celebrated in Ixtapalapa, Santa Ana Tlacotenco (Milpa Alta), Tláhuac, Santiago Tepalcatlalpan (Xochimilco), and San Bernabé Ocotepec (Contreras) with music, processions, dances, fireworks and fairs. March 17.
- **Birthday of Benito Juárez:** March 21 is an official holiday.
- **Festival del Centro Histórico:** This two-week cultural celebration, held each April in the Centro, features concerts, theater performances, art exhibits, seminars, dance,

COURTESY OF MEXICO TOURISM BOARD/CARLOS SANCHEZ

The Semana Santa festival often involves dressing up in elaborate costumes like these "Roman soldiers."

gastronomical events, and activities for children. This festival usually coincides with an especially beautiful time of the year in Mexico City when the jacaranda trees are in full bloom. Dates vary from year to year.

- **Feria de Nieves:** Santiago Tulyehualco (Xochimilco). Exhibition and sale of ice creams and *nieves* (Mexican ices), from the usual favorites to more exotic flavors, including mole, tequila, and *nopal*. Dates vary from year to year.

- **Semana Santa:** Easter Week or "Holy Week" (usually in April, sometimes in late March) is second only to Christmas as the most important holiday period of the year. One of the most prominent Semana Santa customs is breaking *cascarones,* colored eggs stuffed with confetti, over the heads of friends and family. Besides attending Mass on Good Friday and Easter Sunday, many Mexicans take this opportunity to go on vacations. Mexican beach resorts can be overcrowded this week with a large influx of both Mexicans and North Americans.

The Passion Play is reenacted at Ixtapalapa, a *colonia* nine kilometers southeast of the Zócalo. A young man portrays Christ and a young woman becomes Mary—both must be locally born virgins. On Good Friday, around 150 people gather in Ixtapalapa's central plaza to watch the Christ figure suffer mock beatings and a real crown of thorns. Then the young man must drag a 80-kilogram wooden cross for a distance of four kilometers to the summit of Cerro de la Estrella, a hill considered sacred since the prehispanic era. There he will be tied to the cross and ritually "crucified" before his attendants carry him back down the hill (and to a hospital to make sure he's still healthy).

May

- **International Worker's Day:** May 1 is an official holiday.

- **Cinco de Mayo:** This festival commemorates the defeat of an attempted French invasion at Puebla de los Angeles on Mexico's Gulf of Mexico coast in 1862. It features music, dance, food, and other cultural events. In the capital, the biggest celebration is held at Ixtapalapa. May 5.

- **Mother's Day** (Día de las Madres): May 10.

June
• **Navy Day:** June 1 is an official holiday.

July
• **Día de Santiago:** This fiesta for St. James is held in the Plaza de las Tres Culturas, where a great number of groups gather to perform their folkloric dances, wearing traditional costumes. Fireworks, art exhibits, and a handicrafts market are also on hand. July 25.

August
• **Commemoration of the Defense of Mexico and the Fall of Tenochtitlán:** At the Plaza de las Tres Culturas, the handsomely costumed *concheros* and many other groups entertain with dances to celebrate the temporary victory of the Aztecs over the Spaniards before the fall of Tenochtitlán. Aspects of the celebration are also held on elegant Paseo de la Reforma, in the Zócalo, and in front of the monument to Cuauhtémoc—the Aztec Emperor who led his armies in defense of the city. August 13.

September
• **Mexican Independence Day** (Fiesta Patria de la Independencia): Also called *diez y seis* (sixteen), since it falls on the 16th, this holiday celebrates the country's independence from Spain, as announced in 1810 by Father Hidalgo in the town of Dolores, Guanajuato. Festivities actually begin on the 15th and last two days, with fireworks, parades, *charreadas,* music, and folkdance performances. Activities in Mexico City are centered on the Zócalo, where at 11 P.M. on the 15th, the president of Mexico—and the crowds congregated on the square below—call out Father Hidalgo's cry for independence—*El Grito.* There is a huge parade through the Centro Histórico on the 16th. September 15 and 16.

October
• **Día de la Raza:** Celebrated as Columbus Day north of the border, in Mexico, it commemorates the founding of the Mexican "race" *(raza)* as heralded by the arrival of Columbus in the New World. October 12.

November
• **Día de los Muertos:** The Day of the Dead is Mexico's third most important holiday and corresponds to Europe's All Saints' Day except that it's celebrated on the 1st and 2nd of November instead of only the 1st. Some of the festivities are held in cemeteries, where children clean the headstones and crucifixes of their deceased relatives *(los difuntos)* and play games unique to this fiesta. In some areas the faithful spend an entire day and night beside the family graves. Roadside shrines throughout Mexico are laid with fresh flowers and other tributes to the dead. Offerings of *pan de los muertos* (bread of the dead) and food and liquor are placed before family altars on behalf of deceased family members, along with papier-mâché or sugar skulls *(calaveras)* and skeletons. Short plays are occasionally performed in local theaters or large cemeteries, especially the melodrama *Don Juan Tenorio,* in which a murderer finds redemption through his victim's ghost. Colorful remembrances, with smaller crowds, are held in San Lucas Xochimanca (Ixtapalapa), Santa Cecilia Tepetlapa (Xochimilco), and San Antonio Tecómitl (Milpa Alta). This holiday is also referred to as Fiesta de Todos los Santos (All Saints' Festival) and Festival de los Fieles Difuntos (Festival of the Deceased Faithful). November 1 and 2.
• **Día de la Revolución:** The anniversary of the 1910 Revolution is an official holiday. November 20.

December
• **Día de Nuestra Señora de Guadalupe:** The feast day of the Virgin of Guadalupe, Mexico's patron saint. Special Masses are held that day throughout Mexico. The nearest Sunday to the 12th also features special events, such as mariachi Masses, food booths, and games. The celebrations at the Basílica de Nuestra Señora de Guadalupe, in northern Mexico City, are particularly well attended, and the *basílica* becomes an annual focus of pilgrimage, especially among Mexico's Amerindians. It's also called Fiesta Guadalupana. December 12.

- **Las Posadas:** Beginning on December 16; Mexicans hold nightly *posadas*—candlelight processions terminating at elaborate, community-built nativity scenes—in commemoration of the Holy Family's search for lodging. The processions continue for nine consecutive nights. Other activities include piñata parties where children break open hanging papier-mâché figures filled with small gifts and candy. Churches large and small hold continuous Christmas Masses beginning at midnight on the 25th (Día de la Navidad, or Christmas).

Las Posadas culminates on January 6, which is Día de los Santos Reyes (literally, Day of the King-Saints), referring to the story of the Three Wise Men. On this day Mexican children receive their Christmas gifts, and family and friends gather to eat a wreath-shaped fruitcake called *rosca de reyes* (wreath of the kings) baked especially for this occasion. Hidden inside each *rosca* is a small clay figurine *(muñeco)* that represents the infant Jesus. While sharing the *rosca* on this day, the person whose slice contains the *muñeco* is obliged to host a *candelaria*, or Candlemas party, on February 2, for everyone present.

At the *candelaria*—which commemorates the day the newborn Jesus was first presented at the temple in Jerusalem—the host traditionally displays a larger Christ-infant figure and serves tamales and *atole*, a thick, hot grain drink flavored with fruit or chocolate.

Shopping

Mexico City has been an entrepôt of trade for many centuries—even before the legendary markets of Tlatelolco that so dazzled the Spanish conquistadors, with produce from across the Aztec empire sold in orderly stalls under vigilant imperial guards. Markets still thrive today all over this huge city, selling anything you can imagine, and they are joined by the luxury shops of Polanco with the latest imported fashions, specialized block-long strips of stores in the Centro (like the booksellers of Donceles or the electronics shops on República de Uruguay), and street ven-

dors handing a bouquet of divine-smelling gardenias for $0.75 cents through your car window as you're waiting at a red light. If you want it in D.F., you can buy it.

Shoppers will find plenty of places to buy arts and handicrafts from across Mexico. Mercado Ciudadela, near the Centro, and the crafts market in the Zona Rosa are good places to start, but better quality can be had at the weekend markets in Coyoacán and San Ángel, or at a number of upscale shops throughout the city.

Apart from the places discussed in this chapter, consider

Mexico City's Best

M Best Bookstore: With a large selection of Spanish-language literature, **Librería Gandhi,** with branches in the Centro and Coyoacán, is one of the best bookstores in the city (page 157).

M Best Quality Handicrafts: If you're looking for top-quality handicrafts, never mind the price, head to one of the government-run **FONART** stores. They carry some of the finest, well-made traditional artwork you can find anywhere in Mexico, including ceramics, jewelry, and weavings (page 158).

M Best Ceramics: In Polanco, a branch of the famed Puebla ceramic makers **Uriarte Talavera** is where you'll find beautiful (but pricey) dishware with the shop's distinctive designs (page 158).

M Best Place to Buy Tequila: There's any number of stores with extensive tequila selections in Mexico City, but one particularly good one is **La Naval** (page 158).

M Best High-End Shopping: You'll find all the top international fashion shops, including Luis Vuitton, Salvatore Ferragamo, and Hermès on the upscale **Avenida Presidente Mazaryk** (page 159).

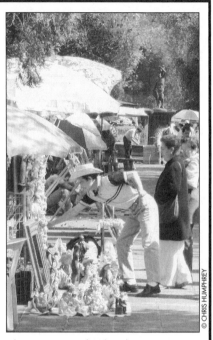

© CHRIS HUMPHREY

shoppers at a weekend market

M Best Budget Handicrafts: A maze of little walkways, **La Ciudadela** market has more than a hundred little shops selling all kinds of handicrafts. These aren't necessarily the most finely crafted goods available, but prices are low (bargaining is expected) and the huge selection makes it an easy place to buy some last-minute gifts (page 160).

M Best Art Market: Housed in a colonial-era building off San Ángel's main square, **Bazar Sábado** might be the best place in the country to buy artwork. This Saturday market gathers several dozen of

the finest artisans in the city. Prices are not cheap, but the paintings and crafts available are well worth it (page 163).

M Best Herbal Remedies: Looking for a love potion to charm someone or a talisman to ward off bad luck? Then head directly to the bustling **Mercado Sonora.** This isn't a tourist destination, but it is an amazing spectacle, with squawking birds (many of them endangered species) and all sorts of mysterious powders and liquids (page 165).

taking a shopping trip to one of the cities and towns around Central Mexico, where you'll often find a better selection and lower prices. Puebla is a great destination for handicrafts, particularly for the renowned Talavera dishware, and Taxco is justly famed for its silver jewelry. (For details on these and other shopping destinations outside Mexico City, see the *Excursions* chapter.)

What to Buy

TEXTILES AND CLOTHING

Mexican Indians still produce prehispanic-style textiles such as the *huipil* (sleeveless tunic) and *quechquemitl* (close-shouldered cape) in the States of Morelos, Guerrero, Oaxaca, and Chiapas, and on the Yucatán Peninsula. Another *yucateco* specialty, the cool *guayabera* shirt worn by men in the tropics worldwide, is made in Mérida. The nearby weaving center of Tixkokob produces the country's finest hammocks.

Mexico's famous *rebozos* (shawls) come from San Luis Potosí, while the finest serapes and *jorongos* (ponchos) are made in Saltillo and Zacatecas, amid Mexico's largest wool-producing region.

Among the many types of embroidered, woven, and beaded shoulder bags produced throughout Mexico, those of the Huicholes in Jalisco, Nayarit, and Durango are the most popular. Also often sought are bright, psychedelic Huichol yarn paintings.

The States of Zacatecas, Durango, Nuevo León, and Tamaulipas produce the finest *charreada* costumery—sequined sombreros, embroidered *charro* jackets, and tight-fitting, *concho* (shell)-studded trousers.

CERAMICS

Mexico boasts an astounding number of potters and pottery styles, natural legacies of ancient Amerindian ceramic traditions. Among the most highly valued by collectors are polychromatic Pueblo-style ceramics from Chihuahua's Casas Grandes area, green-glazed pots from Michoacán, rainbow-hued vessels and black Zapotec jars from Oaxaca, and Puebla's famous tin-glazed Talavera plates and bowls. Potters immigrating from Talavera de la Reina in Spain settled in Puebla, where they fashioned majolica-inspired pottery that became known as Talavera. Although the best pieces still hail from Puebla, much Talavera today comes from potters' workshops in Dolores Hidalgo, in the State of Guanajuato. Usually the place of origin will be marked on the bottom of the piece, but after a while you may be able to tell the difference without checking the inscriptions.

Smaller ceramic pieces fashioned into brightly colored human and animal shapes—some functioning as candelabras or receptacles, others purely decorative—are everyday folk art throughout the country.

The enamel used to color-finish some Mexican ceramic products may contain lead. This doesn't usually pose a health problem for decorative pieces, but if you plan to use Mexican pottery as cooking or eating utensils, you should buy articles *sin plomo* (without lead) to avoid accidental lead ingestion. Although cynics point out that Mexicans have been using leaded utensils for centuries without any perceived harm to themselves, it doesn't hurt to be on the cautious side. Nowadays many Mexican ceramicists create lead-free products whose characteristics surpass those of traditional enamelware and which are available at accessible prices. As recommended by FONART (Fomento de las Artesanías), such pieces may be marked EBT-SP, signifying *esmalte baja temperatura sin plomo* (low temperature enamelware without lead).

JEWELRY

Well-crafted silver *(plata)* jewelry is plentiful and relatively inexpensive throughout Mexico. The finest work comes from Taxco, Guanajuato, and Zacatecas. Look for ".925" stamped into silver products; this means they're 92.5 percent silver,

M
Shopping

the highest quality. You'll also come across *alpaca,* an alloy of copper, nickel, and zinc that looks like silver and costs a third to a half less than the real thing.

The best gold *(oro)* jewelry is said to come from Oaxaca, where Zapotec women regard gold adornments as the most important source of portable wealth. Most pieces are fashioned from 12-carat gold, though some may feature 24-carat plating.

Elaborate earrings, bracelets, and necklaces strung together from semiprecious or nonprecious materials such as turquoise, amber, beads, bone, and onyx have been popular throughout Mexico since the artist Frida Kahlo painted herself wearing prehispanic jewelry. Though fashioned mostly in the central and southern states, this jewelry is sold all over the country.

LEATHERWORK AND SADDLERY

Mexico is home to many expert leatherworkers, a tradition inherited from Spain. Workers in the ranching areas of northern Mexico—particularly the States of Zacatecas, Coahuila, Nuevo León, and Tamaulipas—produce the best belts, bolo ties, boots, leather jackets, gloves, chaps, spurs, bridles, and saddles.

BASKETS AND HATS

A wide range of plant materials are used to fashion Mexican baskets, including palm strips, agave fibers, grass, pine needles, and henequen. High-quality baskets *(cesta, canasta)* are handwoven by the Seri, Yaqui, and Papago Indians of Sonora; the Tarahumara of Chihuahua; and the Mixtecs of Oaxaca. Seri baskets are woven so tightly they're capable of holding liquids; the Seri once used large baskets as rafts to cross the Río Colorado.

Rural Mexicans and Amerindians make and wear an incredible variety of hats, from the wavy-brimmed but stiff Texas-style headgear in Chihuahua to the flat-brimmed, round-crowned sunbusters of the Yucatán. A Mexican hat blocker can reshape just about any woven, natural-fiber hat to fit your head.

WOOD

Wood-carving thrives as a folk art applied to everyday housewares as well as decorative objects. Orangewood combs from Oaxaca, guitars from Michoacán, and cedar *rebozo* boxes from San Luis Potosí are some of the more notable wood arts. Many different Mexican Indian cultures throughout Mexico fashion finely carved and lacquered wooden masks for use in tribal ceremonies; most of the masks seen in souvenir shops are knockoffs produced by carvers in Guerrero or Michoacán.

OTHER CRAFTS

Retablos, religious paintings on wood or tin, are commonly found near religious centers. Lacquered gourds and boxes from Guerrero, Michoacán, and Chiapas represent Mexico's finest lacquerwork.

Ironwork, another legacy of the Spanish, is a specialty of Central Mexico, though wrought-iron furniture, gates, doors, and windows are common throughout the country.

Alebrijes are brightly painted, fantastically shaped animal-like sculptures carved of wood or fashioned from papier-mâché. The very first *alebrijes* were created in Mexico City by Pedro Linares, who created the figures after they appeared to him in a series of dreams, or nightmares, during a long illness. Seeing that the figures sold well among tourists and collectors, residents of Oaxaca later took up the craft and today the pieces are available throughout Mexico.

Glasswork is a popular purchase in Mexico for foreign tourists. Most handicraft shops carry a variety of colored or tinted glass sets.

To get an inkling of the full range of arts and crafts in Mexico, visit the Museo Franz Mayer and Museo Nacional de Culturas Populares (see the *Arts and Entertainment* chapter for more information).

Where to Shop

ANTIQUES

Plaza del Ángel Antiques Center (Centro de Antigüedades) (off Calle Hamburgo in the Zona Rosa, 10 A.M.–8 P.M. daily) brings together more than 30 stores selling antique furniture, paintings, art objects, silver, and other articles—much of it high-end goods from the 19th century. Most shops can arrange shipping anywhere in the world. Some shops have more erratic hours. On Saturday and Sunday, a flea market in antiques, typically featuring more than 100 exhibitors, convenes in the open hallways of the plaza (10 A.M.–4 P.M.).

BOOKSHOPS

In the Centro Histórico, the best overall bookshop for both English- and Spanish language books is **Ⓝ Librería Gandhi** (Av. Juárez 4, tel. 5510-4231, www.gandhi.mx.com). Gandhi also sells audio CDs. Gandhi has several other branches, including one in Coyoacán (Av. M. A. de Quevedo 134, tel. 5661-0911) that features an upstairs café. The **American Bookstore** recently moved to a smaller space at Bolívar 23, just south of Madero, and doesn't have the excellent selection it used to, but you'll find a decent collection of English-language novels and history books.

The bookstore on the ground floor of the **Palacio de Bellas Artes** is chock-full of English- and Spanish-language books on art. Most of Mexico City's larger art museums contain similarly oriented bookshops.

Calle Donceles in the Centro is lined with shops selling used books east of Calle Palma Norte, more or less behind the Catedral Metropolitana. **Librería Hermanos de Hoja** is good for art books; **El Mercader de Libros** has a large general-interest selection; and **El Laberinto,** across the street, is also good hunting grounds.

In San Ángel, **Librería Miguel Ángel Porrúa** (Amargura 4, tel. 5616-2705), near the Plaza del Carmen, is a bookstore that also happens to be a publisher of finely bound and printed books

on Mexican history and art. Very little in English is available, but if you read Spanish and are interested in these fields, you'll find plenty to spend your money on.

The Roma has one of the best art bookstores in the city, **Librería Pegaso** (Casa Lamm, Orizaba 99, tel. 5208-0171). Nearby, along Avenida Álvaro Obregón, is a string of stores with both new and used books. Two right next to each other are **Através del Espejo** (A. Obregon 118A, tel. 5264-0246), and **Librería Ático** (A. Obregón 118B, tel. 5584-7627). In the Condesa is **El Péndulo** (Av. Nuevo León 115, tel. 5286-9493, www.pendulo.com, 9 A.M.–11 P.M. Mon.–Fri., 9 A.M.–midnight Sat., 9 A.M.– 10 P.M. Sun.), with an excellent selection of Spanish-language books. El Péndulo also has a store in the Zona Rosa (Hamburgo 126, tel. 5208-2327).

If you read Spanish and are interested in literature on Mexican history, archaeology, or culture, stop into the **Librería del Instituto Nacional de Antropología e Historia** (Córdoba 43, tel. 5514-0420, 9 A.M.–6 P.M. Mon.–Fri., 9 A.M.–3 P.M. Sat.), in the Roma.

Most branches of **Sanborns** carry a limited selection of Spanish- and English-language books, newspapers, and magazines.

Tower Records (Pabellón Altavista, Calzado Al Desierto los Leones 52, Colonia San Ángel, tel. 5616-5267) carries a good selection of books and magazines in English.

CIGAR SHOPS

Cigar smokers will love Mexico City, which abounds in places to indulge one's taste for brown torpedoes. Apart from the shops mentioned below, most of the upscale hotels and several shops at the airport sell cigars from Cuba, Mexico, and elsewhere in Latin America (cigars from the Dominican Republic and Honduras can be very good).

In the Centro, **Little Havana Cigar Shop** (Av. San Jerónimo 630, tel. 5568-1891) is a Cuban specialist. **La Hoja del Tabaco** a busy side street in the Centro's commercial district

(Uruguay 12, tel. 5518-5200), also in the Centro, emphasizes Mexican brands but also carries *Cubanos*.

La Casa del Habano (Plaza Mazaryk mall on Av. Mazaryk, tel. 5282-1046), in the upscale Polanco neighborhood, is a little pricey, but they have a decent selection, especially of Cubans.

In the Roma, **Los Puros de la Roma** (Zacatecas 184, between Monterrey and Tonalá, tel. 5264-4076) specializes in Cuban cigars starting from $5. Just up the street is **Puros Churchill** (Zacatecas 172, tel. 5584-0239), a small cigar factory using leaf from Veracruz, Eastern Mexico. Factory tours (in Spanish) can be arranged by calling in advance. It also has a small store in front.

Note that if you're planning on bringing Cuban cigars to the U.S., you'll be violating the American trade embargo against Cuba. If U.S. customs finds a couple of cigars during an inspection of your luggage, the usual practice is to confiscate them, nothing more, although you're legally liable for a very stiff fine. When I got nabbed with three lovely Romeo y Julieta Churchills, I pleaded in vain with the customs

agent that they were for me and my two brothers for a wedding, but he was unsympathetic and shredded them before my eyes. If you try to smuggle in a full box or more, you might be in for trouble.

HANDICRAFTS

The best places to buy handicrafts are generally the markets in Mexico City, as well as in several cities and towns in the Mexico City vicinity, like Puebla, Taxco, Tepoztlán (see the *Excursions* chapter for details). In terms of stores in the city, the best place to start is FONART's **Museo de Artes Populares** (Av. Juárez 89, tel. 5521-0171, 10 A.M.–7 P.M. Mon.–Sat.), near the Alameda; it's a combination handicraft museum/store. The merchandise—silver, onyx, pottery, baskets, textiles, and more—is of excellent quality; prices are nonnegotiable and fairly steep. **M FONART** (Patriotismo 691, tel. 5563-4060, 9 A.M.–8 P.M. Mon.–Sat., 10 A.M.–7 P.M. Sun.) has another slightly larger branch in the south part of the city.

The offices of the art magazine *Artes de México* (Córdoba 69, in the Roma, tel. 5208-3205 or 5525-5905, www.artesdemexico.com, 10 A.M.–3 P.M. and 4–5:30 P.M. Mon.–Fri.) has a small but good handicrafts shop. The store also carries back issues of the magazine, which features informative articles on different Mexican arts and handicrafts.

Top-quality (and pricey) Talavera ceramics from Puebla can be bought at **M Uriarte Talavera** (Alejandro Dumas 77, tel. 5282-2849, www.uriartetalavera.com.mx, 10 A.M.–7 P.M. Mon.–Fri., 10 A.M.–5 P.M. Sat.), a Polanco store marketing the products of the famed Puebla workshop.

LIQUOR AND WINE

Mexico City offers an abundance of places selling *licores* and *vinos*. One of the best places to buy fine-quality alcohol by the bottle in central Mexico City is **M La Naval** (Av. Insurgentes Sur 373, at Michoacán, tel. 5584-3500, 8 A.M.–9 P.M. Mon.–Sat.), in the Condesa. Not only does the store have a great selection of tequilas and wines, but they also carry some excellent cheeses, meats, and other delicacies. Downtown, and less expensive, is **La Europea** (Ayuntamiento 21, tel. 5512-6005), with another store in Polanco (corner of Arquimedes and Horacio). Also downtown is **Los Viñedos** (Ayuntamiento 14). Should you be looking for a bottle in the Zona Rosa, you could do worse than **Licores La Central** (Florencia 70, at the corner of Liverpool).

CDS AND TAPES

Mixup, the best Mexican-owned chain retailing CDs and audio cassettes, has branches at Calle Génova 76, between Liverpool and Londrés, in the Zona Rosa; Isabel la Católica and Madero, in the Centro Histórico; Galerías Insurgentes, in Colonia Felix Cuevas; and at Plaza Loreto, in San Ángel. Most stores are open 9 A.M.–midnight Mon.–Sat., 9 A.M.–10 P.M. Sun.

Even better, but in the south of the city, is **Tower Records** (Pabellón Altavista, Calzado Al Desierto los Leones 52, Colonia San Ángel, tel. 5616-5267, noon–9 P.M. Sun.–Thurs., noon–11 P.M. Fri. and Sat.), with CDs from all genres of Mexican and international music. The book section stocks everything from Octavio Paz to Aztec histories. Tower formerly had a store in the Zona Rosa, and the company said they plan to reopen one near there soon.

Librería Gandhi also stocks a good CD collection, especially for American jazz and Mexican folk.

Mercado El Chopo (see *Markets*) is the place to go for alternative Mexican rock, as long as you don't mind bumping through crowds of young folks adorned with wild haircuts, heavy makeup, and plenty of leather.

MUSICAL INSTRUMENTS

You can buy Mexican-made guitars and other stringed instruments at three shops on Calle Bolívar in the Centro: **ABC Musical Instrumentos** (Bolívar 62, tel. 5512-0159), **Hollywood Music Center** (Bolívar 46, tel. 5521-8028), and **Music Club Bolívar** (Bolívar 86, tel. 5709-6005).

HIGH-END CLOTHING AND APPAREL

If you find yourself with the need or desire to peruse the latest in expensive fashion clothing and accoutrements, head to **Ⓜ Avenida**

SANBORNS ALL OVER

Multiple generations of Mexican families have grown up with Sanborns department stores—and their attached restaurants—during the nearly 100 years the company has been in existence. With well over a hundred branches throughout the Mexican republic, Sanborns has set the standard for Mexico-based retail chains and still enjoys a higher profile than any imported franchise.

It all began in 1903, when American brothers Walter and Frank Sanborn founded the Farmacia Americana in Mexico City to fill a perceived market for international pharmaceuticals in a nation where most people still relied on herbal remedies—many of which were, and still are, very effective, but many of which could also be classified as quackery.

Around 1919 the Sanborn brothers moved their growing business into the prestigious Casa de los Azulejos (House of Tiles) in the Centro Histórico and expanded services to include a pharmacy, gift shop, curios shop, and elegant tea salon—thus creating Mexico's first department store.

Today the typical department store operated by Sanborn Hermanos, S.A. (owned by Carlos Slim, the richest man in Latin America) integrates the services of a Mexican restaurant, bar, and large retail store with departments offering books, magazines, games, sweets, jewelry, fashion accessories, arts and crafts, audio and video equipment, baked goods, and, of course, a pharmacy. Newer on the scene has been the establishment of Sanborns Café outlets, which focus on food service only. Menu choices and prices at all Sanborns restaurants tend to be the same, a consistency that Sanborns regulars—Mexican businesspeople, upper-middle class families, and tourists—have come to count on.

Ⓜ Shopping

Presidente Mazaryk in the **Polanco** neighborhood, near Chapultepec Park. If Rodeo Drive has a Mexican equivalent, this is it. You'll find **Louis Vuitton** (Av. Presidente Mazaryk 406, tel. 5282-1178), **Salvatore Ferragamo** (Av. Presidente Mazaryk 440, locales 2 and 3, tel. 5281-4333), **Hermès** (Av. Presidente Mazaryk 422, tel. 5282-1178), **Corneliani** (Av. Presidente Mazaryk 310, tel. 5280-5905), **Mont Blanc** (Av. Presidente Mazaryk 440, local 4, tel. 5280-8359), and **Soho** (Av. Presidente Mazaryk 191, tel. 5281-1707), among many others.

The **Condesa** also has a number of fashion clothing stores, but they're usually a bit more alternative in style. Most shops are located amidst all the sidewalk cafés near the intersections of Tamaulipas, Vicente Suárez, and Michoacán streets. **Gryphos** (Ensenada 6, near the corner of Vicente Suárez, tel. 5553-1515) and **Kosiuko** (Juan Escutia 80, tel. 5553-0292) are two worth checking out.

DEPARTMENT STORES

The most convenient place to buy most department store goods is **Sanborns,** a chain of stores (each with a cafeteria attached) located in all corners of Mexico City, and indeed the entire country. You'll find everything from leather belts to televisions to imported personal grooming goods. **Liverpool** and **Palacio de Hierro** are two much larger, full-scale department stores with a full line of imported and domestic products.

You'll find branches of both stores in the Centro, Polanco, and Roma, as well as on Avenida Universidad in the south of the city.

MISCELLANEA

A string of **computer shops** along República de Uruguay, between Bolívar and Eje Central Lázaro Cárdenas in the Centro, sell just about any hardware or software available in Mexico. Calle Carranza, running east off Eje Central in the same general vicinity, holds several stores specializing in **sporting goods** and **camping equipment.** Overall, Ruben's is the best place for camping gear; Marti is best for sports gear.

Two booths selling traditional **Mexican calendars,** including reproductions of the late Jesús Helguera's colorful idealized scenes of early-20th-century Mexico and the ubiquitous Aztec warriors bending over swooning Aztec maidens, can be found on either side of Callejón de Filomena Mata.

Right behind the Catedral downtown are three stores next to one another specializing in **religious art,** where you can pick up that Virgen de Guadalupe poster you've always been looking for: El Vaticano and La Exposición, both at Guatemala 20, and La Catedral, at Guatemala 26.

Two very well-stocked **paper** and **art supply** stores in the Centro are Lumen (República del Salvador 66, 9 A.M.–7 P.M. Mon.–Sat.) and Lozano (República del Salvador 48, 9 A.M.–7 P.M. Mon.–Sat.).

Markets

ᴍ LA CIUDADELA

A few blocks south of the Alameda, la Ciudadela (Balderas at Ayuntamiento, 9 A.M.–6 P.M. daily) is the best all-around place in the Centro Histórico if you're looking for a great variety of Mexican handicrafts in one place. In addition to all the usual things, Ciudadela's complex of vendor booths is especially good for leather goods, ceramics, silver jewelry, and blankets. The quality here is not the always the best, which is fine for

buying trinkets to give as gifts. If you are looking for a top-quality handicraft, be sure to look closely, and don't be surprised if you don't find the level of workmanship you are after. For example, although several stalls sell hammocks, it's impossible to find the tightly woven and large-sized hammocks you'll find sold on the coasts. Toward the southern end of the market, almost an annex to the main complex, is a luthier's shop with lots of handmade guitars. Bargaining is expected. Balderas is the nearest

EL BARRIO BRAVO DE TEPITO

Tepito is, with no exaggeration, the most famous neighborhood in all of Mexico. This relatively small area just north of the Eje 1 Norte from the Centro, is the legendary poor neighborhood of thieves, drug dealers, prostitutes, street gangs, and world-champion boxers; of the most outrageous of Mexico's wildly creative slang; and of the most bravado-filled *cabrones* (an offensive word for "tough guys") you'll ever run across.

But most of all, it is the land of commerce, Mexico City's ultimate capitalist neighborhood. Here you can find just about anything in the thousands of small shops and market stands lining the labyrinth of narrow streets and alleys. Or you can, at least, if you ask the right people, carry yourself well, and are discrete. Some of the merchandise for sale in Tepito is stolen, and some is simply second-hand, but most of it is *fayuca,* imported goods smuggled over the U.S. border free of taxes and sold for very low prices. The authorities have been raiding Tepito literally since colonial times, to no avail, as any trip through the thriving market will immediately tell you.

Tepito was, according to most historical accounts, a small market area in the time of the Aztecs, and the name is thought to come from the Náhuatl term *tepitoyótl* meaning "small neighborhood" (although an amusingly literalist version has it deriving from *"te pito,"* or "I blow the whistle on you"). During the colonial era, when the Crown's monopoly on trade made smuggling a major industry, Tepito's location near the main northern gate to the city made it the perfect place to sneak goods in and out.

The protectionists PRI-led governments that governed Mexico from the 1940s to the 1980s, with their tight restrictions on imported goods as a way to boost domestic production, was a huge boon to the *fayuqueros* of Tepito. It was during this time that the neighborhood began to gain its national fame. A number of Mexican boxing greats came out of Tepito in the 1950s and 1960s, the first being Raúl "El Ratón" Macías, one of 15 children of a Tepito shoemaker, who became

bantamweight (53.5 kilos) world champion in 1953. He was a humble man who was favored by the PRI and prone to saying he owed everything "to my manager and the Virgin of Guadalupe." Much more in the Tepito style was Rubén "El Púas" Olivares, who became world champion in a fight in Los Angeles in 1969, and then became an antiestablishment hero who liked to smoke weed and listen to rock music; he also openly criticized the PRI and the Catholic Church.

One ex-boxing trainer, asked by a journalist why he thought Tepito had produced so many great boxers, didn't mince his words. "Well, the neighborhood is a battleground, everyone's fucked in terms of money. We all live in *vecindades* [several houses built around a communal patio], so the little kids are fighting there right from the start. And then when they're a little older, they go out on the streets ready to fight whomever. Everyone around here knows the phrase: *'camarón que se duerme, ahí lo plancharon'* [the shrimp that sleeps just got flattened]."

This last phrase sounds funny, but even more so when you know that it's a typically *tepiteño* twist of the original, more poetic *"camarón que se duerme, se lo lleva el corriente"* (the shrimp that sleeps gets taken by the current).

Tepito—which does not technically exist as a *colonia,* or official city demarcation—was the subject of a number of movies during Mexico's golden era of cinema and was even the setting of one of the all-time classics in urban anthropology, Oscar Lewis' *Children of Sánchez* (1961).

Appropriately for a barrio of this character, the favored saint is rather low on the Vatican's list of approved objects of veneration. The Santa Muerte (Saint Death) is a life-sized statue of the skeleton of a woman carrying a scythe in one hand, often wearing a feathered hat, and bedecked in jewelry. The cult of the Santa Muerte is followed across the country by thieves, drug runners, and other underworld types, but only in Tepito do they openly hold Santa Muerte ceremonies (once a month, at midnight, on the aptly named Calle Bravo) and parade the statue through the streets. As one Tepito

(continued on next page)

Shopping

EL BARRIO BRAVO DE TEPITO (cont'd)

merchant told a reporter, "We are all hard people, and we live hard lives. But she accepts us all. She understands us because she is a *cabrona* like us."

But when Mexico's economy began to open up to international trade again in the 1980s and 1990s, the *fayuca* of Tepito no longer earned as much money. Creative *tepiteños* continue wheeling and dealing, branching out into pirate videos and CDs, rip-offs of brand-name clothing, and, increasingly, drug dealing. Police raids still come and go, and contraband merchandise and drugs are impounded, but Tepito goes on, hard and fast as always. When director Tony Scott was filming *Man on Fire* with Denzel Washington in Mexico City, he thought it would be the perfect place for some of the "mean streets" scenes. And indeed they would have been, but maybe a little too much so: The city authorities refused to guarantee the safety of the film crew, so they moved elsewhere.

Santa Muerte, Tepito's patron saint

Metro station. Parking is available, on the side street adjacent to the market.

La Ciudadela is actually the large building (originally a tobacco factory) opposite a small park from the market. Along Calle Balderas, on the edge of the park, is a sidewalk **flea market** with all sorts of random goods for sale, including music, used clothing, and handicrafts.

MERCADO DE ARTESANÍAS SAN JUAN

Also known as Mercado de Artesanías Xochicalco or La Casa de las Flores, this renovated handicrafts market (at Ayuntamiento and Aranda, 9 A.M.–7 P.M. Mon.–Sat., 9 A.M.–4 P.M. Sun.), along the east side of Plaza de San Juan, stands on the site of one of Mexico City's oldest colonial-era markets. It reopened in 1999 as a cooperative venture among Mexican artisans, but it's still feeling its way in terms of quality. Prices are good, especially if you bargain, but the selection is not quite as varied as at La Ciudadela. The nearest Metro station is San Juan de Letrán.

Nearby **Mercado de San Juan** (between Pugibet and Luis Moya, 6 A.M.–5 P.M. daily) offers a good selection of fruits, vegetables, meats, and Mexican delicatessen items.

MERCADO INSURGENTES

In the center of the Zona Rosa, between the streets of Liverpool and Londrés, just off Florencia, is this indoor crafts market, which is popular among tourists for its convenient location. You'll find much of the same merchandise here as at La Ciudadela, although both quality and prices can be a bit higher. The many lunch stands on the side of the market are great for inexpensive lunches.

MARKETS IN SAN ÁNGEL AND COYOACÁN

These two southern colonial-era neighborhoods are very popular destinations for Mexicans on the weekend, attracting numerous vendors to set up stalls selling all variety of handicrafts and art. In San Ángel, **M** **Bazar Sábado** sets up evey Saturday in a 17th-century stone edifice along the northwest side of Plaza San Jacinto. This is one of the finest craft and art markets in the city, where talented artisans sell handcrafted items such as jewelry, pottery, leather, and clothing. Some of the more successful artists selling the highest-quality crafts maintain regular shops here. Spurred by the success of the market, artists without a stall inside have taken to spreading out their wares across the plaza, making the entire area one big art market (10 A.M.–7 P.M., Sat. only). Bargaining is not well received inside the main market, but haggling is more accepted outside.

There's also a huge craft market in Coyoacán on weekends; it's perhaps not quite as refined as in San Ángel but is quite good nonetheless and is certainly less pricey. It's located just off Jardín del Centenario, and you can go in either through the Sanborns or off Calle Aguayo. The market started off relatively modest, but it seems to be getting bigger each year. Jardín del Centenario is also packed with a variety of vendors (adding to the pedestrian traffic jams) on the weekends. A group of Huichol indigenous people from northwestern Mexico sell their traditional handicrafts from the south side of the square, just in front of the Entre Vero restaurant.

CENTRO ARTESANAL BUENA VISTA

Several blocks north of Reforma on Avenida Insurgentes Norte, near the railroad station, this sprawling market (Aldama 187, 9 A.M.–5 P.M. daily) houses an incredibly large selection of everything made or sold in Mexico, much larger than La Ciudadela and with some goods of better quality (if you look). The only drawback is that it's a bit out of the way. The best option for getting there other than taxi is to go via Metro the Buenavista station and walk a couple of blocks. Don't walk toward Insurgentes from the Metro, walk the other way (east)—there's a huge sign over the building that's easy to spot.

MERCADO EL CHOPO

Just north of Centro Artesanal Buena Vista on the same street, the *rockero* street market of El Chopo (10 A.M.–5 P.M. Sat. only) has become *the* place for Mexican punks and rockers to hang out. It's in a warehouse district behind the Buena Vista train station on Insurgentes Norte; walk up Eje 1 Norte to Calle Aldama, turn left (north), and follow the crowd of rockers into the market area. More than 200 vendors sell all kinds of Mexican and Latin rock cassettes and CDs, with sections that specialize in thrash metal, hard-core punk, and rarities such as out-of-print Three Souls in My Mind (El Tri) records with psychedelic covers. Bootleg live cassettes are also available and even tolerated by many Mexican artists (Joselo Rangel, of the band Café Tacuba, says it was on the basis of the number of bootlegs sold at El Chopo that they got their first record contract). Rock paraphernalia—T-shirts, jewelry, tattoo artistry, even hair-dyeing stands—are also on hand.

MERCADO LA LAGUNILLA

About 10 blocks northwest of the Zócalo, just south and north of the Eje 1 Norte, is a cluster of three market buildings known collectively as La Lagunilla, favored by lower-middle class shoppers. Off the east side of Calle Allende, the building marked "1" stocks clothes, while building 2 focuses on inexpensive wooden furniture and lighting accessories. Building 3, north of Eje 1 Norte at República de Chile and Libertad, specializes in food products. All sorts of other merchandise trades hands in the shops and streets around the market buildings.

On Sunday, a flea market, or *mercado de pulgas,* that is known as La Lagunilla sets up on the *lateral* (side lane) along the east side of Paseo de la Reforma just north of the Eje 1 Norte, and on a few side streets heading east into Tepito from Reforma. Although the prices are not as rock-bottom as they once were, it's a great place to wander around for an hour or two and check out the heaps of old books, toys, silverware, movie posters, antique and

M Shopping

not-so-antique furniture, as well as all manner of other paraphernalia spread out on the streets and sidewalks. The side streets are quite safe—just don't walk all the way to their ends, where they meet the rough neighborhood of Tepito. The nearest Metro station is Garibaldi.

ROMA FLEA MARKET

If you want a taste of what the weekend flea market at La Lagunilla is like, but you don't want to walk near the rough neighborhood of Tepito, walk around the weekend street market along the pedestrian median (called a *camellón*) in the middle of Avenida Álvaro Obregón between Frontera and Orizaba, in the Roma. This is a very low-key, positively civilized market. Most vendors make little effort to flog their wares but are happy to talk if you ask questions. The market is small, and prices are a little higher than elsewhere, but it's a nice to walk through, even if you don't buy anything. Part of the merchandise consists of antiques and collectibles, as in La Lagunilla, but you'll also find artists selling their paintings and a number of different handicrafts. It makes a good excuse to come to visit the Roma, a lovely neighborhood to spend half a day. The market is open weekends only until around 5 P.M.

MERCADO DE LA MERCED AND MERCADO DE SONORA

One of the largest retail and wholesale markets in Mexico, **La Merced** (6 A.M.–6 P.M. daily) covers an entire block between the streets of Santa Escuela, General Anaya, Rosario, and Cerrada del Rosario in Colonia Merced Balbuena, near the Ex-Convento de la Merced (from whence it got its name). For most of the nearly two centuries since independence from Spain, La Merced was the city's principal marketplace and was the centerpiece of a bustling commercial neighborhood. In 1983 the city inaugurated the Central de Abastos farther south, and it soon superceded La Merced in the wholesale business. But La Merced is still going strong, and many *capitalinos* (citizens of

The weekend market in Roma is small, but not as hectic as other markets.

© CHRIS HUMPHREY

the capital) still consider it the quintessential Mexico City market.

Across Avenida Fray Servando Teresa de Mier from La Merced is **M** **Mercado Sonora,** the so-called "witches' market" of tourist brochures. Mexicans flock here to buy herbal remedies, love potions, talismans, and other assorted psycho-spiritual balms. The market also does a booming trade in endangered plants and animals, for which it is routinely raided by the police.

Should you be interested in visiting either market, it's best to take the Metro to the Merced station rather than walk. The distance from the Zócalo may not be long, but the neighborhoods are run-down and dirty.

LA CENTRAL DE ABASTOS DEL DISTRITO FEDERAL (CEDA)

Covering about four square kilometers, La Central de Abastos is said to be the "heart" that pumps the food into that great "body" that is Mexico City and the surrounding Valle de México. An armada of up to 17,000 cargo trucks docks at this huge complex each day, handling an estimated 24,000 tons of fruits and vegetables that represent no less than 40 percent of Mexico's national harvest, along with 3,600 tons of dry groceries and other provisions.

CEDA was founded in 1992 to supply food wholesale and retail services that had outgrown Mercado de Merced in the north, and purportedly to create more cooperative and equitable leasing opportunities for vendor and *bodega* (warehouse) space. Although not a mainstream tourist attraction by any means, if you want to see the largest food market in the country, this is it. In the southeast part of the complex, a nine-hectare seafood section called La Nueva Viga displays virtually every kind of fish from all over the country, far more than any one Mexican port.

In addition to the food markets, the central corridors of the *bodegas* contain 18 banks representing 10 Mexican banking institutions, along with a number of small businesses—truck repair shops, tire shops, stationery stores, post and telegraph offices, travel agencies, pharmacies, bakeries, medical clinics, record stores, money-changers, restaurants of all types, beauty shops, perfume stores, video stores, dry cleaners, clothing stores, tortilla factories—in short, everything essential to maintain this city within a city. The nearest Metro station is La Viga.

Recreation

If all that city living has got you in need of some sport, fear not, there's a myriad of ways to sate the craving. The outdoor-adventure enthusiast has really an embarrassment of possibilities, ranging from climbing glacier-covered 5,000-meter peaks, rock climbing up six pitches of 5.11 sport climbing, mountain biking for literally hours or days through endless pine-forested countryside, paragliding and hang gliding, and heart-stopping white-water river rafting through jungle-clad canyons. Those less addicted to adrenaline will find endless destinations for more relaxed hikes through picturesque countryside, with Aztec ruins, colonial-era monasteries, or even monarch butterfly sanctuaries among the many destinations to choose from.

Guides for specific adventure sports are discussed throughout this chapter, but for general outdoor excursions, readers can look to www.amtave.org, the website of the Mexican Association of Adventure Tourism and Ecotourism, with links to many different adventure travel guide companies and lots of other good information besides. **Mochilazo** (tel. 5239-5485, www.mochilazo.com.mx) is one company geared toward younger adventure travelers, with all sorts of trips available, including rock climbing, paragliding, caving, and white-water rafting.

Those more inclined toward spectator sports will find plenty to keep them entertained, too. Soccer, or *futból*, as it's called here, is the ruling passion in Mexico, and Mexico City has three

© CHRIS HUMPHREY

Mexico City's Best

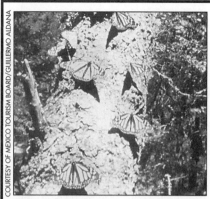

monarch butterflies

M Best Hiking and Mountain Biking: On the flanks of El Ajusco, outdoor enthusiasts will be happy to find **San Nicolás Totolapan,** a community-managed forest reserve. For a nominal fee, hikers and bikers can roam over 150 kilometers of well-maintained and guarded trails, or take guided naturalist walks for a bit more (page 168).

M Strangest Place to Go Rock Climbing: You have to drive through the industrial neighborhoods of northern Mexico City, but when you arrive to **Parque Ecológico El Cantil,** you'll see that although the surroundings are less than bucolic, the wall of 25-meter cliffs offers dozens of great top-rope and even a few trad routes ranging in difficulty from 5.8–5.12 (page 171).

M Best Place to Go for a Jog: The **Primera Sección (First Section) of Chapultepec Park** is crisscrossed with paths through grassy meadows and groves of trees and around a couple of small lakes—an ideal and safe place for a run away from all the traffic. Better to come during the week, though, as the park fills up on weekends (page 176).

M Best Public Golf Course: The golf courses within the city itself are all private, but one good public course just south of Mexico City is the reasonably-priced **Campestre Cocoyoc** (page 176).

M Best *Fútbol* Stadium: The 120,000 seat Estadio Azteca is quite a spectacle if you can grab a seat for a national team match, but for most regular league games, the better bet is the lively **Estadio Universitario** in the national university (page 177).

M Best Place to Lay a Wager: For a lazy afternoon of sipping drinks and betting on the ponies, head out to **Hipódromo de las Américas.** With bets allowed as low as a dime, you don't need to be a big spender to participate (page 180).

M Least P.C. Way to Spend the Afternoon: Fox-hunting may be a thing of the past in Britain, but bullfighting is alive and well here in Mexico. It's definitely not for everyone, but it is certainly a most unusual, ritualistic spectacle. The big shows are held at the **Monumental Plaza de Toros México** (page 182).

torero on horseback

stadiums where you can watch local league games and the national team. Baseball also has a following in D.F., as does bullfighting (not for the squeamish!), horseracing, and *lucha libre,* as the colorful professional wrestling is known here.

HIKING AND MOUNTAINEERING

The mountains of Central Mexico offer plenty of opportunities to get some fresh air, exercise, and adventure within a couple of hours' drive or bus ride. In this section are some suggestions of locations; see the *Excursions* chapter for more details on hikes and guides in specific places.

Hiking

The mountain parks at the southwestern edge of the Valle de México—Ajusco, Los Dinamos, Desierto de los Leones, and La Marquesa—still (despite logging and pollution) support sizable patches of pine and oak forests and are crisscrossed with dirt roads and trails. Hiking to the top of **El Ajusco** (3,930 meters), the prominent peak looming over the south of the city (it's clearly visible most days straight down Avenida Insurgentes), is a stiff but not too lengthy hike—doable if you're reasonably fit and acclimatized. It also makes a good hike to prepare for longer treks up the higher peaks. The only drawback is that it's not the safest place to wander around—more than a few robberies have been reported in the forests around Ajusco over the years. If you go on weekends, when there are plenty of folks around, it should be no problem. But it's best not to go during the week, and never go hiking alone (it's dangerous for accidents more than anything else).

To get to the start of the hike, take the Camino Al Ajusco from the Periférico Sur, which leads directly to the park (buses are available from the Estadio Azteca light rail stop). As the road approaches Ajusco it forks and makes a complete circle around the mountain in about 20 kilometers. At the high point in the road, right at the place where a paved side road branches off out of the valley toward Toluca, is a trail leading to the top of the peak in a one- or two-hour steep climb.

Be sure to bring enough warm clothes, as the mountaintop is frequently chilly and the weather is unpredictable. Don't underestimate the altitude either; it can really hit you.

For those looking for something a little more low-key and safer than Ajusco, go no further than **M San Nicolás Totolapan** (km 11.5 on the Picacho-Ajusco road, tel. 5630-8935, www.parquesannicolas.com.mx, 8 A.M.–4:30 P.M. Mon.–Fri., 7 A.M.–4:30 P.M. Sat.–Sun.), a community-run forest park. The 2,300-hectare reserve, along the sides of a mountain ridge between 2,700 meters and 3,740 meters, is better known for mountain biking but also has trails reserved for hikers and has guided trips (in Spanish) oriented toward local flora and fauna and the community's reforestation work. Contact the park for more information on guided trips. If you just want a relaxed stroll, show up and pay the $1 hiking fee.

Another good place for hiking near Mexico City is at **Parque Nacional Desierto de los Leones,** northwest of Ajusco. Although most visitors limit themselves to walking around the grounds of a lovely colonial-era monastery and the woods nearby, those seeking more energy expenditure should look for the turnoff to **Cruz Blanca,** .8 kilometer up the road from the monastery in the direction of San Ángel, on the right-hand side. A 1.5 kilometer hike up a dirt road will take you to a guard station and picnic area, and from here, dirt roads continue further into the forest, uphill along a river valley. Continuing straight uphill will eventually (roughly two hours, or less if you hoof it) come out at the top of the mountain ridge forming the southwest corner of the Valle de México. From the top of the pass, other dirt tracks head off farther to the west and south, but it's better to return to Cruz Blanca the way you came, as some robberies have been reported in more remote areas near here.

For about three months each winter, roughly between early December and early March, millions of **monarch butterflies** take up residence on a few particular pine-forested patches of mountainsides in the western part of the State of México and eastern Michoacán. Taking a hike up to these "sanctuaries" and seeing the forest completely covered with a pulsating blanket of orange-and-black butterflies is a magical experience. One of the easiest sanctuaries to access is in the mountains just above Valle de Bravo, where visitors can find guides to take them up the hour or so hike (horses are available also) to the butterflies. (See the *Excursions* chapter for details.)

The adventure company **Mochilazo** (tel. 5239-5485, www.mochilazo.com.mx) runs a wide variety of tours in Central Mexico, including trips to see the butterflies and bird-watching trips at Ajusco. You can either join regularly programmed trips or, if you have a group, make up your own trip.

Farther away from Mexico City are many patches of lovely forest that are safe for walkers. Among the many popular places to hike are Parque Nacional El Chico, near Pachuca; the mountains above Tepoztlán, in Morelos; and the spectacular forested countryside around Valle de Bravo, west of Toluca in the State of México. (See the *Excursions* chapter for more details on these areas.)

Mountaineering

Altitude addicts will be pleased to hear of several challenging peaks in the vicinity of Mexico City. Two very good Spanish-language websites with lots of links and contact information for mountaineering in Mexico are the national university's www.montanismo.org.mx (with information in Spanish on a variety of outdoor skills courses at reasonable prices) and the privately run www.xp-mexico.com. The latter also has lots of information on other outdoor adventure sports, such as rock-climbing and mountain biking.

Popocatépetl (5,465 meters) was once

GREEN HOLDOUTS

Amazingly enough, 37 percent of Mexico City's territory (the city proper, not the entire valley) still consists of open land, mostly in the southern parts of the capital. Pine and oak forests cover 18 percent of the city, while cultivated lands make up 13 percent, and 6 percent serves as pasture land, meadows, or city parks.

The remaining forests in Mexico City are almost entirely concentrated in the Milpa Alta, Tlalpan, and Magdalena Contreras delegations, on the steep mountains and narrow gorges in the south and southwestern parts of the valley. These forests are crucial for the continued health of the valley, as the trees help generate oxygen, and their roots collect desperately needed groundwater to replenish the dwindling aquifers.

Unfortunately, the forests have not fared well and face eventual extinction from clandestine logging and the continual encroachment of *paracaidistas* (parachutists), squatters who take up residence on the hilly outskirts of the city as if dropped from above.

But the effects of Mexico City's air pollution on the forests have been worse still. The winds in the valley blow from northeast to southwest, thereby sweeping much of the airborne pollution right into these forests. After decades of accumulating heavy metals and other toxins, the immune defenses of the forests have weakened, opening them up to repeated infestations by burrowing insects and other pests.

Between hunting and pesticide spraying, the pests' only natural predator, the woodpecker, has been driven to virtual extinction. The other technique used to prevent the pests from spreading has been to fell swaths of infested trees. Some observers claim such actions are a veiled attempt to justify logging for profit.

One stubborn local environmentalist, Dr. Luis Manuel Guerra, has taken on the lonely task of trying to reintroduce woodpeckers to the forests. Other efforts include the development of naturalist activities in the forests of Ajusco, Los Dinamos, La Marquesa, and Desierto los Leones, offering economic incentives to local people to help protect the forests. One great example of this is the community-run park of San Nicolás Totolapan near Ajusco, worth a visit if you have the time and inclination to get out of the city for an afternoon.

probably the most popular climb in the country, but volcanic rumblings have kept that mountain off-limits since 1994, and it will remain so for the foreseeable future. For the latest on Popo's rumbles, see www.cenapred.unam.mx/mvolcan.html. However, the adjacent **Ixtaccíhuatl** (5,230 meters) is open for climbers. It presents a nontechnical but very exhausting one- to two-day climb across mostly rock, with glaciers near the summit.

Between the cities of Puebla and Tlaxcala, east of Mexico City, is **La Malinche** (4,462 meters), an extinct volcano rising well above the treeline but low enough to be free of snow. Climbable in one full day without too much strain, this is a good acclimatizing hike for higher climbs or just for enjoying a serious, strenuous hike but without having to worry about snow and ice. Also a good way to taste high altitude without a major expedition is hiking up the **Nevado de Toluca,** a huge extinct volcano, the crater of which is accessible by dirt road. Hike up to the crater rim in an hour or less for fantastic views (weather permitting). It's possible to hike all the way around the crater (two to four hours), but there's lots of loose rock and precarious spots, so beware.

(See the relevant sections of the *Excursions* chapter for more details on climbing Ixtaccíhuatl, La Malinche, and Nevado de Toluca.)

Farther east is the granddaddy of them all, **Pico de Orizaba** (5,611 meters), a major climb across a steep glacier—not to be taken lightly. Climbers start the trip from the town of Tlachichuca, Puebla, on the western flank of the mountain. Pico de Orizaba falls outside the range of this book—for more information, call one of the shops or guide companies listed in this chapter. For detailed information on any of the three peaks, buy a copy of *Mexico's Volcanoes: A Climbing Guide,* by R. J. Secor, revised in 2001.

Mountain Guides

If you're looking for a guided trip up one of these peaks, there are several options. One U.S. company that has been running trips to Mexico for more than 20 years and has an excellent reputation is the **Colorado Mountain School** (341 Moraine Ave., P.O. Box 1846, Estes Park, CO 80517, tel. 970/586-5758 or 888/267-7783, fax 970/586-5798, www.cmschool.com), which offers a package trip from the U.S. to climb Ixta and Pico de Orizaba. An 11-day two-peak trip costs $2,250 per person.

The national university UNAM has a mountaineering club that offers guided trips, as well as classes (in Spanish). Contact the club at www.montanismo.org.mx. The umbrella website www.amtave.org is also a good place to find local guiding companies, which tend to open and close frequently in Mexico City.

One well-established guide company is **Río y Montaña** (tel. 5292-5032 or 5292-5058, www.rioymontana.com), offering two-night trips up either Ixtaccíhuatl ($220 per person) or Pico de Orizaba ($300 per person). Local telephone information is in Spanish only; contact U.S. operators through their website to book their trips in English.

Corporative Retto (San Pedro Cholula, Av. Cinco de Mayo 602, tel. 222/296-2470, www.corporativoretto.com), based in Cholula, Puebla, has trips up Ixtaccíhuatl, as well as La Malinche and Cofre de Perote (in Veracruz, near Pico de Orizaba), and mountain bike trips, parachuting, rafting, and a variety of other adventure sports, mainly in the state of Puebla. They offer climbing courses as well.

A smaller company, **Teporingo's Expediciones** (on the plaza in Amecameca, tel. 597/978-0349, teporingo_ex@yahoo.com.mx), offers less-expensive guided trips just to Ixtaccíhuatl.

Mountain Gear Shops

Probably the best-stocked rock- and ice-climbing shop around Mexico City is **Vertimania** (Patriotismo 899, Colonia Mixcoac, tel. 5615-5230 and Frederico de la Chica 11B, near the Plaza Satelite shopping center, tel. 5393-5287, www.vertimania.com.mx, 11 A.M.–8 P.M. Mon.–Fri., 11 A.M.–6 P.M. Sat.). It rents high-quality crampons for $9 per weekend, and ice axes for $7 per weekend.

Also with good gear for sale (not for rent) is **El Séptimo Grado** (Fernando Montes de Oca 61, in the Condesa, tel. 5553-3777, www.elseptimogrado.com). The owner here is a good climber and is knowledgeable about places to climb and guides.

Two of the gear shops, Vertimania and El Séptimo Grado, can help find guides for rock-climbing trips.

Also renting gear is **Aguayo Deportes** (Coahuila 40, tel. 5574-9683, www.clubalpino-mexicano.com.mx, 10 A.M.–7 P.M. Mon.–Fri., 10 A.M.–3 P.M. Sat.), a small shop in the Roma that rents ice axes and crampons and sells a variety of mountaineering gear.

Deportes Rubéns (Venustiano Carranza 17, tel. 5518-5636, www.dscorp.com.mx/rubens, 10 A.M.–7:30 P.M. Mon.–Sat.) rents rather worn ice axes and crampons, but no boots, for $11 a set per weekend, plus a $42 cash or voucher deposit. The store sells a decent selection of outdoor clothing, backpacking supplies, and some climbing gear, both Mexican and imported.

ROCK-CLIMBING

Rock-climbing has not reached the fanatical level in Mexico that it has in the U.S., Europe, and elsewhere, but a determined and ever-growing community of climbers has established several areas with well-defined, often bolted climbs. There's an interesting non-elite (in fact, anti-elite) subculture of urban climbing in Mexico, which you can check out if you go to the bouldering places around Ciudad Universitaria or to the El Cantil climbing park, in the north of the city.

Wherever you go climbing, don't forget to bring sunscreen, as the sun can be scorching at this altitude, especially if you want to take off your shirt.

The best climbing in the city itself—in fact a thoroughly bizarre place to find such good cliffs—is at **N** **Parque Ecológico El Cantil** (Av. Ticoman, 8 A.M.–6 P.M. Tues.–Sun.). This park, built around a ring of exposed rock jutting up out of the valley floor, is located in a dirty, semi-industrial neighborhood in Northern Mexico City. Despite the unappealing surroundings, the rocks have several dozen bolted, top-rope, and trad routes ranging from 5.8 to 5.12, some fully 25 meters high. I was told the rock is volcanic, but

© CHRIS HUMPHREY

doing the balancing act up a delicate 5.10 at Parque Ecológico El Cantil in Northern Mexico City

it's smooth and hard, nothing like the hardened lava climbing in the south of the city. It's popular on weekends and is a great place to come if you don't have enough time to get outside of the city.

The entrance to the park is watched over by a policeman, who makes sure everyone signs in. Kudos to whichever city official thought of that, because climbers feel quite safe in what would otherwise be a sketchy neighborhood for such things. The policeman also keeps an eye on the small parking lot, and it's customary to give him a small tip ($1 or so) if you park there. To get there, drive or take a taxi up Insurgentes Norte, and turn on Avenida Ticoman. The park is right near Cinemex Ticoman. By public transport, take the Metro to Indios Verdes and hop on any *colectivo* (minibus) marked "Ticomán."

Not far from El Cantil, near the Instituto Politécnico Nacional, in the north part of the

M Recreation

city, is the rock gym **Escalódromo Carlos Carsolio,** (Técnicos Mexicanos 18, Colonia Santa María Ticomán, tel. 5752-7574, www.escalodromo.com, 2–10 P.M. Tues.–Fri., 9 A.M.–7 P.M. Sat., 9 A.M.–5 P.M. Sun.). The easiest way to get there is get to Metro Indios Verdes, and from there take any *colectivo* marked "Ticomán." Get off at the Restaurant Galeón Español—the gym is directly behind the restaurant. Entrance is $6 for unlimited use of 1,200 square meters of climbing walls. For the first visit, equipment is provided free of charge; after that, either bring your own or rent shoes for $2.50 and a harness for $2. Four-hour introductory classes are available for $27.

Several of the lava chunks out in the Espacio Escultórico in Ciudad Universitaria, in southern Mexico City, are great for bouldering, although the lava rock can be rough on the fingers. Rivaling El Cantil for bizarre location, although not as good for the actual climbing, is a few routes up volcanic rock in a housing complex in Copilco, not far from the university.

Peñasco de los Perros, a rocky outcrop near La Marquesa park on the road between Mexico City and Toluca, is a great place for beginning and intermediate climbers to set up some basic top-ropes of varying difficulty. Most of the routes are also bolted, if you want to practice your sport leads. A 60-meter rope is needed to top-rope some of the harder and longer routes.

To get there, continue up the highway toward Toluca, past La Marquesa 2.4 kilometers farther to a turnoff on the right, leading another .8 kilometer to Salazar. From the village, ask for the road to Los Perros. Take this dirt track heading north into a valley and, after arriving at a fork (1.6 kilometer from the beginning of the track), take the right-hand turn, and you'll be facing Los Perros, a couple of hundred meters away across a field. You'll have to take a cab or walk if you don't have a car, as buses don't come out this way.

Leaving the car in a dirt lot to the left of the road, right at the base of the outcrop (there appear to be no problems with theft here), walk up a steep trail into the pine forest to the base of the 25–35 meter pitch. A scramble up a narrow trail leads to the top of the rock, where you'll find several anchors, as well as a few boulders to rope off of if you don't trust the anchors. Bring plenty of anchor rope, as you may have to hang the anchor to get the climbing rope all the way down to the ground, especially if you only have a 50-meter rope. Facing the rock from the bottom, the crack to the left is the easiest climb (a 5.7), while the few farther to the right have more difficult entries and are more like 5.8–5.11. A dozen quick draws will be plenty to lead all the routes. The most difficult route is the farthest to the right.

On weekends you may well have to wait your turn. Los Perros is very popular because it's easy to reach and suitable for novice climbers. It's better to come during the week if possible, when you'll likely have the place to yourselves. Be sure to take a long break at the top to enjoy the views out across the mountain peaks and forests. Without a car, visitors can get to Los Perros by taking a *pesero* (green-and-white bus) marked "Salazar" from Metro Juanacatlán to the town, and from there, either walking or taking a taxi out to the rocks.

Many more bolted routes (no top-ropes possible here) are found at **Los Dinamos,** a narrow gorge in the southwest part of the Valle de México, in the Magdalena Contreras *delegación* (one of 16 large subdivisions in the city). Much of the rock face on the western side of Los Dinamos gorge is covered with dozens of climbing routes, many of them bolted. Routes range mostly from 5.9 to 5.12B, with lots of cracks and overhangs. The cliff directly opposite the Segundo Dinamo parking lot is dotted with climbers every weekend. More bolted routes are found downriver by the Primer Dinamo, while the climbs up at the Cuarto Dinamo are mostly bolt-free for the trad climbers out there.

Climbers have generally not had problems with theft (although hikers and bikers have), but its best to keep an eye out when climbing here.

Look for the road to Los Dinamos turning off the Periférico highway not far past San Ángel, posted for Magdalena Contreras. Catch buses there from Metro stations Miguel Ángel de Quevedo or the Copilco.

A bit farther afield, above the city of Pachuca, two hours northeast of Mexico City, is **Parque Nacional El Chico,** one of the premier climbing areas near the capital. A jumble of rocky outcrops and ridgelines, El Chico is a great place to camp for a few days and try your hand at a few of the dozens of mostly 5.8–5.9 routes (though more complicated multirope pitches are also available). (See the *Excursions* chapter for more information.)

Another location that has a very good reputation for climbing (and also as a safe place for camping) is Jilotepec, in the Estado de México roughly northwest of Mexico City. Ask around at climbing shops or at the rock-climbing gym if you want to go there.

Courses, Gear Shops, and Guides

Mochilazo (tel. 5239-5485, www.mochilazo .com.mx) runs both rock climbing courses and guided trips. The courses are $250 per person for a six-session course, culminating in climbing the six-pitch Peñon de Bernal (transport not included). One-day trips near Mexico City run $45 per person for a group of six (transport not included).

For shops with rock climbing gear, see the *Mountain Gear Shops* section. Two of the gear shops, Vertimania and El Séptimo Grado, can help find guides for rock-climbing trips.

MOUNTAIN BIKING

Central Mexico, and the mountains on the south side of Mexico City in particular, are crisscrossed with top-notch mountain bike trails and dirt roads, where you can bike for miles through pine and oak forest up to mountain ridge tops above 3,000 meters. Close to the city, probably the safest and most accessible places for biking are the community-run San Nicolás Totolapan at Ajusco and Parque Nacional Desierto de los Leones.

San Nicolás Totolapan, (km 11.5 on the Picacho-Ajusco road, tel. 5630-8935, www.parquesannicolas.com.mx, 8 A.M.–4:30 P.M. Mon.–Fri., 7 A.M.–4:30 P.M. Sat.–Sun., $2 admission), a local *ejido* (communal farm), has cordoned off about 2,300 hectares of hillside crossed with over

150 kilometers of dirt roads and trails, ranging in altitude from 2,700 to 3,740 meters at its highest point, Montaña Nezehuiloya. The *ejido* patrols the forest, making it quite safe for hiking and biking. Some trails are for bikes only, others for walkers only, and some are for both. Bikes are usually available for rent on weekends at the park, but get there early if you want to get one, as they go fast. Better to bring your own. The park is often held up as a model for other ecotourism projects in Mexico involving local communities.

Parque Nacional Desierto de los Leones, along the mountaintops in the west-southwest corner of the valley, is also a great place to ride and is generally quite safe. From the park's monastery along the main road, continue half a mile further in the direction of San Ángel and look for a dirt road turnoff on the right-hand side leading to **Cruz Blanca,** a ranger station of sorts. This is as far as unauthorized motor vehicles can go, and in fact it's probably better to park at the monastery and ride or walk up the dirt road, roughly 1.5 kilometers to the ranger station.

From Cruz Blanca, a dirt road used only by hikers and the occasional park vehicle winds parallel to a river valley, until a point where the road meets the river and forks, one branch crossing the river and the other continuing steeply up the mountain.

On the other side of the river, the trail climbs uphill briefly, then meets an old dirt road that has been closed off, winding along the side of the hills, without gaining or losing altitude for perhaps five kilometers, finally coming out at Valle de los Conejos, near La Marquesa. This is a great place for bike riding or a long run in the woods. About halfway out along the road is an army camp, which means it's quite safe between Cruz Blanca and the camp.

However, at the far end of the road, toward Valle de los Conejos, a few robberies have been reported in recent years, so it's best to turn around near the army camp. At the far end of the road is a great downhill mountain bike track leaving from the end of the dirt road out to the highway at Valle de los Conejos. Other single-tracks descend from this road too and eventually come

Recreation

out on the Mexico City-Toluca highway, not far from La Marquesa.

Back at the river junction, the main dirt road from Cruz Blanca continues steadily uphill, staying on the left (east) side of the river valley, to the top of the mountain ridge forming the southwest corner of the Valle de México. It's a steep slog, taking an hour or two to the top, depending on your lungs and legs, but the descent on bike is fast and fun. You can hike to the top of a nearby hilltop and catch the views (and your breath).

From the top of the pass, other dirt tracks head off farther to the west and south. If you stay left at the pass and continue down, staying left all the way, you'll come out at the forest camp on the dirt road between the monastery and Cruz Blanca—a wicked ride. Other roads from the pass lead further east to Los Dinamos and Ajusco. Although these are fun roads for riding if you like to explore, they pass through more isolated stretches of forest and are thus a bit more risky in terms of running into the odd *bandito* (bandit). If you come up this way, plan for a long ride, and come with water, some food, and a sweater or jacket in case of cold. Most riders stick to returning to Cruz Blanca the way they came up (which is a great downhill on a bike, anyway).

To get to the park, **Camino al Desierto** runs from the Toluca highway near the neighborhood of Cuajimalpa to San Ángel. Unless you're in the south of the city, the best way in for those driving motor vehicles is via the Toluca highway. A bus runs from the Metro Barranca del Muerto station up to the monastery on Saturday and Sunday only 6 A.M.–5 P.M. Bikers without a car would have to hire a taxi from the city, which would cost $10–15 at least.

More extensive forests and trails for mountain biking are found around the flanks of Ixtaccíhuatl volcano, at Parque Nacional El Chico in Hidalgo, or in the countryside around Valle de Bravo, State of México (see the *Excursions* chapter for details). You'll also find some good trails around Chiluca, in the northwest of Mexico City (follow Avenida Lomas Verdes from the Periférico to get there). For more information on these routes, check out www.xinte.com.

Guides

The best people to go to for guided mountain bike trips in Central Mexico are **Mountain Bike Mexico** (tel. 5846-0793, www.mtbmexico.com), who offer a range of trips, from one-day excursions in the mountains around Mexico City ($120 per person) to multiday trips through amazing countryside in Veracruz and Guanajuato ($500–700 per person, everything included).

Another good company, with lots of regularly scheduled trips near Mexico City, ranging from beginner to expert in difficulty, is **Solo Montaña** (tel. 5678-1151, www.ruedapormexico .com), with one-day trips running around $65 and two-day trips around $130. **Mochilazo** (tel. 5239-5485, www.mochilazo.com.mx) also runs a variety of mountain bike trips in the mountains around Mexico City.

Río y Montaña (tel. 5292-5032 or 5292-5058, www.rioymontana.com) runs three-night trips to the northern Oaxaca mountains for $450 per person, as well as overnight trips to San Miguel Regla, near Parque Nacional El Chico in Hidalgo ($190 per person). It's best to book the trips through their website.

Unfortunately, none of these companies currently rents bicycles themselves, although Mochilazo's owner said he may start to rent in the future. I've been unable to find (and I've looked for years) anywhere in Mexico City that rents mountain bikes.

Bike Shops

If you're just looking for an inexpensive mountain bike to thrash around on either in the city or the hills, a couple dozen shops sell Benotto (the local brand) bikes for $100–150 on Avenida San Pablo near the intersection of Avenida Circunvalación. Don't be surprised by all the prostitutes hanging out in between the bike shops—it's a seedy neighborhood but safe during the day.

Deportes Martí (Venustiano Carranza 19, tel. 5221-1636, and San Luis Potosí 214, tel. 5264-5085, www.marti.com.mx), a well-known general sporting goods store, has now started carrying a decent selection of mountain bikes, including a number of imported brands.

One of the city's best mountaineering and climbing shops, **Vertimania** (Patriotismo 899, Colonia Mixcoac, tel. 5615-5230 and Frederico de la Chica 11B, near the Plaza Satelite shopping center, tel. 5393-5287, www.vertimania .com.mx, 11 A.M.–8 P.M. Mon.–Fri., 11 A.M.– 6 P.M. Sat.) also now carries a good selection of high-quality mountain bikes and gear.

WHITE-WATER RAFTING AND KAYAKING

The slopes of the Sierra Madre Oriental mountains dropping down to the Caribbean shores are home to a number of exceptional white-water rivers, including the Río Pescados, Río Filobobos, and Río Santa María. They are mainly located in the State of Veracruz and are thus beyond the scope of this book, but rafting is a popular excursion for adventure-minded Mexicans and foreigners staying or living in Mexico City. The main base for most rafting companies is Jacomulco, a little village in a beautifully lush river valley, about a 40-minute drive from Jalapa, the capital of the State of Veracruz. Pico de Orizaba, the highest peak in Mexico, looms right in the background, as does the smaller but still impressive Cofre de Perote.

While the rafting around Jacomulco is spectacular, the trip out to the Río Filobobos, a couple of hours' drive north of Jalapa, is really worth the trip. Not only is the jungle denser and more remote-feeling, but you can break the raft trip partway and explore an ancient Totonac city in ruins right on the banks of the river.

Most trips are two-day packages, with food, lodging at Jacomulco, two river trips, and extras like *temazcal* (Aztec-style sauna) and jungle tours included, for around $180–300 per person. Less-expensive day trips without lodging and the extras can be arranged. It helps your bargaining position if you have a group already put together.

A number of companies offer guided rafting trips in Veracruz and San Luis Potosí, including: **Mexico Verde** (tel. 279/832-3730, toll free in Mexico 800/362-8800, www.mexicoverde .com); **Río y Montaña** (tel. 5292-5032 or 5292-5058, www.rioymontana.com); **Eccosports** (Felix Cuevas 224B, Colonia Del Valle, Mexico City, tel. 5559-3560, www.eccosports.com.mx); and **Aventurec** (Galería Las Animas, Local P-9, Puebla, tel. 222/231-2725, www.aventurec.com).

FLYING

Valle de Bravo is the most popular place in Central Mexico for hang gliding and paragliding, with steady thermals created out over the lake and perfect launch and landing sites.

The best-known company for paragliding and hang gliding is **Alas del Hombre** (Plaza Valle, Local 22 and 24, Fray Gregorio J. de La Cuenca, www.alas.com.mx, tel. 726/262-6382 or 726/262-0934), with nearly 30 years' experience flying around Valle de Bravo and elsewhere in Mexico. They offer courses for both hang gliding and paragliding, tandem flights, and guided tours—all with certified instructors. A 30-minute glide down in a tandem with an instructor costs $130 on weekends and $100 during the week (minimum age seven). Take a windbreaker, sports shoes, and a camera. There are also weeklong courses for those planning to stay in town for a while. The basic introductory paragliding course includes eight days of training over four weekends and costs $1,100–1,500 per person, depending on how many people sign up for the course.

One U.S./Mexican company that runs hang gliding and paragliding trips to Mexico is **Fly Mexico** (tel. 512/467-2529 or 800/861-7198 in the U.S., in Valle de Bravo 726/262-2449, www.flymex.com); courses for $695 (paragliding) or $895 (hang gliding) for one week, all included except airfare. Student trips cost more if you're not a certified flier already.

Hot-air balloon rides are also available around Mexico City with at least two companies: **Globo Aventura** (tel. 5662-4023, www.globoaventura.com), out of Tenancingo in the State of México; and **Sunrise Ballooning Club** (tel. 5782-3414 in Mexico City) in Yautepec, Morelos.

Recreation

HORSEBACK RIDING

In the forest parks around Mexico City, such as Desierto de los Leones, La Marquesa, and Ajusco, local men are out on weekends at the main parking lots with fairly docile horses for rent, usually $5–10 an hour. A great place to take guided horseback trips is in the mountains above Tepoztlán, south of Mexico City, with a well-managed ecotourism company. Near Valle de Bravo, in the State of México about a 2.5-hour drive west of Mexico City, tourists can visit a monarch butterfly sanctuary in the pine forests on horseback from the village of Los Saucos; migration season is between November and March (peaking in January).

(For more details on riding near both Tepoztlán and Valle de Bravo, see the *Excursions* chapter.)

BOATING

Unless you want to go all the way down to the ocean, the closest place to do any sailing is Lake Avándaro, at Valle de Bravo. This three-by-seven-kilometer lake, created by a dam built in the 1940s, is a favorite of yachties and, to a lesser degree (so far), windsurfers. (See *Valle de Bravo,* in the *Excursions* chapter, for more information.)

JOGGING AND WALKING

If you're looking for a good place in the city to go jogging, walking or in-line skating, the roads and pathways of the **M Primera Sección (First Section) of Chapultepec Park** are quiet, safe, and well away from traffic (5 A.M.–4:30 P.M. Tues.–Sat.). The Segunda (Second) and Tercera (Third) sections are more isolated and consequently not as safe. Directly behind the Anthropology Museum, across Avenida Gandhi, is a small forested park with a one-kilometer jogging path that is marked every hundred meters. Smaller parks—including **Parque México,** in the Condesa, or **Parque Hundido,** on Insurgentes Sur—are other daytime options. If you can make your way up to **Parque Nacional Desierto de los Leones,** southwest of Mexico City, you'll find plenty of forest trails and dirt roads, and lots of other trail-runners on weekends.

GOLF

While Mexico City itself has a number of golf courses, they are basically all members-only. However, there are a number of courses not too far away that accept the general public with green fees. Apart from the courses mentioned here, see www.mexgolf.org for listings of other courses around Mexico City.

South of Mexico City, about a 15-minute drive southeast of Tepoztlán on the road to Cuautla, is **M Campestre Cocoyoc** (at Hotel Hacienda Cocoyoc, tel. 735/356-1132, www.cocoyoc.com.mx), an 18-hole course charging $55 during the week (no tee time needed) or $77 on weekends (afternoon only for nonmembers, and expect to wait). Golf carts are $21 and caddies charge $10, plus tip.

Rancho Avandaro (eight kilometers above Valle de Bravo on the Toluca road, tel. 5282-1212 or 5280-4774, www.grupoavandaro.com.mx) charges $50 for the use of their lovely nine-hole course.

GYMS AND EXERCISE LOCATIONS

A couple of the luxury hotels in the city, particularly the Nikko and the Camino Real, have excellent health spas and tennis courts. Unfortunately, at last report they were only open for guests and gym members. You may want to call to see what the current status is. The more devious travelers may feel confident enough to bluff their way in, but that's a personal call.

Assuming you want to follow the straight and narrow, about the best gym available with daily rates is **Sports City** (two locations: Altamirano 46, in San Ángel, tel. 5550-6860, and Miguel de Cervantes Saavedra 397, in Polanco, tel. 5580-0716). At $45 a day, or $20 a day if you go with a member, it's far from cheap, but they do have 25-meter swimming pools, all variety of exercise equipment, and a steam room and sauna. A monthly membership is $450.

Another option, although just with weights and machines (no pool), is **Gold's Gym** (Homero 440, in Polanco, tel. 5203-4385), which charges $375 for a package of 10 visits.

Most neighborhoods have many other less-expensive gyms that cater to the nonwealthy, where you can often get in for $10 or so for a single visit. Asking around at your hotel is a good place to start looking.

Ciudad Deportiva is a huge sports complex with dozens of tennis and basketball courts and ball fields; it's open to the public. It's in central-eastern Mexico City, near the highway exit to Puebla; the easiest way to get there is hop the Metro and get off at the Ciudad Deportiva station. Hoops players can usually get a decent pickup game of basketball there on weekends. The complex also has a great track, but it appears to be open for special events only.

RUGBY

Yes, if you can believe it, there's actually a rugby league in Mexico City, comprising perhaps half expatriates of various countries (France, England, Argentina, U.S.) and half Mexicans. They usually have two seasons, one in the fall and one in the spring, with a couple of 10-a-side tournaments as well. Quality of play is not top-notch (I played for a couple of years, if that gives you any indication), but it is good and has been improving dramatically in the past few years. Games are held at Dos Ríos, a group of sports fields just below the town of Huix-quilucan, in the State of México near the highway to Toluca. If you'd like to watch a game or join a team, see www.mexrugby.com for more information.

SPECTATOR SPORTS

For general information on Mexican sports, nothing can top *El Afición,* a daily newspaper sold at any newsstand and devoted to all types of professional athletics, but principally to the sacred orb, *fútbol.*

Soccer

Soccer (or *fútbol,* as it's called here) is by far Mexico's favorite sport, and the sports fan may want to go catch a league game during the two-part, winter-summer seasons—one between August and January and the other between March and June. Tickets cost $2–10, depending on the seat, and are best bought at the stadium ticket office the day before the game, or the same day. If the tickets sell out (although they usually don't), a vociferous crew of *revendedores* (scalpers) can be found selling tickets for a markup. It's also possible to buy tickets for most games through TicketMaster (tel. 5325-9000, www.ticketmaster.com.mx), which can be picked up at any Liverpool department store or MixUp music store.

Mexico's largest stadium is the 120,000-seat **Estadio Azteca** (Calzada de Tlalpan 3465, tel. 5617-8080), in the southern part of the city, home of Las Águilas del América and Los Rayos de Necaxa (both owned by media giant Televisa). Call for times or check in the sports section of local papers for upcoming games. The massive iron sculpture presiding over the stadium entrance is called *Red Sun* and is one of American artist Alexander Calder's more famous pieces.

Also in the south is **Ⓜ** **Estadio Universitario** (Insurgentes Sur just south of Eje 10 Sur at Ciudad Universitaria), home to the UNAM Pumas. While it's not always among the best teams in the league (although it has been doing very well the last couple of years, under the coaching of former star Hugo Sánchez), going to see a Pumas game at Estadio Universitario is always good fun, as the *porras* (fan clubs) of the Pumas are well known for their elaborate and often hilarious chants and cheers.

The closest stadium to downtown Mexico City is **Estadio Azul** (just off Insurgentes Sur at Holbein, Colonia Ciudad de los Deportes), right next to the Plaza México bullfighting ring. This is home to the Cementeros de Cruz Azul, the second-most popular team in the city after América.

Other teams in Mexico City are the Potros de Atlante, which seems to be shuffled around to different stadiums but mostly plays at Estadio

Ⓜ Recreation

LUCHA LIBRE

Outrageously camp, surreally choreographed, wildly acrobatic or just plain silly: Whatever your opinion of *lucha libre*, the sport's popularity among Mexicans is undeniable. Filling wrestling auditoriums big and small across the country to watch local amateurs or international stars from as far afield as Japan and Scotland, more live spectators watch *lucha libre* in Mexico than any other sport, including soccer.

Bouts are often rowdy affairs, with the wrestlers strutting about the ring and gesticulating or shouting to the excited fans as the opening bell draws near. Once the fight begins, spectators, including

A *rudo* takes a *técnico* to task at the Arena México.

housewives, children, and the elderly, cram closer to shout encouragement or abuse at the heaving hulks. In the smaller auditoriums particularly, they can save themselves the effort as the sweating combatants—complete with tights, masks, and capes—many times end up grappling with each other in the front and sometimes even the back rows of seating.

The fights are hammily staged, but that doesn't mean the sweat, and sometimes blood, is not real, or that the blows are not hard. Equally, the spectacular agility of the wrestlers, especially the lighter weights, is impressive. Professional wrestlers

are frequently injured, occasionally seriously. Broken necks are rare but not unheard of. Wrestlers are not usually well paid, and all but the very best also have day jobs.

Wrestlers divide into two categories, the clean-cut *técnicos* and the surly *rudos,* roughly corresponding to the good guys and the bad guys respectively. The idea is that the *técnicos* are better looking, more skillful, and just plain decent types. The *rudos* are more ruthless and frequently "cheat" in a crude and highly visible fashion. Whacking opponents over the head with various props is a predictable crowd-pleaser. Referees are also routinely strangled, poked in the eye, or dumped out of the ring by *rudos*. Both *técnicos* and *rudos* have no shortage of fans.

A working-class sport, *lucha libre* is often looked down on by Mexico's elite. *Lucha libre* venues are usually down-at-the-heel places with a distinctly blue-collar clientele. That's part of the charm. Nevertheless, *lucha libre's* influence is so pervasive in Mexico that it has even crept into politics and onto the big screen. Famously, Superbarrio is a Mexico City activist who first donned wrestling attire in the 1980s to campaign against poverty and bureaucratic corruption. Meanwhile, El Santo, the archetypal *técnico* and Mexico's most popular grappler back in the 1950s and 1960s, made a series of cheesy lead appearances in eponymous low-budget flicks that many camp aficionados still regard as classics.

Arena México (at Dr. LaVista and Dr. Lucio in Colonia Doctores, tel. 5588-0508), a short walk east of the Cuauhtémoc Metro station, has *lucha libre* every Friday night 8:30–11 P.M., usually four or five fights; tickets are $5–7. On Saturday the arena hosts boxing matches 6:30–10 P.M.; tickets are $6–10. Although the neighborhood around the arena is not the best (watch out after dark), inside it's surprisingly clean and nonthreatening. Also surprising: Although beers are on sale, the crowd does not tend to get overly drunk here.

In the Centro Histórico is **Arena Coliseo** (República de Perú 77, near República de Chile, tel. 5526-1687), with five *luchas* every Tuesday starting at 8:30 P.M. and Sunday starting at 5 P.M. Admission costs $3–5.   —*Contributed by Simeon Tegel*

Recreation

Azteca; and Toros Neza, with its stadium in the rough eastern suburb of Nezahualcóyotl. Toros Neza slid down to the Primera A division a couple of years back (despite hiring Brazilian Bebeto to help it) and is currently struggling to return to the top league.

Often the best matches to watch are the big rivalries, such as the *Superclásico* each season between the Chivas of Guadalajara and América, and the cross-town match between the city's two most popular teams, América and Cruz Azul. In recent years Pumas, Cruz Azul, Atlas of Guadalajara, Los Diablos Rojos of Toluca, and América have consistently been among the best and most fun teams to watch.

Attending a match in Mexico is a remarkably relaxed affair, especially for those accustomed to European football matches. Fans from opposing teams often sit right next to each other and exchange mock-angry commentary throughout the game. Actual fights among fans are very rare, though like most fans in the world, they take great glee in flinging whatever they can onto the field, particularly rolls of toilet paper.

Among the several Internet sites related to Mexican soccer are www.femexfut.org.mx (the official league site); www.futbolmundial.com.mx (general information); www.seleccionmexicana.com.mx (national team); www.esmas.com /clubamerica (Águilas del América); www.pumasunam.com.mx (Pumas de UNAM); www.chivasdecorazon.com.mx (Chivas de Guadalajara); www.cruz-azul.com.mx (Cruz Azul). If you poke around, you'll find some hilarious sites dedicated to trashing the Águilas del América, who are sort of the Yankees of Mexico: They are by far the richest and most hyped team, but they are also the most hated team in the country.

Baseball

Although it can't quite compare to soccer, *béisbol* is extremely popular in Mexico, particularly in the northern part of the country but also in the center and south. Mexico has two leagues, the Liga del Pacífico, which plays in the northwestern part of the country, and the Liga Mexicana de Béisbol, which fields teams pretty much every-

where else. The Liga Mexicana has 16 teams, of which two are from Mexico City: the Tigres Capitalinos and the Diablos Rojos. Because of falling attendance, the Tigres now play in the nearby city of Puebla, which is a shame, because their venerable old stadium in Mexico City was a great place to watch a game. The Diablos Rojos— perennial playoff contenders—play at the Foro Sol (tel. 5639-8722), which seats 26,000 spectators and is in Ciudad Deportiva, right at the junction of the Viaducto and the Circuito Interior, in the eastern side of the city. Tickets run between $1.50 and $8, a bargain for an afternoon of kicking back, watching a game, and having a beer. The season is between March and July, with the playoffs in August. Sunday games are held at noon; on other days, it's either 4 or 6:30 P.M. For more information, see the team website at www.diablos.com.mx, or the league website at www.lmb.com.mx.

Charreada

Decreed the national sport of Mexico in 1933 by presidential edict, the *charreada* (rodeo) is more popular in Mexico than bullfighting. *Charreadas* are staged in skillet-shaped *lienzos charros* (*charro* rings) by private *charro* associations to demonstrate equestrian and ranching skills, much like the U.S. counterpart, which was inspired by the *charreada*. Though open to everyone, *charrería* (the *charro* art) is a rather expensive pastime, requiring the maintenance of trained horses and elaborate clothing, somewhat analogous to polo in the Anglo world.

Unlike in American rodeo, *charros* and *charras* (gentleman and lady riders) compete for team, not individual, awards. Each team fields six to eight people, who singly or in combination perform a series of nine *suertes* (maneuvers or events); upon completion of all *suertes*, the team with the most points wins. *Charreada* points are usually scored for style rather than speed. Live mariachi music adds drama and romance.

The **Asociación Nacional de la Charrería** (Izazaga and Isabel la Católica, tel. 5512-2523) can tell you where to find *charreadas* in or near the capital, or you check with the Mexico City tourist office.

Horse Racing

Mexico City's only horse-racing track is the **Hipódromo de las Américas** (Av. Industria Militar just west of the Periférico, beyond Polanco, in Colonia Lomas de Sotelo, tel. 5387-0600, www.hipodromo.com.mx). The 1.5-kilometer oval course is a diverting place to spend an afternoon, tipping drinks in one of the various bars, watching the horses and riders parade around and race, and of course placing a few bets to keep the excitement up. The officials at the betting windows are usually all too happy to explain the general betting rules to a novice. Races are held Thursday 5:30–10 P.M. and Friday through Sunday 3–8 P.M. The entrance fee is $2 general admission or $5 for box/mezzanine seating. The minimum bet is $0.10. By public transport, get off at either Chapultepec or Auditorio Metro stations and look for buses marked "Hipódromo" driving west on Paseo de la Reforma.

BULLFIGHTING

Alternately called *la corrida de toros* (the running of bulls), *la fiesta brava* (the brave festival), *la lidia de toros* (the fighting of bulls), or *sombra y sol* (shade and sun, in reference to the stadium seating), the bullfight can be perceived as a sport, an art, or a gory spectacle, depending on the attitude of the observer.

To the aficionado, the *lidia* is a ritual drama that rolls together courage, fate, pathos, and death in one symbolic event. But no matter how you may feel toward the bullfight, it is undeniably an integral part of Mexican history and culture.

History

Mexico City's first bullfight took place in the Plaza Mayor (as the Zócalo was then called) on August 21, 1529, to commemorate the eighth anniversary of the fall of Tenochtitlán. Between 1554 and 1810, bullfights were held in the adjacent Plaza Voladores (currently the Corte Suprema de Justicia). By the 18th century, they were also held on the south side of the Alameda, and in the 19th century, at the now defunct Plaza de Toros San Diego (near the current site of the Monumento a la Revolución).

El Toro

The bulls used in the ring, *toros de lidia* (fighting bulls), are descendants of wild Iberian bulls that for more than four centuries have been bred especially for their combative spirit. They're not

baiting the bull at the Monumental Plaza de Toros México in Tlaxcala

COURTESY OF MEXICO TOURISM BOARD

trained in any way for the ring nor goaded into viciousness, but as a breed, they are naturally quick to anger. The fighting bull's neck muscles are much larger than those of any other cattle breed in the world, making the animal capable of tossing a torero and his horse into the air with one upward sweep.

Bulls who show an acceptable degree of bravery by the age of two are let loose in huge pastures in Zacatecas, San Luis Potosí, or Guanajuato to live as wild beasts until they reach four years, the age of combat. By the time *el toro* (the bull) enters the ring, he stands around 127 centimeters high at the withers (higher at the shoulder, but they aren't measured there, because the neck muscle expands to varying degrees when the bull is preparing to attack) and weighs 500 kilograms or more.

El Torero

The bullfighter is rated by his agility, control, and, as surprising as it may seem to the uninitiated, his compassion. The torero who teases a bull or who is unable to kill it quickly when the moment of truth arrives is considered a cruel brute. In order to be judged a worthy competitor by the spectators, he must excel in three areas: *parar,* or standing still as the bull charges (as opposed to stepping away from the bull, even as little as an inch)—only the cape and the torero's upper body should move; *templar,* or timing and grace—the movements must be smooth, well timed, and of the right proportion; and *mandar,* or command, the degree to which he masters the entire *lidia* through his bravery, technique, and understanding of the bull, neither intimidating the animal nor being intimidated by it.

Standard equipment for the torero is the *capote de brega,* the larger cape used in the first two-thirds of the *lidia;* the *muleta,* a smaller cape used during the final third; the *estoque,* or matador's sword; and the *traje de luces,* or suit of lights, the colorful torero's costume originally designed by the Spanish artist Goya.

La Lidia

The regulated maneuvers, or *suertes,* followed in a bullfight date from 18th-century Spain. Anywhere from four to eight bulls may appear in a *corrida* (though there are typically six), and one torero is on hand for every two bulls scheduled. The order of appearance for the toreros is based on seniority. Toreros who have proven their skills in several bullfighting seasons as *novilleros* (novice fighters) are called *matadores de toros* (bull killers). Ordinarily each torero will fight two bulls; if he is gored or otherwise put out of action, another torero will take his place, even if it means facing more than his allotment of bulls.

Each *lidia* is divided into three *tercios,* or thirds. In *el tercio de varas,* the bull enters the ring and the matador performs *capeos,* a cape maneuver that doesn't expose the matador's body to the bull's horns but is meant to test the bull or lead it to another spot in the ring. He then "lances," a cape maneuver that exposes the matador's body to the horns and brings the bull closer to him, while two horsemen receive the bull's charge with eight-foot *varas,* or lances. The *varas* have short, pyramid-shaped points that are aimed at the bull's neck muscle but do not penetrate very deeply on contact.

In *el tercio de banderillas,* the bull's shoulders receive the banderillas—26-inch wooden sticks decorated with colored paper frills, each tipped with a small, sharp, iron barb. They can be placed by the matador himself or more often by hired assistant toreros (called banderilleros when performing this function). Placed in pairs, up to six banderillas may be stuck into the bull, varying in number and position according to the needs of the individual animal.

The final round of the *lidia* is called *el tercio de muerte,* the third of death. The main activity of this *tercio* is *la faena,* the work, involving cape and sword, during which a special set of passes leads to the killing of the bull. For the first two *tercios* there is no time limit; for the last, however, the matador has only 15 minutes within which to kill the bull, or else he is considered defeated, and the bull is led from the ring (where it is killed immediately by the plaza butcher).

In a good *faena,* a matador will tempt fate over and over again, bringing the bull's horns close to his own heart. The time for the kill arrives when the bull has so tired from the *faena* that it stands still, forelegs squared as if ready to receive the sword. Then, with his cape the matador must draw the bull into a final charge while he himself moves forward, bringing the sword out from under the cape, sighting down the blade, and driving the blade over the horns and between the animal's shoulders. A perfect sword thrust severs the aorta, resulting in instant death. If the thrust is off, the matador must try again until the bull dies from one of the thrusts.

If the matador has shown bravery and artistry, the crowd will let him know with its applause; an unusually dramatic performance will see lots of hats and flowers thrown into the ring.

Monumental Plaza de Toros México

Often referred to by its shorter name, Plaza México (Agusto Rodín 241, Colonia Ciudad de los Deportes, just west of Insurgentes Sur), Mexico City's bullfighting stadium is the largest and best-outfitted in the world. Begun in 1944 as part of a huge sports complex that was to include a bullring, soccer stadium, tennis courts, *frontón* (jai alai court), and restaurants, the project was suspended after the *corrida* and soccer stadiums were finished. The plaza was inaugurated on February 5, 1946, with a *cartel* (program) that featured the legendary Luis "El Soldado" Castro, Manuel "Manolete" Rodríguez, and Luis Procuna. The stadium can hold an astounding 41,262 spectators. For more information on upcoming shows in Mex-

ico City and elsewhere in the country, see www.fiestabrava.com.mx.

Monumental Plaza de Toros México's main bullfighting season is in the winter (Nov.–Feb.), with full-fledged matadors pitted against the largest and most ferocious bulls. May to September is reserved for *novilladas,* in which *novilleros* (novice bullfighters) fight *novillos*—younger, smaller bulls.

It's usually a good idea to buy tickets for a *corrida* in advance if possible. Check with the tourist office to find out whether they're available, since it's not unusual for an event to sell out (in which case you might still be able to buy a ticket—at higher prices—from a scalper, or *revendedor*). Spectator sections are divided into the *sol* (sunny side) and *sombra* (shaded side), then subdivided according to how close the seats are to the bullring itself. The *sol* tickets aren't bad, since the *corrida* usually doesn't begin until around 4 P.M.; bring a hat, sunglasses, and sunscreen, plus plenty of pesos for beverages (tequila and beer are usually available, along with soft drinks).

Corridas or *novilladas* alternate irregularly between Saturday and Sunday but always begin at 4 P.M. Ticket offices are open to special pass holders Thursday and Friday only; the general public must buy their tickets Sat.–Sun. 9:30 A.M.–1 P.M. and 3:30–7 P.M. Ticket prices range $1–10 in the *sol* section or $2–20 on the *sombra* side.

For scheduling details, check local newspapers, call Plaza México directly at tel. 5563-3961, or simply go by the stadium and ask at the ticket office.

Accommodations

Places to stay in Mexico City run the gamut, from spartan hostels to no-nonsense business hotels to plush inns in historic surroundings. In the expensive to premium categories, you can pretty well request and receive any service you desire. In the shoestring and budget classes, make sure you know what you're getting before moving in. If it's important to you to have a window, look before accepting a room. Check for security, too—is there a safe deposit box or some similar place to leave your valuables while touring? Though the weather in Mexico is usually mild, it can get cold at night in the winter; check for heat or ask for plenty of blankets. In the summer, it can get warm on occasion, so consider looking for air-conditioning or a fan.

Mexico City's Best

Best Budget Accommodation: Hugely popular with the backpacker crowd, **Hostal Moneda** is well-known for its inexpensive but clean dorm rooms and slightly more expensive private rooms. It's a great spot to meet other travelers, too (page 186).

Best Colonial Inn: Originally built in 1660 as an inn for monks, the **Best Western Hotel de Cortés** is certainly a historic building. The tranquil two-story courtyard makes a great place for a drink even if you aren't staying there (page 189).

Most Socially-Aware Hotel: Near the Monumento a la Revolución, the **Casa de los Amigos** is a Quaker-run hostel that rents out dorm beds to all sorts of interesting travelers, including many who are socially active in non-governmental organizations in Latin America. You can meet some interesting people cooking up dinner in the communal kitchen (page 189).

Most Charming Hotel: In a quiet neighborhood just north of Paseo de la Reforma is **Casa González,** a cluster of little buildings spread out across a grassy yard. This inexpensive little inn is a lovely oasis in the middle of the city, where you can sit on their quaint patio to wind down from the day (page 190).

Best Luxury Hotel: There's a number of world-class hotels in Mexico City, but the **Hotel Four Seasons** is the *crème de la crème*. Rooms here are homier than most luxury spreads, which is perhaps why it's favored by the international business crowd. The courtyard is a popular breakfast spot for local politicians and power brokers (page 191).

Most Artistic Hotel: Designed by architect Ricardo Legorreta, the **Camino Real Mexico City** is a truly bizarre cubist structure. As you wander the

Camino Real Mexico City

COURTESY OF CAMINO REAL MÉXICO CITY

spacious hallways, check out the art works by Rufino Tamayo, Alexander Calder, Pedro Coronel, Davíd Alfaro Siqueiros, and Gunther Gerzo (page 192).

Best Chic Hotel: The ultra-modern, sleek **Hotel Hábita** is nothing if not stylish. The rooms feature clean lines and elegant simplicity. On the rooftop is an open-air bar called El Área, usually filled with the local jet set (page 193).

Best Quaint Hotel: Built in a Porfiriato-era mansion in the Roma neighborhood, **La Casona** has only 30 rooms, each decorated with period furniture and lacy curtains. It's a relaxed, quiet alternative to the busier high-rise hotels along Paseo de la Reforma (page 194).

Best New Hotel: Housed in a lovely mansion in the Condesa, the chic **Condesa df**, with the help of imaginative designer India Mahdavi, is an innovative new hotel with all the modern amenities. Rooms are distributed around the sides of a triangular-shaped building, with a rooftop deck and a dining area in the central patio (page 195).

CHOOSING AN ACCOMMODATION

Where to Stay

Despite the great variety of accommodations that the city offers, hotel locations remain concentrated in only a few areas, mainly in the Reforma–Zona Rosa–Centro Histórico area and along busy boulevards radiating from the center. Most travelers on a tight budget opt to stay in the less expensive and centrally located hotels downtown and near the Monumento a la Revolución. Downtown and near the Zona Rosa, there are a good supply of midrange and higher-priced hotels, and the real luxury spots are found mostly in the Zona Rosa and Chapultepec/Polanco. The Roma and Condesa neighborhoods, two of the more happening parts of town these days, have a couple of new places worth considering but are ripe for more rooms. Coyoacán and San Ángel could also use some convenient accommodations—there's nothing available within 10 blocks of the center of either area, due in large measure to strict zoning regulations.

Rates

Accommodations values, surprisingly, are among the best of any city in Mexico, probably because competition is keen. Except toward the high end, room rates tend to be moderate, if not downright cheap, to begin with, but you may be able to save still more money by planning your stay for certain times of the year or days of the week.

The more expensive hotels along Reforma or in Polanco generally have a range of prices for different types of clients and time/date of stay, and the prices quoted in this chapter are often the most expensive, last-minute rates. Even in the priciest hotels you can often get some kind of a discount, especially at certain times of the year, if you arrive late at night, or if the hotel isn't filled. Rates are also invariably much lower over the weekend for higher-end places. A few more possibilities: **American Automobile Association** (AAA) members generally can get 20 percent off. If you carry a **business card,** ask for a business discount. If you make **reservations** from the airport hotel desks, they frequently offer packages for a little less than the going rates. Or just ask for a discount after they quote a price. Obviously, it won't always work, but occasionally discounts come to those who ask. More upscale hotels often have better rates available on their website.

At hotels in the Centro Histórico or at tourist-oriented hotels anywhere in the city, there's no difference between weekend and weekday stays.

Whatever the walk-in rate, you can occasionally bargain the price down at midrange and less-expensive hotels, except during peak periods such as Christmas or Easter. When checking in, be sure to inquire whether the room rate includes breakfast—occasionally it does. Asking for a room without breakfast *(sin desayuno)* is an easy way to bring the rate down, or simply ask if there's anything more inexpensive available *("¿Hay algo más barato?")*. You can usually count on finding cheaper breakfasts outside the hotel.

Taxes and Surcharges

Unless otherwise noted, the prices listed in this guide do not include the 15 percent IVA (value added tax) and 2 percent city lodging tax. Some of the more expensive hotels also tack on a 10 percent service charge. Be sure to ask, before checking in, whether tax and service are included in quoted rates.

Centro Histórico

You'll find plenty of hotels in the Centro to suit almost any price range, particularly in the area from the Zócalo west to Eje Central. Budget travelers in particular will find a number of good deals to choose from, all conveniently located. Those looking for a bit more pampering have a few decent options, but if you're looking for a top-quality luxury hotel, head to the Zona Rosa or Polanco.

UNDER $15

Two hostels have opened in downtown, which are great options for budget travelers. Both are well managed and receive rave reviews from the backpacker crowd. The first is **Ⓜ Hostal Moneda** (Moneda 8, tel. 5522-5821 or 5522-5803, www .hostalmoneda.com.mx, $10–12 per bed in a dorm room or $25 for a private double room; HI (Hostelling International) members receive a discount. The hostel features 90 beds distributed in three-bed and four-bed communal rooms, as well as private double and triple rooms. Downstairs is a kitchen, washing area, and Internet station, and on the roof is a small terrace café with great views. The location, just half a block east of the Zócalo, couldn't be better for exploring the Centro. The owner works with an adventure travel company that offers hiking, biking, and rafting trips in Central Mexico. Breakfast is included in prices.

On the other side of the Zócalo, right behind the Catedral, is **Hostel Catedral** (República de Guatemala 4, tel. 5518-1726, www.hostelcatedral.com, $12 for dorm bed with HI or International Student I.D. cards, $15 without, $30 d for one of five private rooms, $37 d for a nicer private room with a small terrace). Slightly more upscale than the Hostal Moneda, the Catedral has 204 beds in dorm-style rooms with wooden floors, lockers, and new furniture. A few rooms have views out front toward the Catedral. Coin washing machines and a small kitchen are available for guests. Downstairs is a pool hall, Internet café, travel agency, and patio restaurant. A buffet breakfast is included in the room price.

Of the downtown hotels, **Hotel Zamora** (Cinco de Mayo 50, tel. 5512-1832, with shared bath $11 s and $13 d, with private bath $15 s and $17 d) is a longtime favorite among the backpacker crowd, with 36 rooms in four stories around a small interior patio. The tiled building is kept clean but can be noisy.

Hotel Buenos Aires (Motolinía 21, tel. 5518-2104, $12 s, $15 d, less with shared bath) occupies an ancient two-story colonial building just off Cinco de Mayo. The rooms are surprisingly decent, considering how tattered the outside of the building looks. All rooms have TVs and high ceilings.

$15–30

Four blocks southwest of the Zócalo, in a rambling old five-story building across from the Templo de San Agustín, the **Hotel Isabel** (Isabel la Católica 63, tel. 5518-1213, fax 5521-1233, $19 s, $25 d, less with shared bath) is popular with young foreign travelers. The 74 rooms have high ceilings, private or shared baths, TV, and phone. Exterior rooms are less stuffy than interior rooms but also noisier. A restaurant and bar are on the premises, and the staff speaks English.

Around the corner from the Isabel, on the other side of the Templo San Agustín, is **Hotel Monte Carlo** (República de Uruguay 89, tel. 5521-2559, $18 s, $20 d, less with shared bath) offers 60 rooms housed in what used to be part of the Augustinian convent. With the recent interior makeover (pink paint-job and all), it's hard to notice the colonial flavor, but the rooms do have high ceilings. Famed authors D. H. Lawrence and Somerset Maugham both stayed here in the early 20th century. Parking is available.

Four blocks west of the Zócalo in an older, four-story building, **Hotel Principal** (Bolívar 29, tel. 5521-1333, $19 s, $22 d with one bed, $27 d with two beds, less with shared bathroom) features basic, clean rooms with TV and phone. It's a known favorite among backpackers.

On a pedestrian street three blocks west of

the Zócalo, **Hotel Lafayette** (Motolinía 40, tel. 5521-9640, $15 s, $18 d) is a rather unattractive modern structure on the corner of 16 de Septiembre, but its TV-equipped rooms are a fair value and popular with many low-budget Mexican tourists. The interior rooms are a bit claustrophobic, but the exterior ones are well lit, and the pedestrian-only street is quiet after dark. Laundry services are available.

$30–50

Behind the Catedral Metropolitana, and half a block from Templo Mayor, **Hotel Catedral** (Donceles 95, tel. 5518-5232, fax 5512-4344, www.hotelcatedral.com, $38 s, $44 d, junior suites $53) is a clean, modern, and very comfortable place with a friendly and helpful staff. Another major plus: all local calls are free, and you can make data as well as voice calls, unlike at many Mexico City hotels that cost much more. The hotel features a good restaurant and bar, as well as a travel agency—all on the ground floor. One drawback is the traffic on Donceles in front of the hotel, which can be quite thick during rush hour; keep this in mind if you're planning to catch a taxi to the airport or bus station.

Hotel Gillow (Isabel la Católica 17, tel. 5510-2636, www.hotelgillow.com, $42 s, $48 d with one bed, $54 d with two beds) is run by the same owners as the Hotel Catedral and has 103 clean if somewhat characterless rooms, each with private bath and TV. The hotel is conveniently located just off the Zócalo, and the restaurant is good.

Hotel Capitol (Uruguay 12, between Eje Central and Bolívar, tel. 5518-1750, fax 5521-1149, $33 s/d, $39 d with two beds) has a distinctly sanitized, chain-motel feel despite being housed in a colonial-era building with an inner courtyard. The decor is less than elegant, but the rooms are functional.

$50–75

Tulip Inn Ritz Mexico (Madero 30, tel. 5130-0169, fax 5518-3466, www.tulipinnritzmexico.com, $80 s/d, sometimes with packages as low as $60 s/d) has 117 recently remodeled rooms with carpets, cable TV, bathtubs, and lock boxes. The seven-floor hotel has a rooftop terrace restaurant with room service available. A buffet breakfast is included in the price.

$75–110

If you are looking for a bit of comfort in the Centro, the **Best Western Hotel Majestic** (Av. F. Madero 73, tel. 5521-8600, fax 5518-3466, U.S./Canada tel. 800/528-1234, www.majestic.com.mx, $105 s/d, suites $160, rooms facing the Zócalo cost more) might be the place for you. The rooms are small, but the location on the Zócalo is hard to beat. The patio restaurant is a fine spot for a meal overlooking the square, whether or not you're staying at the hotel.

Also right on the west side of the Zócalo, with its entrance on Cinco de Mayo, is the **Holiday Inn Select** (Av. Cinco de Mayo 61, tel. 5521-2121, toll free in Mexico 800/009-9900, www.holidayinnzocalo.com.mx, $85 s/d, up to $150 for the master suite). Opened in 1998, this hotel has 110 rooms that are a bit cramped but well stocked with new furniture and accoutrements, and the service is very good. Like the adjacent Hotel Majestic, the Holiday Inn has a rooftop patio restaurant, a good spot for a bird's-eye view of the square.

Alameda Central

UNDER $15

Across the street from a lively square rests **Hotel del Valle** (Independencia 35, tel. 5521-8067, $12 s, $14 d, $17 t). The rooms are a little musty and dark, but the hotel restaurant is always teeming with locals and travelers. A remarkably tacky bar adjoins the eatery.

$15–30

Hotel Conde (Pescaditos 15, tel. 5521-1084, $17 s or d, $20 t) offers a good value—clean, bright, efficient rooms with tile baths. The hotel's lounge includes an upright piano, TV, and several sofas for relaxing. Parking is available.

The 87-room **Hotel San Diego** (Luis Moya 98, tel. 5510-3523, $17 s, $18 d, $28 t) is yet another affable and affordable option on Luis Moya. The street boasts a number of these medium-sized cheapies. This one offers room service and a central garden.

Hotel Fornos (Revillagigedo 92, tel. 5521-9594, fax 5510-4732, $22 s/d) has a large, gated parking-lot entrance on Luis Moya. The hotel has a busy bar and restaurant and offers rooms with hot tubs for a premium.

$30–50

Hotel Fleming (Revillagigedo 35, tel. 5510-4530, fax 5512-0284, $30 s, $36 d, $39 t) features 80 rooms, 20 junior suites with hot tubs, ample parking, and a decent coffee shop. It's very clean and a good bargain.

With a modern facade and a welcoming sculpture-and-cactus garden, the **Hotel Marlowe** (Independencia 17, tel. 5521-9540, fax 5518-6862, $35 s, $41 d, $45 t) offers 120 newer rooms, including some with terraces.

The clean, friendly **Hotel Monte Real** (Revillagigedo 23, tel. 5518-1149, fax 5512-6419, $40 s, $45 d) is an efficiently run, crisply decorated venue with a restaurant/bar and a 24-hour

café stuffed with Mexican handicrafts. There's an interior courtyard, though it's not accessible to guests, and the 135 rooms have satellite TVs but are a bit cramped. Parking is available.

A block north of the Alameda, **Hotel Hidalgo** (Santa Veracruz 37, tel. 5521-8771, $26 s, $34 d, $37 t, $39 quad) has 100 clean, modest rooms with large bathrooms. The hotel is in a slightly funky neighborhood, but the service is very good.

Hotel Bamer (Av. Juárez 52, tel. 5521-9060, fax 5510-1793, $48 s, $53 d) has been a traveler's old-reliable for years. The hotel faces the Alameda and is within walking distance of many attractions. Rooms and suites are spacious and have comfy beds; some also have sweeping views of the Alameda. A small *tabaquería* (tobacco shop) sells essentials, a lobby bar dispenses libation, and a brightly lit cafeteria is open daily 7 A.M.–11 P.M.

A bit out of the way, on a side street past Balderas, is **Hotel Ambassador** (Humboldt 38, tel. 5518-0110, $35 s, $45 d), a 150-room midrange hotel with serviceable though slightly worn rooms. They have a restaurant that offers a decent breakfast, but it's better to go right next door to Fonda Santa Anita, a great and inexpensive traditional eatery, for lunch.

$50–75

A refreshing combination of modern convenience and Mexican decor, the **Hotel San Francisco** (Luis Moya 11, tel. 5521-8960, fax 5510-8831, $50 s/d, $52 t) is half a block from the Alameda's southern esplanade. The hotel's lobby boasts bright, modern Mexican murals and rustic seating. The rooms, including suites with large balconies (some with Alameda views), are spacious and tasteful.

Another good value is the modern **Hotel Metropol** (Luis Moya 39, tel. 5510-8660, fax 5512-1273, $51 s, $60 d), two blocks south of the Alameda. The 160 clean rooms have telephones and new color TVs, and hotel service is generally very good. The hotel has a restaurant/bar and travel agency, as well as room service.

$75–110

The **☒ Best Western Hotel de Cortés,** (Av. Hidalgo 85, tel. 5518-2184, fax 5512-1863, U.S./Canada tel. 800/528-1234, www.bestwestern.com/reservations/mx, $108 s/d, $154 suites), opposite the northwest corner of the Alameda, has lots of historical ambience. Originally built in 1660 as the Hospice of Saint Nicolás Tolentino of the St. Augustine Hermits, it was originally dedicated to providing housing and food for the poor. Closed for several years following Mexican Independence, the building reopened in 1860 as a hostel for traveling tradesmen on local market days. The owners inaugurated the Hotel de Cortés in 1943, and today it offers 27 rooms and suites along with a small restaurant/bar and a beautiful courtyard dining area. Corner suites feature separate sitting areas; a few nonsmoking rooms are available. Although the rooms are nothing spectacular, the beautiful two-story terra cotta–colored courtyard, with its fountain, lush foliage, and caged songbirds, is a lovely place to have a relaxed meal. *Trovadores* (strolling musicians) often perform in the afternoon. The 2 P.M. check-out time is another plus.

OVER $110

Dominating the southwest corner of the Alameda is the towering new **Sheraton Centro Histórico** (Av. Juárez 70, tel. 5130-5252, fax 5130-5255, U.S./Canada 800/325-3535, www.sheraton.com/centrohistorico, $120 s/d and up). Built in 2002, the 457-room Sheraton was one of the first private concerns to sign on to the city government's efforts to revitalize the Alameda and Centro neighborhoods. The 24-story building has a stylishly interesting facade. The thoroughly modern, comfortable rooms offer a high-speed Internet connection, a flat-screen television with video games, and suites with Jacuzzis and kitchenettes. The hotel also has a fitness center, a wine bar and a lobby bar, and business and convention centers—and even a heliport.

Right next door to the Sheraton is the more modest **Fiesta Inn** (Av. Juárez 76, tel. 5130-2900, fax 5130-2910, U.S. 800/343-7821, www.fiestainn.com, $135 s/d, $160 suites). Its 140 rooms are cheerfully painted and decorated, and the hotel has a restaurant, business center, and a gym. A room designed for disabled guests is also available.

Paseo de la Reforma and Zona Rosa

Because of its central location, the availability of services, and the relatively easy access to transportation, the Reforma/Zona Rosa area makes a good base from which to tour Mexico City. The hotels in the Zona Rosa and on Reforma fall toward the higher end of the scale, while attractive midrange accommodations can be found just off Reforma, both near the Monumento de Colón and behind the U.S. embassy. Budget travelers will find plenty of low-priced hotels of varying quality in the few blocks between the Monumento a la Revolución and Avenida Puente de Alvarado.

UNDER $15

Near the Monumento a la Revolución, **☒ Casa de los Amigos** (Ignacio Mariscal 132, tel. 5705-0521, fax 5705-0771, www.casadelosamigos.org, $9 for dorm bed, $20 s or $25 d for small private rooms) is run by Quakers and often serves as a base for people doing social work in Mexico and Central America. Don't worry, they don't proselytize, and it can be a good place to meet some very interesting travelers. You are asked not to bring alcohol into the hostel. Reception closes at 10 P.M., so arrive before that on your first night. Guests may also use the kitchen, which can help save pesos. There is a minimum stay of 4 days and a maximum stay of 15 days per month. One studio double with a small kitchen rents for $35.

Nearby but of a very different social milieu is **Hotel Oxford** (Ignacio Mariscal 67, tel. 5566-0500, $11 s, $13 d), which serves as a part-time brothel. But it remains popular with backpackers because it offers reasonably clean, inexpensive rooms. It has a decent, funky little bar inside for late-night drinks, and occasional inebriated guitarists play melancholy *trío* laments.

Just up the street from the Oxford is **Hotel Pennsylvania** (Ignacio Mariscal 101, tel. 5703-1384, $13 s, $14 d), which is also worn but functional for those on a budget.

$15–30

One block from the Monumento a la Revolución, **Hotel Edison** (Thomas A. Edison 106, tel. 5566-0933, $20 s, $22 d) is a modest, inexpensive hotel. Each of the carpeted rooms has a writing desk, TV, telephone, and chairs with well-worn cushions. Check your mattress, as some are severely mushy. Parking is available.

Almost opposite Casa de los Amigos is the modern **Hotel Texas** (Ignacio Mariscal 129, tel. 5705-5782, $19 s, $22 d, $26 d with two beds), with an attached parking lot.

$30–50

Casa González (Río Sena 69, at Río Lerma, tel. 5514-3302, fax 5511-0702, $35 s, $50 d) is a small inn consisting of a cluster of colonial and postcolonial houses close to the U.S. and British embassies. The owner and his family still live in one wing, and staying here is a little like staying in an old, rambling home. The separate buildings, each painted a cheerful white with blue trim and containing several rooms, are situated around a landscaped courtyard. Several of the 22 rooms have their own little patios, which make lovely spots to sit outside, relax, and listen to the birds sing. It's best to call ahead for reservations. Off-street parking isn't available at the hotel, but there's a public pay lot next door.

Hotel Corinto (Vallarta 24, tel. 5566-6555, fax 5546-6888, $40 s/d) is a 10-story, 155-room building one block south of the Monumento a la Revolución. The modern rooms are a bit on the small side but comfortable and a good value, with a tiled bath, TV, and phone. Parking is available, and the hotel also has a small pool.

$50–75

A couple of blocks north of Reforma, the 150-room **María Christina** (Río Lerma 31, tel. 5566-9688, fax 5566-9194, www.hotelmariacristina.com.mx, $57 s, $63 d, $54–61 suites) is a reliable hotel in a four-story colonial-style building featuring interior gardens frequented by midrange travelers. The large suites are a good value, and each is furnished with a wet bar. The attached coffee shop is popular with guests and nonguests alike. The hotel bookshop has a good selection of international magazines.

The 148-room **Hotel Bristol** (Plaza Necaxa 17, tel. 5208-1717, fax 5533-6060, $63 s, $72 d, up to $100 for penthouse suites) is behind the U.S. embassy, three blocks from Paseo de la Reforma and near the Zona Rosa. Recently remodeled, the rooms are very clean and modern

gold-domed Hotel Imperial on Paseo de la Reforma

with air-conditioning and large TVs. Amenities include a restaurant, bar, free parking, and an efficient staff.

About halfway between the Zona Rosa and the Alameda is a good option for those who want to do their own cooking: **Mi Casa** (General Prim 101, tel. 5566-6711, $47 s, $54 d, suites up to $65) is an inexpensive apartment-hotel with 27 modern rooms equipped with full kitchens. It's located about halfway between the Zona Rosa and the Alameda.

$75–110

The 12-story **Casa Blanca** (La Fragua 7, tel. 5096-4500, fax 5096-4510, U.S./Canada tel. 800/905-2905, www.hotel-casablanca.com.mx, $90 s, $110 d) is a thoroughly modern hotel with 270 pastel rooms, each with wall-to-wall carpeting, subdued fluorescent lighting, marble-tiled baths, comfortable chairs and tables, piped-in music, and air-conditioning. A rooftop pool and bar overlook the city.

Right next to the Monumento El Colón, well-located in between the Alameda and the Zona Rosa, is **Hotel Imperial** (Paseo de la Reforma 64, tel. 5705-4911, www.differentworld.com/mexico, US$97 d). Decorations in the 60 rooms, distributed around a Guggenheim–style, multi-level interior atrium, are a little on the chintzy side, but they are comfortable and well kept. The hotel restaurant specializes in Spanish cuisine.

OVER $110

The premier high-end choice for international businesspeople is the **M̄ Hotel Four Seasons** (Paseo de la Reforma 500, tel. 5230-1818, fax 5230-1808, toll-free in Mexico 800/906-7500, www.four seasons.com/mexico, $290 s/d, $340 suites). In an eight-story neocolonial building at the western end of Reforma, the rooms are unusually homey, filled with plants and comfortable furniture, and the courtyard café is a lovely spot for breakfast. The hotel restaurant is frequented by politicos and businessfolk negotiating deals.

A pink granite-and-glass structure on the western section of Reforma, with hints of art deco lines, **Hotel Marquis Reforma** (Paseo de la Reforma 465, tel. 5229-1200, fax 5229-1212, U.S. tel. 800/235-2387, Canada tel. 877/818-5011, www.marquisreforma.com.mx, $265 s/d, $320

© JORGE ARANA

The statue of Christopher Columbus points out the better rooms in the Fiesta Americana.

suites) contains 208 rooms and 84 suites with soft-toned modern styling and vaguely antique-looking furniture. All rooms have data ports and faxes, and cellphone rental is available. Female guests can choose to room on a floor reserved for women only. On the premises are the stylish international restaurant La Jolla, a bar, and a gym with sauna and hot tub.

In front of the Monumento de Colón, the venerable **Fiesta Americana,** (Paseo de la Reforma 80, tel. 5140-4100, fax 5140-4101, www.fiestaamericana.com, $120 s/d) does well with the middle-class business crowd. Rooms are large and comfortable, and the restaurant has a good reputation for quality Mexican food. On the downside, telephone lines in guest rooms do not have data transmission capability. The hotel got some time in the spotlight in 2000, when then-presidential candidate Vicente Fox stayed there during most of his successful campaign.

Galería Plaza (Hamburgo 195, tel. 5230-1717, fax 5207-5867, www.brisas.com.mx, $160 s/d, $260–290 suites) is a luxury favorite in the middle of the Zona Rosa, with 439 elegantly decorated rooms, each with a marble bathroom and all the amenities. The hotel's Île de France restaurant is frequently recommended.

The concrete and steel **Hotel Marco Polo** (Amberes 27, tel. 5080-0063, fax 5080-1448, U.S. tel. 800/310-9693, www.marcopolo .com.mx, $137 s, $153 d) sits near the heart of the Zona Rosa on a quiet side street just off Reforma. The 60 carpeted rooms have a somewhat postmodern feel, and the staff do their best to pamper guests. A restaurant and piano bar can be found on the hotel's ground floor.

Chapultepec and Polanco

The area around Chapultepec and Polanco has some of the finest and most expensive hotels in the city, favored by many businesspeople and wealthier tourists. Low-budget travelers won't find anything in their price range here.

OVER $110

A short distance from the edge of Chapultepec, the Ricardo Legorreta–designed **M Camino Real Mexico City** (Av. Mariano Escobedo 700, tel. 5263-8888, U.S./Canada tel. 800/722-6466, www.caminoreal.com/mexico, $130–230 s/d, up to $310 for executive floor) fills the corners of its unique whitewashed, cubist building with a flamboyant selection of modern art, including a Rufino Tamayo mural in the lobby and masterworks elsewhere by Alexander Calder, Pedro Coronel, David Alfaro Siqueiros, and Gunther Gerzo. Wandering around the palatial corridors of the five-story main building, lined with banquet halls and bars, one could be forgiven for forgetting that it's a hotel. The 713 airy rooms, decorated in solid colors, are practically hidden in the corners of the hotel, which also boasts three swimming pools, four rooftop tennis courts (il-luminated for night play), and an excellent health club available to nonguests for $10 per visit. The hotel has several restaurants and bars to choose from, including a branch of Le Cirque, one of the best French restaurants in Mexico.

Just off Paseo de la Reforma, opposite the first section of Chapultepec, three more of Mexico City's best hotels dominate the skyline. The 38-story tower of **Hotel Nikko México** (Campos Eliseos 204, tel. 5283-8700, fax 5280-9191, U.S./Canada tel. 800/645-5687, www.hotel-nikkomexico.com.mx, $130–210 s/d, $245 executive rooms, $600 suites) is visible from much of the city on a clear day. The Nikko boasts a complete business center, health club with pool and tennis courts, a golf driving range, several restaurants and bars, and a wealth of other amenities. The 745 rooms are rather standard looking, considering the price.

Right next door to the Nikko, the **Presidente Inter-Continental Mexico City** (Campos Eliseos 218, tel. 5327-7700, fax 5327-7730, U.S./Canada tel. 800/327-0200, www.interconti.com, $160–240 s/d, $325 executive rooms) was built in 1977, making it the oldest of the park hotels. A multistory pyramid lobby topped with an im-

COURTESY OF CAMINO REAL MEXICO CITY

Camino Real Mexico City

mense skylight never fails to impress. The 660 rooms, though not exceptional, are well equipped, and executive suites equipped with Internet connections and fax machines are available. The hotel has a "gourmet center," with seven restaurants featuring different world cuisines, including the superlative Au Pied de Cochon French restaurant, open 24 hours a day, and the Balmoral tea room, with English-style high tea and snacks.

A half block from the Nikko and Presidente, at Campos Eliseos and Andrés Bello, the **JW Marriott** (Andrés Bello 29, tel. 5999-0000, fax 5999-0001, U.S./Canada tel. 888/813-2776, www.marriott.com, $190–265 standard rooms, $295 executive rooms) is considered by many to have the best rooms of the "big three." The Marriott has 300 rooms, 20 suites, and a reputation for top-notch service.

A relative newcomer to the area is the **Fiesta Americana Grande** (Mariano Escobedo 756, tel. 5281-1500, toll free in Mexico 800/504-5000, U.S. tel. 800/343-7821, www.fiestaamericana .com, $190 s/d, up to $400 for the standard suite). A complement to the venerable Fiesta Americana on Paseo de la Reforma, this sleek new tower houses 203 rooms and 14 suites, with a full spa and business center and three executive floors.

A change from the high-powered high-rise hotels, though even more pricey, is **Casa Vieja** (Eugenio Sue 45, tel. 5282-0067, fax 5281-3780, www.casavieja.com, $350–$850, depending on which suite you choose), a converted late-19th-century mansion ideally located in the center of Polanco along a quiet side street. The 10 rooms all have a kitchen, stereo, fax machine, desk, and satellite TV and are decorated in Mexican style with bright solid colors, tiles, woven rugs, and wooden furniture. Corporate rates and other discounts are frequently available.

Also a change of pace, but of a very different variety, is **M Hotel Hábita** (Av. Presidente Masaryk 201, tel. 5282-3100, www.designhotels.com, $195 s, $225 d, $315 suites). A member of Small Luxury Hotels and Design Hotels, Hábita is done up in an ultramodern style, with lots of glass and sleek styling. Each of the 36 carpeted rooms is elegantly simple, with futons and a small terrace. Suites are only slightly larger than the regular rooms. Each room has direct Internet data ports, and the hotel has a business/conference center. On the roof is a glassed-in exercise room and open-air pool, as well as a popular hipster lounge bar called El Área. The restaurant downstairs is very good and often frequented by nonguests.

Insurgentes Sur

As Condesa and Roma have been a bit off the tourist track (until now, at least), not a lot of hotel options are to be found in these neighborhoods. But the section of Álvaro Obregón between Insurgentes and Cuauhtémoc, Roma's main drag, has a few decent lower-priced hotels to choose from. There are only three higher-end places here, but they are all very nice in their own way, making this area an alternative to the posh hotel districts of Reforma or Polanco.

$15–30

The bright pink **Hotel Colonia Roma** (Jalapa 100, at Álvaro Obregón, tel. 5584-1396, $19 s/d) offers 50 small, carpeted rooms with TV and telephone.

Three blocks east is **Hotel Monarca** (Álvaro Obregón 32, tel. 5584-0461, $19 s/d), an unattractive five-story building which nonetheless has inexpensive and decent rooms. It's popular among middle-class Mexicans.

$30–50

An excellent midrange hotel in the Roma Norte is **Hotel Parque Ensenada** (Álvaro Obregón 13, tel. 5208-0052, www.hotelensenada.com.mx, $44 s, $52 d, $60 suites), with 140 comfortable, carpeted modern rooms, each equipped with bedside fan, small fridge, TV, and phone. The hotel staff is efficient and friendly.

Hotel Milan (Álvaro Obregón 94, tel. 5584-0222, fax 5584-0696, $30 s, $37 d, $45 for a larger room) has a remarkably ugly facade, but the rooms are modern and very livable. The hotel has a restaurant/bar and parking.

Just barely in the Condesa, right on Insurgentes but with easy access to Parque México, is **Hotel Roosevelt** (Insurgentes Sur 287, tel. 5208-6813, $37 s/d, $42 with king-sized bed). The hotel, with 75 modern rooms, each with cable TV and telephone, has a sanitized, motel-like feel. A reasonably priced coffee shop and parking garage are on the ground floor.

At the eastern edge of the Roma, near the Centro Medico Metro station, is **Hotel Lisboa** (Av. Cuauhtémoc 273, tel. 5574-7088, fax 5564-9862, toll free in Mexico 800/710-2856, www.hotellisboa.com.mx, $43 s, $48 d). It's in a retro, 1970s-looking, white, eight-story tower and has 130 rooms that are clean and unremarkable but functional and well maintained. The more expensive rooms have balconies facing south across the city, but the traffic from Avenida Cuauhtémoc below detracts a bit from the view.

$50–75

A block north of Hotel Lisboa and in from Avenida Cuauhtémoc is the similar but slightly nicer **Hotel Benidorm** (Frontera 217, tel. 5584-9899, fax 5574-8743, www.benidorm.com.mx, $61 s/d, $80–110 suites).

OVER $110

In a residential area of the Roma neighborhood, near the Zona Rosa, **La Casona** (Durango 280, tel. 5286-3001, fax 5211-0871, www.hotel-lacasona.com.mx, $150 s/d with breakfast) is housed in a refurbished late-19th-century mansion. The small but luxurious hotel contains a very good café-restaurant, a gym, services for business travelers, and 30 rooms filled with wooden writing desks and lacy curtains.

A new place in the Roma, wonderfully located right on the quiet little Parque Luis Cabrera, is **Casa de la Condesa** (Plaza Luis Cabrera 16, tel. 5574-3186 or 5584-3089, fax 5592-5681, www.extendedstaymexico.com, studios $100 per day or $500 per week, suites $110 per day or $550 per week), which rents out apartment-style units with fully equipped kitchens, daily housekeeping, and computer data ports (for an extra fee). Choose between

COURTESY OF THE CONDESA DF

Condesa df

the smaller studio apartments or the full-size rooms with separate dining, living, and bedrooms. Try to grab a room on the higher floors facing the park, as they have porches with hammocks. There's no need to worry about traffic noise here.

A great new addition to Mexico City's hotel market is **Condesa df** (Av. Veracruz 102, tel. 5241-2600, www.condesadf.com, $165–395 s/d), run by the same owners as Hotel Hábita, in Polanco. A fine old triangular-shaped *casona* (old mansion) built on a corner property just off Parque España has been intriguingly remodeled to house 24 rooms and 16 suites, all done in a sleek, minimalist style. The top floor rooms, with patios, are more expensive. Also upstairs is a steam room and hot tub, while the restaurant (with excellent food) is in the building's central patio. The staff are bilingual and very efficient.

Coyoacán and San Ángel

This part of the city has a major dearth of good hotels, with none at all in the central areas of either neighborhood because of zoning laws. In recent years some city officials, backed no doubt by the local business community, have attempted to change the laws, but as yet the residents have successfully resisted the change.

While it makes it hard on the tourists, it certainly keeps the neighborhood more pleasingly residential. The best option is to stay elsewhere in the city and visit during the day, but if you really want to stay in the area, there are a couple of acceptable hotels on Calzada de Tlapan near the Metro Tasqueña station, the southern terminus for Metro Line 2.

Also near this area is the Terminal Central del Sur bus station. It's a relatively short taxi or bus ride to Coyoacán and San Ángel to the west.

$30–50

The best moderately priced choice is the modern, 128-room **Hotel Finisterre** (Calz. de Tlapan 2043, tel. 5689-9544, fax 5689-9720, $30 s, $38 d, $44 d with whirlpool bath).

$75–110

Hotel Royal Plaza (Parroquia 1056, Colonia Santa Cruz Atoyac, tel. 5605-8943, fax 5688-2229, toll free in Mexico 800/009-1000, $110 s/d), located just off Avenida Universidad a few blocks north of the Circuito Interior, is the only upscale hotel in this part of the city. The 130 rooms are all spacious and well appointed (although the artwork over the beds is a little dodgy). The hotel has both a cafeteria and a more formal restaurant, and it offers babysitting services to those traveling with small children. It's about a 15-minute drive (depending on traffic) to the Terminal Sur bus station and 10 minutes to the center of Coyoacán.

A bit less expensive, but not as nice either, is **Hotel Cibeles** (Calz. de Tlalpan 1507, tel. 5672-2244, $80 s/d), offering unremarkable rooms equipped with cable TV and air-conditioning in a modern building. The hotel has a restaurant with room service and a bar.

OVER $110

Technically in the Colonia Del Valle but very close to Coyoacán, is **Suites Coyoacán** (Av. Coyoacán 1909, tel. 5534-8353, fax 5534-4013, www.suitescoyoacan.com, $120 s/d, $830 per week, $3300 per month). Designed for businesspeople with extended stays in Mexico, this feels more like a private, colonial-style housing compound than a hotel. Each of the nine suites comes equipped with a high-speed Internet connection, full kitchen, direct telephone, and reserved parking. The more expensive suites also come with a VCR, stereo sound system, and microwave. The hotel has 24-hour security and can arrange for taxis and laundry service.

Near the Airport and Bus Terminals

$15–30

Hotel Brasilia (Av. de Los Cien Metros, tel. 5587-8577, $27 s/d) is just two blocks from Terminal Central del Norte—walkable if you don't have too much luggage. The hotel is no great shakes, but it's more than adequate for an overnight stay if you come in late or need to leave early and don't have time to get into town for a nicer place. The hotel has a restaurant attached. (For places near Terminal Central del Sur, see the *Coyoacán and San Ángel* section in this chapter.)

$30–50

The closest decent low-priced hotel near the airport is **Hotel Aeropuerto** (Boulevard Aeropuerto 380, tel. 5785-5888 or 5785-5851, $40 s/d one bed, $50 d two beds), just across the Circuito Interior from the airport. To get there on foot, walk all the way past the domestic terminal, follow the street around to the left past the Metro station entrance, and cross the Circuito Interior via the nearby pedestrian bridge. The hotel, with 52 basic rooms with TVs and telephones, is right on the far side of the bridge.

OVER $110

Connected to the domestic terminal (near Sala B) via a pedestrian bridge is the **Camino Real Aeropuerto** (Puerto México 80, tel. 3003-0033, fax 3003-0034, www.caminoreal.com, $205 s/d) a 583-room monster of a hotel with a very pleasant, leafy lobby. Guests (and the general public, for $10) have access to a full health club and indoor pool. The hotel has four restaurants, a pizza parlor, a bar, a 24-hour café, and a 24-hour business center. Even if you don't spend the night in the hotel, the coffee shop is a much nicer place to spend layover time than comparable facilities at the airport. Camino Real took this hotel over from Marriot, the former owners, at the beginning of 2004.

The **Airport Hilton** (tel./fax 5133-0505, www.hilton.com, $150 s/d) is actually built on top of the international terminal—take the elevator up to the fourth floor, and you will be in the lobby. The 129 rooms all have a separate phone line for computers. Carlos' Place Bar is a good place to sip a drink, watch planes take off and land, and also keep track of incoming flights if you are waiting for someone.

Across the Circuito Interior highway from the airport, next door to Hotel Aeropuerto, is **Hotel Jr Plaza** (Boulevard Aeropuerto 390, tel. 5785-5200 or 5785-6500, $130 s/d). It's not as nice as the hotels at the airport itself but is nonetheless decent if you want to save a few dollars.

Excursions from Mexico City

Roads radiate from Mexico City in all directions, providing ample opportunities for daytrippers and weekenders to explore the region. This chapter covers the major cities and sights within about two or three hours' drive from Mexico City, maximum; many destinations are not more than an hour away.

It's amazing how much variety you'll find in Central Mexico, just a short trip from the capital. Several different prehispanic ruins, most notably Teotihuacán but also more obscure sites like Malinalco, Cacaxtla, or the Baños de Nezahualcóyotl, are easy day trips, as are jewels of colonial architecture like the Catedral in the city of Puebla, the 15th-century monastery at Huejotzingo, or the colonial art museum in Tepozotlán.

No matter which way you leave the city, the scenery is dramatic, with highways winding up the steep mountains flanking the Valle de Mexico, passing through pine forested parks dotted with lakes and meadows. These are favorite spots for *chilangos* (capital dwellers) to escape for a day of fresh air. Don't forget to pull over on the highway stops lined with little restaurants selling mushroom soup, *tacos de cecina,* (cured-meat tacos) and some of the best blue-corn *quesadillas* you're ever likely to have.

Adventure-sport enthusiasts will be gratified to hear that they can have a blast putting themselves in danger's way in a variety of ways, including rock and ice climbing, mountain biking, paragliding and hang gliding, and

Best Excursions

Talavera ceramics of Puebla

Most Impressive Aztec Ruins: Right outside of Mexico City stands one of the greatest prehispanic cities in all the Americas, **Teotihuacán,** dominated by the towering Pyramid of the Sun. This ancient city housed 200,000 people at its height, rivaling its contemporary, Rome (page 199).

Best Place to Pitch a Tent: In the hills outside of Pachuca, **Parque Nacional El Chico** is full of idyllic meadows in the pine forest, perfect for pitching a tent. This safe area is full of trails for taking walks or bike rides and old mining villages to explore. The adventurous can even take find guides to take them on rock climbing trips on the mountaintop cliffs (page 212).

Best Roadside Food: Up at **Tres Marías,** a village in the mountains between Mexico City and Cuernavaca, hungry travelers can feast on some of the most scrumptious *antojitos* in one of the dozens of little restaurants lining the road. Try a *quesadilla* with *flor de calabaza* (squash flower), a taco of *cecina* (cured, flattened beef), or a *sopa de hongo* (mushroom soup), all at criminally low prices (page 220).

Best Views by Car: As long as there's no snow, follow the dirt road winding up to the extinct crater of **Nevado de Toluca** (4,691 meters). Enjoy the fantastic views across the mountains of central Mexico, or if you get motivated, hike up to the crater rim (page 239).

Best Hidden Getaway: There's a myriad of little-known towns to explore near Mexico City, but **Malinalco** is particularly charming. Tucked into a narrow, lush valley, this *pueblo* has a huge and beautiful early colonial monastery right in the middle, and an unusual prehispanic temple cut into a nearby mountainside (page 242).

Best Arts and Crafts: The silversmiths of Taxco are second to none, but for overall variety of *artesanís,* the shops and markets in and around Puebla are better. Take a walk through **El Parian,** a market housed in a former 18th-century warehouse, thronged with stalls selling Talavera pottery, woven indigenous *rebozos* (shawls), silver cowboy accoutrements, and *alebrijes* (animal-like sculptures carved of wood or fashioned from papier-mâché) (page 264).

Best Colonial Monastary: Built by one of the first Catholic missionaries to arrive in Mexico in the early 16th century, the monastery **Huejotzingo** near Puebla is at once a monument to the dedication of these Spanish friars and a testament to the indigenous spirit. The elaborate artwork decorating the stone facade contains many prehispanic symbols. Inside, the *retablo* (altarpiece) is one of the loveliest in Mexico (page 272).

Excursions

white-water rafting. There are also endless kilometers of quiet mountain paths for hiking, and quiet walks through patches of forest literally blanketed with monarch butterflies in their winter home.

But be sure to catch your breath and take the time to enjoy a day (or three, or ten) *puebleando,* a wonderful Mexican verb meaning something like "wandering around small towns." Dozens of towns and villages dot the countryside, some with little hidden treasures like a gorgeous baroque chapel or a 17th-century hacienda converted into a museum. Others don't have anything in particular to do but are nonetheless fine places to stroll through the town market to buy a *torta* and fresh fruit juice, then head over to the *zócalo* (main square)and sit down on a bench to take in the atmosphere along with your snack, remembering in a flash exactly what it is you love about Mexico.

When leaving from or returning to Mexico City from visiting the destinations in this chapter, choose your times carefully. Nothing's worse than having a lovely, relaxing weekend in some bucolic spot, and then getting caught in endless Sunday afternoon traffic on your way back to the city, leaving you even more frazzled and stressed than when you left! Friday afternoons leaving town and Sunday afternoons and evenings returning are the worst, so if you can schedule your trip to avoid these times, you'll be happier.

Guided Trips

While most visitors will want to make trips on their own and explore, the Mexican government Instituto Nacional de Antropología e Historia (INAH) offers various trips every weekend to destinations around Mexico City. The trips, called Paseos Culturales de INAH, typically cost $33 per day (8 A.M.–8 P.M.), with transportation, guide, and entrance fee to sites included. All the prescheduled trips are in Spanish, but special trips can be arranged with English-speaking guides for groups (minimum 10 people). For more information, contact the INAH office in the Museo Nacional de Antropología (tel. 5553-2365 or 5553-3822, www.inah.gob.mx). Information on the tours was at last report only in the Spanish version of the website, not the English version.

One private tour operator with a variety of different trips throughout Central Mexico is **Rebozo Ecoturismo** (Mexico City tel. 5550-9080, www.marlene-ehrenberg.com.mx). This company is focused as much (if not more) on cultural tourism, with trips geared around certain town festivals or markets, or to see different kinds of local dances or taste local cuisines. (For companies with adventure-sport trips in Central Mexico, see the *Recreation* chapter.)

North of Mexico City

⋈ TEOTIHUACÁN

Little is known about the people who built the ancient city of Teotihuacán, one of the largest, most impressive archaeological sites in the Americas. During the city's heyday it was Mesoamerica's most powerful social and political hub. The structures were built between 100 B.C. and A.D. 250, accommodating as many as 200,000 people and forming the largest and most sophisticated city in the Western Hemisphere and comparable with its contemporaries in the Roman Empire. During its height, the influence of the Teoti-

huacáno empire was felt throughout Mesoamerica. Whatever civilization produced Teotihuacán lasted roughly until the 7th century A.D., but despite its obviously complex technology, left behind no writing system or any other hints as to who built the city. It is clear from the types of artifacts excavated within the pyramids and temples that the builders of Teotihuacán were a heavily militarized society, not unlike the later Toltecs and Aztecs. More than 1,200 human skeletons have been discovered amid the ruins, all of them thought to have been sacrificial victims.

Archaeologists believe a four-chambered

Excursions

lava-tube cave in the Valle de Teotihuacán prompted the choice of location for the construction of the original monuments. Considered places where gods and ancestors emerged, as well as doors to a magical underworld, caves played an important role in Mesoamerican religion. Teotihuacán's Pyramid of the Sun was built directly over the cave in the 2nd century A.D.

The site flourished until about A.D. 750, when it was abandoned and set afire. Some researchers suggest the calamity may have been a war between Teotihuacán and Cacaxtla, a smaller contemporary city in nearby Tlaxcala. Over the centuries, pyramids, citadel, temples, palaces, plazas, and paved streets remained deserted and forgotten until the Aztecs arrived in A.D. 1200. Recognizing the site's formidable history, the Aztecs named the ruins Teotihuacán, or "place where gods are born." The Aztecs used Teotihuacán as a pilgrimage center; according to Aztec legend, the sun, moon, and universe itself were created here. Though awestruck by the city's size, the Aztecs probably knew less about the site than we know today.

The most visited archaeological site in Mexico, it is also among the world's most researched and excavated archaeological sites—"loved to death" according to some. Even though it is a national icon and a major center of tourism, government support has been ambivalent and commercial exploitation of Teotihuacán has been ongoing. UNESCO has designated the ruins a World Heritage Site, and the World Monuments Fund added them to its list of the world's 100 most endangered monuments in 1998, noting that a permanent conservation program and tourist management plan are badly needed. In an ominous sign of how effective that is came with the news that retail giant Wal-Mart was opening a store only a kilometer from the edge of the archaeological zone.

La Ciudadela (The Citadel)

Across from the visitors center is a fortresslike enclosure in the geographic center of the city, measuring about 400 meters on each side and with estimated room for 100,000 people. Archaeologists surmise that this area, called the

Main Plaza, may have been the designated place for many ritual performances. At the southeast end of the plaza is the famed **Templo de Quetzalcóatl,** a striking construction decorated with amazing stone carvings of serpent heads. Although not as tall as either the Sun or Moon pyramids, the elaborate carvings on the Templo de Quetzalcóatl attest to its ritual importance. While the sculptures on three sides of the pyramid have been destroyed, a protective platform built by the *teotihuacanos* themselves (for unknown reasons) on the front has protected the artwork on that side.

The remains of 137 people were found buried here. They were apparently sacrificed, their hands tied behind their backs, during the construction of the pyramid. Scholars believe they were killed as part of a warfare cult that was regulated by the position of Venus in its 584-day celestial cycle. Many of these individuals wore collars made of imitation human jawbones with teeth carved from shell, as well as several real maxillae and mandibles. The corpses were placed in pits with more than 2,100 pieces of worked shell and numerous obsidian blades and points.

Next to the pyramid are two large palaces that may have been living quarters or offices for the city's rulers.

Calzada de los Muertos (Avenue of the Dead)

This causeway, now probably about half the length of when the city was in its heyday, runs north-to-south between the visitors center (at the south end) and the Pyramid of the Moon (at the north end). It received its ominous name from the Aztecs, who apparently believed the structures lining the causeway contained the graves of giants who had died and become gods. Modern archaeologists instead believe these buildings were ancient residential complexes.

Pirámide del Sol (Pyramid of the Sun)

This is one of the largest, most impressive pyramids in the world. As it now stands, the pyramid (actually five stepped platforms) measures 225 meters on each side and just under 70 meters in

TEOTIHUACÁN

To Otumba

Excursions

PLAZA OF THE MOON

PYRAMID OF THE MOON

PALACE OF THE QUETZAL BUTTERFLY

NORTHWEST ENTRANCE

TEMPLE OF THE MYTHOLOGICAL ANIMALS

PUMA MURAL GROUP

STREET OF THE DEAD

To San Juan Teotihuacan

TEPANTITLA

PYRAMID OF THE SUN

ATETELCO

YAYAHUALA

ZACUALA

MUSEUM

VIKING GROUP

EAST ENTRANCE

TETITLA

SUPERIMPOSED BUILDINGS

132D

San Juan River

To Mexico City

SOUTHWEST ENTRANCE

TEMPLE OF THE FEATHERED SERPENT

CIUDADELA

0   200 yds

0   200 m

MOON

© AVALON TRAVEL PUBLISHING, INC.

Pirámide del Sol, Teotihuacán

the Ciudadela was one of the principal ritual areas in the city. Built later than the other principal monuments in the city, the Pyramid of the Moon is 46 meters high and not as steep a climb as the Pyramid of the Sun, but the views over the city and surrounding countryside are still great. When approaching the pyramid along the Avenida de los Muertos, note how the outline of the structure mirrors that of Cerro Gordo, the mountain behind it.

Visitors Center

Back at the south end of the site, the visitors center holds a museum, several craft shops, a bookstore, a restaurant, and restrooms. The 2nd-floor restaurant (9 A.M.–midnight Mon.–Fri., 11 A.M.–11 P.M. Sat., 10 A.M.–6 P.M. Sun.) enjoys a captive audience so is a bit overpriced.

Tips and Information

Wear good walking shoes—the Avenue of the Dead alone stretches about four kilometers. A hat, sunblock, and water are musts to carry with you. Remember, you are at an altitude of 2,300 meters; unless you're accustomed to this, take the steep stairs slowly. The site is open daily. The best time of day to visit the site (8 A.M.–5 P.M. daily, admission $3.80) for pictures and peace is 8 A.M., when the ticket-takers open the gate. The tour buses start arriving around 10 A.M. Weekends are the busiest, especially on Sunday, when admission is free. A parking fee is also charged. For more information, see the website http://archaeology.la.asu.edu/teo.

Getting to Teotihuacán

The ruins lie about 50 kilometers northeast of Mexico City. To get there by bus from Mexico City, look for the sign **Autobuses Sahagun** at the northwest end of the Terminal Central del Norte. Buses leave the terminal every 30 minutes 5 A.M.–6 P.M.; the trip to Teotihuacán takes about an hour. You want the bus marked "Los Pirámides," otherwise you may end up at the nearby city of San Juan Teotihuacán. To return to the city, catch your bus at the entrance gate of the museum. The last bus leaves the main entrance at 6 P.M.

height. Two tunnels burrowed by modern researchers into the core of the pyramid, however, indicate that it was first 215 meters on each side and 63 meters high and was later enlarged to its current height. The hike up is steep and—on the frequent dusty, hot days—exhausting. Take your time, but be prepared for some fantastic views on a clear day. The stark, unadorned lines of the pyramid add a certain austere grandeur to the imposing structure. A temple once stood atop the pyramid, but it has long since been destroyed.

In 1971, a long stairway was discovered that ended in a four-chamber lava cave 100 meters long under the pyramid. Archaeologists believe the cave was considered by the city's builders to be a sacred entryway to another world, which is why they chose the location to build their largest pyramid.

Pirámide de la Luna (Pyramid of the Moon)

At the north end of the Calzada de los Muertos is the Pyramid of the Moon, centered on the Plaza of the Moon, which along with the Main Plaza at

COURTESY OF MEXICO TOURISM BOARD/NADINE MARKOVA

TEOTIHUACÁN'S VIOLENT PAST

For many years, archaeologists had theorized that Teotihuacán was a relatively peaceful society, especially compared to the bloody excesses of the later Aztecs. In part this was because of the lack of artistic depictions glorifying human sacrifice and war. But recent excavations underneath the 1,900-year-old Pyramid of the Moon are changing that view.

In 1999, a burial chamber containing what may be the remains of a retainer of an early Teotihuacán ruler was discovered in the Pyramid of the Moon by an excavation team led by American and Mexican archaeologists. Inside the chamber, which has been dated to 150 B.C., the team found the skeleton of an adult male who had been bound and sacrificed. Surrounding the skeleton were more than 400 burial offerings, including obsidian and greenstone figurines, ceremonial obsidian blades and spear points, pyrite mirrors, and conch and other shells, along with the remains of eight hawks or falcons,

two jaguars, a wolf, a puma, and various serpents, all of which may have been buried alive. The buried individual is thought to be a royal retainer, and archaeologists were hoping to find a royal tomb in the center of the pyramid when they completed their excavations in 2002. In 2000, the same researcher team came across the skulls of 17 sacrificial victims who had been beheaded.

While evidence of sacrifice had been found previously at Teotihuacán, the location of these discoveries indicates the practice was much more central in the city's ceremonial life than previously thought. Nonetheless, despite being one of the most studies sites in Mesoamerica, much remains to be learned on the traditions of the mysterious city. Archaeologists hope that, much like in the Mayan cities of Palenque and Copán, deeper excavations will reveal earlier tombs that might shed further light on the traditions of the people who lived in Teotihuacán.

If you're driving from Mexico City to Teotihuacán, you have a choice of toll-free México 132D or the toll road *(cuota)*, México 85D. The toll road usually has lighter traffic and is quicker.

Acolman

Along the free road to Teotihuacán from Mexico City, and easily visible from the toll road, is the 16th-century Augustinian church and monastery complex of Acolman (tel. 595/957-1644, 9 A.M.–6 P.M., admission $3), noted for its fine Plateresque facade and the churchyard cross in front, carved with a mix of Catholic and Amerindian motifs. Inside the cloister are a series of religious murals. The fortresslike monastery makes a great stop-off while visiting Teotihuacán, especially if you've got your own car. By public transport, you can either take the local (not direct) bus between San Juan Teotihuacán and Indios Verdes Metro stop in Mexico City, or hop a *colectivo* (small bus) from Teotihuacán ruins headed toward "Ecatepec" and alight right next to the monastery for $0.80.

TEXCOCO

A large, dusty town northeast of Mexico City, on what used to be the eastern shores of the nearly vanished Lake Texcoco, Texcoco is not much to see itself, but it has three interesting sites to visit nearby, little seen by foreigners: Molino de Flores, Universidad de Chapingo, and the Baños de Nezahualcóyotl. Texcoco was founded originally around A.D.1200 by the Toltecs and later became the seat of the Acolhua empire, which was one of the principal allies of Aztecs. The city reached its height under Acolmiztli Nezahualcóyotl (1402–1472), the famed king of Texcoco. Not only was he a brilliant poet (his verse remains powerful to modern readers), but he was also a budding monotheist and a superlative engineer. It was Nezahualcóyotl who designed the complex of dams controlling the interlocking lakes of the valley (which were destroyed by Cortés during the conquest). Because of its importance, Augustinian monks established one of the first missions in Mexico nearby at Acolman, just off the highway to Teotihuacán.

The hills to the east of Texcoco, forming part

of the valley of Mexico, remain a heavily indigenous area, populated by Nahua farming communities. In many of these villages, the residents still don't speak Spanish. Ruins from the prehispanic era are found all over this little-explored region. San Miguel Coatlinchan, a village in the hills southeast of Texcoco, is the original site of the Tlaloc statue that now sits outside of the Museo Nacional de Antropología. Although the statue was taken decades ago, the villagers are still reputed to be extremely angry that their rain god was stolen by the government. A 16th-century church and convent in town is worth a visit. Another nearby village with many ruins around is San Luis Huexotla.

Nowadays Texcoco is a primarily agricultural town, and to celebrate that, the town holds the annual **Feria del Caballo.** Formerly the party was held just before Easter (Semana Santa), but in 2004 they shifted to a week in late November and early December, where they plan to keep it from now on. This blowout bash, known as "La Cantina Más Grande de México" (The Biggest Party in Mexico), features horse shows, bullfights, lots of good food, and lots of *ranchera* music.

There are plenty of restaurants in Texcoco should you want to grab a meal on your way through town. One right on the plaza is **Oasis del Naturismo** (7 A.M.–9 P.M. daily), a good place for breakfasts, light meals, or fruit drinks.

To get to Texcoco, take a Primera Plus or one of several other bus lines leaving every basically constantly from the TAPO eastern terminal in Mexico City. The 15-minute ride costs $2. By car, take the Circuito Interior, and look for the exit to Texcoco (Via Rápida Texcoco) just north of the airport. The toll costs $2 but is definitely worth it rather than struggling through the maze of back roads and slums on the free road.

Universidad de Chapingo

Three kilometers south of Texcoco is this university, one of the premier agricultural schools in the country. The university, started in 1923, is not a particular attraction in itself, although the grassy grounds are nice enough. But in one of the main buildings is the **Capilla Riveriana** (tel. 595/952-1500 or 595/952-5189, www.chapingo.mx,

10 A.M.–3 P.M. Mon.–Fri., 10 A.M.–5 P.M. Sat.–Sun., admission $3 for foreigners or $1 for Mexicans) chapel painted by famed Mexican muralist Diego Rivera between 1924 and 1927. The socialist proclivities of Rivera are much in evidence here, with hammer-and-sickle symbols throughout the murals. Also prominent is an earth mother theme, possibly a nod to the school's agricultural focus. Check out the wooden doors at the entrance, carved by Abraham López according to a design by Rivera. A guide offers a complete tour of the chapel and the adjacent building (a hacienda dating from 1690) for free during the week, and there are audio-guides for rent on weekends for $1. Check out the prehispanic stone carving in the entrance to the hacienda. To get to the university from Texcoco, hop a *microbus* (small bus) from downtown for $0.50, or take a taxi for about $3.

Parque Nacional Molino de Flores

The ruins of this 16th-century hacienda (9 A.M.–2 P.M. Mon.–Fri., 11 A.M.–5 P.M. Sat.–Sun.), three kilometers east of Texcoco in a small, tree-filled valley, is now a park frequented on weekends by local folks. The old hacienda was originally built in 1567 to produce cloth, and 20 years later it became a wheat mill. The mill passed through a variety of hands over the next centuries and continued functioning until the 1910–1920 Mexican Revolution. It was expropriated by the government in 1937.

Some of the hacienda buildings have been restored, while others remain in ruins, but all are very beautiful and well worth a visit to get an idea of what life might have been like on a hacienda. Free guided tours are available but in Spanish only. The park is mobbed on weekends, so it's best to come during the week. Taxis from downtown Texcoco cost $2.50, or you can hop a bus for $0.50.

Baños de Nezahualcóyotl

These ruins (10 A.M.–5 P.M. daily, free admission), surprisingly impressive considering how little-known they are, cover a hill just above the town of San Nicolás, about six kilometers east of Texcoco. Whether they were built by Nezahual-

Baños de Nezhualcóyotl, near Texcoco

cóyotl himself or not is not certain, but one can be sure he made use of them. To get to the ruins, formally known as Zona Arqueológica de Tetzcotzinco, either take a bus from Texcoco to San Nicolás ($1) or a taxi ($3.50). By car, follow the road to Molino de Flores, and just before arriving at the park, look for a right turn continuing uphill. From this junction it's three kilometers to San Nicolás. There is no gate per se, and when I went there was no one watching over the site, either. I had no problems and saw nobody threatening, but it's probably better to come on weekends when there are more folks around.

Right at the entrance to San Nicolás, a dirt road to the right leads to a modern public swimming pool (where you can leave your car if you came in one). Just behind the parking lot, a dirt road leads uphill; it quickly becomes a footpath. Passing a carved cave, you will come to a rebuilt staircase leading to the first stone bath, facing west over the valley. Here you can continue uphill to more baths or take side paths winding around the hillside. Wherever you go, you'll find carved stones and baths all over the place. On the back (east) side are the reconstructed ruins of a major

temple built into the hillside, as well as the remains of a causeway and aqueduct leading up into the mountains. More ruins are found continuing east. Visiting these ruins definitely makes for a great alternative day trip from Mexico City instead of going to the same tourist destinations as everyone else. On your way back down, you might consider taking a refreshing dip in the public pool for $3 adults, $2.50 kids under 12.

TEPOTZOTLÁN

Known for its magnificent churrigueresque convent and church, Tepotzotlán also holds a cobbled-street colonial city center—mostly unspoiled either by modernization or chic restorations—and the country's largest and most complete colonial history museum. Very popular with *capitalino* (capital city) tourists, the small town makes a good day-trip destination from Mexico City, about an hour away (43 kilometers) by bus from the Terminal del Norte. If you're driving up from the capital, take México 57D about 37 kilometers north toward Querétaro. The well-marked turnoff to Tepotzotlán lies just before the tollbooth.

Templo de San Francisco Javier and Plaza Hidalgo

This single-towered Spanish church and the attached convent form the nucleus of the town's tourist attractions. The simple early baroque side *portada* (entry) facing the main street corresponds to the first stage of the construction of the church, 1670–1682, and is topped by a niche containing an image of San Ignacio de Loyola. The front entry facing the Plaza Hidalgo is classic late baroque, or *churrigueresco,* and was crafted between 1760 and 1762. This much larger facade consists of many *estípites* (sculpted columns) filled with saints—I lost count at 22. San Francisco Javier, of course, stands in the main niche, right above a rosette window.

Sunday is a very popular time to visit the plaza and church, not just for Mass but to visit the food vendors who fill the plaza in front. The plaza and area surrounding the church and convent were restored by INAH in 1993–1994.

© CHRIS HUMPHREY

M Excursions

Excursions

sombreros for sale in front of the Templo de San Francisco Javier, Tepotzotlán

Museo Nacional de Virreinato

This large and very impressive museum (tel. 5876-0245, 9 A.M.–6 P.M. Tues.–Sun., admission $3.80) occupies a magnificent ex-convent that once served as a Jesuit college of Indian languages. The convent chapels, cloisters, library, refectory, kitchen, and other spaces were constructed between 1606 and 1767, and the overall three-story stone structure is considered an excellent model of the evolution of Spanish colonial architecture in Mexico. Even if you're not especially interested in the art contained in the museum, the convent architecture alone—with its thick walls, complex passageways, arched cloisters, and heavy wood-paneled doors and windows—is worth seeing. On the 3rd floor is a terrace overlooking the town.

Several areas of the building conserve the convent's original art, which was extensive in and of itself, and in 1964, when INAH converted the ex-convent into a national museum, the collection was further enriched with religious art pieces from the Catedral Metropolitana in Mexico City. A few rooms are devoted to the history

of Mexico's conquest, with displays of Spanish armor and weaponry. Other rooms contain an extensive collection of colonial textiles, including a display of religious garments worn by monks, nuns, and priests. There's no shortage of gold and silver, and you'll see vestments woven with these precious metals, plus candlesticks, chalices, and crucifixes of silver and gold inlaid with precious stones. Also worth noting are the collections of religious calligraphy, furniture, porcelains, and ceramics.

The selection of religious paintings rivals that of the Museo Nacional de Arte in Mexico City, added to which is a very ample supply of religious sculpture. A *capilla domestica* (domestic chapel, once meant for the use of convent residents only) on the ground floor contains exquisite *retablos* (altarpieces) and religious paintings.

Restaurants

On the upper floor of the old convent attached to the church, **La Osteria del Convento de Tepotzotlán Restaurant Bar** ($4–6 per entrée) offers "prehispanic" delicacies such as *gusanos de maguey* (cactus worms) and *escamoles* (ant larvae), as well as such familiar central Mexican dishes as *chiles en nogada* (stuffed chiles in a nut sauce), *crepas de huitlacoche* (corn fungus crepes), *queso fundido* (Mexican-style fondue), *caldo tepotzotlán* (a local soup), and *fajitas de pollo* (chicken fajitas), plus a long list of tequila brands.

At the opposite end of the plaza in front of the church is a row of restaurants, including **El Rancho Restaurante Bar.**

Food vendors on Plaza Hidalgo, in front of the Templo de San Francisco Javier and the Museo Nacional del Virreinato, sell *huaraches* (corn snack in the shape of a sandal) and other *antojitos* (snacks) as well as *pulque curado* (fermented cactus juice).

Shopping

If you're setting up house in Mexico City, Tepotzotlán is a good place to look for rustic wooden furniture, custom wrought iron, and terra-cotta pottery. Opposite the plaza in front of the church are a few *artesanía* (artisan) shops.

TULA ARCHAEOLOGICAL SITE

Tollan, today known as Tula, was founded in the 10th century, after the decline of Teotihuacán and well before the arrival of the Aztecs. Evidence suggests that refugees from Teotihuacán caused a rapid increase in Tula's population. It is possible that the city was the capital of the Toltec-Chichimeca Empire. And though this was a powerful nation, it never grew as large as Teotihuacán, although it was a sizeable city. At its peak, archaeologists believe, Tollan covered an area of 13 square kilometers and held a population of 60,000.

Scholars believe Tollan was engulfed in a great fire that destroyed much of the city, and by A.D. 1125, the empire began to decline. Sacked and looted by outsiders, Tollan was abandoned before A.D. 1200. The Aztecs, who arrived in the Valle de México shortly thereafter, considered the Toltecs their ancestors.

Little is left of the once-great city (9 A.M.–5 P.M. daily, admission $4), which is not as frequently visited as nearby Teotihuacán. Despite the dusty desolation of the place, locals (and a few foreign New Age disciples) claim the site emits spiritual forces. The main attraction of Tula is the **Pyramid of the Morning Star** or Templo de Tlahuizcalpantecuhtli. The top of the pyramid is the resting place for four massive stone warriors known as the **Atlanteans,** for which Tula is famed. Each warrior is 4.6 meters tall, wears a butterfly-shaped breastplate and feathered headdress, and holds an *atlatl* (spear thrower) in one hand. Around the sides of the pyramid are reliefs of eagles eating human hearts, as well as coyotes, jaguars, and imaginary creatures.

Other structures at the site feature carvings of snakes, skeletons, and richly dressed nobles. If you look closely, you can see remnants of the paint that once covered the carvings. A ball court here is identical in size to one at the archaeological site of Xochicalco, in Morelos. Some speculate that this is the original Mesoamerican ball court, where the "game" or "tournament" was conceived.

The site entrance fee includes parking and entrance to a small museum. Vendors sell soft drinks and souvenirs. A tourist information module provides some basic information 9 A.M.–4 P.M. next to the Municipal Palace (closed Mondays) of the nearby town of Tula, also known as Tula de Allende.

Accommodations

Most visitors to Tula are day-trippers from Mexico City, but if you have a keen interest in exploring the archaeological site, or if you're just looking to stay in a place where tourists rarely spend the night, Tula is well provided for.

$15–30: Near the center of town, **Hotel Cuellar** (5 De Mayo 23, tel. 773/732-2920, $25 s, $30 d) offers 48 basic, small, but clean rooms that open onto a brick-laid parking area and garden. **Hotel Catedral** (Zaragoza 106, tel. 773/732-0813, $21 s, $5 per added person) offers similar quality rooms with cable TV, parking, and an open, street-front lobby.

$30–50: The most modern rooms in town are to be found at **Hotel Sharon** (Callejon de la Cruz 1, tel. 773/732-0976, $37 s/d, $45 d/t). A large facility with banquet areas and restaurant, the hotel has 120 rooms and helpful staff, and is less than 10 minutes' walk from the archaeological site.

Restaurants

If you're planning a day trip to Tula and looking for a quick bite on the walk to the ruins, try **Pizzas In/Out** (Melchor Ocampo 20, pizzas $2–5). The restaurant serves good Mexican food as well as hand-tossed pizzas and a dozen different types of burgers. There's another location on Hidalgo between Moctezuma and Zaragoza.

Taquería Parrillada Country (on Melchor Ocampo in front of Pizzas In/Out, entrées $2–6) serves tacos, burgers, and good Mexican entrées in a down-home setting with checkered tablecloths and friendly service. The restaurant's second location faces the town plaza between Leandro Valle and Hidalgo.

Across the street from Hotel Catedral is **Chicas Tortas,** a lively sandwich shop with loud music open into the evening.

Cafetería-Nevería Campanario (Zaragoza across from the church) is an excellent choice for well-made coffee drinks or a light meal.

Excursions

For a more local experience, head to the **Plaza del Taco,** a cavernous "taco mall" on the corner of Colegio Militar and 5 de Mayo. Vendors operate individual stalls selling various specialty tacos—but don't expect anything fancy; this is strictly wooden benches and meat-laden tortillas.

Helados Bing (on Melchor Ocampo between Hotel Sharon and the pizzeria) is an ice-cream shop that also sells snacks, soft drinks, and good coffee.

Getting There

Autotransportes Valle del Mezquital (tel. 5567-6791 in Mexico City and 773/732-9600 in Tula) run buses to Mexico City's Terminal Central de Autobuses del Norte for Tula every 30 minutes, 7 A.M.–9 P.M.; the fare is about $4.50. The bus will drop you off in town; you can either walk the three kilometers to the site (about 15–20 minutes), flag a cab, or take the minibus marked "Tlahuelilpan." You might want to make arrangements with your cab or the minibus to be picked up for the return to town. The last bus to Mexico City leaves Tula at 8 P.M.

If you're coming by car, take México 57 from Mexico City toward Querétaro. At Tepotzotlán it becomes a toll road, México 57D. Continue till you see signs on the right directing you to Tula; this road is México 126, which takes you right through town. Look for signs directing you to Las Ruinas; from town the sign says Parque Nacional Tula.

PACHUCA

The state capital of Hidalgo lies in the Sierra Madre Oriental, an important part of Mexico's silver belt. Mining has driven the local economy since before the Spanish arrival in 1534, and it continues to be the most important industry. The hills above the city have been worked off and on for centuries and are riddled with mine shafts and ancient slag heaps. The region still produces more than a million ounces of silver a year.

Most visitors find themselves in Pachuca either to visit Fototeca, Mexico's national photography archive, or because they're on their way to Parque Nacional El Chico.

Around the Centro

Pachuca is a town of narrow, twisting streets climbing steep hillsides. Though not brimming with architectural treasures, it's certainly worth spending a couple of hours admiring buildings in the *centro* (center).

The center of town is the broad **Plaza de la Independencia,** punctuated by the 40-meter-high **Torre del Reloj** (Clock Tower), decorated with four carved statues and a carillon imported from Austria. The **Casa Colorado,** built in the 18th century, is now the city's law court, while the 17th-century **Las Casas** formerly served as a hall for storing the *quinta real,* or royal fifth—the percentage of the area's mined wealth automatically owed to the Spanish crown.

At the modern **Palacio de Gobierno** (in the civic center a few blocks from the Plaza de la Independencia) you'll find a statue of Benito Juárez by Juan Leonardo Cordero and murals by Pachucan painter Jesús Becerril.

South of the plaza and west of the civic center, **Parque Hidalgo** is a favorite Sunday haunt for Pachucans out for a stroll, vendors, and mariachis. On Avenida Guerrero near Salazar is the large enclosed **Mercado de Barreteros.**

Centro Cultural de Hidalgo/Fototeca

A 10-minute walk southeast of the Plaza de la Independencia leads to the former monastery of San Francisco, which has seen many different residents during its 400-year existence, including monks, horses, and criminals. The Conde de Regla, who made a fabulous fortune in local silver mines, is buried in the adjoining church. Today the Instituto Nacional de Antropología e Historia (INAH) runs a fine group of museums in the old ex-convent.

The **Museo Regional de Historia** (tel. 771/714-3989, 10 A.M.–6 P.M. Tues.–Sun., free admission) displays archaeological and ethnological artifacts representing the Huastec, Aztec, Toltec, Otomi, and northern Amerindian cultures. You'll see displays of folk art, crafts, everyday utensils, and traditional dress.

On the 2nd floor of the ex-convent is the **Museo Nacional de Fotografía** (tel. 771/719-1274 or 771/714-3653, same hours as the Museo

Regional, free admission), a small but interesting collection of historical Mexican photography, from early daguerreotypes to Antonio Casasola's famed Revolution-era pictures to the work of modern photographers such as Graciela Iturbide and Nacho López.

In the same building as the photography museum but with a separate entrance is **Fototeca** (tel. 771/714-3653, fax 771/713-1977, www.sinafo.gob.mx, fototecnacional@inah.gob.mx, 8 A.M.–3P.M. Mon.–Fri.), where INAH has cataloged 1.2 million photographs on computer and can search for them by photographer, date, location, or subject. The Fototeca will make 8- by 10-inch prints of any of its photographs for $34, plus reprint permission fees if required. It's best to call ahead and arrange an appointment so a staff member can help you run a search. If you have the information needed, photos can be ordered by phone and delivered to you by courier for an additional charge.

Accommodations

$15–30: Two blocks below the plaza, **Hotel Noriega** (Matamoros 305, tel. 771/715-1555, $20 s, $25 d) offers 40 large, clean rooms in an old colonial building, popular with the occasional young traveler who comes to Pachuca. Though not as nice as the Noriega and a bit more expensive, **Hotel de los Baños** (just off the plaza at Matamoros 205, tel. 771/713-0700, $23 s, $27 d) has decent low-priced rooms.

$30–50: Hotel Emily (Hidalgo at the corner of Plaza de la Independencia, tel. 771/715-0849, $32 s, $40 d) is one of the better places in the town center (though still nothing special), with a restaurant and parking. Also on the square is **Gran Hotel Independencia** (Independencia 116, tel. 771/715-0515, $40 s/d, $45 d with two beds), remodeled in 2001. Each of the 35 simple, brightly painted rooms around the spacious open patio has a phone and TV. The rooms in the front of the building have a small balcony.

$110 and above: Out on the highway exit to Mexico City is **Hotel Fiesta Inn** (Carr. México–Pachuca km 85.5, tel. 771/717-0700, fax 771/717-0726, $140 s/d, $150 junior suite), a modern hotel with an adjoining nine-hole golf course. The hotel has a restaurant and bar, and guests have access to a gym, tennis courts, and a pool at a nearby health club.

Restaurants

Pachuca's regional food specialties include *mixiotes,* tamale-type ingredients baked in maguey leaves; *barbacoa,* lamb wrapped in maguey leaves and baked underground; and *escamoles,* fried ant eggs. The large numbers of British miners who lived in Pachuca at the end of the 19th century introduced *fútbol* (soccer) to Mexico and also brought with them the tradition of pasties. Here called *pastes,* these little pies stuffed with minced meat and vegetables are found all over Pachuca and surrounding towns. They make a great inexpensive midday snack.

A number of small cafés surround the town center. On the side of the Plaza de la Independencia at Matamoros is **Restaurante La Blanca** (8 A.M.–11 P.M. daily), a cafeteria-style restaurant with inexpensive meals and snacks.

Excellent homemade tacos, with nine fillings to choose from, can be found at the cozy **Mesón de Los Ángeles Gómez** (Guerrero 723, just up from the Plaza Juárez, 9 A.M.–11 P.M. Mon.–Sat.). During the day you can buy breakfasts, *comidas corridas* (set meals), and snacks, and it starts serving tacos in the evening. **Hotel Noriega** also has a decent dining room.

Helados Santa Clara at the side of the square on Matamoros, and another branch on Allende, serves good ice cream, sweets, and even a decent espresso.

Information

The municipal tourist office (ground floor of the Monumento Reloj on Allende, tel. 771/718 4454 or 771/718-4605, 9 A.M.–3P.M. Mon.–Wed., 10 A.M.–6 P.M. Thurs.–Sun.) offers a selection of decent printed information, but only in Spanish. The **state tourist office** (Av. Revolución 1300, tel. 771/711-4150 or 771/718-4454) is a fair way out of the center of town and not convenient for pedestrians.

Excursions

Services

The post office is at Juárez and Iglesias.

Several banks in the *centro* will change money and have internationally connected ATM machines.

The Hospital General is on Avenida Madero, on the road toward Tulancingo, while Farmacia del Pueblo is at Matamoros 205.

There's a *lavandería* (laundry) at Centro Comercial Constitución L-14, and an Internet café on Calle Doria.

Getting There

From Mexico City, México 85D (toll road) is a good way to get out of Mexico City quickly, and the toll to Pachuca costs $4.

To get to Pachuca's **central bus station,** hop the bus that leaves from in front of the tourist office on Allende. Several lines run buses all day to Mexico City's Terminal del Norte ($5). **Ovni** offers frequent buses 7 A.M.–7 P.M. to Tula ($4). **ADO** (tel. 771/713-2910) runs four buses daily to Poza Rica ($9.80) and two daily to Tampico ($25). **Estrella Blanca** (tel. 771/713-2747) departs every hour for Querétero ($12). The same company (but a different phone number for information, tel. 771/719-1131) also runs the direct bus to the Mexico City airport 15 times daily for $8. **Primera Plus** (tel. 771/713-3303) offers frequent buses to Puebla ($7), as well as two daily to Jalapa ($12) and Veracruz ($18).

PARQUE NACIONAL EL CHICO

In the hills above Pachuca is Parque Nacional El Chico, a densely pine-forested park covering 2,700 hectares, with campsites, hiking and mountain-biking trails, and fishing holes. El Chico has a reputation for being exceptionally safe and *tranquilo* (tranquil), making it an attractive place to enjoy the outdoors, and camp if you like, close to Mexico City. Just remember to bring warm clothes as it can get surprisingly chilly, especially at night if you're sleeping in a tent. Within the park is the old mining village of Mineral del Chico, perched on a mountain plateau high above Pachuca, with beautiful views.

Rock-Climbing

El Chico is best-known among Mexicans as one of the premier rock-climbing playgrounds near Mexico City (not to be confused with Potrero Chico, a much larger rock climbing area near the northern city of Monterrey), with several dozen bolted routes up the many rock formations in the park. Most routes rate 5.7–5.9. The two hardest routes are 5.12. **La Ventana,** the 150-meter tower reaching the highest point in the park, has three routes up it ranging between 5.8 and 5.10.

A fine place to start looking around for climbing routes and to talk to other climbers is the parking lot around the **Albergue Alpino Las Ventanas,** a hostel of sorts where you can crash with a sleeping bag on weekends, on the south side of the main road running through the park. Right behind the building is a rock formation aptly named **La Botella** (the bottle), a 40-meter, free-standing rock with a couple of 5.7–5.8 routes. Behind La Botella are cliffs with dozens of bolted routes of varying difficulty.

One good place to inquire about local guides for rock-climbing and bungee jumping is **Restaurante Las Güeras** (Morelos s/n, tel. 771/715-2941), in Mineral del Chico.

Camping, Hiking, Biking

Apart from rock-climbing, the park is a wonderful place to wander about in the forest, breathe the crisp clean air, and enjoy the views. Several small valleys make great campsites, and locals charge only $2 for permission to pitch a tent. You can also leave your car at the Albergue parking lot for $1.50 and hike up to pitch a tent on the ridge above, with a lovely view overlooking the park and surrounding countryside. The Albergue itself has simple cots in a dormitory room to sleep in on weekends only for $3.50 per person. Just across the road is a small restaurant and store, also open weekends only. Remember to take warm clothing.

Mountain bikers will also find a couple of decent trails descending different sides of the hill from the area around the Albergue. One great (though slightly hairy, especially if it's wet) trail descends from the south side of the main road, shortly before reaching the Albergue coming from Pachuca, and comes out after a hair-raising ride to a small reservoir by the village of **Estanzuela.** From here you can ride the paved road a couple of steep kilometers back up to the Albergue.

Other trails head downhill from the north side of the road near the Albergue through the woods to Mineral del Chico, and then return uphill on the paved road to the Albergue.

Accommodations

In Mineral del Chico, **Posada El Amanecer** (Morelos 3, tel. 771/715-4812, $65 s/d) has rooms in a converted convent.

At km 19 of the Pachuca–Mineral del Chico road, just before the entrance to Mineral del Chico on the left-hand side, is **Hotel Paraíso** (tel. 771/715-5654, $105 s/d), a modern hotel with good services and panoramic views of the rivers in the valley below.

You can also find a number of houses renting rooms or entire cabins in the area at the state government website, www.hidalgo.gob/hoteles.

Restaurants

The food market in Mineral del Chico is a great place to have breakfast, lunch, or a snack, and it claims with some justification to have the best view of any market in the country. Try the beef-and-onion stuffed *pastelitos, mole rojo, arroz con leche,* or *chiles rellenos.*

Two restaurants in Mineral del Chico that offer unadorned but well-cooked meals for around $6 per entrée are **Las Güeras** (Morelos s/n, tel. 771/715-2941, 9 A.M.–8 P.M. daily) and **La Morenita** (Jardín Hidalgo 25, tel. 771/715-2055, 9 A.M.–10 P.M. Mon.–Sat., until 6 P.M. Sun.). Las Güeras is also a good place to find guides for rock-climbing and bungee jumping.

Getting There

To get to El Chico by car, take the highway leaving Pachuca toward Tampico. About 15 minutes from the city you'll see a paved road angling off to the left, clearly marked El Chico. Turn here and continue driving several kilometers into the park. This road continues all the way through the middle of the park to the town of **Mineral El Chico,** an attractive mining village that has become a favorite weekend spot for Pachucans.

Regular minibuses run between Mercado Benito Juárez in Pachuca and Mineral del Chico; the fare is about $1 for the whole ride, or less to get dropped off at the Albergue. The last minibus descends to Pachuca at 7 P.M. In Pachuca, catch the buses at the north end of town, where the Viaducto turns into the highway leading to Tampico. Buses leave the central bus station in Pachuca for Mineral del Chico three times a day.

Cuernavaca

Nicknamed the "City of Eternal Spring" for its balmy climate, Cuernavaca was first founded as a city of the Tlahuica people, named Cuauhnáhuac (Place at the Edge of the Forest). It fell quickly to Spanish swords in 1521 and was granted to Cortés by the Spanish crown as one of his *encomiendas* (land grants).

Cortés was the first of many Mexico City residents to keep a vacation home in Cuernavaca; his was built out of the ruins of the city pyramid.

Many of Mexico's most powerful politicians and businesspeople, not to mention a few well-known drug traffickers, have built luxury villas here, giving a whole new meaning to the term "weekend getaway."

While you won't see much of Cuernavaca's wealthy residents, who are safely ensconced behind their mansion walls, the city center area is a very popular day trip for Mexico City residents, and it is mobbed on weekends and national holidays. The city also hosts about 20 Spanish-language schools and a correspondingly large contingent of foreign-language students.

If you read Malcolm Lowry's *Under the Volcano* and hope to find the village of Quauhnahuac in which the fictional consul passes a singular day, you will be disappointed. With a population of

To Mexico City
and Tepoztlán

RICARDO LINARES

LAS MAÑANITAS

G FARIAS

LÓPEZ MATEOS

VICTORIA

To Teopanzolco
Archaeological Site

FLECHA ROJA
TERMINAL

ARISTA

NO

REELECCION

GUERRERO

MATAMOROS

AV. MORELOS

MARKET

DEGOLLADO

ARAGON LEON

SALINAS

MORROW

HOTEL COLONIAL

ARTEAGA

ZARCO

RESTAURANT VIENES

BANAMEX

BBVA

TEJADA

Jardín
Juárez

CAFÉ LA
PARROQUÍA

GUTENBERG

HOTEL ESPAÑA

POZOLERÍA
EL BARCO

L. RAYON

JUAN

SALAZAR

CUAUHTEMOC

Jardín
Borda

MARCO POLO

Plaza de
Armas

MVP INTERNET

LA STRADA

HIDALGO

POST
OFFICE

HOSTERÍA DEL SOL

PALACIO DE CORTÈS/
MUSEO REGIONAL CUAUHNAHUAC

PALACIO
MUNICIPAL

CATEDRAL DE
LA ASUNCIÓN

HOTEL
HORTENSIAS

HANDICRAFT MARKET

LAS CASAS

ATLACOMULCO

MUSEO
ROBERT
BRADY

GAIA

METZAHUALCOYOTL

ABASOLO

AUTOBUSES PULLMAN
DE MORELOS TERMINAL

LA POSADA
MARÍA CRISTINA

MOTOLINEA

HUMBOLDT

HOTEL
PAPAGAYO

GALEANA

JUAREZ

LEYVA

To Museo de la
Herbolaría

OBREGON

WAH-YEN

CUAUHTEMOTZIN

ESTRELLA ROJA
TERMINAL

CUERNAVACA

LA FONTANA
PIZZA

GONZALES

BOCANEGRA

PALMIRA

AV. MORELOS

HIMNO

NACIONAL

TOURIST OFFICE

ESTRELLA DE ORO
TERMINAL

0   250 yds
0   250 m

To Temixco, Taxco,
and Acapulco

more than one million, Cuernavaca has grown dramatically in the past few decades, adding several kilometers of nondescript concrete neighborhoods surrounding the colonial city center.

One very good website with information on Cuernavaca and the entire state of Morelos is www.morelostravel.com.

ORIENTATION

Although Cuernavaca covers a lot of territory these days, most places of interest to visitors are within easy walking distance of the two adjacent central squares, the Plaza de Armas and Jardín Juárez.

If possible, try to avoid visiting Cuernavaca on weekends, when the city center is invariably crowded with Mexico City tourists. If you do come on weekends, be prepared for tremendous traffic returning to Mexico City on Sunday afternoon and evening.

SIGHTS

Plaza de Armas and Jardín Juárez

Plaza de Armas is the larger of the two plazas in the center of town. The tree-lined plaza is continually bustling with locals and visitors sitting on the many benches, reading papers, chatting with friends, or just watching the world go by.

Next to the plaza, smaller Jardín Juárez features a late-19th-century kiosk designed by French architect Alexandre Gustave Eiffel, who also designed Paris's famous Eiffel Tower.

Palacio de Cortés/ Museo Regional Cuauhnáhuac

Begun by Cortés in 1522, this austere, intimidating structure has more the look of a fortress than a luxury palace—a reminder that the Spaniards lived in fear of Indian uprisings. Cortés lived between here and his palace in Mexico City until 1540, when he returned to Spain.

COURTESY OF MEXICO TOURISM BOARD/GUILLERMO ALDANA

kiosk on Cuernavaca's Jardín Juárez

Since then, the building has served variously as a prison and the state legislature and now contains a museum of colonial and prehispanic artifacts.

After viewing the museum collection, head upstairs to see the Diego Rivera mural on the 2nd floor, tracing the history of Cuernavaca from the Spanish invasion to the present. The mural was paid for by U.S. Ambassador Dwight Morrow, who kept a house in Cuernavaca during his three years in Mexico. On the ground floor are the barely visible remains of the ancient pyramid destroyed by Cortés to build the palace.

The palace (tel. 777/312-8171, 9 A.M.–5 P.M. Tues.–Sun., admission $3.50) stands at the southeast end of the Plaza de Armas. A shop on the premises offers an excellent selection of books on history, as well as some art and travel in Mexico; it's open 11 A.M.–8 P.M.

Catedral de la Asunción

Opposite the Jardín Borda at the corner of Hidalgo and Morelos, Catedral de la Asunción (tel. 777/312-1290, 8 A.M.–8 P.M. daily) was built by Spanish architect Francisco Becerra, under Cortés's orders, beginning in 1529. Becerra, who also designed the Palacio Cortés, gave the church a similarly intimidating, unadorned facade. Keep an eye out for the ominous-looking skull and crossbones over the main entrance, as well as a dramatic, Japanese-style painting inside depicting the martyring in Japan of Mexico's first saint, missionary San Felipe de Jesús. The painting (artist unknown) was discovered during remodeling work in the 1950s. For a taste of Catholicism with a singularly Mexican flavor, attend the mariachi Mass Sunday at 10:30 A.M. or 8 P.M.

On the other side of the cathedral courtyard is the smaller **Templo del Tercer Orden,** a newer baroque-style church with an ornate gilded altarpiece.

Museo Casa Robert Brady

Originally part of the cathedral cloister, the Museo Casa Robert Brady (Netzahualcóyotl 4, tel. 777/314-3529, 10 A.M.–6 P.M. Tues.–Sun., admission $3.50) is an unusual private art museum containing the collection of an American who lived in Cuernavaca for 24 years but who

had an eye for works of art from around the globe. The house, known as Casa de la Torre, contains an eclectic collection of more than 1,000 works of native art from the world over, as well as colonial antiques and a number of paintings by well-known artists such as Frida Kahlo, Rufino Tamayo, and Miguel Covarrubias. Spanish-speaking guides are available all day, but call in advance for tours in English.

Jardín Borda

Silver-mining empresario José de la Borda built this mansion and surrounding garden (tel. 777/318-1038, 10 A.M.–5:30 P.M. Tues.–Sun., admission $1, free Sun.), which also served briefly as a holiday home for Emperor Maximilian and his wife, Carlota. Several of the rooms the ill-fated couple used have been restored and now house a small museum and occasional art exhibits.

The artificial "lake" is perhaps less lovely than in its former glory days, but the gardens are a lush haven in which to relax in the middle of the city. The entrance is on Morelos at Hidalgo, across from the cathedral.

Next door stands the pretty 18th-century **Iglesia de Nuestra Señora de Guadalupe,** which is also burial place of José de la Borda.

Palacio Municipal

Adjacent to Jardín Borda, the 19th-century town hall contains a museum (Morelos 265, 9 A.M.–6 P.M. Mon.–Fri., free admission) displaying 20 paintings by Salvador Tarasona, each depicting a different facet of Morelos history (with a heavy emphasis on prehispanic life).

La Casa del Olvido/ Museo de la Herbolaría

This small house and garden (Matamoros 200, tel. 777/312-3108, 10 A.M.–5 P.M. daily, free admission) about 1.5 kilometers southeast of the town center, received its nickname, "The House of Forgetting," because of a brief stay by Emperor Maximilian in the summer of 1866. For a few short weeks here, Maximilian consorted with Margarita Lefuisamo Sedano, the gardener's wife, avoiding his own fiercely ambitious, slightly unhinged wife, Carlota, and the unpleasant realities of his precarious situation as leader of Mexico. Maximilian hadn't really wanted to come to Mexico in the first place (Carlota convinced him to do so), and once here, he managed to alienate everyone with his well-intentioned but half-baked liberal ideas. He was deposed and executed the following year. Who can blame him for coming to this little spot and wishing it would all go away, if only for a short while?

Today the house holds a modest museum devoted to Indian folk medicine.

Teopanzolco Archaeological Site

In what is now the neighborhood of Colonia Vista Hermosa northeast of the city center, you can see the remains of a Tlahuica pyramid, with an Aztec pyramid built around it (10 A.M.– 5 P.M. daily, admission $3.50). The first pyramid was built around A.D. 1200, while the second was still in progress when Cortés appeared on the scene. The site is located on Avenida Teopanzolco, cross street Usumacinta, close to Avenida Río Mayo. To get there, hop a Ruta 4 *combi* (minibus) from Avenida Morelos in the city center.

ARTS AND ENTERTAINMENT

Nightlife

The pedestrian street Fray Bartolomé de las Casas has several outdoor bars very popular with young folks both local and foreign to gather, shoot the breeze, and have a drink. A few of the places, such as **Eclipse,** have live music of varying quality.

Long-time nightlife stalwart **Barba Azúl** (Pradera 10) has been recently remodeled and continues to draw the crowds for the thumping techno music. It charges a cover of $10; drinks are $4–7 each. Latin music lovers should drop in at **Zúmbale** (Bajada de Chapultepec 13, Colonia Chapultepec, tel. 777/320-5344), where a live band keeps the salsa dancers swinging Thursday to Saturday. **Rumba** (Paseo del Conquistador 178, Colonia Lomas de Cortés, tel. 777/313-0831) also has live Latin music Friday to Saturday from 10 P.M. until late.

Live performances of music and theater are often staged at the **Teatro de la Ciudad** (Morelos and Rayon), the **Teatro Ocampo** (on the *zócalo),* and **Jardín Borda.** Ask at the tourist office for upcoming shows.

Golf

The city's several golf courses are all private, although some of the higher-end hotels can arrange access for you. Expect to pay $50 weekdays and up to $150 on weekends for greens fees. Local courses include **Club de Golf de Cuernavaca** (Vivero 1, Colonia Club de Golf, tel. 777/312-0600), **Club de Golf Tabachin** (Fracc. Tabachin, tel. 777/312-3845), and **Club de Golf Santa Fe,** on the highway to Acapulco, about 20 minutes south of Cuernavaca.

Tennis

Many of the more expensive hotels in Cuernavaca have courts, and two public courts can be found on Domingo Diez. You can also rent courts by the hour at the following places: **Tennis Palace** (Paseo del Conquistador 903, Colonia Lomas de Cortés, tel. 777/313-6500, $10 per hour), **Villa International de Tenis** (Chalma 702, tel. 777/380-0507, $18 per day, two adults), and **Calinda Racquet Club** (Francisco Villa 100, tel. 777/101-0350, $20 per person, for the time you want).

Water Sports

Just eight kilometers down the free highway toward Taxco, **Temixco** (tel. 777/325-0355, 9 A.M.–6 P.M. daily, $12 admission adults, or $8 kids up to 1.25 meters tall) is a *balneario* (Mexican bathing resort) with pools everywhere you look. It has 22 pools, filled with slides and other water games, as well as a wave pool. It's lots of fun on a hot day. The resort occupies a former hacienda that started as a sugar plantation owned by Martin Cortés, son of Hernán, and then served as a fort during the Mexican Revolution. Vestiges of the old hacienda are still seen around the complex. The Ruta Temixco *combi* from Calle Galeana in Cuernavaca will take you there. If you're driving, follow the toll highway toward Acapulco and turn off on the Las Brisas exit.

ACCOMMODATIONS

As a long-time holiday city, Cuernavaca has a wide range of hotel options, from modest-but-decent rooms near the plaza to luxury spreads on the outskirts of town. If you plan on coming to town over a weekend, or especially during a *puente* (a three or four day holiday weekend), it's best to make reservations a couple of weeks in advance to be sure of having a room. Prices tend to the expensive side because of Cuernavaca's popularity with both foreign and Mexican visitors.

$15–30

Hotel Colonial (Aragón y León 104, two blocks from the *jardín,* tel. 777/318-6414, $24 s/d, $35 d with two beds) is nice for the price. However, rooms vary widely in quality, so look first. All rooms have a TV.

A large, friendly place, with a restaurant inside, is **Hotel España** (Morelos 190, at the corner of Rayon, tel. 777/318-6744, $24 s, $28 d). The 30 tile-floored rooms are spacious and airy, with fans and TV.

Hostería del Sol (Las Casas 5, Plazuela del Zacate, tel. 777/312-4152, $20 s/d, $, $120 s by the week, including breakfast or lunch) has 10 rooms (some with views) in a lovely old house, often taken by language students. It offers discounts for stays of a week or more.

$30–50

Hotel Hortensias (Hidalgo 13, tel. 777/318-5265, $27 s, $31 d) is a small family-run hotel in the center of town set around an interior courtyard; rooms have cable TV.

$50–75

Hotel Papagayo (Motolinea 13, a short walk from the plaza, tel. 777/314-1711, hotelpapagayo@prodigy.net.nx, $46 s, $60d) has 73 tidy rooms with linoleum floors in a brick building. The hotel has a swimming pool, playground, and parking lot in the central area. Breakfast is included in room rates.

On a quiet street up against Jardín Borda, **Hotel Ilebal** (Chula Vista 7, tel. 777/318-2725, $68 s/d) has 35 rooms with TVs, safe deposit boxes, and terraces. The hotel has a friendly, helpful staff and a hot tub and pool for guests.

Named in honor of the Malcom Lowry novel set in a fictionalized Cuernavaca, **Bajo El Volcán** (Av. Humboldt 119, tel. 777/312-4873, www.tourbymexico.com/bajoelvolcan, $70 s/d) has 28 tiled rooms; some have terraces. The patio features a medium-size pool. Rooms in the newer section of the hotel boast a view of the river and fields. Breakfast is included with the price of room.

$110 and Above

Just east of the Mexico City highway, **Hacienda de Cortés** (Plaza Kennedy 90, Atlacomulco, tel. 777/316-0867, fax 777/315-0035, www.haciendadecortes.com, $137 s/d, $170 junior suites, $240 suites) is just what it purports to be: an old hacienda built by the legendary conquistador, on the outskirts of Cuernavaca just off the highway to Tepoztlán. Occupied briefly during the Revolution by the equally legendary Emiliano Zapata, and later destroyed, the hacienda lay in ruins until the 1970s, when it was restored. The 22 rooms are quite a good value if you don't mind staying outside of Cuernavaca. The gardens and outdoor pool are a great spot to relax.

The cozy, 14-room **Posada María Cristina** (Blvd. Juárez 300, one block from the Palacio de Cortés, tel. 777/318-5767, www.mariacristina.com, $130–180) offers colonial atmosphere with amenities including a swimming pool, lovely gardens, and an excellent restaurant. Suites with king-sized beds and hot tubs are available.

Near the entrance to the Mexico City–Acapulco freeway, about a five-minute drive from the city center, **Calinda Racquet Club** (Francisco Villa 100, tel. 777/101-0350, fax 777/101-0359, www.hotelescalinda.com.mx, $175–230) is for folks who really want to play tennis. The colonial-style building is surrounded by beautiful gardens and has all the amenities you expect at a luxury hotel. Rooms offer a variety of layouts, including separate sitting areas.

Camino Real Sumiya (Colonia José Parras, in Jiutepec, near the highway exit to Tepoztlán and Cuautla, tel. 777/329-9888, fax 777/329-9889,

U.S./Canada reservations 800/7-CAMINO, www.caminoreal.com, $225 s/d, or up to $465 for a top suite) offers a taste of the Orient here in Central Mexico. The main part of the hotel was carried across the ocean in pieces from Japan under the direction of heiress Barbara Hutton, whose fine art collection graces the walls of the Kabuki Theater. The hotel has 163 rooms looking onto acres of Japanese-style gardens and walking paths. One restaurant, **La Arbolera** (7 A.M.–11 P.M. daily) features an international menu, while the other, **Sumiya** (noon–midnight Wed.–Sun.) is highlighted by excellent Japanese cuisine.

Las Mañanitas (Ricardo Linares 107, tel. 777/314-1466, fax 777/317-5483, www.las-mananitas.com.mx, $251–378) a 15-minute walk from the city center, is considered one of the best hotels in Mexico. The verdant grounds, in addition to the resident peacocks and other tropical birds, feature an elegant swimming pool and plenty of intimate nooks to sit and enjoy the refined ambience. The relaxing hotel bar is a great place to unwind even if you're not staying at the hotel. The hotel has only 20 suites, and service is superb. Only American Express credit cards are accepted.

RESTAURANTS

While not known for any particular regional cuisine, Cuernavaca has a large selection of quality Mexican and international restaurants catering to visitors and part-time residents.

Cafés
For breakfast and light meals, or just a cup of strong coffee, check out **Café La Parroquía** on the east side of Jardín Juárez, with tables out on the sidewalk.

Mexican
About a block from the *zócalo,* **Pozolería El Barco** (I. Rayon 5F, tel. 777/313-2131, 11 A.M.–midnight) specializes in *pozole,* a flavorful hominy stew with your choice of pork or chicken (vegetarian upon request).

Las Gaoneras (Av. Domingo Diez 1880, tel. 777/313-2604, 1–9 P.M. daily) is a popular restaurant for its hearty meat cuts, *chiles en nogada,* soups and other tasty Mexican cuisine.

A classic old-time Cuernavaca restaurant that first opened its doors in **La India Bonita** (Dwight Morrow 15, tel. 777/318-6967, 8 A.M.–10 P.M. Tues.–Thurs., 9 A.M.–11 P.M. Fri.–Sat., 9 A.M.–6 P.M. Sun.), named in reference to Emperor Maximilian's reputed lover. Favorite dishes include the *India Bonita* soup with squash flower and corn and the *cecina de Yecapixtla,* pork meat pounded flat and served with beans, fresh cheese, avocado, *nopal* cactus, and corn tortillas.

Just off the *zócalo* is **Gaia** (Benito Juárez 102, tel. 777/312-3656, lunch and dinner Mon.–Sat., lunch only Sun.), serving good-quality contemporary Mexican cuisine with a Mediterranean touch at midrange prices. The restaurant is housed in a beautiful old colonial mansion that was once owned by the legendary Mexican comedian Mario Moreno, better known as Cantínflas (English-speakers may remember him as David Niven's side kick in "Around the World in 80 Days"), who supposedly convinced artist Diego Rivera to paint the mural in the swimming pool. Try the portobello mushroom stuffed with spinach, corn, and pepper as an appetizer, or the salmon in a sauce of apricots and chipotle.

Las Mañanitas (Ricardo Linares 107, tel. 777/314-1466, noon–5 P.M. and 7–11 P.M.) serves good (though pricey) food and cocktails on a very relaxing terrace overlooking the hotel gardens. It always has a fresh seafood meal of the day, as well as other specials.

International
A couple of blocks from the *zócalo,* **Wah-Yen** (Blvd. Benito Juárez 20, tel. 777/318-9648, 2–9 P.M. daily) serves a good plateful of Cantonese-style Chinese food at moderate prices.

A more upscale Chinese option is **Log Yin** (Morelos 46, in Colonia Acapatzingo, tel. 777/312-4142, 1–10 P.M. Mon.–Thurs., 1–11 P.M. Fri.–Sat., 1–8 P.M. Sun.), with specialties such as pork or vegetable dim sum or spicy shrimp with baby corn, mushrooms, and nuts.

La Strada (Salazar 38, tel. 777/318-6085, 1:30–11 P.M. Mon.–Thurs., 1:30 P.M.–midnight Fri.–Sat., 2–6 P.M. Sun.), in a 300-year-old

Excursions

building at the rear of the Palacio de Cortés in the city center (go to the left of the building and then almost to the bottom of the stairs), serves very respectable Neapolitan-style Italian food at moderate prices. Specialties include calamari in white wine and *medaglioni La Strada,* beef in red wine with purple onion.

Another popular Italian restaurant is **Marco Polo** (Hidalgo 30, right in front of the cathedral, tel. 777/312-3484, www.marco-polo.com.mx, 1–10:30 P.M. Mon.–Thurs., 1 P.M.–midnight Fri.–Sat., 1–10 P.M. Sun.). The upstairs dining room is always packed, often with foreign visitors, enjoying the relaxed ambience and decent food. It serves a good cappuccino to top off your meal too. Don't go in a rush, as service is less than stellar.

At **La Fontana Pizza** (Juárez 19, Colonia Centro, tel. 777/314-3040, and Calzada de los Reyes 14, tel. 777/317-9310, noon–midnight daily) you can go in and enjoy a pizza, pasta, or *troncos* (baked sandwiches)—or have your food delivered.

PRACTICALITIES
Tourist Information
The Morelos state tourist office (Av. Morelos Sur 187, tel. 777/314-3872 or 777/314-3920, 8 A.M.–5 P.M. Mon.–Fri., 10 A.M.–3 P.M. Sat.–Sun.) stocks lots of literature in English, including information on the city's language schools and archaeological sites. The website www.morelostravel.com offers a wide variety of helpful information in Spanish.

The city runs small tourist booths in the bus stations (10 A.M.–5 P.M. daily), but with limited information. Staff at the municipal tourism office in the Palacio Municipal on the plaza (tel. 777/318-7561) are also helpful and armed with up-to-date information.

Services
The main post office (8 A.M.–7 P.M. Mon.–Fri., 8 A.M.–1 P.M. Sat.) is on the south side of the plaza, next to the government palace.

For Internet access, head to **MVP Internet** (Gutenberg 2, just off the plaza, tel. 777/314-

4567, 9 A.M.–9 P.M. Mon.–Sat., 10 A.M.–9 P.M. Sun., $0.50 a minute).

Bancomer, on the Jardín Juárez, and Banamex, on Matamoros at Arteaga, just north of the Jardín Juárez, exchange dollars or traveler's checks at good rates.

Hospital General (Domingo Diez at Guadalajara, tel. 777/311-2209 or 777/311-2262) has some English-speaking doctors. **Farmacia Cuernavaca** (Dr. Goméz Azcarte 200, right next to the Hospital General, tel. 777/311-4111) is open 24 hours.

Language Schools
Cuernavaca has dozens of language schools. For a complete list of schools and prices, contact the local tourist office. Prices start around $250 per week for one-on-one classes or $135 for classes with five people.

Four of the better-known schools are the following: **Center for Bilingual Multicultural Studies** (Apdo. Postal 1520, Cuernavaca, Morelos 62000, tel. 777/313-0402, fax 777/317-0533, U.S. tel. 800/932-2068, www.uninter.com.mx/spanish, admission@bilingual-center.com); **Cuauhnáhuac Escuela Cuernavaca** (Apdo. Postal 5–26, Cuernavaca, Morelos 62051, tel. 777/312-3673, fax 777/318-2693, U.S. tel. 713/292-1614, www.cuauhnahuac.edu.mx); **Cemanahuac** (San Juan 4, Colonia Las Palmas, tel. 777/318-6407, www.cemanahuac.com); and **Spanish Language Institute** (tel. 800/552-2051, fax 309/692-2926, www.langlink.com), run by Language Link of Peoria, Illinois.

GETTING THERE
By Car
If you're coming from Mexico City, you'll leave from the southern part of that city either by México 95 *libre* (free) or 95D *cuota* (toll). For the most part the two run parallel to each other, but the narrow, truck-filled free road takes considerably longer, often more than two hours. The toll road, which costs $6, is a fine open highway. Whichever road you take, consider making a snack stop at **M** **Tres Marías,** a roadside village high in the mountains; it's famed for ex-

cellent *cecina* (flattened, cured beef), *sopa de hongo* (mushroom soup), quesadillas, and other Mexican treats. At Tres Marías is a turnoff east to a mountain lake park called **Laguna de Zempoala,** a popular forested picnic spot for weekenders from the city.

By Bus

Four different bus companies serve Cuernavaca, each from a separate terminal.

Autobuses Pullman de Morelos has two terminals in Cuernavaca, one in the center of town, at the corner of Abasolo and Netzahualcóyotl, tel. 777/314-3650; and a large, efficient station at Casino de la Selva, northeast of the *centro,* at Plan de Ayala 102, tel. 777/318-4638. The company runs buses to Mexico City's Terminal Tasqueña every 15 minutes 4:30 A.M.–9:40 P.M. for $5.80, or Executive Service (with coffee and cookies) for $6.80. A direct bus to the Mexico City airport (20 daily) costs $10.

Estrella de Oro (Morelos Sur 900, tel. 777/312-3055), whose terminal is 1.5 kilometers from the center of town, also has frequent buses to Mexico City for the same price. It also has regular departures to Acapuclo ($22), the last one leaving at 10:30 P.M. If you don't want to flag a taxi, take a local bus going up the hill on Morelos; you can get off at the city center.

Flecha Roja/Estrella Blanca (Morelos 503, at Arista, tel. 777/312-8190) has buses to Taxco ($4.25, 12 buses daily) and Mexico City ($5.80, 20 buses daily).

From its terminal about eight blocks from the city center, **Estrella Roja** (Galeana 401, at Cuauhtemotzín, tel. 777/318-5934) runs buses to Cuautla and Puebla 6 A.M.–7 P.M. for $3.50 and $12, respectively.

To get to Tepoztlán, hop one of the frequent-but-slow buses leaving from the market on Avenida López Mateos, just northeast of the city center.

GETTING AROUND

It's easy to get around Cuernavaca on foot; most of the main tourist attractions are within walking distance of the center of town. Local buses to different parts of the city cost about $0.30. Street

taxis are inexpensive and usually quite safe, but after dark, it is advisable to call a *sitio* (radio) taxi. One reliable service is **Radio Taxis** (tel. 777/317-3766 or 777/317-3776). Taxi prices increase after sunset.

Car Rental

Car rental agencies in town include **Hertz** (Av. Emiliano Zapata 611, Colonia Tlatenango, tel. 777/313-1607); **Solar Auto** (Av. Benito Juárez 45, Colonia Las Palmas, tel. 777/312-2588); and **Deguer Rent-A-Car** (Av. Morelos Sur, on the corner with Galeana, Colonia Las Palmas, tel. 777/318-5466).

NEAR CUERNAVACA
Xochicalco Archaeological Site

About 42 kilometers southwest of Cuernavaca, this hilltop ruin was once a city populated by at least 10,000 people. Archaeologists place the apogee date at A.D. 700, a time when the lights were going out in so many other cultures of Mexico. Scientists continue to find hints of Olmecs, Toltecs, and Maya among the ruins.

The most outstanding structure here is the **Pyramid of the Plumed Serpent,** marked by intricate geometric patterns and stone reliefs of sinuous serpents and men with plumed headpieces. On the back side of the main acropolis is a tunnel leading to a cave used by the priests of Xochicalco as a kind of subterranean observatory; a long vertical shaft dug by hand let full sunlight into the cave only on two days a year, when the angle of the sun was perfectly aligned with the shaft. The priests used these fixed dates as a reference point to check the accuracy of their calendar. Guides waiting at the entrance to the tunnel will give you an informative tour. They don't charge a fee, but tips are expected.

Be sure to bring water and a sun hat, especially if you go in the dry season, as the ruins (tel. 777/312-5955, 10 A.M.–5 P.M. daily, admission $4) can get scorching hot. During the rainy season, views from the hilltop across the surrounding lush mountains are lovely. Admission includes entrance to a small museum (at the parking lot) that provides background on

M
Excursions

COURTESY OF MEXICO TOURISM BOARD/CARLOS SANCHEZ

the ruins of Xochicalco, southwest of Cuernavaca

the site; you'll appreciate the ruins more if you visit the museum first. If you want to bring a video camera in, you'll pay an extra $3.50.

To reach Xochicalco from Cuernavaca by car, drive south on México 95 or 95D to the turnoff past the town of Alpuyeca. Continue past the town of El Cabrito and turn north on the paved road (signed Xochicalco). To get to Xochicalco via public transport, catch a **Pullman de Morelos Laser** bus from Cuernavaca to Coatlan, and from here take a $2–3 taxi up to the ruins. Alternatively, hop a 2nd-class bus from the Cuernavaca market directly to the ruins for a mere $1. The last bus returns to Cuernavaca from the ruins at 6 P.M.

Lago Tequesquitengo

About 40 minutes south of Cuernavaca off the highway to Acapulco, this lake is a favorite among locals for picnicking, swimming, and waterskiing. To get there without a car, take a bus with Pullman de Morelos from Cuernavaca to Jojutla, and take a short taxi from there to "Tequis," as it's commonly known.

Parque Acuático Las Estacas

A great spot for cooling off on a hot afternoon, especially during the week when it's not so crowded, is this water park (tel. 734/345-0077 or 734/345-0159, or in Cuernavaca 777/312-4412, www.lasestacas.com, admission $11), five kilometers from the small town of Tlaltizapán. Built around a small, crystalline river draped in jungly flora, with grassy meadows to relax on, Las Estacas has been the scene of several Mexican and U.S. movies, including one of the Tarzan series (1967) and, more recently *Beat,* with Keifer Sutherland and Courtney Love.

To get there, take a Pullman de Morelos bus from Cuernavaca ($2) or from Terminal Tasqueña in D.F. ($7 direct) to the town of Jojutla, and from there take either a minibus or taxi to Las Estacas. By public transportation the trip can be quite slow, especially the minibus part. If you're driving, take the highway to Cuautla from Cuernavaca, and at the town of Yautepec turn south to Jojutla–Tlaltizapán.

The nearby town Tlaltizapán was the general headquarters of Emiliano Zapata during the Mexican Revolution. The building now holds the **Museo de la Revolución del Sur** (Museum of the Southern Revolution). Nearby is an impressive 17th-century sugar hacienda, **Ex-Hacienda de San Francisco Temilpa,** worth a visit if you're coming this way.

Tepoztlán

Tucked into a lush valley up against a wall of cliffs about 30 kilometers northeast of Cuernavaca, Tepoztlán enjoys a ruggedly beautiful setting. It is the mythical birthplace of the Mesoamerican god Quetzalcóatl, and the town is steeped in Indian tradition. Older residents still speak Náhuatl, and the town's biggest festival of the year (the night of September 7 and the following day) honors Ometochtli, the god of *pulque,* drunkenness, and fertility.

For centuries a sleepy little village, Tepoztlán has in recent years developed into both a favorite weekend getaway for Mexico City residents and a budding artist community with a vaguely hippie/New Age feel. Although the people of Tepoztlán (frequently shortened to "Tepotz" by the weekender crowd) seem content enough with all the cafés, art shops, and weekend visitors, they keep tourism on their own terms. When wealthy developers tried to build a golf course outside of town in 1995, residents decided that was too much. They deposed the town government that had backed the project, organized a committee to run the town, and eventually saw the project canceled. If you ask Mexicans about this, either from D.F. or from Morelos, no one seems surprised. Tepoztecos are known to have plenty of spunk and character, especially those who live in smaller villages in the hills around Tepoztlán, and they fiercely resisted the expropriation of communal lands and scorned the offer of underpaid service sector jobs.

The town center of Tepoztlán turns into one big market on weekends. The many shops sell all variety of jewelry, art, and clothing from around the world, while locals sell Mexican handicrafts in outdoor stalls on the streets and in front of the church.

The **Auditorio Ilhuicalli** (Av. 5 de Mayo, tel. 739/395-0673) can give information about *danza folklórica* (folkloric dance), concerts, and other musical events, which take place most weekends and holiday periods. The official state tourism website includes useful and up-to-date information on the town at www.morelostravel.com/destinos/tepoztlan.

ORIENTATION

A small town nestled into one end of a narrow valley, Tepoztlán itself is quite easy to negotiate on foot. The main road leading into Tepoztlán from Cuernavaca and Mexico City is called Avenida 5 de Mayo until after it passes the town square, where it becomes Avenida del Tepozteco, dead-ending at the beginning of the trail up to a small pyramid in the hills. The pyramid, perched on a shoulder of one of the mountains directly behind town, can be seen from the town center.

Branching off 5 de Mayo to the right (east) next to the plaza, Avenida Revolución descends past the church and out of town on the free road toward Oaxtepec.

SIGHTS

Apart from the church and pyramid described below, among the town's main tourist activities are shopping in the weekend handicrafts market or simply enjoying a walk around town. (For information on hikes in the nearby hills, see *Near Tepoztlán*)

Capilla de Nuestra Señora de la Asunción

Tepoztlán's imposing church and adjacent Dominican monastery seems more like a castle than a religious complex, reflecting the tenuous situation of the Spanish missionaries when the church was built in the mid-16th century. Although it is simply decorated inside, the church's facade is adorned with interesting sculptures of both Spanish and Amerindian designs. The Christmas midnight Mass, held in the candlelit courtyard, is a lovely experience even for non-Catholics.

A Dominican monastery, **Ex-Convento de la Natividad** (10 A.M.–5 P.M. Tues.–Sun., free

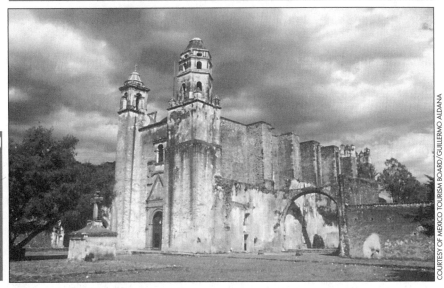

COURTESY OF MEXICO TOURISM BOARD/GUILLERMO ALDANA

Capilla de Nuestra Señora de la Asunción

admission) has been restored and now serves as a regional museum with five rooms.

Museo Arqueológico Colleción Carlos Pellier

This small museum (Pablo González 2, 10 A.M.–6 P.M. Tues.–Sun., admission $1) at the rear of the church houses a tasteful though poorly displayed collection of prehispanic pottery from Totonac, Aztec, Maya, Zapotec, and Olmec cultures, from the collection of poet Carlos Pellier.

Pirámide de Tepozteco

Perched on a ledge in the hills 400 meters above Tepoztlán (and over 2000 meters above sea level) is a 10-meter-high pyramid dedicated to Ometochtli, the Aztec god of plenty and the legendary creator of *pulque.* The pyramid itself is not much to see, but the chance to hike up into the hills and catch views of the Tepoztlán valley below make it well worth the trip.

From town it's a hike of about two kilometers to the pyramid (9:30 A.M.–5 P.M. Tues.–Sun., admission $3.50). Although plenty of nonathletes make their way up the narrow and at times steep 1.2-kilometer trail, be prepared for a good hour's workout. Wear sturdy shoes and avoid weekends, or you'll feel as though you're hiking up with the entire population of Mexico City.

ACCOMMODATIONS

If you don't have a reservation on the weekend, it's unlikely you'll find a room in Tepoztlán. During the week it's usually no problem to show up without reservations, at least at the less-expensive hotels.

$15–30

At the bottom end of the price scale is the conveniently located **Hospedaje Mely** (Av. 5 de Mayo 25, tel. 739/395-3719, $18 for 2 people, $28 for 4). The friendly family rents out eight spartan but relatively clean rooms—three with two beds. It often has space even on weekends.

$50–75

A major step up is the family-run **Posada Ali** (Netzahualcóyotl 2C, tel. 739/395-1971, $50 s/d, or $60 for a larger bed), a rustic little place with decent rooms; they used to be a lot less expensive but have increased in price along with the town's tourism. Breakfast is available for a bit extra.

$110 and Above

Hotel Nilayam (Calle de las Industrias 6, tel. 739/395-0523, toll free in Mexico 800/221-5903, fax 739/395-0503, www.nilayam.com, $100 s, $120 d) offers a full health spa with massage, sauna, pool and *temazcal* (an Aztec sauna). Rooms in the large concrete (not overly attractive) building are modern and clean, and prices include a buffet breakfast at the vegetarian restaurant.

By far the best hotel in town is **La Posada del Tepozteco** (Paraíso 3, a block above the square, tel. 739/395-0010, fax 739/395-0323, www.tepozteco.com, $137 s/d with breakfast). Many of the 20 rooms and seven suites offer great views overlooking town and valley. The garden patio is a supremely pleasant place to sip a drink and contemplate the beautiful scenery. This is a fine place to come and enjoy a meal with a view, even if you don't stay in the hotel.

In the village of Amatlán, at the eastern edge of the Tepoztlán valley, is **Hostal de la Luz** (Carr. Tepoztlán– Amatlán km 4, tel. 739/395-3374, fax. 739/395-0323, www.hostaldelaluz.com, $280 per person per weekend, all included). It's a high-end spa offering concerts, workshops, and yoga included in the price, along with three meals. The conference complex offers lovely views, which guests can contemplate in meditation chairs set in bay window alcoves, and it blends appealingly with the environment.

Camping

About three kilometers west of town, against the foot of the mountains, you can pitch a tent at **Mextitla** for $4 per person. Showers and food are available. The hills behind the camp are a popular spot for hiking and rock-climbing.

RESTAURANTS

Budget travelers should check out the *mercado* (market), where several *loncherías* (lunch restaurants) offer healthy and inexpensive *co-*

midas corridas (set meals). One of the stalls even offers a vegetarian meal. Or for a light snack, choose from the piles of magnificent produce grown in this lush region. The avocados are particularly sublime.

Downhill from the plaza, **Lilah's** (Av. Revolución 60, tel. 739/395-0387, 1–6 P.M. Thurs., 1–9 P.M. Fri.–Sun., entrées $4–10) serves remarkably well-prepared and healthy food in a small courtyard patio. Run by three sisters, the restaurant offers pita and submarine sandwiches, pasta, salads, and vegetarian dishes, as well as a few treats such as grilled tuna or Cornish hen.

At the end of Avenida del Tepozteco, right at the foot of the hills in a house set amidst a jungle of trees and plants, is **Restaurant Axitla** (tel. 739/395-0519 or 739/395-2555, 10 A.M.–7 P.M. Wed.–Sun.). It's well worth the 10-minute walk from the square for the extensive menu of tasty, reasonably priced meals, both Mexican and international. Specialties include *chile jaral,* a wide chile pepper stuffed with shredded beef and raisins, and lamb cooked in a zucchini sauce. All dishes come with a tasty salad. You can dine in the pink, high-ceilinged dining room overlooking the trees and river, or al fresco. A lone guitar player adds to the atmosphere weekend lunchtimes. Special arrangements can be made ahead of time for groups to eat after regular closing time.

For classic, well-prepared Mexican specialties, go to **Colorines,** (Av. al Tepozteco, three blocks north of the plaza, tel. 739/395-0198, 9:30 A.M.–7:30 P.M. Mon.–Fri., 8:30 A.M.–8 P.M. Sat.–Sun., entrées $4–6). The ambience is colorful and cheerful, and the food is authentic, hearty, and moderately priced. It has the added advantage of being open throughout the week, unlike many local restaurants.

The classiest restaurant in town is **El Ciruelo** (Zaragoza 17, behind the market, tel. 739/395-1203 or 739/395-1037, 1:30–6 P.M. Wed.–Thurs., 1–11:30 P.M. Fri.–Sat., 1–7:30 P.M. Sun., entrées $8–12), which features an outdoor patio with views of the mountains, an elegant atmosphere, and creative cuisine. Dishes include *enchiladas de pato* (duck enchiladas), chicken breast in mole and plum sauce, beef fajitas with nopal, and *chiles rellenos* stuffed with seafood and bathed in a goat-cheese sauce. The bill can run up quickly, especially with drinks and desserts.

Far at the other end of the glamour spectrum, but a gem of its own kind nonetheless, is the shabby little **Pulquería Alejandro Gómez** (Av. Del Tepozteco 23, closes 8 P.M. or thereabouts), where the daring can sample *pulque* either *natural* (plain) and *curado* (flavored in a number of ways, including *betabel*, or beet, and *avena*, or oat) for only $.70 cents a cup. Despite the lamentable condition of his customers stumbling over steps and bumping into doorposts, the owner Gómez is a great source of information on this curiously viscous fermented cactus beverage, and his *pulque* tastes (and feels!) good.

GETTING THERE
By Bus
Autobuses Pullman de Morelos (Av. 5 de Mayo, tel. 739/395-0520 or in Mexico City 5549-3505) runs regular buses every 40 minutes to and from Terminal Tasqueña in Mexico City 8 A.M.–7:30 P.M. for $5. The best option is to catch more-frequent buses to and from the *caseta* (tollbooth) above town, for the same price. The ten-minute taxi to and from the *zócalo* will cost you 15 pesos, or less if you share with more travelers. You rarely have to wait even 10 minutes to hop any passing 1st-class bus headed for Mexico City.

By Car
The two-lane free road between Cuernavaca and Tepoztlán, which passes through farmland and several villages, takes about a half-hour to drive. Most auto-equipped tourists coming to Tepoztlán from Mexico City take the Cuernavaca toll highway ($6), turning off before Cuernavaca onto a branch toll road west to Tepoztlán ($1.90). It's also possible to drive to or from Mexico City via a lesser-known but lovely highway, which cuts across the mountains east of Tepoztlán and arrives in Xochimilco. The drive takes longer than on the toll road, but if you're not in a hurry, the forests

and mountain views are worth it. Be prepared for heavy traffic from Mexico City to Tepoztlán on Friday afternoons, and even worse going the other way on Sunday afternoons.

NEAR TEPOZTLÁN

Forming the dramatic backdrop to Tepoztlán is the **Sierra del Tepozteco,** a jagged formation covered in dense vegetation. Above and behind the Sierra del Tepozteco rise the volcanic mountains forming the southern part of the Valle de México, which in this region is protected as the **Parque Nacional Corredor Chichinautzin.** Both ranges offer plenty of hiking opportunities for the adventurous.

One great and safe way to tour deep into the mountains is to take a horseback trip with **Cabalgatas** (Los Ocotes, km 1.5 of the road to San Juan, tel. 739/395-4246, cabalgatastepoztlan@yahoo.com.mx), a well-run tour company based in a ranch just outside of town. They offer weekend trips ($120 per person with food included, two people minimum and five maximum), with a short ride Saturday, a camp-out in tents with a bonfire at night, then a nine-hour trip far up into the mountains on Sunday. You'll pass through a number of different microclimates and see some fantastic views. Shorter and longer trips can be arranged without difficulty, and English-speaking guides are available.

San Juan
Perched on a high plateau in the Tepozteco mountains, San Juan is a Náhua town of farmers surrounded by pine forest, about 10 kilometers by road from Tepoztlán. San Juan is a good place to take a walk in the woods, either farther up into the national park or down to Tepoztlán; ask around in town for good places to go hiking. Following an old set of railroad tracks between Mexico City and Cuernavaca, passing through San Juan, is one recommended way.

To Tepoztlán, one can either follow the old railbed down from San Juan, then turn off on a path down to the Tepoxteco pyramid, or go farther east from San Juan to the next valley, where a trail descends to the Mextitla campground just outside of Tepoztlán. Either hike would take a couple of hours—ask for directions in San Juan to find the trail entrances.

Those interested in trying a traditional Náhua sauna (temazcal) should consider trying the one in San Juan. Run by several Náhua women in a local community center, the temazcal is open on Saturday only, from early morning until early afternoon. The ladies are very friendly and helpful—if you speak some Spanish they'll tell you a great deal about the tradition of the temazcal. Clothing is optional, and visitors may get in or out of the large, mud-baked chamber as often as they like. Bathers are wrapped in blankets afterward and even served a bowl of delicious vegetable soup. The experience is perhaps not for everyone, but it's definitely interesting and physically rewarding. The cost is $14 per person.

Buses run between Tepoztlán and San Juan every hour or so and cost about $0.50, while a taxi runs around $3.

Amatlán

Another town that serves as a good place to start hiking into the mountains is Amatlán, at the far eastern edge of the Tepoztlán valley. Amatlán has in recent years become a favorite spot for artists and alternative-lifestyle types from Mexico City and elsewhere to build houses. There's a hotel catering to this crowd as well. It's possible to hike from Amatlán up several different trails to different points in the Sierra Tepozteco, with great views of the valley and of Volcán Popocatépetl to the east. However, it is wise to stick to main trails, don't go alone, and keep your wits about you, as robberies have occurred.

Regular combis leave Tepoztlán for Amatlán ($0.50), or you can take a taxi for $3–5, depending on how rich you look.

Taxco

Soon after Cortés founded Taxco in 1529, the Spaniards discovered silver here and began mining in earnest. One of the city's hills, Cerro Barmeja, holds what was known as the King's Shaft, supposedly the oldest Spanish mine on the continent. The Taxco mines yielded vast quantities of silver—most of the country's supply came from here. But the veins were worked over so completely and efficiently that the city soon became a silver ghost town. It remained so for centuries, until American William Spratling opened a workshop in 1929 and began creating attractive original silver art designs. Since then the city has served as the locus of the most skilled silversmiths in Mexico, which accounts for its nickname as the "silver city."

SIGHTS

The city itself is built on and between seven hills covered by a maze of cobblestone streets. The steep, narrow streets climb up, down, and about, twisting in and out of the hilly landscape and occasionally opening up to reveal intimate plazas and cooling fountains. You need to watch your step when exploring this city on foot, as there's barely room for both cars and pedestrians on the steep, windy streets. Visitors with physical disabilities may have a rough go of it.

Although the maze of streets can be confusing at first, most of the main sites, as well as shops, hotels, and restaurants, are all close to the center of town. The main drag, a section of the México–Acapulco highway, is Avenida Presidente John F. Kennedy, frequently known by locals as Avenida de los Plateros. The main part of town is basically uphill from Avenida Kennedy, so if you get lost, just go downhill to reorient yourself.

Taxis are cheap in Taxco, with a normal fare within the city not exceeding $1.50. If you need to call for a cab service in advance, drivers with **Sitio Cuauhtémoc** (tel. 762/622-7444) work around the clock.

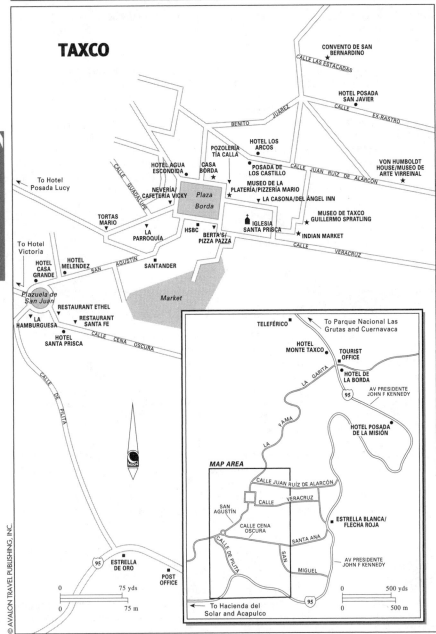

TAXCO

CONVENTO DE SAN BERNARDINO
CALLE LAS ESTACADAS
HOTEL POSADA SAN JAVIER
CALLE
EX-RASTRO
BENITO   JUAREZ
HOTEL LOS ARCOS
POZOLERÍA TÍA CALLA
CASA BORDA
POSADA DE LOS CASTILLO
CALLE JUAN RUIZ DE ALARCÓN
VON HUMBOLDT HOUSE/MUSEO DE ARTE VIRREINAL
HOTEL AGUA ESCONDIDA
CALLE GUADALUPE
MUSEO DE LA PLATERÍA/PIZZERÍA MARIO
NEVERÍA/CAFETERÍA VICKY
LA CASONA/DEL ÁNGEL INN
To Hotel Posada Lucy
Plaza Borda
MUSEO DE TAXCO GUILLERMO SPRATLING
TORTAS MARIO
LA PARROQUIA
HSBC
IGLESIA SANTA PRISCA
BERTA'S/PIZZA PAZZA
INDIAN MARKET
To Hotel Victoria
HOTEL MELENDEZ
SAN AGUSTÍN
SANTANDER
CALLE   VERACRUZ
HOTEL CASA GRANDE
SAN
Plazuela de San Juan
Market
RESTAURANT ETHEL
LA HAMBURGUESA
RESTAURANT SANTA FE
HOTEL SANTA PRISCA
CALLE CENA OSCURA
CALLE DE PILITA
MOON

MAP AREA

TELEFÉRICO
To Parque Nacional Las Grutas and Cuernavaca
HOTEL MONTE TAXCO
TOURIST OFFICE
HOTEL DE LA BORDA
LA GARITA
95
AV PRESIDENTE JOHN F KENNEDY
LA FAMA
HOTEL POSADA DE LA MISIÓN
LA
CALLE JUAN RUIZ DE ALARCÓN
CALLE   VERACRUZ
SAN AGUSTÍN
ESTRELLA BLANCA/FLECHA ROJA
CALLE CENA OSCURA
SANTA ANA
CALLE DE PILITA
SAN
MIGUEL
AV PRESIDENTE JOHN F KENNEDY
95

95
ESTRELLA DE ORO
POST OFFICE

0   75 yds
0   75 m

0   500 yds
0   500 m

To Hacienda del Solar and Acapulco

Iglesia Santa Prisca

A fine example of both churrigueresque architecture and art, the church is a study in 18th-century detail, with an ornate pink facade punctuated by two steeples and a tiled dome. The oval relief on the facade depicts the baptism of Jesus. On the inside, you will see twelve magnificent altars of hand-carved wood, covered with 22-carat gold leaf. In a room at the back, you'll see magnificent paintings by Miguel Cabrera—a famed Zapotec Indian colonial artist—amid a bewildering assortment of gold leaf, sculptures, and nooks. One painting is said to be unique in the world for its depiction of the birth of the Virgin Mary.

The church (open daily) took seven years to complete and was paid for by rich miner José de la Borda. At the back is a small museum shop (9 A.M.–7 P.M. Mon.–Sat., 10 A.M.–5 P.M. Sun.).

wood carvings inside Iglesia Santa Prisca, Taxco

COURTESY OF MEXICO TOURISM BOARD/CARLOS SANCHEZ

Plaza Borda

A shady spot under ancient laurel trees, Plaza Borda is a rare flat spot in the center of town. Bordering the square are Iglesia Santa Prisca and some lovely old buildings containing a variety of gift shops—look for colorful woven baskets, Guerrero masks, local paintings, and of course silver. The plaza also holds court to an array of restaurants, which are generally mediocre and overpriced but have glorious views.

Museo de Taxco Guillermo Spratling

The two top floors of this museum (Delgado 1, tel. 762/622-1660, 9 A.M.–6 P.M. Tues.–Sat., 9 A.M.–3 P.M. Sun., admission $2.40), on Plazuela Juan Ruíz de Alarcón behind Iglesia Santa Prisca, house a fine collection of prehispanic art from Guerrero and Central Mexico, gathered by William Spratling during his years in Mexico. Downstairs is an exhibit hall for temporary art displays.

Museo de la Platería

Aficionados of Taxco silver should definitely pay a visit to this small museum next to the Iglesia Santa Prisca, which traces the history of silver mining and craftsmanship in Taxco, and in Mexico as well. Several of William Spratling's most famed designs are on display here. The museum, which is run by a Taxco silversmith, has labels in Spanish only. However, at last report the museum was being remodeled with no clear information available on what admission price and hours will be when it reopens. It's worth going by to check, if you are in town.

Casa Humboldt/ Museo de Arte Virreinal

Originally built in the late 18th century as a private home, this meandering building (Calle Juan Ruíz de Alarcón 6, a block and a half from the plaza, tel. 762/622-5501, 10 A.M.–6 P.M. Tues.–Sat., admission $1.50) served as a guesthouse in later years and reputedly was where Baron Alexander Von Humboldt stayed when he came through Taxco in the 19th century. Now it's an interesting religious art museum.

Excursions

Casa Borda

Right next to the Iglesia Santa Prisca on the plaza is this mansion (10 A.M.–7 P.M. daily) built for the Borda family in the mid-18th century. Now it's the town Casa de la Cultura (House of Culture), often with art shows by local artists. It houses a small café on the 1st floor that serves breakfast and lunch at reasonable prices.

Town Market

Beside the Iglesia Santa Prisca, this market is chockablock with stalls hawking all manner of food, herbal remedies, and clothes. Some of the streets are so steep, you feel you could navigate them more safely sliding down on your behind than walking.

"Indian" Market

Directly behind Santa Prisca, near the entrance to the Spratling Museum, is a cheerful, cluttered market run by Indians who descend on Taxco from their villages in the hills above, and from far around the state. This offers the best bargains for strands of semiprecious stones, laquered boxes and trays, grimacing jaguar and angel masks, wooden salad bowls, and brightly painted pottery, and some textiles are sold for a fraction of their going price in Mexico City. It's open daily until about 5 P.M.

The Teleférico (Cable Car)

At Los Arcos, at the north end of town, a Swiss-built cable car takes passengers up 240 vertical meters to the top of a bluff overlooking the city. The cable car runs daily 8 A.M.–7 P.M.; the fare is $3 round-trip, $2 for children. Views are predictably spectacular. At the top you'll find the pricey Hotel Monte Taxco, with a restaurant, disco, bar, shops, gym, spa, pool, horseback riding, and a golf course.

Rancho Spratling

The former workshop of William Spratling and current studio of some of Taxco's finest craftsmen is well worth the half-hour trip south of town. Directly off México 95 at km 177.5, the ranch (8 A.M.–1 P.M. Mon.–Sat., free admission) includes the accessible workshop where fine silver is crafted by artisans, a museum depicting Spratling's life, and a showroom of work.

ARTS AND ENTERTAINMENT
Nightlife

Taxco's most alternative bar is **Cafe Sasha** (opposite Hotel Los Arcos in Calle Juan Ruiz de Alarcón, 8:30 A.M.–1 A.M. daily). A decent restaurant by day, at night Cafe Sasha becomes a hip place to sink tequilas and listen to reggae, drum 'n' bass, and world music.

Berta's Bar (next to the Santa Prisca church and adjacent to Pizza Pazza, tel. 762/622-0172, 11 A.M.–8 P.M.) is something of a local institution and a great place to meet locals and travelers alike. It was opened in the 1930s by Berta, a Taxco resident, for whom a specialty house drink—made of with tequila, honey, lime, and mineral water—is named.

If you get the urge to play pool while in Taxco, the closest place around is **La Estación.** The bar and burger joint is one floor below El Corcel Negro, at Cuauhtémoc 8, between Plaza Borda and Plazuela de San Juan.

Taxco's trendiest disco is **Passagge** (Av. de los Plateros 34, from 11 P.M. Thurs.–Sat.) where the deejays spin an eclectic mix of pop, techno, and salsa. Entrance is $6–8 depending on the night.

Semana Santa

The Holy Week festival begins on the week before Easter. On Palm Sunday, the first procession begins in the nearby village of Tehuilotepec, when an image of Jesus is placed on the back of a donkey and carried to Taxco. Candlelight processions take place in town every following night, with hooded *penitentes* making their peregrination (many flagellating their backs raw, or carrying heavy bundles of brambles) to the Iglesia Santa Prisca. On Holy Thursday, in front of Santa Prisca, the Last Supper is performed by the locals, and the major procession takes place from 11 P.M. until the early hours. After that things calm down, although there are other, smaller processions on Saturday morning and Sunday.

Fiesta Alarconia

The last three weekends in May are devoted to a festival honoring Taxqueño Juan Ruíz de Alarcón, a writer during the colonial era. Art exhibits, band concerts, Alarcón plays, and other cultural presentations take place all over town.

Feria Nacional de la Plata

The last week in November each year is dedicated to Taxco's most famous product, crafted silver. Hundreds of artists enter a contest overseen by a panel of judges, who choose what they consider to be the year's best silverwork. This is a great opportunity to see some of the country's most creative silver craftsmanship.

SHOPPING

Taxco offers some of the finest silver creations in Mexico and has more than 2000 silver shops. You can find bargain-basement prices at the market on the corner of the plaza (to the left as you exit Santa Prisco), but don't expect quality workmanship there. A better option is **Linda de Taxco** (Plaza Borda 4 and 5, tel. 762/622-3172). Besides silver you can purchase items with unusual mixtures of silver and ceramics, or silver, brass, copper, and ceramics.

The bulk of the town's shops are in the city center, and while the ones closer to the plaza tend to be more expensive, these are also some of the best or more original. When buying a piece, always look for the ".925" stamp on the back, which ensures authenticity, and be sure to spend some time comparing prices before buying.

Pineda's Taxco (Plaza Borda 1, tel. 722/622-3233, fax. 762/622-4150), right next to Santa Prisca, showcases the work of Bruno Pineda and brothers, with high-quality workmanship and original designs.

Alejandro Viveros is another high-end silversmith-owned shop. Expect unique designs at this Patio de las Artesanías location. Other good shops are **Platería Evelyn** (Plazuela de San Juan 15, tel. 762/622-4961) and **Magic .925** (Benito Juárez 15, tel. 762/622-5660).

ACCOMMODATIONS

Budget travelers will not find a whole lot of options in Taxco, as the hotels cater mainly to midrange and upmarket visitors. It's a good idea to make reservations, as rooms can also sometimes be scarce. Parking can be a hassle in Taxco, so if you're driving, look for a hotel with a parking lot.

$15–30

Hotel Casa Grande (Plazuela de San Juan 7, tel. 762/622-0969, fax 762/622-1108, $20 s, $30 d, $36 t, $410 q with private bath; $15 s, $24 d, $27 t, with shared bath) offers 23 clean rooms. Ask for a quiet room on one of the higher floors or at the back. The hotel's restaurant and bar, **La Concha Nostra,** overlooks the plaza, which makes up for the softish beds and slightly funky bathrooms. Tacos, pizzas, and quesadillas are all good.

$30–50

Posada de Emilia Castillo (Juan Ruíz de Alarcón 7, tel. 762/622-1396, fax 762/622-1762, $35 s, $40 d, $45 t) is a finely restored mansion from the colonial era with 15 rooms—a great place to stay in the center of town. There are plants, flowers, and handpainted murals every place you look. A statue of La Virgen de Guadalupe guards the stairwell.

Hotel Los Arcos (Juan Ruíz de Alarcón 4, a block down the hill from Plaza Borda, tel. 762/622-1836, fax 762/622-7982, $38 s, $44 d, $50 t) was originally built as a monastery in the 16th century. The hotel is decorated with plenty of tile and has a great rooftop terrace. The 21 rooms, each with private bath, are simply furnished and have comfortable beds facing a verdant interior courtyard.

Hotel Posada Lucy (Carlos J. Nibbi 8, tel. 762/622-1780, $25 s, $50 d, $60 t, $80 q), a few streets north of the Plazuela de San Juan, offers 30 rooms with adjoining baths between them. Pleasant gardens surround the narrow rooms. Parking is available.

Hotel Santa Prisca (Cena Oscura 1, on Plazuela de San Juan a couple of blocks west of

Plaza Borda, tel. 762/622-0080, fax 762/622-2938, $30 s, $45 d, $50 t) has 30 small but comfortable rooms around a patio and fountain. Grab one of the many English-language books from the library and enjoy a drink at the hotel's hole-in-the-wall bar. A section of the hotel is newer, with larger rooms and rambling junior suites. The dining room serves decent food.

Hotel Melendez (Cuauhtémoc 6, tel. 762/622-0006, fax 762/622-0613, $37 s, $40 d, $49 t) is home to 32 newly decorated rooms surrounding an interior courtyard. Kitschy, brightly painted butterflies hover beside iron balconies in some of the rooms; other rooms open onto seating areas.

A beautiful garden surrounds **Hotel Posada San Javier** (Ex-Rastro 6, tel. 762/622-3177, fax 762/622-2351, $38 s, $41 d, $44 t), with a swimming pool as centerpiece. This villa-style hotel features three terraces and quaint rooms, as well as spacious suites at reasonable prices. Parking is available.

$50–75

Hotel Agua Escondida (Plaza Borda 4, tel. 762/622-0726, fax 762/622-1306, $60 s, $75 d, $90 t without TV; $57 s, $72 d, $87 t with TV) enjoys a great location right on the Plaza Borda. The 50 rooms are freshly painted with decorative garden motifs, and at least half now offer cable TV. Each has a private bath. Amenities include a rooftop terrace and snack bar, adjacent restaurant, video arcade, and a pool. Expect a crowd on weekends.

Hotel Victoria (Carlos Nibbi 5 and 7, tel. 762/622-0004, fax 762/622-1014, $58 s/d, $80 t) has some of the best views of Taxco and is only a five-minute walk from Santa Prisca. The 60 spacious rooms have cable TV and private bath. There is a private dining room apart from the pleasant restaurant, which offers great views from inside and outside. Parking is available, and pets are allowed.

$75–110

Hotel de la Borda (Cerro del Pedregal 2, opposite the junction of Av. Kennedy and Calle La Garita, tel. 762/622-0225, fax 762/622-0025, www.hotelborda.com, $85 s, $85 d, $100 t) is where J.F.K. and Jackie honeymooned, enjoying panoramic views from its large-windowed suites. Recently restored to its former glory, it offers 120 large clean rooms and suites with charming balconies, a restaurant, a large sparkling pool with a view, and free parking. The themed Revolución bar offers the classic "Berta" and other cocktails.

$110 and Above

Hotel Posada de la Misión (Cerro de la Misión 32, just off Av. Kennedy, tel. 762/622-0063 or 762/622-5519, fax 762/622-2198, www.posadamision.com, $150 s, $170 d) has 150 colonial-style rooms with private baths, and suites with fireplaces are available. On the premises you'll find one of the town's most elegant restaurants, an open air chapel, banquet hall, silver workshop, large pool and gardens (adorned by Juan O'Gorman's 1956 mural dedicated to the last Aztec Emperor Cuauhtémoc), beauty salon, and shops. Parking is available, and ask about tours to ex-haciendas by horse-drawn cart. Room prices include breakfast and dinner.

Hacienda del Solar (off México 95 south of town, opposite the tourist information office, tel. 762/622-0587, $140 d) is an intimate hotel surrounded by beautiful views of the surrounding mountains. Balcony rooms and suites are available. Amenities include a pool, tennis court, gourmet restaurant La Ventana de Taxco, and strolling musicians. Children under 12 are not allowed.

The 156-room **Hotel Monte Taxco** (tel. 762/622-1300, fax 762/622-1428, $155 s/d, $175 t) has a choice location, perched on the top of a bluff on the north end of town near México 95. The hotel offers guests (and nonguests) a nine-hole golf course, tennis courts, horseback riding, steam baths and massage, a fitness center, three restaurants, bars, and a club.

RESTAURANTS

Tacos, Light Meals, and Comidas Corridas

The cozy **La Hamburguesa** (Plazuela de San Juan 5, tel. 762/622-0941, 8 A.M.–midnight

Thurs.–Tues., burgers $3–5, entrées $7–11) serves cheap burgers and tacos *al pastor* (pork cooked on a vertical spit), as well as complete meals. The piano bar gets lively in the evenings.

Lovers of *pozole* (a heart stew with a base of hominy) will be thrilled to find the **Pozolería Tía Calla** (Plaza Borda 1, downstairs, on the left facing Santa Prisca church, tel. 762/622-5602, $3 a bowl), probably the best eatery in town. In addition to the huge, inexpensive bowls of green, red, or white pozole, you have a choice of hearty authentic Mexican fare at friendly prices.

For more than 40 years, the **Restaurant Santa Fé** (Hidalgo 2, just down from Plazuela de San Juan, tel. 762/622-1170, 8 A.M.–10 P.M. daily, entrées $5–7) has been serving good, inexpensive food. Check out the *comida corrida* for $6.

Restaurant Ethel (Plazuela de San Juan 14, tel. 762/622-0788, 9 A.M.–9 P.M. daily, entrées $5–7) charges similar prices for *comidas corridas* and specializes in good *antojitos*.

Nevería/Cafetería Vicky (8 A.M.–10 P.M. daily) has a balcony that faces Plaza Borda. It's a great place to go for an excellent coffee drink or ice cream. The restaurant also serves affordable tacos, burgers, and beer.

For great views and low prices check out **Borda's Cafe** (next door to Restaurant Paco, most snacks $3–6). The funky hole-in-the-wall grills cheap burgers and hot dogs and serves excellent ice cream, as well as mixed drinks and beer.

For fresh, local *tortas*, go to **Tortas Mario** on Callejón de las Delicias (*tortas* $1–2), where the cook/owner will help you practice your Spanish.

Mexican and International

A small dining room and seemingly endless patio corners confront the visitor at **La Casona** (Celso Munoz 4, tel. 762/622-1071, 8 A.M.–8 P.M. daily, entrées $8–12). Located beside the Iglesia Santa Prisca, the restaurant offers a panoramic view of Taxco.

Restaurant El Adobe (Plazuela de San Juan, tel. 762/622-1416, 8 A.M.–midnight daily, entrées $6–10) is also good and a bit less expensive, with specialties such as *queso adobo* (melted cheese with herbs and veggies) or the *enchiladas oaxaqueños*.

With a direct view of the Santa Prisca church

through floor-to-ceiling windows, **Restaurant/Bar Paco** (on the Plaza Borda, 1–10:30 P.M. daily, entrées $5–11) is a pleasant place to spend the afternoon, with live music varying from Spanish guitar to synthesizer classics.

Del Ángel Inn (Celso Muñoz 4, 2nd floor, tel. 762/622-5525, ext.2, entrées $9–16), formerly a 10-room guesthouse, is now an elegant culinary haven. Steaks and meat-oriented dishes stand out in this patio-geared restaurant, though vegetarian Mexican meals are also available.

White tablecloths will greet you at **La Parroquia** (Plazuela de Los Gallos 1, tel. 762/622-3096, entrées $10–15), as well as a menu replete with international favorites and Mexican specialties.

La Pagaduría del Rey (Colegio Militar 8, tel. 762/622-0075, 1:30–9:30 P.M. daily, entrées $8–20) is a hacienda-style restaurant just north of the city center. A serene setting both indoors and out, the high-end restaurant serves everything from fettuccine to filets.

La Ventana de Taxco (Hacienda del Solar, about seven minutes south of town on the highway to Acapulco, tel. 762/622-0587, 8 A.M.–10 P.M. daily, entrées $8–15) gets high marks from *Bon Appétit*. The homemade chicken ravioli is a house specialty. The view is one of the best in town. Reservations are recommended, especially on weekends.

Pizza

The best pizza in town is at **Pizza Pazza** (tel. 762/622-5500, 10 A.M.–midnight daily, $3–10 per pizza), next to the church on the plaza. Apart from the excellent and reasonably priced pizzas, the menu includes pastas and other Italian dishes. Do your best to get a window seat for a good view of the plaza.

You'll find **Pizzería Marios** in an indoor square at Plaza Borda 1. The menu includes cheese fondue, good-sized pies, and spaghetti dishes. A nice terrace faces the plaza.

PRACTICALITIES
Tourist Office

Taxco has two tourism offices (who don't, for some odd reason, seem to like each other, at last report): the state tourist offices (tel. 762/622-2274, 9 A.M.–3:30 P.M. Mon.–Fri., 9 A.M.–1 P.M. Sat.) and the federal tourism office (tel. 762/622-0798, 9 A.M.–7 P.M. daily). Both are on Avenida de los Plateros (Avenida John F. Kennedy), but the latter is closer to the center, just 50 yards from the Hotel Posada de la Misión.

Medical Emergencies
For medical attention, call the Red Cross (tel. 762/622-3232); Hospital Adolfo Prieto (tel. 762/622-0121); or Clínica Santa Cruz (tel. 762/622-3012).

Post Office
The post office (8 A.M.–7 P.M. Sat., 9 A.M.–1 P.M. Mon.–Fri.) has a branch below the *ayuntamiento*, or town hall, on Benito Juárez.

Language Courses
The **Centro de Enseñanza para Extranjeros** (tel. 762/622-0124, www.cepe.unam.mx), a branch of Universidad Nacional Autónoma de México (UNAM), offers six-week intensive Spanish courses for $375. Food and accommodations are extra, but the school can often set up rooms with local families. Call for starting dates.

Banks and Money Changing Services
Banco Santander and HSBC have 24-hour ATMs and cash travelers checks during normal banking hours. Banco Santander is on Calle San Augustín between Plaza Borda and Plazuela de San Juan, while Bital is in Plaza Borda next to the Iglesia Santa Prisca.

Internet
There are several Internet cafés within a stone's throw from Plaza Borda. Try **La Estación** (on Cuauhtémoc, just 50 meters from the square, 10 A.M.–midnight), or **Moloko Plus,** opposite.

GETTING THERE
By Bus
Taxco has two bus stations, both on Avenida de los Plateros (Avenida John F. Kennedy). The **Estrella Blanca/Flecha Roja station** (tel.

762/622-0131), near the intersection of Calle Santa Ana about halfway through town, runs 1st-class buses to Terminal Tasqueña in Mexico City more than 10 times daily, $9; to Acapulco once daily, $15; and to Cuernavaca frequently, $4. Frequent and less-expensive 2nd-class buses go to the same destinations, as well as Toluca and Chilpancingo.

More comfortable and organized, **Estrella de Oro** (near the exit to Acapulco, tel. 762/622-0648) offers 6–10 1st- and 2nd-class buses to the same destinations for about the same prices. Buses also stop at the Hotel Posada de la Misión, which has a small ticket office (6:30 A.M.–8 P.M.) in the lobby.

NEAR TAXCO
Parque Nacional Las Grutas de Cacahuamilpa
These extremely impressive caves comprise 15 interconnected chambers spanning 12 kilometers. About two kilometers are accessible to casual tourists, with concrete footpaths and dim overhead lighting—a flashlight wouldn't hurt, though, to help see places the lighting doesn't reach, and also because power cuts are not unknown! Several of these "rooms" are quite massive—fully 70 meters tall and equally wide, filled with stalactites, stalagmites, and other stone formations. Guided tours leave every hour 10 A.M.–5 P.M. and cost $3, or $2 for kids up to 12 years old. You must go with a guide, but not all guides speak English. Often it's very crowded, especially on weekends, although the caves are vast enough and the path easy enough to follow that escaping from the group is safe and easy. For a side trip, take the path branching to the right before arriving at the mouth of the caves, which leads to a place where the river flows into a 60-meter cave entrance. Minibuses (known in Mexico as *combis*) marked "Las Grutas" leave from in front of the Taxco terminal to the caves roughly every hour throughout the day and cost $1.50 for the approximately 50-minute trip. If you're driving, take the highway east out of town toward Toluca and Cuernavaca, turn north on México

55 (toward Ixtapan de la Sal and Toluca), then watch for the marked turnoff, about 30 kilometers from town.

Ixcateopan

This beautiful mountain village, whose winding streets are hewn out of local marble stone, is held to be the birthplace of Cuauhtémoc. The last Aztec leader was tortured and killed by Cortés's men in Tabasco, but local myth has it his bones were secretly brought home and buried here. A much publicized excavation last century uncovered some charred remains, and these are now displayed in a church, **La Iglesia de la Asunción,** that has been converted into a small museum. While controversy remains as to the veracity of these lugubrious artifacts, you are advised to suspend disbelief and enjoy the mythology while here.

The other attraction, related in matters of prehispanic pride, is **Museo de la Resistencia Indígena** (information in Taxco, tel. 762/622-3927), or the Museum of Indigenous Resistance. This treasure trove of information on the conquest of New Spain is presented from the Indian point of view (all displays are labeled in Spanish).

The best day to visit is on a Sunday, when the local market brings together the best of regional produce, from rare wild mushrooms to unusual sweet breads and *pulque,* a weirdly viscous fermented cactus alcohol. Ixcateopan has one of the oddest regional delicacies, *tortas de nieve* (ice cream bread rolls) sold on the main street leading up to the church.

Ixcateopan is roughly 25 kilometers westsouthwest of Taxco as the crow flies, but a lot longer over the windy mountain roads. *Combi* buses run between Ixcateopan and Taxco every 25 minutess until 7 P.M. daily from a bus stop opposite Taxco's Estrella de Oro station. The journey takes just under two hours and costs $2.20.

Toluca and Vicinity

The capital of the State of México, Toluca, lies 67 kilometers west of Mexico City. Perched in the mountains at an elevation of 2,680 meters, it's the country's highest state capital. Toluca is a large and growing industrial city not frequented by tourists, but the city center still has a few buildings and parks from its colonial past.

SIGHTS

Most of Toluca's sights of note are clustered around the broad, open Plaza de los Mártires or the adjacent Plaza Garibay and can easily be visited on foot. A block south of the Plaza de los Mártires, right behind the cathedral, are the *portales* (arched colonnades) where Tolucans come to eat, shop, and pass the time of day. The square boasts the most *portales* of any city in Mexico. The principal *portal,* with 44 arches, is **Portal Madero,** which runs in front of Avenida Hidalgo. **Portal Constitución,** on the east side, has 38 arches, and **Portal Reforma,** the smallest of the three, with 36 arches, is on the west side. Between the *portales* and the cathedral is a small, hidden square, with a round, simple chapel in the middle.

Plaza de los Mártires

Several colonial buildings, most built of the local dark volcanic stone, face the central plaza, including the **Catedral de la Diocesis de Toluca,** begun in 1573 and finished in 1797. The church is one of the largest in the country and sports a rather severe neoclassical facade with two rows of columns. Facing the principal altar on the right side is a *portada* (entranceway) leading into a separate but adjacent church. For years the entrance was blocked off, but it was recently reopened. Other buildings in the plaza include the adjacent neoclassical **Palacio Municipal,** and, on the far side, the 18th-century **Templo de la Santa Veracruz.** Half a block west is the visually interesting modern **Teatro Morelos,** a brick cube ringed by copper arches.

Excursions

Cosmo Vitral Jardín Botánico

This botanical garden (9 A.M.–5 P.M. Tues.–Sun., admission $1.25), at the eastern end of Plaza Garibay, lies within the walls of a 19th-century market building sporting 54 stained-glass panels. The panels—created by Leopoldo Flores over a period of three years—portray the story of humanity. The blazingly colorful glass art makes a fine backdrop for the garden's 400 different species of plants and flowers from Mexico, Central and South America, Africa, and Asia.

Museums

Eight kilometers west of the city center, the Centro Cultural Mexiquense (Mexican Cultural Center) is an impressive complex holding three museums that contain some of the state's finest exhibits: **Museo de Antropología, Museo de Culturas Populares,** and **Museo de Arte Moderno** (Blvd. Reyes Heroles 302, 9 A.M.–5 P.M. Tues.–Sun., admission $2 for all three museums). The creatively designed buildings (the art museum looks like a spaceship sunken into the earth) comprise one of the finest cultural institutions in the country. Among the highlights are a huge, colorful "tree of life" from Metepec, and artwork by famed Mexican painters such as Siqueiros, Rivera, and Orozco. English-speaking guides are available. Get there via bus (Línea 2 de Marzo) or taxi. Opposite the complex is the imposing Tec de Monterrey University Toluca campus.

On Calle Santos Degollado, find the 16th-century **Templo del Carmen** and, just to its west, the **Museo de Bellas Artes,** (tel. 722/215-5329, 10 A.M.–6 P.M. Tues.–Fri., 10 A.M.–3 P.M. Sat.– Sun., admission $1), which houses paintings and sculptures from the 16th to the 19th centuries. Around the corner on Nicolás Bravo are three small art museums: **Museo Felipe Santiago Gutiérrez, Museo José María Velasco** and **Museo Taller Nishizawa** (10 A.M.–6 P.M. Tues.–Sun., free admission).

Other museums (of limited interest to casual tourists) include the **Museo de Numismática** (Hidaglo Pte. 506, tel. 722/213-1927), about currency and money, and **Museo de Ciencias Naturales** (Parque de los Matlatzincas, no telephone), a natural history museum.

stained-glass windows of Cosmo Vitral Jardín Botánico

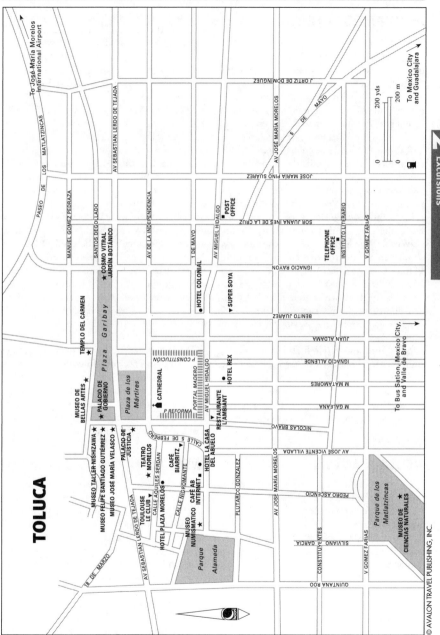

ACCOMMODATIONS

$15–30: At the **Hotel Rex** (Matamoros Sur 101, tel. 722/215-9300, $22), you'll find 40 basic, unremarkable rooms. **La Casa del Abuelo** (Hidalgo Pte. 404, tel. 722/213-3642, $20 s, $25 d, $5 extra Sat.–Sun.) is a good deal in spite of the bizarre pink, Gaudíesque building that houses it, and it is often full as a result. Apart from basic, clean rooms, the hotel has private parking.

$30–50: Two blocks east of the *portales* (arched colonnades), **Hotel Colonial** (Hidalgo Ote. 103, tel. 722/215-9700, $35 s, $40 d) is about the best low-priced option. The hotel's 33 spacious rooms, each with TV and telephone, have high ceilings and wooden floors. Beware of rooms facing the street, as they can be noisy. Parking is available. At a higher price and comfort level, though in an unattractive modern building, **Hotel Plaza Morelos** (Aquiles Serdán 115, tel. 722/215-9201, $40 s, $45 d) is next to the Teatro Morelos, in the town center. The 57 rooms, though a bit small, are clean and carpeted. Each has a TV and telephone. A parking lot and restaurant are downstairs.

$110 and above: High-end rooms can be found at **Hotel Fiesta Inn** (Paseo Tollocan Ote. 1132, tel. 722/276-1000, www.posadas.com.mx, $140 s/d, $188 junior suites), with 140 rooms and four suites with all the amenities, as well as an indoor pool, gym, restaurant, meeting rooms, and a business center.

RESTAURANTS

For snacks, head to the *portales* in the city center, where you'll find a couple of bakeries and plenty of vendors selling tamales and *atole* (a sweet, warm corn drink).

If you're looking for fresh juice, a *torta,* or a *comida corrida,* the health-food restaurant chain **Super Soya** (Juárez 111, half a block off Hidalgo, 8 A.M.–9 P.M. Mon.–Sat., 10 A.M.–7 P.M. Sun.) is a good option.

Coffee Station, in the *portales,* is an American-style café with espresso drinks, salads, croissants, yogurt, and baguette sandwiches at midrange prices.

Café Biarritz (Nigromante 200, facing the side of the *catedral,* tel. 722/214-5757, 8 A.M.–11 P.M. Mon.–Fri., 8 A.M.–8 P.M. Sat.–Sun.) is a good and inexpensive diner-type café with a large menu of standard Mexican meals, as well as fish and seafood. Similar is **Restaurant L'ambiant** (Hidalgo 231, opposite Portal Madero, tel. 722/215-3393, 9 A.M.–9:30 P.M. daily), with odd, bluish lighting (the "ambiant," perhaps?).

Toluca is known for its excellent cuts of meat and sausage, and one good place to give them a taste is **Las Costillas de Venustiano** (V. Carranza 201, at Aldama, several blocks south of the town center, tel. 722/270-4036, noon–2 A.M. daily, $3–5 for tacos, $5–12 for most entrées). An unpretentious place with tables in front of a big grill and TVs invariably showing a soccer match (especially if the beloved Diablos of Toluca are playing), it serves an excellent *arrachera* (flank steak) plate with beans, guacamole, and tortillas for $11. Also on offer is a variety of tacos and *alambres* (meat stir-fry), as well as the *chorizo mero toluca campeón,* a sausage named in honor of the soccer team's recent championship victories.

For a cold beer and a game of pool, chess, or backgammon, check out **Toulouse Le Club,** (at the corner of Aquiles Serdán and Pedro Ascencio, two blocks west of the cathedral, until midnight Mon.–Sat., until 10 P.M. Sun.). This relaxed spot is welcoming for old and young alike, and women will also feel comfortable here.

INFORMATION AND SERVICES

The state tourism office (Av. Robert Bosch and Av. 1 de Mayo, tel. 722/275-8108 or 722/275-8109, 9 A.M.–6 P.M. Mon.–Fri.) is in the city's industrial zone behind the Nestlé factory. Although they are not prepared to deal with the general public and it is not worth the effort it takes to get there, the official website is has some good information: www.edomexico.gob.mx/sedeco/turismo/home.html (and then click on "destino" for the destination you are interested in).

The main **post office** (9 A.M.–5 P.M. Mon.–Fri., 10 A.M.–2 P.M. Sat.) is at the corner of Hidalgo and Sor Juana Inés de la Cruz.

GETTING THERE

Flecha Roja (tel. 722/217-0285) and **Caminante** (tel. 722/217-0152) both offer buses between Toluca and the Terminal Observatorio in Mexico City every five minutes 5 A.M.–9 P.M. for $3.50. Caminante also has direct buses to and from the Mexico City airport 17 times daily for $8.50 (4 A.M.–8 P.M.). **Primera Plus** (tel. 722/217-3485) runs buses to Morelia, six times daily, 2nd class ($14); Guadalajara, six times daily, 1st class ($34); and Querétaro, every hour, 1st class ($12). **Transportes Frontera/Estrella Blanca** (tel. 722/217-1174) sells tickets for Taxco ($7) and Acapulco ($27) on Primera Clase; to Monterrey ($58) and Nuevo Laredo ($76) on Turistar Ejecutivo; and to Monterrey ($55) and Nuevo Laredo ($69) on regular 1st-class Futura buses. **ETN** (tel. 722/217-7308) runs luxury buses to Guadalajara ($49), San Luis Potosí ($32), and Querétaro ($17); all twice daily. It also has 20 buses a day to Mexico City's Observatorio station ($4.50).

México–Toluca–Zinacantepec y Ramales (tel. 722/217-1596) has frequent buses throughout the day to Valle de Bravo ($4.20). **TMT** runs frequent buses to El Oro ($5.70). **Tres Estrellas del Centro** has frequent buses to Teotenango ($0.80), Ixtapan de la Sal ($3.50), and Malinalco ($4).

Once in Toluca, look for buses marked "Centro" if you're heading into the city center. To get back to the bus terminal, catch one of the buses on Morelos (near Juárez, two blocks from the *portales*) marked "Terminal." The terminal is about two kilometers southeast of the town center. A taxi to/from the center costs $2.

To leave the center of town by car, take Avenida Benito Juárez until it dead-ends into Paseo Tollocan, which exits toward Mexico City to the left (east) or to Valle de Bravo to the right (west).

NEAR TOLUCA

Teotenango Archaeological Site

The ominous-looking hilltop complex of Teotenango (9 A.M.–5 P.M. Tues.–Sun., admission $1.50), 25 kilometers south of Toluca, was established first by the local Teotenanca tribe, who were conquered by the Matlatzinca people in A.D. 1200. The Matlatzincas (whose name means "net-users" in Náhuatl, a reference to the people's frequent use of fishing nets) were in turn defeated by the Aztecs in 1477. One of the more fascinating artifacts found was a stone jaguar eating the sun, thought by some archaeologists to depict a solar eclipse. Other structures include a large ball court and several large, squat temples. At the bottom of the hill, where you pay your $1.50 admission, you'll pass a small museum holding some of the artifacts found during restoration.

The site is just under a kilometer from the town of Tenango de Arista (also known as Tenango del Valle), which is serviced by frequent buses from Toluca ($10 with Tres Estrellas del Centro) and easily reached by bus-and-taxi combination. From Tenango tourists may either walk or take a $1.50–2 taxi to get to the ruins. The town itself is a pleasant place to wander around for an hour or so to get a taste of rural life in the region. It's also known for its excellent *barbacoa* (lamb barbeque) and *carnitas* (pork), which can be found in several restaurants or at the local market.

Nevado de Toluca

The 4,691-meter Nevado de Toluca, sometimes called by its Náhuatl name, Xinantecatl (zee-nan-te-KAHT-el), is an inactive volcano with two small lakes in its crater. It is the fourth-highest mountain in Mexico. Tourists can drive up into the crater on a dirt road offering spectacular views, as long as it's not snowing (hence the name, *nevado,* which roughly translates to "snowy one"). From the crater it's another 500 meters or so of scrambling up to the actual crater rim. The 2- to 4-hour hike around the crater rim can be fun, but it is exposed and entails scrambling up lots of boulders and scree, so don't undertake it lightly. The daring can climb part way around the rim and plunge down the steep scree slopes into the crater, sliding meters with each step and descending in just moments what it took so long to slog up. The best sliding chutes are from between the two highest points on the crater rim. Those who agree with Falstaff on discretion being the better part of valor can content themselves with hiking an hour or less up to the crater rim for the fantastic views (weather permitting).

If possible, come during the week, as the crater turns into a mob scene on some weekends, with competing radios, football games, and even a couple of taco stands. The weather is very changeable up on the mountain, so come prepared for anything from sunburn-level sun to freezing cold, snow, and high winds. The mornings usually have the best views, and if you're lucky, you can see all the way across Mexico City and spot Popocatépetl, Ixtaccíhuatl, and Pico de Orizaba in the distance.

In the late 1990s a Mexican development company had grandiose plans of building a ski resort on the mountain, but such ideas were put on hold by the local campesinos, who have part controlling rights of the forest. Apparently they feared that the necessary artificial snow-making would destroy their crops, or perhaps they just didn't like the idea of chopping up their mountain. At any rate, repeated protests put the project on indefinite hold.

To reach Nevado de Toluca by car, take México 134 heading west from Toluca. At km 19, in the midst of pine forest, take México 3 south toward Texcaltitlán. Continue 7.3 kilometers, with great views of the volcano, to the dirt road turning off up the mountain, just past the village of **Raices.** From this turn, it's another 19 kilometers of dirt road east to the crater, first through pine forest, and then above the tree line. Buses to Texcaltitlán and Sultepec can drop you at the turnoff, where you can hitch up on weekends. During the week there's very little traffic.

Part of the way up the road you'll pass a large *albergue* (hostel) with 200 bunk beds, hot water, and a kitchen. It's noisy on weekends but certainly cheap at $5 per night. Camping is allowed anywhere on the mountain except in the crater, but be sure to be well prepared for the cold.

El Oro

Right on the border with the State of Michoacán, 94 kilometers northwest of Toluca via Atlacomulco, is this old mining town nestled into a hillside. Missionaries from the nearby Rancho de Guadalupe found chunks of gold around 1700, but it wasn't until the late 19th century that large-scale mining began, much of it undertaken by foreign miners. Although not a major destination for tourists, it's worth a day trip if you're interested in an offbeat place. There are no hotels to stay in in town, so plan on returning to Toluca or Mexico City by the end of the day.

The very friendly folks at the local tourist office, in the white and red **Palacio Municipal** (tel. 711/125-0036 or 711/125-0099, ext. 26, 9 A.M.–5 P.M. Mon.–Fri., 10 A.M.–4 P.M. Sat.–Sun.) will happily take you on a tour of the town themselves if they aren't too busy, as they are eager to promote El Oro as a tourist destination. Main sites include the *palacio* itself, built in 1910, with an elegant old meeting hall on the top floor. Around the corner is the ornate **Teatro Juárez** (9 A.M.–5 P.M. daily), with four columns in front of its stone facade. The public is welcome to wander around; ask the workmen to turn the lights on for you if they are off. Several other buildings dating from the town's heyday are worth a look, including the old **Oro Club,** now housing a BBVA bank. In the old railway station, a block uphill from the theater, is a collection of artisans selling their wares, including ceramics and woodwork.

A 10-minute walk above town is the **Museo de la Minería del Estado de México** (10 A.M.–6 P.M. Tues.–Sat., 10 A.M.–3 P.M. Sun., free admission), with lots of weird old mining gear, photos of the town during the mining boom, and rusted sculptures of two heroic-looking miners and a woman sitting outside. During the week there's often no one around at all. Views over the town are good from the museum, making it a good excuse for a walk even if the exhibits don't do much for you.

A couple of kilometers outside of town is the **Presa Brockman,** a small lake created by a dam, popular among locals as a place to picnic on weekends.

Several unpretentious eateries in town offer good food. One of the better ones is **Los Girasoles** (one block up from the theater, on the 2nd floor of a building formed by a fork in the road, 8 A.M.–8 P.M. Tues.–Sun., entrées $4.50), run by a friendly matron who takes good care of her clients with very tasty *comidas corridas.* Downstairs is a bakery.

TMT and **Caminante** buses run several times a day between El Oro and Toluca ($5) and Terminal Observatorio in Mexico City ($8).

IXTAPAN DE LA SAL

Thermal springs are the attraction at Ixtapan, a low-key spa/resort of about 25,000 people, 117 kilometers from Mexico City. The mineral baths scattered around town have made Ixtapan a favored weekend getaway for people from Mexico City, Toluca, and Cuernavaca. All the locals will cheerfully tell you that the water is radioactive and can cure whatever ails you. More scientifically, the water comes out of the spring at 40.8°C, with a salt and mineral content of almost 10,000 parts per million. If your hotel doesn't have private baths, you can take a dip at the **Ixtapan Spa** (Mexico City tel. 5254-0500, www.ixtapan.com, 8 A.M.–7 P.M. daily), right at the entrance to town coming in from Toluca, with pools ranging between 32°C and 38°C, as well as regular swimming pools, for $14 adults or $6 for kids under 10. The **Balneario Municipal,** at the corner of Allende and 20 de Noviembre in the center of town, charges a mere $2.50 for a hot bath or $8 for a massage.

Between Ixtapan and Toluca, the highway passes very lovely stretches of countryside, with many hillside towns specializing in growing flowers. Two towns worth a visit if you're coming through in your own car are Santa Ana and Tenancingo.

Accommodations

Hotels in town tend to be of the all-inclusive variety, offering package rates that include room, meals, and spa services.

$15–30: One of the less-expensive places in town is **Hotel Mari's** (right across from the municipal spa at Allende 7, tel. 721/143-0195, $25 s/d), a family-run place with its own restaurant. There is double or triple occupancy only, unless there are not many visitors in town and you can negotiate. Breakfast is an extra $4. **Hotel Don**

Isidro (Av. Juárez Norte, one street down from the Ixtapan Spa, tel. 721/143-0315, $25 s, $35 d) is also a decent low-priced option.

$75–110: Hotel Casa Blanca (Juárez 615, tel. 721/143-0036, $80 d with three meals) has a warm (not hot) pool and a restaurant that stays open all day. Rooms are spread around the one-level complex, with tropical plants everywhere.

$110 and above: A new upscale hotel outside of town, **Rancho San Diego** (Mexico City tel. 5254-7491 or Ixtapan 721/143-4000, www.ranchosandiego.com.mx, $175 d with private mineral bath, $155 d without, a bit less during the week) offers all-inclusive stays with plenty of activities to keep you entertained, such as tennis, rappel, waterslides, mountain biking, or just relaxing on the many patios and enjoying the atmosphere. The complex is interestingly designed, with modern-style buildings painted in earth tones with wood beams.

Restaurants

Check out the string of restaurants on Avenida Juárez Norte between the Ixtapan Spa and town. One good one is **Restaurante Los Arcos** (most entrées $4–8), where you can get a filling set three-course meal for $6, or order entrées from the menu.

Practicalities

Tres Estrellas del Centro runs buses between Terminal Observatorio in Mexico City and Ixtapan de la Sal every hour 7 A.M.–7 P.M. ($7), and to Toluca ($3.30).

Tourist information can be found at the bus station, 1.5 kilometers from town on the road toward Taxco.

For information on Ixtapan and the surrounding areas, either visit or call the **local tourist office** (near Hospital General on highway to Tonatico, tel. 721/141-1450, www.edomexico .gob.mx/sedeco/turismo/ixtapan/ixtclima.html).

Las Grutas de la Estrella

Past Ixtapan, about 17 kilometers down the road toward Taxco, is the turnoff to Las Grutas de la Estrella (10 A.M.–6 P.M. Tues.–Sun., $2 admission), or Star Caves, carved out of a limestone mountain by millennia of rushing water. Take a wander in an impressive series of caverns and side chambers, replete with bizarre rock formations. Through parts of the cave rushes the Río Zapote, which in the height of the rain season can flood the caverns. The caves were first explored thoroughly in 1956, revealing an altar to Tlaloc and other prehispanic artifacts. To get there by bus, take a Tres Estrellas bus from Ixtapan toward Taxco and get off at the turnoff for the caves ($2).

MALINALCO

Set amidst dramatic scenery in a remote corner of the mountains between Toluca and Cuernavaca, Malinalco is well worth the trip just to see this not oft-visited region, as well as to check out the 16th-century convent in the center of town and the impressive archaeological site on a hill just outside. Because of its natural beauty and bucolic ambience, Malinalco has become a popular spot for Mexico City residents to have a weekend home.

Malinalco was a strategic spot dominating a mountain pass and was not conquered by the Aztecs until shortly before the arrival of the Spaniards. The Aztec ruins are thought to have been a means of impressing the local population with the empire's dominance. After the Spanish conquest, a mission of seven Augustinian monks made their way to Malinalco in 1540 to begin evangelization of what was considered an important region. Malinalco also served as a strategic site during the Mexican Revolution, when it was used as a base by Zapata's troops.

Ex-Convento de la Transfiguración

Dominating the center of town is this impressive Augustinian monastery dating from the 1540s. Similar in style to the convent in Tepoztlán, the church itself (dedicated to San Salvador) is unadorned and fortresslike, while the cloister to the side is in two levels around an open garden. Decorating the walls of the cloister are very beautiful murals of flowers and animals. Visitors are free to wander around both the church and the cloister at no charge. Note an obviously prehispanic carved rock sitting on a stump in front of the church.

trimming flowers for holiday decorations in the Ex-Convento de la Transfiguración

Malinalco Archaeological Site

This famous temple complex sits on a bluff about one kilometer west of the town of Malinalco, all uphill on a dirt road. The small but impressive site (9 A.M.–5:30 P.M. Tues.–Sun., admission $3) was built by the Aztecs starting in 1501, although archaeologists believe they built on a preexisting temple. The six monuments are carved directly out of the mountain rock, which was the only time the Aztecs used this technique. The principal structure is the **Temple of the Eagle,** thought to have been where Eagle and Tiger Aztec warriors were initiated into their cult. Two carved ocelots flank the steep stairway up to the circular temple, which has a carved eagle in the center and jaguars around it. Views from the ruins across the town and surrounding countryside are magnificent. The long stairway up to the ruins is a bit of slog, but it's broken up with interesting write-ups (in three languages: English, Spanish, and Náhuatl) on the site itself and local history, culture, and environment. Taking in a video camera costs $3 extra.

Visible from the stairway up is **Rincón de San Miguel,** a small chapel with prehispanic ruins to one side. This is the where the town holds its annual festival on September 29. According to the guards at the main ruins, the hillsides around Malinalco are littered with unexcavated ruins. If you'd like to take a walk in the hills, one place to go is up the cobblestoned road past the turnoff to the ruins, which soon becomes a footpath across the mountains to the town of Tenancingo, about 15 kilometers away.

Accommodations

One low-priced spot right in the center of town is **Hotel Santa Monica** (Hidalgo 109, tel. 714/147-0031, $20 s/d, or $35 for two double beds with TV), with simple rooms around a garden courtyard. Prices are a bit less during the week.

Not as good a deal, but acceptable in a pinch, is **Posada Familiar** (just down from the convent on Av. Juárez, tel. 714/147-0345, $17 s/d), with clean rooms but somewhat lumpy beds. It has an inexpensive *comedor* also.

Restaurants

Calle Guerrero, leaving from the small square in front of the church up toward the archaeological site, has several good restaurants on it. One of the best is **Las Palomas** (Guerrero 104, tel. 714/147-0122, until 6 P.M. Mon.–Thurs., until 11 P.M. Fri.–Sat., until 8 P.M. Sun., entrées $3–7), with tables around a small garden. Specialties include trout cooked with *epazote* (a pungent herb also known as Mexican tea) and *hoja*

santa (herb) spices and chicken breast with cheese and plum sauce. Prices are reasonable, and quality is very good. Another popular place is **Los Miranda,** three blocks up from the square on Calle San Juan.

Two kilometers south of town is a large trout farm, where you can fish yourself if you like or buy a tasty cooked trout from one of the several small restaurants nearby.

Practicalities

Tres Estrellas del Centro (Mexico City tel. 5264-3739) runs buses between Malinalco and Toluca ($3) and Terminal Observatorio in Mexico City ($6) regularly throughout the day.

The quickest route to drive to Malinalco from Mexico City is to take the Toluca highway and turn south at La Marquesa, following signs to Chalma. You'll also see signs to the Club de Golf Malinalco. The drive takes 1.5–2 hours. It's also possible to drive from Malinalco to Cuernavaca through beautiful, wild mountain country, but the road is in poor condition, so expect to go slowly.

Tourist information can be found in the small office right on the higher of the two downtown squares (9 A.M.–4 P.M. daily, www.edomexico.gob .mx/sedeco/turismo/malinalc/malclima.html).

Chalma

About 11 kilometers east of Malinalco, set amid forests and gorges, is the church of **Nuestro Señor de Chalma.** The 16th-century sanctuary was built at the site of an ancient sacrificial center, after the "miraculous" appearance of a crucifix on the site in 1533. The church is one of the most venerated pilgrimage sites in Mexico.

Valle de Bravo

Beautiful Valle de Bravo—often shortened to "Valle"—lies 147 kilometers west of Mexico City and 84 kilometers west of Toluca and serves as a playground for wealthy city dwellers who flock here on weekends. Perched on a hillside above Lago Avándaro (Lake Avándaro), the ex-colonial town is crisscrossed by serpentine cobblestone streets lined with whitewashed stucco houses topped with red-tile roofs and draped with brilliant flowers and bougainvillea.

Actually a dammed reservoir created in the 1940s across a former river valley, Lago Avándaro measures three kilometers across by seven kilometers wide and is invariably dotted with dozens of small yachts and motor boats skimming the cool waters, particularly on weekends.

The gorgeous surrounding pine-forested mountains make a great outdoor venue for hikers, mountain bikers, and nature lovers in general. And as it happens, thermal conditions over the lake and nearby countryside make the area one of the premier locations in Mexico for hang gliding and paragliding. Right above town is a butterfly reserve, one of the best places in Mexico for visitors to see the legendary migrating monarch butterflies during the winter.

ORIENTATION

Valle is divided into two distinct sections, the main center of town up on the hilltop around Plaza Independencia, and a second neighborhood down on the lakeshore and toward the road exit to Avándaro and Toluca. Most of the less-expensive hotels, bike shops, government offices, the market, the bus station, and many restaurants are in the center of town. Down at the docks are a few of the better and more expensive restaurants, a couple of sport shops, and of course the lake. Visitors without wheels may find themselves trudging up and down the steep but short hill between the two with regularity, or you can flag down a passing cab for about $3, or $0.50 cents if you share, which is common practice in Valle. From the dock, a small road follows the lakeshore north, bypassing the town center.

The road leading downhill to the dock from the plaza will eventually take you to the main exit toward Toluca. Just outside of town, a road branches off to the right, leading to **Avándaro,** where many wealthy families maintain holiday homes. Leaving town in the other direction, to the north, a secondary highway passes the Avándaro dam and takes a longer and windier route back to Toluca.

While Valle doesn't have much in the way of tourist sights in town, the **Centro Joaquín Arcadio Pagaza** (Pagaza 201, 10 A.M.–6 P.M. Tues.–Sat., 11 A.M.–7 P.M. Sun., free admission) frequently hosts small exhibitions by Mexican and international artists. A couple of blocks below the plaza, the Centro was once the home of Joaquín Arcadio Pagaza (1834–1918), a famed Mexican poet and translator born in Valle de Bravo.

RECREATION

With its large reservoir and encircling mountains, Valle is an outdoor recreation haven. While most Valle visitors live in Mexico and have their own gear, some rental equipment is available.

Water Sports

The going rate to rent motorboats on the lake is about $28 for an hour's touring, or $45 to go waterskiing (skis included). However, an affordable treat ($15, seating 8 people) is to hire a speedboat at **Los Pericos** (tel. 726/262-0558), the first of Valle de Bravo's two floating restaurants. Fishing trips (perch and bass are plentiful) can also be arranged. To find a pilot, continue past the municipal dock south on the main street and look for a turnoff to the right leading down to a small marina. Be prepared to negotiate.

With a regular stiff breeze and just enough room to get up to full speed, Lago Avándaro is popular for small racing yachts and holds frequent regattas. While boat rentals are not easy to come by, it is possible to take racing classes if you're going to be in the area for a few weeks. The **Club Vela Santa María** (Marina Nacional 201, tel. 726/262-1012 or in Mexico City tel. 5606-4778) offers classes in a single-mast, twin-sail Ventura 21-footers for $70 per class, four classes minimum.

Mountain Biking and Hiking

The pine forests and hills spreading in all directions from around Lago Avándaro are idyllic for taking long hikes or mountain bike rides along old dirt roads or narrow trails. The countryside in this area is generally safe, but robberies have occurred, so stay aware and don't head off alone. When in doubt, ask for information at the bicycle shops or at the municipal tourism office, where you can also arrange biking or hiking guides.

If you're just after a short stroll and a view of town, walk up Calle Depósito, off Bocanegra behind the church, which leads up to a fine lookout spot in the trees. Another good walking destination is to **La Peña,** a rocky outcrop jutting up right from the lakeshore on the northern end of town. On your way up to the rocky peak (with great 360-degree views over the lake and surrounding area), you can take a look at some of the mansions of wealthy Mexicans, some of which have very interesting architecture. Local rock climbers have set up a few routes at the top of La Peña.

A great spot for a longer hike or bike ride is the ridgeline directly behind town. The easiest way to get up into the forest is to follow Calle Bocanegra from behind the church straight out of town without making any turns. After the road leaves town, it heads uphill and eventually turns to dirt. Look for a well-beaten trail on the right side just before reaching a crest in the road, about one kilometer from where the pavement stops. This trail follows the ridge several kilometers south, with the town and lake to your right, and eventually arrives at **La Torre,** a peak used as a takeoff point for hang gliders and paragliders. Before the trail reaches La Torre, several other trails descend to the right back into town. From La Torre a dirt road winds about 14 bumpy kilometers through forest and farmland back to the main highway coming into Valle from Toluca, about five kilometers above town. To find the turnoff to this road (used by all the paragliders on their way to launch) coming from Valle, look for a dirt road on the left about 200 meters below the Pemex station, signposted S.M. Acatitlán.

Another fine area for getting into the woods is past the **Velo de Novia** (Bride's Veil), a 35-meter waterfall in Avándaro. To get there, take the road to Avándaro, pass through the small town center, and follow signs for Avándaro Spa. After passing the *glorieta* (traffic circle), look for a street to the right called Vega de Valle. Follow this a few hundred meters until you see a dirt lot on the right with a few food stands. If you have a car, park here and follow trails walking down to the waterfall or continuing around the lake. A regular taxi from Valle to the entrance to Velo de Novia will charge $2.50, while *colectivos* run $1.

Many longer trips are available in the surrounding mountains. One great multihour bike ride is to get a car ride up to the high point in the road heading back from Valle de Bravo toward Toluca; take a left-hand turn at a dirt road heading into a broad open meadow, called **Corral de Piedra.** From here trails and dirt roads wind way down the mountains through forest and remote farmland all the way back to Valle de Bravo.

Should you prefer to go on an organized trip rather than plunge off into the wilds on your own, or if you need to rent a bike, two shops operate in Valle. **Cletas** (16 de Septiembre 200,

tel. 726/262-0291, 10 A.M.–8 P.M. daily) rents bikes for $3 per hour or $15 a full day, or takes people on 2- to 4-hour rides for $12 per person. The friendly owner Carlos Mejía speaks a little English and will give bikers tips on where to go. He'll also give your bike a quick tune-up for $4.

A block down from the plaza, **Pablo's Bikes** (Pagaza 103, tel. 726/262-3730, 10 A.M.–3 P.M. and 4–8 P.M. Mon.–Wed., 10 A.M.–8 P.M. Fri.–Sun.) rents bikes at similar prices ($4 per hour, $20 per day) and also organizes rides.

Monarch Butterfly–Watching

Valle de Bravo was receiving seasonal vacationers for quite some time before Mexico City residents started showing up. Flocks of millions of monarch butterflies *(mariposas monarcas)* fly annually down from Canada to spend the winter in the western part of the State of México and nearby Michoacán. Walking through forests covered with a brilliant blanket of brightly colored, constantly moving butterflies is a magical experience, not to be missed if you're in the area from December to February. At last count the monarchs wintered at 57 separate sites on the slopes of 11 volcanoes in Central Mexico. Check the Monarch Watch website (www.monarchwatch.org) for blow-by-blow descriptions and best dates for viewing.

As the forests that provide winter homes for the monarchs are increasingly threatened by logging, the Mexican government has created a series of protected areas. One reserve is about 20 kilometers from Valle de Bravo, near Los Saucos, a small roadside village. Keep an eye out for **Restaurant Las Tres Vírgenes**—that's Los Saucos. Just beyond the village toward Toluca, on weekends during the butterfly season, you'll see men with horses on the side of the road; they are offering inexpensive visits to the reserve. A 1.5-hour trip will set you back $20 for a guide and $15 for a horse (if you want one)—considerably less expensive than the better-known sanctuaries in Michoacán.

The Valle de Bravo municipal tourism office (Porfirio Díaz and Zaragoza, three blocks northwest of the plaza, tel. 726/262-1678, www.valledebravo.com.mx, 9 A.M.–7 P.M.

MIGRATION OF THE MONARCHS

The migration of millions of monarch butterflies of up to 2,000 or more miles from the U.S. to their winter homes in Central Mexico is one of the great natural wonders of the animal world. Seeing them in their nesting zones on a dozen mountainsides in Michoacán and the State of México, turning the pine forest into a shimmering mirage of gold and black, is an experience not to be missed if you're there between November and March.

Monarch butterflies *(Danaus plexippus)* are native to North and South America, although they started showing up in many parts of Asia in the early 19th century, probably brought over on boats from the Americas. The North American subspecies *Danaus plexippus plexippus* is divided into two main populations by the continental divide. Those west of the Rocky Mountains flutter off to about 25 nesting sites along the coasts of California for the winter, while those east of the Rockies winter either in Florida (where there's also a year-round population—the smart and lazy crowd) or take the long voyage down to Mexico to flee the cold.

The journey south to Mexico begins from summer breeding grounds, which stretch across a wide swath of eastern and central United States and Canada. The monarch resides in patches of wild milkweed plants, which provide their nourishment as well as a toxin called cardenolides, which render the butterflies poisonous to many would-be predators. Monarch eggs hatch after about four days, followed by the roughly two week larval stage, which is when most of their growth occurs, and then finally the pupae stage, when they transform into adult butterflies.

Nonmigrating monarchs live only a few weeks, meaning two or three generations pass during the course of the summer. The migrating monarchs, born in the early fall, live far longer, as much as nine months, redirecting part of their life energies from breeding to sustaining their bodies during their voyage. For many years, until they were discovered by the scientific community in 1975, the winter home of the these monarchs was a mystery.

How exactly the tiny monarchs, spread across such a huge area, convene into migrating convoys of millions and navigate their way to an area of only about 20 hectares in Central Mexico, two or three thousand miles from their birthplace, "may be one of the most compelling mysteries of animal ecology," as scientists Karen Oberhauser and Michelle Solensky put it. A myriad of theories have been put forth on monarch navigation—including visual clues, like river valleys or mountains; following the earth's magnetic fields with an internal compass; using the sun, moon or stars, infrared energy perception, internal circadian clocks; or some combination of them all.

However they manage it, around about November 1, the monarch begin arriving in Central Mexico. Because of the date, coinciding with the Mexican Day of the Dead festival, local traditions have long believed the monarchs to be the spirits of dead children returning home. The butterflies first spread out around mixed forests at lower elevations, but gradually, over the course of November, they congregate in a dozen nesting sites located at around 3,000 meters in dense stands of oyamel fir trees. Favored locations for nesting sites are relatively steep hillsides, invariably with a southerly or southwesterly exposure, and often near a small stream. Exactly how to count how many butterflies are nesting in a given site is still a matter of debate among scientists, but 10 million per hectare is a frequently used estimate.

In early March, those who survive the winter begin dispersing and fluttering north, but in less dense groups then when they came down. Often the butterflies mate right before leaving Mexico, and lay their eggs and die in the southern United States, leaving it to their offspring to reach the summer nesting sites by May.

Environmental Degradation Threatens the Monarchs

Monarch populations have fluctuated dramatically in the 12 years since they have been tracked systematically. But the winter of 2004–2005 was particularly bad, with 75 percent fewer butterflies than the previous year, according to study by the World Wildlife Foundation and the Mexican government. The government, long stung by criticism of its record in protecting the

(*continued on next page*)

MIGRATION OF THE MONARCHS (cont'd)

butterfly habitat, promptly put most of the blame on the loss of butterfly habitat in the U.S. and Canada.

Although the government was criticized as trying to put the blame off on its neighbors, there is scientific justification to their claims. Milkweed is routinely destroyed by farmers in many parts of North America, sometimes on purpose and sometimes inadvertently with herbicides and insecticides that their genetically engineered crops are resistant to. A new type of genetically engineered corn contains Bt toxin, designed to kill a common corn pest; it may also be affecting the monarchs. The declining numbers of monarchs counted on their way south at major stopover points like Cape May, New Jersey and Chincoteague, Virginia does suggest that summer breeding grounds are shrinking.

Although these are unquestionably major problems, the situation in Mexico is more critical because of the extreme concentration of the monarch habitat, across just a dozen mountaintops in a very limited area. Here the dense oyamel forest on which the monarch depends is being steadily whittled away at by poor campesinos, who are logging to feed their families—a difficult but familiar dynamic in many parts of the developing world. According to one study, 44 percent of the dense, mature forest in the area frequented by the monarchs was destroyed between 1971 and 1999. The government created a reserve in 1986, and then

expanded it in 2000 to a current size of 56,259 hectares, but with limited patrolling and the constant pressure of poverty, logging continues. Other creative NGO-led efforts including setting up a system to pay those with logging permits not to log. However, payments of only about $150 a year per family are not likely to put an end to the problem, as the frequent whine of the chainsaw in the forests attest to.

The forest doesn't even have to be totally destroyed to become compromised as a shelter for the fragile butterflies. The removal of just a couple of trees is enough to break the forest canopy, opening the front door to the butterflies' home in the middle of winter, as it were, letting in the rain and cold. Particularly harsh storms in the region, like the ones during the winter of 2001–2002, have killed as much as 80 percent of the population of some winter sanctuaries.

Therefore tourists should be sure to use local guides, and don't begrudge the cost! These guides, and their families living at the edges of the forest, are literally the first line of defense for the monarchs, and they have mixed feelings about the whole thing. Mexicans generally love the butterflies as much as the many entranced foreigners—as evidenced by the many Mexican tourists you'll see in the sanctuaries. But as even a superficial look around the surrounding countryside villages reveals, these are very poor areas indeed, sustained mainly by meager farming and remittance from the many local people who've traveled to Mexico City or the United States for work.

So while government proclamations to create the reserve (out of, locals never tire of pointing out, communal lands they had owned for centuries) may be well intentioned, the only real way to save the forest homes of the monarchs is to make it worth the while of the people who live there. Visitors like you and I can have a greater impact than any environmental campaign, simply by paying a decent price for a guide into the reserve, and maybe even having some food or a drink at a roadside eatery near the reserve, owned by local campesino families. And the more of us that go, the better—the butterflies are a sociable bunch, they don't mind the company, as long as you keep your voice down.

© ELENA PAPPAS

one of Mexico's regular winter visitors

Mon.–Fri., 9 A.M.–2 P.M. Sat.) can also set you up with guides. Longer trips in the forests can be arranged without difficulty. If you don't see anyone on the road, ask in Los Saucos for a guide. The best month to visit is January, when the southward migration is mostly complete; it's best to visit during the week when there are fewer people around. In years when there are more butterflies than normal (as in 2001–2002), you'll see clouds of monarchs all the way down along the highway itself, along with local policemen waving cars to slow down as they pass through the area. And up in the forest, at "butterfly central," the sight is really staggering: about an acre of forested mountainside literally blanketed in butterflies, to the point where it's hard to actually see the trees they are covering. If you sit still long enough, they'll start covering you, too!

Flying

While the thought of leaping into space and expecting to fly gives some of us visions of Icarus's ill-fated jaunt, hundreds of apparently sane people do just that each year from **La Torre,** the rocky peak behind Valle de Bravo. The equipment is of course much improved from the days of swan feathers and wax: modern wings of choice are either stiff-wing hang gliders or the newer paraglider, a type of soaring parachute. The debate continues to rage over which one is safer, but there's no doubt that paragliding is easier to learn and the equipment is more compact and convenient to transport, and thus more popular with beginners.

Near the lake, **Alas del Hombre** (Plaza Valle, Local 22 and 24, Fray Gregorio J. de La Cuenca, tel. 726/262-6382 or 726/262-0934, www.alas .com.mx) has nearly 30 years of experience flying around Valle de Bravo and elsewhere in Mexico. They offer courses for both hang gliding and paragliding, tandem flights, and guided tours—all with certified instructors. A 30-minute glide down in a tandem with an instructor costs $130 on weekends and $100 during the week (minimum age seven). Take a windbreaker, sports shoes, and a camera. There are also weeklong courses

for those planning to stay in town for a while. The basic introductory paragliding course includes eight days of training over four weekends and costs $1,100–1,500 per person, depending on how many people sign up for the course.

One U.S./Mexican company that runs hang gliding and paragliding trips to Mexico is **Fly Mexico** (tel. 512/467-2529 or 800/861-7198 in the U.S., in Valle de Bravo 726/262-2449, www.flymex.com); courses cost $695 (paragliding) or $895 (hang gliding) for one week, all included except airfare. Student trips cost more if you're not a certified flier already.

EVENTS

The town's two major festivals are the **Fiesta de la Santa Cruz** (May 3), better known locally as *la feria de Santa María,* and the **Fiesta de San Francisco** (October 4). These events maintain many old Mexican traditional games and dances, as well as elaborate fireworks. If you plan to come on these dates, or on a weekend, make sure you make hotel reservations well in advance.

ACCOMMODATIONS

While Valle doesn't have a huge selection of hotels, there are a number of good inexpensive options and a few lovely high-priced spreads. Rates are sometimes lower during the week. If you plan to visit on a weekend, and especially during holidays, be sure to make reservations.

$15–30

The best low-priced place to stay in town is **Posada Girasoles** (right on the main square at Plaza Independencia 1, tel. 726/262-2976, $22 s, $33 d, $3 extra for a TV). The hotel is small, but the brick and plaster rooms are quite spacious and spotless, with nice powerful showers to boot. It's a good deal.

An excellent midrange option, with not much in the way of amenities but lots of character, is **Posada Casa Vieja** (Juárez 101, tel. 726/262-0338, $21 s/d without TV, $31 s/d with TV Sun.–Thurs., $31 s/d without TV, $42 s/d with TV Fri.–Sat.). In a converted hacienda built more than 200 years ago and run by descendants of the original owners, the whitewashed rooms with wooden roofs and brick floors (no phones) spread around a tree-filled courtyard and are surprisingly affordable. If you come during the week it's less expensive, and you might even have the place to yourself. Parking is available.

$50–75

Right on the plaza, **Cueva de León** (Plaza Independencia 2, tel. 726/262-4062, fax 726/262-1361, $63 d, $87 t, king-sized $103) features 14 rooms around a small interior courtyard filled with lots of hanging plants. The brightly painted rooms, with lots of pink trim, all have air-conditioning and color TVs. King-sized rooms have Jacuzzi baths. The attached dining room has mediocre food (for the price) but a nice small balcony overlooking the square.

Hotel las Bugambilias (Av. 16 de Septiembre 406, tel. 726/262-1966, $65 s/d) offers clean but very small rooms in a motel-like complex with parking. Rooms each have two double beds and cost the same for one to four people—a good value with four, but not so great for one person.

$110 and Above

The most upscale place in the center of town is **Hotel Los Arcos** (Bocanegra 310, tel. 726/262-0042 or 726/262-0168, $120 s/d, $130 t), with 24 wood-beamed rooms and suites, each equipped with TV and working fireplace, around an interior garden area with a small pool.

An activity-oriented "therapy center" is the plush **Avándaro Golf and Spa Resort** (Vega del Río s/n, tel. 726/266-0200 or 726/266-0370, Mexico City 5282-1212, fax 5280-0092, www.hotelavandaro.com, $155 s/d, up to $445 for Suite Monarca). Composed of a hotel, health complex, and 18-hole golf course, the resort is secluded amid the pine forests in the town of Avándaro, southwest of Valle de Bravo. Rooms are spacious and bright, and the facili-

ties include a palatial pool, seven tennis courts, a full spa, and the golf course. Guests must still pay an additional $18 to use the spa or $180 for the golf course, while the pool is included in room price. Nonguests may pay $16 to use the spa but are not allowed in the pool or on the golf course.

The adventure travel company Río y Montaña have built a new forest lodge, **Rodavento** (km 3.5 Valle de Bravo Los Saucos, tel. 726/251-4815 or in Mexico City 5292-5032, www.rioymontana.com, $1,300–1,800 for 5–7 days, all included) above Valle de Bravo. Here tourists can take part in a number of different outdoor activites, including kayaking, paragliding, mountain biking, or just enjoying the greenery. The hotel is kind of an updated cabin-style construction out of brick and wood; it integrates well into the lush surroundings. Rooms are comfortable and well kept. Check out the *temazcal* out back, where you can sweat out your toxins in a traditional indigenous sauna and follow it up with a massage. Although they are geared toward longer stays, they will sometimes accept clients for one or two nights, depending on how busy they are.

RESTAURANTS

If you visit Valle during the week, note that many restaurants are open only Thursday through Sunday, which means your options will be a bit limited on other days. Generally the less-expensive eateries are clustered around Plaza Independencia, while the more pricey restaurants are found down toward the docks.

Tacos, Tortas, and Comidas Corridas

At the southeast corner of the Plaza Independencia, on Bocanegra with Pagaza, two stalls offer excellent stand-up fare, perfect for breakfast or a midmorning snack. A great way to start your day from around 8:30 A.M. is the fresh *jugo de naranja con piña* (orange with pineapple juice) with *barbacoa de puerco* (steamed pork). Less than a dollar will get you a big dollop on a double tortilla. Note that the makeshift stall closes when food sells out, which happens well before

Mexican lunchtime begins, so get there before midday to avoid disappointment.

Several small stands in the market, one block from the plaza, sell inexpensive breakfasts and *comida corrida* daily until 5 P.M.

Open from 2:30 P.M. until late, head to el Callejón del Arco one block west of the main church near the corner of Independencia and Juárez near to the market. This is a little cobblestone street that everyone knows as *el callejón del hambre* (hunger alley) because of the wonderful beef tacos cooked up here on makeshift stands for under $1 a serving. For some of the finest *tacos de barbacoa* you're likely to find, go to the first stall on the right as you enter the market, where you'll see a crowd gobbling down this local specialty either *sencillo* (single) or *con copia* (literally, "with copy;" i.e., with two tortillas) daily while supplies last.

El Tortón, on Plaza Independencia next to Posada Girasoles, whips up decent ham, chicken, or sausage *tortas* for $1.50. It also has a stand down by the dock next to La Oveja Negra.

La Michoacana (on Plaza Independencia opposite the church) is the place for fruity ice-lollies, some of the best being *zarzamora* (blackberry) and *zapote* (a sweet, inky black fruit). The custom is to go and pick up a bag of *campechanas* (thin sugary pastries) sold on every corner of the zócalo and stroll around, taking alternate bites of ice and pastry.

Mexican

La Michoacana (Calle de la Cruz 10, just off Pagaza, tel. 726/262-1625, 8:30 A.M.–11 P.M. daily, entrées $4–8), not to be confused with the ice cream shop on the plaza, serves great traditional Mexican dishes such as *sopa de tortilla* (tortilla soup), *cecina* (a type of dried beef), trout, and for the adventurous, *gusanos de maguey* (cactus worms). Meals are moderately priced, and the dining room's windows offer fine views overlooking the town and lake.

A very good, inexpensive local eatery is **Los Churros de Valle** (corner of 16 de Septiembre and Vergel, two blocks from the plaza), with a small but tasty menu, much of it made with

ingredients from the owner's farm. Specialties include a great artichoke dip, hearty soups, and of course the namesake *churros,* a sugary pastry served with hot chocolate.

Right across the street is another good place for inexpensive meals, **Mi Vallecito** (9 A.M.–10 P.M. daily), serving quesadillas, trout, beef dishes, and buffet meals.

Serving the best inexpensive food down by the lake is **La Oveja Negra** (tel. 726/262-0572, 9 A.M.–7 P.M. Tues.–Sun., entrées $2–6), in front of the town dock. Breakfasts, including some creative egg dishes, run $2–4, while a variety of entrées—pasta, meats, shrimp, and salads—cost a bit more.

Trout and Other Seafood

Just about every restaurant in town serves the locally famous *trucha,* or trout. One popular low-budget place is **La Cascada,** a small restaurant on the road between Valle de Bravo and Avándaro, on the roadside next to a waterfall.

A much more upscale spot is **Los Veleros** (Salitre 104, tel. 726/262-0370, 1 P.M.–midnight Fri.–Sun., entrées $9–15), an exceptionally fine restaurant specializing in seafood (but also serving salads and meat dishes) in a beautiful old house. Diners may sit either in one of the interior rooms, decorated with pictures and drawings of sailboats, or on one of the outdoor balconies overlooking the lawn and garden.

Restaurant Santa María del Lago (Marina Nacional 201, tel. 726/262-1012, 8 A.M.–11 P.M. Fri.–Sat., 8 A.M.–6 P.M. Sun., entrées $7–13) is set in a large stone building right on the edge of the lake. The 2nd-floor dining room and terrace have fine views of the lake and of the many paragliders who land right nearby on weekend afternoons. Apart from *huachinango* (red snapper), giant shrimp, trout, and other seafood, the restaurant also offers a tasty chicken or vegetable kebab.

If you like waterborne dining, **Los Pericos** (at the municipal dock, tel. 726/262-0558) specializes in fish and seafood. You pay a little extra for swaying about while you eat, but the views across the lake are worth it.

Italian

Tramezzino (Salitre 104C, tel. 726/262-4082, 4–11:30 P.M. Fri., 1–11:30 P.M. Sat., 1–7 P.M. Sun., $11 medium pizza, $20 large) serves very tasty pizzas and pastas in a spacious, somewhat upscale dining room and courtyard that fills up regularly on weekends with out-of-town visitors. They also deliver.

Coffee and Snacks

The **Italian Coffee Company** (Coliseo 104, 10 A.M.–10 P.M. daily), a chain coffee shop that started in Puebla, has a new place at a block above the plaza, with very good coffee, sweets, and a decent ham and cheese croissant for a light breakfast.

ENTERTAINMENT

La Pila Seca, at the corner of Pagaza and Santa María, near the entrance to town, is a chilled-out bar with good music and comfortable places to sit. It's popular with the alternative crowd living in or visiting Valle. A similar spot is **Bar de los Artistas** (Bocanegra 303), a couple of blocks off the plaza. It's slightly more upscale but still relaxed and sometimes has live music.

Lagartos Bar (Fray Gregorio J. de la Cuenca 6, 726/262-6691) offers live music on Saturday nights, when it is open until midnight. It is a good place to meet people, providing a friendly atmosphere for a drink and a snack, especially around dusk most evenings.

PRACTICALITIES

For information, tourist maps, and pamphlets, stop in at the very helpful and friendly **Municipal Tourism Office** (Porfirio Díaz and Zaragoza, three blocks northwest of the plaza, tel. 726/262-1678, www.valledebravo.com.mx, 9 A.M.–7 P.M. Mon.–Fri., 9 A.M.–2 P.M. Sat.) The tourism office also has a module on the lakeside (10 A.M.–6 P.M. daily).

The Valle **post office** (9 A.M.–4 P.M. Mon.–Fri.) is on the corner of Pagaza and Calle de la Cruz, a block down from the plaza toward the dock.

Computel (on the plaza opposite the side of the church, 7 A.M.–8:30 P.M. daily) offers long-distance phone and fax service.

Internet service is available at **Tiempo en Línea** (Calle de la Cruz 100, 10 A.M.–9 P.M. Mon.–Sat., noon–7 P.M. Sun., $1.60 an hour), a block below the plaza.

Banamex, HSBC, and BBVA, all within two blocks of the plaza, change dollars and traveler's checks, and each has an ATM. On Saturday the **banks** are open 10 A.M.–2 P.M. only.

On San Vicente, a couple of blocks down from Pagaza toward the lake, is an inexpensive, no-name **laundry service** (9 A.M.–2 P.M. and 5–8 P.M. Mon.–Sat.)

Librería Arawi (Coliseo 101, tel. 726/262-2557, 9:30 A.M.–3 P.M. and 5–9 P.M. daily), on the plaza, sells magazines and newspapers, some in English.

Medical

The police can be reached, if you can believe it, via a lawyer's office (tel. 726/262-1126).

Clínica Santa Fe (Nicolás Bravo 203, tel. 726/262-0018), a block south and west of the plaza, offers 24-hour medical attention.

The Cruz Roja ambulance service can be reached at tel. 726/262-0391.

Farmacia Santa Juanita (Nicolás Bravo 103, at the corner of San Vicente, tel. 726/262-1065) is open 24 hours a day.

Shopping for Food

If you're renting a place in Valle and are looking for supplies, the first place to start is of course the **market,** one block from the plaza at the corner of Juárez and Porfirio Díaz. For more luxury goods, including a great selection of wines, cheeses, and other expensive treats, head to **La Europea** (Santa María 114), down near the lake.

GETTING THERE
By Bus

Zinacantepec (16 de Septiembre just past Zaragoza, tel. 726/262-0213) runs buses once an hour from Valle de Bravo to Toluca and

Valle de Bravo is one of the few places in Central Mexico to go sailing.

Terminal Observatorio in Mexico City between 6 A.M. and 6 P.M., charging $3 to Toluca (one hour and 45 minutes) and $6.50 to Mexico City (two hours and 45 minutes). It also runs two direct buses to Mexico City per day, leaving in the afternoon ($9).

By Car

Two roads leave Valle de Bravo to Toluca, the windier and slower México 48 and the faster and more scenic México 134, which passes near Nevado de Toluca. Be prepared for lots of traffic on weekends.

GETTING AROUND

Collective taxis running between Valle and Avándaro leave regularly from Pagaza, right next to the plaza, for $1, while other taxis go to Colorines across the dam from Avenida 16 de Septiembre, just off Juárez, also for $1.

Popocatépetl and Ixtaccíhuatl

The second- and third-highest mountains in Mexico, Popocatépetl (5,465 meters) and Ixtaccíhuatl (5,230 meters) form the southeastern lip of the Valle de México. On clear days in Mexico City, the two snowcapped peaks can be seen in the distance from a number of tall buildings in the city center.

Until a decade ago, climbing Popo was probably the most popular mountaineering adventure in Mexico. In December 1994, however, the formerly dormant volcano began intermittently belching clouds of smoke and ash. The peak is still off-limits to climbers, even though it calmed down at the end of 2003. For updated information on the volcano's activity, look on the Internet at www.cenapred.unam.mx/mvolcan.html.

The **Paso de Cortés,** between the two volcanoes, is a destination in itself for the brisk air and amazing views. It's also the take-off point for an Ixtaccíhuatl climb and is reached by driving or busing 48 kilometers from Mexico City to Amecameca, a large town at the base of the

mountain. Driving from Amecameca to the pass, you will probably have to pass an army checkpoint and show some identification.

PASO DE CORTÉS

Visitors who don't want to hike up to the high peaks might like to wander the many trails around the Paso de Cortés between the two peaks. Be sure to bring plenty of warm clothing, as it can be bitter cold and windy. The pass is so called because Cortés came through here from Cholula on his way to conquer the Aztec capital of Tenochtitlán. On the way, two of the Spanish soldiers reputedly climbed up Popo and descended into the crater to get sulphur for gunpowder (apparently not a big deal for those unbelievably hardy Spaniards), which would make them the first nonindigenous people to scale the mountain, and the first recorded climbers.

On weekends, several food stands offer quesadillas and other snacks at the parking lot in

Excursions

the pass, and a visitors center can provide some information on the volcanoes. The **Albergue Alzomoni,** by the radio towers just off the dirt road leading to La Joya, rents beds for $2 a night, with very minimal facilities (reserve with CONANP offices in Amecameca, tel. 597/978-3829). The lodge, atop a hill with great views of both peaks and the valleys below, can be crowded on weekends.

Getting There

Although no buses drive the 30-kilometer potholed road to the Paso de Cortés from Amecameca, taxis in Amecameca are accustomed to taking up weekenders for a negotiable fee, usually around $15 per car. If you did bring a car and don't mind a few bumps, consider continuing down the dirt road on the far side—it leads down through the forest to Cholula (46 kilometers) and on to Puebla (10 kilometers farther), where you can take the highway back to Mexico City. Driving up through Amecameca, enjoying the views at the pass, and returning to Mexico City via Cholula (with a stop at the convent at Huejotzingo) makes a great day trip.

CLIMBING IXTACCÍHUATL

Ixtaccíhuatl is still open for climbing and presents more of a challenge than Popo did. While the single cone of Popo required a steep hike of four to seven hours to reach the peak, the most common route up the broken, jagged Ixta, replete with false summits along the way to test your resolve, takes a solid seven to ten hours.

Below is only a general overview of what the route is like, and it does not pretend to serve as a blow-by-blow guide. Climbers should take a certified guide. The climb, while not particularly difficult in a technical sense, is nonetheless extremely dangerous for getting lost on the vast mountain terrain and getting caught unprepared in bad weather. Only very experienced and well-prepared climbers should attempt the route without a guide. Whether you go with a guide or not, it's very important (and legally required) to register with the Amecameca offices of CONANP (Plaza de la Constitución 9B, tel.

climbing Ixtaccíhuatl, with Popocatépetl in the background

© CHRIS HUMPHREY

597/978-3830), the National Commission for Protected Areas, which administer the Izta-Popo park and is in charge of organizing rescue teams in case of emergency. Usually someone in the office speaks English.

For more detailed route-finding information on Ixtaccíhuatl or other Mexican volcanoes, buy a copy of R. G. Secor's guide, *Mexico's Volcanoes,* 3rd edition (Seattle: The Mountaineers, 2001). The official government website (in Spanish) contains excellent updated information and maps: http://iztapopo.conanp.gob.mx /infor_turis.php.

La Joya Route

By far the most frequented route up Ixta begins at La Joya (4,000 meters), a dirt parking lot perched on the southern flank of the mountain, reached by a seven-kilometer dirt road from the Paso de Cortés. The road is passable by passenger car most of the year but can get treacherous in the rainy season. No buses go to either the Paso de Cortés or La Joya, so if you don't have wheels, you'll have to hire a taxi in Amecameca ($24 per carload).

camping shelters on Ixtaccíhuatl

© CHRIS HUMPHREY

In profile Ixta looks something like a sleeping woman, and climbers have labeled parts of the mountain accordingly. The La Joya climb starts at "Los Pies" (the feet) and continues up "Las Piernas" (the legs) to the brutally steep "Rodillas" (knees). From there it crosses the snowfields of "La Barriga" (the belly) at a more gentle grade to reach the mountain's summit atop "El Pecho" (the breast). Although it's not so steep, the last stretch across the icefields is really a rude shock for most people, who frequently give everything they have up Las Rodillas, thinking the summit is not much further. It's also extremely bright when sunny, so hopefully you thought to bring your sunglasses, or you might have to turn back. From El Pecho, the views down onto the rock formation of "La Cabeza" (the head) are spectacular.

One popular schedule for climbing is to arrive at the parking lot at La Joya in the afternoon or evening, sleep until around 2 A.M. in your car or a tent, then climb most of the way up in the darkness, arriving at the peak sometime between 8 and 11 A.M. and returning to the parking lot in the early afternoon. Leaving at this ungodly hour provides spectacular sunrise views and ensures that the ice on the peak is hard, making it easier and safer to cross. The drawback is the possibility of losing your way if you're unsure of the trail.

If no one in your group has been on the mountain before, or if you just think getting up so early is for the birds, leave La Joya in late morning or early afternoon and spend the night about halfway up the mountain (at 4,750 meters) in a pair of climbing huts just below the "Knees." Although rudimentary, the huts are safe from the weather and will keep you warm enough if you have a good sleeping bag and pad. They can get crowded on weekends in the dry season, so if you go then, it's better to have a tent on hand, just in case. Another consideration is the altitude—if you're not acclimated, it's often better to knock out the climb in one shot rather than try to sleep at the huts, where the thin air can make for a miserable night.

Although the trail is well worn, it zigzags back and forth across a long ridge leading northward up to the summit—sometimes on the Mexico City side of the mountain, sometimes on the Puebla side—and can at times be difficult to spot among the jumble of rocks and gravel. Go slowly and avoid energy-consuming detours.

Should you have no particular burning desire to go to the summit, a hike halfway up to the huts (either spending the night or returning the same day) crosses over only dirt and rock, not ice, and requires no special climbing equipment. The hike is still very arduous, especially with the altitude, and takes five to eight hours round-trip.

Equipment and Safety Precautions

If you hike Ixta in the dry season (December to April), you can generally get away with just bringing an ice axe for emergencies, as the only stretches of ice you'll have to cross are mostly flat. The rest of the year you'll also need crampons. A rope is generally not needed. Check with a climbing shop in Mexico City (see the *Recreation* chapter) for current snow conditions. As with any mountain climb, keep a close eye on the weather, and come prepared with waterproof, warm clothes in case things take a turn for the worse.

Visiting climbers may be disheartened to see Mexicans young and old tromping gleefully past them on the trail, while they rest, wheezing, against a convenient rock. But don't forget, most of these locals live in Mexico City (which has an elevation of 2,240 meters) and are well acclimated. Don't just fly in from sea level or thereabouts and expect to hike up to the peak without a care. Even those who have spent some time in Mexico City may get struck by a splitting headache, fierce vomiting, and possibly worse. Should these symptoms befall you, the quickest remedy is a fast descent. Drinking plenty of water while climbing can help keep altitude sickness at bay.

Though not a technically challenging climb, this is a very large mountain and should not be taken lightly—don't go unless you have some experience climbing or you're with an experienced group leader. **Socorro Alpino** has a rescue crew at La Joya on weekends in case of problems, and someone is always around who can call for help at the ranger station at the Paso de Cortés. The closest medical help is the hospital at Amecameca.

Guides

Colorado Mountain School, (341 Moraine Ave., P.O. Box 1846, Estes Park, CO 80517, U.S.A., tel. 970/586-5758 or 888-267-7783, fax 970/586-5798, www.cmschool.com) offers a package trip from the U.S. to climb Ixta and Pico de Orizaba. A 11-day two-peak trip costs $2,250 per person.

Two local guide groups that offer less-expensive trips up Ixta are **Río y Montaña** (tel. 5292-5032 or 5292-5058, www.rioymontana.com) and **Teporingo's Expediciones** (on the plaza in Amecameca, tel. 597/978-0349, teporingo_ex @yahoo.com.mx). Río y Montaña organizes all sorts of adventure trips around Mexico, including their popular rafting trips to Veracruz, while Teporingo's is a smaller outfit specializing in hiking, mountaineering, and mountain bike trips in the volcanos of Central Mexico. Both companies have more than 10 years' experience.

A third company that run guided trips to the volcanos is **Corporative Retto** (San Pedro Cholula, Av. Cinco de Mayo 602, tel. 222/296-2470, www.corporativoretto.com), based in Cholula.

Getting There

Get on the Puebla highway leaving Mexico City, then take the turnoff marked Cuautla–Amecameca. After going through a $1.50 toll, a sec-ondary highway continues 22.5 kilometers to Amecameca. One kilometer beyond Amecameca, a road turns left (east) and snakes its way 30 kilometers up the mountain to the Paso de Cortés, accessible by either car or taxi from Amecameca. By bus, ride from Terminal TAPO in Mexico City to Amecameca and take a taxi (see the *Amecameca* section for details).

Elsewhere on Ixta

The pine-forested flanks of Ixta are crisscrossed with dirt roads, giving access to the mountain from several different directions besides the Paso de Cortés.

On the Mexico City–Puebla highway, at the road's highest point above the valley of Mexico, 21 kilometer from the toll gate leaving Mexico City, is the roadside village of **Llano Grande,** where you'll see a couple of dozen food stands and stores. Look for an archway on the north side of the highway—a dirt road turns in here and continues 10 kilometers up the northern side of Ixta, where it runs into a large meadow at 3,350 meters, with a forestry research station managed by the Universidad de Chapingo. From here secondary dirt tracks continue up the side of the mountain to a second, higher meadow with fantastic views of the peak, as well as down toward Cholula on the east side and toward San Rafael and Amecameca to the west. The climbing routes up Ixta from here all go by the "Head" of the mountain and are more technical, so don't attempt them without a guide.

While the forests on this side of Ixta are lovely for hiking and mountain biking, don't park your car near the village of Llano Grande, as robberies and assaults have been reported. Instead drive all the way up the dirt road as far as the research station, and leave the car there, where it's generally safe. This is, nonetheless, a very remote area, so there is always some risk.

North of Amecameca, on the eastern side of Ixta, is the village of **San Rafael,** the takeoff point for another approach to the summit. Robberies have been reported recently around San Rafael, so at the moment it's not advisable to venture over this way.

AMECAMECA

On the way to the Paso de Cortés from Mexico City is Amecameca (2,475 meters), a mountain town with clean brisk air (dress warmly). The market and picturesque town square, with the bright red **Iglesia de la Asunción** on the east side, are fun to explore for an hour or two. It's also a good place to grab a meal or pick up supplies before heading up the mountain. The best season to visit the town is after the rains have finished, usually towards the end of October, until May, when the views are razor sharp. It is very cold at night in the winter months, so take coats and scarves.

Just west of town is a hilltop park known as **El Sacramonte** (Sacred Mountain), with two chapels on top. Each year on Ash Wednesday, the townsfolk carry a decorated image of Christ—supposedly made in 1521—in a candlelight procession from one of the churches to the nearby burial cave of Fray Martín de Valencia, who is said to have been the leader of the first group of missionaries to the area.

Another attraction just before arriving in town from Mexico City, on your left, is **Hacienda de Panoaya,** (km 58 Carr. Fed. Mex–Cuautla, tel. 597/978-2670 or 597/978-2813, 9 A.M.–7 P.M. Tues.–Sun.), which has been converted into a museum, zoo, and restaurant complex. The museum contains a small volcano museum (Sat.–Sun. only, admission $2 adults, $1 children), and the restaurant serves good venison steaks.

Amecameca holds a **Feria de la Nuez** (Nut Fair) in August.

A new tourism office (in the Presidencia Municipal, tel. 597/978-0028 or 597/978-0345, www.amecameca.gob.mx) provides visitor information and ideas for day trips or weekend visits. It's best to visit in person, as their website doesn't have much information.

The best place to get information on the volcanos, and also very good for finding hiking, biking, or climbing guides, is the CONANP (Plaza de la Constitución 9B, tel. 597/978-3830), the National Commission for Protected Areas, which administer the Izta–Popo park.

Getting There

Transportes Volcanes runs buses every 15 minutes or so, 5 A.M.–10 P.M., between Terminal TAPO in eastern Mexico City and Amecameca; the fare is $1.80. Taxis from Amecameca's plaza to Paso de Cortés cost around $15 per carload, or $24 to La Joya, although prices vary.

Puebla and Vicinity

The Spanish founded the city of Puebla in 1531 as an intermediate supply depot and resting point between the port of Veracruz and the Mexican capital. Puebla became an important trading center in the colonial era, and the route from Mexico City to the coast via Puebla is still one of the country's main commercial arteries.

The capital city was laid out in the neat grid pattern typically employed by the Spanish. The historic city center is full of ornate colonial buildings replete with magnificent stonework, gold leaf, and Puebla's distinct signature, **Talavera tile,** which decorates rooftops, church domes, walls, and much else besides. Those with an eye for architecture will enjoy the city's plentiful baroque churches and churrigueresque facades.

The **Cinco de Mayo** holiday, one of Mexico's greatest celebrations, originated in Puebla, when on May 5, 1862, a ragtag Mexican army beat back the invading French. The French were eventually victorious, but Mexicans still celebrate Cinco de Mayo as a day of national pride and independence.

Today Puebla is the fourth-largest city of Mexico, with a population of about 1.5 million people. The city's colonial architecture provides a backdrop for bustling commerce, thick traffic, cafés, bars, shops, shoppers, museums, students, and scores of tourists. Agriculture, tourism, and the production of ceramics are major industries, and Puebla is also home to Mexico's Volkswagen factory, responsible for

Excursions

© AVALON TRAVEL PUBLISHING, INC.

the *bochitos* (Beetles) seen all over Mexican roads, as well as the sleek "new Beetle" so popular in the U.S. Tragically for those with a soft spot for the ubiquitous *bochitos,* they have been discontinued, although they'll surely be lots of them still running for years to come.

SIGHTS
Orientation

Puebla was the first Mexican town built from a master plan rather than around an existing Indian city. With a few exceptions, streets running north–south are called *calles,* and those running east–west are called *avenidas.*

The intersection at the northwest corner of the *zócalo* forms the center of town for purposes of street labeling. Here, Avenida Reforma/Palafox (east–west) meets Avenida 16 de Septiembre/5 de

Mayo (north–south, one of the exceptions mentioned above). Coming from the west, Avenida Reforma becomes Avenida Palofax east of this intersection. Coming from the south, Avenida 16 de Septiembre becomes Avenida 5 de Mayo north of this intersection.

Even-numbered *avenidas* lie north of Avenida Reforma/Palafox; odd-numbered *avenidas* lie to the south. On the west side of Avenida 16 de Septiembre/5 de Mayo, all *avenidas* are labeled with the suffix "Poniente" (west), abbreviated to Pte.; on the east side, they're all labeled "Oriente" (east), shortened to Ote.

Even-numbered *calles* lie east of Avenida 16 de Septiembre/5 de Mayo; odd-numbered *calles* lie to the west. On the south side of Avenida Reforma/Palafox, all *calles* are labeled with the suffix "Sur" (south), while on the north side they're all labeled "Norte" (north), or Nte.

The historic section of town is bounded by Boulevard Héroes del 5 de Mayo on the east, Calle 11 on the west, Avenida 18 on the north, and Avenida 11 on the south. Most sites of interest to visitors are within easy walking distance of the cental plaza. A few destinations, such as Railway Museum, Uriarte Talavera, and the Ex-Convento de Santa Mónica, are a bit further afield and are best visited by taxi or *colectivo.*

Taxis in Puebla do not use meters, so check the cost before you board. One taxi company you can call for a car is **Radio Taxi** (tel. 222/243-7055 or 222/243-7212).

Plaza

The city center (call it the *zócalo,* the plaza, the Plaza de la Constitución, or the Plaza de Armas) faces the cathedral and is bordered on three sides by the original broad stone *portales* (arches). The buildings exhibit a variety of architectural styles from across the centuries: baroque, churrigueresque, neoclassic, herreresque, and renaissance. The 16th-century arches lining the plaza house sidewalk cafés, restaurants, shops, and newspaper stands. The broad *zócalo*—once a bustling 19th-century marketplace—is an island of tranquility with shady trees, benches, and a bandstand.

Catedral de la Inmaculada Concepción

On the south side of the *zócalo,* you can't miss the cathedral, widely considered one of the most beautiful churches in México (no small compliment). The twin-towered and tile-domed cathedral, begun in 1575 by Francisco Becerra and completed in 1664, shows medieval, renaissance, and baroque styles on the facade, and even a few neoclassical hints on the inside, for example Manuel Tolsá's marble and onyx altar. Inside, past the lovely carved wooden doors, visitors will find 14 gilded chapels filled with religious paintings, relics, and sculptures, as well as a 12-meter-high pipe organ.

One tale about the church says the enormous 8.5-ton bell was placed in the bell tower by angels. How else would it have gotten up to the top of the 73-meter tower? The second tower has no bell, because it was feared that the weight would cause the structure to sink into the ground. A tower tour is offered every day at 11 A.M.; English-speaking guides are usually available.

Casa de la Cultura

Formerly the archbishop's palace, the Casa de la Cultura (Avenida 5 Ote. 5, next door to the tourism office, tel. 222/246-3186, 222/232-1227, or 222/232-4647) was built in 1597. The palace housed the colleges of San Pablo, San Pedro, and San Juan in the 17th and 18th centuries. In 1891 it became the Governor's Palace, and in 1973 it was reconstructed. Inside you'll find a movie room, exhibition space, workshops, and restrooms.

Up a flight of marble stairs to the 2nd floor is the **Biblioteca Palafoxiana,** one of the oldest libraries in the Americas. In 1646, Bishop Juan Palafox y Mendoza donated the first 5,000 volumes, including works of philosophy, theology,

an 18th-century Santo Domingo statue at Museo de Arte Virreinal San Pedro

© CHRIS HUMPHREY

Excursions

and history. The books cover a wide variety of scholars; many are in Greek and Latin, others in Hebrew and Sanskrit, and some were printed as early as the 15th century.

In 1773 Bishop Francisco Fabian y Fuero constructed the library, a parallelogram 43 meters long and 12 meters wide, covered by five domes on six Doric arches. Shelves of white cedar, divided into 2,472 sections, hold 50,000 volumes. Check out the revolving *atril,* or lectern, used to consult various books at once. It's really an amazing, unique sight, something out of *The Name of the Rose* or *Harry Potter,* and well worth a visit.

Iglesia de Santo Domingo de Guzmán

Three blocks north of the plaza on 5 de Mayo lies what remains of a fine baroque Dominican monastery (10 A.M.–12:15 P.M. and 4:30–8 P.M. daily), consecrated in 1690. Inside the exceptional **Capilla del Rosario,** the walls are covered with gilded ornate carvings, tiles, and cherubs.

Iglesia de San Cristóbal

Another baroque beauty—this one is on Calle 4 Norte at Avenida 6 Oriente. The interior is similar to that of the Capilla del Rosario. The elaborate relief figures are very well done but not gilded.

Other Churches

Puebla has around 60 churches, many dating from the colonial era. Church buffs might want to take a look at **Iglesia de San José** (nine blocks north of the plaza, at Av. 18 Ote. and Calle 2 Nte.) and the adjoining tile-domed **Capilla de Jesús.** The church's interior is inaccessible but worth a look from the outside.

The churrigueresque **Templo del Tercer Orden y Ex-Convento de San Francisco** (Av. 14 Ote. 1009, at Blvd. Héroes del 5 de Mayo) was begun in 1535 and completed in 1667. The principal dome is an eight-sided star. *La Virgen de la Conquistadora,* the statue of the Virgin that according to legend accompanied Cortés on his battles of conquest, is also here—an ominous sight for those who can imagine the scenes the small statue witnessed.

Other churches worth a visit are **Iglesia de la Compañía** (Av. Palafox at Calle 4 Sur), **Iglesia del Carmen** (Av. 16 de Septiembre at Av. 17 Ote.), and **Iglesia de la Santa Cruz** (Av. 14 Ote. and Calle 14 Sur), built at the site of Puebla's first Mass, in 1530.

Museo de Arte Religioso Santa Mónica

This religious museum (Av. 18 Pte. 103, on the corner with 5 de Mayo, tel. 222/232-0178, 10 A.M.–4:30 P.M. Tues.–Sun., admission $2.50) was founded as a convent in 1610. With the laws of the Reforma, promulgated by President Benito Juárez in 1867, the Catholic nuns of this convent literally went underground and remained hidden there until they were discovered in 1935. The building then was converted into a museum. Visitors can walk through narrow halls, winding stairways, hidden passages, and look through a secret window where the nuns watched Mass in the adjacent church. The museum entrance is through a private home, as it was when the convent was in operation. Kids will get a kick out of the velvet paintings with hands and faces that seem to change position when you view them from different angles, the neat spiral staircase, and the creepy cold crypt.

Museo Amparo

This restored colonial mansion (Calle 2 Sur 708, tel. 222/246-4646, www.museoamparo.com, 10 A.M.–5 P.M. Wed.–Mon., admission $2.50), three blocks from the *zócalo,* showcases an extensive collection of prehispanic and colonial art. The displays are labeled in Spanish and English, with push-button recordings (headsets cost $2). The museum's restaurant and shop are both very good.

Museo de Arte Virreinal San Pedro

Puebla's newest museum (Calle 4 Nte. 203, tel. 222/246-6618, 10 A.M.–5 P.M. Tues.–Sun., admission $2) is dedicated to colonial religious art. Housed in the former Hospital de San Pedro, the museum has a permanent exhibit of art from the many churches around the city, displayed in a fine two-story stone building around a

DOWNTOWN PUEBLA

Excursions

© AVALON TRAVEL PUBLISHING, INC.

courtyard with lovely exhibition spaces. Note several fine carved sculptures of saints, including the imposing San Cristóbal holding the baby Jesus. One of the rooms traces the construction of the building itself (begun in 1556) and its operation as a hospital.

Museo Bello y González

José Luis Bello, a businessman who amassed a fortune, spent his riches on this seemingly endless collection of elegant furnishings and art from throughout Mexico, Europe, and Asia. The museum (Av. 3 Pte. 302) displays all manner of art and collectibles, including porcelain, glass, Talavera ceramics, wrought iron, religious vestments, clothing, locks, and even original sheet music by Beethoven. The museum was closed awaiting restoration when we last visited, so ask at the state tourism office if it has reopened yet. When last open, guided tours were available in Spanish (English guides by appointment), and museum hours were 10 A.M.–4:30 P.M. Tues.–Sun.; admission will be around $2.

Museo de Artesanías Santa Rosa

This museum (Calle 5 Nte. 1201, in the ex-convent of Santa Rosa, tel. 222/246-2471, 10 A.M.–4:30 P.M. Tues.–Sun., admission $1.50) houses the Talavera-tiled kitchen with huge cauldrons and other earthenware utensils where legend has it that Dominican nun Sor Andrea de la Asunción created the first *mole poblano.* One of Mexico's most famed dishes, this mole has more than 25 ingredients, including a variety of spices, chiles, and chocolate. Mexican art is displayed on two floors, and a gift shop offers a selection of local handicrafts.

Museo del Estado Casa de Alfeñique

The intricate baroque facade of this building (Av. 4 Ote. 416, tel. 222/232-0458, 10 A.M.–4:30 P.M. Tues.–Sun., admission $2) is a classic example of *alfeñique* architectural style, named for a white sugar candy made in Puebla. Built in 1790, it now houses the state museum, with old manuscripts related to Puebla history, ethnography on different indigenous groups in the state, and colonial clothing (including the original *china poblana*

dress). Parts of the museum were closed for renovation when we visited.

Casa de los Muñecos (House of Dolls) or Museo Universitario

The top floor of this house (Calle 2 Nte. at Av. Palafox) is famous for its facade. It is decorated with caricatures of the town fathers, who refused to let the owner add the 3rd floor. After going to Mexico City and getting the necessary permission, the owner exacted his vengeance on his opponents by making fun of them in stone. The building suffered extensive interior and exterior damage during a recent quake, though restoration is under way.

Barrio del Artista

Across the alley from the Teatro Principal, check out the Barrio del Artistas, an exhibition hall that in former years housed the fabric spinners of the local clothing industry. Nowadays it's used by local artists as a workshop and selling space. It's open daily.

Zona Cívica del Cinco de Mayo

Three kilometers northeast of the *zócalo,* at Blvd. Héroes del 5 de Mayo, is a complex of parks and museums on the site of the Battle of Puebla, which gave birth to the Cinco de Mayo fiesta. The **Fuerte de Loreto,** built in 1821, was the center of the battle; 2,000 Mexicans led by General Ignacio Zaragoza tried to defend the fort against an attack by 6,000 French troops. The fort is now a museum (10 A.M.–4:30 P.M. Tues.–Sun., admission $2.50) that contains dioramas of the battle, photos, drawings, and paintings. Cinco de Mayo is celebrated here each year with a major military and school parade.

Also at the complex are a modern planetarium, a children's museum called Museo Imagina and the Museo de Antropología (10 A.M.–4:30 P.M. Tues.–Sun., admission $2.50 to each museum).

Museo Nacional de los Ferrocarriles Mexicanos

Choo-choo buffs should not fail to come to the railroad museum (Calle 11 Nte. 1005, at Av. 12 Pte., tel. 222/232-4988 or 222/246-0395,

10 A.M.–5 P.M. Tues.–Sun., free admission) to study the collection of spiffed-up trains that have been put out to pasture. The antique steam engines and rail cars are open for visitors to examine and explore. Kids will have a ball climbing in and around the 50 rail cars, some of which have special bunk-bed lookouts where guards kept watch for *bandidos* (bandits). In some of the cars visitors find pictures and displays illustrating the history of Mexican trains since 1837.

Africam

At this zoo (tel. 222/281-7000 or 222/236-1212, in Mexico City 5575-2731, www.africamsafari.com, 10 A.M.–5 P.M. daily, admission $10 adults, $9 children 12 and under), about eight kilometers from town, you can take a safari ride through 6,075 hectares inhabited by wild animals, including giraffes, antelope, ostriches, rhinoceros, guacamayas, lions, pelicans, bears, hippos, chimpanzees and blue-eyed Bengal tigers. A boat trip and llama rides for children break up the tour at a halfway area (called "Mombasa"). All of this is before you reach the children's area, which is prettily arranged in walkable segments that include a Bat Cave, a resplendent Butterfly House, cages of hopping toucans, and a good look at the tiger cubs. To make the most of a visit, take at least four hours, if not more. As Sunday is the busiest day, it's a good idea to plan your visit for a Saturday or, if possible, during the week. Arrive early. Buses for Africam leave the Central Camionera (CAPU, north of the city at Calle 11 Nte. and Blvd. Atlixco) three times daily. A taxi to the park costs about $8.

ARTS AND ENTERTAINMENT

Theaters

Teatro Principal (Calle 6 Nte. at Av. 8 Ote., tel. 222/232-6085) and **Teatro U.A.P.** (Calle 4 Sur 104) both offer performing-arts events. For a schedule, check at the tourist office.

Nightlife

La Cantina de los Remedios (Juárez 2504, tel. 222/249-0843) is one of the most typical and popular drinking holes on Avenida Juárez. You may have to line up to get in on Thursday to Saturday night, and the bar will be crowded, but the atmosphere is kicking.

For a taste of the bohemian life in Puebla, visit **El Convento de las Carolinas** (Av. 3 Oriente 403). This gallery, live music venue, bar, and *antojería* (snack restaurant) is popular with the local literati as well as young people.

La Leyenda Restaurant and Bar is more bar than restaurant and conveniently located next to Vittorio's. This hole-in-the-wall caters to a young crowd, and the music is invariably techno. There are lots of small rooms to hide in, and drinks are reasonable at $1–4.

Teorema Librería Cafe (Reforma at Calle 7 Nte., 7 A.M.–1 A.M.) is a bookstore and coffeehouse that transforms itself into a hip nightspot come dark. Don't forget your black turtleneck.

Both the Juárez area and the road from Puebla to Cholula (eight kilometers) are home to several of the area's discos. Most don't get started until about 11 P.M. It's best to ask around to find out which discos are the current favorites.

Sports

Soccer packs in the locals during the season (September to December and January to May) at Estadio Cuauhtémoc (Calz. Ignacio Zaragoza 666, tel. 222/226-2166).

For **bullfights,** go to Plaza de Toros El Relicario, near the fort in the Zona Cívica de 5 de Mayo. The season is late November and December, and also during the city fair, in late April through May. A *lienzo charro* (Carretera Tehuacán Poniente 1032, tel. 222/283-6308), or rodeo ring, holding 4,000 people hosts *charreadas* (rodeos). *Charrería* is big in Puebla, and *charreadas* are held most Sundays.

SHOPPING

Puebla is an outstanding shopping city, filled with stores selling fine Talavera tile, pottery, onyx, handicrafts from surrounding regions, wool and cotton clothing, amate fiber paper, and a myriad of other artwork and handicrafts.

the famed Talavera ceramics of Puebla

Excursions

El Parian

A former 18th-century clothing warehouse, El Parian (Calle 8 Norte btwn. Av. 2 and Av. 6 Oriente), today houses rows of shops selling all manner of handicrafts. If you're looking for good quality Talavera and don't mind the price, check out **Centro de Talavera La Colonial** (Av. 6 Ote. 11, tel. 222/242-2340). Also in the Parian, an up-and-coming workshop with factory tours for the public is **Talavera Armando's** (Av. 6 Ote. 408, on the corner with 6 Nte., tel. 222/242-3455, 10 A.M.–6 P.M.).

Uriarte (Av. 4 Pte. 911, tel. 222/232-1598, www.uriartetalavera.com.mx) is not in El Parian, but it is nonetheless one of the most famed Talavera shops in the city. The shop, which opened its doors in 1872, has excellent guided tours.

Amozoc

If you've always had the cowboy fantasy and want to indulge in all the accoutrements, take a short bus ride out to this small town, 17 kilometers due east of Puebla on the free highway to Tehuacán. Here you'll find superb craftsmen in dozens of shops fashioning what is reputed to be the finest ornamental silver and ironware for Mexican *charro* outfits. Particularly famous are the spurs, but they also make dagger handles, buckles, and *mancuernos,* which are chained brooches worn on clothing, saddles and reins. Prices are not cheap, but the quality is excellent.

Markets

Callejón de los Sapos (Av. 7 Ote. and Calle 4 Sur, three blocks south and one block east of the *zócalo*),is a quiet antique district during the week, but converts into a bustling flea market on weekends, especially Sundays.

Mercado Municipal (Calle 11 Nte. and Av. 4 Pte.), a sprawling indoor market, is chockablock with all manner of foods from the region.

Market Days

Market days at a few of the surrounding cities can be an expedition of discovery. In **San Martín Texmelucan,** it's Tuesday; in **Huejotzingo,** it's Saturday; in **Cholula,** it's Wednesday and Sunday; in **Tepeaca,** it's Friday; and in **Tehuacán,** it's Saturday. **Puebla** has a market day every day.

ACCOMMODATIONS

Under $15

Hotel Victoria (Av. 3 Pte. 306, tel. 222/232-8992, $13 s/d) offers basic, rundown rooms without TV.

With two branches in town, **Hotel Catedral** (Catedral 1 at Av. 3 Pte. 310, tel. 222/ 232-2368 or 222/232-5089, and Catedral 2 a few blocks west on 3 Pte., tel. 222/232-8416, both $10 s without TV, $12 s with TV, $14 d) offers private and shared rooms and baths at cheap prices. Some of the rooms are cabin-style, with two stories and grubby makeshift kitchens.

$15–30

A better value is **Hotel Teresita** (Av. 3 Pte. 309, tel. 222/232-7072, $18 s, $22 d), with 47 rooms with TV and tiled bathrooms.

Gran Hotel San Agustín (Av. 3 Pte. 531, tel. 222/232-5089, fax 222/232-5089, ext. 600, $21 s/d with continental breakfast) is a friendly place with clean rooms.

A beautiful garden juxtaposed with garish, whorehouse decor mixes the sublime with the ridiculous at **Hotel Virrey de Mendoza** (Reforma 538, tel. 222/242-3903, $25 s, $30 d).

Hotel Provincia Express (Reforma 141, tel. 222/246-3557 or 222/246-3642, $21 s, $28 d) is on the main drag closer to the plaza and has very tidy rooms at great prices. The building dates to the 17th century and has lovely hand-painted tiles and decorous hallways.

Hotel San Miguel (Av. 3 Pte. 721, tel. 222/242-4860, $23 s, $30 d) has a modern facade and a bright clean lobby. The rooms are a little dank and on the monastic side but are good value for the increased cleanliness and security.

$30–50

A dramatic step up in quality is **Hotel Imperial** (Av. 4 Ote. 212, tel. 222/242-4981, $34 s, $49 d). This spacious hotel has 65 large rooms, each with TV, telephone, and private bath. Amenities include a restaurant, pool table, parking lot, hot water all day, and bicycles for free use. Anyone carrying a copy of this guide (not a photocopy) gets a 30 percent discount, making it that much better a value. Breakfast is included.

At **Hotel Santiago** (Av. 3 Pte. 106, tel. 222/242-2860, fax 222/242-2779, $37 s, $47 d), the staff may go a bit overboard in their use of cleaning products, but the sparkling rooms and sterilized bathrooms of this modern hotel are nothing to scoff at.

$50–75

Hotel Royalty (Portal Hidalgo 8, tel. 222/242-0204, $49 s, $64 d) offers 45 rooms and an outdoor café under the *portales*. The hotel and café face the *zócalo* and make for a lively atmosphere. The colonial building's interior is lovely, although rooms are somewhat small.

Hotel Colonial (Calle 4 Sur 105, tel. 222/246-4612, $47 s, $57 d), a block from the plaza (and across from its own picturesque little square), is convenient for exploring downtown. The rooms are fairly large, and some have balconies, wood floors, and tile baths. The good restaurant has a gorgeous stained-glass ceiling. Parking is available.

You'll find nice rooms at the **Hotel Palace** (Av. 2 Pte. 13, tel. 222/232-2430, $41 s, $55 d). The adjacent restaurant, El Sardinero, was being remodeled last time we visited. King-sized rooms for just a few dollars more have better light and a street view.

$75–110

Hotel Lastra (Calzada de los Fuertes 2633, tel. 222/235-9755, www.hotellastra.com.mx, $85–160 s/d) has 66 pleasing rooms of differing sizes with spic-and-span bathrooms.

Just one block north of the *zócalo* is **Hotel Posada San Pedro** (Av. 2 Oriente 202, tel. 222/246-5077, fax 222/246-5376, $98 s/d). Housed in a 16th-century building, the hotel is a good mix of interesting architecture and modern amenities, such as the interior courtyard pool, hot tubs, restaurant, and bar.

$110 and Above

One of the more interesting high-end hotel options is **Mesón Sacristía** (Calle 6 Sur 304, tel. 222/246-6084, www.mexicoboutiquehotels .com/meson sacristia, $150 s/d, $190 suites), in the vicinity of Los Sapos. Each of the hotel's nine rooms is individually appointed with fabulous antiques and collectibles such as a 1940s-era typewriter turned into a bedside lamp. An antique store, the lovely Restaurante Sacristía, and Bar El Confesionario are all within the 18th-century building that houses the hotel. Live music plays evenings until midnight, except for Sunday.

Equally elegant is the sister hotel **Mesón Sacristía de las Capuchinas** (Av. 9 Ote. 16, tel. 222/242-3554, www.mesones-sacristia .com, $150 s/d, $190 suites), a converted convent. Thick monastic walls ensure silence and privacy, and antiques are for sale. Rates for both hotels include a la carte breakfast and courtesy car wash.

Hotel Puebla Marriott (Hermanos Serdán 807, tel. 222/223-8300, www.marriott.com, $148 s/d) is one of the better hotels outside of the city center. The 192-room modern hotel has a good restaurant, bar, pool, and car service.

The modern yellow tower of the **Best Western Hotel Real de Puebla** (Av. 5 Pte. 2522, tel. 222/230-0122, toll free in Mexico 800/227-2700, $125 s/d) is on the west side of the city. Amenities include a pool, spa, workout room (you can schedule time with a personal trainer), dining room, cocktail lounge, coffee shop, and a lobby bar. The tan-colored rooms feature minibars, satellite TV, twin double beds, plush carpets, and beautifully appointed tile bathrooms. Suites are available. Ask for a room with a panoramic view of the city.

The **Camino Real Puebla** (Av. 7 Pte. 105, tel. 222/229-0909, toll free in Mexico 800/901-2300, www.caminoreal.com, $180 and up), downtown, is not what you might expect if you've seen other hotels in the chain. There is no swimming pool or tennis courts here, just top-quality rooms in the late-16th-century Ex-Convento de la Concepción. Amenities include two restaurants and a bar; for alfresco eating and drinking, tables are placed outside on the central patio—a very pleasant place on a sunny day.

The **Holiday Inn** (Av. 2 Ote. 211, tel. 222/223-6600, www.holidayinnpuebla.com.mx, $134 s/d, $17 per extra person) has 78 recently remodeled rooms in an elegant old French-colonial building one block from the plaza. A white-linen restaurant (San Leonardo), bar, rooftop pool, and parking lot are on the premises. Rooms have hand-painted bed frames, and the lobby is decorated with antiques and Oriental rugs.

RESTAURANTS

Puebla is noted for its exceptional cuisine. In addition to mole, which everyone here will tell you was first made at the Santa Rosa convent, several other local specialties are worth a try. *Mixiotes* are made by wrapping barbecued meat (beef, pork, lamb, or goat) and spices in a maguey leaf (not edible) and steaming. *Tinga* is a meat (pork or chicken, usually) and vegetable melange, sort of half salad, half stew, and delicious. *Chiles en nogada* consists of pork-stuffed green *poblano* chile peppers in a white sauce of crushed walnuts, decorated with pomegranate seeds. The patriotic colors of the dish (red, green, and white) make it popular around Independence Day, September 16. *Taco árabe* is a Middle Eastern version of the taco—a pita bread wrapped around meat cooked on a spit. **Tacos Tony** (Av. 3 Pte. 149, tel. 222/232-0675) is a good place to try one.

Mexican

For an outdoor seat and a good strong cup of coffee, the **Cafe Aguirre** (Av. 5 de Mayo 4) is a good choice any time of day. For a solid meal, try **La Princesa** (Portal Juárez 101, tel. 222/232-1195), where the breakfasts, appetizers, and *comidas corridas* are all reasonably priced and hearty. This side of the plaza has several restaurants, including **Restaurante Cafe El Vasco,** specializing in Spanish dishes, including good Valencian paella.

The sidewalk café at **Hotel Royalty** (Portal Hidalgo 8, tel. 222/242-0202) is a relaxing spot for cocktails or a nice meal, though prices are slightly high.

Restaurant Bar Casa Real (Av. 4 Ote. 208, tel. 222/246-5876), two blocks from the *zócalo,* is open for breakfast, lunch, and dinner and serves local specialties such as mole, *chalupas, chiles en nogada,* and a large selection of meats. Prices are moderate. On weekends (and some weeknights), live music is presented; shows start at 9 P.M.

Legendary **Fonda de Santa Clara** (Av. 3 Pte. 307, tel. 222/242-2659, and Av. 3 Pte. 920, tel. 222/246-1952, 8 A.M.– 10 P.M. daily, entrées $5–15) is a popular and often noisy restaurant serving traditional regional food. Try the *mixiotes, tingas,* or *mole poblano.* The adventurous can even order *gusanos de maguey en salsa borracha* (maguey worms in tequila sauce). The menu is available in English.

Restaurante Típico La China Poblana's (one block south of El Parian at Calle 6 Nte. 1) offers a small storefront room with three tables next to the kitchen and a larger dining room in the rear. It's decorated with local plates, masks, clothing, and a life-sized China Poblana. The food is very good, but there's no written menu, so be sure to ask carefully. Double-check your order and the price if your Spanish is weak.

Plazuela de los Sapos, on the southeast side of the city's center, is another good arena for restaurants. The small plaza and its surrounding streets are home to several trendy restaurants and good, cheap eateries, as well as interesting home-furnishing shops to browse in. **El Resguardo de los Ángeles** (Calle 6 Sur 504, tel. 222/246-4106), **La Guadalupana Restaurante** (Av. 5 Oriente 605, 222/242-4886), and **La Bella Elena** (Calle 6 Sur 310, tel. 222/242-0702) are a few of the nicer spots for drinks or dinner, all offering local and international dishes for $5–12.

The west side of town, Calle Juárez in particular, offers the city's largest array of high-end Mexican, European, and Asian restaurants. Cruise this strip in a taxi and you'll be sure to find what you're looking for if you've had enough of the historical district. **La Cava** (Av. Juárez 2302, tel. 222/248-5839, entrées $8–18) serves good-quality international (including pastas, salads, steak and seafood) food in a mellow, refined ambience with good service.

International

At **Vittorio's Pizzería** (Portal Morelos 106, tel. 222/232-7900, 7 A.M.–midnight daily, pizzas $4–12), you can enjoy a cappuccino or espresso outside, or stay indoors if it's cold. If you haven't had a Mexican-style pizza yet, here's your chance. And if you haven't had your share of mole already, the restaurant offers a pizza version. The menu also includes pasta, salad, and *típico* (typical) fare, and food can be delivered.

Restaurante Chesa Veglia (Av. 2 Ote. 208, tel. 222/232-1641, 1–11 P.M. daily, entrées $5–12) serves good Swiss food, including cheese, meat, and chocolate fondues.

Vegetarian

Two vegetarian restaurants run by the same group are close to the city center. **Barra Vegetariana La Zanahoria** (Av. 5 Ote. 206, tel. 222/232-4813) and **El Vegetariano** both sell veggie versions of fast food and Mexican specialties, as well as wheat germ and bulk health-food products.

PRACTICALITIES

Tourist Office

The state tourism office (Av. 5 Oriente 3, tel. 222/246-2044, www.puebla.gob.mx and www.turismopuebla.com.mx, 9:30 A.M.–8:30 P.M. Mon.–Sat., 9 A.M.–2 P.M. Sun.) has a very friendly and helpful staff—many have a good command of English, and their love of the beauty and culture around them is evident. Maps and directions are cheerfully provided, and three-hour tours (in English) are available for around $40 (prices vary and are negotiable). One excellent guide is Misael Neri, reachable at extensions 2205 and 2206. It's better to use the official Sectur guides rather than the freelance guides who seek clients in the bus station and in downtown.

The municipal tourist office (Av. Palafoax and Calle 2 Norte, tel. 222/246-1580, 9 A.M.–8 P.M. Mon.–Fri., 9 A.M.–5 P.M. Sat., 9 A.M.–3 P.M. Sun.), in the Palacio Municipal on the plaza, can also be helpful with city information.

Communication

The post office (corner of Av. 5 Oriente and 16 de Septiembre, 8 A.M.–8 P.M. Mon.–Fri., 9 A.M.–1 P.M. Sat.) is in the Archbishop's Palace; it isn't well marked.

There is no shortage of Internet places close by. One is on Calle 2 Sur, between 5 and 7 Ote. ($1 per hour).

Money

Several banks scattered about the center of town exchange both dollars and travelers checks and have ATMs. Try **BBVA** (Av. 3 Pte. 116) and **Banamex** (Av. Reforma 135). A *casa de cambio* (exchange booth) in the Pasaje del Ayuntamiento between Palafox y 2 Ote., is another good place if you don't feel like waiting in bank lines.

Medical

Hospital UPAEP (Av. 5 Poniente 715, tel. 222/246-6099 or 222/246-6464) is a hospital option. **Farmacia del Ahorro** (at 2 Nte. with 2 Ote. tel. 222/231-3383) is the main chain of pharmacies in the center. One centrally located pharmacy is **El Fenix del Centro** (Av. 4 Pte. 111, tel. 222/242-1974) and (5 de Mayo 803, tel. 222/242-2361).

Car Rental
Rent a car from **Budget** (Av. Juárez 1914, tel. 222/232-9108) or **Easy Rent A Car** (7 Sur at the corner of 41 Pte., tel. 222/243-9100 or 222/211-1413).

GETTING THERE

By Car
The modern toll road (México 150D) goes from Mexico City clear to Veracruz and avoids larger cities. To Puebla it is 120 kilometers—90 minutes by bus, and usually less if you are driving. There are two *casetas* (tollbooths) that charge about $6 and $4. The free road crosses the same mountain pass but can be difficult to follow leaving Mexico City, and it is also very congested. Coming into Puebla, the free road is slow as it passes through several towns, but it also gives an excuse to stop at the impressive monastery at Huejotzingo.

By Bus
CAPU, the large Puebla bus station, is north of the city at Calle 11 Norte and Boulevarde Atlixco. From the station, you can get to the city center on a *combi* marked "Centro" ($0.40) or a *sitio* taxi ($3). Ignore taxi touts. Here, 1st- and 2nd-class buses depart for Mexico City's Terminal TAPO almost constantly, all day and night, with lines ADO, Cristóbal Colón, Estrella Roja, and Estrella Blanca (tel. 222/249-7561, $8 for 1st class, $5 for 2nd class).

There are now hourly departures from Terminal Sur (Tasqueña) in Mexico City with **Cristóbal Colón** (tel. 5544-9008 in Mexico City). **Estrella Roja** (tel. 222/249-7099) runs the express bus direct from the CAPU to the Mexico City airport (every hour 3 A.M.–6 P.M.) for $13. **ADO** (tel. 222/225-9001 or 5133-2424 in Mexico City) offers 1st-class buses to Jalapa ($10), Veracruz ($17.50), Mérida ($74), Cancún ($89), Oaxaca ($22) and elsewhere in the southeast of the country. **Cristóbal Colón** (tel. 222/249-7327 or 222/225-9007) runs 1st-class

buses to Tuxtla Gutiérrez in Chiapas ($52). **Autobuses Unidos** (tel. 222/225-9004) offers 1st- and 2nd-class buses to Veracruz ($16) and elsewhere. **Estrella de Oro** has frequent buses throughout the day to Cholula and Huejotzingo.

Tickets for ADO, Cristóbal Colón and Autobuses Unidos, and many other bus lines throughout the country as well, can be bought at Ticketbus (tel. 5133-2424 in Mexico City or 800/702-8000 nationwide, www.ticketbus.com.mx). Buying tickets online is a very efficient way to go.

CHOLULA

The major population center in the region of Mexico where Cortés arrived was Cholula, and the Spaniards stopped here on their way between Tlaxcala and the Aztec capital in Tenochtitlán. The local leaders planned a secret revolt, which was discovered by Cortés's Tlaxcalan allies. The Cholulans paid with their lives, one of the more sordid episodes of the Spanish conquest. The tranquil scene today belies the dramatic bloodbath of the Amerindians that took place in Cholula, when 6,000 warriors were slaughtered in one day.

Cortés was so incensed by the Cholulans' almost successful ploy that he vowed to build a Catholic church in Cholula for each day in the year. He didn't quite make it, but there are at least 39.

Cholula was the base for the first Franciscan friars who came to convert the native people of New Spain. In 1524 the Franciscans established themselves on the former temple of Quetzalcóatl, where soon they began to build the Convent of San Gabriel, or San Gabriel's Friary (1540). This is still a functioning monastery—about 15 to 20 Franciscan monks still live in one part of the premises.

Cholula had, and still has, the largest ancient structure in the Americas, the Great Pyramid of Tepanampa. It covers 18 hectares, is 60 meters high, and has a volume of three million cubic meters. Cholula lies 10 kilometers (and about a 20-minute drive) west of Puebla.

The liveliest time to visit Cholula is on week-

COURTESY OF MEXICO TOURISM BOARD/GUILLERMO ALDANA

the church atop the Gran Pirámide de Tepanapa, with Popocatépetl in the background

ends, when you will catch the Sunday market and live music in restaurants on evenings. Even better, try to catch one of the town's many festivals, especially *la feria de San Pedro* (first two weeks of September), which includes *la bajada de la Virgen,* when the Virgin of Remedies is carried down from her church atop the pyramid and stays a night in each of the town's neighborhoods (normally from September 1 to 9). Other good festivals are *la feria de San Andrés* (in the week around November 30) and the ritual of Quetzalcóatl (March 21).

Around the Zócalo

On the east side of the *zócalo* is the fortresslike **Ex-Convento y Iglesia de San Gabriel** (San Gabriel Monastery), with its Moorish look and 49 domes. The Franciscan ex-convent is one of the original 12 built after the conquest. Construction began in 1549 and was completed in 1571. During the 16th and 17th century, this was a major religious center, where massive baptism and confession ceremonies were held. Check out the entrance door, with 122 Roman nails,

each a different design. On the north side of the *zócalo,* you'll find **Parroquia de San Pedro,** which dates to 1641. In 1986, the monks agreed for part of the building to be renovated and converted into the Franciscan Library. When the Anthropology Department of the Universidad de las Américas began the work on the library, they found the stairs outside (near the ramp, parallel with the arches) were actually part of the pyramid of Quetzalcóatl. This is located in the *Portal de Peregrinos,* or the Pilgrim's Arcade—a series of round arches to the north of San Gabriel's huge atrium, where the pilgrims slept before going to Mass. With 17 *portales,* it has the largest number of arches of any Portal de Peregrinos in the Americas. For more information, contact the library (tel. 222/261-2395) or the Universidad de las Américas (tel. 222/229-2084, http://biblio.udlap.mx/portal/english/).

Gran Pirámide de Tepanapa

If it weren't for the church sitting on top, you might never realize this large hill is actually the largest pyramid in the continent (by volume), with a base measuring 450 meters on each side. About the same age as Teotihuacán, the Great Pyramid of Tepanampa of Cholula was in use before the birth of Christ.

As was the custom in ancient Mesoamerican civilizations, seven structures were superimposed over the original pyramid. The whole process, from original pyramid to seventh structure, spanned 600 years. Because of the massive pyramid, Cholula was also referred to as *Tlachihualtepetl* (hill made by hand, in Náhuatl) in the past.

On the far side of the pyramid from the main road is the entrance to the Gran Pirámide de Cholula archaeological zone. The pyramid was first explored in 1931 and the archaeologist in charge decided to excavate two tunnels to prove that *el cerrito* (the little hill), as many still call it, was an archaeological monument. In the process, he also discovered altars with offerings, floors, walls, and buried human remains.

Guides are available at the pyramid (Calzada San Andrés at Calle 2 Nte., tel. 222/247-9081, 10 A.M.–5 P.M. daily, admission $3), and it's a good idea to hire one; you'll see and appreciate more than if you go it alone in this lighted, subterranean maze. The guides charge about $6. Excavations continue today. About eight kilometers of tunnels have been dug, but only a section is open to the public.

Follow the signs to the small site museum (half a block further down the road away from the *zócalo*), containing early chisels and blades, female fertility icons, and polychromatic ceramics, for which the area is famed. There is also a replica of the 50-meter-long mural of *The Drinkers* that depicts people drinking *pulque* in loincloths, headdresses and masks. The mural is one of the largest in the continent, but the original, located in a large building on the **Gran Plaza** to the south of the pyramid, has been protected so that its colors are not further damaged by the elements, and is not open to public view. Information in English outlines prehispanic funerary customs, the introduction in Postclassic period (A.D. 800 to 1521) of the practice of human sacrifice, and the custom of cranial deformation. Entrance to the museum is included in the admission price. Flash/video camera use costs $3 more.

To get to the beautifully gilded **Capilla de la Virgen de los Remedios** (1–5 P.M. daily), first built in 1594 and rebuilt after an earthquake in the mid-19th century, turn back the way you came and follow the steep path to the top of the hill. Early and late in the day the views of Popocatépetl are spectacular.

Accommodations

$15–30: The basic **Hotel y Bar Reforma** (Calle 4 Sur 101, tel. 222/247-0149, $20 s/d, $25 d with two beds) has reasonably maintained rooms with private baths a block from the *zócalo*.

$50–75: Hotel Posada Señorial (Cinco de Mayo 1400, tel. 222/247-0049, $58 s/d, $64 t) is a clean, pleasant spot just outside of town on the road back toward Puebla.

Villa Arqeológica, (Av. 2 Pte. 601, tel. 222/273-7900, fax 222/247-1508, U.S. tel. 800/258-2633, www.clubmedvillas.com /cholula, $80 s/d Sat.–Sun., $70 s/d during week) is one of the resorts in the Club Med–owned chain of hotels built near various archaeological zones in Mexico. It's about 15 minutes from the Great Pyramid and offers tennis courts, swimming, and a reasonably good French restaurant.

$110 and above: Hotel Quinta Luna (Calle 3 Sur 702, tel. 222/247-8915, fax 222/247-8916, toll free in Mexico 800/672-8669, www.laquintaluna.com, $160 s, $200 d) is Cholula's newest and best hotel, housed in a converted 17th-century mansion just a five-minutes walk from the *zócalo*. Six luxurious rooms are arranged around a central patio with fountain, where you can eat alfresco or inside. With traditional Mexican and nouvelle recipes, this is also the town's finest restaurant. One of the unusual attractions is the library, built with 17th-century wooden beams. Guests have access to the 3,000 books within (on design, economics, and Mexican artists, as well as a small collection of Spanish- and English-language literature). Each room has flat-screen television, DVD player, minibar, coffee service, and safety box. Rates include an a la carte breakfast.

Restaurants

While not extravagant, the cooking in Cholula is wholesome and cheap, at least by Puebla and Mexico City standards. Service is also much more laid-back and friendly than in the big cities.

The most attractive restaurant under the arches is **Las Mañanitas** (at the end of the *portales,* corner with church, tel. 222/261-2537, 9 A.M.–10 P.M. Sun.–Thurs., 9 A.M.–2 A.M. Fri.–Sat., entrées $2–6). Dishes of the day are advertised on a board outside, while the inviting interior is rustic. Portions are generous, and service is personal. Live music at night is laid back, with lots of friendly chatting. **Los Jarrones,** also in the *portales,* is pretty good too—the *cecina* (salty, thin beef) is a good choice.

One block off the main street, **La Casona** (Av. 3 Ote. 9, tel. 222/247-2776, noon–8 P.M. Mon.–Sat., entrées $2–6) is an attractive restaurant filled with trees and flowers. Take a seat on the outdoor patio (or inside if the patio is full, as it often is on weekends) and enjoy a good-quality, traditional Mexican meal.

La Pirámide (Morelos 416, 1–11 P.M. daily) is another popular spot with locals, offering moderately priced, traditional, regional food.

Cafe Enamorada (9 A.M.–11 P.M. daily) and its adjacent shop frame the southwest corner of the *zócalo;* it's a good spot for outdoor dining. This side of the plaza is full of busy cafés, ice cream parlors, and coffee shops.

The Italian Coffee Company (Portal Guerrero 9A, tel. 222/298-0458, 9 A.M.–10 P.M.) has managed to find its way into this ancient city serving brownies, cakes, and cookies under the arches. There is also **Los Tulipanes,** whose mushroom *antojitos* are not to be missed, and nearby **Restaurant-Bar Los Jarrones** (Portal Guerrero 7, tel. 222/247-1098, 10 A.M.–10 P.M. daily, entrées $3–7) is a charming spot with tasty Mexican food. The breakfast buffet on weekends is a good bargain, and live music at night is loud but tuneful.

Just under three blocks from the pyramid, a pretty little restaurant, **La Lunita** (Av. Morelos, corner with 6 Norte, tel. 222/247-0011, 9 A.M.–9 P.M. daily, entrées $7–12) provides welcome refreshment. Although prices are a little inflated, the *acamayas* (crayfish) are great when in season.

Tacos Tony, (Morelos 212) serves inexpensive *tacos árabes,* a regional style of taco in pita bread.For Mexican fast-food standards, fresh and hot in a bustling and industrious atmosphere, go to **Restaurante Güeros** (Av Hidalgo 101, on a corner of the *zócalo,* tel. 222/247-2188, 9 A.M.–midnight daily, entrées $2–6). Here you can tuck into, or take away, tacos, *cecina, tacos árabes, tortas, tostadas, flautas, pozole,* pizzas, and fish.

Information and Services

The **post office** is at 7 Sur, between 5 Pte. and 7 Pte. You can change money at the **BBVA** or **Banamex** (Av. Morelos on the *zócalo*) which each have ATMs, or nearby at **Casa de Cambio Azteca** (2 Sur, close to the center).

The **Municipal Tourist Office** (Calle 12 Ote, at 4 Nte., tel. 222/261-2393, 9 A.M.–7 P.M. Mon.–Fri., 9 A.M.–5 P.M. Sat.–Sun.) has some information. Further information can be found at http://puebla.magazzine.net.

For medical or emergency services, dial 066, or contact the municipal police (tel. 222/247-7449). One pharmacy in town is **Farmacia Nuestra Señora del Sagrado Corazón** (Av. Hidalgo 103B, tel. 222/247-0398, 9 A.M.–10 P.M. daily).

Getting There

Buses from CAPU bus station in Puebla to Cholula, Huejotzingo, and San Martín depart every 15 minutes (Estrella de Oro) or every half-hour (Estrella Roja) between 5 A.M. and 9 P.M. Minibuses also leave Puebla from Avenida 2 Poniente at Calle 13 Sur, across from the Railroad Museum. Authorized taxis cost around $7 from CAPU to Cholula, and about $9 to return.

If you are driving from Puebla, take Avenida Juárez west, go halfway around the traffic circle (México 190 to Cholula), and continue for about 10 kilometers.

Near Cholula

Just south of Cholula, in the villages of **Santa María Tonantzintla** (also famed for its pottery) and **San Francisco Acatepec,** are two of the country's finest churches from the early colonial period.

West of Cholula, a dirt road heads to the town of **San Nicolás de los Ranchos** and continues up into the forest to reach the **Paso de Cortés,** between the volcanoes of Popocatépetl and Ixtaccíhuatl, about 30 kilometers from Cholula. From here a paved road continues down to Amecameca, and from there on to Mexico City or Cuautla. This road is passable in any decent passenger car—if you don't mind a little dust—and the scenery is fantastic.

Fourteen kilometers northwest of Cholula, on the free highway back to Mexico City (about half an hour's drive) is the dusty town of **M Huejotzingo,** site of a 16th-century monastery dedicated to the Archangel Michael, one of the first built in Mexico and one of the best preserved as well. The mix of indigenous and Christian motifs in the carvings on the church and adjacent cloister are fascinating. Note the ominous carved skulls on the courtyard towers, known as *capillas posas.* Inside, the superb late-16th-century *retablo* (altarpiece) is considered one of the greatest of its kind in the New World. The monastery is open until 5 P.M. daily.

The best times to visit Huejotzingo, if you want a spectacle, are the week around its saint's day—San Miguel, on September 29, which conveniently doubles up with a national cider festival—and carnival, in the early spring, which here culminates on Shrove Tuesday, featuring enactments of battles that combine indigenous history, colonial legend, and sheer fantasy.

Buses are easy to find to and from Huejotzingo. Catch buses on the highway passing frequently for Cholula and Puebla, or go the Estrella Roja office (Nicolás Bravo 3, in the center of town near the monastery, tel. 227/276-0213), to and from the TAPO terminal in Mexico City. The roughly two-hour ride costs $4.

The same road to Huejotzingo branches left and leads to **Calpan,** a poor, rural village famed for the **Ex-Convento de San Andrés Calpan,** an outstanding colonial building. At the entrance you can see the details of the chord of San Francisco, carved carefully in stone, and inside are possibly the best-preserved *capillas posas* in the world. You can see St. Michael with his lance, stepping on the devil, the souls rising from their graves, and many indigenous motifs, including prehispanic flowers and hearts cut open with ventricles on display.

Tlaxcala and Vicinity

Tlaxcala, the capital of the state of the same name, is a beautiful colonial city built on the site of the prehispanic capital of the Tlaxcalteca people. This was the first major Amerindian city seen by Cortés and his band of conquerers as they marched toward the Aztec capital of Tenochtitlán in 1519. After fighting and losing to the Spaniards, the Tlaxcaltecas opted to join the conquerers in fighting the Aztecs, their hated enemies. Cortés and a group of Franciscan monks founded the colonial city in 1520. The first bishopric of the country was established here in 1527, and the chapels of the San Francisco convent were built in 1537. About 120 kilometers east of Mexico City, Tlaxcala still has a population of only around 50,000. Though not possessing the stunning colonial art and architecture of nearby Puebla, Tlaxcala has a number of interesting sites

and is a relaxed place to escape the hectic city, well worth taking a day or two to visit to appreciate the small-town vibe.

SIGHTS

Plaza de la Constitución
In the center of the city, Plaza de la Constitución (also known as the *zócalo*) holds a 19th-century bandstand surrounded by flowers. The nearby octagonal fountain, topped by a carved stone cross, was given to the city in 1646 by Spain's King Philip IV. Adjacent is another large square, the Plaza Xicoténcatl.

Palacio de Gobierno
The 16th-century Palacio de Gobierno, on the north side of the plaza, has suffered a turbulent

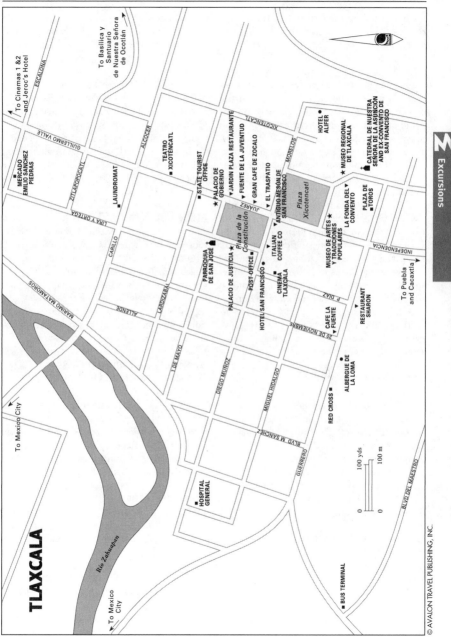

TLAXCALA

Río Zahuapan

To Mexico City

To Mexico City

To Cinemas 1 &2
and Jeroc's Hotel

To Basílica y
Santuario
de Nuestra Señora
de Ocotlán

ESCALONA

GUILLERMO VALLE

ALCOCER

ZITLALPOPOCATL

LIRA Y ORTEGA

CARILLO

LARDIZABAL

ALLENDE

MARIANO MATAMOROS

I DE MAYO

DIEGO MUÑOZ

MIGUEL HIDALGO

BLVD M SÁNCHEZ

GUERRERO

BLVD DEL MAESTRO

20 DE NOVIEMBRE

P DÍAZ

JUÁREZ

MORELOS

XICOTÉNCATL

INDEPENDENCIA

MERCADO
EMILIO SÁNCHEZ
PIEDRAS

LAUNDROMAT

TEATRO
XICOTÉNCATL

STATE TOURIST
OFFICE

PALACIO DE
GOBIERNO

JARDÍN PLAZA RESTAURANTE

FUENTE DE LA JUVENTUD

GRAN CAFE DE ZOCALO

EL TRASPATIO

ANTIGUO MESÓN DE
SAN FRANCISCO

Plaza
de la
Constitución

Plaza
Xicotencatl

HOTEL
ALIFER

MUSEO REGIONAL
DE TLAXCALA

CATEDRAL DE NUESTRA
SEÑORA DE LA ASUNCIÓN
AND EX-CONVENTO DE
SAN FRANCISCO

LA FONDA DEL
CONVENTO

PLAZA DE
TOROS

PARROQUIA
DE SAN JOSÉ

PALACIO DE JUSTICIA

POST OFFICE

ITALIAN
COFFEE CO

HOTEL SAN FRANCISCO

CINEMA
TLAXCALA

MUSEO DE ARTES
Y TRADICIONES
POPULARES

CAFE LA
FUENTE

RESTAURANT
SHARON

To Puebla
and Cacaxtla

ALBERGUE DE
LA LOMA

RED CROSS

HOSPITAL
GENERAL

BUS TERMINAL

0   100 yds
0   100 m

Excursions

history. It was burned during an Indian uprising in 1692 and rocked by an earthquake 20 years later; only the lower part of the facade and interior arches remain of the original structure.

On the 1st floor are a series of murals, by Tlaxcalan artist Desiderio Hernández Xochitiotzin, depicting the history of Tlaxcala since prehispanic times. The work, begun in 1957, is still in progress; it was interrupted for years due to disagreements between Hernández and local politicos on the content of the mural. Hernández Xochitiotzin, now in his 70s, still has one section to complete.

There is a poignant anecdote of Hernández Xochitiotzin, a Tlaxcalan, going to Mexico City many years ago to see Diego Rivera's murals in the Palacio Nacional (in preparation for his work here). The guide sneered at him, saying he "did not give explanations to Indians," and as a response, these murals in Tlaxcala are accompanied by a text, in Spanish, and every section has a title also in Náhuatl.

Tours of the building (9 A.M.–9 P.M. Mon.–Fri.) are available; only flashless photography is allowed.

Parroquia de San José

Across the street from the Plaza de la Constitución, Parroquia de San José (6 A.M.–8 P.M. Mon.–Sat., 7 A.M.–8 P.M. Sun.) dates from early in the 17th century. The Bishop of Puebla dictated the original design, including the mortar images, tiled facade, and lone tower. The dome was damaged in an 1864 earthquake, and the resulting cracks were covered over with the tiles. No flash photography is allowed. Masses go on much of Sunday morning.

Catedral de Nuestra Señora de la Asunción

The cathedral (6 A.M.–2 P.M. and 4–8 P.M. Mon.–Fri., 6 A.M.–7:30 P.M. Sat., 6 A.M.–8:30 P.M. Sun.) is part of the complex of the Ex-Convento de San Francisco, which began construction in 1520. Among the interesting details in the church are heavy cedar cross-beams decorated with stars and the wrought-iron gate of the Virgin's Chapel. In the Capilla de la Tercer Orden is the stone baptismal font first used in 1520 to baptize the four rulers of Tlaxcala. No flash photography is allowed.

Museo Regional de Tlaxcala

Next to the cathedral in the old cloisters of the Ex-Convento de San Francisco, this museum (10 A.M.–5 P.M. Tues.–Sun., admission $3.50) contains exhibits from prehispanic to the independence era, as well as a bookstore and library. Exhibits include a *chac mool* (sculpture of the ancient Maya god) and the original state constitution. Tours are available.

Museo de Arte de Tlaxcala

This new (opened June 2004), modest little art museum (Plaza de la Constitución 21, tel. 246/466-0278, 10 A.M.– 5 P.M. Tues.–Fri., admission $3.50) has three oil paintings and five engravings by Frida Kahlo, collected by a poet friend of hers named Miguel Nicolás Lira. The museum also has temporary exhibits of Mexican art over the centuries, with a special emphasis on artists from Tlaxcala.

Basílica y Santuario de Nuestra Señora de Ocotlán

On a hill above the city is this high baroque church (7 A.M.–7 P.M. daily), with ornate sculptures of the 12 apostles, seven archangels, and other religious figures, framed by plaster columns. Note the star-shaped stained-glass window above the choir depicting the Immaculate Conception. Ask permission before taking pictures.

Plaza de Toros

Dating from the early 19th century, the town bullring (10 A.M.–10 P.M. daily for touring), just off Independencia on Calle Capilla Abierta, is Mexico's oldest existing *plaza de toros*.

Museo de Artes y Tradiciones Populares (Casa de las Artesanías)

In this living museum (Av. Emilio Sánchez Piedras 1, tel. 246/462-2337, 10 A.M.–6 P.M. Tues.–Sun., admission $1), some artisans are on display along with the folk art produced. Exhibits highlight the traditional lifestyle of the region's Amerindian people and include an Otomí kitchen complete with three stone *tlecuil* (stoves) and large cooking vessels, a typical bedroom, designs for *huipiles* (blouses) and *titixtle* (woolen dresses), a *cuexcomate* (for storing corn), and a working *temazcal* (sauna).

Upstairs Otomí women spin wool into yarn using traditional methods and use different types of looms to make sweaters, blankets, jackets, and rugs. Another display shows the making of *pulque*, a regional drink of fermented cactus juice. Throughout the museum are exhibits of local costumes and masks.

In the store downstairs you'll find lots of information about Tlaxcala, including some in English, and local crafts, such as Talavera and walking sticks. A small restaurant offers visitors a taste of traditional Tlaxcalteca cuisine, including *mixiotes, pulque, escamoles* and *gusanos de maguey.*

Santa Ana Chiautempan

This small town, six kilometers east of Tlaxcala, is famous for its woolen textiles and makes a good afternoon outing. After a round of shopping, stop for a look at Santa Ana's two colonial churches, the **Iglesia de Nuestra Señora Santa Ana Chiautempan,** built in 1588, and the **Parroquia de Santa Ana,** finished at the end of the 17th century.

RECREATION
Balnearios

Dotting the countryside around Tlaxcala are many small *balnearios,* or swimming spas, which make good places to cool off. They're usually crowded with Mexican families on weekends, so try to go during the week.

A few near Tlaxcala are **Zacatelco** (18 kilometers out of Tlaxcala by way of México 150 and 119), **Palo Huérfano** (16 kilometers from Tlaxcala via 150 and 119, tel. 246/461-0268), **Los Pinos** (six kilometers from Tlaxcala via 150 and 119, in Santa Ana Chiautempan), and **Santa Lucía** (16 kilometers from Tlaxcala via 150 and 119).

For more information about these *balnearios,* ask at the tourist office.

ENTERTAINMENT AND EVENTS
Regional Fiestas

Fiestas de la Virgen de Ocotlán take place on the first and third Mondays in May. On August 15 look for **Fiesta de la Virgen de la Asunción,** one of the biggest events in the state. The **Feria de Tlaxcala** comes to town the last week of October through the first week of November.

Tlaxcala's colorful carnival (at the beginning of Lent) is famous nationwide, with hundreds of Tlaxcaltecans donning masks and outlandish costumes to join in ancient dances on Shrove Tuesday and the weekends before and after. Dates change from year to year, but the event is always in February or March.

Also renowned throughout the country is the annual running of the bulls in the town of Huamantla, 50 kilometers from Tlaxcala. This Mexican version of the famed Pamplona festival, called the **Huamantlada,** takes place in late August and is great fun to attend (but stay out of the bulls' way!).

Shopping

Bazar del Claustro (Plaza Xicoténcatl 8, tel. 246/462-2258) is a great place to browse for art, jewelry, and other collectibles, although prices can be high. **Museo de Artes y Tradiciones Populares** sells the high-quality textile work of its artisans, but you might find the same quality at a lower price in the town of Santa Ana Chiautempan first. **Mercado Emilio Sanchez Piedras,** a standard town market for food and other necessities, is on the corner of Lira y Ortega and Escalona, four blocks north of the *zócalo.*

For high-end browsing, **La Tlaxcalteca Tendajón Cultural** (tel. 246/462-0014, ext. 24, 10 A.M.–8 P.M. Tues.–Sun.) is amid the row of restaurants beneath the Arcos de Hidalgo on the plaza. Regional music, books, lithographs, textiles, carved wooden sculpture, and reproduction silver pieces are sold here.

ACCOMMODATIONS
$15–30

Albergue de la Loma (Av. Guerrero 58, tel. 246/462-0424, $25 s, $31 d) is small and pleasantly hidden at the top of a long and winding staircase facing the street. The 25 rooms— some with a view overlooking the city—are comfortable and well lit. The restaurant serves inexpensive regional food, with a view over town to contemplate as you eat. Parking is available.

Hotel Alifer (Av. Morelos 11, off Independencia, tel. 246/462-5678, $30 s/d) has rooms of varying sizes, each with double beds, a writing desk, marble-tiled bath, and cable TV. Other amenities include a restaurant/bar and parking.

$50–75

Jeroc's (Blvd. Revolución 4-Bis, tel. 246/462-1577, $53 s, $63 d), a 10-minute drive outside of downtown, offers modern clean rooms with double beds, TVs, and stereo music; the common areas include a pool, tennis courts, gym, conference room, restaurant, and disco.

$75–110

Hotel Posada San Francisco (Plaza de la Constitución 17, tel. 246/462-6022, fax 246/462-6818, www.posadasanfrancisco.com.mx, $80 s, $90 d) faces the *zócalo* and is a large, roomy building with interior courtyards and all the amenities, including a good restaurant—**Piedras Negras**—a billiards room, tennis courts, a boutique, a library, and the **Bar Rancho Seco.**

Hotel Escondida, Hacienda Soltepec (km 3 Carr. Huamantla–Puebla, tel. 247/472-1466 or 247/472-3110, fax 247/472-3109, www.haciendasoltepec.com, $58 d, $68 suites) is in Huamantla, 51 kilometers from Tlaxcala, and is definitely worth looking into if you are looking for a quiet retreat. Named for the 1957 María Felix film shot here, this extraordinary hotel lies 51 kilometers from Tlaxcala city, just outside the quaint town of Huamantla and within view of the Malinche volcano. Inside the stately hacienda you'll find a gleaming gym, large indoor heated swimming pools, steam bath, two squash courts, and a juice bar, as well as 12 rooms and one of the best restaurants in the state.

$110 and Above

Cascada Inn and Spa (10 kilometers out of town on the highway to Apizaco, tel. 246/461-

0000, fax 246/461-0334, toll free in Mexico 800/543-3498, $127 s/d and up) has a drafty old section with iron-railed balconies and high ceilings, and a more standard modern new section. Amenities include tennis courts, heated pool, and room service. The restaurant serves an excellent Sunday brunch for $11 per person, open to nonguests.

RESTAURANTS

Those who like regional cuisine will have no problems eating very well in Tlaxcala, and at very reasonable prices. Specialties include *mixiotes, chiles rellenos al pulque, sopa de haba con nopal* (bean and cactus soup) and *pollo Tocotlan* (Tocotlan-style chicken).

The restaurant at **Hotel Albergue de La Loma** (entrées $3–5)is a good spot to try delicious regional cuisine. For an interesting taste sensation, try *chamorro al pulque,* pork knuckle prepared with *pulque.*

Facing the plaza and shaded beneath the Arcos de Hidalgo are several lovely restaurants with outdoor dining as well as cozy, indoor tables. **El Traspatio** (Plaza de Constitución 8, tel. 246/462-5419, entrées $4–8) is an attractive hideaway behind the restaurant Los Portales and specializes in a *filete de res con huitlacoche* (beef steak smothered in corn fungus sauce) for $6 or *sopa de habas con nopal* ($2.60). Next door is **Gran Cafe del Zócalo,** where the prices and setup are less fancy but the cuisine is similar.

For regional versions of familiar dishes, try the *quesadillas cacaxtla* or the *spaghetti tlaxcalteca* at **Jardín Plaza Restaurante,** in the center of the Arcos.

La Fonda del Convento (Calzada de San Francisco, tel. 246/462-0765, 7 A.M.–9 P.M. daily) is an attractive and intimate restaurant on cobblestone street downtown. It offers regional cuisine in a romantic atmosphere and is open for breakfast.

Restaurant Sharon (Guerrero between Porfirio Díaz and Juárez, entrées $4) has an excellent *comida corrida* for $4, as well as *queso fundido* and *pozole* for $2.

For a good cup of coffee and a snack break, head to **Cafe La Fuente** (Guerrero on the corner of

20 de Noviembre). The small café is upstairs from the gift shop **El Regalito**. Another option for coffee is **The Italian Coffee Company,** at the southern end of the *zócalo*, where you can buy gourmet coffees and sweets to sip there or take away.

PRACTICALITIES
Tourist Information
The state tourist office (tel. 246/465-0960 or 246/465-0968, toll free within Mexico 800/509-6557, www.tlaxcala.gob.mx/turismo) is just off the *zócalo* at the corner of Juárez and Lardizabal. A friendly and helpful staff will give you information and maps.

Communication
The post office is on the Plaza de la Constitución. The telegraph is at Porfirio Díaz 6. Long-distance phones are available at Avenida Juárez 56C (8:30 A.M.–8 P.M.) and under the *portales* at the plaza.

Other Services
Banamex is at Plaza Xicoténcatl 8, and BBVA is at Avenida Juárez 54.

Get your duds cleaned at a **no-name laundry** (Alcocer 30, about two blocks north of the Plaza de la Constitución, 8 A.M.–4 P.M. and 5–7 P.M. Mon.–Fri., 8 A.M.–3 P.M. Sat.).

The **Red Cross** (Allende between Guerrero and Hidalgo, tel. 246/462-0920) offers 24-hour ambulance service. Other medical services can be obtained at **Hospital General** (Av. de La Corregidora, tel. 246/462-0357).

GETTING THERE
By Bus
The **central bus station** is a kilometer from the Plaza de la Constitución. Buses to Mexico City (Terminal TAPO) are with ATAH (tel. 5542-8689 in Mexico City), which has a bus every hour and half or so 6 A.M.–8 P.M., charging $8 for the two-hour ride. Buses to Puebla and Jalapa-Veracruz leave often throughout the day with ADO (tel. 241/417-0085). Minibuses to Apizaco and Huamantla can be found outside the Casa de las Artesanías or in the market.

By Car
From Mexico City take the highway to Puebla and turn off before Puebla toward Tlaxcala. Driving time is roughly 90 minutes, depending on traffic leaving Mexico City. An alternative scenic route, probably an hour longer, is to follow México 136 east out of Texcoco.

CACAXTLA AND XOCHITÉCATL
A small hilltop ruin, for years Cacaxtla was not considered an important site. But in 1975, locals found an immense mural showing a man painted black and dressed as a bird in a polychrome panorama filled with details. The mural caught the attention of representatives of the Instituto Nacional de Antropología e Historia. Using clues from murals and ruins, archaeologists have been busily piecing together what life was like in the 1,100-year-old culture. A few years later, searching for more murals, archaeologists uncovered the related but much older site of Xochitécatl.

The People of Cacaxtla
The archaeological site lies 130 kilometers east of Mexico City, a strategic junction point between traders from the Mayan coastal regions and the central highlands, dominated by A.D. 750 by the city of Teotihuacán. The inhabitants of the region are thought to have been originally Chontal Maya from the Gulf Coast, near the border of present-day Veracruz and Tabasco, who migrated into the highlands shortly before the time of Christ. After they populated several of the valleys around what is today Puebla and Tlaxcala, Cacaxtla rose some time around A.D. 300 as the capital of the region.

Cacaxtla is believed to have ruled over about 200 rural towns and villages, each controlled by a local strongman, or *cacique*. Perhaps because of competition among these many different local leaders, Cacaxtla society was extremely warlike, with the warrior as the most exalted figure in society. These traits are readily apparent when examining the spectacular battle

Excursions

MYSTERIES OF XOCHITÉCATL

Unearthed less than two decades ago, steeped in mystery and deeply entwined with local legend, the prehispanic ruins of Xochitécatl in the State of Tlaxcala can provide one of the most rewarding visits to an archaeological site within a reasonable distance from the capital. The ruins reemerged into the blinding sunlight of this region because archaeologists hoped to find murals similar to those at neighboring Cacaxtla.

They didn't find any impressive polychrome murals, but they found an unusual spiral structure, two lava stone tubs, and a pyramid—perfectly aligned with the Malinche volcano—whose steps were adorned with clay figurines. Curiously, all these figures are female, from babies in baskets to elderly dames with visible crow's feet. There are even pregnant women with holes in their inflated bellies in which little clay fetuses have been inserted.

Unlike its neighbor, Xochitécatl dates from the late Preclassic period, peaking in around 800 B.C. and continuing being in use until around 400 B.C. Then it was inhabited again—no one knows if by descendents of the same ethnic group, or if by newcomers—at the same time as Cacaxtla, in the Epiclassic period (circa A.D. 600–900).

The archaeologist who excavated the site, Dr. Maricarmen Serrapuche, thought the second occupation was by the original group that remembered the sacred place of their ancestors. "But the majority now hold that it was by the Olmec-Xicalanca people, who are believed to have built Cacaxtla," explained Catalina Barriendos, author of a thesis on the Preclassic period of Xochitécatl. "The important thing is we know in the second occupation, the two sites were united."

As with Teotihuacán, no one knows why the site was abandoned, but one reasonable theory is that activities of the Popocatépetl volcano, nearby to the south, could have temporarily stunted the productivity of the fields. It is known that there was some kind of eruption between 100 B.C. and A.D. 100, Barriendos said, and this may have caused mudslides, causing the agricultural population to leave.

Visitors should make their first stop the Museo del Sitio, displaying small clay figurines of images of women—some pregnant, others ancient—which were part of a large offering found on the steps of this site's large pyramid, known as the Pirámide de Las Flores (*xochitl* is Náhuatl for "flower," and *técatl* means "lineage"). Outside the museum there is a very odd assortment of statues and heads, in-

mural. Some believe it may have been an invasion from Cacaxtla that finally toppled the rulers of Teotihuacán and put that city to the torch around A.D. 750. Cacaxtla slid into decline around A.D. 1100.

During its heyday, the white-stuccoed hilltop acropolis looming over the surrounding countryside must have been a striking sight. The ceremonial center measures roughly 1.7 kilometers long by just under a kilometer wide, and contains various platforms, pyramids, palaces, and other buildings. While the structures are impressive to modern visitors—particularly the **Gran Basamento (Great Base)** (now covered with a metal roof), **Templo Rojo** (Red Temple), and **Building A,** the real attraction is unquestionably the amazing mural paintings decorating the walls.

Scholars believe that murals once covered most

of Cacaxtla's exterior, and that they were painted somewhere between 850 and 750 A.D. Motifs common to both Mayan lowland painting and also to those used in nearby Teotihuacán point to Cacaxtla's position as an intermediary of sorts between these two stronger cultures. The brilliant colors of the murals, depicting all sorts of people and creatures, remains shockingly bright considering the intervening centuries.

The largest and most impressive of Cacaxtla's murals, the ***Battle Mural*** (on the north wall of the North Plaza) displays 48 warriors divided into two groups. Those dressed like jaguars appear to be the victors of a battle over those dressed as birds, who are shown wounded or already dead, in gory detail. It's uncertain whether the mural depicts the fighters of Cacaxtla defending against invaders, invading a foreign place themselves, or some other as-yet-unknown event.

cluding a frog looking upwards to the sky, a serpent's tongue, and a head with a lopsided mouth.

"The frog is clearly associated with water," Barriendos said, "and research has showed that facial paralysis, and its cure, was the domain of the water gods."

Water has retained a sacred vale in the surroundings, she said, giving the example of the village of San Miguel de Milagro, on the slopes below Cacaxtla, where people come on pilgrimages to the *santuario* (small church) whose well provides holy water with healing properties.

On the pyramid that faces south, called El Pirámide del Serpiente, is a first monolithic (made of just one stone) tub, which has a drainage hole. It is thought this was used to collect rainwater used in ritual cleansing. The other tub, at the foot of the Pyramid of the Flowers, also has a drainage hole pointing in the same direction, toward Popocatépetl and Ixtaccíhuatl volcanoes, leading Barriendos to think that even the drainage of the water was part of the site's ritual function.

"People here still have a legend that a large serpent lives in the hill of Xochitécatl. Workers say they have seen or heard it and have left in fear. It lives in a cave inside the hill and has gold scales,"

Barriendos said, adding that she has seen small rattlesnakes in the area but nothing so monstrous. "Sometimes it leaves and goes to the Ixta or Malinche volcanoes, both female mountains."

Another potent local legend tells of a *hacendado* (landowner) who fell in love with a beautiful Indian woman who washed her clothes on the other side of the river. He persuaded her to elope and waded across to take her home, but as he carried her back through the water, he realized she had turned into a giant snake, which he dropped and fled. There are two versions of the ending, that he killed the snake, and that she—in her human form—continued to reappear at the edge of the river, washing.

"In either version, the serpent is clearly a woman, Cihuacoatl, the snake goddess," Barriendos said.

The mysteries of this unique sacred place remain far from resolved, but the interaction with living folk invests Xochitécatl with power and intrigue. In addition it is a comfortable site to visit, without too much arduous climbing and with a number of benches set beneath trees so visitors can rest in the shade.

—*Contributed by Barbara Kastelein.*
Barbara is a freelance journalist and travel writer living in Mexico City.

Practicalities

The sites are open seven days a week 10 A.M.–5 P.M.; admission is $4. A snack shop and restrooms are at the entrance to Cacaxtla. Avoid Sundays, as it is free for Mexicans and very crowded. During the week the site is very quiet.

Cacaxtla-Xochitécatl is 19 kilometers southwest of Tlaxcala near the town of San Miguel de Milagro. From there take the "Nativitas" bus from the central bus station. You will find taxis and *colectivos* that will take you to the site. Be prepared for a lot of walking around when you get there, and try to arrive as soon as the site opens.

If you're driving from Tlaxcala city, head toward Puebla on the free highway, which leaves town from near the bus terminal, and follow signs to Nativitas. Once you pass Nativitas, look for a sign about two kilometers out of town; the

road will go to the right and is quite bumpy. Though the distance isn't great, many *topes* (speed bumps) slow you down.

From Mexico City the site is less than two hours' drive. Take the *autopista* (fast highway) to Puebla, and turn off to your left when you reach the factory of Santa Juliana. Signs first point to Xalmimilulco, then you take a right in San Rafael, after which there are clear signposts. From Puebla it is no more than a half hour's drive.

LA MALINCHE

One of the best hiking areas in Central Mexico is Volcán La Malinche (4,462 meters), Mexico's fifth-highest mountain. This extinct volcano is blanketed by thick forest protected by law as **Parque Nacional La Malinche.** Locals usually refer to the mountain by the indigenous version of the name, Malintzi (the "n" is silent). Climbing the peak makes an excellent hike for those who want to experience the high mountains of Central Mexico without dealing with ropes, crampons, and glaciers, and it is also a perfect acclimatization hike for those looking to tackle the higher mountains of Pico de Orizaba, Popocatéptl, or Ixtaccíhuatl.

The trail begins easily, heading up through lovely forest before coming out onto grassy fields below the peak. The last stretch up the sandy, exposed flanks of the mountain is tougher going. Allow three to four hours one-way. The views from the peak are stupendous, as the mountain lies between Popo and Ixta to the west and Pico de Orizaba to the east.

All visitors to the park must pay a $1 admission. The park is open 9 A.M.–5 P.M. daily.

Getting There

Travel east from Apizaco (which is northeast of Tlaxcala) on México 136 about 13 kilometers to a signed junction directing you to Campamento IMSS La Malintzin. The paved road leads to a camp on the side of the mountain, at about 3,100 meters. Drivers will have to pause at an inoffensive little road block, manned by the Coordinación General de Ecología de Tlaxcala, and write down their names and explain the purpose of their visit. From the camp, continue 4.7 kilometers to its end at the trailhead, by the ruins of a building. You may want to leave your vehicle at the camp and walk up the last stretch of road, as some cars have been broken into at the trailhead. Driving from Puebla, take the Highway 150 Puebla–Amozoc, and then Highway 129 to Huamantla, and from there Highway 136 toward Apizaco, and keep an eye out for the signposted turnoff to the park.

To get to La Malinche without a car, catch a bus to either Apizaco or Huamantla, and from there hire a taxi. The price should be $10 one-way, and usually it's no problem to arrange to be picked up. On weekends a bus winds its way around the volcano on bumpy dirt roads and down to the bus terminal in Puebla. Times vary, but the last one usually heads down around 5 P.M.

Camping

Camping is allowed in the forest above the camp for free, or in the camp itself for $2.50 per person. Cabins at the camp, run by the Mexican Social Security Institute (IMSS), cost $50 for a basic cabin sleeping six, or $80 for a cabin sleeping nine. Reservations (necessary for the cabins, but not for camping) can be made by phone, in Spanish, at tel. 246/462-4098 or 246/461-0700, ext. 677.

TOWARD VERACRUZ

Huamantla

East of Apizaco past La Malinche is Huamantla, a midsized agricultural town. Most of the year there's not a lot to attract tourists to Huamantla apart from the attractive 16th-century Franciscan monastery, but every August the town holds the largest "running of the bulls" festival in Mexico over the course of two weeks. Try to get there before the morning of the 15th to see the elaborate and colorful sand paintings that local residents use to decorate the streets before the religious processions begin. For more information on the festival and the town, look at the municipal website: www.huamantla.gob.mx.

Tlaxco

Turning north from Apizaco on the road to Zacatlán (instead of continuing east to Huamantla and Jalapa), a secondary road leads to Tlaxco, about a 30-minute drive from Apizaco across the high plains of Tlaxcala. The town itself is nothing stupendous, but it's a picturesque little Mexican town with an attractive church. The town is well known for its *requesón* and *tenate* cheeses; ask around where to buy some. Nine kilometers west of town on the road toward Hidalgo is the **Hacienda Xochuca,** an old-style ranch that still produces *pulque,* a curious fermented cactus drink for which Tlaxcala and Hidalgo are well known. About 15 kilometers on the road toward Puebla you'll enter the Sierra de Tlaxco, a forest-covered range with some campsites and hiking. By public transport, catch a bus here every hour throughout the day with ATAH from the Terminal TAPO in Mexico City ($9), or from Tlaxcala.

Chignahuapan

On the far side of the Sierre de Tlaxco, right at the edge of where the central plateau ends and begins to drop off down steep canyons to the coast, is Chignahuapan, a small town 65 kilometers from Apizaco. Perched in the very top of one of these canyons five kilometers from town is the **Hotel Baños Termales de Chignahuapan** (tel. 797/971-0313, www.termaleschignahuapan .com.mx, $85 per person), a spa hotel built around a gushing thermal hot spring. The hotel has 75 rooms in two buildings. The rooms are a little faded, but each has its own large bath fed directly from the spring (too hot by itself, you'll have to mix it with the cold for it to be bearable). Down below, built along the river, is a big public pool, as well as a smaller pool and Jacuzzi reserved for guests. The prices might seem steep, but they include three meals, and the restaurant food is hearty and well cooked. The public pools cost $6 per person for the day and are open until 10 P.M.

If you'd like to stretch your legs between lazing about in the hot springs, take a hike up the hillside above the hotel. A good place to start is the high point of the dirt road from town. Just pick a likely-looking trail and head upward. You'll go through small mountain farms owned by humble campesinos who are very friendly, especially if you say *buenos días* with a wave and smile. Further up are patches of forest, and up higher you'll have great views over the landscape. Keep an eye out for the huge maguey cacti all over the place.

If you're without a car, you can catch buses here several times daily from Tlaxcala, or take a bus from Mexico City to Zacatlá, Puebla from the Terminal del Norte, and get off at Chignahuapan.

Excursions

MEXICO CITY ENVIRONMENT

A 7.5 earthquake gently rocks the city. Phone calls will be interrupted and office workers will be ushered outside. But the traffic doesn't stop on the Eje Central and *chilangos* (Mexico City residents) take it as just another day in one of the world's largest cities. Talk about the environment here and residents will regale you with stories of contamination, natural disasters, and environmental neglect.

With its 16 million-plus population, Mexico City has a well-deserved reputation for being overcrowded and overpolluted. Long gone are the days when Carlos Fuentes could title his novel *Where the Air Is Clear.*

Air

Mexico City measures its Metropolitan Air Quality Index (Índice Metropolitana de Calidad de Aire, or Imeca) every hour every day. According to collected stats, air pollution is usually worse on the southern edge of town because the prevailing winds are from the north and the air is trapped by the Sierra Ajusco to the south. The winter months are the worst months for air pollution in the Valle de México, because of fewer and lighter air currents. Cooler air temperatures create thermal inversions, which keep car exhaust and industrial emissions hovering just above ground level, often causing respiratory, eye, and throat irritations.

The United Nations' World Health Organization classifies Imeca readings of more than 100 points as Unsatisfactory, readings of more than 200 points as Bad, and readings of 300 Dangerous. When the Imeca breaks 200 points, the city orders all outdoor activities for primary, secondary, and preschool canceled, as the young are more susceptible to the ill effects of bad air. A Phase One alert (called when the Imeca breaks 250 points) doubles the *Hoy No Círcula* (No Driving Today) policy, and 40 percent of

privately owned vehicles and half of all government vehicles are kept off city streets the following day. Industries are also ordered to reduce their emissions. You can track the daily Imeca readings in most local newspapers or online at www.sima.com.mx/valle_de_mexico. You can also see the most recent reading on the home page of the city government, www.df.gob.mx.

Are the policies working? Anecdotal and statistical evidence suggests that although Mexico City's air is still extremely poor, it is improving. In 2003, air quality was above 100 points for 252 days, compared to 306 in 2000, and the number of emergencies (*contingencias*) has dropped as well. The number of days a year past acceptable ozone levels has fallen from 84 percent in 2000 to 69 percent in 2003 and 56 percent in 2004. Also, the average number of hours the high levels last has fallen from 6.6 hours in 1991 to 1.3 hours in 2004. For recent reports (in Spanish) on air quality, look at the website for the Mexico City Secretaría de Medio Ambiente (Environment Secretariat) at www.sma.df.gob.mx.

The single biggest contributor to D.F.'s haze is the automobile, which accounts for an estimated 70 percent of detectable smog. The *Hoy No Círcula* program, which is supposed to ensure that every registered vehicle stays off the roads at least one day a week, seems to have exacerbated the problem. Instead of using public transport, the city's moneyed classes simply bought second or third vehicles, often cheaper used autos with higher emissions. Since the program was introduced, the number of private vehicles in circulation has soared an estimated 40 percent.

Dr. Mario Molina Pasquel, the Mexican scientist who won the 1995 Nobel Prize for Chemistry, has been working on a plan to reduce PM10 levels, one of the leading pollution causes of health problems, but he's fighting a hard bat-

Know Mexico City

The Land

GEOLOGY

Mexico City takes up half the surface area of the roughly 3,100-square-kilometer Valle de México, a unique land formation in the center of Mexico's volcanic central highlands. Technically not a valley—as it has no natural drainage—the basin is completely ringed by mountains. The worn down, low hills to the north rose 30 million years ago and were followed later by the steep-walled ridges on the east and west. A row of volcanoes to the south first erupted around two million years ago, thus sealing off the basin entirely. Several of Mexico's highest peaks—Popocatépetl (5,465 meters), Ixtaccíhuatl (5,230 meters), Ajusco (3,930 meters), Volcán Tláloc (3,690 meters), and Cerro Pelado (3,670 meters)—rim the valley to the south and southeast.

The valley floor, more than half of which was once covered by a series of broad, shallow lakes, varies between 2,100 and 2,400 meters in altitude and extends roughly 120 kilometers north to south, depending on where you measure from (the northern boundary is a bit vague), and between 40 and 70 kilometers from east to west. While mostly flat, the valley is punctuated by several anomalous mountains, mainly volcanic in origin, such as Cerro de la Estrella, Cerro Chapultepec, and Cerro Tepeyac.

The Valle de México is very active seismically and experiences frequent earthquakes, most of which are generated from the movement of geologic plates toward Mexico's Pacific coast. Because of the interaction between earthquake wave movement and the valley's weak subsoil, Mexico City sometimes feels the effects of a coastal quake more than places closer to the quake's actual epicenter. Such was the case in the 1985 earthquake, which left thousands dead in Mexico City, despite the fact that its epicenter was more than 160 kilometers away.

HYDROLOGY

One of the most vexing problems that people settling in the Valle de México have had to deal with throughout its history is the complex water system. Before humans began making their modifications (originally under the Aztecs), five interconnected lakes in the valley fluctuated dramatically in size throughout the year, depending on rainfall and evaporation rates. The highest of the lakes, Chalco, had the freshest water, while Texcoco, the largest and lowest-lying, was the saltiest.

This constant fluctuation in water levels was a problem for the Aztecs. Because all the best land on the lakes' shores had already been taken by the time they arrived, they settled on an island near the center of the lake. Thus when lake levels rose, their territory shrank on all sides. In the late 15th century, Nezahualcóy-

otl, the poet-king of neighboring Texcoco and an Aztec ally, oversaw the construction of a massive dike dividing Lake Texcoco into two halves, one salty and one fresh, as a means of controlling the annual floods. In addition, a network of canals was built for drainage control and transportation.

As part of his final assault on Tenochtitlán in 1521, Cortés ordered the breaching of the dike to flood the Aztec city. The water level was not high enough at that point to cause the damage he'd hoped for, but in the long run Cortés may have been more successful than he had planned. The Spaniards, not understanding the complexities of the ecosystem, left the dike in ruins when they rebuilt the city, and as a result saw their new colonial capital flooded repeatedly over the next few centuries. After repeated heavy rainy seasons, the entire city once remained underwater constantly for five years in the early 17th century, forcing many inhabitants to abandon their palaces and live temporarily on higher ground at the edge of the valley.

Thus a public works project was initiated that has seemingly continued unabated to this day, digging ever bigger tunnels and canals to completely drain the valley. Although successive colonial governments dug drainage canals, it was not until 1900, with the construction of the Gran Canal de Desagüe (Great Drainage Canal) under the administration of Porfirio Díaz, that the waters of Lago Texcoco were finally emptied almost entirely.

Currently the only major bodies of water in the valley are small tracts of Lago Xochimilco in the south, the lakes in Chapultepec, and the much reduced remnants of Lago Texcoco northeast of the city, in the State of México. The dozen or so rivers that once flowed into the valley mainly from the western mountains—such as Río Mixcoac, Río de la Piedad, Río Tacubaya, and Río Churubusco—still exist but are canalized and sealed under major avenues, eventually draining into one of the five canals on the east side of the city, which in turn flow out of the valley to the northeast.

While only a few patches of lake still exist, flooding remains a yearly occurrence in many parts of the Mexico City metro area during the April–October rainy season. A huge new Drenaje Profundo (Deep Drainage) is on the drawing board and awaiting funding.

The results of all this drainage can be seen in the capital's uneven streets and settling architecture. Because much of the valley's groundwater has been siphoned off, the sandy, unstable soil has sunk dramatically (about 7.5 meters in the last century, currently 15 centimeters a year in places), leaving many downtown buildings comically contorted as different parts sink at different rates. City air is also affected; the dried lakebeds in the northeast part of the valley create swirling clouds of dust that are swept up into the atmosphere and moved to the southwest, directly across the city, by the prevailing winds, worsening the air pollution.

CLIMATE

Although Mexico City straddles the 19th parallel North, thus placing it squarely in the tropics, its 2,240-meter elevation can add a chill to the air, particularly during the December–January winter months, and at times during the summer rainy season due to the cloudy weather. Nights and early mornings can be chilly throughout the year. Generally the city has one of the mildest climates in Mexico—pleasant during the day and comfortable for sleeping at night.

The rains usually begin in April or May and continue sporadically until October. They often abate for two or three weeks in August, usually before the coming of the fall hurricane season. The violent high winds that lash Mexico's coasts during the frequent annual storms do not usually make it to Mexico City, but they can leave skies gray and rainy for days at a time, and sometimes flooding occurs.

Rain levels average 700–1,300 millimeters per year in the southwest mountains, and 400–600 millimeters per year in the more arid central and northern parts of the valley.

El Castillo atop Cerro Chapultepec

© CHRIS HUMPHREY

tle. The plan entails convincing Pemex to recalibrate its refineries to reduce sulphur in fuel emissions, in particular diesel, and implementing new large-capacity, low-polluting buses on dedicated lanes. The government appears to be moving ahead with the bus part of the plan, but time will tell if Pemex can be convinced to change its fuel production techniques. The $3 billion cost of refinery upgrading is meant to be paid for a by a fuel tax. Molina believes that because much PM10 pollution comes from trucks traveling to Mexico City from across the country, only a national-level solution to emissions, rather than only local measures, would have any significant effect.

Water

The city has a seemingly unquenchable thirst for water. Most of the city's water supply is pumped from aquifers beneath the city. The removal of the groundwater has caused some of the buildings to sink more rapidly than usual. The water table has dropped by 32 meters, and the city itself has sunk by seven meters since 1940. The city consumes 3.5 million cubic meters of water every day, twice the level of many industrialized countries. Why? Because up to a quarter of the city's water supply is lost through leaky pipes before it reaches household taps.

About 20 to 30 percent of the city's water is pumped uphill 1,000 meters from the Lerma and Cutzamala Rivers, 100 kilometers to the west. The rest is pumped from underground aquifers. Sewage is disposed of out of town, much to the frustration of outlying communities. Built in 1900, the Gran Canal de Desagüe (Great Drainage Canal) project drove a pipeline through the northern hills to carry human waste and garbage outside the valley. At the beginning of the century, gravity was sufficient to pull the putrid black waters out of town. But as the city began to sink, 11 pumping stations were constructed. Today, another deep drainage system is under construction.

Is There Hope?

A reforestation program along the banks of the dwindling Lago de Texcoco has helped to cut back on dust and to recycle carbon dioxide, and it may also speed efforts to reclaim more rainwater in the lake basin. More creative, low-tech measures recently begun include digging 600 absorption wells in the southern mountain parts of Tlalpan, Milpa Alta, Xochimilco, Magdalena Contreras, and Cuajimalpa *delegaciones*. These will collect rainwater and funnel it underground, which will both reduce the risk of flooding and help replenish the subterranean aquifers. A total of 2000 wells—each costing only $9,000—are to be dug between now and 2008.

Mexico City hosts a number of environmental groups dedicated to raising environmental awareness. Mexican Conservation Learning Network (www.imacmexico.org) is the country's leading clearest house on environmental matters, with news and publications in English and Spanish. The Centro de Ecología y Desarrollo (Cecodes) is one of the more persistent of the academic centers that review environmental issues. Cecodes (www.planeta.com/ecotravel/mexico/ecologia/ecologia.html) produces numerous Spanish-language reports and studies on Mexico City environmental issues. Further information about environmental matters in Mexico City can be found online at www.planeta.com/ecotravel/mexico/df/mexinfo.html.

—Contributed by Ron Mader. Ron is author of the guidebook Mexico: Adventures in Nature *(John Muir Publications, 1998) and is host of the popular Planeta.com environmental travel website, at www.planeta.com.*

Temperature also varies depending on location, ranging from 12°C on average in the western mountains to 16°C in the center of town. The hottest months of the year are usually April and May, when temperatures sometimes hit 30°C in the day, while the coldest are December and January, with daytime temperatures averaging 14°C. Humidity is low to moderate, except during the rainy season.

Air Quality

Mexico City's Metropolitan Air Quality Index (Índice Metropolitana de Calidad de Aire, or Imeca) measures air quality hourly. Although folk wisdom says the air is worse in the winter months than the rest of the year, it really depends on wind patterns, which vary from year to year. (See the sidebar *Mexico City Environment* for more information on Imeca.)

History

PREHISPANIC HISTORY

First Arrivals

Mexico's earliest human inhabitants arrived slowly via the Bering Strait land bridge (which at the time spanned the Asian and North American continents) between 50,000 and 25,000 B.C. Descendants of Asia's late Paleolithic epoch, these nomadic hunter-gatherers dispersed throughout North America seeking food and benign natural conditions. No evidence of any sociocultural organization survives, although remains of hunted mammoth, mastodon, giant bison, and antelope near Puebla suggest humans arrived this far south by 24,000 B.C.

The First Inhabitants of the Valley

Groups of nomads are thought to have first found their way into the valley of Mexico sometime around 20,000 B.C. The advantages of an abundant water supply and the surrounding wall of the mountains—which served both as a natural defense and as a barrier for keeping game near at hand—must have made the valley an appealing place for these wandering bands to settle down and build small villages.

© ELENA PAPPAS

sculpture detail from the Templo de Quetzalcóatl, at Teotihuacán

But this very appeal led to the extinction of the valley's large game between 9000 and 8000 B.C. Over the next several thousand years, the valley's population grew to rely on gathering fruits and grains, especially maize, until the third millennium B.C., when fully agricultural societies established themselves.

As in other parts of the world, this agricultural revolution created profound changes in social organization. Between 1500 and 650 B.C., villages around the edge of the valley's lakes grew in size, particularly in the northeast and in the south. The first full-fledged city to develop was Cuicuilco, centered around a pyramid site that can still be seen at the junction of Insurgentes Sur and Periférico Sur. By 100 B.C. a second city was growing at Teotihuacán in the north, driven by springs, which permitted irrigated agriculture.

The incipient rivalry between the two cities was dramatically cut short sometime in the second century A.D., when Volcán Xitle blew its top and covered Cuicuilco and much of the southeastern part of the valley with beds of lava. Following Cuicuilco's fiery demise, the population of Teotihuacán increased sharply, reaching a height of perhaps 200,000 in A.D. 750. Through a combination of excessive logging and overintensive agriculture, the productivity of the once-fertile valley began to decline (even today the area has remained barren and arid), and the final blow was dealt by successive invasions by northern warrior tribes.

The Toltecs

Just before the end of the first millennium, the Toltecs—a culturally hybrid group dominated by Amerindians from Northern Mexico—established a fortified capital at Tula in present-day Hidalgo, just north of Mexico City. Between A.D. 900 and 1200, Toltec centers developed as far north as Zacatecas and as far south as Guatemala; Toltec influence apparently extended to the post-Classic Maya architecture at Chichén Itzá as well.

The Toltec civilization never reached the heights achieved by Teotihuacán and slipped into decline after A.D. 1200. After suffering successive invasions by warrior tribes from the north, Tula was abandoned in the 13th century.

The Aztecs

In the wake of Tula's fall, control of the valley was divided between several competing communities, with population centers of 10,000–20,000 at Texcoco, Azcapoltzalco, Tacuba, and Xochimilco, as well as dozens of smaller towns. Into this mix arrived yet another northern tribe, the Aztecs, in the mid-13th century. The fiercest warriors Mexico has ever known, the Aztecs claimed to come from an island in the north called Aztatlán or Aztlán (Place of Herons). According to Aztec chronicles, their war god Huitzilopochtli led them to the valley after a century of wandering and gave the tribe a new name, México.

Receiving a cold reception from the tribes already living around the lake, the Aztecs first settled on the insect-infested Cerro Chapultepec in A.D. 1280 and tried to ingratiate themselves to the neighboring Tepanecs by serving as mercenaries. They quickly developed a reputation as bloodthirsty warriors. Around 1300 the Culhuacán, rivals of the Tepanecs, defeated the Aztecs in battle and took the survivors as slaves. After serving for 25 years as Culhuacán mercenaries, the Aztecs were eventually granted their freedom. In a telling sign of their vengefulness and brutality, they tricked the Culhuacán leader into giving them one of his daughters to marry their own ruler. At the Aztec "wedding" ceremony, the guest leader was greeted by the sight of the Aztec high priest wearing the flesh of his daughter.

Still weaker than the Culhuacán, the Aztecs fled to an uninhabited island named Tenochtitlán, in the center of the lake, rather than risk a war they might lose. Legend has it that the sight of an eagle perched on a cactus, a snake in its beak, was the fulfillment of Aztec prophecy, which convinced the tribe to settle there for good. Historians cite the island's natural defenses and the existence of several small freshwater springs on the island as more prosaic reasons.

For a time the Aztecs returned as soldiers for their former Tepanec masters, but the fourth Aztec king, Itzcoatl, overthrew the Tepanecs in 1428 and, along with the leaders of nearby city-states Texcoco and Tlacopán, established the Triple Alliance to rule over the valley. Aztec hegemony in the alliance was implicit from the start and grew stronger over the next century.

Under Itzcoatl's mid-15th-century successors, all historical records belonging to other tribes were destroyed to cement the Aztec perspective of the Valley of Mexico, which revered the Toltecs as their spiritual ancestors and downplayed their nomadic past. Moctezuma I (1440–1469) embarked on an expansionist program that brought the Huastec and Mixtec regions under Aztec control, and under Aztec monarch Ahuitzotl (1486–1502), all of Central Mexico fell under Aztec sway, except for the fierce and copper-equipped Tarascan warriors of Michoacán and the doughty Tlaxcaltecas to the east, who would later prove key in the Spanish conquest.

Far from tempering their bloody ways as they grew in power, the empire Aztecs took their formerly modest practice of human sacrifice and occasional cannibalism to staggering heights. Historians continue to argue about the accuracy of the incredible number of victims Spanish chroniclers reported killed in single ceremonies (in the tens of thousands), but the Aztecs unquestionably sacrificed on a huge scale, reputedly believing it necessary to feed the sun with blood so it would rise each day.

Conquered by such a culture, vassal states obeyed the Aztecs from fear rather than loyalty. Tribute demanded by the Aztecs included gold, copper, gemstones, jade, amber, rubber, jaguar skins, tropical feathers, and chocolate. Apart from these material goods, other tribes were required to send victims for sacrifice. Even nominal Aztec enemies such as the Tlaxcaltecans and the Cholulans were forced into mock battles known as "flower wars," in which soldiers were rarely killed; instead they were taken as prisoners to have their hearts ripped out a few days later by Aztec priests.

The glittering city of Tenochtitlán was the heart of the great empire, an island command center measuring roughly three kilometers square and linked to the mainland only by four causeways that could be easily blocked from attack. Adjacent to Tenochtitlán, and eventually linked to it by continual landfill projects, was the smaller island of Tlatelolco, the empire's principal market center.

Tenochtitlán was laid out in an orderly grid pattern and crisscrossed by a system of canals, which allowed for drainage during the flood season and also provided the principal means of transportation. The Spanish conquistadors (mostly young provincials with limited educations) who saw Tenochtitlán before they destroyed it were in utter awe of the pervasive cleanliness and order.

As the conquistador Bernal Díaz del Castillo put it in his book, *The Conquest of New Spain:*

> . . . *we were struck with admiration and said that it all seemed like enchanted things from the book of Amadís, seeing the great towers and buildings which they had built in the water all made of plaster and stone, and some of our soldiers asked if what they saw was a dream, and how marvelous it was the things that I write about here, because it made one amazed. I don't know how to describe it, seeing things never heard of, never even dreamed of.*

In 1519, with a population of perhaps 250,000, Tenochtitlán was arguably the greatest city on earth.

SPANISH CONQUEST AND COLONIZATION
The Spanish Entrada
In the wake of Columbus's momentous voyage in 1492, the Spaniards quickly took over several Caribbean islands, principally Hispaniola and Cuba. In 1518, Cuban Governor Diego Velázquez chose a 34-year-old Spaniard named Hernán Cortés from Medellín, a town in the poor province of Extremadura, Spain,

La Malinche, Hernán Cortés's indigenous interpreter and lover, remains Mexico's symbol of both national and feminine treason.

to lead what was intended as a reconnaissance expedition to the Mexican coast.

Cortés, who at the time was working as a secretary for Velázquez, had other ideas in mind. The expedition of 530 soldiers landed in what is now the Gulf Coast State of Veracruz on April 20, 1519. After destroying his ships and convincing his men to risk all for glory, he made his way over the next several months to Tenochtitlán, gathering Aztec enemies as his allies along the way. According to many accounts, the superstitious Aztec Emperor Moctezuma II apparently became convinced that Cortés was the embodiment of the plumed serpent god Quetzalcóatl, who according to legend would return from the east. Because of this, or perhaps because of Cortés' clever diplomacy through Aztec messengers, Moctezuma eventually allowed the Spaniards into his city as protected guests when they finally arrived at Tenochtitlán in November of 1519. Through sheer force of personality and a series of psychological tactics, Cortés assumed a bizarre sort of mental control over Moctezuma, who was soon doing the bidding of the Spaniards and keeping them safe from an increasingly restive and angry Aztec elite.

While Cortés was away on an expedition to the coast, to fight off a group of rival conquistadors who had sailed from Cuba, the less subtle Pedro de Alvarado led a slaughter of Aztec nobility who were performing a ceremony that apparently he didn't like the looks of. Cortés hastened back, but the damage was done, and the already unhappy populace rallied to expel the Spaniards from the city on July 1, 1520, known as the *noche triste* (sad night).

Cortés had hoped to hand over Tenochtitlán intact, as a sparkling jewel to the Spanish crown, but after several months of regrouping their forces, organizing allies around the valley, and building a flotilla of lake boats, the conquistadors mounted a brutal 90-day siege and then invaded the city. The Aztecs, already weakened by the diseases brought by the Spaniards and starving to death, fought to the bitter end under the iron leadership of a young warrior named Cuauhtémoc, who is today a national hero in Mexico.

To take the city, the conquistadors were forced to destroy it block by block, eliminating the high redoubts from which the Aztecs flung down rocks and spears, until eventually the remaining defenders, refusing to surrender, were killed in the main plaza of Tlatelolco. Cuauhtémoc was captured, tortured to reveal hidden stashes of gold (of which none remained—the Spaniards lost most of it during the *noche triste*), and was later executed by Cortés on a pretext.

Nueva España

Facing the rubble of Tenochtitlán, Cortés contemplated establishing the new colonial capital on the edge of the lake, but in the end chose to rebuild the old Aztec city, partly for defensive reasons, but also for the symbolic significance: in many ways, the Spaniards aimed to merely replace the Aztecs as the rulers of the already existing empire system. So under the direction of Alonso García Bravo, a new city was laid out atop the old, utilizing much of the original Aztec street plan.

While the new conquerors often rationalized their right to rule Mexico on the grounds that they were converting the natives to Christianity, missionary zeal was hardly their only motive. Early Aztec gifts of gold and silver had tantalized the treasure-seeking Spaniards, and silver strikes in Taxco in 1522 presaged the fabulously rich mining industry that would form the basis of the colonial economy, and in fact that of all Europe as well.

All of the immense quantities of silver mined in New Spain passed through *la ciudad de México*—as the capital was soon called—on its way back to Spain. On top of this, the Mexico City merchants had an official monopoly on all trading in the colony. As a result of these convenient, royally granted advantages, the city grew immensely wealthy and came to be known throughout Europe as *la ciudad de los palacios* (the city of palaces).

With the decline of the silver industry, Mexico City stagnated in the late 17th and early 18th centuries, but the last decades of the 18th century saw a burst of reformist zeal under the new Bourbon kings, who appointed a series of activist viceroys, the colonial governors. Viceroy Conde de Revillagigedo ordered the creation of a master plan for the city's development, calling for all manner of urban improvements—including an overhaul of basic infrastructure such as sewage and street lighting and building new, tree-lined avenues outside downtown (such as La Viga and, later, Paseo de Bucareli).

MEXICO CITY AFTER INDEPENDENCE

Independence and Early Instability

Mexico's struggle for independence from Spain began on September 16, 1810, when Padre Miguel Hidalgo y Costilla gave his famous *grito de la independencia* (independence shout) from a church in Dolores, Guanajuato. Mexico City, which depended on the colonial trade monopoly

for its living, remained a royalist holdout during the struggle, firmly opposed to independence. Hidalgo's anarchic rebellion, with racial and class overtones, was quickly put down, and independence was not consummated until royalist officer Agustín Iturbide switched sides and cut a deal with rebel Vicente Guerrero in 1821. Iturbide was appointed emperor of the new republic, but his reign lasted only two years before he was overthrown by another junta that established a federal republic called Los Estados Unidos de México—the United States of Mexico—in 1824. Under this republic, named for the México (Aztec) tribe originally defeated by the Spanish, the 22 provinces of New Spain were divided into 19 states and four territories.

Over the next six years the Mexican republic endured two more coups; it wasn't until 1829 that all Spanish troops were expelled from Mexico. In 1833 Antonio López de Santa Anna, a megalomaniac, opium-addicted general in charge of enforcing the expulsion of Spanish troops, seized power and revoked the Constitution of 1824. Mexico in many ways was cursed by Santa Anna, who was a brilliant, charismatic general but utterly uninterested in the difficult tasks of administering a new nation. Santa Anna was in and out of power for the next decade, switching sides repeatedly between the feuding liberals and conservatives. The former favored reigning in the power of the church and proceeding with modernist reforms, while the latter felt that the only way for the country to survive was to maintain the social structure with a strong church and central government.

While Mexico was engrossed in this bitter infighting, its neighbor to the north was increasing its control on the Mexican territory of Texas and eyeing other territories covetously. In 1847, on a flimsy pretext, U.S. President James Polk ordered the invasion of Mexico, which ended with the U.S. occupation of Mexico City for 10 months. It was during this battle that six young military cadets, defending the Castillo de Chapultepec from the invading gringos, reputedly leapt to their deaths from the castle ramparts rather than surrender. For their Quixotic heroism, the six are remembered in Mexican history as the Niños Héroes, the Child Heroes. As a result of the unequal and unjust war, Mexico ceded almost half of its territory to the United States.

Juárez and Maximilian

Santa Anna returned to power after the war, but he was finally overthrown in 1855 by a Zapotec lawyer named Benito Juárez. The new president and his liberal allies promulgated a constitution in 1857 and passed laws restricting the financial powers of the Church; all Church property save for Church buildings had to be sold or otherwise relinquished. These actions infuriated conservatives and, not surprisingly, the Church, and led to the War of Reform, with self-appointed governments in Mexico City and Veracruz vying for national authority. A reactionary opposition group took control of Mexico City, and fighting continued until 1861, when the liberals won and Juárez was elected president.

Once in power, Juárez promptly enacted the Reform Laws, dispossessing the Church of its property, a turn of events that would change the face of Mexico City. Much of the downtown area was at that time covered by large monasteries and convents, including San Agustín, San Francisco, Santo Domingo, and La Merced. After seizing the properties, city officials demolished parts of these religious compounds, running new streets through and walling off the old churches. While remnants of the old convents and monasteries still stand, none in the Centro Histórico are intact.

Between 1863 and 1867, Mexico was governed by Austrian Emperor Maximilian, installed by an invading French army and supported (initially at least) by Mexican conservatives. Maximilian's rule was brief: once he had alienated his conservative supporters by well-intentioned but half-baked liberal reforms, they withdrew their backing, and the liberal rebels under Juárez defeated his armies and executed Maximilian. But the modernist-minded emperor made a lasting mark on the city. Unhappy with the cold, gloomy palace on the Zócalo, Maximilian and his wife moved to and remodeled the Castillo de Cha-pultepec, now a popular tourist sight. To link the new palace with downtown, the Paseo de la Reforma (originally the Paseo de la Emperatriz), now the city's broadest boulevard, was laid out. He also overhauled the Zócalo itself, decorating it with trees, benches, and a Parisian-style kiosk.

MODERN MEXICO CITY
The Porfiriato

Juárez defeated the hapless Maximilian in 1867 and again took power, governing Mexico until his death in 1872, when political opponent Porfirio Díaz succeeded him. Díaz thoroughly dominated Mexico for the next 28 years, governing with a brutal and efficient authoritarianism, modernizing the country's education and transportation systems, and opening the doors wide for foreign investors and speculators.

Although originally from rural Oaxaca, Díaz became so attached to Mexico City's pomp and ceremony that by the end of his regime he rarely left the city, a factor that took the formerly wily ruler out of touch with the country as a whole. He spent lavishly on city infrastructure, overhauled the police force, and did his best to convert the wealthy neighborhoods on the western side of the city into little pockets of Europe. The poor shantytowns east were ignored entirely, except when he unleashed the police on their inhabitants whenever they ventured into the "good" parts of town.

It was under Díaz that Mexico City began to systematically expand beyond the Centro Histórico. The first neighborhoods established outside downtown were Guerrero and San Rafael, north and west of the Alameda, in the 1850s and 1860s. Under Díaz, this trend accelerated, first with the development of San Cosme and Santa María de la Ribera farther west, and later Juárez and Cuauhtémoc on either side of the newly chic Paseo de la Reforma, and the Colonia Roma just to the south.

Interestingly, this division of the city between the wealthy west and poor east has continued to the present day. The likeliest explanation for the split, which began early in the colonial era, is that the elite were trying to keep as far away as possible from the floodwaters of Lago Texcoco, which lay on the east side of the city.

The Mexican Revolution

By the early 20th century, it was obvious that the gap between rich and poor was increasing, caused by the extreme procapitalist policies of the Díaz regime and the lack of a political voice for workers and peasants. Following the annulment of elections won by opposition candidate Francisco I. Madero in 1910, the Mexican Revolution unleashed itself upon the country, and 10 years of warring between different factions followed, until Sonoran General Álvaro Obregón established control in 1920.

As during the independence wars, Mexico City remained on the side of the conservatives throughout the conflict. The populace gave no sign of rising to defend Madero when General Victoriano Huerta staged a coup d'etat and had the liberal president executed in early 1913. In retaliation for this apathy, when guerrilla leader Pancho Villa took the capital (which he loathed) in 1915, he staged an elaborate ceremony to shame the city elite, forcing them to rename Plateros, the wealthiest street in the Centro, to Francisco I. Madero, in honor of Villa's slain hero.

Mexico City under the PRI

Despite its antirevolutionary inclinations, there was never any doubt that the city would remain the heart of Mexico's political, social, and economic life. With the creation of a stable, single-party government under the Institutional Revolutionary Party (PRI), the capital embarked on a new path of explosive growth that has continued to the present day.

After the rule of General Álvaro Obregón (1920–1924) and General Plutarco Elias Calles (1924–1934), Lázaro Cárdenas was elected president in 1934. Cárdenas, a mestizo with Tarascan Indian heritage, was handpicked by Calles, who hoped to remain the power behind the throne, but he was quickly disabused of this notion. Cárdenas instituted the most sweeping social reforms of any national leader to date, effecting

significant changes in education, labor, agriculture, and commerce. Because of his humble ways and his evident desire to improve the lot of the average Mexican, he is revered to this day throughout the country.

Cárdenas didn't devote a lot of attention to Mexico City in his reformist drive, but the reforms themselves would end up having a major impact on the capital. The new offices created to manage the myriad new programs would eventually lead to the Mexican "super state," a massive, bloated bureaucracy located entirely in Mexico City: "The dreams of the revolution, converted into a nightmare of centralization," as one historian put it.

Further catalysts to growth came from falling investment in the countryside and from policies encouraging all manner of new industry to spring up in Mexico City. Rather than trying to locate these factories outside of the city, successive governments actively encouraged them to stay, offering tax breaks and promising to build necessary infrastructure if industries would locate in northern suburbs such as Naucalpan, Azcapotzalco, Tlanepantla, and Ecatepec.

The lack of jobs in the countryside and the new industry in Mexico City kicked off waves of migration to the capital, which doubled the population in 20 years, from 906,000 in 1920 to 1,757,000 in 1940. To cope with its new residents, the city expanded in all directions. And as is immediately apparent when you fly over Mexico City, this expansion took place with very little planning or forethought. The government turned a blind eye to the impromptu settlements set up by rural immigrants, which would eventually become entire cities in their own right, and freely gave out permits to build new, upscale neighborhoods for the wealthy. First Colonia Condesa was the "in" place in the 1930s, and it was soon followed by Polanco and Lomas farther west in the 1940s.

The Post–World War II Boom

The dynamics of centralization and rural migration accelerated in step with Mexico's economic growth levels during and after World War II.

The construction of the new national university complex in the south of the city in the early 1950s, and the expansion of Avenida Insurgentes to connect it to the city center, led to the buildup of the entire southwestern quadrant of the city in just a few short years. Wide open fields south of Roma were quickly converted into the Del Valle and Nápoles neighborhoods. In the early postwar years the formerly outlying villages of Mixcoac, San Ángel, Tacuba, Tacubaya, and Coyoacán were formally incorporated into the city limits.

To the north, the industrial areas promoted by the government spurred the building of ever-greater numbers of houses, to the point where the remaining open land between them and the city itself soon disappeared entirely as the *mancha urbana* (urban stain) spread across the entire valley. When the middle-class suburb Ciudad Satelite was built with great optimism in the late 1950s, it was surrounded by open land, but in the intervening years the city gobbled it up completely, sprawling all the way to Tepozotlán, by the entrance of the tollway to Querétaro.

The poor, rural immigrants flooding into the city didn't have money to buy property or houses, and so they simply erected shantytowns in the less desirable, eastern side of the valley, once under the waters of Lago Texcoco. Over the years these *ciudades perdidas* (lost cities) have converted into increasingly permanent cities themselves, with infrastructure and local government. The classic *ciudad perdida* is Ciudad Nezahaulcóyotl (Ciudad Neza for short), which saw its population increase from 65,000 in 1960 to 650,000 in 1970 to 1,233,868 in 1995, making it one of the largest cities in the country.

Immigration has fallen off somewhat in recent years, and city and federal governments make a lot of noise about controlling city growth, but the overall dynamic appears to have changed little. If anything, the changes under way due to NAFTA and the privatization of the communal farms will only drive more people out of rural Mexico, and if these migrants can't get to the United States, they'll come to Mexico City.

One example of the continuing relentless city growth can be seen in Chalco, in the southeastern corner of the valley. Still a farming community with miles of open fields, Chalco is now being "colonized" by immigrants from Ciudad Neza, and urban researchers say it's just a question of a few years before new roads are built, power lines are put in, and the new communities are regularized.

Government

Colonial Era

During the Spanish colonial era, Mexico City was governed as an *ayuntamiento,* the traditional Spanish form of town council. While subservient to the royal authorities, the *ayuntamiento* was a power to be reckoned with in colonial affairs.

The capital government became a *municipio* (roughly equivalent to a county in Anglo-American administrative systems) after independence from Spain, and was declared the official seat of the federal government. City authorities managed to maintain a limited autonomy throughout the turbulent decades until the arrival of Porfirio Díaz, who centralized its authority (along with the rest of the country's) in his hands.

Under the PRI

In 1928, the revolutionary government of President Álvaro Obregón revoked the city's status as a *municipio,* creating the Distrito Federal, whose mayor was appointed directly by the president. The new entity encompassed what was previously the *municipio* of México and several outlying communities, converting them into 16 *delegaciones,* so named because their leaders were delegated by the federal government.

While these centralizing reforms were ostensibly intended to help modernize the city, in reality they created a bloated, incredibly inefficient, and numbingly corrupt bureaucracy. Taking care of any sort of *tramite* (official procedure) was an exercise in frustration, unless you were willing to pay the *mordida* (literally, "the bite," a bribe) to speed up matters. Any kind of government contract became an opportunity for graft. The entire patronage system was managed by the long-ruling Institutional Revolutionary Party (PRI).

After seven decades as a badly managed appendage of the federal government, Mexico City's political reform began in 1989 with the birth of the Asemblía de Representantes del Distrito Federal (ARDF), housed in the old federal Congress in the Centro. After arduous negotiations, the city took its first step in modern democracy by voting for the first full elections of the assembly and mayor on July 6, 1997.

The PRD in Government

The election was a watershed. With 47 percent of the vote, Cuauhtémoc Cárdenas won by almost double the number of his closest competitor, the PRI's Alfredo del Mazo (25 percent). Carlos Castillo Peraza of the center-right Partido Acción Nacional (PAN), who was early on thought to be the likely winner, finished with a distant 15 percent.

And on top of that, Cárdenas's leftist Partido de la Revolución Democrática (PRD) swept every single assembly district in direct vote. The PRI, PAN, and the smaller parties were able to capture seats only by proportional representation. With this overwhelming mandate, joyously expressed in the victory celebration in the Zócalo on election night, Cárdenas's possibilities seemed limitless.

But the euphoria evaporated quickly. Given only a shortened term of three years and facing a city with an array of complex problems, the Cárdenas administration was bound to fall short of public expectations. In addition, the federal government retained control of city finances, and during the 1999 federal budget debates in Congress, in a last-second jab at Cárdenas, the PAN and PRI factions denied a request to issue 10 billion pesos in debt, hamstringing the city budget.

Cárdenas, a former PRI member who had left the party to pursue democratic reforms, was also criticized for acting too cautiously and refusing to

negotiate with the other parties. While the new government, filled with idealistic young reformers, clearly made some efforts to clean up bureaucracy in the *delegaciones* and fight corruption in the police, it did not manage to seize its golden opportunity as dramatically as it might have. Cárdenas's dour, uncommunicative style did not help the city government's poor public image.

In the 2000 elections, when the PRI finally lost the presidency after seven decades in power, the PRD again easily won in Mexico City under Andrés Manuel López Obrador, irreverently known as *el pejelagarto,* "the alligator mayor," because of his origins in the coastal state of Tabasco. A fiery leftist politico who made his name fighting the PRI in Tabasco, López Obrador has had a mixed record running the city. As with Cárdenas, he is seen as setting himself up to run for president in 2006, and he has been very public in his criticisms of President Fox. The mayor has scored some political points through a program offering increased pension payments to the elderly poor and by building a second story along a congested stretch of the Periférico highway. Some progress has been made on both corruption and crime, the two issues Mexico City residents are most concerned about, but a series of scandals in which people close to López Obrador were caught on videotape apparently accepting bribes has put a dent in his popularity.

Whatever the success of López Obrador, the PRD is firmly established as a major force in Mexico City politics, winning a majority of the 16 now-elected (formerly appointed) delegation heads. On a national level, the PRD remains riven with internal disputes and muddled on its platform, but in the city, it has found a niche. It seems appropriate: the PRD has a knack for street-level organization and is clearly focused on helping the poor, attributes that lend themselves well to city politics. The PAN, predictably, has better luck in the wealthier areas of the city, while the PRI seems to have lost its way in Mexico City, although this could change under the leadership of López Obrador's old Tabasco rival, PRI president Roberto Madrazo.

Economy

As it has for centuries, Mexico City controls a far larger share of the country's economy than any other region. During the colonial era, the wealth came primarily from the monopolies held by Mexico City merchants on imports and exports between the colony and Europe. After independence from Spain, but especially under the rule of the PRI since the Revolution, a large part of the country's new industry was located in the city, which only accentuated the already-growing dominance of the capital.

Since the 1970s, Monterrey and Guadalajara have been developing industrial bases of their own, and in more recent years, smaller cities such as Puebla, Querétaro, Aguascalientes, and Toluca have started industrializing as well. Mexico City completely controls the financial sector, as it is home to the stock exchange and all major banks and insurance companies, and it plays a major role in the service economy. As it is the location of essentially all federal government offices, government jobs are also a major factor in the economy. In short, the Distrito Federal continues to dominate the national economy.

Employment and Wages

Because Mexico City is such a magnet to migrant workers from the countryside, it has a higher unemployment rate than the national average, despite the city's overall economic strength. The official unemployment figures—4.2 percent in 2004—don't even come close to reflecting reality. With such a high proportion of the population participating in an informal, unregistered economy, accurate numbers are extremely difficult to come by.

Fully three quarters of Mexico City's jobs are in the service and commerce sectors, while just under a quarter are in industry and manufacturing. The retail sector accounts for 20 percent of employment, followed by transport at 8 percent and wholesale commerce at 7 percent.

Wages tend to be higher than the national average. The city is in the highest of the three national minimum wage brackets, with a daily minimum wage of just over $4.

No look at the Mexico City economy would be complete without mentioning the legendary armies of *ambulantes,* the informal street vendors seen all over the city, their wares spread out on the sidewalk. Guesses on the number of city *ambulantes* vary wildly, but they certainly number in the tens of thousands. As they have for generations, many new immigrants to the city begin their new urban lives hawking their modest wares from any street corner not already occupied by another seller.

For years the *ambulantes*—organized into disciplined groups that voted for the PRI and could be relied on to show up at progovernment rallies—were protected by the city police, despite the occasional crackdown. But driven in part by a desire to clean up the downtown area, and also because of the severe increase in *ambulantes* in the wake of the 1994–1995 crisis, city authorities have begun regular patrols to evict the vendors. These have stepped up in the last few years, such that the Centro has far fewer *ambulantes* than it did in past years.

DID YOU KNOW?

Mexico City's population, best estimate: 17.8 million

Number of registered cars and buses in the city: 2.6 million

Daily driving trips within the city: 29.2 million

Number of hotel rooms: 25,000

Hospitals: 344

Museums: 161

Art galleries: 106

Streets: 90,000

The People

Population

Accurate population statistics for Mexico City are notoriously difficult to obtain. Between 1990 and 1995 alone, the metropolitan area added 1.5 million residents, or about 20,000 per month. The official Mexican government does the estimate for the population of México D.F., the Federal District proper, and if you include the more densely populated *municipios* immediately adjacent to D.F. in the State of México, then the number rises to 17.8 million. These are the most up-to-date numbers from the most recent census (in 2000), and any more current numbers you see are only estimates.

You'll hear a figure of 20 million bandied about with reference to the Federal District combined with the entire population of the State of México, which wraps around the top two-thirds of the district. By either reckoning, this makes the metropolis not only Mexico's largest city, but one of the largest in the world. In terms of city limits proper, Buenos Aires is actually more populous than the D.F., but it doesn't come close in terms of metropolitan area.

According to the most recent statistics from the government's Institute of Statistics, Geography, and Information (Instituto de Estadísticas, Geografía e Información, or INEGI), the Federal District's population density averages about 5,600 people per square kilometer. Figures for the individual 32 states vary considerably, of course, ranging from very low rates in the States of Baja California Sur, Chihuahua, Sonora, Campeche, Durango, and Coahuila (each with fewer than 15 inhabitants per square kilometer) to the State of México, where there are 571 inhabitants per square kilometer. If we combine the densities of the State of México and the Distrito Federal—each of which account for about half the metro area's total population—then the density for the whole is 3,085 people per square kilometer. Compare with Mexico's overall average density of just 48 per square kilometer, and you'll get an idea just how intensely urbanized the city is, although it's less packed than Hong Kong (6,364 per square kilometer) or Singapore (5,460 per square kilometer).

INEGI claims that the total population of Mexico stands at 99 million, which means that the D.F./México metro area harbors approximately 17 percent of the nation's inhabitants. Whether you count the percentage as low as 15 percent or as high as 20 percent (parlor estimates of 25 percent cannot be substantiated), this helps Mexico City meet the classic sociological definition of a primate city; i.e., one in which more than 10 percent of a nation's inhabitants live. Economic factors such as Mexico City's disproportionate share of national wealth (around 35 percent) and the fact that a preponderance of goods produced in the country as a whole end up in Mexico City complete the definition of urban primacy.

It's worth noting that Mexico City's growth has slowed considerably since the 1970s, when its population was expanding at an average rate of 4.5 percent per annum. Such vigorous growth came as a result of the dynamic social and economic environment that prevailed in the postwar era. Mexico's relative isolation in matters of international trade forced local manufacturers to concentrate on the internal market and, in particular, on the country's main center of consumption: Mexico City. This propelled the creation of an infrastructure whereby all the major routes of communication converged on the capital. The centralist attitude of the government also played an important role in this inward development.

Interestingly, the slowing overall growth masks two distinct trends: all the population growth of the past 30 years has been in the outer edges of Mexico City, while the population of the inner core has been declining steadily. The combined population of the Cuauhtémoc and Miguel Hidalgo *delegaciones* dropped from 1.5 million in 1960 to 850,000 today. By contrast, the outer edges of the city are still growing, while the adjacent areas outside the city limits are growing faster still.

The city's population in the 1980s grew at only .7 percent each year, well below both the national annual rate (2 percent), and the overall urban rate of growth (3.7 percent). The city now is Mexico's slowest-growing metropolitan area.

Anecdotal newspaper stories suggest that for the first time the city's population may be flattening out, or even declining. While this has yet to be confirmed by census figures, it is true that an increasing number of younger professionals are moving to nearby cities like Querétaro and putting up with the long commute to escape the stressful life of the city.

Mestizaje

In Spanish colonial Mexico City, the most privileged class was the *gachupines,* pure-blooded Spaniards born in Spain, followed by *criollos,* pure-blooded Spaniards born in Mexico; mestizos, those of mixed Indian-Spanish blood born in Mexico; and *indios,* pure-blooded Indians. In many cases the Spanish lumped together *indios* and mestizos as *indígenas.* One of the ironies of the colonial caste system was that "pure-blooded" Spaniards were themselves descended from a 700-year mixing of Moors and Iberians, the conquerors and the conquered—a pattern the Spaniards repeated in the New World.

The caste system still exists in a subtler and

Know Mexico City

WHO'S BIGGER?

It is often claimed that Mexico's capital is "the largest city in the world," yet after a relatively exhaustive research into existing records, I could find no set of statistics that would back this claim. According to the International Data Base of the U.S. Bureau of the Census, part of the U.S. Department of Commerce (a government department with a keen interest in tracking foreign population statistics for trade purposes), a ranking of the world's largest urban "agglomerations" places Mexico City in the number-two position, following Tokyo. According to this list, the Mexico City agglomeration numbered an estimated 27.8 million in the year 2000, while Tokyo was counted at 29.9 million, less than two million ahead of Mexico City. A second study, published by World Gazeteer, listed Tokyo in first place with 31 million, New York/Philadelphia (a rather generous lumping!) second with 29.9 million, and Mexico City third with a mere 20.9 million.

Another authoritative source, the United Nations Center for Human Settlements (HABITAT), published a report in 1996 with a very different ranking. According to this report, Mexico City contained an estimated 11.2 million in 1975—ranking it number four for that year—and was expected to reach 18.8 million by the year 2015. This latter projection would bring Mexico City down to a standing of 10th for that year. In first place for both HABITAT lists, again, was Tokyo (19.8 million in 1975; 28.7 million in 2015).

The apparent discrepancies among all these estimates can be explained by the fact that different organizations are tracking different statistical entities, from the 16 *delegaciones* of the Distrito Federal all the way to the entire Valle de México, which measures roughly 120 by 65 kilometers, or more than 7,000 square kilometers.

A middle-ground approach says that *la Ciudad de México*—or Zona Metropolitana de la Ciudad de México (ZMCM)—covers the Distrito Federal plus 21 *municipios* (a *municipio* is roughly equivalent to "county" in Anglophone countries) in the adjacent State of México. Using this definition, the Mexican Instituto Nacional de Estadística, Geografía e Informatica (INEGI) estimates the entire metro area to be at 17.8 million, a number that many independent observers consider the most realistic. According to the 2000 INEGI census, the population of the city proper is 8,591,309, which makes it the 11th most populous city in the world.

more simplified form throughout Mexico today. The national government recognizes *mestizaje* (mestizoism, or "mixing") as the root cultural characteristic of Mexico, yet distinguishes between two kinds of mestizos, the *indomestizos* of the south, "in whom indigenous characteristics predominate," and the *euromestizos* of the north, "in whom European traits prevail." Also recognized are smaller groups of *afromestizos* from the south gulf coastal regions, particularly Veracruz, where toward the end of the colonial era the Spanish imported African slaves to fill labor shortages caused by the rapidly shrinking local population.

No statistical ethnic breakdown of the capital appears to be available to the public. However, according to the Mexican government, *mestizos* represent roughly 55 percent of the population of the whole nation. Caucasians are believed to represent another 14 percent; with 6 percent *indígenas,* that leaves 25 percent of the nation unaccounted for. An exact national ethnography obviously isn't one of the government's objectives. The Central Intelligence Agency claims a more exacting set of statistics: *mestizo* (Indian-Spanish), 60 percent; Amerindian or predominantly Amerindian, 30 percent; Caucasian or predominantly Caucasian, 9 percent; other, 1 percent. Others break the population down with different numbers—it all depends on who gets slotted into which category, which in the end is a largely unscientific decision.

Representatives of virtually all 56 Amerindian groups recognized by the government can be found in Mexico City, along with many of the 90 officially cataloged native languages. Altogether around 100,000 inhabitants of the Mexico City metro area speak Amerindian languages, more than in any other city in the Americas.

Most numerous are the Náhua or Náhuatl-speaking people of Puebla, Veracruz, Hidalgo, Guerrero, Tlaxcala, Morelos, México, and San Luis Potosí. Most often described as progeny of the Aztecs, today's Náhuatl speakers are actually descendants of a number of disparate tribes whose individual languages were lost to the lingua franca of the Valley of Mexico.

Class Differences

The estimated distribution of wealth among *indomestizos, euromestizos,* and *afromestizos* remains roughly the same as it was when Mexico achieved independence from Spain. The *indígenas* occupy the statistical bottom, a colonial legacy that's still the standard throughout present-day North, Central, and South America.

While Indian values are publicly extolled, in practice almost anything labeled *indio* is considered low caste. Political and economic power remains concentrated in the hands of an elite group of "pure" European descent, a social stratum sometimes referred to as the "Thousand Families."

RELIGION

Between the 16th and 19th centuries, Spanish missionaries indoctrinated the original inhabitants of the Valle de México in the ways of Roman Catholicism. That Catholicism is now the nation's majority religion is an amazing achievement, considering it was laid over a vast variety of native belief systems in existence for thousands of years. About 90 percent of the population call themselves Catholics; Mexico is the second-largest Roman Catholic nation in the world after Brazil.

Mexico's Protestant population consists mostly of Indians in the South missionized by North Americans in the 19th and 20th centuries. There are very few Protestants in Mexico City, which is considered the nation's most stalwart Catholic base after Guadalajara. Although many Spanish Jews arrived in the early days of European migration to Mexico, the Spanish Inquisition forced most to convert to Catholicism. Still, many more *capitalinos* (citizens of the capital) identify themselves as "nonreligious" than in any other city in Mexico. The Mexican Constitution of 1917 guarantees freedom of religion; Church and State are strictly separated.

Mexican Catholicism

Mexican Catholics tend to be devout practitioners of their faith. Mexican Catholicism, however, has its own variations that distinguish the religion from its European predecessors. Some differences are traceable to preexisting Indian spiritual traditions absorbed by the Catholic faith, and as such are localized according to tribe.

One variation common to all of Mexico is the Virgin of Guadalupe cult, which began in 1531 when a dark-skinned Virgin Mary appeared before Juan Diego, an Aztec nobleman formerly named Cuauhtaoctzin, in a series of three visions at Tepeyac, near Mexico City, previously a sacred Aztec site dedicated to the goddess Tonantzin. According to legend, in the third vision the Virgin commanded Diego to gather roses and present them to the local bishop, requesting that a church be built in her honor. When the devout Diego unfolded his rose-filled cloak, both he and the bishop beheld an image of the dark-skinned Virgin imprinted on the garment. This was deemed a miracle, and church construction commenced at once.

Today, many Mexican churches are named for Our Lady of Guadalupe, who has become so fused with Mexican identity that the slogan *¡Viva Guadalupe!* is commonly used at political rallies. The affectionate Mexican nickname for Guadalupe is La Morenita, "Little Dark One." She has become, as Mexican American cultural commentator Richard Rodriguez puts it, the "official private flag of Mexico," and one way in which Catholicism has been absorbed by native cultures rather than vice versa. The official feast day for Guadalupe, December 12, is fervently celebrated in Mexico City and throughout the country. (For more information, see the entry on the Basílica de la Virgen de Guadalupe in the *Sights* chapter.)

Mexican Saints

The legion of saints worshiped in Mexico runs the gamut of Catholic history. Three native saints warrant special mention. San Felipe de Jesús (1527–1597), a Franciscan friar, became Mexico's first Catholic martyr when he was killed while performing missionary work in Nagasaki, Japan. His martyrdom was officially recognized by the Church in 1627, and in 1629 Mexico named him the patron saint of the *virreinato* (the viceroy-

© CHRIS HUMPHREY

a carved wooden statue of Saint Cristóbal at Puebla's Museo Virreinal

alty; i.e., the Spanish administration in Mexico). Santa Rosa de Lima (1586–1617), a Dominican nun, was canonized as a saint in 1671 and thus became the first *santa americana* (American female saint) within the Catholic tradition. After years of controversy, Juan Diego, the Aztec nobleman who saw the vision of the Virgen de Guadalupe, was declared a saint in 2002.

LANGUAGE

Mexico is the largest Spanish-speaking country in the world. The type of Spanish spoken in Mexico is usually referred to as Latin American Spanish, in contrast to the Castilian Spanish spoken in Spain. Still, the Spanish here differs significantly from that of even other Spanish-speaking countries in the Western Hemisphere. Many Anglicisms have crept into the Mexican language. For example, the common Latin American Spanish term for car is *coche,* but in Mexico you'll often hear *carro.*

While English is occasionally spoken by merchants, hotel staff, and travel agents in the Centro and in wealthier suburbs, first-time visitors are often surprised by how little English one hears in Mexico City compared to what might be encountered at popular beach resorts in Mexico. Outside areas of the city frequented by tourists, it's relatively rare to encounter anyone who speaks more than a few words of English.

Hence it's incumbent upon the visitor to learn at least enough Spanish to cope with everyday transactions. Knowing a little Spanish will not only mitigate communication problems, it will also bring you more respect among the local *capitalinos,* who quite naturally resent foreign visitors who expect Mexicans to abandon their mother tongue whenever a gringo approaches. Out of courtesy, you should at least attempt to communicate in Spanish whenever possible. (See the *Spanish Phrasebook* for a list of useful words and phrases and for a guide to pronunciation. Also see the information on Spanish language courses in Mexico and recommended reference works.)

Mexican Spanish, and especially Mexico City Spanish, is extremely rich with slang expressions, unique tones of voice, and hilarious wordplay. It is unquestionably one of the richest types of Spanish spoken anywhere, and one that is immediately recognizable to any other Spanish-speaker (who usually react with a smile), both because of its distinct character and also because of the prevalence of Mexican television throughout Latin America. (See the *Chilango Slang* phrasebook for more details.)

Getting There

AIR

Aeropuerto Internacional Benito Juárez

Mexico's airport, in the eastern part of the city near the exit toward Puebla, has two terminals, domestic and international. As you enter from the Circuito Interior, the domestic terminal comes first. Inside the domestic terminal, a wall between Gates B and C features a mural (thoroughly ignored by the thousands of travelers swarming below it every day), by Juan O'Gorman, illustrating the history of flight, from an Aztec nobleman eyeing the wings of a bat with curiosity to the Wright brothers and Charles Lindbergh.

Both terminals have several fast-food joints and restaurants of mediocre quality where you can get a bite to eat, as well as a few newsstands, several ATMs, and plenty of money-exchange booths. One of the latter, Tamibe, in the arrival hall for international flights, is open 24 hours. Also in the international terminal is a 24-hour Servitel telephone office for long-distance calls. For general airport information, call tel. 5571-3600. In the international terminal is a 24-hour **Internet Café** ($2 for 15 minutes,

$4.25 for an hour). Both Conaculta (the government culture institute) and INEGI (the government map and information service) have stores in the national terminal.

The airport is well past its capacity, despite a half-billion-dollar expansion project that should be completed by the time this book is printed. A few years back the government planned to open a new airport not far northeast of the current location, not far from an old lakebed near Texcoco. However, a small group of local farmers protested, and the whole issue got lost in a swamp of politics from which it appears unlikely to emerge. A second proposed location, near Tizayuca in Hidalgo, was deemed too far away to be viable. Instead, nearby regional airports like Toluca, Puebla, and Querétaro are gearing up for international traffic. Continental inaugurated the first international nonstop flights from Houston to Toluca and Puebla in 2004, and more are expected.

Airlines

The principal domestic airlines flying from Mexico City to other destinations in the country include Aero California (Paseo de la Reforma 332, tel. 5207-1392 or 5207-0068); Aeromar (tel.

5133-1111 or 800/704-2000, www.aeromar .com.mx); AeroMexico (Paseo de la Reforma 80, tel. 5133-4000 or 800/021-4000, www.aeromexico.com); Aviacsa (Paseo de la Reforma 195, tel. 5716-9004, www.aviacsa.com.mx); Mexicana/Aerocaribe (Paseo de la Reforma 312, tel. 5448-0990 or 800/502-2000, www.mexicana.com.mx); and Republicair (Thiers 148, Colonia Anzures, tel. 5203-8090, www.republicair.com.mx).

The following airlines service the North American market: Air Canada (tel. 5208-1883, www.aircanada.com); America West Airlines (tel. 5511-9788 or 800/235-9292, www.americawest.com); American Airlines (tel. 5209-1400, www.aa.com); Continental Airlines (tel. 5283-5500 or 800/900-5000, www.continental.com); Delta Airlines (tel. 5279-0909 or 5202-1608, www.delta.com); Northwest Airlines (tel. 2122-1300 or 2122-1305, www.nwa.com); and United Airlines (tel. 5627-0222 or 800/003-0777, www.ual.com).

To fly elsewhere in Latin America, contact Aerolineas Argentinas (tel. 5523-7154, www.aerolineas.com.ar) for Argentina; Lan Chile (tel. 5566-5211 or 800/700-7600, www.lanchile.com) for Chile or other South American destinations; Lloyd Air Boliviano (tel. 5591-1134 or 5535-3734, www.labairlines.com) for Bolivia; Taca (tel. 5553-3366 or 5211-6640, www.taca.com) for Central America; and Varig (tel. 5280-9192 or 800/907-8800, www.varig.com.mx) for Brazil.

To Europe and elsewhere, contact Air France (tel. 5627-6060, www.airfrance.mx); Air New Zealand (tel. 5208-1708, www.airnz.co.nz); Alitalia (tel. 5533-5590, www.alitalia.it); British Airways (tel. 5387-0300 or 5785-8714, www.britishairways.com); El Al Israel Airlines (tel. 5545-3317 or 5545-33190, www.elal.co.il); Iberia (tel. 5130-3030 or 5130-3000, www.iberia.com); Japan Air Lines (tel. 5242-0149 or 5242-0154, www.jal.co.jp); KLM (tel. 5726-0149 or 5563-1254, www.klm.com); Lufthansa (tel. 5230-0000, www.lufthansa.com); Qantas (tel. 5628-0547 or 5628-0548, www.qantas.com.au); and Swiss International Airlines (tel. 5511-5074, www.swiss.com).

Arriving

When flying into Mexico City, your first airport stop is immigration, where you will fill out a tourist card if you don't already have a Mexican visa. While tourists are eligible to stay for six months, immigration agents will arbitrarily stamp the card with as many days as they feel like (often 60 days), meaning you'll have to go to an immigration office to renew it if you plan to stay longer. However, if before they've had a chance to stamp your card, you say authoritatively *"Ciento ochenta días, por favor"* (One hundred and eighty days, please) they'll usually give it to you. Once they start writing, don't bother to say it, as they apparently never rewrite a card once they've already started.

After immigration, you'll proceed downstairs to collect your luggage from baggage claim and pass through the customs station, where you may be randomly chosen for inspection.

If you are waiting to meet someone arriving on an international flight, be prepared to wait an hour or so (occasionally less, often more), along with a hundred or so others outside the glass doors past the customs checkpoint. While the bar at the Freedom restaurant looks like a great vantage point to wait for someone, the staff will only let you sit there if you order a meal.

Departing

Almost all departing international flights leave, logically enough, from the international terminal, but a few leave from the domestic terminal if the plane has a stopover in another city (such as Guadalajara or Cancún) while flying out to another country. Check with your airline by phone beforehand to be sure. When you depart Mexico, be sure to bring your tourist card, as you will be asked for it before leaving the country.

It's very important to leave enough time, as the lines to get tickets and check bags can be very lengthy at times, as can the second line upstairs to go through security before heading out to the gate. The security officials are entirely unsympathetic to pleas of those who are close to missing their flight and want to go to the front of the line. So if you want to have a meal before going through security (the restaurants are better outside than near the gates), check how the line looks to be sure you have enough time.

The duty-free shops in the international terminal have a large selection of tequila, cigars, and other consumer goods.

To and From the Airport

Metro: If you're arriving in Mexico City between 6 A.M. and midnight and don't have a lot of baggage, you could take the Metro into town from the Terminal station, a short walk up the sidewalk from outside the domestic terminal. It's a lengthy ordeal, but saves a $12–17 taxi ride for those pinching their pesos.

Taxi: No city buses service the airport, making taxis the only option besides the Metro to get into town. Because of the very high incidence of robberies by street cabs at the airport, tourists should use only the authorized airport taxi service. They are not cheap compared to other taxis in Mexico City, but there's not much alternative. Buy a ticket from the taxi service window, in the international terminal right where passengers are let out after the customs checkpoint. There are two windows: Be sure to go to the one with regular taxis, not the large Suburban vans that are considerably more expensive, and the window attendants have been known to refrain from telling this fact to foreign tourists. These vans are a reasonable option if you have a large group of people or a whole lot of luggage.

Fares are based on how far your destination is from the airport—a map next to the window tells you which zone you're going to (assuming you know the city well enough to find it). Regular taxis costs $12 to the Centro; $12 to the Alameda area, Roma, and part of Paseo de la Reforma; $16 to Condesa or the Zona Rosa; $17 to Polanco or Coyoacán; and $19 to San Ángel or farther west along Paseo de la Reforma.

Chauffeured cars (seating four) and vans (seating eight) are also available to nearby cities such as Pachuca ($60 car, $65 van), Toluca ($67 car, $76 van), and Puebla or Cuernavaca ($70 car, $80 van).

Bus: There are no city buses to the airport, but there are bus companies that offer a number of direct routes from the airport to several nearby cities. As there are no bus offices at the airport, you simply exit the domestic terminal near Sala D and buy a ticket on the bus when it arrives. Pullman de Morelos drives to Cuernavaca 21 times a day 6:30 A.M.–11 P.M. for $10. Estrella Roja drives to Puebla 40 times a day 6 A.M.–midnight for $13. Primera Plus goes to Querétaro 15 times daily 7 A.M.–10 P.M. for $20. Caminante goes to Toluca 17 times daily 7 A.M.–11 P.M. for $8.

Driving: The airport is just off the eastern side of the Circuito Interior ring highway, which is easily accessible from most major neighborhoods in the center, west, and south of the city. The best route from most neighborhoods frequented by tourists is from the Viaducto, an east–west highway across the center of the city that has an exit on to the Circuito just south of the airport. However, the turn off the Viaducto is badly marked and easy to miss, so beware—it's a left-hand exit. The airport exit from the Circuito is clearly marked. The entrance road first passes between the domestic terminal (on the right) and the domestic parking terminal (on the left). Another 500 meters beyond on the right side is the international terminal, with its parking lot just beyond, also on the right side. Returning to the city, just loop back around to the left at the crossover past the international terminal and either bear to the right to get on the Circuito heading north or stay in the middle and cross over the Circuito to the southbound side. Go southbound to get to the Viaducto—again, the turnoff is a bit tricky. Taking the Circuito northbound is a quicker route to get to Polanco and nearby neighborhoods.

BUS

Mexico's top-notch bus system has dozens of competing companies offering first- and second-class buses throughout the country at very reasonable prices. First class has more comfortable seats, fewer stops, and, whether you like it or not, videos. The screens are usually spaced every four or five seats, so request a seat as far as possible from one if you don't want to watch. Second-class buses are 20 to 40 percent cheaper, but they're not as comfortable and always take longer, as they stop at seemingly every town on the route.

For trips to nearby major cities (such as Puebla, Toluca, Cuernavaca, or Guadalajara), there's usually a departure every 15 minutes or so throughout the day, so travelers can safely show up at the bus station whenever is convenient and not have to wait very long. If you are going to destinations with less frequent service, want a particular seat, or are traveling during the holidays, it's best to get your ticket beforehand. The easiest way to do this for most bus lines is through **Ticket Bus** (tel. 5133-2424 or from outside Mexico City toll free tel. 800/702-8000, www.ticketbus.com.mx), a central reservation service for basically all of the main bus lines in Mexico. It has nearly 40 offices around the city where you can go to buy tickets. Some convenient ones are: Isabel la Católica 83, in the Centro, tel. 5709-9985; Paseo de la Reforma 412, near the Diana monument, tel. 5207-9437; and Puebla 46, in the Roma, tel. 5511-2916. Alternatively, although less convenient, you can go to the bus station and buy a ticket the day before your departure. For smaller bus lines to less-frequented destinations, you may have to go to the terminal itself a day beforehand. (For the Mexico City telephones of several of these bus lines, see the *Excursions* chapter, but reservations with small companies are iffy, even if you can get through.)

First-class bus companies include Omnibus de Mexico (tel. 5719-2397 or 5567-5858, www.omnibusdemexico.com.mx) for Northern and Central Mexico; Estrella Blanca/Turistar (tel. 5729-0707, www.estrellablanca.com.mx) for Northern, Central, and Western Mexico; Primera Plus/Flecha Amarilla (tel. 5567-7887 or 5567-7176, www.flecha-amarilla.com) for Western and Central Mexico); Estrella de Oro (tel. 5549-8520 or 5549-8521, www.estrelladeoro.com.mx) for Cuernavaca, Acapulco, Taxco; ADO (tel. 5133-2444 or 5785-9659) for southeastern Mexico; and Cristóbal Colón (tel. 5700-1089 or 5133-2400, www.cristobalcolon.com.mx) for Oaxaca and Chiapas.

Luxury bus line ETN (tel. 5273-7155 or 5277-6529, www.etn.com.mx) offers very comfortable reclining seats and nonstop rides at a premium cost, but it's worth it for a long haul. ETN serves North-Central Mexico. Another luxury line, this one serving Oaxaca, Chiapas, Veracruz, and other parts of the southeast, is UNO (tel. 5522-1111, www.uno.com.mx).

For connections to destinations within the U.S., talk to Greyhound (Amores 707-102, Colonia Del Valle, tel. 5543-1511 or 5669-0986, www.greyhound.com.mx).

Terminals

Mexico City has four intercity bus terminals at the four main highway exits out of the city, corresponding to the cardinal points of the compass. Each is accessible by Metro, and all have authorized taxi services on arrival. It's always better to take an authorized taxi than the ones on the street, because bus stations are prime scouting sites for taxi thieves.

Terminal Central del Norte (North Terminal) (Av. de los Cien Metros 1907, tel. 5587-5973): Take Metro Line 5 to Terminal Norte station. From this station, there's bus service to Querétaro, San Miguel de Allende, Guanajuato, Zacatecas, Chihuahua, Monterrey, and Tijuana.

Terminal Central del Sur (South Terminal), also known as Terminal Tasqueña (Av. Tasqueña 1320, tel. 5689-9795): Take Metro Line 2 to Tasqueña station. This terminal offers buses to Cuernavaca, Acapulco, Taxco, and Ixtapa/Zihuatanejo.

Terminal Poniente (Western Terminal) (Av. Sur 122, tel. 5271-4519): The Metro stop is Observatorio. From this station there are departures to Toluca, Valle de Bravo, Morelia, Guadalajara, and Puerto Vallarta.

Terminal Oriente (Eastern Terminal), also known as Terminal TAPO (Calz. Ignacio Zaragoza 200, tel. 5762-5977): Take Metro Line 4 at the Morelos station or Line 1 at San Lázaro station. Buses depart to Puebla, Veracruz, Mérida, Cancún, Palenque, San Cristóbal de las Casas, and Tapachula.

CAR

From the United States, Mexico City can be reached in 12–48 hours of reasonably sane driving, depending on which route you take. The shortest route (about 12 hours) is to cross the border at Laredo, Texas, taking México 85 to Monterrey, then México 57 on to Saltillo, San Luis Potosí, and Querétaro, all on good highway and almost entirely free of tolls. Other, longer routes extend from Ciudad Juárez on México 45 through Chihuahua, then México 49 on to Gómez Palacio, Zacatecas, and San Luis Potosí (two days, best broken for the night somewhere between Zacatecas and Saltillo); the northwest highway from California and Arizona (México 15) passes through Hermosillo, Mazatlán, Tepic, and Guadalajara (Tepic or Mazatlán are about a day's drive from D.F.).

In many places along Mexican highways drivers can choose between the free *(libre)* or the toll *(cuota)* road. The toll highways can be pricey, but the pavement is excellent and traffic is much lighter than on the congested free roads. However, some free roads, especially in the northern deserts, are wide open and fast, and if you get to know which ones are good, you can save a good chunk of money without sacrificing much time. But don't drive on the free roads at night if you can avoid it, and if you do, be cautious.

The highways connecting Mexico City to Guatemala (via Tapachula, 16–20 hours of driving) and Belize (via Chetumal, 20–24 hours of driving) are in worse condition than the northern roads and should be driven only during the day.

Try to avoid arriving in Mexico City on Sunday afternoon and evening, as the highways are invariably jammed with weekenders heading home. Conversely, Friday afternoon is about the worst time to try to leave the city.

Insurance

It's very important to carry a Mexican liability insurance policy on your vehicle when driving in Mexico. No matter what your own insurance company may tell you, Mexican authorities don't recognize foreign insurance policies for private vehicles in Mexico.

At least minimum liability vehicle insurance is now required by law in Mexico. Without it, a minor traffic accident can turn into a nightmare. Short-term—as little as one day's worth—insurance can be arranged at any of several agencies found in nearly every border town between the Pacific Ocean and the Gulf of Mexico.

One of the most popular, and reliable, Mexico insurers is **Sanborns Mexico Insurance** (P.O. Box 310, McAllen, TX 78505, tel. 956/682-6677 or 800/222-0158, fax 956/686-0732, www.sanbornsinsurance.com), which has offices in or close to virtually every town along the U.S.–Mexico border except Tijuana and some of the smaller border crossings. Sample coverage for a vehicle insured at a value of $20,000–25,000—plus $50,000 property damage, $80,000 liability, and medical payments of $2,000 per person (up to $10,000 per occurrence)—costs around $12 per day or around $800 per year to drive anywhere in Mexico.

For long-term visits, better deals can sometimes be negotiated from other sources, especially for drivers who will be making more than one trip into Mexico each year. Some agencies in Mexico offer annual policies in which you're only charged for those days you're actually in Mexico. Of course, this requires a trip south of the border to obtain such a policy in the first place, so you'll need a day or two's worth of border insurance for the trip. Whichever policy you choose, always make photocopies of the policy and keep originals and copies in separate, safe places.

Driving To/From Querétaro

Take Paseo de la Reforma west out past Chapultepec to the Periférico, turn north on the Periférico, and follow it all the way past Satelite and Tlanepantla, keeping an eye out for Querétaro signs. It's also possible to follow the Eje Central north from downtown, but this is sometimes more complicated and with more traffic. Returning to the city, stay on the Periférico around the northwest side of the city and either get off at Paseo de la Reforma (for Polanco, the Zona Rosa, and the Centro) or continue farther south on the Periférico for San Ángel and Coyoacán.

Driving To/From Toluca

Paseo de la Reforma and Avenida Constituyentes (a major avenue parallel to Reforma but farther south) both lead to free and toll highways to Toluca. The toll road costs $5 for the 10-mile stretch to La Marquesa (one of the most expensive tolls in the country for the distance), where it meets back up with the free road. If you're not in a rush, take the free road and save your pesos. Coming in from Toluca, keep an eye out for signs directing you to Reforma (for Polanco, Paseo de la Reforma, or the Centro Histórico) or Constituyentes (for Condesa, Roma, or anywhere in the south of the city).

Driving To/From Cuernavaca

Both Avenida Insurgentes and Calzado Tlalpan (the southern extension of Pino Suárez, the road on the east side of the Zócalo) lead directly to both the free and toll highways to Cuernavaca. Tlalpan is usually faster. The Periférico ring road also connects with the highway exit in the south part of the city. The $6.50 toll highway to Cuernavaca bypasses the windy, scenic, and slow free road. Arriving in the city, watch for the major junction as you come out of the hills and enter the valley, the right-hand fork leading to Tlalpan and downtown, and the left-hand one to Insurgentes, San Ángel, Coyoacán, Roma, and Condesa.

Driving To/From Puebla

Navigating your way from the Centro through to the market neighborhoods to the eastern exit of the city is no simple task. It's often easier to head south along Pino Suárez and Tlalpan, turn off on the Viaducto Miguel Alemán heading east, and follow the signs to Puebla. It's also possible to follow Avenida Chapultepec east (farther on, it's called Avenida Fray Servando) to Calzado Izazaga and the highway to Puebla, but a couple of turns are confusing, and traffic is usually bad. From the west and south of the city, take Viaducto Miguel Alemán.

Coming into the city, paradoxically, it's a bit of a trick to find the entrance to the Viaducto, whereas following Izazaga and then Fray Servando into the city center is fairly straightforward. Once you learn the Viaducto entrance, however, it's the quickest way to get into most of the center, south, and west parts of the city.

The toll road to Puebla costs $5 and allows you to avoid all the curves and slow trucks on the free highway.

Driving To/From Teotihuacán and Pachuca

Getting out on the highway to the ruins northeast of Mexico City, as well as to Pachuca, couldn't be simpler: just get on Avenida Insurgentes north and keep going straight. At the first tollbooth, Pachuca drivers stay to the left, while those going to Teotihuacán stay to the right. Coming back is just as easy.

TRAIN

At last report, there was no passenger train service operating out of Mexico City. The last routes, to Apizaco in Tlaxcala and to Veracruz, have all been discontinued. If for some reason you need to get to the train station anyhow, it is on Avenida Insurgentes Norte in Colonia Buenavista (Metro station Buenavista).

The federal government announced in 2004 that it would support the construction of a proposed high-speed train linking Mexico City to Guadalajara via the thriving *Bajío* cities of Querétaro, Celaya, and León. The total trip would take roughly 2.5 hours at 250 kilometers per hour for $90, if all goes as planned (a big if!), making it a great improvement over the 6.5-hour, $55 bus ride. It will, however, take several years to build, so make do with the bus or fork out $140 for the plane ride in the meantime.

Getting Around

Getting around Mexico City is cheap, efficient, and—with a little caution—safe. Within each neighborhood, walking is the best way to see everything; attractions are usually concentrated in each of the city's most popular areas.

To cover more ground, the options available include bus, taxi, and Metro. Those who have their own wheels will find negotiating the city not as daunting as might be expected, unless they're unlucky enough to be caught in one of the political demonstrations that frequently snarl the city center.

BUS

The most common of Mexico City's several bus types is the *pesero,* a medium-sized, box-shaped bus painted white and green. Fares ($0.20–0.50) depend on how far along the route you are going—ask and pay when you get in. To signal a stop, push the button above the rear door, and if that doesn't work, call out *"baja, por favor"* (stop, please) in a loud voice. *Peseros* tend to stop anywhere, not just designated stops. These buses can be extremely crowded during peak hours, and pickpockets are common, so watch out if you're standing.

The larger buses, some of them double-long, cost a bit more ($0.40) but are more comfortable and stop less often, and only at official stops. Some of the express buses running down Insurgentes stop only every kilometer or so. In some areas, particularly farther out from the city center, *combis* or *colectivos* (shared Volkswagen buses) are common.

To find the right bus for your destination, start by looking at the placards posted in the front window. These invariably only state the end of the line, so you most likely will have to ask drivers if they are going your way, and if not, which bus you should take.

At the end of each Metro line, huge corrals of buses depart for destinations around the edge of the city.

METRO

Many visitors, expecting the worst, find themselves pleasantly surprised by Mexico's clean and efficient Metro system. At a cost of $0.25 per ride, the 11 lines *(líneas)* of the Metro move an average of five million people around the city each day. Just about all of the city's major sites, hotels, bus stations, and the airport are accessible from the system.

The Metro stations are well lit and generally safe. Directions are indicated by the last stops at each end of each line, so you must know where you want to go in between these stops. Metro maps are posted on the walls of all stations. Signs marked Correspondencia indicate the walking route to take to transfer train lines—look for the name of the station at the end of the line in the direction you are going. For example, if you go into the Zócalo station and want to ride to Metro Revolución, go in the direction of "Cuatro Caminos" and get off at the Revolución station. There is no charge to transfer lines as often as you like, as long as you don't leave the Metro system. Try to buy several tickets in advance if you're going to use the Metro, as ticket booth lines can sometimes be very long. Operating hours vary slightly according to day of the week and the line, but they're roughly 6 A.M.–midnight, or until 1 A.M. Saturday nights.

For destinations beyond the reach of the Metro system, get off at the station farthest out in the direction you're going, then go outside where fleets of microbuses are parked and ask which one to take.

A *tren ligero* (light rail train) extends Metro service into the southern part of the city, from the Tasqueña Metro station as far south as Xochimilco.

A new elevated train line, heading from downtown northwest from Garibaldi past Tacuba to Naucalpan, Satelite, and beyond, was at last report the next Metro line planned.

For more information about the Metro, see its website www.metro.df.gob.mx.

Customs and Safety

Metro users are not known for their politeness, with people getting in at stations often shoving past others trying to get off. British travelers will no doubt be infuriated by the local habit of standing on the left side of the escalators, thus blocking those who are trying to walk. Mexicans who find their path blocked, however, stop walking and wait for the end of the ride with the resigned aplomb for which Mexico City is legendary; they don't even consider asking the person in front to move.

Foreign women, particularly those unaccompanied by a man, can expect plenty of looks at the least and very possibly some groping as well if the train is crowded—many female travelers avoid using the Metro if they're alone because of all the tiresome unwanted attention. Pickpockets are also rife on the Metro—after taxi robberies, the most common form of crime foreigners will run across is probably losing their wallet on the Metro.

These annoyances aside, the Metro is generally safe and easy to use, particularly if you don't try to use it during the morning and afternoon rush hours (7–9 A.M. and 6–9 P.M.). At peak hours in some stations, the front couple of cars may be designated for women and children only—look for special roped-off lines, marked with signs.

TAXI

Taxis in Mexico City come in two varieties: roving taxis, hailed from the street, and various *sitio* taxi companies, based at a certain station and reached by telephone.

Street Taxis

The most common are the green and white taxis, often Volkswagen Beetles but increasingly other makes and models also, equipped with taxi meters *(taxímetros)*. Metered taxis hailed from street corners in Mexico City have a bad reputation, and not without reason. Armed muggings are not uncommon, and foreigners are unquestionably a high-risk group. It's not recommended to take street taxis unless you really have to. Expats who get to know the city well, and have a good command of Spanish,

© CHRIS HUMPHREY

Flagging street cabs down is a fairly high-risk proposition in Mexico City—better to call a *sitio*.

may feel more comfortable taking street cabs, but most tourists will want to avoid them.

A much better idea, for essentially the same price and just a couple of minutes' extra time, is to take a *sitio* taxi, either by walking to a nearby taxi stand or calling one of any number of *sitio* companies and having them pick you up .

Should you decide to take a street taxi, check that the driver has a *tarjetón,* or identification card, keep the window rolled up and door locked (most robberies involve an accomplice jumping in when the taxi stops), and give clear directional instructions to the driver. Also be sure the driver turns on the meter as soon as you start driving. If possible, try to have small bills when taking rides around town, as taxi drivers often don't have change. Tipping is not expected.

After 10 P.M. taxis are legally allowed to charge 20 percent above the meter reading. Some have special meters with a night setting, while with others you simply have to calculate the extra amount—ask when you get in. If it's late taxi drivers may refuse to turn on their meter and will instead want to negotiate a price. Although this is technically illegal, it's common practice. Also, all rides going outside the city limits into the State of México cost extra. Note the amount the meter reads when leaving the Distrito Federal—all charges incurred after entering the State of México are doubled, then added to the amount accumulated on the meter while still in D.F.

Sitio, Radio, and Hotel Taxis

If you need to take a taxi in the city after dark, or you need one during the day and don't want to risk a street cab, a safer alternative is a *sitio* (pronounced SEE-tee-yoh) taxi. These are taxis attached to a permanent taxi stand, or *sitio.* You'll find taxi *sitios* in various parts of the city, and you can recognize them by a short line of taxis, all painted the same color, with the name of the *sitio* emblazoned on the side. Often a curbside kiosk stands nearby where dispatchers log the taxis in and out.

Radio-dispatched *sitios* reached by telephone, with service to and from anywhere in the city, are

considered to be the safest of all. Some are expensive, while others are very reasonable—check how the fare is calculated when you call. Sometimes it's a flat fee per route, sometimes it's a taxi meter plus a certain amount, and sometimes it's by kilometers. If you plan on using a lot of *sitio* taxis, it's not a bad idea to buy a Ladatel telephone card, so you can call them from public telephones.

Taxi Mex (tel. 5519-7690 or 9171-8888) is a reliable *sitio* service charging the *taxímetro* plus $1.25 during the day; add another 20 percent after 10 P.M. Similarly reliable is **Delta** (tel. 5551-3176 or 5771-5862).

Servitaxi (tel. 5516-6020 or 5516-6025) has taxis charging according to a taxi meter plus $2. Call the central operator and they will radio for the nearest taxi, or call one of the neighborhood bases: Centro (tel. 5526-2300), Reforma (tel. 5566-1060), Polanco (tel. 5282-1428), Condesa (tel. 5553-5059), Insurgentes Sur/Del Valle (tel. 5687-8819), Coyoacán and Mixcoac (tel. 5534-3861), and Roma (tel. 5574-7356). Two other companies with similar rates are **Radio Taxi** (tel. 5674-6120 or 5674-6620) and **Servicios Ejecutivos Sitio 144** (tel. 5654-3083 or 5649-0657).

A very good unmarked taxi service charging by kilometer (rather than with a taxi meter) is **Radio Elite** (tel. 5660-1122 or 5593-3440).

Most high-end hotels have a cab service; these are the most expensive cabs, but they're quite safe, and fares are usually posted. The cars are usually unmarked, four-door Fords, and the drivers often speak some English (some are licensed guides as well). There may also be a taxi *sitio* near your hotel; ask the doorman to point one out.

Cars with Drivers

If you plan on driving around the city a lot and don't want to deal with taxis, or you are looking for a private driver for any other reason, one excellent and reliable company is **Limorent** (tel. 5277-2304), which will provide an English-speaking driver (on request) and a car fitting four for $280 for an entire day. Longer and shorter rentals can also be arranged.

Two other companies offering chauffeur service around the city and elsewhere, with bilingual drivers, are **Transportación Turística y Ejecutiva Chapultepec** (tel. 5516-0850 or 5516-0770, www.mexicolimorent.com.mx) and **Arguba** (tel. 5523-2973 or 5687-0617).

CAR

Driving in Mexico City is certainly not for the faint of heart. Nevertheless, those who have driven in other large, chaotic cities will find Mexico City negotiable, as long as proper caution is taken and a few basic principals are kept in mind.

One essential factor to peaceful driving in the city is to choose your hours carefully. Mornings (8–10 A.M.) can be very congested, while midday traffic is usually fairly reasonable until around 3 P.M. During the week, midafternoon and early evenings are the worst, particularly on the main commuter routes in and out of the city and in the Centro. Traffic begins to dissipate around 9 P.M., or earlier in the city center. The worst traffic of all is Friday afternoon, and even worse still if it's a *viernes quincena,* a Friday that coincides with the twice-monthly payday. Unpredictable demonstrations in various parts of the city—but particularly on Paseo de la Reforma, on Paseo Bucareli, and in the city center—also regularly tie up traffic.

Navigation

As might be expected, learning your way around an urban area of several million inhabitants can be a bit confusing, but being familiar with a couple of major avenues can help you stay oriented. Avenida Insurgentes is the longest boulevard in the city and is a major north/south route crossing Mexico City. To the northeast, Insurgentes takes you to the exit for Pachuca and Teotihuacán, while to the south it continues past San Ángel to UNAM and the exit to Cuernavaca and Acapulco.

Paseo de la Reforma is a broad avenue punctuated by large traffic circles (called *glorietas*) running northeast–southwest. Originally Reforma ran between the Alameda and Chapulte-

pec, but now it extends west to the exit to Toluca and northeast to the Basílica de Guadalupe.

The city is circled by two ring highways, the inner Circuito Interior and the outer Periférico. The Circuito makes a complete loop, although it changes names (Río Churubusco, Patriotismo, Revolución, and Circuito Interior) along the way. The Periférico, however, extends only three-quarters of the way, with the northeast section (between the highway exits to Querétaro and Puebla) unfinished.

Cutting across these two loops is a grid of *ejes,* axis roads running in one direction with traffic lights (somewhat) timed, either east–west or north–south. *Ejes* are numbered and given a reference of *norte* (north), *sur* (south), *oriente* (east), and *poniente* (west). Hence the Eje 2 Norte is the second east–west road north of the center of the city, and the Eje 3 Norte runs parallel to it, several blocks north, etc. Other important roads that are not technically *ejes* are the east–west Viaducto Miguel Alemán and the south-to-center Avenida Tlalpan, both of which are major, two-way arteries with few stoplights.

Finding specific addresses in the city can be tricky. The best tool is the *Guía Roji,* a bright red book of maps and indexes of the city. It can be found in Sanborns and is sold on many street corners for $8. When driving, don't expect to see street signs placed in logical places, and be ready to ask for directions frequently. And always try to know the name of the *colonia* (neighborhood) where your destination is located.

Hoy No Circúla

In an effort to reduce the number of cars driving in the city, hence reducing air pollution, the city enforces a ban on each vehicle during the week based on the final digit of its license plate, a program known as *"Hoy No Circúla"* (literally, Don't Drive Today, but often translated as Day without a Car). Foreign-registered cars are not exempt from the program. Failure to comply can result in fines of up to $80, or less if you are inclined to negotiate with the police officer who catches you. The ban is enforced 6 A.M.–10 P.M. five days a week. The schedule is as follows.

Monday: No driving if final digit is 5 or 6
Tuesday: No driving if final digit is 7 or 8
Wednesday: No driving if final digit is 3 or 4
Thursday: No driving if final digit is 1 or 2
Friday: No driving if final digit is 9 or 0
Saturday and Sunday: All vehicles may drive.

In the last couple of years the city has enforced a new double ban when the pollution hits certain levels (250 points on the Imeca scale) as an emergency measure, but enforcement has been erratic.

Local cars are required to have a decal bearing either a "0," "1," or "2." A "0" means the car is exempt from any days off, regardless of the license number, because it has passed emissions tests. A "1" requires the car to not circulate on one day, regardless of the conditions; and a "2" means the car cannot circulate on two days of the week during a pollution alert. Foreign-registered cars are not required to have these decals or to pass emissions inspections.

Drive to Survive

The best advice I can offer for how to survive the roads of Mexico City is to remain watchful and alert at all times. Expect anything to happen. Most drivers usually follow the rules of the road (at least in a general sense), but you can't always rely on that. Drivers will pull out at inopportune moments, cut across in front of you to make a turn, drive the wrong way down a one-way street—all the while fully assuming you will get out of their way. Many intersections on side streets don't have stop signs in either direction, and the decision of who goes first seems to be the one who appears more determined. In the many *glorietas* (traffic circles), the standard rule of the person in the circle having right-of-way does not pertain. Expect drivers to come barreling into the circle without even looking to their left to check traffic. Aggressive driving is not a tendency but a basic necessity. For example, the quaint notion of taking turns when two lanes merge is

laughable here, and if you're on a highway entrance ramp in rush hour, you just have to jam the front of your car in and make them give room, or you'll never get in the lane.

Mexico City drivers are aggressive in general, but some are worse than others and bear watching out for. The *pesero* bus drivers, in particular, are legendary for swinging their green-and-white machines around the streets with great abandon, expecting everyone to get out of their way. Be prepared for taxis to slow down unexpectedly and veer across several lanes to pick up a potential passenger. Perhaps worst of all are the armored cars—high-speed tanks, really—piloted by sunglass-wearing toughs who think that because they are driving money and guns they are free to chug through red lights, make illegal U-turns, and perform all sorts of other lovely stunts.

Officials

If your car has foreign plates, you may attract an inordinate amount of attention from Mexico City's various police forces, particularly the brown-uniformed *tránsito* police—either on foot, in patrol cars, or on venerable, stylish (and sometimes barely functioning) Harley-Davidson motorcycles. If your car is in Mexico legally, the papers are in order, and you haven't broken the law, all will be well. Insist that you have done nothing wrong, and you should be allowed to go on your way.

If you did break the traffic rules in some way, you may find yourself being threatened with going to the *delegación,* the precinct house, if you don't pay a "fine" there and then. How you react to this will depend on your own moral compass, as well as how much of a hurry you are in. Fed up with the perennial corruption of the police, some Mexicans have taken to refusing to pay bribes (known as *la mordida,* "the bite"). Foreign visitors may well wish to take this road also—it's certainly the scrupulous thing to do. And because you are a foreigner, and also because the policeman will not want to bother taking you down to the *delegación,* you may well be let off with just a warning. If you opt to make a quick getaway, you should be able to get away from basic traffic violations with a 50- or 100-peso note ($5–10) or less, depending on your negotiating talent. The option of actually going down to the *delegación* is a several-hour ordeal (trust me, I've gone through it).

More serious than the *tránsitos* are the Policía Fiscal Federal, the Finance Secretariat police, who drive new-model blue pickup trucks and sometimes pull over foreign cars to check that their papers are in order. Again, if the papers are all fine and up-to-date, you'll have no problems whatsoever. If they are not, however, the car will be impounded, and you will go through a lengthy, nightmarish ordeal to get it out again. And don't think about offering *mordidas* to these guys.

A welcome change from all the spooky policemen are the men and women in bright yellow uniforms driving motor scooters around the city, forming part of the new Apoyo Vial road-assistance program. Apoyo Vial takes care of all sorts of traffic and vehicle problems, basically doing most of what traffic police are supposed to do. Don't be surprised if you run across a busy intersection and see Apoyo Vial workers energetically and efficiently directing traffic while a group of *tránsitos* lounge around their patrol car, smoking cigarettes and eyeing the traffic lazily.

Parking

Parking is an entire industry in Mexico City, employing many thousands of men (and occasionally women or children) who watch over certain stretches of sidewalk. As you pull up to park, they will hustle over and wave you into the spot. When you leave, they will again wave you out and expect a small tip in return. This can vary from $.50 for a short stay in a normal area, up to $2–3 for spots near crowded parts of the city or during events. The custom is to merely acknowledge them when you park your car, and then when departing get in, have them guide you out of the spot whistling and waving vigorously with their hand, and then you roll down your window and hand them the coins as you drive off. While they have no particular right over that part of the sidewalk and probably wouldn't do anything if you didn't pay on leaving, the general custom is to pay them. And they will in fact watch out for your car.

The next rung up the parking ladder is the *estacionamiento,* a type of parking lot found all over the city. Pull in, give the attendant your keys in return for a ticket with the time punched on it, and pay (usually $.75–1.50 an hour). Don't leave valuables in the car. The attendant will expect a small tip of a couple of pesos after he drives the car up for you to leave.

Outside crowded clubs, bars, and restaurants, clients frequently leave their cars with a valet for $2–5.

Parking meters, called *parquímetros,* are installed only in a few areas of the city, particularly around the Zona Rosa and Paseo de la Reforma. Should the meter expire, the parking cops will eagerly slap a "boot" onto your wheel, which is costly and time-consuming to have removed.

Car Rentals

You'll find many car rental offices throughout the city and in the airport. Also, many agencies have rental desks in the bigger hotels. The major agencies are generally very expensive compared to U.S. prices. A small car with unlimited mileage will run $50–80 a day, sometimes less if you shop around or have some kind of discount. Major U.S. companies operating in Mexico include **Avis** (branches at the airport, Leibniz 83 near Hotel Camino Real, and Paseo de la Reforma 308, tel. 5588-8888 or 800/707-7700, www.avis.com.mx); **Budget,** (at the airport, tel. 5784-3011 or 5784-3118; Hamburgo 68 in the Zona Rosa, tel. 5533-0451, www.budget.com.mx); and **Dollar** (at the airport, tel. 5208-4313 or 5513-0128; Av. Baja California 111, in Colonia Roma, tel. 5564-6479 or 5564-6489, www.dollar.com.mx).

Some of the best car rental bargains are arranged before you leave home. It's always worth checking for discounts linked to airline mileage clubs and Costco/Price Club cards.

A myriad of local rental agencies offer cars at lower prices than the U.S. agencies. One good agency I've used several times is **Casanova Renta de Automoviles** (Chapultepec 442, right near Metro Sevilla, tel. 5514-0449 or 5207-6007; Patriotismo 735, in Colonia Mixcoac, tel. 5563-7606 or 5598-4814, www.casanovarent.com.mx), offering a no-frills (not even a cigarette lighter!) Nissan Tsuru (a simple four-door sedan) for around $40 a day with 200 kilometers mileage, or $45 with unlimited mileage, or $30 a day for a

smaller Chevy. The agency is used to dealing with foreign renters, and someone who speaks English is always on hand. Another good local agency is **Fresno Rent A Car** (at the airport, tel. 5784-4030 or 5785-3951; Dr. Andrade 246, in the Centro, tel. 5588-3809; Monterrey 324, in the Roma, tel. 5584-2443). There are many more in the yellow pages, and it's worth calling around to compare rates.

Visas and Officialdom

TOURIST PERMITS AND VISAS

Tourist Permits
Citizens of the U.S. or Canada (or of 38 other designated countries in Europe and Latin America, plus Singapore) visiting Mexico solely for tourism are not required to obtain a visa. Instead they must carry validated tourist cards (*forma migratoria turista*, or FMT), which aren't actually cards but slips of paper. Although you can get FMTs at any Mexican consulate, it's not necessary to arrange them before going to Mexico—just show up at the airport or the border, and it will be taken care of with minimal hassle. The tourist card is valid for stays of up to 180 days and must be used within 90 days of issue. Your card becomes invalid once you exit the country—you're supposed to surrender it at the border—even if your 180 days hasn't expired. If you'll be entering and leaving Mexico more than once during your trip, you should request a multiple-entry tourist card, available from Mexican consulates only.

To obtain the FMT you need proof of citizenship—a birth certificate (or certified copy), voter's registration card, certificate of naturalization, or passport. A driver's license doesn't qualify, but it is helpful to back up a birth certificate.

Once you cross the border or land at the airport in Mexico City, your tourist card must be validated by a Mexican immigration officer. You can arrange this at any *migración* office in Mexico (many *municipio* seats have them), but it's accomplished most conveniently at the border crossing itself. At airports you pass through im-

migration, where an officer stamps your paperwork with the date of entry and the number of days you're permitted to stay in Mexico.

In mid-1999, the Mexican government began collecting a 150-peso fee (around $16) from all tourists entering the country. If you fly in, this fee is tacked on to your airfare. If you arrive by land, you can pay this fee at any bank in Mexico. The bank issues a receipt, which you must show when you leave the country.

Before 1991, Mexican regulations required children under the age of 18 crossing the border without one or both parents to carry a notarized letter granting permission from the absent parent or both parents if both were absent. This regulation is no longer in effect, but it's best for unaccompanied minors or minors traveling with only one parent to be prepared for all situations with notarized letters. In cases of divorce, separation, or death, the minor should carry notarized papers documenting the situation.

In reality, minors with tourist cards are rarely asked for these documents. Children under 15 may be included on their parents' tourist card, but this means that neither the child nor the parents can legally exit Mexico without the other.

Tourist Visas
Tourists from countries other than the 40 countries for which no visa is necessary need to obtain tourist visas in advance of arrival in Mexico. If you apply in person at a Mexican consulate, you usually can obtain a tourist visa on the day of application, although for some countries it can

take a couple of weeks. Requirements include a valid passport, a round-trip air ticket to Mexico, three photos, and a visa fee of $29.

Foreign visitors who are legal permanent residents of the U.S. do not need visas to visit Mexico for tourism. A free tourist card can be obtained by presenting your passport and a U.S. residence card to any travel agency or at the airport or border crossing.

Business Travel

Citizens of Mexico's NAFTA (North American Free Trade Agreement) partners, the U.S. and Canada, are not required to obtain a visa to visit Mexico for business purposes. Instead you can receive a free NAFTA business permit (*forma migratoria nafta,* or FMN), which is similar to a tourist card, at the point of entry (border crossing or airport); it's valid for 30 days. At the port of entry (the Mexico City airport if you arrive by air), you must present proof of nationality (a valid passport or original birth certificate, plus a photo identification or voter registration card) and proof that you are traveling for "international business activities," usually interpreted to mean a letter from the company you represent, even if it's your own enterprise.

Those who arrive with the FMN and wish to stay over the authorized period of 30 days must replace their FMN with an FM-3 form at an immigration office in Mexico. The FM-3 is valid for a period of up to one year, for multiple entries, and may be extended. Note that the FMN is not valid for anyone working during their time in Mexico, for either a foreign or Mexican company.

Citizens of non-NAFTA countries who are visiting for business purposes must obtain an FM-3 visa endorsed for business travel, which is valid for one year.

Visitors to Mexico coming as part of human rights delegations, aid workers, or international observers should check with a Mexican embassy about the current regulations.

Overstays

If you overstay your visa and are caught, the usual penalty is a fine of $50 for overstays up to

TOURIST INFORMATION BOOTHS

Aeropuerto Internacional de la Ciudad de México
Llegada Nacional Local 9
tel. 5786-9002
7 A.M.–8:30 P.M. daily

Bellas Artes
Av. Juárez and Angela Peralta
tel. 5518-2799
9 A.M.–6 P.M. daily

Centro
Next to Catedral
9 A.M.–6 P.M. daily

Chapultepec
In front of Anthropology Museum
Paseo de la Reforma
tel. 5286-3850
9 A.M.–6 P.M. Tues.–Sun.

Terminal TAPO
tel. 5784-3077
9 A.M.–6 P.M. daily

Terminal Tasqueña
Door 3
tel. 5336-2321
9 A.M.–6 P.M. daily

Zona Rosa
Paseo de la Reforma and Florencia
tel. 5522-1849
9 A.M.–6 P.M. daily

100 Metros
Terminal de Autobuses del Norte
tel. 5719-1201
9 A.M.–6 P.M. daily

a month. After that the penalties become more severe. It's rare that a Mexican border official asks to see your FMT or visa when you're leaving the country. Your main risk comes if you get into trouble with the police somewhere in Mexico and they ask to see your immigration documents. Having expired papers will only further complicate your situation in such cases, so the best policy is to stay up-to-date in spite of the apparent laxity of enforcement.

Pets

Dogs and cats may be brought into Mexico if each is accompanied by a vaccination certificate that proves the animal has been vaccinated or treated for rabies, hepatitis, pip, and leptospirosis. You'll also need a health certificate issued no more than 72 hours before entry and signed by a registered veterinarian.

Since 1992 the requirement that the health certificate be stamped with a visa at a port of entry or at a Mexican consulate has been repealed. The certificate is still necessary; the visa isn't.

Visitante Rentista and Inmigrante Rentista Visas

FM-3 visas may be issued to foreigners who choose to live in Mexico on a "permanent income" basis. This most often applies to foreigners who decide to retire in Mexico, though it is also used by artists, writers, and other self-employed foreign residents. With this visa you're allowed to import one motor vehicle as well as your household belongings into Mexico tax-free.

The basic requirements for this visa are that applicants must forgo any kind of employment while living in Mexico and must show proof (bank statements) that they have a regular source of foreign-earned income amounting to at least $1,000 per month (plus half that for each dependent over the age of 15; e.g., $1,500 for a couple). A pile of paperwork, including a "letter of good conduct" from the applicant's local police department, must accompany the initial application, along with an immigration tax payment ($60) and various applications fees totaling about $75.

The visa must be renewed annually, but the renewal can be accomplished at any immigration office in Mexico. After five years in Mexico, you have to start over again or move up to the FM-2, or *inmigrante rentista* visa, which has higher income requirements and signifies an intent to stay longer. After five years on an FM-2, an *inmigrante rentista* is eligible to apply for *inmigrado* status, which confers all the rights of citizenship (including employment in Mexico), save the rights to vote and hold public office.

Many foreigners who have retired in Mexico manage to do so on the regular 180-day tourist visa; every six months they dash across the border and return with a new tourist card (issued at the border) on the same day. This method bypasses all the red tape and income requirements of the retirement visa. If you own a home in Mexico, however, some local immigrations officials may interpret the law to mean that you must have an FM-2 or FM-3 visa—not an FMT or tourist visa—to be able to stay in that home for any period of time whatsoever. Although it's clear from a straight reading that Mexico's immigration laws do not require any special visas for home ownership, each immigration district behaves like an individual fiefdom at the mercy of the local immigration chief.

Monthly income requirements for both *rentista* visas are keyed to the Mexican daily minimum wage (400 times minimum wage for the FM-2, 250 times for the FM-3), hence figures may vary according to the current dollar–peso exchange rate.

CUSTOMS

Entering Mexico

Officially, tourists are supposed to bring only those items into Mexico that will be of use during their trip. This means you can bring in practically anything as long as it doesn't appear to be in large enough quantities to qualify for resale.

Technically speaking, you're not supposed to import more than one still camera, one movie camera, and one video camera, and no more than 12 rolls of film or blank videocassettes for each. Anything more is supposed to require permission from a Mexican consulate. In everyday practice, however, Mexican customs officials rarely blink at more film or an extra camera or two. Professional photographers and others who would like to bring more cameras and film into Mexico can apply for dispensation through a Mexican consulate abroad. Regarding audio equipment, you're limited to one CD disc player and one audio cassette player (or combo), two laserdiscs, and up to 20 CDs or recording cassettes. Other per person limitations include one musical instrument, one tent and accompanying camping gear, one set of fishing gear, two tennis rackets, five "toys," and one sailboard.

Other limits are three liters of liquor or wine, two cartons (20 packs) of cigarettes, 25 cigars, or 200 grams of tobacco.

Other than the above, you're permitted to bring in no more than $300 worth of other articles. You will be subject to duty on personal possessions worth more than $300, to a max of $1,000, except for new computer equipment, which is exempt up to $4,000.

Auto Permits

Foreign-registered motor vehicles—cars, trucks, motorcycles, RVs—do not require permits for border-town visits of less than 72 hours. For longer visits, you *must* obtain a temporary vehicle importation permit at the border if you're going anywhere besides Baja California Norte and Sur, Puerto Peñasco, or Golfo de Santa Clara. To receive a permit, you simply drive your vehicle to a Mexican customs office at an official border crossing and present a valid state registration or similar document certifying legal ownership, a driver's license, and a credit card issued outside Mexico. If you're leasing or renting the vehicle, you'll also need a copy of a rental/leasing contract with the owner. If the vehicle belongs to someone else, such as a friend or relative, you must present a notarized letter from the owner giving you permission to take the vehicle into Mexico.

Once the Mexican customs officials have approved your documents, you'll proceed to a Banjército (Banco del Ejército, or Military Bank) office attached to the customs office, where your credit card account will be charged $11 for the permit fee. Once the fee is charged to your credit card or the appropriate bond paid, the permit is issued, and a hologramic sticker is affixed to your front windshield. Make sure the validity period equals that of your tourist card or visa. You may drive back and forth across the border, at any crossing, as many times as you wish until the permit expires.

It's now possible to start the paperwork for car papers at the Banjército website (www.banjercito.com.mx) or at several consulates in the U.S., including Chicago, Dallas, Los Angeles, San Francisco, and Phoenix. Further information on the process (in Spanish, unfortunately) is available at the customs website: www.aduanas.sat.gob.mx.

Always carry your vehicle import permit when driving in Mexico. The permit may be checked at interior immigration checkpoints, and the police may ask to see it during routine checks or stops. Tourists who wish to renew their vehicle permits in Mexico City (only possible if your tourist permit or tourist visa has been extended) need to go to the Hacienda office at the airport.

Returning to the U.S.

Visitors returning to the U.S. from Mexico may have their luggage inspected by U.S. customs officials. The hassle can be minimized by giving brief, straight answers to their questions (e.g., "How long have you been in Mexico?" "Do you have anything to declare?") and by cooperating with their requests to open your luggage, vehicle storage compartments, and anything else they want opened. Sometimes the officers use dogs to sniff luggage and/or vehicles for contraband and illegal aliens.

Nearly 3,000 items—including all handicrafts—made in Mexico are exempt from any U.S. customs duties. Adults over 21 are allowed one liter (33.8 fluid ounces) of alcoholic beverages and 200 cigarettes (or 100 cigars) per person. Note that Cuban cigars may not be imported into the U.S., and customs will confiscate the cigars if discovered. An estimated 9 out of 10 cigars sold as Cubans in Mexico are fake anyway, so it's not worth the hassle. All other purchases or gifts up to a total value of

$400 within any 31-day period can be brought into the U.S. duty-free.

The following fruits and vegetables cannot be brought into the U.S. from Mexico: oranges, grapefruits, mangoes, avocados (unless the pit is removed), and potatoes (including yams and sweet potatoes). All other fruits are permitted (including bananas, dates, pineapples, cactus fruits, grapes, and berries of all types).

Other prohibited plant materials are straw (including packing materials and items stuffed with straw), hay, unprocessed cotton, sugarcane, and any plants in soil (this includes houseplants).

Animals and animal products that cannot be imported include wild and domesticated birds (including poultry, unless cooked), pork or pork products (including sausage, ham, and other cured pork), and eggs. Beef, mutton, venison, and other meats are permitted at up to 50 pounds per person.

Returning to Canada

Duty-frees include 200 cigarettes (or 50 cigars or 250 grams of tobacco) and 1.14 liters of booze. Exemptions run from C$20 to C$500 depending on how long you've been outside Canada. To reach the maximum exemption of C$500, you must be gone at least one week. Because Canada is also signatory to NAFTA, customs legalities will change over the next decade.

Returning to the U.K.

Duty-frees include 200 cigarettes (or 50 cigars or 250 grams of tobacco) and one liter of beverage with an alcoholic content of over 22 percent or two liters under 22 percent, plus two liters of wine. The total exemption runs £136.

Returning to Australia

Duty-frees include 200 cigarettes (or 250 grams of tobacco, including cigars) and one liter of alcohol. The total exemption runs $400.

Customs Regulations

Customs regulations can change at any time, so if you want to verify the regulations on a purchase before risking duties or confiscation at the border, check with a consulate in Mexico before crossing,

or look on the customs website (in Spanish): www.aduanas.sat.gob.mx.

As NAFTA proceeds with scheduled decreases in trade tariffs among the U.S., Canada, and Mexico, expect a steady loosening of customs regulations in all directions until 2009, when all import tariffs are supposed to be erased.

CONDUCT AND ETIQUETTE

Time and Appointments

Of the many stereotypes of Mexican culture, the one about the Mexican sense of time being highly flexible is probably the most accurate. The reasons are too numerous and complex for the context of this book; read *The Labyrinth of Solitude*, by Octavio Paz, for a glimpse of an explanation. That said, it's important to realize that the so-called *mañana* attitude is nothing more than a generalization; in many cases Mexican individuals are every bit as punctual as Americans, Canadians, or northern Europeans—especially when it comes to doing business with them.

If you make an appointment with a Mexican for dinner, a party, or other social engagement, the actual meeting time may end up being an hour or two later than actually scheduled. As with business engagements, if the person involved has dealt frequently with Americans, Canadians, or northern Europeans, this might not always be the case. But even then, 30 minutes late is considered actually more polite than arriving at the indicated hour. Also, Mexicans will typically accept an invitation rather than decline, even if they don't plan to attend the scheduled event. Within the Mexican social context, it is usually worse to refuse an invitation than not to show up. To avoid disappointment, prepare yourself for any of these scenarios.

When hiring any sort of guide, you can expect a modicum of punctuality—Mexicans in the tourist industry usually adapt themselves to the expectations of American and European tourists.

La "Hora" de la Comida

The stereotypical siesta, where everyone goes off to sleep for a couple of hours in the afternoon, is fast becoming a thing of the past throughout Mexico. Nevertheless, a vestige of the siesta is preserved in the operating hours for offices and small businesses, which are typically closed 2–4 P.M. or 3–5 P.M. The first hour is reserved for *comida*, the midday meal, while the second hour is for relaxing or taking care of personal business. While to Americans and Canadians two hours may seem like a long lunch hour, the fact is that Mexican offices and businesses generally stay open much later than in the U.S. or Canada, until 7 or 8 P.M.

No matter what hours are posted for small businesses, the actual opening and closing times may vary with the whims of the proprietors. This is also true for tourist information offices. Banks usually follow their posted hours to the minute.

Terms of Address

Mexicans frequently use titles of respect when addressing one another. At a minimum, *"señor"* will do for men, *"señora"* for married women, and *"señorita"* for unmarried women or girls.

Professional titles can also be used for variety and to show additional respect. *Maestro* (master) or *maestra* (mistress) are common and can be used to address skilled workers (cobblers, auto mechanics, seamstresses, etc.) and any teacher except those at secondary schools and colleges or universities, who are *profesores* (men) or *profesoras* (women).

College graduates are *licenciado* (men) or *licenciada* (women), while doctors are *doctor* or *doctora*. Some other professional titles include *arquitecto* (architect), *abogado* (attorney), *ingeniero* (engineer), and *químico* (chemist).

Body Language

Mexicans tend to use their arms and hands more during verbal communication than do their American, Canadian, or northern European counterparts. Learning to read the more common gestures can greatly enhance your comprehension of everyday conversations, even when you don't understand every word being spoken.

One of the more confusing gestures for Amer-

icans and Canadians is the way Mexicans beckon to other people by holding the hand out, palm down, and waving in a downward motion. Holding the palm upward and crooking the fingers toward the body—the typical American or Canadian gesture for "come here"—is a vaguely obscene gesture in Mexico.

Extending the thumb and forefinger from a closed hand and holding them about a half-inch apart means "a little bit" in the U.S. and Canada, but in Mexico, it usually means "just a moment" or "wait a minute" (often accompanied by the utterance *"momentito"*). The wagging of an upright forefinger means "No" or "Don't do that."

Mexicans commonly greet one another with handshakes, which are used between the sexes and among children and adults—in fact, with everybody. Mexican males who are friends will sometimes greet one another with a handshake, followed by an *abrazo* (embrace), and completed with another handshake, and urban women may kiss one another on the cheek. Foreigners should stick to the handshake until they establish more intimate relationships. Handshakes are also used upon parting and saying farewell.

Dress

Mexicans are relatively tolerant of the way visitors dress. Nonetheless, invisible lines exist that—out of respect for Mexican custom—shouldn't be crossed. In Mexico City almost no one ever wears shorts; although this is mainly because of the cool year-round climate, it also demonstrates that *capitalinos* tend to be more formal in dress than Mexicans in many other cities, especially compared with coastal cities.

Upon entering a church or chapel in Mexico, men are expected to remove their hats. Many Mexican males will also remove their hats when passing in front of a church. More tradition-minded Mexican women will cover their heads when inside a church, but younger women usually don't, and foreign females aren't expected to. Shorts, sleeveless shirts/blouses, sandals, or bare feet are considered improper dress for both men and women in churches, even for brief sightseeing visits.

Money

CURRENCY

The unit of exchange in Mexico is the peso, which comes in paper denominations of 20, 50, 100, 200, and 500. Coins are available in denominations of 5, 10, 20, and 50 centavos, and 1, 2, 5, 10, and 20 pesos.

Prices

The N$ symbol (standing for "new pesos" to differentiate from pre-1993 "old pesos") is sometimes, though rarely these days, used for indicating peso prices. Much more common now is the $ symbol for pesos. While it's highly unlikely you'll ever confuse dollar and peso prices because of the differing values, you should ask when in doubt. Because dollar prices tend to fluctuate less, in this book, I refer to all prices in U.S. dollar terms.

Because coins smaller than one peso are often scarce, payments are sometimes rounded off to the nearest peso or at least to the nearest 50 centavos. For a marked price of $8.55, for example, you actually have to pay only $8.50; for a $8.75 price you may have to pay $9. Any denomination over $50 is difficult to break, so change them at every opportunity to secure a good supply of smaller notes and coins.

Dollars vs. Pesos

A few commercial establishments in Mexico City will take U.S. dollars as well as pesos. Paying with pesos, however, usually means a better deal when the price is fixed in pesos; if you pay in dollars for a purchase quoted in pesos, the vendor can determine the exchange rate. If a bottle of boutique tequila, for example, is marked at $280, and the bank rate is $10 per dollar, you'll pay $28 for the tequila with pesos changed at the bank. However, if you ask to pay in dollars, the vendor may charge $30.

Devaluation

The Mexican peso has had a tumultuous history in the past 30 years, but since 1998, the currency has been remarkably stable, even gaining

value at times, despite floating freely in the international market. In 2000 it was one of the only currencies in the world to gain value against the U.S. dollar, although it has subsequently slid somewhat, even though the dollar itself has lost value against many other currencies. But the combination of a floating currency, restrained spending policies, and a strong, independent central bank have combined to avoid dramatic plunges in the currency's value. At last report, the peso was around 11.5 to the dollar.

CHANGING MONEY

In general, though changing money is not at all difficult in Mexico City, the most hassle-free way to get pesos is to use an ATM card, which are widely accepted in Mexican banks and invariably offer the best and most up-to-the-minute exchange rate. Almost all Mexican banks are now owned by foreign banks, meaning the ATMs are all connected to most international networks.

Banks

Banks that handle foreign exchange generally accept a wide range of foreign currencies, including the euro, English pounds, Japanese yen, and Canadian dollars. Either cash or traveler's checks are accepted, though the latter usually guarantee a slightly better exchange rate. The main drawbacks with banks are the long lines and short hours—9 A.M.–3 P.M. Mon.–Fri., but the foreign-exchange service usually closes about noon–12:30 P.M. With privatization, some banks are extending their hours.

Casas de Cambio

The second-best exchange rate, generally speaking, is found at the *casa de cambio,* or private money-changing office. The *casa de cambio* (also called *servicio de cambio*) either knocks a few centavos off the going bank rate or charges a percentage commission. It pays to shop around for the best *casa de cambio* rates, as some places charge considerably more than others. The rates are usually posted; *compra,* always the lower figure, refers to the buying rate (how many pesos you'll receive per dollar or other foreign currency), while *vende* is the selling rate (how many pesos you must pay to receive a dollar or other unit of foreign currency). As with banks, the difference between the buying and selling rates is the moneychanger's profit, unless it charges a commission on top of it.

Moneychangers are usually open much later than banks; some even work evening hours, which makes them immeasurably more convenient than banks. U.S. dollar currency is generally preferred, though many *casas* will also accept Canadian dollars. However, Canadians should always keep a reserve supply of U.S. dollars for instances where Canadian currency isn't accepted. Moneychangers usually accept traveler's checks.

One of the better *casas de cambio* in the **Centro is Casa de Cambio Plus** (opposite the south side of the Alameda on Av. Juárez, 9 A.M.–7 P.M. Mon.–Fri., 9:30 A.M.–1:30 P.M. Sat.). Others in the Centro Histórico include **Casa de Cambio Tiber** (Madero 27, 9 A.M.–5 P.M. Mon.–Fri., 10 A.M.–2:30 P.M. Sat.) and **Casa de Cambio Velasco** (Gante 12B, 9 A.M.–5 P.M. Mon.–Fri., 10 A.M.–2 P.M. Sat.).

The bank exchange booths at the Mexico City airport offer regular bank rates and are open long hours (some stay open 24 hours), so the airport is a good place to change some money on arrival. You'll also find ATMs in the airport.

Credit Cards, Debit Cards, and ATM Cards

Plastic money (primarily Visa and MasterCard, and to a lesser extent, American Express) is widely accepted at large hotels, restaurants catering to tourists or businesspeople, car rentals (you can't rent a car without a credit card), and shops in tourist centers. Usually card displays at the cash register or on the door will announce that *tarjetas de crédito* (credit cards) are accepted. If in doubt, flash one and ask *"¿Se aceptan tarjetas de crédito?"* (Do you accept credit cards?) or simply *"¿Está bien?"* (Is it OK?). A reference to *efectivo*

means cash. Many shops and some hotels, however, add a 3 to 6 percent surcharge to bills paid with a card.

Cash advances on credit card accounts—a very useful service for emergencies—are available at Mexican banks. Keep in mind, however, that most credit card companies charge a much higher interest rate for cash advances.

Many banks now accept MasterCard or Visa debit cards ("cash" or "check" cards), as well as ATM cards on the Plus or Cirrus systems. Using such cards to obtain pesos from ATMs in Mexico is a much more convenient way to carry travel funds than using traveler's checks. Some banks that issue ATM cards charge transaction fees for use of another bank's ATMs; check with your bank to see how much they are. Most Mexican banks now charge nominal fees for withdrawing cash from their ATMs by using a card from another bank.

Travelers Checks

If you decide to bring travelers checks, **American Express** is the most recognized type you could carry. Should you lose your Amex checks, or should you need to buy more, go to the American Express office (Paseo de la Reforma 350, at Lancaster, tel. 5207-7204 or 5207-7049, 9 A.M.–6 P.M. Mon.–Fri., 9 A.M.–1 P.M. Sat.). Amex maintains a 24-hour hotline, tel. 5326-3625, for reporting lost or stolen checks or credit cards.

MONEY MANAGEMENT
Estimating Costs

Inflation in Mexico is running under 10 percent per annum, and barring major international financial crisis, it will likely stay that way. Nevertheless, I've used dollar prices in this book on the belief that this will fluctuate less. This doesn't mean that there won't be any increase in prices by the time you arrive. A couple of phone calls to hotels for price quotes should give you an idea how much rates have increased, if at all; this difference can be applied as a percentage to all other prices for a rough estimate of costs.

Students and seniors can frequently obtain discounts on the admission to many tourist sites—be sure to ask, and have your credential in hand.

Tipping
A tip of 10 to 15 percent is customary at restaurants with table service unless a service charge is added to the bill. Luggage handling at hotels or airports warrants a tip of $0.50–1, or the equivalent in pesos, per bag. A few hotels maintain a no-tipping policy; details will be posted in your room. The tipping of chambermaids is optional according to Mexican custom—some guests tip, and some don't. Remember that these folks typically earn minimum wage; even a small tip may mean a lot to them.

Taxes
An *impuesta al valor agregado* (IVA, or value-added tax) of 15 percent is tacked onto all goods and services, including hotel and restaurant bills as well as international phone calls. Although by American standards this may seem high, this tax hike brings Mexico more in line with other countries that employ such value-added taxes.

Hotels add a further 2 percent lodging tax. Some hotel rate quotes include taxes, but to make sure, you might ask *"¿Se incluyen los impuestos?"* (Are taxes included?).

Bank Accounts
For long-term stays in Mexico—six months or more—visitors might consider opening a Mexican bank account. Now that peso deflation has been virtually halted, a peso account seems quite safe. While the 1994–1995 devaluation devastated the banking system, no depositors ever lost their savings. Essentially all Mexican banks are now owned by foreign companies, and many offer dollar- and even euro-denominated accounts now.

Tips for Travelers

STUDYING IN MEXICO
Spanish Language and Mexican Culture
Mexico City is an excellent place to study Spanish. In the first place, the level of spoken Spanish in the city is among the highest in the country, and just as important, it's a very friendly and open city, where Mexicans generally don't hesitate to speak to strangers, whatever their nationality. This isn't necessarily the case in other state capitals in Mexico.

Since 1921, the Universidad Nacional Autónoma de México (UNAM) has operated the Centro de Enseñanza para Extranjeros (CEPE), a special division of the university dedicated to teaching Mexican history, culture, and language. The programs enjoy a very good reputation and are divided among six departments: Spanish, Art History, History, Social Sciences, Literature, and Chicano Studies. The popular Spanish courses generally run three hours per day. Sessions run year round, although the summer session, which combines language with cultural and historical studies, is the most intensive. A sampling of courses offered in the summer session include Mexican Art, Popular Culture in Xochimilco, Traditional Medicine in Xochimilco, Traditional Mexican Dance, 20th-Century Mexican Theater, History of Modern and Contemporary Mexico, History of Science in Mexico, Myth and Rationality in Contemporary Mexico, Mexican Literature, Contemporary Mexican Women Writers, Images of Mexico through Literary Texts, Chicano-Latino Community in the United States.

UNAM also runs special training programs for teachers of Spanish as a Second Language (SSL). For all courses, tuition is reasonable, and CEPE can arrange housing either with local families or in dormitories. For further information contact CEPE-México (Apartado Postal 70–391, Ciudad Universitaria, 04510 México D.F, tel. 5622-2470, fax 5616-2672, www.cepe.unam.mx). UNAM/CEPE also has a branch in Taxco

(CEPE-Taxco, Ex-Hacienda El Chorrillo, Apartado Postal 70, 40200 Taxco, Gro., México, tel./fax 762/622-0124).

Universidad La Salle (Benjamin Franklin 65, Colonia Condesa, tel. 5728-0500, www.ulsa.edu.mx) offers good, inexpensive Spanish group classes and is closer to the center of the city than UNAM.

The city of Cuernavaca, an hour's drive south of Mexico City, is a very popular place for foreigners to take intensive Spanish courses for several weeks. (For more information, see the *Excursions* chapter.)

EMPLOYMENT IN MEXICO CITY

A great many foreigners find themselves looking for ways to get by in Mexico City for a couple of months or a couple of years. Because it is one of the principal capitals of the Americas, and because it is uniquely linked to the United States economy through NAFTA, Mexico City is brimming with business activity. Apart from the ideas mentioned below, would-be residents could try contacting their embassy and asking if they have information on work opportunities in Mexico. The U.S. Chamber of Commerce (Lucerna 78, near Paseo de la Reforma, tel. 5724-3800, www.amcham.com.mx) maintains some information on jobs with U.S. companies in Mexico.

Teaching English

The most popular way of making cash for footloose visitors is teaching English at one of the literally hundreds of English schools in Mexico City. Hours are flexible, and pay is usually around $7–10 an hour. The trick is to put together enough hours to make a decent living and to make sure the school pays you regularly (some are notoriously shifty in this regard). A livable, though hardly luxurious, wage is $800–1,000 a month.

While some schools require a TEFL (Teaching English as a Foreign Language) certificate, most do not. Schools generally pay certified teachers better, and often they are able to arrange private classes on the side.

Angloamericano (tel. 5658-6700 or 5659-2148, www.angloamericano.com.mx), which has schools in Polanco, Coyoacán, and Satélite, has received decent reviews from foreign teachers. Apart from English, it sometimes needs teachers for French, German, and Italian.

Harmon Hall (tel. 5211-2020, www.harmonhall.com) has schools all over the city (in fact, all over the country) and is always looking for teachers, but its pay scale is among the lowest.

To find others, just open the yellow pages and start calling around. Beware that at some of the smaller schools, payment can sometimes be unreliable.

Journalism

As the number-one media center in Latin America, Mexico City can be an excellent place to get a start as a reporter. The favored place for inexperienced writers to get a foot in the door used to be the *News*, an English-language daily that has recently closed its doors (to the nostalgic chagrin of many a veteran, myself included). Nowadays the only major publication in English is the *Herald* (www.mexiconews.com.mx), published jointly by *El Universal* and the *Miami Herald*, although *Business Mexico, Latin Trade, Latin Finance*, and many other outlets are still frequently on the lookout for freelance writers, especially if they can cover business news.

Mexican newspapers are often in the market for part-time translators. If your Spanish is good (and it better be if you want to translate!), pick up copies of all the major newspapers and start calling around.

APARTMENTS

Compared to large cities in Europe and America, housing in Mexico City is reasonable in price. Wealthier residents tend to live in Polanco and farther west along Paseo de la Reforma, in the Bosques and Lomas neighborhoods. San Ángel and Coyoacán are also more upscale, though less so than the foregoing, while Roma and Condesa are favored by younger expatriates who can afford the steadily rising rents. Del Valle, south of Roma

EMBASSIES IN MEXICO CITY

Argentina
Blvd. M. Avila Camacho 1, 7th floor
Lomas de Chapultepec
tel. 5520-9430 or 5520-9431

Australia
Rubén Dario 55
Polanco
tel. 5531-5225
www.mexico.embassy.gov.au

Austria
Sierra Tarahumara 420
Lomas de Chapultepec
tel. 5251-9799 or 5251-1606
www.embajadadeaustria.com.mx

Belgium
A Musset 41
Polanco
tel. 5280-0758 or 5280-1133

Belize
Bernardo de Gálvez 215
Lomas de Chapultepec
tel. 5520-1346 or 5520-1274

Bolivia
Insurgentes Sur 263, 6th floor
Roma
tel. 5564-5415 or 5264-6169

Brazil
Lope de Armendariz 130
Lomas de Virreyes
tel. 5202-7500

Canada
Schiller 529
Polanco
tel. 5724-7900
www.dfait-maeci.gc.ca/mexico-city

Chile
Andres Bello 10, 18th floor
Polanco
tel. 5280-9682 or 5280-9689

Colombia
Paseo de la Reforma 379
Lomas de Chapultepec
tel. 5525-0277

Costa Rica
Río Po 113
Cuauhtémoc
tel. 5525-7764 or 5525-7765

Cuba
Av. Presidente Masaryk 554
Polanco
tel. 5280-8039
www.embacuba.com.mx

Denmark
Tres Picos 43
Lomas de Chapultepec
tel. 5255-4145
www.danmex.org

Ecuador
Tennyson 217
Polanco
tel. 5545-6013 or 5250-4999

El Salvador
Temistocles 88
Polanco
tel. 5281-5723

Finland
Montes Pelvoux 111
Polanco
tel. 5540-6063
www.finlandia.org.mx

France
Campos Eliseos 339
Polanco
tel. 5282-9700 or 5282-9840
www.francia.org.mx

Germany
Lord Byron 737
Polanco
tel. 5283-2200
www.embajada-alemana.org.mx

Greece
Sierra Gorda 505
Lomas de Chapultepec
tel. 5520-2077 or 5202-2310

Guatemala
Av. Explanada 1025
Lomas de Chapultepec
tel. 5520-9249 or 5540-7520

Honduras
A. Reyes 220
Hipódromo Condesa
tel. 5211-5250 or 5515-6689

India
Musset 325
Polanco
tel. 5531-1002 or 5531-1085

Indonesia
Julio Verne 27
Polanco
tel. 5280-5748 or 5280-6863

Israel
Sierra Madre 215
Lomas de Chapultepec
tel. 5201-1500 or 5201-1555

Italy
Paseo de las Palmas 1994
Lomas de Chapultepec
tel. 5596-3655
www.embitalia.org.mx

Jamaica
Schiller 326, 8th floor
Polanco
tel. 5250-6804

Japan
Reforma 395
Cuauhtémoc
tel. 5514-5459
www.embjapon.com.mx

Netherlands
Vasco de Quiroga 3000
Santa Fe
tel. 5258-9921

New Zealand
Jaime Balmes 8
Polanco
tel. 5283-9460

Nicaragua
Prado Norte 470
Lomas de Chapultepec
tel. 5540-5625

Norway
Virreyes 1460
Lomas de Chapultepec
tel. 5540-3486 or 5540-3487

Panama
Horacio 1501
Polanco
tel. 5580-5648 or 5557-2793

Paraguay
Homero 415, 2nd floor
Polanco
tel. 5545-0405 or 5545-0403

Peru
Paseo de la Reforma 2601
Lomas de Reforma
tel. 5259-0239 or 5570-2443

Philippines
Paseo de las Palmas 1950
Polanco
tel. 5251-9760

Portugal
Alpes 1370
Lomas de Chapultepec
tel. 5520-7897

República Dominicana
Guatemala 84
Centro
tel. 5522-7409

(continued on next page)

Know Mexico City

EMBASSIES IN MEXICO CITY (cont'd)

Romania
Sófocles 311
Los Morales
tel. 5280-0197 or 5280-0447

Serbia Montenegro
Av. Montañas Rocallosas 515 Ote.
Lomas de Chapultepec
tel. 5259-1332 or 5520-2523

Slovac Republic
Julio Verne 35
Polanco
tel. 5280-6544 or 5280-6451

South Africa
Andres Bello 10
Polanco
Tel. 5282-9261 or 5282-9262

Spain
Galileo 114
Polanco
tel. 5282-2974 or 5282-2982

Sweden
Paseo de las Palmas 1375
Lomas de Chapultepec
tel. 5540-6393

Switzerland
Paseo de las Palmas 405, 11th floor
Lomas de Chapultepec
tel. 5520-3003

Turkey
Monte Libano 885
Palmas
tel. 5282-5043

United Kingdom
Río Lerma 71
Cuauhtémoc
tel. 5207-2449
www.embajadabritanica.com.mx

United Nations
Av. Presidente Masaryk 29
Polanco
tel. 5250-1231

United States
Reforma 305
Cuauhtémoc
tel. 5080-2000
www.usembassy-mexico.gov

Uruguay
Hegel 149, 1st floor
Polanco
tel. 5254-1163 or 5531-0880

Venezuela
Schiller 326
Polanco
tel. 5203-4233 or 5203-4435

along Insurgentes, is also a quiet residential neighborhood with many apartment buildings. Colonia Cuauhtémoc, north of Paseo de la Reforma, has both inexpensive and higher-end apartments. Real penny-pinchers (or those fascinated with relentless urbanity) might consider checking out the many old, lovely buildings in the Centro.

Rents for a midrange, two-bedroom apartment in the Condesa/Roma/Cuauhtémoc areas run around $700–1,400 a month, while Polanco apartments easily run $2,000–3,000. In the Centro, decent places can be found for as low as $300–700.

Word of mouth is the best way to find a good apartment, but failing that, the ads in *Segunda Mano* (a weekly classifieds publication) will give you plenty of places to start. The daily ads in *El Universal* are also extensive. Another good technique is to choose a neighborhood you want to live in and prowl the streets looking for *se renta* signs on buildings.

Red Tape

Most apartment contracts in Mexico City are fairly standard affairs, usually just a template bought at a local stationery store with the names, dates, and numbers filled in. Contracts usually extend by the year, although most landlords are amenable to shortening it if you notify them well in advance, and especially if you arrange for someone to take your place. If not, you may lose your deposit.

Landlords commonly request first and last months' rent, as well as an unusual requirement: a *fiador,* someone who owns property in Mexico City who is willing to sign a paper making themselves responsible for the rent if you do not pay.

Needless to say, many foreigners have a hard time finding a *fiador.* The options are twofold. The best plan is to try to convince the landlord that you are a responsible person, perhaps offering to pay a couple of months ahead of time. Long used to Mexican tenants who go for months without paying (and who are very difficult to evict under Mexican law), landlords are often very well disposed toward potential non-Mexican tenants, as they have a reputation for paying on time. Thus they may sometimes waive the *fiador* requirement.

However, if the landlord is rigid, or if a real estate company (rather than an individual) is managing the apartment, the only option if you don't have a *fiador* is to buy a *fianza,* or a bond, from a local bank, which serves as your guarantee. The amount of the bond depends on the apartment rent but will run at least a few hundred dollars.

Utilities

Usually water is included in the rent, while tenants pay for electricity. This minimal fee can be paid at local banks if paid before the due date but only at the offices of Luz y Fuerza del Centro if you're late. It can take several days to reconnect after being cut off.

Water heaters and stoves invariably run on gas, which is either supplied from a tank attached to your building (in which case you will be charged each month) or sold in 30-kilo tanks ($14) to individual tenants from gas trucks that circulate a couple of days each week.

If a phone line is already installed, you will often have to buy it from the previous tenant or the landlord (usually $100–200). If the apartment has no line, you'll have to go down to the local TelMex office, wait in line for an hour or two, and pay $150 to get a new personal telephone line or $300 for a commercial telephone line. Company workers will usually come to your apartment one or two weeks later to install the line. While TelMex has a monopoly on local service, clients may choose among several long-distance providers.

Health and Safety

By and large, Mexico City is a healthy place. Sanitation standards, particularly in the areas most tourists are likely to visit, are relatively high compared to many other parts of Latin America.

FOOD AND WATER

Visitors who use common sense will probably never come down with food- or water-related illnesses while traveling in and around Mexico City. The first rule is not to overdo it during the first few days of your trip—eat and drink with moderation. Shoveling down huge amounts of tasty but often heavy Mexican foods along with pitchers of margaritas or strong Mexican beer is liable to make anyone sick from pure overindulgence. If you're not used to the spices and different ways of cooking, it's best to ingest small amounts at first.

Second, take it easy with foods offered by street vendors, because this is where you're most likely to suffer from unsanitary conditions. Eat

Know Mexico City

only foods that have been thoroughly cooked and are served either stove-hot or refrigerator-cold. Many visitors eat street food without any problems whatsoever, but it pays to be cautious, especially if it's your first time in Mexico. One rule of thumb is to eat street food only where you see a lot of other clients, which is a good indication of quality and also means there's a lot of turnover, so the food isn't sitting around a long time. Squeezing lots of the ever-present limes over food also helps kill germs.

Hotels and restaurants serve only purified drinking water and ice, so there's no need to ask for mineral water or to refuse ice. Tap water, however, should not be consumed except in hotels that have a water-purification system—if so, you'll be informed by a notice over the washbasin in your room. Just about every grocery or convenience store sells bottled purified water *(agua purificada)*. Water-purification tablets, iodine crystals, water filters, and the like aren't necessary for Mexico travel unless you plan on extensive camping.

Turista

People who've never traveled to a foreign country may undergo a period of adjustment to the new gastrointestinal flora that comes with new territory. There's really no way to avoid the differences wrought by sheer distances. Unfortunately, the adjustment is sometimes unpleasant.

Mexican doctors call gastrointestinal upset of this sort *turista* because it affects tourists but not the local population. The usual symptoms of *turista*—also known by the gringo tags "Montezuma's Revenge" and "Aztec Two-Step"—are nausea and diarrhea, sometimes with stomach cramps and a low fever. Again, eating and drinking in moderation will help prevent the worst of the symptoms, which rarely persist for more than a day or two. And if it's any consolation, Mexicans often get sick the first time they go abroad too.

Some Mexico travelers swear by a preventive regimen of Pepto-Bismol, begun the day before arrival in the country. Opinions vary as to how much of the pink stuff is necessary to ward off or

tame the evil flora, but a person probably shouldn't exceed the recommended daily dose. Taper off over the second week, until you stop using it altogether.

If you come down with a case of *turista*, the best thing to do is drink plenty of fluids. Adults should drink at least three quarts or liters a day, a child under 37 kilograms at least a liter a day. Lay off tea, coffee, milk, fruit juices, and booze. Eat only bland foods—nothing spicy, fatty, or fried—and take it easy. Pepto-Bismol or similar pectin-based remedies usually help. Some people like to mask the symptoms with a strong over-the-counter medication such as Imodium AD (loperamide is the active ingredient), but though this can be very effective, it isn't a cure. Only time will cure traveler's diarrhea.

If the symptoms are unusually severe (especially if there's blood in the stools) or persist for more than one or two days, see a doctor. It could be a case of amoebic or bacterial dysentery. Most hotels can arrange a doctor's visit, or you can contact a Mexican tourist office or your consulate for recommendations.

SUNBURN AND DEHYDRATION

Sunburn probably afflicts more Mexico visitors than all other illnesses and injuries combined. This might sound ridiculous. But trust me, the sunlight can be very strong at the Valle de México's generally high elevation, especially if you go to high mountain areas and have fair skin. For outdoor forays, sun protection is a must, whatever the activity. The longer you're in the sun, the more protection you'll need.

A hat, sunglasses, and plenty of sunscreen or sunblock make a good start. Bring along a sunscreen with a sun protection factor (SPF) of at least 25, even if you don't plan on using it all the time. Apply it to *all* exposed parts of your body—don't forget the hands, top of the feet, and neck. Men should remember to cover thinned-out or bald areas on the scalp. Sunscreen must be reapplied after swimming or periods of heavy perspiration.

It's also important to drink plenty of water and/or nonalcoholic, noncaffeinated fluids to avoid dehydration. Alcohol and caffeine—including the caffeine in iced tea and colas—only increase your potential for dehydration. Symptoms of dehydration include darker-than-usual urine or inability to urinate, flushed face, profuse sweating or an unusual lack thereof, and sometimes a headache, dizziness, and general feeling of malaise. Extreme cases of dehydration can lead to heat exhaustion or even heatstroke, in which the victim may become delirious and/or convulse. If either condition is suspected, get the victim out of the sun immediately, cover with a wet sheet or towel, and administer a rehydration fluid that replaces lost water and salts. If you can get the victim to a doctor, all the better—heatstroke can be very serious.

ALTITUDE SICKNESS

Some visitors who fly into 2,240-meter Mexico City airport experience mild altitude sickness shortly after arrival. Symptoms include headache, shaky stomach, breathlessness, and general malaise. The body needs time to acclimate to the change in barometric pressure and lesser amounts of oxygen. Those afflicted need to take it easy for a while: no running, no climbing pyramids, no alcohol. The city's polluted air may exacerbate symptoms. Those with medical problems relating to the heart or lungs should probably consult with a doctor before even considering a trip to Mexico's higher climes. Some people find it takes them two or three days to fully adjust to the elevation when flying in from places at or near sea level.

Altitude sickness strikes some people at elevations as low as 1,600 meters. Others don't feel a thing until they reach much higher elevations. Above 3,000 meters, acute mountain sickness (AMS) can occur—headache, loss of appetite, lethargy, shortness of breath, and insomnia are all pronounced. You're not likely to experience AMS unless you climb the higher volcanoes outside Mexico City. If you think you've been stricken, descending at least

300–600 meters should result in immediate relief. You can usually avoid AMS with a slow, step-by-step ascent. The climber's adage is to sleep no more than 300 meters higher than the place you slept the night before.

MEDICAL ASSISTANCE

The quality of basic medical treatment, including dentistry, is relatively high in Mexico City; ask at a tourist office or at your embassy for recommendations. Large hotels usually have a doctor on staff or a list of recommended physicians in the neighborhood. Sectur's 24-hour hotline, tel. 5250-0123, may also be able to offer suggestions. Polanco is the best area for private medical clinics, where a consultation will run $25–60. Another good option is to call the Hospital ABC, which has a referral service for quality doctors of different specializations.

An ambulance may be summoned via Cruz Roja (Red Cross) by dialing tel. 065 or 5557-5757.

Hospitals

Hospital American British Cowdray (ABC) (Calle Sur 136, No. 116, tel. 5230-8000 or 5230-8161, www.abchospital.com), at the corner of Avenida Observatorio, south of Bosque de Chapultepec in Colonia Las Américas, is considered the best hospital in the city.

Another well-regarded hospital is **Hospital Español** (Ejército Nacional 613, in Polanco, tel. 5255-9700 for ambulances and 5255-9600 general information, www.hespanol.com).

Emergency Evacuation

Over the years, several American companies have offered emergency 24-hour airlift service (accompanied by licensed physicians and nurses) from anywhere in Mexico to U.S. hospitals. Few have lasted more than a year or two. Two of the longer-running operations are **Air Evac Services, Inc.** (2630 Sky Harbor Blvd., Phoenix, AZ 85034, U.S.A., toll-free in the U.S. and Canada tel. 800/421-6111, www.airevac.com) and **Advanced Aeromedical Air Ambulance**

Service (P.O. Box 5726, Virginia Beach, VA 23471 U.S.A., tel. 757/481-1590 or toll-free in the U.S. and Canada 800/346-3556, http://aeromedic.com).

SAFETY CONCERNS

Until relatively recently, Mexico City enjoyed a reputation for being one of the safest large cities in the Americas, if not the world. The image suffered a reversal after the economic crisis of 1994–1995, when the peso plummeted, unemployment soared, and some urban residents began resorting to robbery as a way to make up income shortfalls—or to lash out at the crisis, if you take the psychological explanation. In both cases, before and after 1994–1995, the image was exaggerated. Mexico City was never as free from crime as, for example, Tokyo or Zurich, and nowadays it's nowhere near as bad as Nairobi or Bogotá, not to mention most large metropolitan areas in the United States.

To put things into perspective, FBI statistics indicate that Washington, DC by comparison has a crime rate 230 percent above Mexico City's, while Los Angeles crime indices are 94 percent higher, New York's 63 percent higher, and Detroit's 292 percent higher. On the other hand, there is general agreement that crime increased substantially (most experts estimate a 35 percent increase) since the 1994–1995 economic crisis and has improved marginally if at all since the new opposition-led administrations after 1997.

According to Mayor Andrés Manuel López Obrador, car thefts have declined from 155 a day on average in 1995–1997 to 95 on average in 2000–2004, while murders fell from 2.9 a day to 2.0 a day over the same period. Reported crimes (always a dodgy statistic, but somewhat revealing nonetheless) fell 6.2 percent in 2004 from the previous year.

But the sad truth is, Mexico City residents go about their daily lives with a sense of insecurity, and they don't have much confidence in the po-

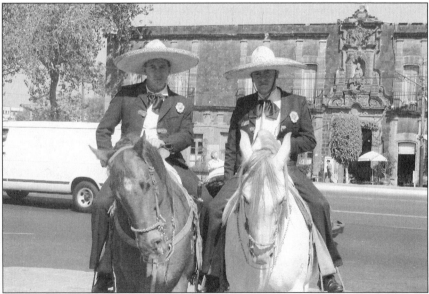

policias charros (cowboy cops) in the Alameda, with Hotel de Cortés in the background lice to help them. A horrific example was the lynching of two policemen in 2005 in a poor neighborhood in the south of the city by the townspeople, who suspected them of being part of a kidnapping ring. It turns out, even more horribly, that they were wrong, but their reaction was an example (extreme, no doubt) of how little faith city denizens have in the authorities.

Precautions

In general, visitors to Mexico City should take the same precautions they would when traveling anywhere in their own countries or abroad. Keep money and valuables secured, either in a hotel safe or safe deposit box, or in a money belt or other hard-to-reach place on your person. Keep an eye on cameras, purses, and the like to make sure you don't leave them behind in restaurants, hotels, or campgrounds. At night, lock the doors to your hotel room and vehicle. Don't ever take taxis from the street, instead call an inexpensive *sitio* to pick you up.

Take extra caution after dark, when certain districts that are safe during the daytime—such as the Centro Histórico—become a little riskier. Walking alone in the less-populated streets of the historic center after 9 P.M. is not a great idea. Even more touchy are areas north, northwest, and east of the Centro Histórico. Polanco, the Zona Rosa, the Roma, and the Condesa all seem to fare better after dark, though even in these areas you should stay alert. Stick to well-lighted areas and keep a steady, determined-looking pace. The centers of San Ángel and Coyoacán are relatively safe to walk around both day and night.

It's a good idea to carry limited cash and credit cards—no more than you need for an outing—when moving about the city. Don't wear expensive-looking clothes or jewelry. If confronted by someone intent on robbing you, don't resist. The only instances of violence I've heard about occurred where the robbery victims tried to resist.

If you'll be using ATM machines as a source of cash, using off-street machines, such as those found inside many department stores (including Sanborns), is a good idea.

When riding the Metro or public buses, watch out for pickpockets, particularly when these modes of transport are crowded.

Help

"060" is the city's emergency telephone number for reporting criminal acts. It is designed to facilitate the reporting of crimes committed against tourists and residents alike. When an individual calls this number, a representative of the Ministerios Públicos Moviles (Mobile Justice Department) reports to the scene of the crime or, when tourists are involved, to their hotel to register the complaint.

One city attorney general's office fairly accustomed to dealing with foreigners is the **Procuraduría General de Justicia** (Av. Juárez 60, tel. 5346-8742), on the south side of the Alameda. They don't always have English-speakers here, but sometimes they do, and regardless they will try to help if you've had some problem. The office is open 24 hours a day.

Sectur (tel. 5250-0123 or 5250-0151) maintains a 24-hour traveler's aid hotline for emergencies of all kinds.

Legal Matters

All foreign visitors in Mexico are subject to Mexican legal codes, which are based on Roman and Napoleonic law updated with U.S. constitutional theory and civil law. The most distinctive features of the Mexican judiciary system, compared to Anglo-American systems, are that the system doesn't provide for trials by jury (the judge decides) nor writs of habeas corpus (though you must be charged within 72 hours of incarceration). Furthermore, bail is rarely granted to an arrested foreigner—for many offenses, not even Mexican nationals are allowed bail. Hence, once you're arrested and jailed for a serious offense, it can be very difficult to arrange release. The lesson here is: Don't get involved in matters that might result in your arrest. This primarily means anything having to do with drugs or guns.

The oft-repeated saw that in Mexico an arrested person is considered guilty until proven innocent is no more true south of the border than north. As in Canada, the U.S., and most of Europe, an arrested person is considered a criminal *suspect* until the courts confirm or deny guilt. You have the right to notify your consulate if detained.

If you get into trouble with Mexican law, for whatever reason, you should try to contact your consulate in Mexico. Sectur and state tourist offices can also help in some instances. These agencies routinely handle emergency legal matters involving visiting foreigners; you stand a much better chance of resolving legal difficulties with their assistance.

Services and Information

COMMUNICATIONS

Postal Service

The Mexican postal service, though mostly reliable, is relatively slow. Delivery time has been shortened by 75 percent since 1989, the year a full government subsidy for Sepomex (Servicio Postal Mexicana) was discontinued and the Ministry of Communications and Transport ordered the agency to become self-sufficient. Average delivery time between Mexico and the U.S. or Canada is about 10 days, while to Europe you must figure two weeks. Mail sent to Mexico from outside the country generally reaches its destination more quickly.

Most post offices *(correos)* in Mexico City accept general delivery mail. Have correspondents address mail in your name (last name capitalized), followed by "a/c Lista de Correos," the *colonia* name, and the postal code (e.g., CHRIS HUMPHREY, a/c Lista de Correos, Col. Condesa, México 06140 D.F., México). Mail sent this way is usually held 10 days. If you want your mail held up to 30 days, substitute the words "Poste Restante, Correo Central" for "Lista de Correos" in the address (e.g. CHRIS HUMPHREY, a/c Poste Restante, Col. Condesa, México 06140 D.F., México). Because delivery time is highly variable, it's best to use poste restante just to be safe.

In small towns and villages, residents often don't use street addresses, simply writing the addressee's name followed by *domicilio conocido* (known residence) and the name of the town or village. Even in large towns and cities, addresses may bear the name of the street without a building number (*sin número,* abbreviated as "s/n"), or will mention the nearest cross streets (e.g., *ent. Abasolo y Revolución,* or "between Abasolo and Revolución)."

The Mexican post office offers an express mail service (EMS) called Mexpost. International rates are relatively high; a Mexpost express letter to the U.S. or Canada, for example, costs $16; to Europe, $20. Mexpost claims to deliver almost anywhere in Mexico within 48 hours and to major cities around the world within 72 hours. A Mexpost parcel cannot exceed 1.05 meters along any one dimension and cannot weigh more than 20 kilos. The **main MexPost center** (Netzahualcóyotl 109, tel. 5709-9606), in the Centro, offers packing services.

Some individual post offices with convenient locations include:

Palacio Postal (Eje Central Lázaro Cárdenas and Tacuba, opposite the Palacio de Bellas Artes, 9 A.M.–6 P.M. Mon.–Fri.)

Zócalo (Plaza de la Constitución 7, 9 A.M.–2:30 P.M. Mon.–Fri.)

Zona Rosa (Londrés 208 at Varsovia, 9 A.M.–5 P.M. Mon.–Fri., 9 A.M.–1 P.M. Sat.; adjacent MexPost EMS office open 9 A.M.–2 P.M. and 2:30–4 P.M. Mon.–Fri., 9 A.M.–1 P.M. Sat.)

Paseo de la Reforma, (Paseo de la Reforma 77, 9 A.M.–5 P.M. Mon.–Sat.)

Colonia Cuauhtémoc (Río Misisipi 58, 9 A.M.–3 P.M. Mon.–Fri., 9 A.M.–1 P.M. Sat.)

Colonia Condesa (Aguascalientes 161, 9 A.M.–5 P.M. Mon.–Fri., 9 A.M.–1 P.M. Sat.)

Roma (Álvaro Obregón 31, 9 A.M.–7 P.M. Mon.–Fri., 9 A.M.–1 P.M. Sat.)

Polanco (Galileo 245, 9 A.M.–5 P.M. Mon.–Fri., 9 A.M.–1 P.M. Sat.)

San Ángel (Dr. Gálvez 16, 9 A.M.–5 P.M. Mon.–Fri., 9 A.M.–1 P.M. Sat.)

Coyoacán (Higuera 23, 9 A.M.–5 P.M. Mon.–Fri., 9 A.M.–1 P.M. Sat.)

Courier Services

Several courier services operate in Mexico City. In our experience, DHL and UPS seem to offer the lowest prices and best services. MexPost, the express delivery offered by the Mexican Postal Service, is less expensive and a bit slower. All of the couriers listed here offer packing service. Each of these central offices has many branches and offers home pickup: DHL Internacional de México (Paseo de la Reforma 76, tel. 5345-7000, www.dhl.com); Federal Express (Insurgentes Sur 899, Col. Nápoles, tel. 5228-9904, www.fedex.com); MexPost (Palacio Postal, Eje Central, Col. Centro, tel. 5729-3500); UPS de México (Insurgentes Sur 667, tel. 5228-7900, www.ups.com).

The courier Estafeta Mexicana (Hamburgo 213, Zona Rosa, tel. 5270-8300), was recently made an official agent of the U.S. postal service, which makes for reliable, lower-priced service to the U.S.

American Express

Amex cardholders can pick up mail at the American Express office (Paseo de la Reforma 350, México 06600 D.F., México, tel. 5207-7204, 9 A.M.–6 P.M. Mon.–Fri., 9 A.M.–1 P.M. Sat.).

Telephone Services

The national telephone company, **TelMex,** was privatized in 1990 and has improved its services considerably over the last several years. Local phone calls are relatively cheap—a local phone-booth call costs only one peso—as are long-distance calls *within* Mexico. If you can find a working phone—many public phones seem permanently "out of order"—connections are usually good, though you may have to wait a while to get through to the operator during busy periods such as Sunday and holidays.

If you don't want to use a phone booth or a hotel phone (hotels usually add their own surcharges to both local and long-distance calls), you can make a call during business hours from a TelMex office or from a private phone office or *caseta de teléfono,* often set up in the corner of a local shop. Like hotels, private telephone offices add surcharges to calls.

Probably the best option to make local calls and long-distance calls within Mexico is the public pay phone service called **Ladatel** (acronym for Larga Distancia Teléfono), with phone booths where you can pay for local and/or long-distance calls with a *tarjeta de teléfono* (phone card) issued by TelMex. You can buy these cards in denominations of 20, 30, and 50 pesos at many pharmacies, convenience stores, supermarkets, bus terminals, and airports.

In 2001, the Mexican government overhauled local area codes in the entire country, a process that left many people extremely confused about what number to dial, especially from outside Mexico. The numbers in this book all include the new area codes, but in case you need to check a number, see www.cft.gob.mx/frame_camp.html for a complete list of the new area codes. Unlike most of the rest of Central Mexico, Mexico City has a two-digit area code (55) followed by an eight-digit phone number. To dial a Mexico City number from elsewhere in Mexico, call 01-55-5234-5678. All other locations covered by this book have a three-digit area code followed by a seven-digit phone number. For example, to dial a number in Cuernavaca from Mexico City, call 01-777-318-1234.

If you have a calling card number for Sprint, AT&T, MCI, or Bell Canada, you can use them to make long-distance calls within Mexico or

Know Mexico City

to another country. Each of these has its own access code for direct dialing.

To direct dial an international call via TelMex, dial 00 plus the area code and number for a station-to-station call, or 09 plus area code and number for a person-to-person or other operator-assisted call. Long-distance international calls are heavily taxed and cost more than equivalent international calls from the U.S. or Canada.

The appropriate long-distance operator can place a collect call on your behalf or charge the call to your account if you have a calling card for that service. If you try these numbers from a hotel phone, be sure the hotel operator realizes the call is toll-free; some hotel operators use their own timers to assess phone charges.

Since the deregulation of Mexican telephone service, several private, U.S.-based long-distance phone companies have set up their own phone systems—not just the lines and service but actual pay phones—in Mexico to take advantage of undiscerning tourists. The English-language signs next to the phone usually read "Call the U.S. or Canada Collect or With a Credit Card" or "Just Dial Zero to Reach the U.S. or Canada." Often a company operates under several different corporate names in the area, charging at least 50 percent more per international call than TelMex, AT&T, MCI, or Sprint—as much as $10–20 for the first minute, plus $4 each additional minute, even on weekends. A percentage of these charges usually goes to the hotel or private phone

TELEPHONE CODES

Long-distance operator (national): 020
Time: 030
Directory Assistance (Mexico): 040
Police, Red Cross, Fire: 060
International operator: 090
Long-distance direct dialing from Mexico via TelMex:
    station to station (in Mexico): 01 + area code + number
    person to person (in Mexico): 02 + area code + number
    station to station (U.S. and Canada): 001 + area code + number
    person to person (U.S. and Canada): 09 + 1 + area code + number
    station to station (other international): 00 + country code + area code + number
    person to person (other international): 09 + country code + area code + number
    noninternational U.S. 800 number: 001 + 880 + number (be aware these are not
                  free calls when dialed from Mexico)
Access numbers for other long distance companies:
    MCI: 01-800-021-8000 or 001-800-674-7000
    AT&T: 01-800-288-2872 or 001-800-462-4240
    Sprint: 01-800-234-0000 or 001-800-877-8000
    Canada Direct: 01-800-123-0200

    To call Mexico direct from outside the country, dial your international access code + 52 + number. Example: to call the number 5155-0631 in Mexico City from the U.S., dial 011 (international access code) + 52 (Mexico country code) + 55 (Mexico City code) + 5155-0631 (the phone number in Mexico City). The Mexico City area code "55" is the only two-digit area code in the regions covered by this book; all others are three digits.

    Help: Sectur (the Ministry of Tourism) maintains a 24-hour traveler's aid hotline for emergencies of all kinds: 5250-0123 or 5250-0151. If you're dialing from outside Mexico City, call 01-800-903-9200.

office offering the service. At most private phone offices, it's much cheaper to use TelMex (or a well-known international company such as AT&T, MCI, or Sprint), even if you have to pay a service charge on top of the rates, than to use these fly-by-night U.S. companies. If you're concerned about economizing, always ask which company is being used before you arrange an international call through a hotel or private phone office.

For international service, calling collect often saves hassles. In Spanish the magic words are *por cobrar* (collect), prefaced by the name of the place you're calling (e.g., *"a los Estados Unidos, por favor—por cobrar"*). This will connect you to an English-speaking international operator. For best results, speak slowly and clearly. You can reach an international operator directly by dialing 090.

In 1999 the "5" was added to the regular seven-digit numbers in D.F., so that now you must dial an eight-digit number. Some listings for Mexico City businesses still use the old seven-digit numbers; if you see a listing in the city for 256-1720, then you'll have to dial 5256-1720. Many new phone numbers begin with a different digit, not always "5."

Email and Internet Access

If you're bringing a computer and modem to Mexico with hopes of staying on the infobahn, online options are limited to a handful of local Internet service providers and a few international ones. Band rates can be slow, bottlenecked by low bandwidth and line interruptions in the Mexican phone system. With fiber optic on the way in many parts of the country, this could change rapidly, though much depends on the kind of equipment installed at any given town linked with fiber optics.

America Online and AT&T offer local access phone numbers in Mexico. Mexico's own TelMex/Prodigy is the most widely used local service. Long-term visitors can try their luck with local ISP accounts (the average cost is $10–20 a month), but most people prefer using AOL, AT&T or TelMex/Prodigy over anything else available in Mexico so far.

INTERNET CAFÉS

Because so few Mexicans own their own computers and/or have an Internet connection, public places to surf the Web have been multiplying throughout Mexico City. Travelers should have no problem at all finding places to log on. If the ones listed below are not satisfactory, just ask at your hotel for other suggestions.

Downtown
Escuela Superior Lafoel, Donceles 80 at the corner of República de Brasil, tel. 5512-3584, 10 A.M.–8 P.M. Mon.–Sat., $2.20 an hour

Zona Rosa
Coffee Mail, Amberes 61, 9 A.M.–10 P.M. daily, $2 an hour

Java Chat, Génova 44-K, tel. 5525-6853, 9 A.M.–11:30 P.M. Mon.–Fri., 10 A.M.–11:30 P.M. Sat., $2.20 an hour

Monumento a la Revolución
Intermedios, Puente de Alvarado 70, right near the corner of Arriaga, 10 A.M.–11 P.M. daily, $0.50 for 15 minutes

Condesa
Cafenaut, Ensenada at Vicente Suárez, 10 A.M.–10 P.M. Mon.–Fri., 11 A.M.–8 P.M. Sat., 2–6 P.M. Sun., $2 an hour

ADN, Campeche 280, tel. 5584-1894, 10 A.M.–7 P.M. Mon.–Fri., $2 an hour or $1 for half-an-hour

Roma
W@ll Internet, Orizaba 39, tel. 5511-1749, 10 A.M.–8 P.M. Mon.–Fri., 10 A.M.–4 P.M. Sat., $1.50 an hour

Coyoacán
Hippie Net, Madrid 68, 10 A.M.–8 P.M. daily, $2 an hour

A very convenient option for many travelers and businesspeople is the use of pre-paid Internet access cards, which you can then use through a dial-up modem from a computer connected to a regular telephone line. The most well-known of this type of card is **Todito Card** (tel. 5447-8864 in Mexico City, www.toditocard.com), which can be activated either for a set amount of minutes—300 minutes is $4, for example, or 1.3 cents a minute, and it gets less expensive per minute the more you buy. Conversely, you activate the card to provide unlimited access for a certain number of days, which can be very useful for travelers; $4 is good for 5 days and $10 is good for 15 days, and two months goes for $30. Email service is available as well if you need it, and the service works in several dozen cities across Mexico. They can be purchased online before you travel, or in a number of chain stores like Oxxo, Gigante, Superama, and Liverpool. Reportedly Yahoo is about to launch a similar new service in Mexico.

Cybercafés where you can log on using public terminals to send and receive email or browse the Internet are multiplying in Mexico City. No doubt more public Internet access points will appear over the next few years. All allow access to any Internet-based emailing such as Yahoo! or MSN Hotmail, or you can go through TelNet to check your account back home if you prefer, and provided you know the ins and outs of TelNet.

Library

The **Biblioteca Benjamín Franklin** (Liverpool 31, Colonia Juárez, tel. 5080-2733, www.usembassy-mexico.gov/biblioteca, 11 A.M.–7 P.M. Mon.–Fri.), a block away from its previous location, is an excellent library run by the U.S. Embassy, but it's open to anyone over 16 years of age. To check out books, you're required to show proof of residence in Mexico City and wait several days to get a card, but anyone is allowed to browse the periodicals or books at in the library.

The largest library in Mexico City, and indeed the entire country, is the **Biblioteca Nacional de México** (tel. 5622-6800, bibional .bibliog.unam.mx, main collection 9 A.M.–8 P.M. daily) at the Centro Cultural Universitario at UNAM, in the south of the city. Anyone over 16 with a current photo identification is welcome to peruse the over one million volumes in the general collection, but only accredited researchers can access more specialized collections.

A specialized collection on the history of Mexico and the Americas is located at the **Instituto Mora** (Plaza Valentín Gómez Farías 12, tel. 5598-3777, www.institutomora.edu.mx, 8 A.M.–7 P.M. Mon.–Fri., 8 A.M.–3:30 P.M. Sat.), in Colonia Mixcoac.

MEDIA

Newspapers

Among the national Spanish-language dailies, *Reforma* is widely considered the most informative and objective, and *El Universal* isn't bad either. *La Jornada* and *Uno Más Uno* lean well toward the left, while *El Financiero* is oriented toward business and politics. The latter also appears in a weekly English-language edition available at various Mexican consulates and cultural centers in the U.S., Canada, and Mexico. You can buy these newspapers at any of the many street-corner newspaper kiosks around the city, with the exception of *Reforma,* which (because of a dispute with the newspaper union) is sold by vendors on street corners or in convenience stores only. Even if your Spanish is minimal, city newspapers are worth a glance for current information on museum exhibits and local cinema.

With the venerable English-language paper the *News* now out of business (the end of an era!), the current best option is the *Herald,* an English-language paper printed by *El Universal* and the *Miami Herald. USA Today* and the *International Herald Tribune* are sometimes sold in hotel lobbies or bookstores.

Downstairs from the Club de Periodistas de México Prensa Nacional y Internacional (International and National Press Club), **La Torre de Papel** (Filomeno Mata 6A, in the Centro Histórico, 9 A.M.–6 P.M. Mon.–Fri.,

9 A.M.– 3 P.M. Sat.) sells more than 300 daily newspapers from around Mexico, plus about 50 from other countries (mainly the U.S. and Europe). **La Casa de la Prensa** (Florencia 57, 8 A.M.–10 P.M. Mon.–Fri. and 8 A.M.–4 P.M. Sat.–Sun.; Hamburgo 141, 8 A.M.–10 P.M. Mon.–Fri. and 1–9 P.M. Sat.– Sun.), a shop with a large magazine section and daily U.S. and European newspapers, has two branches in the Zona Rosa. In Polanco, **The Coffee Bar** (at the intersection of Temistocles and Presidente Mazaryk) has a similarly large selection. Newsstands at the airport carry the *New York Times,* the *International Herald Tribune,* the *Financial Times, El Pais* from Spain, and several Mexican newspapers.

The stores mentioned also carry many international magazines from the U.S. and Europe. Any Sanborns store is also a good place to look.

Magazines

In English, *Latin Trade* (www.latintrade.com) is heavily focused on business stories. The U.S. Chamber of Commerce puts out a magazine in Mexico City called *Business Mexico,* also heavily oriented toward business and finance; it's available in Sanborns around the city. In Spanish, *Proceso* (www.proceso.com.mx) is the leading muckraking magazine. Its stories on Mexican political machinations, though occasionally a bit over the top on conspiracy theory, are often excellent. Two glossy weekly magazines are *Milenio,* which also has good international news stories, and *Cambio.*

A new entrant on the Mexico City magazine market is *D.F.,* the first really good magazine of the city itself, in all its glory. The biweekly magazine has a clear appreciation for the underlying weirdness of Mexico City, with features and short stories about slices of city life, generally written in an intelligent and funny style. The restaurant and entertainment listings in the back are the best of any magazine in the city. Their laconic motto, which you've got to love, is *"20 milliones de chilangos no podemos estar equivocados"* (20 million Mexico City residents can't be wrong). Another new monthly magazine, *Chilango,* is

similar but caters to a more upscale, *fresa* (slang for "rich kid") readership.

Television

Mexican TV offers a mix of American dramas and sitcoms dubbed in Spanish and Mexico's own versions of the same formulae. Mexico's famous *telenovelas*—soap opera series that run several months rather than several years—are exported all over Latin America.

Many hotels and motels maintain their own satellite dishes with as many as 50 channels from Mexico and the U.S. CNN International is widely available. The main movie channels in Mexico City are Cine Latino (Spanish), USA Network (English), Fox (English), Multicinema (mixed), De Película (Spanish), Multicinema (mixed), and Cinema Golden Choice (English).

Radio

Mexico City boasts hundreds of AM and FM stations. Most of the music stations play Mexican Top 40, but for visitors interested in authentic *música mexicana,* we can recommend several stations. Morena FM 89.7 FM broadcasts traditional *romanticismo,* romantic songs by such crooners as Luis Miguel, Alejandro Fernández, Tania Libertad, and Juan Gabriel.

Radioactiva 98.5 FM is an alternative rock/Top 40 station presenting a mix of English and Spanish groups, with a greater emphasis on English. For *grupera,* La Zeta 107.3 FM is the one to listen to, and for *tropical,* try Sabrosita 100.9 FM. Radio Uno 104.1 FM plays salsa daily 3–4 P.M. and 9–10 P.M.

One of the better radio news programs with news 24 hours a day is Formato 21, 790 AM.

MAPS

The government statistics institute, **Instituto Estadísticas, Geografía e Información (INEGI)** (Balderas 71, tel. 5512-8331, 9 A.M.–8 P.M. Mon.–Fri.; and at Patriotismo 711, tel. 5278-1000, www.inegi.gob.mx) sells a variety of maps, as well as statistical yearbooks and other information resources. They also have a small store at the airport's domestic terminal.

Mexico City Maps

Most casual Mexico City visitors will find the free fold-out map designed by the Mexico City Tourist Department quite adequate for their needs. The foldout pamphlet has maps of the Centro, Reforma/Chapultepec/Polanco/Condesa, San Ángel, Coyoacán, the Metro, and a broad sketch map of the entire city. It's well made, easy to read, and printed on fairly sturdy paper that will hold up better than most paper maps. You can pick them up at any of the tourist information booths around the city, if they haven't run out (see the sidebar *Tourist Modules* for addresses).

If you're planning to take up residence in the capital, you'll want to go a step further and get the thick *Ciudad de México Area Metropolitana* street atlas published by Guía Roji, which has a scale of 1:22,500 and costs around $10 if you buy it in D.F., or around $16–20 abroad. This one covers every corner of the Distrito Federal and includes two complete indexes, one by street name and one by *colonia*. Guía Roji also publishes a simple two-sided folding street map ($4 in Mexico City, up to $9 abroad), *Ciudad de México,* with a scale of 1:30,000, but it's really not a very good map. Another Mexican-made sheet map of similar quality is Pronto's *Ciudad de México,* which costs about the same as the Guía Roji sheet map.

Highway Maps

Among the many Mexico maps available to visitors who will be taking excursions outside Mexico City, two are particularly well suited to general-purpose Mexico road travel. One is published by the American Automobile Association (AAA) and is available from most AAA offices; maps are free to members, about $4 to the general public. The excellent graphics on this map make it easy to read, and it's accurate and detailed enough for most Mexico auto trips. The map's coverage extends well into the U.S. border states. Distances are marked in kilometers for Mexico, miles for the United States.

Those planning to spend time on Mexico's back roads should buy a Mexican road atlas. The best available is the annual 127-page *Guía Roji por las Carreteras de México,* published in Mexico but available through Treaty Oak (P.O. Box 50295, Austin, TX 78763, U.S.A., tel. 512/326-4141, www.treatyoak.com) and Map Link (25 E. Mason, Santa Barbara, CA 93101, U.S.A., tel. 805/965-4402, fax 805/962-0884, www.maplink.com), as well as many travel bookstores abroad and in Mexican department stores. This atlas contains 38 double-page maps with a scale of 1:1,000,000 (1 inch equals 25 kilometers), along with color graphics to indicate forests and woodlands, deserts, and marshlands. Best of all, the atlas includes a fairly complete network of unpaved roads, villages, and *ejidos* that don't appear on the AAA or any other large-scale, single-page maps. Another plus is that the atlas includes 15 city maps.

Guía Roji also publishes state maps at 1:800,000 scale, simple to read and adequate for most purposes.

Topographical Maps

Because differences in elevation often determine backcountry route selection, hikers, kayakers, mountain bikers, and off-road drivers should consider using topographical maps. You can obtain these in advance from Treaty Oak or Map Link in the U.S., or in Mexico from INEGI.

TOURIST INFORMATION

Mexico City has its own tourist office, the **Secretaría de Turismo de la Ciudad de México** (Av. Nuevo León 56, 9th floor, in Colonia Hipódromo Condesa, tel. 5286-9077, fax 5286-9022, www.mexicocity.gob.mx). For the most part this is an administrative office, so if it's information you need, you're better off visiting one of the several tourist suboffices *(módulos de información turística)* around the city and at the airport (see the sidebar *Tourist Modules* for addresses). These small offices usually stock a variety of free brochures, maps, hotel and restaurant lists, and information on local activities, and are staffed by Mexicans who are trained to handle visitor queries. Some speak very good English, others not.

The federal government also operates a national tourism secretariat, the **Secretaría de Turismo de México** (Av. Presidente Mazaryk 172, México, D.F. 11570, tel. 5250-0151 or 5250-0123, in the U.S. 800/482-9832, fax 5250-6610, www.mexico-travel.com). Again, this office isn't much good with walk-in requests, and they don't have information on the city itself, just the rest of the country. Their telephone service, however, can be quite useful for answering basic questions.

WASHING YOUR DUDS

If you're tired of trying to wash those blue jeans in your sink (nightmare job) and want to have someone else clean the grime out of your clothes, you'll be pleased to hear getting your washing done in Mexico City is easy and inexpensive. Coin-operated laundries are not common in Mexico—instead you normally drop your clothes off one day and pick them up either later that same day or the following day. Usually prices are charged in kilos, with a minimum of three kilos for wash, dry, and fold. If your clothes need special treatment, be sure to tell the owners first.

Below are four places we've found that are reliable. There are many more in every *colonia* in the city, and many hotels will wash clothes for a fee also.

Lavandería Automática Esmafga, Mesones 42, Colonia Centro, tel. 5709-0278, 10 A.M.–6 P.M. Mon.–Sat.

Lava Jet, Danubio 119B, Colonia Cuauhtémoc (near Paseo de la Reforma), tel. 5207-3032, 8:30 A.M.–5:30 P.M. Mon.–Fri., 8:30 A.M.–4 P.M. Sat., English spoken, $6 for first three kilos

Lavandería Automática Edison, Edison 91, near Monumento a la Revolución, 10 A.M.–7 P.M. Mon.–Fri., 10 A.M.–5 P.M. Sat.

Lavandería Del Río, Jalapa 99, Colonia Roma, tel. 5511-2538, 8 A.M.–7 P.M. Mon.–Sat., 8 A.M.–2 P.M. SUN., $4 for three kilos

Translators and Interpreters

AHPLA Institute (Juan Escutia 97, Colonia Condesa, tel. 5286-9016, www.ahpla.com).

Berlitz de México (Eugenio Sué 316, Colonia Polanco, tel. 5545-0644 or 5545-0650, www.berlitz.com.mx).

Koiné (Bajío 335–104, Colonia Roma Sur, tel. 5264-6787 or 5564-5256, koinetraductores@prodigy.com.mx).

Recursos Técnicos para Conferencias (Eugenia 13–602, Colonia Nápoles, tel. 5543-5011 or 5543-3517).

Traducciones Willy de Winter (Horacio 528–404, Colonia Polanco, tel. 5545-5764 or 5254-7446, willywinter@infosel.net.mx).

TIME, POWER, AND MEASUREMENTS
Time

Mexico City time coincides with central standard time in the U.S. and is six hours ahead of Greenwich Mean Time (GMT -6), from the last Sunday in October to the last Sunday in April each year. From April 25 to October 26 Mexico changes over to central daylight saving time (GMT -5).

Looking at the whole country, there are three time zones. The State of Baja California Norte runs on Pacific Standard Time (GMT -8 or GMT -7); the States of Baja California Sur, Sonora, and Sinaloa follow mountain standard time (GMT -7 or GMT -6); and the rest of the states are on central standard time (GMT -6 or GMT -5). This means you should set your timepieces an hour ahead when crossing the above zone boundaries going east, or back an hour when crossing west.

Time in Mexico is commonly expressed according to the 24-hour clock, from 0001 to 2400 (one minute past midnight to midnight). A restaurant posting hours of 1100–2200, for example, is open 11 A.M.–10 P.M. according to the 12-hour clock popular in the United States. Signs in Mexico may be posted using either system.

Business Hours

The typical small business will be open Monday to Friday (plus Saturday for retail businesses) 9 A.M.–2 P.M., then closed until 4 or 5 P.M., and then reopened until 7 or 8 P.M. Official government offices typically maintain an 9 A.M.–7 P.M. schedule, with a 2–3 P.M. lunch hour.

Banks are open Monday to Friday 8:30 A.M.–3 P.M., but remember that the foreign exchange service usually closes about noon (probably to lock in the exchange rate before afternoon adjustments). A few competitive banks have extended their hours as late as 5 P.M.

Electricity

Mexico's electrical system is the same as those in the U.S. and Canada: 110 volts, 60 cycles, alternating current (AC). Electrical outlets are of the American type, designed to work with appliances that have standard double-bladed plugs. Small towns in some rural areas may experience brief interruptions of electrical service or periods of brownout (voltage decrease). In a few villages, gasoline-powered generators are the only sources of electricity and they may be turned off during the day.

Measurements

Mexico uses the metric system as the official system of weights and measures. This means the distance between Nogales and Mazatlán is measured in kilometers, cheese is weighed in grams or kilograms, a hot day in Monterrey is 32°C, gasoline is sold by the liter, and a big fish is two meters long. The conversion chart at the back of this book will help Americans make the conversions from pounds, gallons, and miles to kilos, liters, and kilometers when necessary.

Chilango Slang

The Spanish spoken in Mexico is lined with a rich vein of colloquialisms, slang expressions, and turns of phrase. Most Mexican slang originates from working-class neighborhoods in the capital (particularly Tepito), but it's then frequently picked up by middle class and wealthier youth, from where it moves into general popular culture and is transmitted by the media to the rest of the country. In fact, because Mexican soap operas are by far the most popular in Latin America, people from other Spanish-speaking countries tend to understand a lot more Mexico City slang than would normally be expected.

A crucial aspect of understanding Mexican Spanish is getting into the world of the *albur,* a sort of pun made at the expense of another. When a group of Mexican men are standing around talking, you'll notice one after the other is constantly taking turns trying to twist someone's last phrase into something that will crack everyone else up. The trick is to make everyone laugh, but using clever phrasing, never just a straight insult or put-down.

As in Cockney English, another trick is to use words that sound similar to well-known swear words, thus making the meaning more acceptable, and more humorous, in polite company.

Rare is the foreigner who masters local slang enough to take part in this generally good-natured word competition, but it's entertaining to try. Keep in mind that everyone wants to laugh and will be looking at you expectantly when you open your mouth, so even if you're not sure what you're about to say, do it with the right expression and tone, and you might be able to pull it off.

Glossary

a huevo—definitely, for sure

a toda madre—excellent

a todo mecate—similar to *a toda madre,* but softer, as *"madre"* has a slightly vulgar connotation when used in this sense

aguas—watch out!

ahí nos vidrios—a twist ("we'll windows") on *"ahí nos vemos"* ("we'll be seeing each other")

banda—people, as in *mucha banda,* meaning a lot of people

bailar lola—to screw something up, make a mess of it

bicla—bicycle

cámara—same as *simón*

cantar oaxaca—to vomit

carnal—very good friend, a "brother"

chamba—work

chale—multipurpose exclamatory interjection ("really? wow! no way! right on!"); often used as *"chale, mano"*

chela—beer

chesco—soft drink

chilango—someone from Mexico City

chingar—to "screw" somebody, in both meanings of the word

chingón—really excellent

ciego—100 pesos

cualquier hijo de vecino—"some son of a neighbor," a softer way of saying *"hijo de puta"* (son of a slut), an insult

cuero—handsome, good-looking

de pelos—excellent

desvelar—to stay out late

diegos—10 pesos

douglas—two pesos

en un ratón—in a while, a twist on *"en un rato"*

está del nabo, está de la fruta—it sucks

está cañón—a tough situation, a twist on *está cabrón,* which means the same but is more vulgar

está grueso—literally, "it's fat," but meaning, "wow, heavy, that's serious"

fajar—to make out, to kiss

faxear—variation of *fajar*

fresa—literally "strawberry," meaning a prissy, a snotty rich kid

gabacho—American

guácala—gross

guacarear—to vomit

guarra, guarura—bodyguard

güey—dude, guy; common throughout Mexico, but used every other word by young *chilangos,* and even *chilangas*

hojaldra— same as *ojete,* but softened slightly

hueva—a drag, something boring or tedious

jefe, jefa—father, mother

jetón—asleep

jipiteca—Mexican hippie

la julia—the police van

la neta—the best, or also the truth, the real deal

la pura neta—even better

la puritita neta—better still

lana—"wool," i.e. money

mamón—stuck-up, arrogant person

mano—short for *hermano* (brother) and the Mexican equivalent of "Bro"

milanesa—1,000 pesos

melón—1,000,000 pesos

móchate—pass it along already, give me one, or give me some (often *"móchate, güey"* or *"móchate, cabrón"*)

naco—someone with bad taste

nave—literally boat, but slang for car

ni madres—no way, not a chance

no mames—vulgar, meaning "no way, get out"; invariably said as *"no mames, güey"*

no manches—means the same as *mames,* but twisted at the end to make it sound less crude

ojete—a strong, vulgar insult

órale—exclamation, "right on, wow"

pachanga—big party

pacheco—stoned (i.e., smoking marijuana)

pedo—literally "fart," but meaning either "drunk" (*"está bien pedo"*) or a problem, i.e., ¿*que pedo*? (what's the problem?) or *no hay pedo* (no problem)

pendejo—vulgar, insulting adjective, i.e., idiot

pepino—a jerk

perro—as an adjective, something very difficult

perro—as a noun, a guy who sleeps around a lot

pinche—a vulgar adjective, i.e., *"¡Abre la pinche puerta!"* ("open the @#@!!%@ door!")

pitufos—literally "smurfs," meaning the blue-uniformed police

ponerse punk—to get mad, as in *"no te pongas punk,"* don't get mad *que mal viaje*—what a drag, what a bad trip

¿que hongo?—literally "what mushroom?," a play on *¿que onda?*

¿que milanesa?—what's up?

¿que onda?—what's up?

que oso—literally "what a bear," but meaning "what a fool," i.e., "what a ridiculous spectacle they're making of themselves"

¿que pasión?—twist on *¿que pasó?* or what's happening?

¿que pedo?—same as above

¿que pez mi acuaman?—same as above

que poca madre—"can you believe that?" but with an indignant tone

¿que te picó?—literally, "what bit you?," meaning, "what's the matter?" or "what's your problem?"

quiúbule—also what's up? Usually, *"quiúbule, cabrón"* or *"quiúbule güey"*

rajar—a verb, meaning to back out of doing something, to bail

reventón—big party

rola—a tune, a song

se puso hasta atrás—he/she got thoroughly drunk

se puso hasta las chanclas—he/she got thoroughly drunk

simón—a play on the word *sí* (yes), but more hip and current; combination of "I agree" and "right on"

tamarindos—the *tránsito* police, with brown uniforms

tirar la onda—try to pick up on someone

tostón—50 pesos

tranzar—to deceive somebody

varos—pesos (i.e., *"cuesta diez varos"*—"it costs 10 pesos")

vientos—"winds," right on

vientos huracanados—"hurricane winds," excellent

vientos huracanados aztecas—"Aztec hurricane winds," completely superb

vientos huracanados del pacífico—same as above

Spanish Phrasebook

PRONUNCIATION GUIDE

Spanish pronunciation is much more regular than that of English, but there are still occasional variations.

Consonants

c—as 'c' in "cat," before 'a', 'o', or 'u'; like 's' before 'e' or 'i'

d—as 'd' in "dog," except between vowels, then like 'th' in "that"

g—before 'e' or 'i,' like the 'ch' in Scottish "loch"; elsewhere like 'g' in "get"

h—always silent

j—like the English 'h' in "hotel," but stronger

ll—like the 'y' in "yellow"

ñ—like the 'ni' in "onion"

r—always pronounced as strong 'r'

rr—trilled 'r'

v—similar to the 'b' in "boy" (not as English 'v')

y—similar to English, but with a slight "j" sound. When standing, alone it's pronounced like the 'e' in "me".

z—like 's' in "same"

b, f, k, l, m, n, p, q, s, t, w, x—as in English

Vowels

a—as in "father," but shorter

e—as in "hen"

i—as in "machine"

o—as in "phone"

u—usually as in "rule"; when it follows a 'q' the 'u' is silent; when it follows an 'h' or 'g', it's pronounced like 'w,' except when it comes between 'g' and 'e' or 'i', when it's also silent (unless it has an umlaut, when it again pronounced as English 'w'

Stress

Native English speakers frequently make errors of pronunciation by ignoring stress; all Spanish vowels—a, e, i, o and u—may carry accents that determine which syllable of a word gets emphasis. Often, stress seems unnatural to nonnative speakers—the surname Chávez, for instance, is stressed on the first syllable—but failure to observe this rule may mean that native speakers may not understand you.

NUMBERS

0—*cero*
1—*uno* (masculine)
1—*una* (feminine)
2—*dos*
3—*tres*
4—*cuatro*
5—*cinco*
6—*seis*
7—*siete*
8—*ocho*
9—*nueve*
10—*diez*
11—*once*
12—*doce*
13—*trece*
14—*catorce*
15—*quince*
16—*dieciseis*
17—*diecisiete*
18—*dieciocho*
19—*diecinueve*
20—*veinte*
21—*veintiuno*
30—*treinta*
40—*cuarenta*
50—*cincuenta*
60—*sesenta*
70—*setenta*
80—*ochenta*
90—*noventa*
100—*cien*
101—*ciento y uno*
200—*doscientos*
1,000—*mil*
10,000—*diez mil*
1,000,000—*un millón*

DAYS OF THE WEEK

Sunday—*domingo*
Monday—*lunes*
Tuesday—*martes*
Wednesday—*miércoles*
Thursday—*jueves*
Friday—*viernes*
Saturday—*sábado*

TIME

While Latin Americans mostly use the 12-hour clock, in some instances, usually associated with plane or bus schedules, they may use the 24-hour military clock. Under the 24-hour clock, for example, *las nueve de la noche* (9 P.M.) would be *las 21 horas* (2100 hours).

What time is it?—*¿Qué hora es?*
It's one o'clock—*Es la una.*
It's two o'clock—*Son las dos.*
At two o'clock—*A las dos.*
It's ten to three—*Son tres menos diez.*
It's ten past three—*Son tres y diez.*
It's three fifteen—*Son las tres y cuarto.*
It's two forty five—*Son tres menos cuarto.*
It's two thirty—*Son las dos y media.*
It's six A.M.—*Son las seis de la mañana.*
It's six P.M.—*Son las seis de la tarde.*
It's ten P.M.—*Son las diez de la noche.*
today—*hoy*
tomorrow—*mañana*
morning—*la mañana*
tomorrow morning—*mañana por la mañana*
yesterday—*ayer*
week—*la semana*
month—*mes*
year—*año*
last night—*anoche*
the next day—*el día siguiente*

USEFUL WORDS AND PHRASES

Mexicans and other Spanish-speaking people consider formalities important. Whenever approaching anyone for information or some other reason, do not forget the appropriate salutation—good morning, good evening, etc. Standing alone, the greeting *hola* (hello) can sound brusque.

Hello.—*Hola.*
Good morning.—*Buenos días.*
Good afternoon.—*Buenas tardes.*
Good evening.—*Buenas noches.*
How are you?—*¿Cómo está?*
Very Good.—*Muy bien.*
And you?—*¿Y usted?*
So-so.—*Más o menos.*
Thank you.—*Gracias.*
Thank you very much.—*Muchas gracias.*
You're very kind.—*Muy amable.*
You're welcome.—*De nada* (literally, "It's nothing.")
yes—*sí*
no—*no*
I don't know.—*No sé.*
It's fine; okay—*Está bien.*
Good; okay—*Bueno.*
please—*por favor*
Pleased to meet you.—*Mucho gusto.*
Excuse me (physical)—*Perdóneme.*
Excuse me (speech)—*Discúlpeme.*
I'm sorry.—*Lo siento.*
Goodbye—*adiós*
see you later—*hasta luego* (literally, "until later")
more—*más*
less—*menos*
better—*mejor*
much, a lot—*mucho*
a little—*un poco*
large—*grande*
small—*pequeño, chico*
quick, fast—*rápido*
slowly—*despacio*
bad—*malo*
difficult—*difícil*
easy—*fácil*

He/She/It is gone; as in "She left," "He's gone"—*Ya se fue.*
I don't speak Spanish well.—*No hablo bien el español.*
I don't understand.—*No entiendo.*
How do you say. . . in Spanish?—*¿Cómo se dice. . . en español?*
Do you understand English?—*¿Entiende el inglés?*
Is English spoken here? (Does anyone here speak English?)—*¿Se habla inglés aquí?*

TERMS OF ADDRESS

When in doubt, use the formal *usted* (you) as a form of address. If you wish to dispense with formality and feel that the desire is mutual, you can say *Me puedes tutear* (you can call me "tu").

I—*yo*
you (formal)—*usted*
you (familiar)—*tú*
he/him—*él*
she/her—*ella*
we/us—*nosotros*
you (plural)—*ustedes*
they/them (all males or mixed gender)—*ellos*
they/them (all females)—*ellas*
Mr., sir—*señor*
Mrs., madam—*señora*
Miss, young lady—*señorita*
wife—*esposa*
husband—*marido* or *esposo*
friend—*amigo* (male), *amiga* (female)
sweetheart—*novio* (male), *novia* (female)
son, daughter—*hijo, hija*
brother, sister—*hermano, hermana*
father, mother—*padre, madre*
grandfather, grandmother—*abuelo, abuela*

GETTING AROUND

Where is. . . ?—*¿Dónde está. . . ?*
How far is it to. . . ?—*¿A cuanto está. . . ?*
from. . . to. . . —*de. . . a. . .*
highway—*la carretera*

road—*el camino*
street—*la calle*
block—*la cuadra*
kilometer—*kilómetro*
north—*norte*
south—*sur*
west—*oeste; poniente*
east—*este; oriente*
straight ahead—*al derecho; adelante*
to the right—*a la derecha*
to the left—*a la izquierda*

ACCOMMODATIONS

Is there a room?—*¿Hay cuarto?*
May I (we) see it?—*¿Puedo (podemos) verlo?*
What is the rate?—*¿Cuál es el precio?*
Is that your best rate?—*¿Es su mejor precio?*
Is there something cheaper?—*¿Hay algo más económico?*

single room—*un sencillo*
double room—*un doble*
room for a couple—*matrimonial*
key—*llave*
with private bath—*con baño*
with shared bath—*con baño general; con baño compartido*
hot water—*agua caliente*
cold water—*agua fría*
shower—*ducha*
electric shower—*ducha eléctrica*
towel—*toalla*
soap—*jabón*
toilet paper—*papel higiénico*
air conditioning—*aire acondicionado*
fan—*abanico; ventilador*
blanket—*frazada; manta*
sheets—*sábanas*

PUBLIC TRANSPORT

bus stop—*la parada*
bus terminal—*terminal de buses*
airport—*el aeropuerto*
launch—*lancha; tiburonera*

dock—*muelle*
I want a ticket to. . . —*Quiero un pasaje a. . .*
I want to get off at. . . —*Quiero bajar en. . .*
Here, please.—*Aquí, por favor.*
Where is this bus going?—*¿Adónde va este autobús?*
roundtrip—*ida y vuelta*
What do I owe?—*¿Cuánto le debo?*

FOOD

menu—*la carta, el menú*
glass—*taza*
fork—*tenedor*
knife—*cuchillo*
spoon—*cuchara*
napkin—*servilleta*
soft drink—*agua fresca*
coffee—*café*
cream—*crema*
tea—*té*
sugar—*azúcar*
drinking water—*agua pura, agua potable*
bottled carbonated water—*agua mineral con gas*
bottled uncarbonated water—*agua sin gas*
beer—*cerveza*
wine—*vino*
milk—*leche*
juice—*jugo*
eggs—*huevos*
bread—*pan*
watermelon—*sandía*
banana—*banano*
plantain—*plátano*
apple—*manzana*
orange—*naranja*
meat (without)—*carne (sin)*
beef—*carne de res*
chicken—*pollo; gallina*
fish—*pescado*
shellfish—*mariscos*
shrimp—*camarones*
fried—*frito*
roasted—*asado*
barbecued—*a la parrilla*

breakfast—*desayuno*
lunch—*almuerzo*
dinner (often eaten in late afternoon)—*comida*
dinner, or a late night snack—*cena*
the check, or bill—*la cuenta*

MAKING PURCHASES

I need. . . —*Necesito.* . .
I want. . . —*Deseo.* . . or *Quiero.* . .
I would like. . . (more polite)—*Quisiera.* . .
How much does it cost?—*¿Cuánto cuesta?*
What's the exchange rate?—*¿Cuál es el tipo de cambio?*
May I see. . . ?—*¿Puedo ver.* . . ?
this one—*ésta/ésto*
expensive—*caro*
cheap—*barato*

cheaper—*más barato*
too much—*demasiado*

HEALTH

Help me please.—*Ayúdeme por favor.*
I am ill.—*Estoy enfermo.*
pain—*dolor*
fever—*fiebre*
stomach ache—*dolor de estómago*
vomiting—*vomitar*
diarrhea—*diarrea*
drugstore—*farmacia*
medicine—*medicina*
pill, tablet—*pastilla*
birth control pills—*pastillas anticonceptivas*
condom—*condón, preservativo*

Suggested Reading

DESCRIPTION AND TRAVEL

Barros, José Luis. *Encuentros en la ciudad de México.* Miguel Ángel Porrúa, Grupo Editorial 1997. Collection of historic writings on the capital by such illustrative figures as Hernán Cortés, Thomas Gage, Guillermo Prieto, Miguel León Portilla, early Catholic friars, and others. Spanish only.

Gerrard, A. Bryson. *Cassell's Colloquial Spanish: A Handbook of Idiomatic Usage.* New York: Macmillan, 1980. Not as out of date as the publication year might suggest, Cassell's explains common *vulgarismos* (slang) used in Mexico, Central America, and South America; *píldora,* for example, is recognized as "the pill" in Mexico, but it refers to cocktail frankfurters in Argentina.

Legorreta, Jorge. *Guía del Pleno Disfrute de la Ciudad de México.* Mexico City: Jorge Legorreta/Metrópolis, 1994. This thin, spiral-bound guide to city nightlife, written by Mexico City politician Jorge Legorreta and

oriented toward *capitalinos* rather than tourists, is a gem. Sadly out of print, the *Guide to the Full Enjoyment of Mexico City* contains critiques and descriptions of many classic Mexico City restaurants, cafés, cantinas, *pulquerías,* cabarets, burlesque shows, dance halls, and other nocturnal pursuits. Spanish only.

Martinez, Ruben. *The Other Side: Notes from the New L.A., Mexico City, and Beyond.* Vintage Books, 1993. A stimulating account of the growing pan-Latino culture extending from Los Angeles to El Salvador, with plenty of pop culture information on Mexico City.

O'Reilly, James and Larry Habegger, eds. *Travelers' Tales Mexico.* San Francisco: Travelers' Tales, 1994. If you only read one piece of travel literature on Mexico, make it this one. Forty-eight essays by travel writers, natural historians, journalists, and ecologists present a kaleidoscopic view of Mexico's mystery, beauty, tragedy, and internal contradictions.

Ryan, Allen, ed. *The Reader's Companion to Mexico.* New York: Harcourt Brace and Company, 1995. Contains 26 literary excerpts from works on Mexico—the oldest dates to 1888, the latest 1985—published by Katherine Ann Porter, Graham Greene, Paul Theroux, Langston Hughes, Paul Bowles, D. H. Lawrence, John Steinbeck, and a number of lesser-known authors. A full chapter is devoted to essays on Mexico City.

HISTORY AND CULTURE

Arnold, Caroline. *City of the Gods: Mexico's Ancient City of Teotihuacán.* New York: Clarion Books, 1994. Illustrated with color photographs, Arnold's readable outing explores the ancient metropolis and extrapolates how the daily lives of the Teotihuacanos might have been.

Bierhorst, John. *The Mythology of Mexico and Central America.* New York: William Morrow, 1990. A good introduction to Mexican mythology, particularly with regard to Mesoamerican cultures.

Caistor, Nick. *Mexico City: A Cultural and Literary Companion.* New York: Interlink Books, 2000. An interesting and extremely atmospheric account of different aspects of Mexico City history and culture, written by someone who is clearly fascinated with the city.

Coe, Michael D. *Mexico: From the Olmecs to the Aztecs.* New York: Thames and Hudson, 1994. This textbook by curator/university professor Coe provides a readable, well-illustrated summary of prehispanic history in Southern Mexico, wisely leaving the Maya for another volume.

Johns, Michael. *The City of Mexico in the Age of Díaz.* Austin: University of Texas Press, 1997. A well-written, well-researched, and ultimately fascinating chronicle of the capital during the rule of dictatorial president Porfirio Díaz.

Kandell, Jonathan. *La Capital: The Biography of Mexico City.* New York: Random House, 1988. A readable chronicle of Mexico's capital city that would have benefited from a sharper focus on the city itself rather than the larger issues in Mexican history that it tends to fall back upon.

Katz, Friedrich. *The Life and Times of Pancho Villa.* Stanford: Stanford University Press, 1998. The larger-than-life bandit revolutionary Villa is portrayed here in all his complexity in exhaustive detail.

Krauze, Enrique. *Biography of Power: A History of Modern Mexico, 1810–1996.* New York: HarperCollins Publishers, 1997. One of Mexico's most respected historians traces the course of Mexican history, principally through the actions of its leaders. Because of his focus on personality, Krauze falls short on portraying the country's social dynamics.

Lewis, Oscar. *The Children of Sanchez: Autobiography of a Mexican Family.* New York: Random House, 1979. A gritty anthropological account of the city, based on the lives of a family whose patriarch works as a waiter at Café Tacuba restaurant.

Oppenheimer, Andres. *Bordering on Chaos: Mexico's Roller Coaster Journey to Prosperity.* Boston: Little, Brown and Co., 1998. Miami Herald reporter Oppenheimer has some engrossing anecdotes on the turbulent times of the Salinas and Zedillo era, though at times he seems overly concerned about illustrating his own involvement with the power brokers rather than focusing on the people and events themselves.

Oster, Patrick. *The Mexicans: A Personal Portrait of a People.* New York: Harper & Row, 1989. Reporter Patrick Foster presents 20 profiles of not-so-ordinary Mexicans, from a streetside fire-eater in Mexico City to a Sonoran *PANista.* Most of those profiled are Mexico City denizens. Despite a nearly overwhelming gloom-and-doom perspective, the essays provide hard information on Mexican politics and social schema.

Paz, Octavio. *The Labyrinth of Solitude: Life and Thought in Mexico.* New York: Grove Press, 1961. Paz has no peer when it comes to expositions of the Mexican psyche, and this is his best prose work.

Preston, Julia and Sam Dillon. *Opening Mexico.* New York: Farrar, Straus and Giroux, 2004. Preston and Dillon, former *New York Times* correspondents in Mexico, is an engrossing successor of sorts to Alan Riding's *Distant Neighbors,* starting in the mid-1980s but focusing principally on the *sexenio* of Ernesto Zedillo and the transition in 2000 with the victory of opposition candidate Vicente Fox.

Quiñones, Sam. *True Tales from Another Mexico: The Lynch Mob, the Popsicle Kings, Chalino, and the Bronx.* Albuquerque: University of New Mexico Press, 2001. An idiosyncratic and entertaining collection of stories from across Mexico, but particularly from the northern border regions.

Reed, John. *Insurgent Mexico.* New York: International Publishers, 1994. Famed American journalist Reed, of *Ten Days That Shook the World* fame, wrote this breathless, entertaining, and unabashedly biased first-hand account of time spent with Villa's troops in Northern Mexico during the Mexican Revolution.

Riding, Alan. *Distant Neighbors: A Portrait of the Mexicans.* New York: Vintage Books, 1986. Riding was the *New York Times* correspondent in Mexico City for six years, and when he finished, he wrote this excellent exposition of Mexican culture and history through 1988.

Rodriguez, Jeanette. *Our Lady of Guadalupe: Faith and Empowerment among Mexican-American Women.* Austin: University of Texas Press, 1994. Explores the Guadalupe myth as the most powerful female icon in Mexican and Mexican American culture and as a symbol of liberation for Mexican Catholic women.

Scarborough, Vernon and David Wilcox, eds. *The Mesoamerican Ballgame.* Tucson: University of Arizona Press, 1991. A well-researched history of the martial sport in all its gory details.

Simon, Joel. *Endangered Mexico: An Environment on the Edge.* San Francisco: Sierra Club Books, 1998. An superb collection of essays on Mexico's precarious environmental situation and the many social factors propelling it, written by a journalist who has traveled far and wide to get his information.

Thomas, Hugh. *Conquest: Montezuma, Cortés, and the Fall of Old Mexico.* New York: Simon & Schuster, 1995. The definitive account of one of the greatest events in history: the meeting of the New and Old Worlds in Mexico in 1519. Detailed and extremely well written.

Womack, John. *Zapata and the Mexican Revolution.* New York: Knopf, 1970. This is considered the classic account of the legendary *caudillo del sur,* Zapata, and his role in the Mexican revolution. A must for anyone interested in understanding Zapata's mythic status in the Mexican pantheon of heroes.

ARCHITECTURE

Opher, Philip with Xavier Sánchez Valladares. *Mexico City: A Guide to Recent Architecture.* Ellipse, 2000. This handy, pocket-sized guide is a good compendium of Mexico City's modern architecture.

FOOD

Adair, Marita. *The Hungry Traveler: Mexico.* Kansas City: Andrews McNeel Publishing, 1997. A pocket-sized Mexican culinary lexicon, with plenty of references to Mexico City and nearby states.

DeWitt, Dave and Nancy Gerlach. *The Whole Chile Pepper Book*. Boston: Little, Brown and Co., 1990. Written by the editors of *Chile Pepper* magazine, this compendium of fact, lore, and recipes is the definitive culinary guide to chiles.

Quintana, Patricia. *The Taste of Mexico*. New York: Stewart, Tabori & Chang, 1993. Written by one of Mexico City's most famous chefs, this is perhaps the most authentic Mexican cookbook available in English. Also available in Spanish as *El Sabor de México*.

Walker, Ann and Larry Walker. *Tequila: The Book*. San Francisco: Chronicle Books, 1994. This small but beautifully bound and printed book contains the definitive history of agave distillate, along with tips on tequila etiquette and recipes for cocktails, *antojitos,* salads, soups, entrées, salsas, and desserts. Humorous anecdotes and place descriptions add to the reading fun.

FICTION

Burroughs, William. *Queer*. New York: Penguin Books, 1987. Set mainly in Mexico City during the Beat era, this autobiographical novel fictionalizes Burroughs's flight to Mexico to avoid drug charges in the United States.

Kerouac, Jack. *Mexico City Blues: 242 Choruses*. New York: Grove Press, 1990. Beat novelist and poet Kerouac often tried to mimic the cadences of jazz in his writing. This work arguably comes closer to that goal than anything else he ever published, and it is evocative of 1950s Mexico City.

Lida, David. *Travel Advisory.* New York: Willam Morrow & Company, 2000. A collection of 10 gritty short stories set in Mexico (several in Mexico City) from an American writer who divides his time between New York and Mexico. Mexico has a bitter history with *americanos* and an even longer history with *malinchismo,* and some of these stories expose—rather than ignore—this essential cornerstone of modern Mexican culture. Lida has an especially good ear for dialogue, which he reproduces partly in Spanish.

Lowry, Malcolm. *Under the Volcano*. New York: Reynal & Hitchcock, 1990. Although when originally published in Canada in 1947 it only sold two copies in two years, Lowry's tale of the alcoholic demise of a British consul in Cuernavaca has become a modern cult classic.

Paco, Ignacio Taibo II. *Return to the Same City.* New York: Mysterious Press, 1996. Mexico City's favorite eccentric Marxist mystery writer resurrects his detective protagonist, Héctor Belascoarán Shayne. While chasing a Cuban arms/drug dealer through D.F., Shayne gives us an insider's glimpse of the city and his existential way of coping with it. The novel's 1993 predecessor, *No Happy Ending,* is also set in *la capital.*

Traven, B. *The Rebellion of the Hanged.* New York: Hill and Wang, 1972. The mysterious B. Traven, author of the more well-known *The Treasure of the Sierra Madre,* here chronicles Amerindian exploitation under Porfirio Díaz in another powerful work of fiction.

Internet Resources

While a substantial number of English-speakers live in Mexico City, the Internet offers paltry resources in English about one of the world's largest megalopolises. Yet for those Mexicophiles who feel the need to stay on top of city politics and tourism, government offices offer content-rich websites for those with some command of Spanish. You'll also find English-language participation in bulletin boards, specialty guides, and an online rating, courtesy of Deja.com.

Keep in mind that websites come and go, and URLs (universal resource locators, or World Wide Web "addresses") change. More websites are included throughout the book on different topics.

Directorio de Comunicación Social
www.precisa.gob.mx

An excellent directory of the entire Mexican government: all branches, the federal and state level, and state-run companies. As well, the site maintains updated lists of foreign embassies, foreign journalists in Mexico, media (radio, television, and newspapers) from across Mexico, universities, and political parties.

Mexico City Government
www.df.gob.mx/

Mexico City's website is well designed and, best of all, there is a great deal of content. If you're interested in city politics and administration, track down the addresses, phone numbers, and emails of the city's precinct leaders or participate in the online chat forums (www.df.gob.mx/foros/index.html) on topics including public security, tourism, and environmental affairs. Mixing thoroughness and creativity, the Mexico City website exemplifies what a government website can be. The only thing missing would be an email mailing list that provided press releases and announcements from specific departments. This information is posted online (www.df.gob.mx/noticias/index.html), but you have to hunt for it.

Mexico City Government Tourism Office
www.mexicocity.gob.mx/

The city's new tourism office has a fairly fancy website with plenty of good links, although descriptions are very limited. Check the Centro Histórico page (www.mexicocity.gob.mx/eng/enjoy/chistorico/index.asp) and the links for museums, theaters, cinemas, and walking tours. You'll also find the addresses for tourism *modulos* around the city (www.mexico city.gob.mx/eng/modules/index.asp) and an archive of city statistics.

Instituto Nacional de Estadísticas, Geografía e Informatica
www.inegi.gob.mx

Inegi is the government statistical institute, and its website (although difficult to navigate) has a wealth of detailed information about the country's population, economy, environment, and much else besides.

Mexican Wave
www.mexicanwave.com

Another general site for travelers, this one geared toward a European audience, but in English, with lots of good information.

Guide2Mexico
**www.guide2mexico.com/
content/mexlinks.htm**

An impressive collection of travelers' resources, including lots of useful links.

Expats
www.mexpat.com

Oriented toward younger expats, especially those living in Mexico City, with lots of information on city events of interest to the expat community. They also have a lively forum.

www.mexconnection.com

Run by a U.S. expat living in Ajijic, Jalisco,

this site has a lot of practical information for expatriates in Mexico.

Centro Histórico
www.viveelcentro.com

As the name implies, this site focuses on the historic center of the city and on ambitious plans to renovate the district.

Mexican Embassy in Washington, D.C.
www.embassyofmexico.org

This is the place to come for the latest Mexican visa information.

Art and History Museums
www.museosdemexico.org

This excellent site contains descriptions and opening hours of every important art and history museum in the capital.

Mexico City Art
www.arte-mexico.com

Online map of the city's many galleries and art museums and listings of current exhibitions and openings.

Intellicast Forecast
www.intellicast.com

This website offers daily weather information.

Newspapers

A number of Mexican newspapers are on the Internet. Reforma (www.reforma.com) is great, but you have to pay to access their site. El Universal (www.eluniversal.com.mx) is free and also good.

Nongovernmental Organizations
http://host.laneta.org

This umbrella site has links to the extensive NGO community in Mexico.

Environmental Information in Mexico City
www.planeta.com/ecotravel/mexico/df/mex info.html

A one-stop information center for anyone interested in environmental issues. This page is frequently updated and is part of the Planeta.com website.

Moon Handbooks
www.moon.com

Moon's website contains occasional excerpts from this book and other Moon titles, ordering information, an online travel newsletter with articles on Mexico, and links to various related sites.

Contributed by Chris Humphrey and Ron Mader, Mexico-based journalist and host of Planeta.com: Global Journal of Practical Ecotourism website (www.planeta.com).

Index

Frida Kahlo

Acknowledgments

First and foremost thanks go to Barbara Kastelein, who did an excellent job updating the *Excursions* chapter of this edition, and for giving some great suggestions for the city as well. David Lida, novelist and journalist extraordinaire, was as usual a source of many tips on city life, as were Ana Morales and Christopher Leroy (congratulations!), Fernando Flores, Luis Briones, Rodrigo Palacios, Eugenio Aburto, Anna Gurney, "El Chapulín" Felix (for, among other things, explaining a myriad of *dichos mexicanos*), and Guadalupe Paz. Thanks to Elena Pappas, again, for some great photos. Thanks again to Joe Cummings for getting me into this gig in the first place, and for work of his that remains in this edition. The editing team at Avalon Travel Publishing—especially my lead editor, Erin Raber, and photo editor, Deb Dutcher (have fun in D.F.!)—both did a top-notch job, and kudos to the design team that came up with the great new layout used in this edition.

U.S. ~ Metric Conversion

1 inch	=	2.54 centimeters (cm)
1 foot	=	.304 meters (m)
1 yard	=	0.914 meters
1 mile	=	1.6093 kilometers (km)
1 km	=	.6214 miles
1 fathom	=	1.8288 m
1 chain	=	20.1168 m
1 furlong	=	201.168 m
1 acre	=	.4047 hectares
1 sq km	=	100 hectares
1 sq mile	=	2.59 square km
1 ounce	=	28.35 grams
1 pound	=	.4536 kilograms
1 short ton	=	.90718 metric ton
1 short ton	=	2000 pounds
1 long ton	=	1.016 metric tons
1 long ton	=	2240 pounds
1 metric ton	=	1000 kilograms
1 quart	=	.94635 liters
1 US gallon	=	3.7854 liters
1 Imperial gallon	=	4.5459 liters
1 nautical mile	=	1.852 km

To compute Celsius temperatures, subtract 32 from Fahrenheit and divide by 1.8. To go the other way, multiply Celsius by 1.8 and add 32.